# World Economics 1
# Comparative Theories and Methods of International and Development Economics

World Economics 1

# Comparative Theories and Methods of International and Development Economics

(A Historical and Critical Survey)

BY

TAMÁS SZENTES

AKADÉMIAI KIADÓ, BUDAPEST

The manuscript of this book has been peer-reviewed by the Committee on Economics of the Hungarian Academy of Sciences, which has strongly recommended its publication.

ISBN 963 05 7967 7 (1–2.)
ISBN 963 05 7984 7 (1.)



Published by Akadémiai Kiadó
P.O. Box 245, H-1519 Budapest, Hungary
www.akkrt.hu



Printed in Hungary

# Table of content

# Foreword

It is already thirty years ago when I was writing the manuscript of my book *The Political Economy of Underdevelopment* in Dar es Salaam, Tanzania, the first edition of which appeared in 1971. This book, which between 1971 and 1988 was published in ten languages and eleven countries, altogether in 15 editions, has been widely used in courses on developing countries all over the world, at universities of more than forty countries. It is still available at most of the university libraries. Thirty years is, however, a long time during which not only the views of an author may change but also the very reality of the topic he was writing about.

Unlike the last chapters of the above book, which concerning the prospects and alternative policies to overcome "underdevelopment" proved to be naive as expressing illusions about "self-reliance", "delinking", and an independent, democratic (non-Soviet type!) "socialism" (such as believed to get birth in Tanzania), the major part of the analysis on the causes, nature and mechanisms of "underdevelopment" seems still valid (fortunately for the book but unfortunately for those countries concerned). More or less the same applies to my criticism of the conventional theories of "underdevelopment", which I need to extend only to their more up-to-date variants as well as to other theoretical views (besides, of course, getting rid of the that time compulsory restraint from criticizing Marxism as well).

Nevertheless, too many and too substantial changes have taken place since that time both in the world of development and in its literature which make my former book rather obsolete and induce me to reconsider my concept, to revisit my "political economy of underdevelopment".

Thirty years ago the economics of development (or the interdisciplinary course called, as in many places, "development studies") was concerned about the underdeveloped economy (and socio-political reality) of developing countries only. Who could be able that time to predict the rise of "newly industrialized countries" from among the developing countries, or the oil crisis with the subsequent world recession caused by a group of developing countries and imposing, together with the suddenly recognized dangers for environment, problems of (sustainable) development also upon the advanced market economies?! Or who was able to foresee, particularly, the collapse and transformation of the so-called "socialist world", i.e. the Soviet bloc, and the end of the "bipolar world" and its cold war?!

All these and other historical changes have, of course, influenced the development of "development studies"; have questioned not only their earlier concepts but also even their former subject and area of research. New problems and dilemmas of development have arisen and also on new levels. New paradigms are born or some old ones reappear in new dresses. The very fact that economics of development is not the same as it used to be (though it has never been a homogeneous discipline with clear-cut frontiers!) seems to induce some scholars to announce its "requiem" while others to celebrate its renascence. Whatever is the case, development literature has been enriched by both theoretical and empirical studies so much during the last three decades that despite the on-going polemies, the obviously divergent views and development policies, or the coming new challenges, time has, perhaps, arrived for drawing some common lessons and conclusions from the past debates and experiences, and for trying to sum up those crystallized concepts resulting from a kind of "constructive eclecticism". Such a situation and such attempts may suggest writing a book (applicable in teaching, too) with seemingly impersonal approaches and more or less balanced viewpoints, presenting an eclectic knowledge. No doubt, I must admit, this is, indeed, one of the reasons why this book is formulated and constructed almost in a textbook-style rather than in a style of a primarily polemizing monograph. (The other reason is that my former books, both *The Political Economy of Underdevelopment* and the *Theories of World Capitalist Economy* were also used as teaching materials despite their hardly didactic, rather polemizing, often too detailed or comprehensive text and difficult style, the inconvenience of which I would like to avoid as much as possible in this case.)

But a monograph even if it aims also to be used as a textbook can hardly be impersonal indeed. Whether intended and confessed by the author or not, it necessarily reflects his (or her) approach, value order, and "philosophy" or "ars poetica" in the very selection of views and data, in the critical or uncritical presentation of concepts or arguments, and even in the formulation of open questions or dilemmas. Bearing this in mind I won't pretend to be "neutral" vis-à-vis the various theoretical theses or practice-oriented paradigms! In this respect I will do the same as in the former books, namely delivering also a critique on them and expressing, of course, my own views as well. I may hope, however, that this will not make me so easily "categorized" into one group of scholars as many years ago, nor my intended orientation towards "constructive eclecticism" will be considered as compromising with principles and values.

When Professor *Paul Streeten*, whom I highly respect, published his articles (1977 and 1985) on the development of development theories, he has greatly honoured me by mentioning my name, rather undeservedly, among illustrious scholars, as probably overestimating my moderate contribution to development theories. But he also "categorized" me among those who attribute "underdevelopment" merely to external forces, to the international system, and believe that the South could be better off without the North. This was perhaps due to the fact that I wrote, indeed, a sharp critique (in the first chapter of my book) against the conventional theories of unilinear development which explain "underdevelopment" merely by internal conditions, but was also contrary to my real perception (also explained in the same book, in its third chapter) which was very similar to Streeten's in pointing to the interactions between external and internal factors. Not to mention that by the date when his second article mentioned above was published, I had already presented my critique also on those radical views blaming merely the international forces of exploitation for the underdevelopment of the developing countries, in my new book *Theories of World Capitalist Economy* in 1985.

As regards "constructive eclecticism", I see the very development of development economics to follow this direction, contrary to any "counter-revolutions" in this field. And it is not surprising at all, partly because the heavy ideological bias stemming from cold war conditions, which has characterized this field of studies for a long time, is to fade away since the end of confrontation between "East" as representing "existing" or "real socialism", and the "West" representing some sort of homogeneous "capitalism", and partly because this should be indeed the natural direction of development of social sciences, in general. For all theories, without exception, are based upon abstraction, looking at the changing reality from different viewpoint, in different time and place, thus not only contradicting but also complementing each other.

The very intention to get rid of ideological biases and the very recognition of the relative value, limited applicability and also of the complementary nature of all theories, will be the guiding rule and principle of this book. Thus, instead of pretending to provide its readers with a ready-made, "final" stock of knowledge, it aims at stimulating only their critical thinking, namely by presenting a critical survey of different theories and also my own views on development and "underdevelopment".

Since, however, the economics of development or the political economy of underdevelopment has extended, in the meantime, to the case of the former "socialist" countries, too, and when investigating their system and system-change I came to the same conclusion as in the analysis of "underdevelopment", namely that no explanation if out of the historical context of world economy and politics can be relevant, I have complemented the topic area of this book with the issue of "comparative economic systems" as well as a historical and critical survey of the theories of *international economics.* And for the views on the "international" or world economy and on national development or economic "underdevelopment" of countries, as well as on "comparative economic systems" have always been interrelated since the very beginning of modern economics, it seemed reasonable to investigate briefly how they have developed from the 16th century to the present.

Thus, unlike my former *Political Economy* which critically surveyed only on the conventional theories of "development economics" since the latter emerged as a special field of study separated from general economics and limited to "underdeveloped economies", this new one has enlarged the scope of the critical survey not only in respect of the topic areas but also in time, and presents, with critical comments, the comparative concepts of the major theoretical schools on national development, economic systems and international economy alike, from Mercantilism to present-day theories. Consequently, this First Volume of *World Economics*, which includes such a historical and critical survey of theories, may hopefully be used as a comprehensive reading in courses of international economics just as well as in those of development economics or economics of comparative systems.

The *second volume* of the book outlines my own views on the world economy as an organic system, on its uneven historical development and accelerating globalisation, on the reasons of the “international development gap”, on the interactions of the external and internal causes of “underdevelopment”, on the rise and failure of “socialism” and on comparative systems within the single world economy. It finally raises questions about the prospects of development on national and world level, points to the new challenges and opportunities as seen at the beginning of the 21st century.

# I.
# Introductory Remarks on Theories in General and their Historical Background

## 1. The nature and limitations of social science theories

1. Social science is necessarily and inherently critical. It cannot do without a permanent critical analysis of the ever-changing social reality and a regular critique of its own developing perceptions on the latter. Radical changes in social reality may not only dispel those illusions attached to the former state of affairs and induce social scientists to revisit their paradigms, but normally give birth also to new theoretical concepts and illusions as well.

2. Social science theories are always products of abstraction and generalization, i.e. of neglecting certain (presumably secondary or tertiary) aspects of social reality in order to focus on one or another (presumably primary) aspect, and of selecting accordingly the common features of the partially observed reality and of drawing general conclusions there from, while disregarding particularities and specificities.

This means that without exception all social science theories are based upon a certain simplification which, on the one hand, makes easier to understand the complex reality, while, on the other, sets limits to their value, validity and applicability. A mere empiricism, however, i.e. a registration only of numerous unconnected facts or data cannot, of course, substitute for theory which in one way or another, more or less correctly or incorrectly orientates us in the masses of the latter. A confrontation between different social science theories in a polemy among their representatives is not only necessary, but also inevitable and useful, as thereby they mutually reveal the weaknesses and induce corrections in each other's concept, but it is also meaningless and irrational in so far as different theories approach the same reality from different angle and shed light on different parts of it, or apply different time and space horizon. In other words, different theories may not only conflict with, but also complement each other. No theory is able to comprehend the entire reality in its full complexity and dynamics.

3. The terminologies created or used by different theoretical schools are also of relative value, full of inconsistencies and contradictions as they necessarily reflect certain biases, limitations and partial approaches of the latter. Many of the terms applied conventionally in "development studies" (including this very term itself) are also questionable, inaccurate, if not misleading. (Such as among many other, the term "world market", "developing countries", "Third World", "United Nations",

"centrally planned vs. market economies", "existing" or "real socialism" vs. "capitalist societies", "self-reliance", "self-sustained growth", "capital vs. labour-intensive" techniques, "delinking", "auto centric development", "economic independence", "national sovereignty", "human rights", "basic needs", "just" or "remunerative prices" and so on...) Those radical changes in reality, shaking the former paradigms and generating new ones suggest a reinvestigation and corrections also in terminology.

## 2. Historical turning points and changes of paradigms

The 20th century has involved several historical turning points, such decisive events and far-reaching revolutionary changes as determining the main trends also in social science, which disproved former assumptions or theses, refused the distinctive paradigms of the previous period, and raised new ones. In most cases the latter while contradicting the former ones have also preserved some-thing from them – in accordance with the dialectics of continuity and discontinuity or the logic of thesis-antithesis-synthesis. In fact none of them has justified a return to those obsolete paradigms already rejected and surpassed in the previous period.

1. Such a historical yard-stick causing a break of continuity also in social science, has been represented e.g. by the Great Crisis and the subsequent rise of fascist systems in a few countries of Europe, leading to the Second World War.

As a consequence the old Classical and Neoclassical visions about the harmonious operation of an uncontrolled, unregulated market, its beneficial "invisible hand" and equilibrium mechanism have been destroyed just as well as the hopes attached to the stability of the former inter-state order in Europe and of the system of parliamentary democracy in less developed or heavily crisis-stricken societies with explosive social tensions.

New paradigms, new theoretical concepts and policies were born, such as the Keynesian idea and recipe of indirect state interventions, demand- and employment-generating public investments, income redistribution for the low-income strata with smaller saving propensity, indicative planning and welfare measures etc. or the paradigm of Welfare State and a new "social contract", the acceptance of social "countervailing powers" in the economy and politics, the full cooptation of social democracy in the Western political systems, the concept of "consumer society" and a post-industrialist era, the programme of (West-) European integration and the reorganization of the international institutional system after the war.

Needless to add how many new illusions had been also attached to these or some other new paradigms, which have been dispelled later, particularly by the global crisis of the 1970s.

2. The post-war process of decolonisation, the rapid collapse of colonial empires and the rise of the "Third World" with its non-aligned movement, anti-imperialist stand and just claim to get more benefits and lose less in the interna-

tional economy and politics, have also brought about considerable changes in views, concepts and paradigms.

The myth of the "civilization mission" of colonial powers has been, of course, totally smashed. The credibility of the conventional views about mutual benefits of international trade, comparative advantages of specialization and internationally equalizing effects of capital mobility on factor supply conditions and income levels etc. has also been seriously undermined in the light of the widening international development gap between North and South.

As a result of decolonisation a number of newly independent countries became UN members, bringing their grave economic problems on the agenda of international negotiations and claiming preferential treatment in trade and finance as well as technical assistance from developed nations. This fact has induced not only the UN bodies to classify countries according to their level of economic development in order to judge which of them deserve and which of them should provide such preferences and aid, but also many scholars to help such a work by comparative analysis of economic development and investigation of the causes of economic development or underdevelopment.

In view of the specificity of the problems faced both by the international community in assisting financially or technically such countries and by the latter themselves in managing economic development and modernization, a new "discipline" called "development economics" (or as a more interdisciplinary field of research: "development studies") has been distinguished from economics in general, and from social science research on the advanced countries.

Almost parallel with the rise of development economics or studies in the late 1940s, early 1950s, the split of Europe into two groups of countries, and the emerging cold war between the Soviet bloc of the so-called "socialist" countries and the Western alliance of developed capitalist nations has given birth to another specific field of studies called "comparative economic systems".

At the same time and to some extent also linked with development economics, a more or less new school in international economics, rooted in some former, quite diverse theoretical streams, has also appeared which gave a critical analysis of the prevailing international economic order, blaming its precedent in colonization or its trade and financial regime for the international development gap and the "development of underdevelopment".

Since then, i.e. since the late 1940s and early 1950s, the development of the economics of development, this increasingly interdisciplinary "discipline" itself, going through various phases while keeping its original controversies between "internalists" and "externalists" or "neoclassicals" and "structuralists", "blues" and "reds" etc., has been illustrating fairly well the changes of paradigms (and illusions) in response to changes in reality.

3. The global crisis of the world economy, coupled temporarily with food and energy crises in the early 1970s, has dispelled the illusion of "three worlds" and the naive belief that the stability of the international economic order and the econom-

ic equilibrium of the developed industrial "first world" or the extensive economic growth of the more or less isolated "second world" could not be threatened and affected by the lasting and deepening crisis of the Third World. The recognition, in the light of the oil embargo and price explosion, of the vulnerability even of the most developed economies, and of those common dangers caused by unilateral actions or seemingly local economic disturbances in any part of the world has put the concept of interdependencies to the fore. The idea of a "single world", the term "one-world problem" (such as population, environment, etc.), the method of a global approach or a "world system approach" (Wallerstein), the studies on global problems and the new or (renewed) paradigms of the Club of Rome have gained wide popularity.

The obvious failure of the Bretton Woods system and the end of the "golden age" (from the point of view of the major developed economies) of the international economy have strengthened the position of the new post-Keynesian critical school of international economics which recommended international reform measures, a concerted indirect regulation of the international market and redeployment processes, a redistribution of incomes and financial resources in favour of the poor, i.e. a sort of application of the Keynesian principles on world level in order to establish a new international economic order, and raised also hopes (or rather illusions) about the implementation of the nicely formulated UN documents on NIEO and the economic rights and duties of the states.

At the same time, owing to the reappearance of classical crisis-symptoms (such as a high rate of unemployment) in the Western economies and the manifest disturbances in the operation of the Welfare State and Western "consumer societies", the concept of underdevelopment of the South has been complemented by the concept of "over development" or "maldevelopment" of the North in the critical social science schools. The Keynesian paradigms have been increasingly attacked and dethroned by a "monetarist counter-revolution" and replaced by neoliberal or "neo-conservative" concepts and policies in most of the Western countries.

The marked differentiation of the Third World, accelerated by the crisis itself, has questioned the interpretation of the Third World as a meaningful unit of analysis and also the simplified version of the concept of centre-periphery dichotomy. New terminological distinctions were made, such as "Fourth" or "Fifth" World and new illusions appeared in respect of the applicability of the model of the newly industrialized countries (NICs or NIEs) or the policy of OPEC.

The slowing down of economic growth and the increasing disequilibria in the economies of the "Second" ("socialist") World, reflecting (besides its own inherent anomalies) also the impact of the global crisis, have undermined the ideology of a separate system of "socialist world economy" and by pointing to undeniable global interdependencies, paved the way, also from this side, for the later transformation in the East.

4. Since the late 1980s and early 1990s it is indeed this very transformation, the disintegration of the Soviet bloc and the systemic changes in the former "socialist"

countries, which have induced a thorough rethinking and revision of former paradigms, theoretical concepts and even terminologies in development economics and in the economics of comparative systems, too.

The final collapse of the “socialist” systems in Eastern Europe has put an end to treating the “socialist” countries as (either positive or negative) exceptions. They have ceased to represent an alternative path of development, namely a non-capitalistic one, whether the latter was supposed to be followed as a successful way of modernization or to be avoided as a blind alley because of its economically inefficient and politically dictatorial methods.

The process of transformation following systemic change in these countries has not only involved far-reaching structural and institutional changes but also raised a historical question: whether they would be able to join (by new ways and efforts of modernization) the group of developed countries, the “North”, or they would join (by falling back to or remaining in the underdeveloped “periphery” of the world economy) the group of developing countries, i.e. the “South”. In other words, development economics has extended also to the former “socialist” countries, thereby having totally lost its original specificity, its limitedness to some group(s) of countries only. It has become (again?) a universal field of studies related to the problems of development of all the countries of the world, as a qualitative process (distinguished from quantitative growth) which requires and involves structural and institutional changes. Moreover, in view of the global(ized) problems of development or its “sustainability” (such as related to the dangers for ecological balance of the Earth, to dangers of environmental pollution, exhaustion of non-renewable natural resources, nuclear or other catastrophes, “overpopulation”, food shortage, or to the international development gap, conflicts between rich and poor nations, international insecurity, terrorism, refugee waves, etc.), development economics has also become universal in the sense of dealing with development of the world as a whole.

# II. Different Approaches to the Economics of the World Economy, National Development and Comparative Systems

## 1. International economics or economics of the world economy? (Perception of the global economy in theories and standard textbooks)

### 1.1. "Global economy" or "international economy"?

The terms "global" or "world economy" and "international economy" have often been used as synonyms in economic literature[1] and university curricula. Apart from the problem of the ambiguities in the definition of "nation" and from the incongruity of the state borders of numerous countries with the geographical frontiers of "nations", such a use of terminology necessarily involves a biased interpretation of the world economy and its relationship with nations.

The rise and development of a more or less global world economy and modern, industrialized national economies in the more or less developed part of the world have been the result of simultaneous, interlinked processes rather than that of two processes following each other. Nevertheless the conventional perception of the world economy as being identified with an "international economy" has been based on the assumption that the latter is a mere derivative of the growth and operation of national economies the development of which has naturally preceded that of the world economy.

Though it cannot be doubted that there has been such a direction of cause-effect relationship between the development of national economies and that of the international economy, the world economy is obviously more than the aggregate of national economies or the trade and financial transactions among them.

---

[1] Mihály *Simai* writes in his recent book [(1994), pp. XVI–XVII.]: "This book looks at the *global system* (or *international system*)". He defines a *system* (I think correctly) "as the entirety of interactions and interdependencies among groups or items within a specified structure or framework". The question may be raised: Which is this specified framework in the case of the world economy, and what groups or items can be identified? The reason why he also uses the terms "global" or "international" as synonyms can be found, perhaps, in the following text explaining also the dilemma about the appropriate unit of analysis: "The global system encompasses the entirety of relationships among those actors that influence processes and changes beyond national frontiers. Operating in a structure characterized by the existence of states, these actors inevitably include the states themselves."

The opposite direction of cause-effect relationship (if acknowledged at all) can hardly be reduced to the growth promoting and welfare effects of an expanding world trade and international specialization or to the growth limiting effect of a contraction of international trade.

The very fact that the growth of international trade and specialization, of these decisive components of the world economy, has been retarding (by its disintegrating effect and terms) the development of modern, integrated and industrialized national economies in several parts of the world, namely in the periphery of the world economy, while promoting it, indeed, in the core areas, shows the point. The blaming, simply, of the local, national political forces for the failure in making use of the opportunities and the assumed "comparative advantages" in international trade to build up a modern industrial national economy, is not an answer to the problem but a sheer over-simplification, even if in most cases their responsibilities cannot be questioned.

Counterarguments which refer to the success stories of quite a few "late-coming" countries having managed by modernization to catch up with the developed ones, may shed light perhaps, if explaining the reasons, on the (historically changing) criteria of catching-up, but at the same time willy-nilly reveal the very *impossibility for all* countries to follow the example and copy the policy of the successful ones. The simplest calculations can easily prove that (in view of the squandering over-utilization of non-renewable resources, overproduction in many fields, pollution of environment, unsustainability of consumption patterns, etc.) neither the available resources of our Earth nor its ecological balance could allow a mass repetition of the national development path of the pioneer countries or the successful late-comers, including the newly industrialized economies. However such instructive their case may be for others, it cannot be a model for *all*[2].

Thus something must be wrong with the conventional perception of the world economy as a derivative and development-promoting factor of national economies.

[2] Besides other reasons (such as the expected consequences of an imagined world-wide spread of the pattern of consumption or the type of urbanization of the few advanced countries in respect of (a) the allocation of waste materials, (b) air, land and water pollution, and (c) reduction of cultivable lands, forests, etc., it is the obvious contrast between the pattern of energy use and the limits as well as the unequal distribution of the available world resources of the predominant types of energy, which makes impossible for the majority of countries to follow the development path of the advanced countries. For example, the US, which involves less than 6 per cent of the world population, is using cca. 30 per cent of all the energy produced in the world, while India with more than 20 per cent of the world population makes use of only 2 per cent of the world energy produced. What would happen if without a radical shift in the patterns of energy production and use, all those less developed countries with an enormous and growing population tried to copy the model of the industrialized countries?! For more details see *The Gaia Atlas* (1985).

## 1.2. The world economy as appearing in the major streams of economic theory: a short summary[3]

The development of economic theories, particularly theories of "international economics", as we shall see in more details later, has always reflected in one way or another the development process of the world economy and the major changes in it, as well as the actual problems or challenges faced by certain countries or groups of countries in practice, i.e. both the time and space dimensions, the historical and local context of economic development[4].

It is not surprising that economic theories have been generated mostly in the more developed countries or those being near to catch up with the latter, and have always manifested more the problems or interests of the countries of their origin than those of others.

This applies not only to the early and primitive theories of modern economics, such as Mercantilism and Physiocratism but also to the first sophisticated economic theory, namely *Classical economics.* Since in their time, i.e. in the period from the early 16th to the first decades of the 19th century the "international" economic relations involved only (even if not exclusively) *trade flows* and the concomitant flows of money as a means of exchange, their perception of the "world economy" and their theses about foreign trade corresponded to the trade position of the countries of their origin, and differed accordingly from each other only in respect of the aim or "base", and the assumed effect of, mutual or exclusive benefits from, international trade.

While the *Mercantilists* (just like their recent followers, the Neo-mercantilists) urging their country to achieve a regular export surplus did not care of the trade deficits of the partners and the international economic disequilibria caused thereby, the *Physiocrats* preferred an equilibrium in international trade (if the latter was necessary or reasonable at all on the base of differences between countries in natural conditions). The representatives of *Classical economics* believed in mutual benefits from international trade based upon absolute or comparative advantages, on differences in absolute or relative labour productivity, and also in an automatic equilibrium mechanism both within the partner national economies and in the international economy under the conditions of free trade. The link between international trade and the growth and operation of the national economy was obvious for them, which implied also a *link* between national (macro) and international economics, and between the latter and their concepts of development. Since they,

[3] In other chapters of this book there will be a more detailed discussion and critique of the theoretical views on the world economy, national development and economic systems of the major "schools" of economics.

[4] For a comprehensive investigation of the history of modern economic theories in general see *Mátyás*, A. (1979). For a critical survey of the theories of international economics only, see *Szentes*, T. (1985).

just like their predecessors and followers, have expressed views on the given or an ideal economic system as well, such a link also appeared, implicitly or explicitly, between, at least, the germs of the economics of development and of comparative economic systems, too.

Though the fact (contrary to the opposite statement of many standard textbooks) that Ricardo did not apply his labour theory of value, the determination of "natural price" by labour input, to the international economy, was already a sign of the split between the rules on international and those on national level, no other separation according to the validity of general rules and principles, between the two distinguished units of analysis has been made yet since that time.

Since the symbiosis of liberalism and the labour theory of value has soon proved to be untenable, the subsequent theoretical streams having the same origin (namely *Classical economics)* but diverging away from each other, either insisted on the principles of liberalism (as e.g. the Neo-classical school) and gave up the labour theory of value, or preserved the latter and turned against the liberal ideas about the harmonious operation of a spontaneous national as well as international market economy (as e.g. Marxism). On the other hand a certain separation (not only distinction) between the various units of analysis has appeared both in the "mainstream" Neo-classical school (namely between micro-, macro- and international economics) and in the opposite, Marxist school (insofar as international trade was considered by Marx himself as an "external factor" influencing the rate of profit, counteracting its falling tendency, and insofar as a separate "world function" of money was also distinguished by him, quite inconsistently, among the various functions).

*Marx* missed to clarify whether his abstract model of the capitalist economy with its cyclical motion, tendencies of overproduction and growing relative inequalities in ownership, exchange and income relations, was to be applied to country or world level, i.e. to the national economies or to the world economy. He made several points in his work which seem to justify the choice of the former, though at the same time he identified the world market as the natural sphere of operation for capital, this very motive force of the system, and pointed also to the world level manifestation of "primitive accumulation of capital". His followers, with rare exceptions (such as e.g. Kautsky) took the level of countries as the primary level of analysis almost for granted, and considered the world level development of capitalism as a derivative of changes within countries (even if presenting a theory of "imperialism"[5] or calling for a world revolution in the name of solidarity of the world proletariat.

[5] The concept of *Lenin* on the five characteristics of "imperialism" illustrates the point as the first two, namely monopolization and the fusion of industrial and banking capital resulting in the rise of a financial capital and oligarchy, are related to the *internal* development of the most advanced countries, while the other three are derived from the first two, moreover, the fifth one, namely the struggle of the powerful states for colonies, is a *directly international* characteristic. See later and *Lenin*, V. I. (1967).

*Marshall,* one of the most famous representatives of the Neo-classical school has elabourated a separate theory of international economics, namely the "pure theory of foreign trade"[6] as separated from the theory on the domestic economy, leaving the question of the links between changes within and between national economies, and that of the domestic determinants of his "reciprocal demand/supply curves" of international exchange rather open and left also unclarified the role of international capital mobility in international trade.

Though the growing importance of the export of capital in shaping the world economy has been recognized (as we shall see later) not only by the Marxian political economy but also by the Neo-classical school, and new theses have been elabourated on the direction and effects of international capital flows, the "pure theory of international trade" has remained intact of the reality of foreign direct investments shaping the production and export structures. The famous *Heckscher–Ohlin theorem* on trade and specialization (which will be discussed later) and also those correcting or complementing the latter (such as the concept of trade based on differences in "tastes" or on the economy of scale or on the "technological gap" and "product cycles", etc.[7]) have simply abstracted from the international mobility of capital and the tendency of its transnationalization.

The *"Keynesian revolution"* has questioned, as we shall see, most of the basic presumptions of the conventional Neo-classical theory (such as the automatic self-correcting equilibrium mechanisms in the product and factor markets with an assumed flexibility of prices determined by and determining both demand and supply, which would always ensure or re-establish a "perfect equilibrium" in the national economies). Keynes himself has contributed a lot to the new approaches, new thoughts not only in respect of anti-cyclical economic policies, methods of indirect state regulations of national market economies but also in respect of the post-second-world-war international economic (particularly monetary) order. Nevertheless the Keynesian theory has preserved (or even reinforced) the primacy of the "macro-economic" unit of analysis, i.e. the concept of national economies as basic units.

Even after the Second World War this *primacy of the national economy* as a basic unit for analysis as well as for action has unambiguously though paradoxically remained characteristic not only in the so-called *"Marxism–Leninism"*, this ideologically distorted and politically manipulated version of Marxism in the countries of the Soviet bloc, but also in the first dominant stream of *development economics*, in the theories of "developmentalism" or "underdevelopment" related to the developing countries.

Though *"Marxism–Leninism"* was born under the aegis of the "world solidarity of proletarians", practically it was apologetically serving the interest of the Soviet

---

[6] See *Marshall, A.* (1923).

[7] On these concepts see e.g. *Salvatore, D.* (1998).

Union and the very "national" endeavours of catching up in isolation with the developed capitalist nations.

Insofar as "underdevelopment" of the developing countries, particularly the newly independent states was explained exclusively or primarily by domestic reasons (such as by unfavourable natural or demographic conditions, lack of capital and entrepreneurial spirit, poor quality of labour, etc. or the "vicious circle" of poverty[8]) and development policy was supposed to copy the model of the Western (or the "socialist") countries, development economics has neglected the reality of global interdependencies of the world economy even more inadmissibly than theories of economics in general.

True, in sharp confrontation with the conventional theories of development, which all have placed emphasis on domestic factors and suggested a unilinear concept of development with universal stages[9], an opposite school of development studies did also appear (originated mainly in the *Latin American school of "dependencia"* and inspired also by post-Keynesian and neo-Marxist thoughts). As we shall see, it has focussed on the external obstacles to development such as the dependent and exploited position of the developing countries – either, historically, within the colonial empires[10] or, as more recently and more generally, within the world economy[11].

From the very beginning this stream had been quite heterogeneous and was soon splitting into different theoretical schools or sub streams, such as the *reformist post-Keynesian school* (Myrdal, Lewis, Singer, Balogh, etc.), which called for reforms, by means of collective regulation of world market prices, in the system of international trade in favour of the developing countries, and the *more radical* "new left" (Emmanuel, Wallerstein, etc.) and *neo-Marxist schools* (Amin, Frank, Dos Santos, etc.) which suggest, as we shall see, the developing countries a policy of "delinking" from the capitalist world economy or (and before) a full transformation of the world system.

By questioning the reversibility of disequilibria in unregulated market economies both on national and international level and by pointing to the cumulating of inequalities under the conditions of unequal exchange and lack of regular income redistribution, etc. the *post-Keynesian school* of international economics has gone obviously much further than the Keynesian theory itself in rejecting or revising the conventional theses and presumptions of the Neo-classical school. However, even

[8] For more details of the concept of "vicious circle" see e.g. *Viner, J.* (1953), and for its critical investigation see the related subchapter of this study.

[9] See e.g. *Rostow, W. W.* (1960a). For a critical investigation of Rostow's theory see the related chapter in this study.

[10] See e.g. *Rodney, W.* (1972).

[11] On the sharp division line between the conventional and the critical theories, i.e. those explaining "underdevelopment" by domestic and those explaining it by external reasons, see e.g. *Paul Streeten's* paper (1977) to which we shall return later.

apart from the ambiguity of "equal" or "unequal" exchange[12], both the treatment of the developing countries as a special case and the suggested reforms of the international economic order only by means of state policies or inter-state cooperation indicate a search for solution which is still based upon the concept of a fragmented world not only consisting of, but also confronting with each other the existing "nations", the individual "national" economies or "nation" states.

The more radical *new left* and *neo-Marxist theories*, while placing the development of underdevelopment into the context of the uneven development of world capitalism[13] and "global accumulation of capital" or a world-wide "trade imperialism"[14], and looking at the underdeveloped economies of developing countries as "sub-systems" of the global economy, have (with rare exceptions) finally concluded on an *international* conflict between groups of countries or states, namely those belonging to the South and those to the North, and visualized a revolt or delinking of the former versus the latter, thereby willy-nilly leaving the transnationalized economic relations and the stratification, across the state frontiers, of the world society out of sufficient consideration.

Nevertheless it was first these new theoretical streams, the post-Keynesian reformist and the above-mentioned radical schools, the representatives of which cast doubts on the relevance[15], or (with an obvious exaggeration) even about the reality, of "national economies", rejected the conventional approach of "country A and country B" of those economists becoming "slaves to the geographers"[16], and put forward the idea of a "world-system approach"[17] and the primacy of "world level analysis", the "pre-eminence of world values", the "unity of world system"[18]. While the rejection of any relevance of national economies as real units for analysis and action is in general an excessive simplification, and so is the interpretation of the unity of the world economy as world-wide trade relations only, the proposed "delinking" policy itself (even if interpreted as a collective policy to be applied by a group of countries, perhaps the entire South) seems to contradict the search for really *global* solution in consonance with a world-system approach.[19]

Parallel with the rise of new concepts and approaches regarding the world economy and with the extension of debates between and within the above streams (as

[12] On this ambiguity see *Szentes, T.* (1985), Part Two, which critically investigates the theory of "unequal exchange" in more details than the related chapter of the present study.

[13] See e.g. Amin, S. (1976) whose views will be discussed in details later on.

[14] See *Emmanuel, A.* (1972). We shall discuss Emmanuel's theory later.

[15] See e.g. *Furtado, C.* (1971), p. 1. – Furtado's views will also be discussed later.

[16] See *Singer, H. W.* (1971), p. 8. – We shall return to Singer's views later.

[17] See *Hopkins, T. K.–Wallerstein, I.* (1977). – Wallerstein's theoretical concept will also be discussed later, in a separate chapter.

[18] See *Amin, S.* (1973). – As already noted, Amin's views will be discussed later.

[19] Not to mention that e.g. *Emmanuel's* theory of unequal exchange as "trade imperialism" involves certain neoclassical elements and illusions about the equalizing effect of international capital mobility if not accompanied by labor immobility.

e.g. on unequal exchange and reforms or revolts), the increasing worries about world demographic growth and ecological dangers, environmental pollution and exhaustion of non-renewable resources[20] as well as about the further widening of the "international development gap" and also about the acceleration of an extending arms race with global militarization, which all undermine even the given, limited security of the world society, have resulted in the formulation of the concept of "global problems", i.e. problems which take global dimensions and cannot be solved but on global level. Research on the future of the world economy and "global modelling" have been strongly encouraged by the latter and by the eruption of the world economic crisis in the early 1970s.

The *crisis of the world economy* was interpreted and explained quite differently in the literature. Even apart from such over-simplifications as those attributing it merely to the unilateral action of OPEC causing a price explosion, many scholars simply considered it as similar in nature to the great crisis of 1929, which originated in and spread from individual national economies, or as a regularly returning phase of long-wave (Kondratieff-type) cycles. However, the crisis of the world economy has manifested itself (perhaps the first time in history) as a global crisis not only in the sense that practically none of the countries was left unaffected by it (not even the still more or less isolated countries of the Soviet bloc) but also in the sense that it was rooted in the global structure of the world economy, in the centuries-old pattern of international division of labour and its post-second-world-war modification, both with built-in disequilibria. It has also reflected the increasing inadequacy of the institutional system for an effective regulation of economic processes. Development problems have ceased to appear as limited to the special case of developing countries only, as confronted to the case of developed nations, which were supposed to be already in the stage of "self-sustained growth".

The realization in the light of the crisis, of the vulnerability even of the most advanced and powerful national economies seemed to provide exceptional opportunity for international, inter-state compromises on large-scale reforms of the "international order", for the efforts to establish a *New International Economic Order*. The recognition of worldwide interdependencies has also induced a great number of interdisciplinary research projects on the global crisis and global policy or governance, too. Nevertheless the hopes and claims for NIEO have soon faded away as most of the developed countries had chosen, instead, a national way of recovering from the crisis at the expense of others, while global studies had still to face the reality of a bipolar world, the split and confrontation of "two systems".

The arguments of the *monetarist counter-revolution* versus the Keynesian recipe of demand-stimulating fiscal (and monetary) policy and inflationary welfare expenditures have been used (or misused rather) to justify the policy of restriction on social budget and international assistance in the advanced countries (coupled

[20] See e.g. the reports of the *Club of Rome*, particularly *Meadows, D. and D.* (1972).

in some of them with increased military expenditures), and to shape a more or less uniform package of measures of stabilization and *structural adjustment* internationally for all the countries suffering balance of payments deficit. In this way the *monetarist school* seems to have reinforced the *national* approach, despite the liberal principles it emphasizes, which suggest free trade and free flows of production factors also on the level of the world economy, thereby the promotion of globalisation without restrictive national policies.

Besides a reinforcement of the national approach, however, *neoliberalism* which, as we shall see later, characterizes the monetarist school as well, has presented an alternative concept of a *new world order* (versus the former idea of a New International Economic Order which was based upon the hope of constructive intergovernmental compromises and inter-state cooperation in regulating the operation of the international economy). Namely the concept of a global integration of markets and transnationalization of capital, i.e. a full and unlimited unfolding of these on-going processes, with a radically reduced economic role and unambiguously market-friendly behaviour of governments all over the world. It visualizes the rise of such a federative world government as promoting and serving, instead of regulating, the above processes[21].

The growing concern about *global problems of survival*, security and development and about the on-going negative-sum-games (such as arms race and global militarization, environmental pollution and ecological destruction[22], international terrorism, etc.) as well as the failure of national policies not only in overcoming global disequilibria but also in ensuring a lasting and full recovery within the national economies concerned (as manifested by a return of recession in the early 1980s and the chronic symptom of higher than "normal" unemployment even in the most successful countries) have kept global studies alive, moreover encouraged them to extend investigation over the non-economic aspects of the "global crisis"[23].

Since the late 1980s and early 1990s global studies have gained a new, exceptionally strong momentum, namely by the *systemic change* in the "East", the former "socialist countries", the collapse of the Soviet bloc and the resulting end of the bipolar world with "two world economic systems"[24]. This has reinforced and

---

[21] On this concept see *Simai, M.* (1992).

[22] See e.g. the *Bruntland Report* (1987.) World Commission on Environment and Development. UN. New York.

[23] See e.g. the *UNU* research project on the global crisis and transformation in 1983–87, which besides the problems of the world economic disequilibria has involved studies also on militarization, security, the state system, etc. See also the UNU project and publication on "New Global Science: From Chaos to Order".

[24] "Since the collapse of the communist regimes in Eastern Europe, international exchange of knowledge and information, training and cooperation are needed more than ever before. The world is experiencing an abrupt change towards *the need for global, political and economic cooperation*. Today many problems can only be solved at a global level." Quotation from *EUR-OP NEWS*. Vol. 4. No. 3. Autumn 1995. p. 3.

made increasingly manifest the link between the economics of the global world economy and national development and the economics of "comparative economic systems".

True, paradoxically enough, the transformation in the "East" has revitalized some disintegrative tendencies as well in the world economy, such as demonstrated by the reappearance of an anachronistic nationalism in several countries of Eastern Europe, by conflicts or even wars between some of the newly created or recreated states in the region or between nationalities, ethnic and religious groups within countries. It has also reinforced the belief in a unilinear road of development, in only one possible "system" for all the individual countries of the world and in their need to accept and simply follow the universal recipe of "structural adjustment". Nevertheless it has opened a new, a unique opportunity for researchers and politicians alike, to look at the world as single (though not homogenous) unit, to apply a *one-world approach* and perceive all the global issues, such as disarmament, reduction of the international development gap, recovery and equilibrium of the world economy, protection of natural environment and ecological balance, security of all nations and protection of all people versus nuclear catastrophes, terrorism, drugs, AIDS, epidemics etc., as really *common* problems of humankind.

As a result, *development economics*, while keeping the country-by-country approach in comparative analyses and insisting on the simplified concept of North-South dichotomy, appears no more a study of a special case, namely that of the developing countries only (in an opposite terminology: a study of the majority case versus the "special case" of the minority, if the latter applies to the few developed countries) or at best relevant for the "capitalist" part of the world economy. It has in fact become a discipline dealing with the problems of development *all over the world,* relevant for all the countries, and necessarily involving non-economic aspects as well, i.e. more interdisciplinary than ever before. At the same time it has gained a new dimension and theme, as manifested in the concept of "sustainable development".

In view of the reunified world community, with the fading away of the concept of "two systems" in the world, the historical challenge to the South to gain and make use of more equal opportunities for a sustainable development appears almost necessarily as a challenge to the entire humankind. Many of the claims and principles formulated in the *Report of the South Commission* [1990] are not any more the reflections of particular interests of a group of countries only but relevant issues for all the peoples of the world.

The rejoining of the former "socialist" countries in the world community and their increased participation in the operation of international organizations seem to promote or facilitate not only the strengthening of multilateralism[25] and the

[25] On a new multilateralism see *Simai, M.* (1994), and *Camps, M.–Diebold, W.* (1986).

extension of inter-state cooperation but also the placing of those global, common problems crossing the state borders of countries on the agenda of international fora. The World Summit for Social Development exemplifies this in 1995, which focussed on the current social problems of the world *as a whole* (particularly those of poverty, alienation, unemployment, social disintegration, marginalization, migration, violence, unregulated transnational activities and global financial markets, institutional breakdowns, media revolution and globalisation of consumerism, dangers for traditional values and cultures, etc.).

A number of new studies have also been published on the *global economy*, on increased globalisation and transnationalization of economic activities and processes, production and consumption patterns, economic and social values, communication and information, cultures and sociological behaviours as well as on global policy[26], on the global management of resources and waste materials, on global control over dangerous technologies, and, in general, on the problems of *global governance*[27], on the incongruence between the globalized economy and the existing international institutional system, and on the possible ways of solution.

While all the recent developments suggest, indeed, a new, revised concept of the world economy, most of the *standard textbooks* of economics at the universities all over the world still reflect the old conventional approach[28], that of *international economics* as shaped by the *mainstream* schools[29]. They start with the *pure theory of trade*, the Classical and Neo-classical concepts of international trade and specialization (no matter how relevant their presumptions are in the real world economy)[30], and present the over-simplified models of equilibrium mechanisms and the various recipes of *balance-of-payments adjustment* (including also the monetarist ones). They outline the theoretically assumed direction and effect of international factor flows (no matter how "perverse"[31] the real flow of capital is) and touch upon, at best, the problem of the international *development gap* (as related to the

---

[26] See e.g. *Altvater, E.* (1993).

[27] See e.g. *Pronk, J.* (1991), *Senghaas, D.* (1993), *Simai, M.* (1994), etc.

[28] Such as assuming independent, sovereign units acting in the world economy. Even one of the best textbooks reflects this over-simplification: "The subject matter of international economics...consists of issues raised by the special problems of economic interaction between sovereign states." *Krugman, P. R.–Obstfeld, M.* (1991), p.3.

[29] See even among the best e.g. *Salvatore, D.* (1998).

[30] As *A. Koshla* (1995) correctly points out [p. 19.]: "The conditions for free markets to function properly are simple but critical: perfect competition, equal access to the factors of production..., institutions that permit the prices to be determined purely by supply and demand, and an economy in equilibrium. None of these conditions actually exist in today's global economy." We should add: what makes the conventional trade theories, indeed, anachronistic and irrelevant in the contemporary world economy, is their abstraction ("for the sake of simplification") from international factor flows, their neglect of the fact that international trade has been primarily shaped by foreign direct investments, particularly by those of the transnational companies.

[31] *Balogh, T.* (1963). We shall return to Balogh's views later.

concept of "immiserizing growth"[32] and the terms of trade indicators) and the issues or institutions only of the international economic order.

An alternative (so badly needed) concept of the world economy, may be based, perhaps, not only on the empirical lessons learnt from the *historical development* of economic processes on world level, but also on a certain reinvestigation of the ideas taught by various *schools of economic theory* which will be discussed in this study. (In the second part of this study we shall also return to an alternative concept of the world economy and its specific characteristics.)

## 2. "Development economics" as defined earlier, with a conventional approach

The late Dudley *Seers*, a world-famous representative of the "Sussex school" and first president of EADI, published an article (1979) under the title: "The birth, life and death of development economics" in 1979. Three years later, Albert *Hirschman*, one of the nine "pioneers of development", also wrote a paper (1982) on "The rise and decline of development economics". In 1987 *A. Bose* was writing about the "requiem" of *development economics* (1987). *Andre Gunder Frank,* who is well known as one of the most critical scholars condemning the prevailing world order, pointed to the "crisis of development thought" in the early 1990s (1991).

Though development economics still exists, moreover several textbooks have been recently published[33], the question still arises: are we witnessing, indeed, the death, decline or perhaps a lasting agony of this field of studies, or, just the contrary, perhaps its rebirth? (The appearance of textbooks does not prove anything as one can say that when a set of theoretical theses or policy-oriented models, supposed to be final, and "ready-made", is incorporated in textbooks, it may testify both the results of progress and the beginning of the end of any science which, by its very nature, requires the *re*-search, i.e. a regular reinvestigation of the ever changing reality.)

In order to answer the above question, we need to clarify:

- what *development economics* means, how it has been interpreted and defined, and whether its definition has proved correct, moreover (as not only directly related to, but also substantially determining its definition),
- what the very term *development* is to mean, how its meaning has changed in time.

This suggests an investigation, at least a short survey, also of: 1. the history of this discipline (or rather this interdisciplinary field of studies), the development of

[32] *Bhagwati, J. N.* (1958).

[33] See e.g. *Todaro, M. P.* (1997), *Grabowski, R.–Shields, M. P.* (1996), *Meier G. M.* (1995), etc. *W. W. Rostow* has noted [(1990), p. 373.] that "development economics in the first half of the 1980s ...exhibited some of the signs of "being ripe for text book treatment"".

"development thought" in history, 2. how it has developed from the very beginning, in the context of the historical development of the economy in reality, on national and world level alike.

According to the most general and *conventional definition* development economics is a field of study on the less developed (developing) countries which for their catching up with the advanced countries need large-scale structural and institutional changes, a "transformation from backward to modern economies" [*Grabowski, R.–Shields, M. P.* (1996), p. 1.].

As *M. Todaro* (1997) expresses this interpretation:

"it is a field of study that is rapidly evolving its own distinctive analytic and methodological identity...It is nothing more or less than the economics of contemporary poor, *underdeveloped, Third World nations*. ...Development economics ...must be concerned with the economic, cultural, and political requirements for effecting rapid *structural and institutional transformations* of entire societies..."[34] [pp. 7–8. – My italics – T. Sz.]. It implies that development economics is supposed to be restricted to the developing countries only, while economics in general, and the "economics of growth" in particular, are relevant for the advanced market economies. Such an interpretation perfectly corresponds to the already anachronistic, but in a certain time predominant, assumption that the advanced industrial countries as having passed the "threshold", the critical stage of historical development (a Rostowian "take off") long time ago, entered the stage of a "self-sustained growth", a quantitative process of evolution without considerable changes in structure and institutions, moreover, enjoy a kind of dynamic equilibrium, too, owing to spontaneous equilibrium mechanisms or to efficient anti-cyclical policies. It may also follow from the above interpretation that modern ("mainstream") economics is not fully applicable as yet in the less developed economies of the developing countries, or even it may be considered as the economics of a "special case" (*D. Seers*) only which represents the tiny minority of the contemporary world.

For example, *Albert O. Hirschman* (1958), among others, has adopted this distinction on the grounds that the structural and organizational changes that turn a traditional economy into a modern one are no longer necessary in the case of advanced industrial countries.

Similarly, *A. Bonne* (1957) expressed the view that economic growth is "a self-induced process of economic expansion" characterized, under given and unchanged institutional conditions, by changes in terms of economic parameters, i.e. by quantitative changes, while "economic development" presupposes a "conscious and active promotion", i.e. institutional changes.

*D. W. Jorgenson* differentiated between the theories of "development" and "growth" on the grounds that "in the theory of development emphasis is laid on the balance between capital accumulation and the growth of population, each adjusting to the other. In the theory of growth the balance between investment and saving is all-important and the growth of population is treated as constant or shunted aside as a qualification to the main argument".[35] (This explanation, however, is already based on a def-

[34] The above definition involves some obviously vague notions. It refers only to certain 'requirements' for 'effecting' only a 'rapid' transformation.

[35] Quoted by *Paukert, F.* (1962), p. 43.

inite, clearly outlined theory, which connects "underdevelopment" with the problem of "population pressure" and "capital shortage". Although, as we shall see later, many have shared this view, we cannot regard it as general and even less predominant.)

While the origin of the above interpretation reflects both a certain theoretical approach and some temporary historical circumstances, to which we shall return, the terminological distinction between "growth" and "development" on a semantic basis is hardly acceptable, because development always and everywhere involves and presupposes the dialectic of quantitative and qualitative changes, of evolution and revolution. Even if a purely quantitative "growth" can be observed in a given place and at a given time within the framework of the existing structure or system, it is not only the consequence of a previous qualitative change but it also inevitably paves the way for a new one. On the other hand, even if the spheres of quantitative and qualitative changes can be distinguished in space within a given period, their separation can be justified only if these spheres represent perfectly separate closed systems. If this is not the case, if they are connected with each other, or if they are just parts of a superior, synthetic process, their separation makes it simply impossible to understand them, as the quantitative changes taking place in the one sphere affect the qualitative changes taking place in the other, and vice versa.

Any way, quite contrary to, or marking only some inconsistencies in, the above terminological distinction, many publications in development economics have, as a matter of fact, appeared under a title referring to "growth". (See e.g. the title of *Leibenstein's book*[36] or *Rostow's*[37], etc.) But even apart from such "inconsistencies", any distinction between the theories of "development" and "growth" can at best only be applied for practical reasons (just like the terms "backward", "less developed", "developing" which are used to designate the ex-colonial or semi-colonial countries), namely to refer to the different conditions of the development process.

The above distinction of development economics as limited to the underdeveloped economies of the developing countries, thus separated from the economics of the assumed "self-sustained growth" of the advanced market economies, may also explain *why* several scholars, particularly those evaluating critically the changes in the advanced countries after the early 1970s, started to speak about the decline, the "death" or "requiem" of development economics. At least three (or four) important changes are to be mentioned in this respect, which could suggest such a conclusion:

(a) the *world economic crisis* of the mid-1970s and the rise or reappearance, in the wave of recession and stagflation, of such problems of disequilibria also in the advanced economies, which obviously put some structural and institutional changes on the agenda even for these countries;

---

[36] *Economic Backwardness and Economic Growth*.

[37] *The Stages of Economic Growth*.

(b) the recognition of such global ecological, environmental and resource-exhaustion problems, as manifested in the first reports of the *Club of Rome*, which induced serious doubts about the applicability or even the sustainability of the idealized model of industrialization and urbanization of the advanced countries, thereby also urging a change in their development path and paradigms;

(c) the "*redeployment*" activity of the transnational corporations, i.e. their global business and investment policy relocating some industrial branches and activities, the effect of which, as manifested in the phenomenon of "run-away" industries and the (rather exaggerated) signs of a "de-industrialization", has also contributed to structural and institutional problems of the advanced countries as well, and to the decreasing efficiency of the indirect economic intervention of the state, the (Keynesian) anti-cyclical government policy in these countries.

Perhaps, as a fourth circumstance, (d) the *integration process* in West Europe and those new challenges the European Economic Community had to face in the process of mutual adjustment of its member countries both structurally and institutionally, can also be enlisted, although these challenges were mainly arising from the above three conditions.

As a consequence of these changes and new conditions or challenges, the very issues of *structural and institutional transformation* were not to be limited any more to the developing countries only, but became somewhat common problems[38] of humanity and appeared as important items also on the policy agenda of the most advanced countries (at least until they managed to overcome the stagflation and monetary disequilibria, rather than mass unemployment, by a restrictive pseudo-monetarist[39] policy). The earlier distinction and conventional separation of development economics as a study of structural and institutional changes required in the developing countries only have therefore lost the original reason. Taking into account the reappearance of grave structural problems of disequilibria in the advanced economies in the 1970s, many scholars came to the conclusion that development economics should be extended to these countries, too[40].

---

[38] See the *Brandt Commission's* report.

[39] Why "Reagenomics" and the economic policy of the Thatcher cabinet should be qualified as a "pseudo-", not a real monetarist concept, is because the reduction of state intervention in the economy and particularly of the welfare expenditures from the central budget was accompanied by an increased role of the government and its enormous expenditures in the military sector (as exemplified by the SDI program in the US and the Falkland adventure of Britain). In many other countries where the monetarist theory has been referred and used for legitimizing a radical cut of welfare expenditures, often in a "shock therapy" and following a universal recipe prescribed by the IMF, it is also forgotten that the neoliberal (Friedman-type) monetarist theory sees, in general, a possibility of overcoming monetary disequilibria not only by reducing the money supply but also by increasing the demand for money via economic growth.

[40] *Dudley Seers*, e.g., provocatively questioned that time whether Britain was also a "developing" country. Since the late 1970s the EADI has encouraged research and discussions on the development experiences and problems also of advanced European industrial countries.

Later on, particularly in the 1980s and 1990s, the assumption of a decline, "death" or crisis of development economics became also linked with and reinforced by some other circumstances and changes. Such as the following:

(a) Practically all of those attempts seeking for an alternative path of development, different from both of the advanced West and of the Soviet-type "socialism", have failed, while the spectaculous success in industrialization and export of a few "newly industrialized countries" in South East Asia, seemed to verify the conventional recipe of "adjustment" and the copying of the model of the advanced market economies, thereby also questioning the meaningful separation of development economics from the general "mainstream" economics.

(b) Under the obvious impact of the "monetarist counter-revolution", a sort of counter-revolution took place also in development economics, which intended to return to the concept of a unilinear development process in which the individual countries are ahead or lagging behind simply in accordance with their own efforts, with their correct and responsible or incorrect, irresponsible government policy and to reinforce the belief in the universal applicability of the "mainstream" economics.

(c) The policy of "conditionalities" of the major international monetary institutions, particularly the IMF, has forced a more or less universal recipe on all the indebted countries, and encouraged the same kind of "structural" (in fact rather a balance-of-payment) "adjustment policy" (instead of a real structural transformation both within the national economies and in the world economy).

(d) Most of the so-called "socialist" systems collapsed at the end of the 1980s and early 1990s, which not only made groundless to treat them as (either positive or negative) exceptions to the general rule, and to exempt them from the applicability of "mainstream" economics[41], but also raised the question, quite important both for themselves and the international community, whether they (or which of them) would be able to join the group of the rich, industrially developed countries or would, instead, increase the number of the underdeveloped countries[42]. In addition, the very transformation of such systems, the so-called "transition", does obviously involve, as a necessity, profound, far-reaching structural and institutional changes, even if somewhat different from those required in the developing or in the advanced countries.

[41] *G. M. Meier* (1995) notes that in contrast to the early development economics which rejected the universal applicability of neoclassical economics and considered it as the economics of a "special case" irrelevant for development policy in the underdeveloped countries, "many economists now emphasize the universality of neoclassical economics and dismiss the claim that development economics is a special subdiscipline in its own right". He quotes *Krueger*, who stated: "the separateness of development economics as a field largely disappears". (p. 88)

[42] In the early 1990s numerous articles were published in the former "socialist" countries which, either with a provocative intention or with a sorrowful realism, qualified these countries as also "developing" ones or posed the question whether they would be "Latin Americanized".

As a result of these changes in reality, development economics has ceased to be related to a limited group of countries only, and its separation from general economics has also become questionable.

As regards "its own distinctive analytic and methodological identity", which may still suggest and justify a separation, one can hardly doubt that a holistic and interdisciplinary approach, i.e. a due attention paid to the global context and to non-economic aspects, such as social relations, cultural and political factors, traditions, and social habits, too, may indeed be a distinctive feature versus the "mainstream" economics as it appears in standard textbooks.

However, it is to be noted that

(a) this holistic and interdisciplinary approach has never characterized the *entire* literature of development economics, has by no means become a general feature of *all* the theories of development;

(b) such a holistic and interdisciplinary approach did appear also in some of the theoretical streams in general economics, and certain obvious signs of it can also be observed nowadays, e.g. in the new streams of political economy and neo-institutionalism;

(c) a distinction is to be made also between the original thoughts and approaches of those scholars whose theoretical theses and methods are considered to constitute the "mainstream", and their over-simplified, often distorted interpretations in the standard textbooks, particularly their politically motivated ideologized versions;

(d) the reason itself of such a distinction, on the whole, may easily disappear once the entire history of economic thoughts, theories of economics is surveyed, including both the original thoughts of those belonging to the "mainstream" and those excluded there from, i.e. if those basic issues, important questions, and policy dilemmas raised by them is compared to those enlisted in the literature of development economics in the narrower sense.

## 3. The meaning of "development", its various, changing interpretation, and the ways, methods of measuring it

The meaning of development economics basically depends, of course, on the interpretation of development itself.

Development is, however, a much more general and broader term than its interpretation in development economics or even in social sciences in general. But apart from the differences in interpretations between evolution in Nature, i.e. development of new species (genetic development in vegetation or in the animal world, fauna) or development of the human body in childhood, and the development of the human society, its economy, science, culture and institutions, etc. – the meaning of development is not only *ambiguous* but also *contradictory*. It is perceived, on the one hand, as a more or less permanent progress towards a higher and higher level, which can never end or lasts until "perfectness" or "stagnation" is reached, or as a temporary progress only in a cyclical or spiral process, which necessarily turns to decline, to death and to the rise, the birth of a new "species" or system, to a new cycle of development.

According, for example, to the Report of the Committee on Historiography of the *Social Science Research Council* of the USA: "Development is any change which has a continuous *direction* and which culminates in a phase that is qualitatively new. The term 'development' should be used to characterize any series of events in thought, action or institutional arrangements which exhibits a directional cumulative change that either terminates in an event marked off by recognized qualitative novelty or exhibits in its course a perceptible pattern of growth[43]."

*Simon Kuznets* (1973) has added: "Stage theory is most closely associated with a uni-directional rather than cyclic view of history. In the cyclic view the stages are recurrent; in a uni-directional view, a stage materializes, runs its course, and never recurs. Even in the process of devolution and decline, the return to a level experienced previously is not viewed as a recurrence of the earlier stage." (p. 243.)

Depending on whether a uni-directional path or a cyclical nature of development is assumed, the views on development are either optimistic, perhaps even utopian, or realistic, perhaps even pessimistic. Development is often taken to mean a process of a predetermined direction, governed by "objective", man-free, perhaps God-determined rules, even fatalistic laws of motion, or as an undetermined, perhaps even random process depending on human decisions, human responses to new challenges also stemming from human actions. It may be viewed as having a straightforward, unilinear direction or as involving some circular motion or round-abouts. Sometimes it is also interpreted as a more or less harmonious, balanced process or, more often, as an uneven process full with contradictions, disequilibria and conflicts. Development may also be related to the whole, the entire entity in question, or to some parts of it only, i.e. approached in a holistic way or with a partial analysis.

In social sciences, thus also in economics and in development studies, the term "development" is often mixed up or linked with the concept of "modernisation". The latter may also have a double, consequently ambiguous, meaning: it may refer, on the one hand, to the efforts and success in following the example of the more advanced, by taking over the most up-to-date achievements of the pioneering agents (countries, enterprises, institutions), and, on the other, to a primary initiative, a first, "pioneering" response to new challenges.

The former interpretation raises the question whether development can always be achieved by copying the practice, the "model" of the more advanced, and if yes, whether it implies also a catching up with the latter, or depending on the historical circumstances of the relationship between the more advanced and the "late-

[43] *Social Science Research Council* (1946), p. 117. – Quoted by *S. Kuznets* (1973), p. 243.

comer", a successful copying is not feasible at all or, despite some development achieved thereby, it perpetuates the development gap between them.

The second interpretation may lead to another dilemma, namely: whether the primary responses of the "pioneers" to the new challenges lead to real solution rather than to aggravation of the very problems manifested in new challenges, and even if yes, whether it proves to be a solution for all, including the less developed partners, or only for the "pioneers" themselves at the expense of the latter or the future generations.

Unlike in Nature, development in human society presupposes, of course, *human activity*. Moreover, while the genetic development and the operation of the "law of selection", serving survival "only", may work spontaneously, the human society seems to be forced to carry on purposefully, to renew consciously its development process for its very survival, to respond thereby again and again to those challenges stemming from the problems mostly caused by itself and its solutions of former problems. Development thus appears as a must for human society, for its survival – as the only chance for it to avoid or postpone a final destruction.

Despite, however, all the real or assumed differences in the meaning of development between "natural" and social sciences, the increasingly recognized interactions between human activities and changes in Nature undermine the separation of development in human society and that in Nature. In so far as human society is considered, correctly, as a *part of Nature*, its development cannot be viewed independently from the changes in Nature, whether they are "autonomous" or "induced" by human activities. In social sciences all issues of development necessarily raise the question: "for whom?", in whose favour and at whose expenses, which may refer to the (unequal) "partners in development" (within and/or between countries) or to different generations. Consequently, development is to be considered in a concrete "space" and "time", and its "level of analysis", the "unit of investigation" has to be clarified.

The actual definition of development in development economics has changed a lot in time, reflecting not only the above variants and the related approaches of different theoretical schools, but also the changes in reality and a somewhat converging trend in theoretical development (see later).

At the time when development economics arose as a distinctive, separate field of study, related to the developing countries only, the interpretation of development and also the methods of measuring it was strongly influenced both by the conventional concept of economic growth and the practical tasks faced by UN bodies to distinguish those less-developed countries needing and deserving international assistance, i.e. to classify countries according to their level of development. This explains why (quite contrary to the distinction between development economics related to developing countries only and the economics of the advanced market economies supposed to be in a "self-sustained growth" process) "economic growth" and "economic development" were often used as synonymous concepts, the rate of development was identified with the rate of growth in GDP, and the level of development was simply measured by the per capita national income or GDP.

Very soon, however, it became clear and revealed that in many countries a mere increase in GDP does not lead to a higher level of development even if the latter is conceived as an increase in per capita GDP only, because of a more rapid population growth, and that a growth in per capita income does not mean development for a whole society, either[44]. Since development was identified with or assumed to require "structural and institutional changes", economic growth became to be perceived as a necessary but not sufficient condition of development[45]. Moreover, contrary to the concept of economic growth as a self-sustaining process in the already advanced countries, a growth in the economy of developing countries could be considered (similarly to a growth of a tumour in human body) as an unhealthy symptom, as an obstacle to development, or at least as a mere quantitative change without the required change in quality, i.e. as a "growth without development".

## 3.1. The per capita national income index

Quantitative, statistical indicators have always been used for measuring and comparing the level of development of countries even if the term "development" is understood as a change in quality, involving structural and institutional transformation, instead of a mere increase in quantity. Among such indicators the most important is, of course, the per capita national income or GDP.[46]

In the late 1950s the most frequently used "statistical frontier" between developed and underdeveloped/developing countries was a $100 per capita national income level, and later on, after considerable depreciation of US dollar, this was also used as one of the criteria of categorizing the poorest developing countries into the group of the "least developed" countries in the early 1970s. This "frontier" has, of course, changed in time, because of changes in the average performance and/or in exchange rates, but even today it is one of the basis of classifying

[44] "The experience of the 1950s and 1960s, when many Third World nations did realize their economic growth targets but the level of living of the masses of people remained for the most part unchanged, signaled that something was very wrong with this narrow definition of development." This led to "the 'dethronement of GNP'". *Todaro, M. P.* (1997), p. 14.

[45] "Economic development involves something more than economic growth. Development is taken to mean growth plus change: there are essential qualitative dimensions in the development process that extend beyond the growth or expansion of an economy". *Meier, G. M.* (1995), p. 7.

[46] *G. M. Meier* (1995) also stresses the importance of this indicator: "If our interest in the development of a poor country arises from our desire to remove mass poverty, then we should emphasize as the primary goal a rise *in per capita real income* rather than simply an increase in the economy's national income, uncorrected for population change." (p. 7.) – One may, of course, pose the question whether mass poverty can be eliminated simply by an increase in the average income?!

countries according to their development level. (For example, the World Bank categorizes all those countries of the contemporary world, having minimum 1 million inhabitants, into four groups today: "low-income", middle-income", "upper-middle-income", and "high-income" countries.)

However important and useful a comparison between countries on the basis of the per capita national income or GDP can be, it reflects, of course, only a *static,* momentary situation, without showing the dynamism of development[47], and measures the *average* level, thereby glossing over the conditions of the production, distribution and utilization of the national income – i.e. the very factors that are of decisive importance from the point of view of the internal possibilities and limitations of development. It cannot show, of course, under what production relations and in what social and economic sectors and branches the national income is produced, who gets hold of it, and for what purposes it is utilized[48].

Thus comparisons based upon this index (or other quantitative indicators) can hardly provide sufficient and unambiguous results[49].

In calculating the per capita national income or GDP a considerable uncertainty follows from the rather unreliable *statistical information* both on the actual level of the gross national product and the real number of population in most of the developing countries[50]. In the economies which involve, beside a kind of "modern" sector also a more or less large-scale traditional subsistence or informal sector[51] it is extremely difficult to measure, even to roughly estimate, the total output[52], because most of the products and services of the subsistence or informal sector as not appearing in an open market cannot be registered at all, and the prices used for adding up the value of the various products and services cannot be but somehow biased or irrelevant prices, derived from the modern sectors or from international markets. Comparisons between the GDP or GNP data of different

[47] *H. Myint* (1964) remarked: "The fact that the underdeveloped countries have lower income levels does not necessarily mean that they also have a lower rate of growth in incomes." (p. 11)

[48] *Ignacy Sachs* (1964) noted: "All the averages per head of population conceal sharp differences in class distribution and regional distribution of the income." (p. 2, footnote 3.)

[49] Among many others, *H. Myint* (1964) also pointed out that the "low income per capita, however important, is only one aspect of the complex problem of underdevelopment and a definition of the underdeveloped countries relying solely on the per capita income criterion is bound to be arbitrary"(p. 10)

[50] *Gunnar and Myrdal* once stated that the statistical data in developing countries are not worth even the piece of paper they are printed. *Myint* (1964) has also noted that "owing to imperfections in basic statistics in calculating both the total national income and the total population, the per capita income figures for many underdeveloped countries are still very crude and liable to wide margins of error". (p. 10)

[51] "When a dual economy exists – with a division between the modern money economy and the traditional indigenous economy – it is also possible for all of the increase in total income to occur in the modern economy, and income per head might still rise, even though there had been no change in the indigenous economy." *Meier, G. M.* (1995), pp. 7–8.

[52] "...The valuation of the output may also be biased insofar as it is valued by market prices that do not reflect external diseconomies or social costs." *Meier, G. M.* (1995), p. 8.

countries may, of course, be biased, as in general, by the choice of the exchange rates, which again in the case of many developing countries do not necessarily reflect real conditions[53]. The situation is not much better in respect of population data, either. The reason is partly related to the large-scale migration[54] across the (often artificially demarcated and poorly controlled, moreover in many cases practically uncontrollable) state borders, and partly to some of those ways and methods[55] the official census is often organized[56].

When the development level of different countries is compared and countries are classified as more or less developed on the basis of their per capita national income or GDP, a further problem arises, namely: how to find a valid yard-stick, where to draw a realistic division line. Whatever point or level is used as a division line, as a "statistical frontier", it is always and necessarily arbitrary. (The same applies to the variant, which expresses the division line in a percentage of the US national income.[57]) And wherever this "frontier" is marked out, there are always some countries, which in view of some more qualitative criteria would belong to groups of countries other than they are categorized by this method.

In the 1960s the calculations of the American economists, *F. Harbison* and *C. A. Myers* (1964) showed that the difference in level estimated on the basis of the per capita gross national product of the most developed and the most underdeveloped groups of countries amounted to only about one third of the difference that existed in the development of "human resources" (i.e. the "production" of skilled personnel.

---

[53] "Intercountry comparisons of levels of income are often misleading when they are made by converting the incomes of the various countries into a common currency...through the use of official exchange rates... Normally the purchasing power of the currency of an LDC tends to be greater than is suggested by its official exchange rate... Purchasing power parities ... – rather than exchange rates – are the correct converters..." – states *G. M. Meier* (1995), p. 17. We have to add that the very calculation of PPP also involves errors. And it is always a debatable question what to put into the consumers' basket and what weights to apply.

[54] In some cases this migration may involve the regular movement of nomadic tribes from one country to the other and back, which causes not only uncertainties in population data but also many problems in public administration, taxation, schooling, parliamentary elections, etc.

[55] Such an obviously misleading method was the counting of the number of huts from a helicopter and multiplying it with an estimated average number of families in those African countries where traditional farming with rotation induced the families to leave their formerly used huts behind and build new one on the spot of cultivation.

[56] As an illustration it is often mentioned that a considerable difference in the registered number of people between the first and the second census in Ghana was mainly due to the fact that the first was carried out by tax officers while the second one by school teachers.

[57] According to *Benjamin Higgins* (1959): "In general, underdeveloped countries in this sense are those with per capita incomes less than one-quarter those of the United States". But he adds: "The choice of 25 per cent of the United States level as the per capita income dividing advanced from underdeveloped countries is, of course, somewhat arbitrary. It can be justified in terms of policy, but it is harder to defend in terms of pure analysis." (pp. 6, 8)

## 3.2. Other comparative indicators of development level

In order to overcome some of the problems or insufficiencies of measuring development by per capita income or GDP, other quantitative methods, other statistical index variants have also been introduced and applied, mostly complementarily to the former. Such are:

- the annual increase in GDP or GNP,
- the rate of growth of per capita income or GDP (GNP),
- the growth rate of "real" per capita income or GDP/GNP (i.e. the nominal/monetary increase in per capita GDP/GNP minus the rate of inflation), or of per capita income corrected for purchasing power parities,
- the share of different branches of economy (agriculture, manufacturing industry, service sector) in GDP and in total employment,
- the percentage level of literacy, schooling, etc.

Classification of countries by using several different criteria such as above, is, of course, more difficult, but the comparisons based on them are always very interesting, informative and undoubtedly more useful. However, they are, at best, reflecting rather than explaining why countries are more, others are less developed. These indicators are also of quantitative rather than qualitative nature and related mainly (though not exclusively) to the economic aspects only of development. Any classification made on the basis of these indicators may put countries with completely different motives and limiting forces of development in the same category. Countries in which far-reaching changes have taken place in the socio-economic structure, institutional, legal and political order may fall into the same category of underdeveloped countries as others with an obsolete, rigid and stagnant system. These classifications reflect the actual levels of the productive forces of countries at a given time rather than those, more essential differences in their social and political conditions (class structures, mass poverty and unemployment or welfare systems, dictatorial regimes or democracies, etc.) which may play decisive role in determining the development potential and level of countries. Nor do they reveal substantial differences in the world-economic position of countries and their asymmetrical interdependencies. Therefore, such comparisons and classifications can hardly offer, or even contribute to, any real explanation for development and underdevelopment.

## 3.3. Further refinement of the concept of "development"

Owing, on the one hand, to the frustrating facts of growing inequalities not only internationally but also within many developing countries, to the disappointing experiences with several development and assistance programs or plans, to the witnessing not only of an increase in mass poverty, hunger and unemployment in a great part of the world but also a conspicuous, extreme income gap in some of the poorest countries, and, on the other, to the debates, polemies and development in theory, the concept of "development" has also changed a lot, somehow shifting away from the economistic, narrow interpretations.

Now it is taken to mean a multidimensional process extending over the entire society, all members and strata of it, involving not only the economy but also the institutional and political system, improving the techniques and skill of production, the cultural and educational level as well as social attitudes and the quality of life[58], the conditions of freedom and free choices, eradicating poverty and inequalities, meeting the environmental challenge and ensuring "sustainability", too.[59]

Consequently, it either implies

- an explicit distinction between "development" in general and "economic development" in particular, i.e. between development of a country, its society, and development of its economy only (and, of course, the same distinction if it is about the world society and its economy only), or
- a recognition of the fact that economic development cannot be isolated from the development of other parts of society, moreover it necessarily involves social, political, cultural, educational, technical and institutional elements as well, because there are no purely economic phenomena and processes in reality.

*Meier's* note seems to reflect and mix up both: He states (1995) that "...the definition that would now gain widest approval is one that defines *economic* development as a process whereby the real per capita income of a country increases over a long period of time – subject to the stipulations that the number of people below an 'absolute poverty line' does not increase, and that the distribution of income does not become more unequal." He adds that the qualitative difference between economic growth and development is "likely to appear in the improved performance of the factors of production and improved techniques of production – in our growing control over nature. It is also likely to appear in the development of institutions and a change in attitudes and values." Finally he concludes that eco-

---

[58] As *M. P. Todaro* (1997) notes, "Even the World Bank, which during the 1980s championed economic growth as the goal of development, joined the chorus of observers taking a broader perspective when, in its 1991 World Development Report, it asserted: 'The challenge of development ...is to improve the quality of life...'." (p. 15)

[59] *G. M. Meier* (1995) in defining economic development also refers to the requirement of "sustainability", i.e. "development that lasts without making future generations worse off through environmental damage". (p. 8) Since "sustainability of development" is obviously a main concern also of the advanced countries and of the entire human society, it is an obvious inconsistency or logical contradiction to define "development" and "development economics" as to relate and be applied only to the developing, poor countries. It is also to be noted, in advance, that "sustainable development" on a world level, i.e. for the world society as a whole, does not depend on ecological, environmental conditions only, but also on the very reduction of the "international development gap".

nomic development "… may be defined as nothing less than the 'upward movement of *the entire social system'*, or it may be interpreted as the attainment of a number of 'ideals of modernization', such as a rise in productivity, social and economic equalization, modern knowledge, improved institutions and attitudes, and a rationally coordinated system of policy measures that can remove the host of undesirable conditions in the social system that have perpetuated a state of underdevelopment". (p. 7.)

*Meier's* definition is, indeed, complex enough, embracing almost all the important, substantial components or symptoms of development. Apart, however, from the incorporation practically of all the main elements of "development" in the term "economic development", and from the mixing up of the determinant components and the symptoms or the results of economic development, it involves certain vagueness and leaves some questions unanswered. For example:

- what does it mean: "a long period of time"?
- is it, indeed, a sufficient stipulation that "absolute poverty" should not increase and income distribution would not become more unequal (instead of speaking also about more equal opportunities and participation in the process of development)?
- what does it mean: "our growing control over nature"? (should we still believe in our ability to control it really?!)
- as regards the development of institutions and changes in values and attitudes, what kind of institutions should develop and how, and what type of attitudes and values should change in which direction?
- what is "upward movement", and what is a "social system"?
- what "ideals" are to be attained, and in what sense, according to what concept of, "modernization"?
- what is "social and economic equalization"?
- what are the "undesirable conditions" and from whose point of view, and is it only some undesirable internal conditions in the social system which have perpetuated underdevelopment, i.e. is the latter due to internal conditions only?!

*M. Todaro* also concludes that development "must be conceived of as a multidimensional process involving changes in social structures, popular attitudes, and national institutions, as well as the acceleration of economic growth, the reduction of inequality, and the eradication of poverty". He attributes three "core values" to development: "sustenance" (i.e. the ability to meet basic needs, which he considers as the necessary but not the sufficient condition of development), "self-esteem" (i.e. "to be a person", "a sense of worth and self-respect, of not being used as a tool by others for their own ends"), and "freedom" (i.e. the ability to choose, and "emancipation from alienating material conditions of life and from social servitude to nature, ignorance, other people, misery, institutions, and dogmatic beliefs"). [(1997), pp. 16–17]

While his interpretation stresses the interactions between economic and non-economic forces[60] in the multidimensional process of development in which economic growth is but one component, his reference to the above "core values of development" seems to combine, on the one hand, certain very concrete tasks to be met (as criteria of any development) indeed in underdeveloped countries, such as to satisfy "basic needs", and, on the other, some quite general (if not utopian) aims of development to be followed by all human societies, such as the emancipation from alienation, which is, indeed, an old dream of social philosophers. It may also be noted that his three "core values" and the "three objectives of development" he specifies (namely "to increase the availability and widen the distribution of basic life-sustaining goods", "to raise levels of living", and "to expand the range of economic and social choices"), which are to some extent overlapping, also involve certain vagueness, some unclarified notions. (How should we interpret and achieve e.g. "the emancipation from social servitude to nature"?! And what kind of "economic and social choices" are to be opened, and for whom?) A more substantial critical remark may be addressed to Todaro's insistence (which reflects a certain inconsistency) that, contrary to the fact that some of the "core values" and "development objectives" are not quite achieved yet even by the most advanced countries, "...development economics focuses primarily on the economic, social, and institutional mechanisms needed to bring about rapid and large-scale improvements in levels of living for the masses of poor people in Third World nations" (only?!). (*Todaro*, 1997. p. 18)

According to *Amartya Sen* (1985) development primarily means the rise and expansion of various "entitlements" for the people rather than a mere increase in their income, and depends on those "capabilities" generated by new entitlements. Consequently underdevelopment, backwardness or poverty "is not just a matter of being relatively poorer than others…, but of not having some basic opportunities of material well-being – the failure to have certain minimum 'capabilities'", such as of being free from starvation, of being adequately sheltered, etc. The question, however, arises: how such "entitlements" come into existence, and how their "minimum" is determined.

The elimination of poverty and large-scale social inequalities as a basic criterion has gained a greater emphasis also in other concepts of economic development, which (quite contrary to the conventional proposition giving priority to economic growth versus a greater equality) may suggest a "redistribution with growth"[61], moreover in opposition to Kuznets' "inverted-U hypothesis", a reduction of the intra-society income gap as even a necessary condition of economic development. The latter is interpreted as leading to increased economic and social welfare for all people.

[60] He notes (1997) that "…in the past …economists …neglected to view the economy as an interdependent social system in which economic and noneconomic forces are continually interacting". (p. 19.) This may be a correct critique on some, undoubtedly quite influential theoretical streams of economics, but without specifying them sounds as an over-generalization.

[61] See e.g. *Ahluwalia, M. S.–Chenery, H. B.* (1974) and also *K. Griffin, K.–Knight, J.* (1989).

"Economic welfare" is distinguished from "social" or "human" welfare since the latter involves not only better material conditions, higher living standard, and "justice in distribution" but also improved social and cultural conditions for all members of society, respected "human rights", moreover the release of personal relations from impersonalising alienation among members of society.

*G. M. Meier* notes (1997): "...even though it is conventional to begin with an increase in per capita real income as the best available overall index of economic development, we abstain from labelling this an increase in *economic welfare*, let *alone social welfare*, without additional considerations of various sub goals and explicit recognition of the value judgements regarding at least the composition, valuation, and distribution of the expanded output." "Economic welfare is but a part of social welfare" (i.e. the former may increase without the latter...). "Economic welfare poses not only the question of *distributive justice*, but also the prior questions of the compositions of the total output that is giving rise to an increase in per capita real income..." "Some aspects of human welfare might suffer if relations that were once personal become impersonal...and the assurance of traditional values disappear". (p. 8)

Here again, certain questions have to be answered or clarified, e.g.: What is "distributive justice"? Which composition of output may give rise to increase in per capita income? What is the difference between "social" and "human welfare"? And if modernization necessarily involves changes in values, attitudes, then how can development imply the assurance of traditional values? Finally, in view of the "personal relations" which existed between slaves and slave-owners, between feudal landlords and serfs, versus the "impersonalised" market relations between employers and wage-earner employees, are, indeed, "personal relations" to be always considered better than "impersonal relations" from the point of view of "human welfare"?!

Besides the "human content" of economic development its "sustainability" is also emphasized. It is widely and increasingly recognized that it is easier to achieve a short-term success in the development process than ensuring it in a longer run, and to keep its ecological conditions unaltered, without worsening them for the future generations.

## 3.4. New indicators of development

The progressing reconsideration of the nature, conditions and criteria of development and its resulting re-definitions (as noted above) have led, of course, to new approaches and new or complementary indicators of measuring it and to new methods of comparing the development levels of countries, to new ways of classifying them accordingly.

It is particularly the various *social indicators* and those measuring "economic" and "social welfare", "absolute" or "relative poverty", "absolute" or "relative deprivation"[62] and social inequalities, income gaps, and *"human development"*, which have gained increasing role in comparative development analyses. Such as:

[62] "Absolute deprivation refers to the denial of an individual's basic needs. Relative deprivation relates to interpersonal gaps in the income distribution within the poor country and to international gaps in standards of living." *Meier, G. M.* (1995), p. 9.

- Death rates and birth rates (per thousands),
- LEB (life expectancy at birth, measured in years),
- IMOR (infant mortality rate: per thousand life births and/or per thousand mortality under 5 years),
- CSPC (calorie supply per capita, daily),
- Number of poor,
- "Poverty line" (the costs of basic necessities, including the cost of minimum adequate caloric intakes and other components of subsistence minimum, which are internationally compared in PPP dollars, and, in principal, also the historically and culturally varying cost of participating in the everyday life of society),
- Headcount index of poverty (percentage share of those poor in the population who live below the "poverty line"),
- Poverty gap (the transfer needed to lift all people above the "poverty line"),
- Number of physicians and hospital beds per thousands,
- PEDU (percentage of age group enrolled in primary education, i.e. net primary enrolment),
- Secondary school enrolment (percentage of age group enrolled in secondary education),
- Income distribution inequalities (measured as a total share of income received by the poorest, e.g. 20, 30 or 40 % of the population, or as the ratio of the share of income received by the richest 10 or 20 % of the population divided by that of the poorest 10 or 20%, etc.), including the indicator of:
- the famous *Lorenz curve* which, fitted to percentile shares, shows the quantitative relationship between the percentage of income recipients and that of income they receive in a given period, normally a year (by measuring in the vertical axis the percentage share of income of those percentiles of population arrayed in the horizontal axis) and the *Gini coefficient* (or "Gini concentration ratio") which measures the relative degree of income inequalities by calculating the ratio of the area (of inequality) between the diagonal (expressing complete equality) and the Lorenz curve to the total area under the line of complete equality (the Gina coefficient ranges from 0 to 1, thus the larger the coefficient, the greater the inequality);
- *the level of living index of UNRISD,* which involved *six physical* indicators of development, measuring the level of nutrition, education, housing, leisure and recreation, health, and security, and also *one monetary* indicator reflecting incomes above subsistence to meet higher needs[63];
- the other, more complex *UNRISD development index* which is based on 18 physical indicators, namely: 1. life expectancy, 2. population in localities of more than 20,000 people as a proportion of the total population, 3. per capita

[63] See *UNRISD* (1966).

consumption of animal proteins per day, 4. combined primary and secondary enrolment as a percentage of the related age groups, 5. enrolment in vocational training as a percentage of the 15–19 age group, 6. accommodation facilities, calculated as an average number of persons per room, 7. average circulation of daily newspapers per thousand inhabitants, 8. number of telephones per thousand inhabitants, 9. number of radio receivers per thousand inhabitants, 10. percentage share of economically active population in the service sector, 11. average labour productivity in agriculture, measured in 1960 US dollars, 12. percentage ratio of the number of adult male labourers in agriculture to the total number of adult male labourers, 13. per capita electricity consumption measured in Kwh, 14. per capita steel consumption in kg, 15. per capita energy consumption in kg of coal, 16. percentage share of manufacturing industries in GDP, 17. per capita value of foreign trade (sum of exports and imports) measured in 1960 US dollars, 18. percentage ratio of the number of salary- and wage-earners to the total economically active population[64];
- the composite *Human Development Index (HDI)* which involves not only 1. the real per capita income measuring the "standard of living", but also such social indicators as 2. "longevity" (measured by life expectancy at birth), and 3. "knowledge" (measured by a weighted average of adult literacy as two-thirds, and mean years of schooling, as one-third), and instead of measuring absolute levels of human development, ranks countries on a scale from 0 ("minimum HDI value" representing the lowest human development) to 1 ("maximum HDI value" representing the highest human development).

## 3.5. Concluding remarks

In the wake of corrections, further elabourations and broadening of the concept of economic development, the more its complexity, its multidimensional nature, the interactions between economic and non-economic factors, and the need of its sustainability have become emphasized, and the more its aim of improving the quality of human life and the opportunities of social choices has been put into focus, the less relevant the former, narrow interpretation of economic development, its limitedness only to developing countries turned out to be. And the more those "structural and institutional changes" qualifying the subject area of development economics came (back) to the agenda of the developed market economies and to the fore of the very transformation process (the so-called "transition") of the former "socialist" countries, the more it became reasonable or even necessary to extend the studies on development to all the countries of the world. And, finally, the more those global problems, including not only environmental pollution, the

[64] See *UNRISD* (1970).

dangers of ecological disturbances, "over-population", exhaustion of non-renewable natural resources, but also the international "development gap", the related dangers of mass famine, epidemics, growing unemployment, refugee floods (the "march from the South"), transnational criminalities, international terrorism, etc., have been recognized, the more the concept of "sustainable development" became related to the world society as a whole.

As a result, development economics seems to have gained not only a substantially and geographically broadened subject area of research but also a new, additional level of analysis, namely the global one.

From the above, and in view particularly of the fact that development economics is getting to deal with or at least to raise some very general issues, social aims and policy dilemmas which cannot be neglected by the economic and social policy of any country, one may conclude that thereby its field of studies has come closer to the core problematic of macro- and international economics and also of some other social sciences in general, which may question, indeed, its separable identity.

Since the issues of national economic development had always been (as we shall see later), in one way or another, the main concern in the history of economic theories, long before the "economics of development" as a separate discipline was born, one may expect a kind of reintegration of it as a special sub-discipline only, in the body of economics in general. In this case its relative specificity will follow, just like that of other sub-disciplines, from the particular issues, from the "problem area" (instead of the geographical area) it deals with.

However, if economics, at least its "mainstream" variant, remains a more or less "purely" economic field of study with an economistic approach, i.e. with the false assumption that the "economic sub-sector" of societies can be studied independently of other sectors, neglecting the "non-economic" factors, then the survival of development economics (or "development studies") with its own identity may be another possible alternative, in which case it is the interdisciplinary approach having gained more or less general acceptance and increasingly shaping the nature of development economics, which would justify its separatedness from economics in general.

Any way, and whichever of these alternatives comes true, the economics of development is going through a sort of metamorphosis, which may imply its renascence rather than its "death".

The same can be expected in the case of "the economics of comparative systems" (or "comparative economic systems") whose history as a separate discipline is not only linked in many ways with that of development economics, but also shows several similarities.

## 4. Comparative economic systems or development through stages of economic growth? (The economics of comparative systems and its link with development economics)

As one of the main (and for a long time predominant) concept of economic development of countries has been the one assuming a unilinear process of development with definable "stages" which may also represent different socio-economic systems, and also because some of those opposite theories pointing to the specific, dependent position of the developing countries and/or to the irrelevance of the developed countries' model, explicitly or implicitly accuse a certain socio-economic system for the international development gap, therefore a certain link between development economics and comparative system analysis has appeared since the very beginning.

Just like development economics as a separate discipline, the economics of comparative systems was "born" after the Second World War, under the same historical circumstances, and thus also heavily influenced earlier by ideological approaches. While development economics has focussed first on the differences between developed and underdeveloped economies in general, and took into account, if at all, the different systems as causes of underdevelopment or as future development alternatives only, the economics of comparative systems concentrated first on the contrast between the existing "capitalist" and "socialist" systems, and considered, if at all, "underdevelopment" as a preceding "stage" and background or as a less developed variant of the two "historical" systems.

Accordingly, very similar approaches, methods of analysis have been applied, at least at the beginning, in both fields of studies: Besides a more or less common interdisciplinary approach[65], a kind of "subtraction approach"[66] characterized the conventional development economics, and a kind of (let's call it as) "contrast approach" the economics of comparative systems, respectively.

The former means that the comparison between developed and underdeveloped (developing) countries is made by "subtracting" the model of a "typical" underdeveloped country from the idealized model of the "typical" developed country, and what appears as a plus (on the side of the latter) explains its higher level development while the minus represents and explains underdevelopment. If a developed country is characterized by a slow population growth, a relative abundance of capital, an expanded and more or less "perfect" market, large-scale supply of skilled labour, well-developed human capital, entrepreneurial spirit, market-

[65] *M. P. Todaro* stresses (1997) that "economic systems...must be viewed in a broader perspective than that postulated by traditional economics." (p. 12)

[66] *Frank, A. G.* (1967).

friendly institutions, etc. then a typical "underdeveloped", developing country suffers a too rapid growth of population, a kind of "demographic explosion", serious shortage of capital, great many market imperfections, scarcity of skilled labour, poor quality of the working population, i.e. undeveloped "human capital", lack of entrepreneurs and entrepreneurial spirit, obsolete institutions and market-distorting state interventions, etc. (See later in more details!)

The "contrast approach" implies, in a very similar way, that whatever is found on one side, its diametrically opposite is to be found on the other side. Consequently various pairs of contradicting features have been used to describe and characterize the two predominant, opposite systems (of which "underdevelopment" appeared as a variant only or as a subject in their "historical struggle"[67]).

One can argue, of course, that whenever we *compare* different phenomena, things or persons, we normally apply such a subtraction (or contrast) approach. What makes, however, such an approach unacceptable, unreal and unscientific in the case of defining (moreover explaining) the (still originally backward, self-reproducing, or "quasi-stable equilibrium") system of underdevelopment of the developing countries as distinctive from the system of the advanced countries (or the former system of "socialism" from that of capitalism) is not only the comparison of idealized (thus also ideologized) entities but also and primarily the very assumption that what are thereby compared are completely separable entities, independent of each other. This assumption (whether explicit or implicit only) contradicting their historical development within the global system of extending and deepening interdependencies, means that "the intellectual question" is taken out of both the historical and global context, i.e. out of the very reality.

Another similarity also appears between development economics and the economics of comparative systems, namely in respect of the doubts about their future. As a result of the collapse of the "socialist" system in the former Soviet bloc, and the subsequent "transition" of the former "socialist" countries concerned into a capitalist system, a certain homogenization of the formerly different systems has appeared as a general tendency, which, unlike the earlier "convergence" visualized in the light of the rise of capitalist welfare states and reform-socialist market economies[68], seems to question the "raison d étre" of a subdiscipline dealing with comparative system analysis.

However, it is a shift in the focus, namely towards the comparison between the different variants within the "same system", therefore only a kind of metamorphosis, rather than a "death", which can be expected in this field of studies, too. Such a metamorphosis would involve a thorough, de-ideologized historical reinvestigation of the real roots and nature of the former, Soviet-type system of "existing socialism" in the context of the global system of the world economy and interna-

[67] See e.g. *Fritz Baade* (1964).

[68] See the concept of "convergence".

tional politics, and as an attempt, a nationalist endeavour of catching up with the advanced countries rather than a really "socialist project" of surpassing capitalism. In view of all the above and of the growing recognition of that socio-economic systems can hardly be evaluated out of the context of development challenges, nor the economic development of countries can be considered independent of the actual variants of the given socio-economic system, a certain merger of development economics and economics of comparative systems may also be expected, along with an increased application, in both, of a world-system approach (without neglecting, however, the still relevant national/country level of analysis and action, i.e. the still important, though relative and limited autonomy of national policies).

# III.
# The World Economy, National Development and Economic Systems as Viewed in Various Schools of Theoretical Economics Before the Second World War

Though development economics as a separate field of studies, "born" after the Second World War, has a very short history, it does not mean that those issues it concentrates on had been neglected in social sciences before. Just the contrary. As a matter of fact, since the very beginning of modern economic thoughts, moreover, since the appearance of the first "germs" of modern economics, the major concern of all the theoretical streams of economics has been, directly or indirectly, explicitly or implicitly, about the source of economic development, the origin of the "wealth of nations", and the ways and means, conditions and factors, promoting agents and policies of development[69] (and very often in the context of a defined or at least an assumed economic system).

This was obviously the reason why *W. W. Rostow*, the author of one of the most famous books in development economics (1960a), when surveying the various theories of economic development (in his terminology: "growth theories") in a more recent book (1990) extends his excellent critical investigation also to the schools of general economics of the past centuries, including the British Classical economics, the Marxian political economy, etc. What seems a bit surprising is that he starts the historical survey with David Hume, i.e. with the Classical economics only, thereby neglecting the very first representatives of modern economic thoughts, namely Mercantilism and Physiocratism. Perhaps it is because he compares the views of the various scholars also on the "basic growth equation" (i.e. in terms of production function), and such a "growth equation" cannot so easily be found in these early schools, particularly in Mercantilism. Rostow makes his comparison in more or less strictly identical terms such as, besides the "basic growth equation", with regard to the views on "population and the working force", "capital and technology", "business cycles", "stages of and limits to growth", and "noneconomic forces".

In the following, our short historical and critical survey of the major pre-second-world-war theoretical schools of economics which have given us relevant thoughts on development issues and/or economic systems, will be less consistent than Rostow's in applying identical "parameters", but tries to focus more on the differences in approach and in the perception or emphasis regarding the nature, the basic

---

[69] For another survey on the history of economic theories related, directly or indirectly, to development economics see e.g. *W. W. Rostow* (1990).

source(s), most decisive factors, motive forces, and results, prospects of development, including its relationship with equilibrium or disequlibrium, equality and justice or inequality and dominance (perhaps exploitation), market spontaneity and/or state interventions, socio-political (system-related) and international conditions.

## 1. Mercantilism and Physiocratism

These early and somewhat primitive variants of the economic theory and policy of the capitalist market economy, born under the 16th and 17th centuries conditions of the great historical transformation leading to the rise of industrial capitalism in Western Europe, first of all in Britain and France, had already raised, and answered in one way or another, some of the fundamental questions and dilemmas of economic development which are still with us in the literature of the post-second-world-war development economics. Such as:

- what the economic development of a nation implies,
- what its motive forces and sources are,
- where and how the "surplus" (an excess over what is needed for survival) can be created and mobilized, consequently
- whether an outward- or an inward-oriented policy,
- whether international trade or domestic production,
- whether the monetary or the real processes,
- whether the merchants (as "development agents") or the producers,
- whether manufacturing industries or agriculture,
- whether equilibrium or disequilibrium, balanced or imbalanced growth, and
- whether State interventions or market spontaneity, etc.

promotes, indeed, economic development, contributes more to national progress, to the increase in "surplus", thus in the wealth, welfare and strength of the nation.

### 1.1. Mercantilism

Mercantilism (as indicated by its very name) has placed the emphasis on the role of merchant capital and trade in the creation of a "surplus". According to this stream of economic theory and policy, the *source* of the growing wealth of a nation, the motive force, the "engine" of its economic development is foreign trade carried out by merchants. This is because the Mercantilists believed that the wealth and power of a nation and its development primarily depend on, and are manifested in, the accumulation of real (golden) money acquired by means of foreign trade in which, and in so far as, a *regular export surplus* (i.e. an active balance of trade) is achieved.

As *John Stuart Mill* has noted (1896): "The restrictive and prohibitory policy was originally grounded on what is called the Mercantilist System, which representing the advantage of foreign trade to consist solely in bringing money into the country, gave artificial encouragement to exportation of goods, and discountenanced their importation." (p. 553)

While domestic trade accomplishing a distribution and exchange of products within the country may enrich at best the merchant stratum of the given nation, at the expense of other social strata, namely the local producers and/or consumers by an "unequal exchange" (by buying at a lower and by selling at a higher price), foreign trade (and internationally unequal exchange) can make the entire nation richer insofar as, owing to the achieved export surplus (or to other methods, including, as witnessed by history, colonial plunder), more money flows into than flowing out of the country.

In order to ensure a regular export surplus Mercantilists strongly advocated an export-promoting policy and import restrictions, i.e. an aggressive *and protectionist trade policy* of the government.

*Thomas Munn* wrote (repr. 1928): "The ordinary means...to increase our wealth and treasure is by *Foreign Trade*, wherein we must ever observe this rule: to sell more to strangers yearly than we consume of theirs in value. For...that part of our stock [exports] which is not returned to us in wares [imports] must necessarily be brought home in treasure [bullion]."[70]

In view of the fact that an active balance of trade could more easily be achieved by exporting industrial products which were not yet produced in other countries, Mercantilists did their best to urge, force or promote the rise of *export-oriented manufacturing industries*. For this reason, too, they considered the active role of the *State* in regulating trade and promoting industrialization as necessary[71]. They did not bother about equlibrium in the economy, moreover in view of the regular export surplus supposed to be a necessary requisite for national development, they presumed a lasting *disequilibrium* in the international economy. Thus, in fact, they presented a concept of "development without equilibrium".

Attributing the growth of national wealth to the accumulation of real money (money with its own, real value, i.e. precious metal), Mercantilism (at least its early variant, the so-called "monetary system") undoubtedly reflected the "money

[70] Quoted by *Salvatore, D.* (1998), p. 27.

[71] Insofar, however, as the government policy which the Mercantilists called for and actually practised, tended to promote a freer activity of merchants and thus the spirit of capitalistic entrepreneurship in a time when feudal institutions, privileges and disorder had been the main obstacles to the latter, they can hardly be blamed as advocates, in general, of dirigism. The resulting *paradox* which follows from the historical conditions has been well noticed by *Alfred Marshall* (1890) who wrote: the "spirit of regulation and restriction which is found in their systems belonged to the age; many of the changes which they set themselves to bring about were in the direction of the freedom of enterprise." (p. 755)

fetish", namely the illusion of money which having arisen from the world of exchanged commodities has become the predominant factor in life. This illusion, however, partly expressed the concrete reality of the capital accumulation process giving birth to capitalism, and partly reflected the effect of fetishism, in general, of a market economy, which by making human relations appear as relations *via* money, has increasingly asserted itself in economic theories.

*Arghiri Emmanuel* (1972a), who seems to have failed to take into account in this respect the works of early Mercantilists and the statements of the advocates of "metallism" on the natural properties and subjective values of precious metals, was inclined completely to acquit Mercantilism of the charge of illusion, and has drawn a line between Mercantilism based, in his view, on reality and the theories of later economics, beginning already with the theory of physiocrat *François Quesnay* who, in his view, was divorced from the world of reality and was playing at constructed models. (pp. XIV–XVII. and XXXVII. fn. 15)

Though as regards the frequent misinterpretation and misappraisal of Mercantilism *Emmanuel* was right in many respects (particularly if we think of such scholars of developed mercantilism as e.g. *Thomas Munn*, and consider the actual survival of Mercantilist policies until quite recently), yet such a dividing line is hardly correct. Emmanuel has passed his judgement too one-sidedly from a single aspect and ignored not only the false transmissions and distortions of reflections of reality in Mercantilism (i.e. the fetish of money, the erroneous absolute primacy of the exchange phenomena, etc.) but also denied the fact that the post-mercantilist theories also expressed, not less than Mercantilism, but under different historical conditions, the actual challenges and interests of the country where they were born.

The rationality of seeking to acquire precious metals from abroad for accumulation, and later to ensure – first as a means and then as an independent objective – a trade surplus, involved the following consideration which was still justified before the transformation of the mode of production, i.e. the unfolding of industrial capitalism: Since apart from oppressive methods the source of wealth of individuals, of acquiring a surplus in money form was an unequal exchange, i.e. a difference between the price at which an individual such as the merchant buys and that at which the latter sells a product, the wealth of a nation, unlike that of individuals, cannot be increased but by an unequal exchange with other nations.

It also reflected the realistic recognition that the inflow of precious metals gave a boost, through the "price explosion" induced by that inflow, to the expansion of the domestic market and commodity production and to the concentration of potential capital, and that the trade surplus achieved by tax-payer merchants proved to be an efficient means to enrich the royal treasury, thereby to strengthen the State and its army, and to ensure a dominant position for the nation versus other nations[72]. (It is to be noted, however, that the growth of the royal treasure did not necessarily contribute to the development of commodity production and a capitalistic market economy, as the case of those countries, such as Spain and

[72] "The mercantilists were under no illusions as to the nationalistic character of their policies and their tendency to promote war. It was *national* advantage and *relative* strength at which they were admittedly aiming." *Keynes, J. M.* (1938), p. 348.

Portugal, has shown, where the accumulated money as potential capital had remained in hoards or wasted by luxurious expenditures instead of being converted into productive investments.)

*John Maynard Keynes* (1936) has pointed to another realistic element of Mercantilism, namely the effect of an active balance of trade on the rate of interest and also on foreign investments: "At a time when the authorities had no direct control over the domestic rate of interest or the other inducements to home investment, measures to increase the favourable balance of trade were the only *direct* means at their disposal for increasing foreign investment; and, at the same time, the effect of a favourable balance of trade on the influx of the precious metals was their only *indirect* means of reducing the domestic rate of interest and so increasing the inducement to home investment." (p. 336) He emphasized the rationality of the aim of ensuring an increased inflow of money, which cuts usury and by reducing the rate of interest and stimulating thereby productive investments may result in a higher level of employment.

The permanent drive of a country with a mercantilist economic policy, for an export surplus necessarily implied a disequilibrium in international trade and conflicts of interest between the trading partners.

According to *Eli Heckscher*, it was "the tragedy of mercantilism" that such a nationalistic aim "was bound up with a static concept of the total economic resources in the world", which suggested a "fundamental disharmony" there and "endless commercial wars".[73]

Mercantilist theory can, therefore, be conceived of as the first theory of "unequal exchange" with the implication of the obvious inequality of the partners in trade. It was also the first advocator of protectionism.

Mercantilism as a theory and as an economic practice eventually became split in a sense. Mercantilism as a *theory* was rapidly fading away.[74] Even if we disregard the response to it in the alternative theory of the Physiocrats, which partly reflected the failure of a mercantilist policy in France, and partly appeared as the herald of Classical economics, Mercantilist theory was soon ousted completely by the latter and the subsequent theories of economics. (It occasionally reappeared implicitly in modified concepts only where and when the State applied forceful or artificial methods to promote the development of industrial capitalism and the process of catching up with more developed nations.) In practice, however, Mercantilism has survived even in the height of free trade and often in the very policy of governments advocating liberalism[75].

[73] Quoted by *J. M. Keynes* (1936), p. 348.

[74] According to *J. M. Keynes* (1936), while the "mercantilists perceived the existence of the problem without being able to push their analysis to the point of solving it..., the classical school ignored the problem, as a consequence of introducing into their premises conditions which involved its non-existence". (p. 350)

[75] "Year after year and decade after decade, the governments of every country in the world have practiced without interruption a policy of protection. This has gone on for centuries. The only break was the brief parenthesis of free trade that began for England in 1846 and ended completely in 1932. ...Leaving aside this brief and insignificant interlude, the normal practice of the world, since the early Middle Ages and even since the Greco-Roman period, to go no further back, has been and still remains protectionism." *Emmanuel, A.* (1972), pp. XIII–XIV.

## 1.2. Physiocratism

Physiocratism was, as a matter of fact, a kind of "counter-revolution" versus Mercantilism, particularly in France where the Mercantilist policy (in Colbert's time) proved to be a failure, not only in the sense of being less successful than in Britain (which was due, among others, to France's obviously much weaker naval and trade position), but also because its forced industrialization policy seriously damaged the French agriculture and hindered its capitalistic transformation (by imposing increased burden on it).

Thus the views of the Physiocrats reflected, indeed, the adverse consequences of the attempts of forced industrialization and severe protectionism of a Mercantilist policy in their country. But they also reflected in a way the transition from the age of merchant capital to that of a capitalist mode of production (even if such a transition seemed to be more promising in agriculture than in industry in France) and to the era of liberalism.

As their name also indicates, the Physiocrats put the emphasis on the physical side of the growth of national wealth, on the *production* of physically useful, consumable products instead of trade, on the physical appearance of the "surplus" as a product in excess of what is needed for subsistence and for the repetition of the production process on the same level. Thus, for them the *source* of economic development was production, namely in *agriculture* where human labour and *Nature* cooperate to create new product (while industries may, at best, change the form only of the created products). "The corner stone of their policy was obedience to Nature."[76] They questioned the rationality of profit-making exchange and accumulation of directly non-consumable money. Trade, in their views, can serve the distribution of products only. Instead of export-orientation the country should develop a preferably self-sufficient economy that (along with a maximum import-substitution) would exchange products with foreign partners only if it is necessary (because of natural conditions) or, perhaps, if import-substituting domestic production of certain commodities is too expensive. A drive for export surplus is totally irrational and uneconomic because thereby the country deprives itself of a part of its consumable output for which what it receives, the money, is not consumable but serves as a means of exchange only. Foreign trade, insofar as it is necessary or economical in terms of absolute cost differences[77], should *be balanced*, just like the national economy itself.

While they had objection or serious reservation versus a money-seeking, export-oriented trade policy, they also pointed out such advantages of participating in international trade with a division of labour as the possibility of acquiring even such consumer goods demanded by the nation's consumers as not producible, for inap-

[76] *Marshall, A.* (repr. 1930), p. 756.

[77] Here we can recognize the first, early concept of international trade based (not only on differences in natural conditions but also) on "absolute advantages".

propriate natural conditions, within the country, and also of economizing on national labour costs by importing goods which are cheaper abroad. As regards the latter consideration their views may be regarded as forerunners of the Classical theorems on international specialization (namely the Smithian concept of "absolute advantages").

The Physiocrats, particularly the most outstanding among them, *Francois Quesnay*, paid particular attention to the conditions of economic *equilibrium*. In his famous "tableaux économiques" Quesnay investigated the circular flows of products and money in the national economy and the preconditions in income distribution, of a repeated process of production in equilibrium. (This was a kind of precedent for the Marxian "reproduction schemes".)

Since State interventions did a lot of harm to the French economy and particularly agriculture in the Mercantilist period, and because, as they believed, the normal flows of products and money do not require such or any interventions, the Physiocrats argued for the free activity of the individual economic actors, and formulated their related concept in the famous idea of "*laissez faire, laissez aller*", which was the first explicit expression of the principle of *liberalism* (as a precedent of Smith's concept about socially beneficial result of the activity of individuals following their own interest, and also about the "invisible hand" of the market).

While in searching for the "natural", "eternal laws" of the economy and society, they strongly believed in the principles of liberalism, and thus rejected, in general, State interventions, protectionism and subsidized industrial development, they were also aware of some possible dangers and harmful consequences of free trade under certain conditions. They referred e.g. to the adverse effect of the inflow of cheaper (American) agrarian products on the domestic production by depressing the price level in the market and thereby also reducing the income of agricultural producers and the rent of landlords (which, in their views, played an important role in the equilibrium mechanism of reproduction).[78]

## 1.3. The major development issues in the controversy of the two schools

In the controversy between the Physiocrats and the Mercantilists somehow we can recognize a certain neglect of the *dual nature*, of the two sides of all economic phenomena and processes, which cannot be isolated from each other. Namely the symbiosis, in each commodity, of a "use value", a "utility", i.e. its physically consumable/usable nature and an "exchange value", i.e. its ability of being exchanged

[78] It is to be noted that it was exactly this effect of free import on the land rent in favor of which *David Ricardo*, the Classical economist so vehemently attacked the landlords who opposed trade liberalism.

for money or other commodities[79]; the coexistence and interactions of the natural, real, physical or technical processes and social, political, cultural, institutional processes. What has made their views rather one-sided, biased, is first of all the over-emphasis of one or the other side of the "same coin", and the presentation of the suggested policy as an exclusive alternative versus another. With a certain simplification we may say that:

- while the Mercantilists concentrated on the *monetary* phenomena of economic life, the Physiocrats on the *real* ones;
- the former looked at the commodities as a means of acquiring money, i.e. as having exchange value, the latter as goods for direct or indirect consumption, as having utility, a "use value";
- the former identified the *surplus* as an increment of money, resulting from exchange, the latter as an increment of output in kind, resulting from production; consequently:
- the former emphasized the role of exchange, *trade* and the activity of the merchants, the latter that of *production* and producers;
- according to the former the source of economic development and wealth of nations is the acquisition, from abroad, of money by unequal international exchange and its accumulation, according to the latter it is the *cooperation of human labour and Nature* in the production of primary commodities;
- the former advocated *export-orientation*, the latter *self-sufficiency* and import-substitution;
- the former gave priority to *industrialization*, the latter to *agricultural development*;
- the former suggested intensive *State interventions* in the economy, the latter an *economic liberalism,* "laisser faire" and *market spontaneity*;
- the former presented a "model" of economic *growth without equilibrium*, the latter elabourated the "model" of a national economy in *equilibrium*;
- the former applied a *stock approach* (in focussing on the accumulation of money), the latter a *flow approach* (in the search for repeated equlibrium in the economy);
- the former urged *protectionist* trade measures, export promotion and import restrictions in order to achieve an *active balance of trade*, the latter a *free and balanced trade* (if any);
- thus the former visualized an international economy *with unequal partners*, unequal exchange and *disequilibria*, the latter with *equality and equilibrium*; and so on...

[79] This "dual nature" of commodities has been thoroughly analyzed and taken into consistent consideration in the abstract model of the capitalist economic system by Karl Marx. (What surprisingly questions this consistency is his vision about a communistic society without money, with production of use values only.)

It is to be noted that as long as the mode of production has basically remained precapitalistic, the "surplus" (if any) could appear and be observed only, indeed, either as a *surplus product in kind*, namely in agriculture (as a positive difference between the quantity of seeds and the harvested product or as a *surplus money* acquired by the merchants in commerce due to the difference between the price at which they sell and the price at which they buy the same product. Later, along with the unfolding of the capitalist, market-oriented and market-governed mode of production in the national economy, with the marked division of society between capitalist employers and wage-earning employees, more precisely and originally between owners of the means of production and those having only their labour power (their ability to work) to sell, the "surplus" created in the production process has also taken a basically monetary form (namely profit or in a more general term, according to the Marxian terminology: "surplus value", as a difference between total revenue of the capitalist owners and their invested capital, or as a difference between the total "new value" produced by the workers and the value of their labour power, respectively).

While in the precapitalistic mode of production, such as in the system of slavery and feudal serfdom, the "surplus" in production (i.e. the "surplus product") had to be appropriated by non-economic violence, by sheer force only, and the "profit" of the merchants had to originate from an unequal exchange indeed, the capitalistic mode of production with personally free labourers has made non-economic violence unnecessary in acquiring profit from the production process, too, and principally integrated the primary source of profits, including those of the merchants, in the latter as a social process of reproduction which can operate even under the conditions of equivalent exchange.

## 2. The Classical School of Economics

### 2.1. General features and common concepts of the Classical School

The views of the representatives of Classical economics were not only much more diversified than those of their Mercantilist or Physiocrat predecessors, but have presented a far more complex perception of the economy in general and its development, involving manifold aspects. Nevertheless, on the basis of certain common elements in their views and by concentrating on their most "typical", characteristic features to distinguish them, with a certain simplification, from other concepts, we may not only note that practically also the same questions of development have been raised and answered in a somewhat different way by them, but also point to those new development issues and dilemmas they have added to the former mainly in view of the new historical circumstances.

One of the basic, distinctive features of the Classical economics (at least, of the concept of its most characteristic representatives, such as Adam Smith and David Ricardo) versus those theoretical streams following it, is that it has still combined the *labour theory of value and the principles of liberalism*, in other words the concept, on the one hand, of "natural prices" (i.e. "values" as centres of market price formation) being determined by the quantity of human labour used in production, from which it could logically follow that incomes are also determined by the labour performed, and, on the other, the belief in the economically rational and socially favourable operation of an unregulated, spontaneous market economy.

Thus, unlike their followers, the Classical economists have attributed equally important role in economic development, in the growth of the "wealth of nations", to human labour (as the source of all values) and to free, spontaneous operation of the market (i.e. to a liberal system). They believed that if individuals can freely pursue their own selfish interests, an "invisible hand" (owing to the spontaneous operation of the market) would coordinate their actions towards social rationality, ensuring efficient allocation of resources, growing welfare and just income distribution, and also that their behaviour would be socially responsible. But unlike their predecessors, they could find the origin of "surplus" both in production (including industrial production) and foreign trade (even without unequal exchange and disequilibrium).

While the Classical economists were quite aware of the need for all the "three factors of production" (Nature, Labour, and Capital), they have put the emphasis in several respects on

- the *human labour* (which could be considered as the source also of capital, namely as producing tools and equipment[80], and whose performance is supported by nature),
- the increase in its productivity (hopefully countervailing the "law of diminishing returns") as following not only from improved techniques (tools and equipment) of production but also from acquired experiences, from "learning by doing", from dexterity, therefore also:
- the role of *specialization*, i.e. the division of labour both within and among nations, which contribute to accumulation of skill and knowledge in production, and may also represent an additional source of "surplus", namely in the *international trade* based on "absolute advantages" (Smith) or particularly "comparative advantages" (Torrens, Ricardo), and bringing about increasing wealth and mutual benefits for all the partners in it without unequal exchange and disequilibrium.

They have also emphasized

- the role of capital accumulation and savings to be stimulated by the acquisition of profits, the importance of "frugality" versus "prodigality" for the development and welfare of society[81], the role of the industrious spirit of active entrepreneurs and all *productive* people in promoting development

[80] This view has reflected not only a historical consideration but also perfectly corresponded to how *Benjamin Franklin* identified human beings as "tool-making animals".

[81] According to *Adam Smith* "...every prodigal appears to be a public enemy, and every frugal man a public benefactor." Smith, A. (1997), p. 441.

(versus idleness of the unproductive ones who hinder it)[82], thus also the priority of "capital versus revenue"[83].

They have believed in the possibility of the combination of

- economic *development and equilibrium* (assuming automatic equilibrium mechanisms both within the national economy and internationally), but have also pointed to
- the conditions of such automatic equilibrium mechanisms within the economy (Say's dogma) and also in international trade, namely for the "price-specie flow mechanism" (Hume);
- the problem of population growth if exceeding the growth of food production (Malthus), which would be limited either by tragic catastrophes or preferably by the increasing living standard and education of the working masses;
- the need for free international trade without tariffs and non-tariff barriers (except some special and temporary cases);
- the contradicting tendencies in *the international exchange ratios* (terms of trade) between primary producing and industrial countries;
- the "rich country–poor country" problem and the somehow different (better or worse) opportunities of the "late-comers" in development;
- the necessary functions of the *State*, of the government in public services, education, health care, security, and also in the correction or limitation, if needed, of the socially undesired effects of the self-interest-governed market mechanism (Smith), etc.

There are, of course, several other, more or less common elements, even in details, in the concepts of the Classical economists. Such as:

1. the *quantity theory of money*, i.e. the derivation of the value, the purchasing power of money from its quantity, and also the determination of the price level (quite contrary to the labour theory of value) by the quantity of money (if its velocity is constant) under a given available volume of commodities (normally, in a closed economy determined by the possible maximum output[84]);

2. consequently the reduction of the role of *money* to its function as a *medium of exchange*, implying practically a "neutral" role of it; and

3. the assumption of *full employment* and full utilization of all the other resources, i.e. all the factors of production[85], suggesting a primary attention

[82] "Unproductive laborers, and those who do not labor at all, are all maintained by revenue..." *Smith, A.* (1997), p. 432.

[83] "The proportion between capital and revenue, therefore, seems everywhere to regulate the proportion between industry and idleness. Wherever capital predominates, industry prevails; wherever revenue, idleness." *Smith, A.* (1997), p. 437.

[84] In modern terminology: when production is carried out along the line of the "transformation curve" (the "production possibility frontier").

[85] In modern terminology: "perfect equilibrium".

focussed on economizing on labour input rather than on extending the use of available but idle factors of production;

4. the premise of *competitive market* without imperfections, i.e. without concentrated powers or monopolies on the side of the supply or the demand[86], and without State interventions, either;

5. the assumption of *perfect mobility* of labour and capital *within* the national economies and of their *international immobility*, thereby reducing the processes in the world economy to those of trade and the related money flows;

6. the involvement in the "model" of the operation of the market economy, both on national and international level, of a more or less implicit assumption of a given technique and equal *technological level* rather than taking into full account of technological progress and inequalities in technological level, thereby practically neglecting the problems of "different factor intensities"[87] and differences in the qualities of factors[88] in income distribution;

7. a certain confusion of the total value (the "natural price") of the gross product and the "new" value (or "value added"), leading (as in the "Smithian dogma") to the perception of the former as a sum of incomes, to the *division of total value to incomes*[89];

8. the (Ricardian) concept of an *income distribution* within the national economy in which the equilibrium level of real wages is basically determined by a *subsistence minimum*[90] (as an enforced adjustment because of demographic tendencies)

---

[86] In modern terminology: "perfect market".

[87] In Marxian terminology: the differences in the "organic composition of capital" which means the ratio of "constant" and "variable capital", i.e. capital invested in the means of production (raw materials, machinery, buildings etc., the value of which is only transferred in the production process, without changes, to the final value of the product) and capital spent on hiring the wage workers (who are supposed to produce all the "new value" over and above the "old" one represented by "constant capital") the value of which turns into a greater "new value" including the "surplus" over the wage cost.

[88] This does not mean that the representatives of Classical economics were not aware of the importance of skill, knowledge and experience of the laborers. Moreover, *John Stuart Mill* (a "late-comer" of the Classical school), for example, explicitly stated (1896): "Things...which are made by skilled labor, exchange for the produce of a much greater quantity of unskilled labor", adding, however, "for no reason but because labor is more highly paid" (p. 279)

[89] "The whole annual produce of the land and labor of every country, or what comes to the same thing, the whole price of the annual produce, naturally divides itself...into three parts; the rent of land, the wages of labor, and the profits of stock; and constitutes a revenue to three different orders of people; to those who live by rent, to those who live by wages, and to those who live by profit." *Smith, A.* (1997), p. 356. Insofar as the new value is supposed not only to be divided in the process of distribution into incomes but also made up by the latter as its *components, this* concept is, of course, inconsistent with the labor theory of value which determines the natural price of each product by the labor input in its production, from which the various incomes (rent, profit and wage) will result in the process of distribution governed by other rules.

[90] "The natural price of labor is that price which is necessary to enable the laborers, one with another, to subsist and to perpetuate their race, without either increase or diminution. ...The natural price of labor, therefore, depends on the price of the food, necessaries, and conveniences required for the support of the laborer and his family." *Ricardo, D.* (1821), p. 50.

and in which the profits representing a residue left over after the payments of other incomes, namely of the workers and the landlords, depend on the wage costs as well as rent (and taxes, etc.), which practically suggest a "zero-sum-game" in national income distribution[91];

9. the assumption of a *natural tendency of the demand to equalize with the supply* in the product market (as formulated in "Say's dogma"[92]) and also in the factor markets, i.e. the demand for labour to equalize with its supply, and the demand for capital (i.e. investments) to equalize with its supply (i.e. savings), leading normally to "equilibrium prices" in all these partial markets because of high flexibility (elasticity) of the interacting variables in the markets;

10. consequently, a more or less general assumption of the *reversibility* of those processes causing (if any and temporarily only) disturbances in the equilibrium mechanisms;

11. and also an assumed reversibility of arising or inherited inequalities in the international economy, with the chance of the poorer, less developed countries to *catch up* with the richer, more developed ones.

It is to be noted, however, that the very problem of different "factor intensities" influencing the relative prices (as well as income distribution) did appear, in one way or another, in the works of the Classical scholars. *David Ricardo* (1821) noted that the "proportions, too, in which the capital that is to support labour, and the capital that is invested in tools, machinery, and buildings, may be variously combined." Thus "the division of capital into different proportions of fixed and circulating capital, employed in different trades, introduces a considerable modification to the rule, which is of universal application when labour is almost exclusively employed in production". He also added that the "principle that value does not vary with the rise or fall of wages, modified also by the unequal durability of capital, and by the unequal rapidity with which it is returned to its employer." (pp. 20, 25)

Namely in the sense that if *wages* exceed the prevailing subsistence level, it is not only the consequent decrease in the demand for labour, but owing to the assumed increase in the birth rate, also the resulting growth in the supply of labour, which restore equilibrium on the level of subsistence minimum. *David Ricardo* noted that in the case when the market price of labour rises above the "natural price", i.e. "that price which is necessary to enable the labourers, one with another, to subsist and to perpetuate their race, without either increase or diminution", "it will not be till after a great addition has been made to the population, that the market price of labour will again sink to its then low and reduced natural price". (pp. 50, 52) With the same logic, it follows, that if wages fall below the subsistence minimum,

[91] *Ricardo* emphasized (1821): "There can be no rise in the value of labor without a fall of profits." (p. 23)

[92] What is called "Say's dogma" is the assumption that supply creates its own demand because all those incomes created in the production of the commodities which constitute supply, are always going to appear as effective demand for, i.e. will be spent on these commodities.

then not only the increasing demand for labour but, due to the increasing death rate of the working population, also the resulting decline in the supply of labour will tend to bring back the wage level to subsistence minimum. *Adam Smith* also referred (1997) to the case when "the funds destined for the maintenance of labour were sensibly decaying" and, consequently, "famine, and mortality would immediately prevail…, till the number of inhabitants in the country was reduced to what could easily be maintained by the revenue and stock which remained in it". (p. 175)

*Marshall* (repr. 1930), by referring to Turgot's work "Sur la Formation et Distribution des Richesses", pointed to that the concept of subsistence minimum wages had originated in the views of Physiocrats, who "… assumed for the sake of simplicity, that there was a natural law of population according to which the wages of labour were kept at starvation limit." According to him, *Adam Smith* "…when he is carefully weighing his words, his use of the terms 'the natural rate of wages', and 'the natural rate of profit," has not that sharp definition and fixedness which it had in the mouths of the Physiocrats". And although "Ricardo's language is… 'was more unguarded', but there is no good cause for attributing to him "a belief in the 'iron law' of wages (pp. 505–508). True, *David Ricardo* (1821) noted "It is not to be understood that the natural price of labour, estimated even in food and necessaries, is absolutely fixed and constant. It varies at different times in the same country, and very materially differs in different countries. It essentially depends on the habits and customs of the people." (p. 52)

*Adam Smith* was, indeed, more explicit in pointing to several conditions other than the subsistence minimum, which may cause lasting deviation of wages from the latter. Besides the bargaining power of workmen, it is the very progress of society, which can bring about a rise in wage level. He noted (1997): "What are the common wages of labour, depends everywhere upon the contract usually made between those two parties, whose interests are by no means the same. The workmen desire to get as much, the masters to give as little as possible. The former are disposed to combine in order to raise, the latter in order to lower the wages of labour. …But though in disputes with their workmen, masters must generally have the advantage, there is, however, a certain rate below which it seems impossible to reduce, for any considerable time, the ordinary wages…" (p. 169 and 170). He added: "It is not the actual greatness of national wealth, but its continual increase, which occasions a rise in the wages of labour. …The liberal reward of labour, therefore, as it is the necessary effect, so it is the natural symptom of increasing national wealth." (p. 172 and 176)

Although Classical economics represents only a tiny part of the enormous theoretical literature of general economics (not to mention development economics in its narrow interpretation), it may deserve a more detailed and longer presentation in this historical survey than other schools because it had actually embraced great many thoughts which were developed into sophisticated formulas later on, and it had practically involved, at least in "germs", all the major concepts and methods which were picked up and elabourated further by subsequent theoretical streams.

(This is why it can be called "classical" indeed, as a *common origin and base* of the subsequent theories, including such opposite theoretical streams as e.g. Neo-Classical[93] and Marxian economics.) There is, however, another (related) reason for giving a bit more details about their views, namely the *variety* of the latter which is much greater than usually assumed or revealed in textbooks, and which may warn us to be careful with any generalization (even such as necessarily appearing in the present text).

## 2.2. On the nature of development and economic system

As regards the nature of development and also of the system in which it may proceed, no doubt, the Classical economists emphasized, in general, the economic content and determinants of the former and the capitalist, private property based, market-governed, liberal nature of the system which provides the best opportunities for development. Accordingly, they are often distinguished as having an "economistic" *approach* to development and human society, and as expressing, consciously or unconsciously, the interests of the emerging new, bourgeois class of capitalists only (or identifying the latter with those of the entire nation). However distinctive such an emphasis on the economic conditions or forces of development and on the active role of private entrepreneurs in their views may be, they by no means neglected the *non-economic*, political, sociological, cultural and institutional factors, conditions or effects of development, nor did they miss to express concern about the working classes or to stress the role of the *governments.*

For illustrative examples only:

*Adam Smith*, while believing in the capitalist market economy based on private ownership and emphasizing the progressive role of self-interest in developing social welfare, also pointed to that "... those exertions of the natural liberty of a few individuals, which might endanger the security of the whole society, are, and ought to be, restrained by the laws of all governments". Moreover, what is so often forgotten is that when he advocated the individuals to follow freely their personal self-interest, he has also added: "without harm to the community not only because of the restrictions imposed by Law but also because ...built-in restraint derived from morals, religion, custom and education"[94]. In his *Theory of Moral Sentiments* he also referred to the moral, non-economic interest of individuals: "How selfish so ever man may be supposed, there are evidently some principles in his nature, which interest him in the fortune of others, and render their happiness necessary

[93] It is to be mentioned that, apart from the application or the rejection of the "labor theory of value", it is not quite easy to draw a division line (except in time) between Classical and Neo-Classical economics, indeed. Moreover, even the "labor theory of value" itself was not applied (or not consistently applied) by all the representatives of Classical economics, either.

[94] Quoted by *Toye, J.* (1987), p. 161.

to him, though he derives nothing from it, except the pleasure of seeing it."[95] Adam Smith has also argued for social equity, and in favour of the poor and also of the workmen: "No society can surely be flourishing and happy, of which the far greater part of the members are poor and miserable. It is but equity, besides, that they who food, clothe, and lodge the whole body of the people, should have such a share of the produce of their own labour as to be themselves tolerably well fed, clothed, and lodged." (p. 181) He also added: "In every different branch, the oppression of the poor must establish the monopoly of the rich, who, by engrossing the whole trade to themselves, will be able to make very large profits." (p. 198) And what he stated, as follows, about the effect of wages on prices, seems very relevant to the criticism of some "modern" theories of prices and unequal exchange: "Our merchants and master-manufacturers complain much of the bad effects of high wages in raising the price, and thereby lessening the sale of their goods both at home and abroad. They say nothing concerning the bad effects of high profits. They are silent with regard to the pernicious effects of their own gains. They complain only of those of other people," (p. 201)

*Thomas Robert Malthus*, who is often considered as careless about the poor, noted: "...unfortunately the working classes, though they share in the general prosperity, do not share in it so largely as in the general adversity. They may suffer the greatest distress in a period of low wages, but cannot be adequately compensated by a period of high wages. To them fluctuations must always bring more evil than good; and, with a view to the happiness of the great mass of society, it should be our object, as far as possible, to maintain peace, and an equable expenditure."[96]

*David Ricardo* (1821), perhaps the most outspoken advocators of providing free opportunities to capitalist entrepreneurs and of those worrying about the decline in the rate of profits, wrote: "The friends of humanity cannot but wish that in all countries the labouring classes should have a taste for comforts and enjoyments, and that they should be stimulated by all legal means in their exertions to procure them. There cannot be a better security against a superabundant population." (p. 54)

*John Stuart Mill* (who appears as an intermediate theorist, not only in time but also in concept[97], between Classical and Neo-Classical schools) was even more explicit in defending the interests of the working population: He wrote (1896): "...the time has come when the interest of universal improvement is no longer promoted by prolonging the privileges of a few..." (p. 477). "If...the choice were to be made between Communism with all its chances, and the present state of society with all its sufferings and injustices; if the institution of private property necessarily carried with it as a consequence, and that the produce of labour should

[95] *Smith, A.* (1776) – quoted by *Skinner, A. S.* (1997), p. 14.

[96] Quoted by *Rostow, W. W.* (1990), p. 64.

[97] In regard to the "labor theory of value" he stated (1896): "The value of commodities...depends principally (we shall presently see whether it depends solely) on the quantity of labor required for their production; including in the idea of production, that of conveyance to the market." (pp. 277–278)

be apportioned as we now see it, almost in an inverse ratio to the labour – the largest portions to those who have never worked at all, the next largest to those whose work is almost nominal, and so in a descending scale, the remuneration dwindling as the work grows harder and more disagreeable, until the most fatiguing and exhausting bodily labour cannot count with certainty on being able to earn even the necessaries of life; if this, or Communism, were the alternative, all the difficulties, great or small, of Communism would be but as dust in the balance." (p. 128)

## 2.3. On the sources and forces of development

In respect of the main sources and decisive factors, motive forces of development, Classical economists, while stressing indeed the role of human labour and the benefits from international specialization, by no means neglected the importance of other factors of production, such as Nature and particularly capital, thus also the role, in national economic growth, of savings and investments, moreover of possible technical progress, nor did they miss to point to possible adverse effects of specialization.

In their concept of economic development as a growth of total output resulting in a growing wealth of the nation, we may practically find the outlines (with all the main elements) of a modern composite production function, in which the growth of the gross national product depends on the changes, influenced by social, cultural and institutional circumstances, in the available quantity and productivity of all the factors of production, and also on the gains, benefits (or losses) from international transactions (at least, in trade).

One may say that the Classical economists have paid equally great attention to the "real" sources of development, i.e. to the factors of production, and to the monetary processes, i.e. to trade, to the exchange of products for money. But in their views the aim of exchange was not merely the acquisition of bullion but instead an increase, by developing mutually favourable trade and economizing on the costs of production, in the available quantity of products for the nation. They rejected Mercantilism, but did not underestimate the role of merchants.

*David Hume*, for example, qualified the merchants "one of the most useful races of men" who play "the central creative function...in terms that embrace domestic as well as foreign trade". He wrote: "Foreign trade, by its imports, furnishes materials for new manufactures, and by its exports, it produces labour in particular commodities, which could not be consumed at home...in most nations, foreign trade has preceded any refinement in home manufactures, and given birth to domestic luxury."[98]

[98] Quoted by *Rotwein, E.* ed. (1955), pp. 13, 22, 52.

Unlike Physiocrats, Classical economists (living already in time of industrial capitalism) did not consider agriculture as the only source of "surplus" production. They emphasized the role in surplus production, also of *manufacturing* industries.

Even *T. R. Malthus*, who was very much concerned about the rural economy, stated that "...it is the union of the agricultural and commercial systems, and not either of them taken separately, that is calculated to produce the greatest national prosperity; ... a country with an extensive and rich territory, the cultivation of which is stimulated by improvements in agriculture, manufactures, and foreign commerce, has ... a various and abundant resources"[99].

*Adam Smith*, while pointing (repr. 1997) to "that the same capital will in any country put into motion a greater or smaller quantity of productive labour, and add a greater or smaller value to the annual produce of its land and labour, according to the different proportions in which it is employed in agriculture, manufactures, and the wholesale trade"(p. 467), has made, nevertheless, (perhaps under the influence of Phyisocrats) a remark in favour of agricultural investments: "It has been the principal cause of the rapid progress of our American colonies towards wealth and greatness, that almost their whole capitals have hitherto been employed in agriculture." (p. 466) On the other hand, he emphasized that the division of labour (and thereby technical progress) is promoted by manufacturing industries more than by agriculture: "The nature of agriculture, indeed, does not admit of so many subdivisions of labour, nor of so complete a separation of one business from another, as manufactures. ... This impossibility of making so complete and entire a separation of all the different branches of labour employed in agriculture is perhaps the reason why the improvements of the productive powers of labour in this art do not always keep pace with their improvement in manufactures." (p. 111)

The representatives of Classical economics have focussed on *human labour* as the primary source of development, which, supported by Nature, by more or less favourable natural conditions, and by the accumulated "stock" (i.e. capital[100]) as a result of saving a part of the produce of labour performed in the past, thus depending on its productivity, determines the annual output and income of society. They have also emphasized the role of *division of labour*, both within and between countries, in the process of development, i.e. in the growth of the "wealth of nations" and in international trade.

Adam Smith, by applying the *labour theory of value* and income distribution, noted (repr. 1997): "The annual produce of the land and labour of any nation can be increased in its value by no other means, but by increasing either the number of its productive labourers, or the productive powers of those labourers who had before been employed" (p. 443). Consequently: "The annual labour of every nation is the fund which originally supplies it with all the necessaries and conveniences of life which it annually consumes, and which consists always either in the immediate produce of that labour, or in what is purchased with that produce from other nations." (p. 104) He has practically presented a production function in which, given the available size of land, the number of workers and their productivity

[99] Quoted *by Rostow, W. W.* (1990), p. 70.

[100] "As the accumulation of stock is previously necessary for carrying on this great improvement in the productive powers of labor, so that accumulation naturally leads to this improvement." *Smith, A.* (repr. 1997), p. 372.

determine the output.[101] By adding that an increase in labourers' productivity may follow not only from increased "dexterity" achieved by specialization, but also from "the invention of a great number of machines which facilitate and abridge labour, and enable one man to do the work of many"[102], he has completed it by technology, by physical capital, too and particularly by a reference to division of labour. *Smith* emphasized that the increase in labour productivity and the improvement of the quality of labour, as well as progress in science, primarily follow from the *division of labour*[103], which is stimulated by and depending on the opportunities of exchange and the size of the market.[104] But Smith made also a remark on the unfavourable effect of specialization on the labourer, namely intellectually, in so far as the latter "has only a simple operation to perform", which may lead to "degenerative and alienating consequences". [105]

In regard to the labour theory of value, *Adam Smith* appeared as not very consistent. While stating (repr. 1887) that labour "is alone the ultimate and real standard by which the value of all commodities can at all times and places be estimated and compared" (p. 136), and that labour "therefore, it appears evidently, is the only universal, as well as the only accurate measure of value, or the only standard by which we can compare the values of different commodities at all times, and at all places" (pp. 139–140), considered the "natural price" of all commodities[106] not only the manifestation of the amount of labour actually performed in their production but sometimes as that of the amount of labour they can purchase, and more often as a sum composed by the incomes of the owners of factors of production, i.e. wages, profit and rent.[107]

---

[101] "The annual produce of the land and labor of any nation can be increased in its value by no other means but by increasing either the number of productive laborers, or the productive powers of those laborers who had before been employed." *Smith, A.* (repr. 1997), p. 443. 107 "The natural price, therefore, is, as it were, the central price, to which the prices of all commodities are continually gravitating." *Smith, A.* (repr. 1997), p. 160.

[102] "This great increase of the quantity of work which, in consequence of the division of labor, the same number of people are capable of performing, is owing to three different circumstances; first, to the increase of dexterity in every particular workman; secondly; to the saving of the time which is commonly lost in passing from one species of work to another; and lastly, to the invention of a great number of machines which facilitate and abridge labor, and enable one man to do the work of many." *Smith, A.* (repr. 1997), p. 112.

[103] "The greatest improvement in the productive powers of labor, and the greater part of the skill, dexterity, and judgment with which it is anywhere directed, or applied, seem to have been the effects of the division of labor." *Smith, A.* (repr. 1997), p. 109.

[104] "As it is the power of exchanging that gives occasion to the division of labor, so the extent of this division of labor must always be limited by the extent of that power, or, in other words, by the extent of the market." *Smith, A.* (repr. 1997), p. 121. It is to be noted that such a direction of the cause-effect relationship as involved in the latter is denied by the very possibility of a division of labor without market exchange and is quite the opposite to the historical experiences which suggest the derivation of exchange and market from the rise of division of labor.

[105] Quotations from Smith's lectures in *Rostow, W. W.* (1990), p. 37.

[106] "The natural price, therefore, is, as it were, the central price, to which the prices of all commodities are continually gravitating." *Smith, A.* (repr. 1997), p. 160.

[107] "Wages, profit, and rent, are the three original sources of all revenue as well as of all exchangeable value." *Smith, A.* (repr. 1997), p. 155.

Smith also pointed (repr. 1997) to the dual nature of commodities, consequently of the world "value", too, i.e. both to the real and the monetary aspects: "The word VALUE, it is to be observed, has two different meanings, and sometimes expresses the utility of some particular object, and sometimes the power of purchasing other goods which the possession of that object conveys." (p. 131)

*David Ricardo* (1821), like Smith, also pointed to the possible difference between the "natural price" of a commodity and its actual "market price": "In making labour the foundation of the value of commodities, and the comparative quantity of labour which is necessary to their production, the rule which determines the respective quantities of goods which shall be given in exchange for each other, we must not be supposed to deny the accidental and temporary deviations of the actual market price of commodities from this, their primary or natural price." (p. 47)

It is to be noted that in the debate on the determination of the value of commodities *Ricardo* somehow modified (1887) his concept, and instead of identifying the value of each commodity with the amount of labour actually performed in its production, stressed that it is only the "relative value" of goods, which in the exchange "is in proportion to labour employed". In his view, "the doctrine is less liable to objections when employed not to measure the whole absolute value of the commodities compared, but the variations which from time to time take place in relative value." Moreover, as facing the problem of the tendency of equalization of the profit rates between industries with different capital/labour ratios, he added: "Cost of production, in money, means the value of labour as well as profits." (p. 176)

*Ricardo* also considered (1821) the physical output as a function of land, capital, and labour, and their joint productivity, while applying the labour theory of value (to determine the "natural price" of all commodities" in view of the primary role of human labour[108]. Smith has explicitly stressed the role played not only by the divi-

[108] *Rostow* (1990) believes that the "critical function of the labor theory of value in Ricardo's Principles is as an alternative device for measuring the key economic variables in uniform, comparable terms", because "...the value problem could not be avoided" by "using corn" (like Smith believed) "as both circulating capital and output permitting the wage rate, productivity, and the profit rate to be measured in real terms, because wage goods consisted of more than corn...". (p. 78)

The *labor theory of value* really seemed to provide a solution to determine the "centre" of prices (i.e. the "value" or "natural price" from which the actual market prices may deviate only in case demand is not equal to supply) without assuming already existing prices, in other words: without a tautology, since all the inputs are measurable "in real terms" indeed, namely in (labor) *time*. However, its application by the Classical economists might have followed from its historical origin and from the fact that in their time it was still relatively easy to trace back the physical capital to the product of human labor, rather than simply from the "measurement problem". While the latter has hardly been solved by the labor theory of value, and tautology (as we shall see in Marx's theory) has not been really avoided thereby, the basic philosophy behind it was rather the recognition of the fact that all the products, all the values, all achievements of society, including capital and technology, accumulated wealth and power, are indeed, directly or indirectly, the products of human labor. (This was obviously the consideration behind the famous "thesis" of the mediaeval Catholic philosopher, Thomas the Saint of Aquinas, namely that "pecunia iuncta cum hominis laborem pecuniam parare potest", which was one of the early formulations of the "labor theory of value".)

sion of labour, and by the increasing skill, both in science and art, of the producers, but also by the "improvements...in machinery", "the better machinery...used in the manufacture of...commodities", "improvements in agriculture", i.e. the role of technological development. He noted: "...improvements in agriculture are of two kinds: those which increase the productive powers of the land, and those which enable us, by improving our machinery, to obtain its produce with less labour". (pp. 81, 42) Contrary to what is so often emphasized in the criticism of his (and other classical scholars') perception of the labour-determined value ("natural price"), namely that only one factor of production is taken into account thereby, Ricardo explicitly stated: "Not only the labour applied immediately to commodities affect their value, but the labour also which is bestowed on the implements, tools, and buildings, with which such labour is assisted." (p. 16) In other words, he just conceived of (physical) capital as also the product of labour performed in the past, i.e. "accumulated labour" (p. 250).

*John Stuart Mill* also presented (1896) a kind of production function in which "the increase of production depends on...Labour, Capital, and Land", and the "degree of productiveness" depends, besides "natural advantages" and "the use of machinery", on the "energy of labour", on the "skill and knowledge", and even on "the moral qualities of the labourers", i.e. on the "qualities of human agents", and also "on the circumstances in which they work" as well as "the diffusion of intelligence among the people" and thus on "popular education", moreover, on the conditions of "security", i.e. "protection *by* the government, and protection *against* the government", too. (pp. 63–71) Thereby, he included among the sources and factors of economic development certain non-economic, social, cultural, moral, and institutional conditions, too, even the social position of women, the security of property, the psychological propensities to save and invest (means and motives to saving", "desire of accumulation"), moreover such organizational structures as implying "combination of labour", cooperation among farmers who are sharing the profits (i.e. "producers' cooperatives"), etc. He emphasizes that "...a human being...[is] possessing productive powers", an "acquired power of body or mind", including "the skill". (pp. 100–116)

*Population growth* was, of course, one of the major concerns of Classical economists, particularly Malthus. But it was conceived by all of them, even by the latter, as of having a double effect, i.e. as being, on the one hand, a source of economic growth, because of the increase in working forces, in number of labourers, and, on the other, as causing a constraint on development, because of decreasing the potential surplus by increasing the required volume of subsistence products.

They assumed that population growth as a "production of people" is also governed, like the production of commodities, by the market, by its price changes, in the sense that increasing wages, exceeding the subsistence minimum, induce an increase in birth rate, while declining wages, falling below the subsistence level, lead to increased mortality, i.e. a decrease in population.

*T. R. Malthus*, while stressing that "...an increase in population is a powerful and necessary element of increasing demand", believed in "the natural tendency of population to increase beyond the funds destined for its maintenance". However, quite contrary to what is attributed to him as a cruel conclusion, namely that only some natural or man-made catastrophes (such as earthquakes, floods or wars, epidemics, misery, etc.) can prevent over-population, and re-establish an equilibrium between the growth of population and the growth of food production, he did refer to other, desirable methods of preventing an excessive growth of population. Such as developing "civil and political liberty", and popular education, teaching "the lower classes of society to respect themselves by obliging the higher classes to respect them", ensuring a "greater degree of respect and personal liberty to single women", and making the smaller families "respectable, virtuous, and happy", i.e. by encouraging a limitation of the family size, in view of the changeable character of human behavior under changes in material and social conditions.

Malthus actually wished to avoid those checks on population growth, which are so often mentioned as his suggested remedies! (In his second edition of the Essay on Population he wrote: "...it appears that in modern Europe the positive checks to population prevail less and the preventive checks more than in past times, and in the more uncivilized parts of the world." Malthus believed that "the nurturing of those institutions plus the cultivation of popular education would maximize the strength of preventive checks to population by teaching 'the lower classes of society to respect themselves by obliging the higher classes to respect them...'."[109]

Although *Adam Smith* expressed his belief (repr. 1997) that population growth, by increasing the "number of useful and productive labourers" may contribute to the wealth of nations, and that the "most decisive mark of the prosperity of any country is the increase of the number of its inhabitants" (p. 173), also pointed to the expectable consequences of the situation when a country is "fully peopled". As he wrote: "In a country fully peopled in proportion to what either its territory could maintain or its stock employ, the competition for employment would necessarily be so great as to reduce the wages of labour to what was barely sufficient to keep up the number of labourers, and, the country being already fully peopled, that number could never be augmented." (p. 197)

*John Stuart Mill* (although stating that "no one has a right to bring creatures into life, to be supported by other people") also emphasized (1896) the need for such preventive measures to avoid "over-population", as the "effective education of the children of the labouring class... and, coincidently with this, a system of measures which shall...extinguish extreme poverty." He pointed to the misunderstanding of "a passing remark of Mr. Malthus hazarded chiefly by way of illustration, that the increase of food may perhaps be assumed to take place in an arithmetical ratio, while population increases in a geometrical...". (pp. 220, 230, 217)

[109] Quotations from *Rostow, W. W.* (1990), pp. 58, 71.

## 2.4. On the effects and prospects of development

Although for the representatives of Classical economics conceived of the capitalist market economy as the natural and best possible system of the economy, which can ensure all the necessary conditions for development as well as equilibrium and welfare for all, intra-society and international justice, this does *not* mean, however, that they were unambiguously optimist about the results, effects and prospects of development.

They have *not* assumed an ever-lasting process of development; nor did they totally exclude the possibility of disturbances, disequilibria or even cyclical phenomena in the spontaneous operation of the market economy, and the rise of undesired social consequences, class conflicts and international inequalities.

In view of the "law of diminishing returns" (at least in primary production) and the assumed tendency of the *falling rate of profits* resulting there from, or of an unfavourably high rate of population growth exceeding the rate of growth of consumer goods production, Classical economists mostly worried about some final *limits* to economic development and visualized a future "stationary state".

*Adam Smith*, taking into consideration of natural endowments, such as soil and climate, and diminishing returns as well as the declining profit rate, pointed to a possible end of the process of development when the economy approaches its "full complement of riches".

He wrote (repr. 1997): "In a country which had acquired that full complement of riches which the nature of its soil and climate, and its situation with respect to other countries, allowed it to acquire; which could, therefore, advance no further...both the wages of labour and the profits of stock would probably very low...". (p. 197) He also noted that "it is in the progressive state, while the society is advancing to the further acquisition, rather than when it has acquired its full complement of riches, that the condition of the labouring poor, of the great body of the people, seems to be the happiest and the most comfortable. It is hard in the stationary, and miserable in the declining state. The progressive state is in reality the cheerful and the hearty state to all the different orders of the society. The stationary is dull; the declining, melancholy." (p. 184)

*Malthus* was primarily concerned about population growth as setting a final limit to the process of economic growth, unless "man's ingenuity and the exploitation of comparative advantage could keep the old evil Diminishing Return at bay."[110]

*David Ricardo* emphasized the "natural tendency of profits to fall", which follow from the rising wage costs caused by diminishing returns in food production[111], and consequently referred also to the future when the country reaches therefore

110 Quoted by *Rostow, W. W.* (1990), p. 71.

111 He wrote (1821): "...in the progress of society and wealth, the additional quantity of food required is obtained by the sacrifice of more and more labor." (p. 66)

the limit of its increase both of capital and population. But in view of some counteracting tendencies, such as technological progress, introduction of new methods or machineries in agriculture[112], perhaps also the slowing down of population growth, and of course the unfolding of international trade based upon "comparative advantages" and providing mutual benefits (by economizing on wage costs, too), he appeared to be rather optimistic in regard to the near future.

*J. S. Mill* also believed in the arrival of the "stationary state", in that "the increase of wealth is not boundless" and "that all progress in wealth is but a postponement of such a stationary state", but he assessed it far less negatively than others. He wrote (1896): "...at the end of...the progressive state lies the stationary state," and "all progress in wealth is but a postponement of this, and that each step in advance is an approach to it". He believed, however, not only in the possibility of its postponement by means of "progress...in the physical sciences and arts, combined with a greater security of property", but also in "that it would be, on the whole, a very considerable improvement on our present condition". Namely, it would involve a "better distribution of property attained, by the joint effect of the prudence and frugality of individuals, and of a system of legislation favouring equality of fortunes", coupled with "human improvement" and "mental culture". (pp. 452–455)

## 2.5. On the equilibrium mechanism within and between national economies

As regards equilibrium and equality, the Classical economists had almost unanimously shared the view about the ability of the spontaneous market economy to remain or regain automatically equilibrium both within the countries and internationally, and also about its ability to provide equal benefits (or opportunities) to all people and nations.

This belief in a harmoniously operating market economy has gained expression not only in Smith's idea about the "invisible hand" of the market and the growth of social welfare resulting from self-interest-oriented activities of individuals, in general, but also and more specifically, in their concept of automatic equilibrium mechanisms and, as regards the international economy, in Hume's famous "price-specie-flow" theorem, as well as in Ricardo's trade theory of "comparative advantages" and mutual benefits.

[112] *Ricardo* noted (1821) that the tendency of the falling rate of profits "is happily checked at repeated intervals by the improvements in machinery connected with the production of necessaries, as well as by discoveries in the science of agriculture, which enable us to relinquish a portion of labor before required", i.e. to counteract or limit the operation of the "law of diminishing returns" in agriculture. (pp. 66–67)

The general (national economic) *equilibrium theory* of Classical economics has included a system of interrelated mechanisms in the "partial markets" (i.e. in product and factor markets), where both demand and supply depend on the same, namely on the price (the price of the products concerned in the product markets, and the price of factors in factor markets) which flexibly responds to any change in the latter:

a) the mechanism involving the relationship between output and labour input, i.e. the production function;
b) the mechanism determining the relationship between the quantity of commodities and that of money, thereby determining the price level (in accordance with the "quantity theory of money")[113];
c) the mechanism regulating the relationship between nominal wages and prices and relating it to changes in the labour market and to population growth, which ensures equilibrium in the labour market at the level of full employment; and
d) the mechanism of the capital market ensuring equilibrium between saving and investment.

These mechanisms (in themselves and also owing to their interlinkages) are assumed to ensure or always restore equilibrium at the highest possible level of output, i.e. under the full utilization of all the available factors of production (full employment), to offset any effects diverting from perfect equilibrium.

A diagrammatical illustration of these mechanisms and their linkages can be found in *Gardner Ackley's* book (1961). Unfortunately in his presentation the propositions and assumptions of the original Ricardian "classical model" are rather intermingled with those of later concepts, as e.g. of the marginal productivity theory. Thus the historical and social context of the development and modification of the theory cannot, of course, be revealed. (In Ricardo's theory the adjustment of the real wage level to the subsistence demographic "laws" ensured minimum, while in the income distribution theory of the neoclassical marginalists it is the wage level corresponding to the marginal productivity of labour, which ensures equilibrium. Ackley presented his functions in accordance with the latter even though Ricardo had nothing to do with such a determination of the wage level.)

Without going into a detailed analysis of such mechanisms and their interlinkages in a system, which would clearly go beyond the scope of our subject, let us see briefly their main features:

The one-factor *production function* reflects a simplified variant of the labour theory of values in Classical economics, with its assumptions about a practically unchanged technical level of production

[113] It is to be noted, however, that insofar as *the link* between golden (or silver) money and paper money was theoretically established (as, e.g. by Adam Smith), the "quantity theory of money" appeared either as logically invalidated by the general theory of all values determined by labor (including the value of gold, as independent of its money function), or as being restricted to the case of *deviation* of the quantity of paper money in circulation, from that of golden money required in the exchange process. In view of the convertibility to gold or silver, of the national currency and its fixed exchange rate that time, the Classical scholars excluded the possibility of such a deviation. For example, *Adam Smith* stated (repr. 1997): "The whole paper money of every kind which can easily circulate in any country never can exceed the value of the gold and silver, of which it supplies the place, or which (the commerce being supposed the same) would circulate there, if there was no paper money." (p. 397)

and a constant (or, in respect of agriculture and mining: a diminishing) return to labour inputs. Consequently, the maximum output can be attained with full employment of the labour force. This is ensured directly by the mechanism of the labour market in which both demand for and the supply of labour depend, on the price of labour, and, in the final analysis, on the real wage level, which is adjusted, in line with the "laws" of population growth, to the subsistence minimum. It is indirectly ensured by the effect of the total output depending on the actual employment level, which determines, through the money-price mechanism and the wage-price mechanism, the equilibrium conditions of the labour market.

It means that if, for example, for some reason temporarily fewer workers are employed than available, this will either lead directly to an increase in output (in view of the resulting higher profits, that is, by having a stimulating effect on the expansion of investments and employment, and being of a directly self-correcting effect), or, as a consequence of the remaining lower level of total output and in accordance with the quantity theory of money, will cause a rise in average prices (an increase in the aggregate price of a smaller output). If the direct self-correcting effect of these reversible changes did not work, or proved insufficient, then a rise in the price level would eventually imply such a fall in real wages, which would restore full employment, either by expanding the demand for labour or, owing to its demographic effect, would eliminate surplus or ensure full employment thereby.

The *money-price mechanism* reflects – as already mentioned – the quantity theory of money, thus the concept of price formation according to a quantitative relationship between commodities and money (in contradiction, as a matter of fact, to the labour theory of value) and also the assumption of a "neutral" role of money in the economy. Money is supposed to function as a *means of exchange* only. Such an assumption leaves not only the problems of the mechanism of credit money[114] out of the equilibrium analysis but also the questions relating to the value formation of the (real) money commodity, and to the accumulation of the stock of money (as a liquid asset) saved but not spent or invested. Thus it ignores the problem of a possible disequilibrium in the capital market, i.e. between savings and investments, and, in general, the very problem of money functioning as capital, as a means of accumulation. In this way, the money-price mechanism is connected not only with the automatism of the labour market and the mechanism of income distribution in respect of labour (by creating a direct relationship between the volume of commodities produced and, under a given stock and velocity of money, the wage level, and through it between the demand for and the supply of labour), but also with the assumed mechanism of the capital market and with the laws determining the return on capital.

The *wage-price mechanism* simply involves the adjustment of nominal wages to the price level determined by the production function and the money-price mechanism. This adjustment is necessary because it takes place on the basis of the real wage level determined on a subsistence level by the labour market mechanism. (Or, conversely, the wage-price mechanism involves the necessary adjustment of changes in the price level to changes in the nominal wage level.) The assumed mechanism of the labour market makes the formation of wages practically independent of the profit formation and connects it exclusively with the demand for and the supply of labour. The underlying laws are assumed to be independent of social class relations, given the production function determined by Nature and the demographic "laws". These assumptions already express the essence of the "iron law of wages" (attributed to the Classical economists), i.e. the false dilemma, divorced from social and political relations, of "either higher wages or greater employment".

Owing to the then still comparatively low level of capital accumulation, to the insignificance, at that time, of the problem of over-saving, to a frequent confusion of the categories of profit and interest, and in general, to the still extensive coincidence of capitalist entrepreneur and owner of capital, the mechanism of the capital market is perhaps the least explicit element of the equilibrium system.

---

[114] It is worth mentioning that *Adam Smith* paid particular attention to the problem arising from a careless practice of some banks when discounting such *bills of exchange*, i.e. credit money, which, if the debtor would not pay, cause a loss of the advanced money of the banks in question. See *Smith, A.* (repr. 1997), Book Two, Ch. II.

A distinction (and also a link) has, nevertheless, been made between profit and interest by the Classical scholars. For example, *Adam Smith* noted (repr. 1997): "According, therefore, as the usual market rate of interest varies in any country, we may be assured that the ordinary profits of stock must vary with it, must sink as it sinks, and rise as it rises." (p. 191) He also added: "The interest which the borrower can afford to pay is in proportion to the clear profit only." "But the proportion between interest and clear profit might not be the same in countries where the ordinary rate of profit was either a good deal lower, or a good deal higher. If it were a good deal lower, one half of it perhaps could not be afforded for interest; and more might be afforded if it were a good deal higher." "As the quantity of stock to be lent at interest increases, or the price which must be paid for the use of that stock, necessarily diminish, not only from those general causes which make the market price of things commonly diminish as their quantity increases, but from other causes which are peculiar to this particular case. As capitals increase in any country, the profits which can be made by employing them necessarily diminish." (pp. 199–200 and 453)

In the Classical equilibrium theory just as the two sides of the labour market, *both supply and demand depend on the same* as being functions of the price of labour, and just like in the product markets both supply and demand depend on the price of products, so both sides of the capital market, namely supply, i.e. the sum of savings, and demand, i.e. the sum of investments, depend on the price of capital, which is the rate of interest. In all these partial markets *prices* are also *perfectly flexible* and respond to any changes in demand or supply.

A relationship, if any, between the real wage level and the level of the real return on capital (interest or profit) is created merely by the given amount of total income (gross output) or, more precisely, by the distribution of the amount left over after the deduction of land rents.[115] This relationship has a one-way direction: the residue left over after the payment of the "natural" (equilibrium) price of labour is the natural return on capital (the "dependent variable" proper).

The latter assumption, i.e. that the return on capital, at given gross output, is a function of wages, seems to be a logical antecedent of those old and "new"[116] theories which interpret wages as an "independent variable"[117].

A few assumptions and propositions of the general equilibrium theory of the representatives of the Classical economics are also included, partly explicitly, partly implicitly, in their theory relating to the *international economy*, while others are excluded from it.

---

[115] *Adam Smith's* income distribution theory, just as his value determination, includes (as already noted) other variants (obviously contradicting his labor theory of value), such as the concept of basic incomes as components of price formation, in which case it is not incomes that depend on price changes (and on changes in "values" behind them) but the other way around. In regard *to rent*, Smith emphasized (repr. 1997) its monopoly nature: "The rent of land...considered as the price paid for the use of the land, is naturally a monopoly price." (p. 249)

[116] See more on this point in the subchapter discussing *Emmanuel*'s theory.

[117] Quite contrary to this assumed general relationship, *Adam Smith* actually pointed (repr. 1997) to cases when profits appeared as independent variable: "In reality high profits tend much more to raise the price of work than high wages." (p. 200)

The labour-value principle, the determination of "natural prices" by the amount of labour absorbed (actually performed in the production of a product)[118], which anyway came into contradiction with the money-price mechanism as an essential element of the equilibrium theory outlined on the basis of the "quantity theory of money", has been neglected in the Classical theory of international economy. So is also the process of international flow of capital and thereby a tendency of the equalization of the rates of profit. (The same applies practically to the "law of diminishing return").

We must note here that the "law of diminishing return", which played such an important role in Ricardo's distribution theory and in the critical explanation of the rising rent of landowners as well as in the arguments for free trade and international division of labour, strangely enough was hardly included among the premises in his theory of international trade and specialization. It has rather been replaced by the assumption of *constant returns to scale,* constant "opportunity costs". This is because the assumption of a general, international validity of the "law of diminishing return" would have made questionable (as in the case of Bastable and others) the benefits from specialization, the rationality of the concentration of production of specific goods in certain countries. The acceptance of an unequal international allocation of the branches of production behaving differently in respect of cost changes (branches with diminishing or increasing returns) would have made doubtful, indeed, the mutually beneficial nature of the international division of labour (as in the case of *Graham* and others).

As regards the *export of capital*, the representatives of the Classical school were aware, of course, of its possibility and actual practice, but they either underestimated its importance, in view of the assumed reluctance of the owner of capital to emigrate or to take the risk of investing abroad, or they reduced its role to a derivative from trade.

*Adam Smith* noted (repr. 1997): "It is of more consequence that the capital of the manufacturer should reside within the country. It necessarily puts into motion a greater quantity of productive labour, and adds a greater value to the annual produce of the land and labour of the society." (p. 464.)

Although referring to the possible "idleness" of capital at home as a reason of its export, Smith practically reduced the function of the latter to trade business: "...the money which ...is annually thrown out of domestic circulation, will not be allowed to lie idle. The interest of whoever possesses it requires that it should be employed. But having no employment at home, it will, in spite of all laws and prohibitions, be sent abroad, and employed in purchasing consumable goods which may be of some use at home." (p. 440)

*David Ricardo* stated (1821): "Experience...shows, that the fancied or real insecurity of capital, when not under the immediate control of its owner, together with the natural disinclination which every man has to quit the country of his birth and connexions, and trust in himself, with all his habits fixed, to a strange government and new laws, check the emigration of capital." (p. 77)

Although for *John Stuart Mill* it was quite obvious (1896) that: "Money is sent from one country to another for various purposes; such as the payment of tributes or subsidies; remittances of revenue to or

[118] "The same rule which regulates the relative value of commodities in one country does not regulate the relative value of the commodities exchanged between two or more countries." *Ricardo, D.* (1821), p. 75.

from dependencies, or of rents or other incomes to their absent owners; emigration of capital, or transmission of it for foreign investment", nevertheless he seemed to share more or less the same view as Ricardo: "...between different countries...there may exist great inequalities in the return to labour and capital, without causing them to move from one place to the other in such quantity as to level those inequalities. The capital belonging to a country will, to a great extent, remain in the country...". (pp. 348, 370)

*International economic relations* – according to their views – comprise the sum of the bilateral trade relations of national economies based upon a mutually favourable division of labour between them. The above discussed elements of the general equilibrium system and the market mechanisms within the individual national economies, ensuring full employment and total investment of all the available savings, i.e. full utilization of all capital, play an important role also in the operation of the international economy.

The "price-specie-flow" (or "gold-flow" or "specie-flow-price level") *mechanism of international equilibrium that* is practically an automatic adjustment of the price levels (thus it may also be called as "automatic price-level equilibrium mechanism") is based upon

a) the premise of "perfect" (full employment) equilibrium within the partner national economies, maintained or restored by the above-described automatism of their partial markets (product as well as factor markets) in which both demand and supply depends on the same, flexibly changing (perfectly elastic) price, and also the interconnection of these partial markets;
b) free trade conditions, i.e. the possibility of free flow of products and money between countries without tariff or non-tariff barriers or other state interventions;
c) the operation of the same ("real"[119], golden) money within the partner countries and in their international exchange relations (or of a money perfectly convertible to gold in fixed exchange rate, i.e. of a "gold standard"), which makes all the prices and price changes directly (or indirectly) expressed in the same money; and
d) the assumed validity of the "quantity theory of money", according to which a change in the quantity of money as well as a change in the quantity of supplied products leads to a proportional change in prices, and vice versa (if the velocity of money does not change).

Consequently, if, for any reasons, in the trade relations between two countries a disequilibrium appears, i.e. one of the countries imports more from the other than exports into it, which means that the latter exports more than imports, then the prices (measured in the same money) will decline in the former and rise in the lat-

[119] "Real money" is often distinguished from "paper money" in the sense that the former is a valuable asset in itself even if not functioning as money, such as gold or silver, while the latter, as a piece of paper has got a negligible value of its own as compared to that attributed to it as money. See also *Smith, A.* (1997), Book Two, Ch. 2.

ter (because the quantity of available products has increased, due to a greater inflow of products, and the quantity of money has decreased, because of its greater outflow from the former country, while the opposite is the case in the latter). Such a change in the prices in both countries will result then in an opposite tendency: the former (trade deficit) country where prices decline will be able to export more and import less than before, while the other (trade surplus) country with her increased prices will import more and be able to export less than before. In such a way the very disequilibrium induces opposite process, which restores equilibrium, which means that the processes are normally reversible, according to this Classical view.

## 2.6. On international trade and specialization

The Classical trade theory, including, of course, both Smith's concept of "absolute advantages" and the theory of Torrens and Ricardo of "comparative advantages", has also reinforced the belief in the harmony of interests if, indeed, the liberal principles of the economy are realized[120].

The *Smithian* concept, the germ of which had already appeared in Physiocrat views[121], was based upon a fairly simple and logical consideration. Namely: if labour productivity in producing a certain product is higher in a country than in another one, while the latter's labour is more productive than the former's in another field of production, then both countries may benefit from a division of labour and trade in which the first country specializes on that product produced with higher productivity, while the second country, following the same rule, also specializes and produces for export, too, the product in which her higher productivity implies an "absolute advantage" vis-à-vis the partner country. (Such a specialization corresponds also to the interest of rationalizing the use of resources and necessarily follows, in the views of Smith, also from the natural process of development[122].

[120] In favor of international trade and trade liberalism, *Adam Smith* made, among others, the following remark: "A country which neglects or despises foreign commerce, and which admits the vessels of foreign nations into one or two of its ports only, cannot transact the same quantity of business which it might do with different laws and institutions." (pp. 197–198)

[121] Another similarity between the views of the Physiocrats and Adam Smith appears in a certain preference of domestic trade versus foreign trade. *Smith* noted (repr. 1997): "The capital…employed in the home trade of any country will generally give encouragement and support to a greater quantity of productive labor in that country, and increase the value of its annual produce more than an equal capital employed in the foreign trade…". (p. 472)

[122] "If the society has not acquired sufficient capital both to cultivate all its lands, and to manufacture in the complete manner the whole of its rude produce, there is even a considerable advantage that the rude produce should be exported by a foreign capital, in order that the whole stock of the society may be employed in more useful purposes." "According to the natural course of things, …the greater part of the capital of every growing society is, first, directed to agriculture, afterwards to manufactures, and last of all to foreign commerce." *Smith, A.* (1997), p. 483.

The (Torrens-) *Ricardian* "law of specialization according to *comparative advantages*" goes further in logic, and suggests a possible trade with mutual benefits for the partner countries even in the case when one of the two countries happens to have higher labour productivity in the production of both products, i.e. when this country can produce both products at lower (labour) costs. Thus this concept is based upon an international comparison of the national costs (measured in labour time) of the same two products (or of the labour productivities in the production of these two products). In other words, it is based upon a comparison between the calculated *relative* labour costs (or relative labour productivities), which implies the revealing (normally by the market which gives signals about prices) of a difference either between the relative (national) costs of the two ($x$ and $y$) products in the two ($A$ and $B$) countries (i.e. $Px : Py$ in country $A$ and country $B$), or conversely: between the relative international cost of each product (i.e. $PA : PB$ of product $x$ and of product $y$), where the relative costs are calculated as the ratios of the cost of $x$ and $y$.

Applying Ricardo's example, this means that if, related to the cost of producing a unit of wine, the comparative cost of making a unit of cloth is lower in England than in Portugal, while, related to the cost of cloth-making, the comparative cost of producing wine is lower in Portugal (or, with another approach, if, computed on the basis of the cost/price level in Portugal, the cost of making cloth in England is lower than that of producing wine, while the cost of producing wine in Portugal, computed on the basis of the cost/price level in England, is lower than that of cloth-making), then it is worthwhile for England to specialize on cloth-making and for Portugal to produce wine for export, too. This is so even if the absolute cost in the case of both products happens to be lower in Portugal, i.e. if this country has an absolute advantage in both products.

It means that if each of the partner countries specializes on that particular product in the production of which enjoys the *greatest absolute advantage* or suffers the *smallest absolute disadvantage,* then, as a result of such an international division of labour, each nation and the world society as a whole will benefit there from[123]. Each country will have available a quantity of products which exceeds its own productive capacities, and total world output (and income) will also increase substantially.

No doubt, if we accept the explicit and implicit assumptions of Ricardo's theory of comparative advantages or to the extent to which they prove, within definite limits in time and space, to be realistic, then this concept may be a suitable tool, a useful practical method not only for analysing the various historical cases of development but also for the development policy of a nation state in regard to stimulating certain export industries and specialization of the national economy.

123 "...it is not a difference in the *absolute* cost of production, which determines the interchange, but a difference in the *comparative* cost." *Mill, J. S.* (1896), p. 348.

Some of these *assumptions*, however, make Ricardo's approach, and the computation method recommended by him static and oversimplified to such an extent that its application is possible only in the short run and within narrow scope and only under some ideal conditions, which remain unchanged. Such assumptions of a static character and effect are, among others, the appraisal of natural conditions practically divorced from the development level of the productive forces, of science, technology[124] and social relations, and the disregard of technological progress and infrastructural development as well as the "internal" and "external economies", which basically influence the production function and cost ratios. In other words, the neglect, in general, of the dynamics of social productive forces in their broad sense, of their effect eliminating comparative disadvantages and disclosing new "dynamic comparative advantages".[125]

It is, for example, extremely oversimplifying (and historically unrealistic) to assume the *full employment* at any time of the factor of production and its unrestricted mobility within the national economy; to assume an unlimited substitutability of concrete varieties of labour and their transferability among the various branches of production, i.e. to assume *homogeneous units* of labour, thereby neglecting the differences in skill, trade and quality of labour[126]; and to assume an identity or even a close correlation between relative price and relative cost ratios[127]; to abstract from the problem of the international comparability of national costs; to assume a neutral nature of money and to neglect debtor–creditor relationships; to forget about the natural constraints on the feasibility of produc-

[124] Although the calculation of comparative costs reflects, indeed, a static approach, i.e. a neglect of technological progress, it is to be noted that *David Ricardo* (1821) had not excluded (in his example, p. 78) the change in the relative costs in case of an improvement in the production process. Moreover, he referred to "the improvements in arts and machinery, which are constantly operating on the natural course of trade" (p. 81). Adam Smith also mentioned (1997) "improvements in machinery" (p.115), but as the results of division of labor which improve "dexterity".

[125] This terminological distinction was clearly made by *Vajda, I.* (1965), pp. 253–254.

[126] Such a neglect, in the theory of international trade and specialization, of the differences in the quality of labor is rather surprising as in another context they are explicitly noted, e.g. by *Adam Smith* (1997): "...if the one species of labor requires an uncommon degree of dexterity and ingenuity, the esteem, which men have for such talents will naturally give a value to their produce, superior to what would be due to the time employed about it." (p. 150) Moreover, *Smith* already referred (like Marx later on) to the time spent on education as an increase not only in the quality of labor but also in its value-creating ability: "There may be more labor in an hour's hard work than in two hours' easy business; or in an hour's application to a trade which it cost ten years' labor to learn, than in a month's industry at an ordinary and obvious employment." (p. 134)

[127] *Arghiri Emmanuel* (1972a) has provided, by the way, convincing evidence by the numerical example of a modified variant of the Ricardian scheme that in the (real) case of differences in the "organic composition of capital" even a slight international deviation of the wage level is sufficient to upset the structure of comparative advantages, more exactly, to cause the international division of labor built upon comparative costs to develop losses for the world as a whole. Moreover, a different change, owing to socio-cultural development, in the "organic composition of labor" in the partner countries may reverse the distribution of comparative advantages. (pp. 245–253)

ing certain products in a country, about the monopoly over some natural resources[128] or about technological monopoly in one or another productive branch of economy; to leave the differences in *consumption patterns*, consumer preferences or their international demonstration effects out of consideration; and, particularly, to disregard the *international flows of capital*.

A serious theoretical deficiency in Ricardo's concept, stemming from the above simplifying premises and the static approach, is the indifference to the size and the inequalities of the developmental potentials of the production structure and endowments of the national economies concerned, thereby neglecting the direct and indirect *structural effects* of the type of specialization, the economic (production) and social linkages and spread effects generated by the latter, and, in general, the differences and changes in the pattern of social relations; in other words the lack of a historical, social and structural approach.

Even those of Ricardo's assumptions which could originally be more or less justified in the given time and place have become anachronistic since his time and irrelevant for other parts of the world. This is the case for example, on the one hand, regarding the abstraction from the international mobility of the factors of production, particularly of capital, and, on the other, regarding the assumption of equal partners, of independent countries entering trade relationship at a relatively identical development level.

It should be added that even if all the premises and the preconditions for applying Ricardo's concept are realized, the question still arises whether the *kind of specialization*, the type of export product and export industry, developed in accordance with and ensuring comparative advantages, would indeed be the best, the most favourable for promoting the development of the national economy in the long run. This is so, because different products, different export sectors do not stimulate equally, do not provide equal opportunities for the improvement of the quality of labour and development of "human capital", for technological progress and for the development, *via* input–output linkages, of the domestic market, which are of primary importance in determining the future development of a national economy.

### 2.6.1. Empirical tests of the Classical trade theory

Though the actual validity of the Classical concept of specialization according to comparative advantages in the historical reality of the world economy can be seriously doubted in view of and because (if not for other reasons as well) quite a

[128] It is worth mentioning that *Ricardo* was otherwise aware of the fact of monopoly prices in certain fields. He noted (1821) about those "commodities, which are monopolized" that "their price has no necessary connnection with their natural value". (p. 234)

number of countries have been actually forced to specialize according to foreign interests, several attempts were made to test it empirically, which have produced useful methods.

Such an attempt was made e.g. by *G. D. A. MacDougal* (1951) who compared relative labour productivities (output per worker) and relative export shares between US and British industries in a given year, and found a positive correlation between a higher ratio of the US productivity to the British productivity in a given industry (i.e. a higher relative productivity of US labour) and a higher ratio of the share of US exports to that of the British exports (i.e. a relative share of US exports) directed to third markets. In other words, the greater was the assumed comparative advantage in the Ricardian sense, i.e. in relative labour productivity, of the US in certain industries relative to the British ones, in most cases the greater was in them the ratio of the US exports to the British ones.

*Béla Balassa* (1965) followed MacDougal's attempts to test the relevance of the Classical, Ricardian thesis. He introduced a new, simple method (without measuring comparative costs) for the evaluation of comparative advantages in international trade, namely the calculation of the index of *"revealed comparative advantages"* (pp. 99–124) The latter has (at least[129]) 2 variants: (a) an RCA index measuring the ratio of the share of a particular product (or industry) in the country's total exports to that in her total imports; (b) another RCA index which measures the share of a particular product (or industry) in the country's total exports relative to the share of the same products (or industry) in total world exports.

If the ratio (calculated according to the above variants) is greater than unity it is supposed to mean that the country realizes comparative advantage in the trade of the product (or industry) in question.

As a matter of fact the *RCA index* (in whichever variant) is unable to reveal indeed which product (or industry) provides comparative advantage to which country. This concept of "revealed comparative advantages" tacitly assumes that countries have *de facto* specialized already according to their comparative advantages and the higher value of an RCA index does reflect *ex post* such a specialization.

Even apart from its neglect of the well-known problem of the various obstacles, restrictions and distortions in reality, such as State interventions, protectionism, tariff and non-tariff barriers, market imperfections, dominance relations between the trading partners, trade diverting and distorting effects, restrictive business practices, cyclical fluctuations and disequilibria, etc. which have often prevented the basic assumptions of the Ricardian (and other) theories from being realized, the RCA concept involves also a methodological weakness. (At least insofar as it is expected to rank unambiguously the various products or industries according to the assumed comparative advantages of individual countries.) It may often happen that the same product or industry in the production and trade of which a given

[129] As a matter of fact, *Béla Balassa* has applied some other variants, too.

country registers the highest RCA index among all the partner countries, i.e. internationally, does not command the highest RCA index among the alternative products or industries within the country concerned, i.e. internally, and *vice versa*.[130]

Despite, however, all their obvious shortcomings the application of RCA indexes may, no doubt, help us by relevant inter-country and inter-industry comparisons in the analysis of the actual patterns of international trade and the structural position of the individual countries in it.

Another concept (or index) is also worth mentioning in the context of the theory of international specialization: the *Maizels index*[131] which is to give us certain information on trade-related "structural adjustment", on whether the direction of changes in the proportions of individual industries in a given country corresponds to its "revealed comparative advantages". The Maizels index measures for the individual industries in a country the rate of growth of their share in the total value added, weighted by their share in total exports. In other words, it calculates the weighted growth rates of sectoral shares in total value added and uses as weights the shares of each sector of production in total exports of the country concerned. Insofar as this index reflects indeed comparative advantages (which as a general assumption is just as doubtful as in the case of the Balassa index) it certainly sheds light on the relationship between change in the domestic production structure and the export specialization.

### 2.6.2. Implications and weaknesses of the Classical trade theory

The Ricardian theory of international division of labour and the above-described "price-specie-flow" mechanism of international equilibrium are, of course, connected with each other[132].

Internationally, the money–price mechanism of the general (national economic) equilibrium mechanism affects, and is connected with, the assumed equilibrium mechanism of the international economy in such a way that the transfer of the surplus quantity of money abroad or its equalization by additional imports of products from abroad (and, conversely, the completion of the less than necessary quantity of money from abroad, or the export of the surplus quantity of products) restores, owing to the price changes induced thereby, both the internal (national economic) equilibrium and the equilibrium of international trade.

---

130 See *Yeats, A. J.* (1985).

131 See *Maizels, A.* (1982), and a reference to it in *Rodrik, D.* (1982).

132 Here again, we may agree with *Arghiri Emmanuel* (1972a) who stated (p. 240) that the derivation from barter and the delimination from money economy of the law of comparative costs in Ohlin, Samuelson and others is a complete misunderstanding of the Ricardian theory. Without the Ricardian money mechanism even the assumed system of international division of labor based on comparative costs cannot unfold and work harmoniously.

Should a large-scale divergence in the national costs of production develop a deficit, owing to purchases from the country with lower production costs, in the trade balance of a country, then on the one hand, the rise, caused by money flow in the price level of the exporting country would diminish the divergence in the cost level and the purchases from it, and, on the other, it would make it worthwhile again for the importing country to develop the least disadvantageous branch of production and to expand the export of its products. In other words, the money–price mechanism is supposed to be also a sort of guarantee that the international division of labour should develop not according to absolute advantages/disadvantages (by winding up the production opportunities of certain countries and condemning them to a lasting deficit) but according to relative, comparative advantages within the limits set by the relative cost ratios.

But this assumed mechanism was based not only on certain simplifying premises and theoretical concepts (such as the quantity theory of money) but has also become increasingly anachronistic and irrelevant, particularly with the mechanism of credit money becoming wide-spread (clearly manifesting that money has functions not only as a means of exchange) and with the development of international capital flows. Under the conditions of capital exports mutually promoting commodity exports and in a world economy in which the international flows of investment capital has become the most decisive factor determining international trade relations, the debtor–creditor relationship has increasingly ceased to be merely a transitory consequence or an attendant phenomenon of trade relations. The phenomenon of cumulative indebtedness of many countries dispels the illusion about the above-described mechanism.

The connection of the assumed mechanism of international commodity and money flows with the commodity–money mechanism based on the quantity theory of money, and the equilibrium mechanism within the national economies concerned, seems to provide a "solution" to resolving the obvious contradiction between the labour theory of value and Ricardo's money theory (in that the more or less than necessary quantity of money not corresponding, at the given velocity of circulation, to the sum of the labour-values of all the products, can be absorbed abroad or complemented from abroad. But on the other hand such a "solution" actually eliminates also the very issue of a price centre in the international economy, i.e. the problem of how "natural prices" (values) are formed internationally. (Anyway, Ricardo explicitly denied the validity of the labour theory of value in international trade.)

The concept, based on the labour theory of value, of an objective centre of world market price formation was replaced[133] by the assumption about two extreme

[133] The causal relationship between the formation of world market prices and the social costs of reproduction was practically excluded from the theory of international economics. As already noted, *Ricardo* himself denied the validity of the labor theory of value in international trade.

("repulsing") points of mutually advantageous exchange facilities, on the basis of the law of comparative costs, and about a possible range of price formation, namely between these two points, either determined accidentally or by the subjective will of the partner with the greatest bargaining power. (Or, it is replaced, as later on in the Neo-classical theory, by the concept of the Marshallian reciprocal demand/supply curves – drawn in a "vacuum" or with the assumption of already existing prices –, the intersection of which is supposed to determine the equilibrium prices and price ratios in the international economy involving only two countries.)

The Ricardian picture or rather his dream of the world economy and international division of labour also included the assumption that the decisions on specialization and allocation of productive resources are supposed to be taken by independent, *sovereign national actors* in view of comparative advantages computed on the level of the national economies concerned. But in reality specialization has developed, as a rule, according to the business interests of private entrepreneurs making decisions on micro-level, and in the case of quite a number of countries the type of specialization was determined by foreign powers under the colonial rule, or foreign companies.

Although certain premises of Ricardo's theory and the validity of his conclusions were questioned and criticized[134] already in his time and later, these critics were registered rather as pointing to the exceptions only to the general rule[135] or as concepts of "paradox".[136] The Neo-classical correction, though it gave up several basic presumptions of Ricardo's theorem, appeared as a further development or modernization of the latter rather than its replacement.

Thus, as we have seen, the Classical theory of international economy drew a rather naive, optimistic picture of the world economy, which has become increasingly unrealistic. It described the latter as always tending to be in equilibrium. It regarded equilibrium as an embodiment of a harmony of interests. It held the international division of labour based upon comparative advantages to be beneficial to all national economies in that it increases, by specialization and trade, the quantity of products available for consumption (without leading to unearned profits and to an uneven rise in the profit rate) and ensures the highest possible level of global welfare. It assumed international immobility of the factors of production

[134] On this point see *Emmanuel, A.* (1972a), pp. 253–256.

[135] See e.g. the concept of *Friedrich List* (1985), which is known in literature as that of the exceptional case of "infant industries".

[136] See e.g. the famous "*Graham paradox*" which refers to the increasing disadvantage of the country, out of two countries engaged in international division of labor and exchange relations with each other, which specializes on a product whose production is subject to the "law of diminishing returns" as against its partner country specializing on another with increasing returns. (As a matter of fact, this so-called "paradox" already involves the possible case of the deterioration of the terms of trade of those underdeveloped countries specialized in primary production.)

and perfectly competitive markets, as well as an independence and equality of the partners trading with each other[137]. As a consequence of neglecting technological progress and taking comparative advantages for granted, as (more or less) static endowments, it practically excluded (at least in the model) the very possibility of comparative advantages changing direction and emerging on the other side. Owing to the neglect of the economies of scale it excluded also the case of the dominant or more rapidly developing partner even from the relationship of the allegedly independent partners.

## 2.7. On possible disequilibria and social inequalities

However optimistic, even naive, the Classical views on the operation of the market economy within a country and also internationally, may appear as ensuring equilibrium, mutual benefits and equality, it has to be noted, that, on the one hand, their concepts and "models" were perhaps expressing their hopes and wishes (a "wishful thinking") rather than an identification of the prevailing contemporary system of the market economy or the world economy with the described ideal one, and, on the other, that besides believing in the ability of the spontaneous market economy to ensure equilibrium and provide equal benefits (or opportunities) to all, the Classical economists often pointed also to some possible disequilibria, even crisis or cyclical phenomena as well as to some cases of social or international inequalities.

For example, *Adam Smith* not only made remarks (repr. 1997) on the case of "over-trading" (when the profits of trade happen to be greater than ordinary, and "the high profits of trade afforded a great temptation to over-trading" (p. 406), but also paid special attention to the disturbances in the monetary and financial system, to the "excessive circulation of paper money" and bills of exchange, to "fictitious" payments by banks, etc. which are caused by "bold projectors" having "in their golden dreams the most distinct vision of...great profit". Thereby, he referred to the role of psychological factors, to (what Keynes called:) "expectations" in the business cycles. – (Book Two, Ch. 2)

*Malthus* pointed to "a phase of widespread unemployment of labour and capital marked by a piling up of unsold manufactures"[138].

---

[137] This does not mean that the Classical scholars completely ignored the fact of colonialization in their economics. *David Ricardo* (1821) also referred to the disadvantages of colonized countries (at least in respect of the direction of trade, but not in respect of specialization itself), and agreed with Adam Smith "who has shown most satisfactorily the advantages of a free trade, and the injustice suffered by colonies, in being prevented by their mother countries from selling their produce at the dearest market, and buying their manufactures and stores at the cheapest." (p. 204) It is to be added, however, that *Adam Smith* did believe in the mutual benefits from international trade, if it is free, which both the industrialized mother countries and their primary producing colonies can gain, without questioning the unequal pattern of division of labor. See *Smith, A.* (repr. 1997), p. 466.

[138] Quoted by *Rostow, W. W.* (1990), p. 58.

*David Ricardo* was also aware of cyclical fluctuations in the market and the possibility of "distress" in trade[139].

*John Stuart Mill*, although rejecting the assumption of the possibility of a "general over-supply", pointed (1821) to the appearance of a "commercial crisis", which is "simply the consequence of an excess of speculative purchases". (p. 340)

The fact or at least the possibility of certain *social conflicts* and *inequalities* have also appeared in the presentation of the Classical theses, not only in relationship to some "abnormal" circumstances or obstacles to the perfect operation of the market economy, but also in the context of its "normal" operation – if not elsewhere, then at least in the theory of distribution.

This is particularly clear in *Ricardo*, who considered "the laws which regulate this distribution" (namely between rent, profit, and wage) "the principal problem in Political Economy"[140], and who often presented the income distribution system in a market economy as a kind of "zero-sum-game" in which the more is received by one the less remains to the other. Accordingly, and in view of the diminishing returns in agriculture which cause an increase in the subsistence minimum wages as well as in the rent paid to the landlord, what remains for profit tends to fall, the tendency of which could be prevented by free import of cheaper food. But in this respect Ricardo revealed an obvious conflict between the interest of the landlords and those of the active participants of the economy, both the labourer class and, particularly the capitalist entrepreneurs.

*Adam Smith*, who expressed similar views on the the tendency of increasing rent and declining profit rate, also pointed (repr. 1997) to a conflict of interest between workers and their employers: "The workmen desire to get as much, the masters to give as little as possible." (p. 169)

*Malthus* also noted: "...unfortunately the working classes, though they share in the general prosperity, do not share in it so largely as in the general adversity. They may suffer the greatest distress in a period of low wages, but cannot be adequately compensated by a period of high wages. To them fluctuations must always bring more evil than good; and, with a view to the happiness of the great mass of society, it should be our object, as far as possible, to maintain peace, and an equable expenditure."[141]

Besides the conflict of interests in distribution, the somehow unequal position and opportunities of different classes are also noted in some places of writings of the Classical economists, e.g. when they pointed to the possibility of a kind of technological unemployment, to the cases when machine throws some workers out of their jobs.

*David Ricardo* wrote (1821): "...the discovery and use of machinery may be attended with a diminution of gross produce; and whenever that is the case, it will be injurious to the labouring class" (p. 238)

*John Stuart Mill* (1896) noted: "...there is in all rich communities a predatory population, who live by pillaging or over-reaching other people" (p. 68)

[139] See e.g. *Ricardo, D.* (1821), pp. 487–491.

[140] *Ricardo, D.* (1821), Preface, p. 5.

[141] Quoted by *Rostow, W. W.* (1990), p. 64.

## 2.8. On the relations between rich, developed and poor, underdeveloped countries

The fact of *international inequalities* appeared in the writings of the Classical economists (if at all) as the legacies of the past, i.e. as the consequences of the former stages of development passed earlier or later by the individual countries, or as following from different natural endowments, rather than resulting from the operation of the market economy on international scene. Nevertheless, and also despite the premise, in their trade theory, of sovereign and more or less equally developed countries entering trade relationship with each other, the problem of interactions between more and less developed nations was also touched upon by them in some places. This problem is related to the issue of international terms of trade (the changes in relative prices), too.

Their views on the position and catching-up opportunities of the *less developed, poorer countries*, and on the relationship between such "late-comers" and the already developed or richer countries were quite diverse, suggesting either specific advantages of the poorer countries or pointing to the disadvantages of the "late-comers" versus the already developed, rich nations in international competition.

*David Hume*, for example, stressed the advantage of lower *wage level* in the poorer, less developed countries, which may make easier their catching up with the richer nations, and play a role in the gradual shift of dynamic industries to new, still less developed areas and referred also to "backlog of hitherto unapplied technology".

He noted that "Manufactures...gradually shift their places, leaving those countries and provinces which they have already enriched, and flying to others, whither they are allured by the cheapness of provisions and labour".[142]

*Malthus* also believed that the development advantages of the industrial countries cannot be lasting, moreover he pointed to the disadvantage of those countries dependent on the import of primary products.

He wrote: "Advantages which depend exclusively upon capital and skill, and the present position of particular channels of commerce, cannot in their nature be permanent." He added: "A country dependent on both food and raw material imports to sustain its people and industry is vulnerable to a wide variety of forces that might reduce its capacity to import from its suppliers; indolence or bad management of resources in the supplying nation; an unfavourable shift in the terms of trade; or, a virtually certain shift in the supplying nation from agricultural and raw material production to manufacturing. Malthus concludes that a balanced system of both agriculture and commerce is optimal."[143]

*John Stuart Mill* believed (1896) in the advantage of less developed economies in trade. "He noted that the countries which carry on their foreign trade on the most advantageous terms, are those whose

[142] Quoted by *Rotwein, E.* (1955), pp. 34–35; and *Rostow, W. W.* (1990), p. 29.

[143] Quoted by *Rostow, W. W.* (1990), p. 70.

commodities are most in demand by foreign countries, and which have themselves the least demand for foreign commodities. From which, among other consequences, it follows, that the richest countries, *ceteris paribus*, gain the least by a given amount of foreign commerce; since, having a greater demand for commodities generally, they are likely to have a greater demand for foreign commodities, and thus modify the terms of interchange to their own disadvantage." (p. 365)

Here we can find the origin of the dubious concept (so fashionable in standard textbook) of the "small countries" enjoying greater benefit from trade.

Quite the contrary, *Adam Smith* held the view that a rich nation with higher level of real wages may enjoy the advantage, versus a less developed, poorer one, not only in respect of a more developed infrastructure and a larger domestic market promoting the division of labour, but also in respect of the wage cost per unit of production.

## 2.9. On the terms of trade

Despite the assumed mutual benefits from international trade based upon "comparative advantages" of all the partners, Classical economists were aware also of the problem of changes in *international price ratios*, i.e. of the possibility of deterioration of the terms of trade for certain countries. However, in view of technical progress (if any) assumed to be more rapid in manufacturing industries, and of that the primary producing sectors, rather than manufacturing industries, are subject more to the "law of diminishing returns", they actually assumed a tendency of increasing relative prices of primary products, i.e. of improving terms of trade for primary exporting countries and a regular deterioration of the terms of trade for the countries exporting manufactured products.

*David Hume* noted that the "arts of manufacture...had made greater progress than the knowledge of agriculture"[144]. *Adam Smith* also assumed that the relative prices of manufactured goods tend to decline, while those of the primary products increase, because of increasing returns in manufacturing industries (where "the same cause,...which raises the wages of labour, the increase of stock, tends to increase its productive powers, and to make a smaller quantity of labour produce a greater quantity of work"). But he also mentioned the disadvantage of those producing and selling "perishable" goods, such as "oranges", as compared to the producers of "durable commodities", because of "a much greater competition" in the case of the former[145]. Such a remark logically suggests the disadvan-

[144] Quoted by *Rostow, W. W.* (1990), p. 25.

[145] "The market price will sink more or less below the natural price, according as the greatness of the excess increases more or less the competition of the sellers, or according as it happens to be more or less important to them to get immediately rid of the commodity. The same excess in the importation of perishable, will occasion a much greater competition than in that of durable commodities...". *Smith, A.* (repr. 1997) p. 159.

tage, at least, of those many underdeveloped countries specialized in the export-oriented production of "perishable" agricultural products.

*Malthus* wrote: "The elementary cost of manufactures, or the quantity of labour and other conditions of the supply necessary to produce a given quantity of them, has a constant tendency to diminish; while the quantity of labour and other conditions of supply necessary to procure the last addition which has been made to the raw produce of a rich and advancing country, has a constant tendency to increase."[146]

According to *W. W. Rostow* (1990) Malthus was nevertheless "quite optimistic about the prospects for sustaining productivity and profits in agriculture. He cites, in particular: improved agricultural machinery, methods of cropping and managing the land, and increased personal exertion by farm labour, noting wide international variations in labour efficiency; the possibility of a rise in domestic prices damped by increased imports; and a decline in the price of manufactures due to improved machinery, which may permit a rise in the money price of agricultural produce without a proportional rise in the money wage rate." (pp. 66–67)

*David Ricardo* also stressed (1821) the problem of diminishing returns in agriculture versus the case of increasing returns in manufacturing industries.

Accordingly he noted: "The natural price of all commodities, excepting raw produce and labour, has a tendency to fall in the progress of wealth and population." (p. 50) As a consequence of diminishing returns in agriculture he pointed to the great reductions in the rate of profit (because of the rise of wage costs) and a rapid rise in rent, rather than a necessary deterioration of the terms of trade. Such a natural tendency of the declining rate of profit could be countervailed, in his view, by the free imports of cheaper food, by "the discovery of new markets" and also by the improvements in machinery, by the better division and distribution of labour, and by the increasing skill, both in science and art, of the producers". (p. 50)

*John Stuart Mill* also shared (1896) the Ricardian view on diminishing return in primary production:

"That the produce of land increases, *ceteris paribus*, in a diminishing ratio to the increase in the labour employed, is a truth more often ignored or disregarded than actually denied." (p. 111) Besides referring to the counteracting forces, such as "the progress of agricultural knowledge, skill, and invention", he clearly exempted manufacturing industries from the effect of the Law of Diminishing Return. "Manufactures are vastly more susceptible than agriculture, of mechanical improvements, and contrivances for saving labour; and it has already been seen how greatly the division of labour, and its skilful and economical distribution, depend on the extent of the market, and on the possibility of production in large masses. In manufactures, accordingly, the causes tending to increase the productiveness of industry, preponderate greatly over the one cause which tends to diminish it... This fact has manifested itself in the progressive fall of the prices and values of almost every kind of manufactured goods". (pp. 114–115) Accordingly, the terms of trade for the primary producing countries should have regularly improved.

[146] Quoted by *Rostow, W. W.* (1990), p. 66.

## 2.10. On the role of the State in a liberal system

It follows from their basic trust in a spontaneous market economy that the Classical economists were very strong advocators of liberalism, and opponents, in general, of the *State interventions* disturbing *market spontaneity* in the economy.

Nevertheless, they have by no means presented such a simple, one-sided view of liberalism as often attributed to them, in respect of the dilemma of whether the spontaneous market or the State can promote development more. Nor they have excluded the possibility of a need for protectionism in trade.

*Adam Smith*, who is considered as the "father" of classical liberalism, while stressing the importance of "natural liberty" and the beneficial operation of the spontaneous market with its "invisible hand", also underlined the need for an active State.

According to him a responsible government has got "the duty of protecting the society from the violence and invasion of other independent societies...the duty of protecting, as far as possible, every member of the society from the injustice or oppression of every other member of it...and, thirdly, the duty of erecting and maintaining certain public works and certain public institutions, which it can never be for the interest of any individual, or small number of individuals, to erect and maintain".

"As for the third function, Smith envisaged education and a wide array of infrastructure investments as legitimate".[147]

Moreover, Smith (1937) actually gave priority to the interest of the society versus those selfish individuals damaging it.

"But those exertions of the natural liberty of a few individuals, which might endanger the security of the whole society, are, and ought to be, restrained by the laws of all governments; of the most free, as well as of the most despotical." (p. 308)

*T. R. Malthus* suggested government actions in organizing public (and private) works in case of unemployment.

He wrote: "...in our endeavours to assist the working classes in the period like the present, it is desirable to employ them in those kinds of labour, the results of which do not come for sale into the market, such as roads and public works."[148]

As regards *trade liberalization versus protectionism*, Classical economists were, of course, in favour of the former, but did not necessarily oppose protectionist measures in all cases.

---

[147] Quoted by *Rostow, W. W.* (1990), pp. 48–49.

[148] Quoted by *Rostow, W. W.* (1990), pp. 61–62.

For example, *David Hume* noted that "there could be circumstances when tariff protection might be justified"[149].

*Malthus* also referred to cases when import liberalization, moreover a free import of agricultural products may lead to unfavourable consequences even for the industrial entrepreneurs and wageworkers. According to him the removal of restrictions on trade and imports of corn and other agrarian goods have contributed to "distress both among capitalists and labourers". But – as *Rostow* notes – "he did not advocate in the transition from war to peace a return to high taxes, large military expenditures, and the imposition of high protective tariffs on grain... He also opposes a radical increase in the issuance of paper money..."[150].

Even *David Ricardo*, the most militant advocator of free trade, of the removal of import restrictions on food products, admitted (1821) that under specific circumstances, such as those after a war, "in a period of emergency" (p. 162), when "...the obstacles to importation are removed, and a competition destructive to the home-grower commences..., [the] best policy of the State would be, to lay a tax, decreasing in amount from time to time, on the importation of foreign corn, for a limited number of years, in order to afford to the home-grower an opportunity to withdraw his capital gradually from the land." He noted: "Notwithstanding, then, that it would be more productive of wealth to the country, at whatever sacrifice of capital it might be done, to allow the importation of cheap corn, it would, perhaps, be advisable to charge it with a duty for a few years." (p. 162)

*John Stuart Mill*, while qualifying (1896) the "doctrine of Protection to Native Industry" "the most notable" among false theories, considered the case of "the interest of national subsistence and of national defence" as providing ground for the protectionist doctrine. Moreover, he stated: "The only case in which, on mere principles of political economy, protecting duties can be defensible, is when they are imposed temporarily (especially in a young and rising nation) in hopes of neutralizing a foreign industry". (pp. 553–556)

## 2.11. On the stages of development and economic systems

The representatives of the Classical economics perceived, in general, the historical process of development as an evolution leading from the early stages (or systems) characterized by primitive activities (such as gathering, hunting and fishing) or primary activities only, to the most developed, industrial system of the economy and society, based upon a spontaneously operating market, a harmonious cooperation of the owners of factors of production as well as of the trading nations, and on the freedom of individuals who act according to their interest and thereby contribute to all-social welfare.

In this perception not only a kind of *unilinear development concept* appears, but also a *confidence* in (or at least a dream about the feasibility of an ideal system of) the capitalist market economy. However, the Classical economists were quite aware, as already noted, of some imperfections of the prevailing system even in their own country, and also of the different position of countries in the evolutionary process of development, moreover, as we have seen, they expressed also their worries about prospects, namely about a "stationary state".

[149] Quoted by *Rostow, W. W.* (1990), p. 30.

[150] Quoted by *Rostow, W. W.* (1990), p. 60.

For example, *David Hume* described the historical process of development as starting from the "savage state" in which people "live chiefly by hunting and fishing"[151] and leading to the stage of agriculture and finally to manufactures.

*Adam Smith* defined the first stage in the historical process of development as "the lowest and rudest state of society", in which the means of subsistence are gathering the "spontaneous fruits of the soil" and hunting, while the second one, which allows larger groupings of people, is that of pasture, based on the domestication of animals, and implying a nomadic way of life. With the latter private property appears as an increasingly decisive factor causing social inequalities and tensions, and making necessary the existence and operation of a central authority, a "civil government", "instituted for the security of property", "for the defence of the rich against the poor". The third stage is the "agrarian" state of society, in which land, instead of cattle, represents the major form of property, tillage is the dominant form of activity, and the communities are settled, not nomadic. It involves a great authority and power in the hands of the proprietors of land and the personal services for them, of those subordinated (yeomanry). The next stage is characterized by the growth of manufactures along with the development of cities and the rise of merchant classes who also invest in land, and tend to employ free wage workers instead of tenants, serfs or slaves. In this stage a regular government operates both in the city and the country, and due to the spontaneous development of agriculture and manufacturing ("the increase and riches of commercial and manufacturing towns") leading to a "great revolution", the "civilized society" carries on a "great commerce...between the inhabitants of the town and those of the country". Service relationships are replaced by monetary relationships, thus dependence is less direct and severe. In such a commercialized economy there are three "great constituent orders": landlords, capitalists and wage labour[152].

*Smith*, as already noted, actually believed that the direction of development follows "the natural inclinations of man", which means that proceeds from agriculture to manufactures, and foreign trade. This would be, in his view (repr. 1997), also a "natural order of things" in every society, which, however, "has, in all the modern states of Europe, been, in many respects, entirely inverted" (p. 483). He also believed that development finally leads to a stationary state, because of limited resources and diminishing returns.

*Malthus* also saw the development process as going through the stages of hunting gathering, stock-raising, agriculture, and leading to commerce-manufacturing society, and was worrying about population growth exceeding the growth of food production.

*David Ricardo*, as already noted, pointed to the "natural tendency of profits to fall" because of diminishing returns and rising wages and rents. In his views, in the

151 Quoted by *Rotwin, E.* (1955), pp. 5–6.

152 See *Smith, A.* (1776), Book No. V. and III. – Quotations from Smith, A. (repr. 1997), pp. 479–520.

advancing state, the rise or fall of wages depends on whether the capital or the population advance, at the more rapid course. But in every society advancing in wealth and population, general profits must fall, unless there are improvements in agriculture, or corn can be imported at a cheaper price.

He also paid attention to the prevailing differences of countries in respect of their economic conditions or development stage, and made conclusions on the recommendable development policies accordingly.

He distinguished three cases: "In new settlements, where the arts and knowledge of countries far advanced in refinement are introduced, it is probable that capital has a tendency to increase faster than mankind: and if the deficiency of labourers were not supplied by more populous countries, this tendency would very much raise the price of labour. Although "it will not long continue so; for the land being limited in quantity, and differing in quality, with every increased portion of capital employed on it, there will be a decreased rate of production."

"In those countries where there is abundance of fertile land, but where, from the ignorance, indolence, and barbarism of the inhabitants, they are exposed to all the evils of want and famine,...a very different remedy should be applied...they require only to be better governed and instructed, as the augmentation of capital, beyond the augmentation of people, would be the inevitable result."

"With a population pressing against the means of subsistence, the only remedies are either a reduction of people, or a more rapid accumulation of capital." "In rich countries, where all the fertile land is already cultivated, the latter remedy is neither very practicable nor very desirable, because its effect would be, if pushed very far, to render all classes equally poor." (pp. 53–54)

*John Stuart Mill* presented (1896) a more detailed picture about historical development, which begins with a stage when the community lives only on "the spontaneous produce of vegetation" (by gathering its products). A more developed phase is represented by hunting and fishing, while the next one results from "the domestication of the more useful animals; giving rise to the pastoral and nomad state, in which mankind do not live on the produce of hunting, but on milk and its products, and on the annual increase of flocks and herds". "From this state of society to the agricultural" the transition was promoted by "the growth of the population", and "inequality of possession". The activity of "a mercantile class" and "a surplus of food beyond...necessary consumption" and its "appropriation" by "the proprietors of the land" employing serfs, paved the way for the rise, mostly from "emancipated serfs", of a class of "artificers" and handicraft manufacture of textiles, leading to a "commercial and manufacturing Europe", to "modern industrial communities". In describing this process of development he refers to the struggle between the nomads and the agricultural communities, between "conquerors and conquered", and also distinguish between the various forms of agricultural-based societies, such as the great empires, city-states, and small town-communities. (pp. 6–12)

*John Stuart Mill* also expressed the view which became quite characteristic of conventional development economics after the Second World War, namely that the various historical stages of economic development could be observed in the contemporary world. By pointing to the differences even among the "industrial communities", i.e. within the same system of the economy, he presented a view, which has come to the fore in the economics of comparative systems more recently, after the collapse of "non-capitalist" systems in Europe. Mill refers to five cases in which the three basic determinants of development (namely: the rate of growth of population, the rate of increase in the capital stock, and "the arts of production" are changing in different ways: " Case 1. Population increases; capital and the arts of production stationary... Case 2. Population stationary; capital increasing; arts of production stationary... Case 3. Population and capital increasing equally, the arts of production stationary... Case 4. Population and capital stationary; the arts of production progress... Case 5. Population, capital, and the arts of production increase together..."[153].

## 2.12. Concluding remarks

As it appears from the above, the representatives of Classical economics have practically pointed, in one way or another, implicitly or explicitly, to almost all of the main conditions, factors and aspects of economic development, including

- its natural conditions and
- the growth of population, i.e. the number of both consumers and producers;
- the conditions of equilibrium both within and between national economies;
- the productivity of labour, depending on specialization, dexterity, skill, education and technical equipment, as a source of surplus both in agriculture and industry;
- savings and capital formation, depending not only on the rate of interest but also and more generally on incomes, and income distribution[154];
- investments, competition and technical progress (science and innovations);
- effective demand[155] both inside and outside the country;

[153] Quoted by *Rostow, W. W.* (1990), pp. 113–116.

[154] *David Ricardo* considered "the laws which regulate...distribution" the "principal problem in Political Economy". *Adam Smith*, like Ricardo, was very much aware of how the actual distribution of incomes can affect savings and thereby development. He wrote: "What is annually saved is as regularly consumed as what is annually spent...but it is consumed by a different set of people. That portion of his revenue, which a rich man annually spends, is in most cases consumed by idle guests, and menial servants, who leave nothing behind them in return for their consumption. That portion which he annually saves is immediately employed as a capital, is consumed in the same manner...but by a different set of people, by laborers, manufacturers, and artificers, who re-produce with a profit the value of their annual consumption..." *Smith, A.* (1937), pp. 321–323. *Malthus*, approaching the problem of income distribution from another aspect, namely from the point of view of effective demand and realization of what has been produced, concludes in an opposite way. He suggests maintaining, "such a proportion of unproductive consumers as is best adapted to the powers of production". Quoted by *Rostow, W. W.* (1990), p. 61.

[155] *Malthus* noted: "If consumption exceeds production, the capital of the country must be diminished and its wealth must be gradually destroyed from its want of power to produce; if production be in a great excess above consumption, the motive to accumulate and produce must cease from the want of an *effectual demand* in those who have the principal means of purchasing...there must be an intermediate point, ...where, taking into consideration both the power to produce and the will to consume, the encouragement to the increase of wealth is the greatest." Quoted by *Rostow, W. W.* (1990), pp. 64–65. (My italics: T. S.)

- international trade and division of labour;
- the trends in relative prices;
- moral, cultural, social and institutional aspects of development, and
- the role and responsibilities of government in a spontaneously operating market economy.

If they, nevertheless, over-emphasized one or the other side of the various issues of development (though far less than so often attributed to them), it was (besides the always limited extent of human knowledge) mainly because of the historical conditions that time in their country, and/or their hopes to point thereby to requisites and desirable changes.

## 3. The Marxian political economy

The economic theory[156] of *Karl Marx* can quite easily be considered as a theory of development at least for three reasons:

1. First, because (apart from its utopian and political-ideological elements) it has also contributed a lot to the theoretical discussion of such *development issues* which are still relevant for the economics of development today, as e.g.:
   - whether the late-comers, the less developed nations can and should follow the example of the more advanced, industrially developed ones (in a unilinear process of development);
   - how the penetration of more developed economic powers such as the colonizers or foreign "working" capital may promote the development and modernization, while also subordinating the economy and exploiting the labour force, of the less developed countries;
   - what positive and negative interactions arise in different phases of development of all the social formations (determined by their "modes of production") between the so-called "social relations of production" (i.e. relations of ownership, division of labour and distribution of incomes), and the most dynamic factor of social and national development, namely the "productive forces", first of all human "live" labour, its quality, skill, knowledge (in modern terminology: "human capital") and the means of production (i.e. technology, capital goods as "dead" labour);
   - what dialectical cause-effect relations develop between the "economic base" (the "mode of production") and the political, legal, cultural and institutional "superstructure" of all societies, and also, in general, between "social existence" and "social consciousness", i.e. between the material life conditions of social strata or nations and their psychological-sociological behaviour or national attitude;

[156] See *Marx, K.* (repr. Vol. I: 1965, Vol. II.: 1967, Vol. III: 1966).

- how the price formation and income distribution in a fully developed capitalist (national or international) market economy are modified by capital mobility;
- how equality (equivalence) and inequality of exchange may accompany, and correspond to each other, and consequently why "equality" is meaningless without questioning: "from what point of view?";
- how market competition, even under the conditions of equivalent exchange, by forcing technological innovations, leads to monopolization;
- what preconditions are needed for a dynamic equlibrium in the (national or world) economy, and
- why, in the absence of the latter, the market economy operates in a cyclical way; etc.

2. Second, because by interpreting all economic phenomena and processes in a socio-political context, it seems to represent the kind of *interdisciplinary approach*, which is, in general, considered as a distinctive feature of development economics born after the Second World War.

3. Third, because it presents an overall concept of the *historical development* of human society.

## 3.1. The Marxian approach to the economy and social development

The Marxian political economy emerged from the "soil" of the British Classical economics, but was also influenced by the German philosophy (particularly Hegel's) and the French "utopian socialists". *Marx,* however, rejected and criticized the Classical concept of liberalism, and the belief in the socially and internationally harmonious operation of the capitalist market economy, while insisted on and elabourated further the labour theory of value as a background concept explaining exploitation even without sheer (non-economic) force.

Marx applied not only a socio-political, moreover *holistic*, i.e. necessarily interdisciplinary approach in his analysis of the contemporary capitalist system, but in addition to the "stock" and "flow" approaches (already applied and combined in the Classical economics) he introduced a "relation approach" by seeking for the lasting relations between members or classes of society or nations behind their position, action or behaviour.

Accordingly, the economy, in his view, consists not only of certain "stock" or endowments, and of certain transactions, in the form of "flows", between the economic actors, but also and more decisively, of "social relations of production and distribution" among the members, classes of society (or nations). *Development* thus means, in his view, both a progress, an evolution of the "productive forces" and changes, from time to time, in the "social relations of production" with the concomitant changes in the institutional, political and legal systems (the so-called "superstructure").

The major, aboriginal, primary "force of production" is *human labour*, the only source of any social value, the creator of capital, and technology. Productive forces include also the "means of production", i.e. "physical capital" (tools, equipment, machinery, etc.) which are, in the final analysis, the products of human labour.

The production process, which is, in a broader sense of the word (thus including even the activity of gathering, hunting and fishing), a prerequisite of the life and survival of all societies, necessarily includes, as a physical process, the work of human labour, the "object of production", such as raw material, which is to be transformed (processed for use or just made available) by human labour, and the "means of production", i.e. the tools, instruments, buildings, machines, etc. used by human labour. Production in all societies must be repeated, but development requires an "extended reproduction", i.e. production on a higher level. Since such an extended reproduction implies not only a mere growth of the output, but also a required process of distribution and a corresponding pattern of the use of products, Marx referred to the process of "social reproduction" which includes distribution and use of products as well.

The "engine" of economic development, a more or less permanent motive force is the progress of "productive forces", i.e. the improvement (by accumulated experiences, skill, education, culture) of the quality and performance of the labour force and the introduction of better techniques, new technologies. But this development of productive forces without which a society can hardly develop, can proceed more rapidly or more slowly, or can even be retarded, depending on the prevailing pattern of the "social relations of production". The latter involve, first of all, the *ownership relations,* namely the pattern of ownership over the main "means of production" (including the land, and "physical capital"), and the *relations of division of labour* within the society or internationally, i.e. the pattern of occupation, trade, activity, specialization, and last but not least, *distribution relations.*

Marx considered the actual pattern of "social relations of production" with the concomitant level of development of the "productive forces" as the "economic base" of society, on which a kind of political, institutional, legal, moral, religious, and cultural "superstructure" is built. Social development must obviously extend over both the "economic base" and the "superstructure" which are in a "dialectical" interaction with each other.

Marx, contrary to the Classical view, stressed the *contradictory nature* of the development process, and considered (like Hegel) the very contradictions as promoting factors of development. He perceived the process of development as a combination of evolution and revolutions, of gradual changes in quantity leading to sudden qualitative transformation, and as a process not only creating newer and newer contradictions but also being pushed forward by them.

Such a contradiction regularly appeared – according to Marx – in the historical development of human societies between their growing productive forces and those social relations of production at the beginning promoting but later on hindering the growth of the latter. Since this contradiction manifests itself socially in the "class struggle" and politically in the struggle between the ruling forces of the "ancient régime" and the emerging revolutionary forces of the oppressed, it finally leads to a revolutionary change, a qualitative transformation of the system, of the so-called "social formation", the "economic base" of which as a "mode of production" involves, besides the forces of production, a certain pattern of social relations of production, while its "superstructure" involves a corresponding power structure with a ruling class.

Strangely enough, *Marx* exempted the future, post-capitalist society, as visualized by him, of this general rule of contradictions. Contrary to all the other, historical social formations, his "communistic society" is supposed to operate without contradictions between social relations and productive forces, without "class struggle" and even without classes and any state power. Thus, unlike the Classical economists who have some worries about the limits of development and a "stationary state", he was fully optimistic about the future society of humankind.

## 3.2. On the nature of commodity and money

*Marx* strongly (and more consistently than his classical predecessors) emphasized the *dual nature*, the two sides of some basic economic categories. He explicitly pointed to

- the physical and the social side of *production* (the former implies the three necessary elements of it: the object of production, the means of production and human labour force, while the latter implies the social relations of production);
- the "use value" (utility) and "exchange value" of *commodity* (the former implies its consumable or usable nature, the latter its ability to be exchanged for another commodity or money), and the mutual determination of them, in the sense that the realization of a commodity depends both on the willingness of a consumer to buy it, for whom it should represent a use value, and the readiness of its producer to sell it, for whom it means an exchange value[157];
- the appearance of the "surplus" in kind[158] as a "surplus product" and its monetary appearance as "surplus value"[159];
- the physical form of *capital* and its monetary form (the former implies primarily the means of production which are separated by monopolistic ownership

[157] See *Marx, K.* (repr. 1966), Part I., Ch. I.

[158] According to the definition of *Adam Smith* (repr. 1997), the "surplus" is "that part of the produce" of the laborer, "which is over and above his own consumption". (p. 126)

[159] See *Marx, K.* (repr. 1966), Part III. and Part IV.

from the labour force, and also temporarily those products, owned by the capitalist, which are waiting for marketing, while the latter implies the accumulated money resulting regularly from appropriated surplus value).

Strangely enough, and as another inconsistency, *Marx* assumed that in the future "communistic society" the products would cease to be "commodities", thus lose their "exchange value", and production would create "use values" only.

*Marx* started his analysis of the capitalist system (without, however, clarifying unambiguously the level, the primary "unit" of analysis, i.e. whether applying the level of nations or that of the world, whether conceiving of "capitalism" as a national or a world system) with the investigation of the most "atomistic", elementary phenomenon of the economy: the *commodity.* From its dual nature, from its two inseparable sides, as having both a "use value" and an "exchange value", he derived not only the birth, the origin of *money* (as a general representative of "exchange value" which acquires several functions) but also the abstract possibility of *disequilibrium* and crisis.

*Money,* which originally and for a long historical period was "real money", i.e. "commodity money" with its own value, such as gold, silver, etc., functions, according to Marx, not only as *a means of exchange* serving to facilitate the exchange of commodities (in which function a "paper money" can substitute for it), but also as a *means of measuring the value* of all commodities (by its own value, even in an abstract comparison), and as a *means of payments* (in case the actual delivery of commodity or performance of work, service, etc. precede or follow in time the transfer of money) and *means of accumulation*, hoarding up, preserving treasure and wealth. In addition to these reasonably distinguished functions of money *Marx added* (1966) a fifth one, namely the function of "world money", which simply refers to the operation of money (actually with the same functions) in international transactions.

While the recognition of several important money functions, other than merely the "means of exchange", and thereby the rejection of the Classical assumption about the "neutral role" of money in the economy, has been, indeed, a great step forward (also a precedent of the Keynesian and modern monetarist concepts), such a categorization of the functions of money according practically to two criteria, one referring to different roles, the other to the "level of action", i.e. to the actual sphere (national or international) where these roles are played, shows an obvious inconsistency, which likely follows from the already noted lack of clarification concerning the "level of analysis" in the Marxian analysis of the abstract model of capitalism.

The realization of the "use value" of a commodity for its consumer or user presupposes the realization of its "exchange value" for its producer (even if it is a direct exchange without intermediaries). Such an exchange requires either the coincidence, in time and measure, of the wish of two partners producing different commodities to acquire the "use value" of the other product by exchanging their own for it in accordance with "exchange values", or in case the functioning of money as a medium of exchange separates buying and selling, an equivalent purchasing power is required on the side of the demand of those wishing to enjoy the "use value" of the commodity, for making realizable its "exchange value" on the side of supply of those wishing to sell it. Since such a coincidence or equivalence is, of course, not guaranteed, a *disequilibrium* in the market may follow from the very nature, the double face of commodity, which as an "abstract possibility" of crisis is reinforced, according to Marx, by the intermediary role of money (i.e. as a medium of exchange), and even more by its functioning as a means of payments (separating not only in space but also in time the two transactions, thereby aggravating uncertainties) and as a means of accumulation or hoarding up (breaking thereby the link between savings and investments).

## 3.3. The labour theory of value and the concept of exploitation

*Marx* distinguished capitalism from all the other, previous systems of economy by its ability to operate without sheer force, non-economic violence, which implies also its ability to appropriate the "surplus" from those who produce it, by a new method, via the market.

Looking for the origin of "surplus value" and for a consistent explanation of the "puzzle" of its rise in any sector of production also in money form, but without such an unequal exchange as assumed by Mercantilists, *Marx* not only applied (repr. 1966) the *labour theory of value* to the factor markets as well, particularly to wage labour, but also elabourated it further.

In the Marxian definition the "value" (the "natural price") of a commodity is equal (not to the actually used amount of labour which was needed in the past to produce it, as assumed by the Classical economists, but) to that amount of labour "socially necessary for its reproduction". It means, first of all and very positively, that a possible change in labour productivity (such as owing to better technology and/or improved skill, education of the labourer) is taken into account, thereby dynamizing the concept itself, and, second, that what matters as determinant is not the individual productivity or the labour cost of a commodity for an individual producer, but the social average, moreover, what the society accepts as necessary. What follows, on the one hand, is that in an equal, "equivalent" exchange each commodity is valued and exchanged according to the average labour cost of its production, behind which a great variety of individual labour costs can be, consequently a producer with a productivity lower, thus with a labour cost higher than the average, must give more labour in exchange for less. On the other hand, insofar as "socially necessary" means "socially accepted" amount of labour, it inevitably makes the Marxian concept tautological, because what commodities, in what quantity and at what level of exchange value the society accepts turns out only in the market, and depends on the already existing prices and incomes.

Though from the logic of the Marxian interpretation of the labour theory of value it would follow that in the evaluation of the output the increasing cost of *re*production should also be taken into account in the case of those branches of production causing exhaustion of natural resources or environment pollution, the national income calculus (the so-called NMP[160]-based calculation), supposed to correspond to the Marxian principle, in the former "socialist" countries completely neglected how much more (live and "dead" labour, i.e. total factor-use) is needed to reproduce the same quantity of product on a polluted or exhausted land, and to "reproduce" the same quality of air, water, environmental, if the latter have been polluted by production.

As it is capitalism which, according to *Marx,* creates as its precondition a class of proletariat, i.e. of wage workers free in double sense (namely, "freed", deprived of the means of production, and free also in mobility and to choose employer), thereby making the "labour force" (the physical and intellectual ability of the worker to perform labour) also a *commodity,* the labour value theory seemed for Marx perfectly applicable to this special commodity, too. Consequently, the value (the "natural price" or centre of price formation) of labour force is supposed to be determined, like that of all other commodities, by the amount of labour "socially necessary" for its "reproduction". But the *specificity* of this commodity versus ordinary commodities lies in its ability to create, if used, more new value than its own. In other words, Marx found the explanation for the rise of "surplus" in any productive activities by pointing to the (potential) difference between, on the one hand, the "new value" (a kind of "value added") of the product which is created (over and beyond the "old" value of the raw materials, machinery, etc., i.e. of the "object" and "means of production") by the worker's labour force, and, on the other, the value of the latter, i.e. the amount of labour socially necessary for the reproduction of labour force (the physical and intellectual ability of the worker to perform labour again, including, of course, the labour costs of all the products and services consumed by the worker and its family, of accommodation, health care and education, etc.).

This value of the labour force, from which the actual market price of labour, i.e. the wage level, may, of course, depending on demand and supply, deviate, is *not* determined by a subsistence minimum, but varies from country to country and from time to time, according to historical, cultural and social conditions, including particularly the bargaining power of labourers versus capitalist employers.

By applying the labour theory of value to the labour force as well, and explaining the origin of the surplus thereby, Marx presented a theory of *exploitation* which finds the social (or international) conflict not simply in distribution (of the already produced goods or incomes, by assuming a "zero-sum-game") but in the inequality of the very position of different classes (or nations) in *ownership relations*. This is because the labourer is economically forced (i.e. by an "economic violence" instead of non-economic, sheer force) to sell his/her labour force only in so far as

160 "Net Material Product".

being excluded from the ownership of the means of production. Consequently, since the basis of exploitation is ownership, those researchers wishing to reveal social or international inequalities must start by finding out: who owns what, and in order to eliminate exploitation the kind of "monopolized", exclusive ownership (i.e. which excludes the majority of people from ownership) has to be replaced by common ownership.

One of the reasons why the Marxian concept of exploitation is questioned nowadays more than ever is the workers' participation in ownership in the advanced countries, the phenomenon of "workers' shares", even if the concentration of property and wealth may have increased despite progressive taxation in many of these countries. Though the Marxian concept places an excessive emphasis on ownership position, which can easily lead to over-simplification of the issue of "exploitation" and inequalities, what may also follow logically from it is a distinction, in general, between those earning their incomes *primarily* from own work, and those whose incomes primarily originate in and depend on accumulated wealth. The question, however, arises, which is more difficult to answer, whether the earned incomes are proportional to the work performed, and what is considered "work" at all.

It is also to be noted that despite the Marxian definition of "social relations of production" involving, besides ownership relations, the relations of division of labour, and income distribution relations as well, the heavy emphasis by Marx on ownership provided an excellent opportunity for the Communist regimes to interpret the "transition from capitalism to socialism" as a change in ownership structure leading to the predominance of state ownership, the opposite variant of which, with the same over-simplification, appears in the wide-spread interpretation of the systemic change today in the former "socialist" countries, namely the "transition from socialism to capitalism" as primarily and decisively determined by privatisation.

### 3.4. On the source of "new value" in a "social process of reproduction"

According to the Marxian concept, the "value" of each commodity is solely determined by the necessary amount of total labour required for re-producing it (i.e. partly that performed in the past, or more precisely to be performed in the production of the means of production *before* the new process of production, and partly that performed, or more precisely to be performed in the new process of production). Insofar as the production process is of a capitalist nature, and, consequently, the capitalist entrepreneur has to invest capital both in buying the material elements of production and in hiring wage workers, it is only the latter part of his capital (called "variable") which can result, accordingly, in a new value with an increment over and above the wage cost, i.e. a surplus-value, while the value of the former part of capital (called "constant") is unchanged but proportionally "transferred" only by live labour to the value of the new product.

"The value of a commodity is equal to the value of the constant capital contained in it, plus the value of the variable capital reproduced in it, plus the increment – the surplus-value produced – of this variable capital."[161].

The "surplus-value" is, thus, the difference between the "new value" created by live labour, and, in principle (insofar as the wage cost is equal to the value of labour power), the value of the labour power, which performed the latter. Its source is (what Marx called) "surplus-labour", implying that "extra" part of the labour actually performed which exceeds the one covering the wage cost, thus required for the reproduction of the labour power of workers. However, the actual size of the surplus value depends, according to Marx, on the very *quality* of labour.

*Marx* made a clear distinction between skilled and unskilled labourer, between complex and simple labour, and considered one unit of the former as equivalent (both in respect of its own value and its capacity of producing new value) to the multiple of simple labour units of unskilled worker[162]. Thus, while stressing the equally new-value-creating capacity of all human labour he did not assume an equal value resulting from the performance of different quality of labour. He pointed to a possible higher value created during the same time by a qualified worker as compared to a lower value by an unqualified. It means that not only its own value, i.e. the cost of reproduction of a qualified labour force is higher than that of an unqualified one (because of the cost of education), but the value of its product, too, moreover, the usually greater difference between the created new value and the own value of a qualified labour may provide the opportunity for both profits and wages to increase. Consequently, Marx did *not* assume a "zero-sum-game" in distribution (like Ricardo and others), i.e. a necessarily opposite direction of changes in the incomes of workers and capitalists.

While speaking, however, about a "social process of reproduction" in a broad sense, including, of course, the reproduction of the most important factor of production, namely human labour, Marx practically limited the value-creating process of production to *material* production only (leaving out the services) and reduced the new-value-creating ability of the labour force to the so-called "productive workers"[163]. This is not only another inconsistency in his theory (though quite corresponding to the Classical concept of "productive labour" and reflecting the histor-

[161] *Marx, K.* (repr. 1966), p. 150.

[162] The germ of such a concept, as we have seen, did already appear in the writings of the Classicals.

[163] It is worth noting that e.g. *Adam Smith* (repr. 1997) also distinguished "productive" and "unproductive" labor according to whether it "adds to the value of the subject upon which it is bestowed", but qualified also those "persons whose capitals are employed in any of those four ways" (namely, "first, in procuring the rude produce...; or, secondly, in manufacturing and preparing that rude produce for immediate use and consumption; or, thirdly, in transporting either the rude or manufactured produce...; or, lastly, in dividing particular portions of either into...small parcels", i.e. in agriculture, in manufacturing industries, in whole sale trade and transport, and in retail trade) as "productive laborers". (pp. 429, 459)

ical conditions, as well), but has also become an extremely false misconcept in the later Marxist literature and policy.

Quite contrary to the logic of Marx's concept of social reproduction and the primary role of human labour in it, particularly to his stress on the quality of labour, in the Marxist literature

1. the original source of new value, thus of surplus, of profits, rents etc. has been, in general, identified with the labour performed in the branches of material production only, even if it implies the production of weapons, drugs, unhealthy goods or environment polluting products, while labour performed even in important services, necessary for the production process itself or for the allocation and distribution of the products, etc. has been, at best, qualified as a (secondary) source of profits, without creating new value;
2. the working class, the "proletariat" which is supposed to create all values and be exploited by the capitalists, has mostly been identified with the "blue-collar workers" (with a 19th-century-type of industrial working class), while the "white-collar workers", technicians, all administrators, qualified and higher-salary employees, particularly the hired managers and other salary-earners, even in the same industries of material production, have been considered as recipients only (even if also exploited) of the new value produced by the former;
3. consequently, and in sharp contradiction to the Marxian emphasis on the reproduction of the human labour force (both in its physical and intellectual qualities) as an organic, and most decisive part of the social process of reproduction, the role played in upbringing, caring, educating of the new labour force, by mothers, physicians, nurses, teachers, scholars, etc. has been qualified as "unproductive labour", thus the incomes received by them, and the expenditures spent on the related social services, including education, public health, science and research, culture, etc. which are investments in "human capital" have been considered (and treated in practice accordingly) as deductions from investable funds, as residuals in the distribution of national income or budget resources.

Such misconcepts have not only made the Marxist views on the "working class" quite anachronistic by the late 20th century, hindering the full recognition of substantial changes in the social structures, class behaviour and the actual composition of the "working class" in the advanced market economies, but have also strongly influenced, or were used to legitimise only, the income and budget policy of the former "socialist" countries, the "egalitarian" wage system and the priority in budget expenditures, of material investments.

Those questions related to the above (mis)concept (such as: who are "productive" in a society?; whose work creates "new value", the source of incomes?; who are recipients only, moreover exploiting appropriators of incomes produced by others?; which branches of the economy and what kind of activities contribute directly to the growth of national income?; etc.) are all belonging to sphere of development theory and policy as well.

Apart from such inconsistencies, even contradictions and misconceptss in Marxism, it is obviously *the human labour*, which is defined as the primary, the most decisive factor of production and source of social development in Marx's theory. For Marx the labour theory of value was not only a price and income determining concept but a basic philosophy and approach.

## 3.5. The Marxian price theory and its international implications

In the Marxian theory the production of *value* and the actual price formation of commodities in a fully developed capitalist market economy is conceptionally distinguished. *Marx* (like his predecessors in the labour theory of value) also postulated that it is human labor only which can create "value", and (unlike most of them) did not consider the value, or "natural price", of commodities as being made up by the costs of individual production factors, such as land, labour and capital, i.e. as formed by its "components".

While, in his views, the value of all commodities is assumed to be the original background and primary determinant of price formation, and the sum of all values is supposed to be determined only by the total amount of labour (socially) required for the (re-)production of them, the actual centre of price formation cannot be the value in all cases, but exceptionally only[164].

The Marxian *price theory* involves several different categories derived from each other, and representing different levels of abstraction. The most abstract category is "value" itself, defined (as noted above) as a "socially necessary amount of labour for reproducing" a commodity. Since "new value" is created by human labour only, it follows from this concept that those industries employing relatively more labourers (in modern terminology: the labour-intensive industries) would produce more new values from which their capitalists (if paying the same wage rate) would get higher profits than those in the "capital intensive" industries.

*Marx* pointed out (repr. 1966) that "in different spheres of production equal portions of the total capital comprise unequal sources of surplus-value, and the sole source of surplus-value is living labour. ...Now, if capitals in different spheres of production, calculated in per cent, i.e. capitals of equal magnitude, produce unequal profits in consequence of their different organic composition, then it follows that the profits of unequal capitals in different spheres of production cannot be proportional to their respective magnitudes, or that profits in different spheres of production are not proportional to the magnitude of the respective capitals invested in them. (pp. 149–150)

[164] *Marx* stated (repr. 1966): "The exchange of commodities at their values...requires a much lower stage than their exchange at their prices of production, which requires a definite level of capitalist development." (p. 177) In regard to the latter he remarked, "that here the theory of value is incompatible with the actual process, incompatible with the real phenomena of production". (p. 153)

He also mentioned that "there is yet another source of inequality in rates of profit. This is the different period of turnover of capital in different spheres of production." (p. 151)

However, in a real market economy of capitalism the *mobility of capital* brings about a tendency of equalization of the returns to capital, i.e. of profit rates.

According to Marx (repr. 1966): "The cost-prices are the same for equal capitals in different spheres, no matter how much the produced values and surplus-values may differ. The equality of cost-prices is the basis for competition among invested capitals, whereby an average profit is brought about." (p. 153)

Therefore, the centre of price formation modifies, shifts to a new category, the so-called "price of production", which, as a modified, converted form of value[165], includes, besides also, of course, the "old value", i.e. "constant capital", the wage cost and as much profit only as corresponds to an average rate of profit – instead of the total "new value" created in the given industry and distributed primarily between wage and profit, While the total sum of "values" and the total sum of "prices of production" are supposed to be equal[166], the price of production in a relatively labour-intensive (in Marx' terminology: "low organic composition of capital"[167]) branch of economy is lower than value, and in a relatively capital-intensive ("high organic composition of capital") branch is higher[168]. It means that an

165 As *Marx* indicated (repr. 1966) his own logic of abstraction in the analysis of price formation: "In Books I and II we dealt with the *value* of commodities. On the one hand, the *cost-price* has now been singled out as a part of this value, and, on the other, the *price of production* of commodities has been developed as its converted form." (p. 163)

166 "As concerns the total social capital, ...the price of production is equal to the value". "Consequently, the sum of the profits in all spheres of production must equal the sum of the surplus-values, and the sum of the prices of production of the total social product equal the sum of its value." *Marx, K.* (repr. 1966), p. 165 and 173

167 "By composition of capital we mean...the proportion of its active and passive components, i.e., of variable and constant capital." *Marx, K.* (repr. 1966), p. 145. *Marx* called "variable" that part of capital which undergoes a metamorphosis in the sense that the wage cost representing the value of the labor power (of workers) is replaced, at the end of the process, by a new value exceeding the latter, thus involving the "surplus value", i.e. the source of profit, while he qualified "constant" that part of capital (spent on raw materials, and means of productions, etc.) which, as a "passive" part, has no change in its original value.

168 The fact of differences in the "composition of capital" was already recognized by the Classical economists. For example, *Adam Smith* stressed (repr. 1997): "Different occupations require very different proportions between the fixed and circulating capitals employed in them." (p. 374) The former meant that part of the capital "employed in the instruments", while the latter "employed in the wages and maintenance of...laboring servants". (pp. 374–375) *Marx* however, criticized the confusion of the distinction between "fixed" and "circulating" capital with that between (what he called:) "constant" and "variable" capital, because, in his views, it is only the latter which marks out the actual source of new value and, thus, of profit, too. He wrote (repr. 1966): "As far as the ratio of the fixed and circulating capital in the composition of capitals is concerned, ...it does not in itself affect the rate of profit in the least." (p. 151)

income-redistribution takes place, in a disguised way, via a shift in price formation in the market, according to the rule: "equal profits for equal investment".

*Marx* distinguished (repr. 1966) the "technical composition" of capital and its "value composition". He wrote: "A definite number of labourers correspond to a definite quantity of means of production, and hence a definite quantity of living labour to a definite quantity of labour materialised in means of production. This proportion differs greatly in different spheres of production... This proportion forms the technical composition of capital and is the real basis of its organic composition. ...The difference between the technical composition and the value composition is manifested in each branch of industry in that the value-relation of the two portions of capital may vary while the technical composition is constant, and the value-relation may remain the same while the technical composition varies. ...The value-composition of capital, inasmuch as it is determined by, and reflects, its technical composition, is called the *organic* composition of capital." (pp. 145–146)

The centre of price formation in a fully developed market economy cannot be "value" because of the flows of capital among the various branches of the economy. Instead, it is the "prices of production".

*Marx* wrote (repr. 1966): "Now, if the commodities are sold at their values, then...very different rates of profit arise in the various spheres of production, depending on the different organic composition of the masses of capital invested in them. But capital withdraws from a sphere with a low rate of profit and invades others, which yield a higher profit. Through this incessant outflow and influx, or, briefly, through its distribution among the various spheres, which depends on how the rate of profit falls here and rises there, it creates such a ratio of supply to demand that the average profit in the various spheres of production becomes the same, and values, are, therefore, converted into prices of production." (pp. 195–196)

*Marx* called attention to that the "prices of production" may actually mislead in respect of the origin of "surplus-value".

He noted (repr. 1966): "The transformation of values into prices of production serves to obscure the basis for determining value itself." "Since in the rate of profit the surplus-value is calculated in relation to the total capital and the latter is taken as its standard of measurement, the surplus-value itself appears to originate from the total capital, uniformly derived from all its parts, so that the organic difference between constant and variable capital is obliterated in the concept of profit. Disguised as profit, surplus-value actually denies its origin, loses its character, and becomes unrecognisable." (pp. 167–168)

The actual *market price* can, of course, differ from both value and price of production, depending on the actual changes in demand and supply, i.e. in their relation. A further price category follows, in Marx's too, from the process of monopolization (in modern terminology: from market imperfections).

The *monopoly price* is nothing more, in the Marxian concept (quite similar to the Smithian one), than a further deviation in price formation away from value and price of production, and a further redistribution via prices, namely between monopolized and non-monopolized branches of economy.

Since all these categories may refer to or be applied to *international prices* and terms of trade, as well, which are of great importance from the point of view of the development potential and policy, it is worth discussing how Marxists approach this issue.

Although *Marx* did not elabourate a theory of international trade, nor did he clarify whether the subject of his political economy was the national or the world economy and whether his general price (value) and income theory would apply to the latter, his followers have produced various interpretations of the Marxian concept of "value" and "price of production" in relation also to international trade, partly on the basis of his rather sporadic (and hardly consistent) statements about international exchange inequalities.

According to one of these interpretations, which tacitly accept the ahistorical assumption of a possible separation (not only in theoretical abstraction but also in history) of the stage of value-determined price formation and the stage of price-of-production-determined price formation, it is a sort of *"international value"* which is the natural centre of price formation in the world market.

The concept of such an "international value" presupposes not only a neglect of capital mobility which (according to Marx) transforms value into "price of production" as the centre of price formation (by equalizing the rates of profit and thereby replacing the "surplus value", i.e. the capitalist's share in the "new value", by an average profit) but also the existence of a single, fully integrated world market of all products the value (as price centre) of which is directly determined by the amount of total labour "socially necessary" for reproducing them, i.e. the internationally average sum of labour inputs "accepted" by the world society as "socially necessary".

Exchange equivalence (the Marxian "law of value") prescribes that all products are exchanged at prices corresponding to their values, i.e. to the socially *average* costs in terms of total labour inputs both of the past as materialized "dead labour" (such as in tools, equipment, machineries) and of the present as "live labour", required for reproduction. Consequently, it is the *average* producers only in each industry (i.e. those producing with an average productivity) who can realize an exchange of equal amount of labour. Those producing above the socially acceptable average cost have to give more own labour in exchange for less labour of others and cannot realize a part of their labour actually performed, as "socially necessary" input, or, depending on the market conditions cannot sell a part of their output as socially demanded production at all, while those producing below the level of average cost can gain "extra profits" as long as other producers, forced by competition, do not catch up with them in productivity (thus also cost level).

All this means that even a theoretical equivalence of exchange, i.e. a perfect operation of the Marxian "law of value", involves *inequalities* among producers, moreover disequalizing tendencies reinforcing the temporary or lasting differences in their production conditions.

A modified version of the same concept of "international value" derives the latter, indirectly, from the assumed pre-existence of national values and defines international value as a weighted or unweighted average of the national values. Apart from the problems of how to weight (if at all) the national values of all or only the internationally traded goods, this concept seems to bring us away from reality even further than the previous one (and backward rather than forward) as it totally disregards the impact of capital mobility on price formation even within nations, or assumes in a contradictory way that the Marxian category of "prices of production" appears only on international level, as derived from that of international values. Exchange is also considered equivalent only if it takes place at such international values. Here again those nations producing at higher than international (weighted or unweighted) average costs necessarily suffer relative loss in exchange.

The same follows from what *Marx* said (without defining the relevance of his "law of value" to the above-mentioned cases) about nations whose social (i.e. overall) labour productivity level is below that of their trading partners, namely about their disadvantage of being forced by the market to exchange more units of their own labour for less units of labour of their more advanced partners.

According to *Marx* (repr. 1966) "...the more advanced country sells its goods above their value even though cheaper than the competing countries", namely those "with inferior production facilities". "In so far as the labour of the more advanced country is here realised as labour of a higher specific weight, the rate of profit rises, because labour which has not been paid as being of a higher quality is sold as such. The same may obtain in relation to the country, to which commodities are exported and to that from which commodities are imported; namely, the latter may more materialised *labour in kind* than it receives, and yet thereby receive commodities cheaper than it could produce them. Just as a manufacturer who employs a new invention before it becomes generally used, undersells his competitors and yet sells his commodity above its individual value, that is, realises the specifically higher productiveness of the labour he employs as surplus-labour. He thus secures a surplus-profit." (p. 238)

Whether such cases of unequal exchange are to be considered as those of non-equivalence or, on the contrary, as corresponding to the requirements of equivalent exchange, depends, of course, on the choice of the primary level of analysis: on whether equivalence is primarily considered on national level and from the point of view of individual nations or on the world level, from the point of view of the world society as a whole.

Whatever is the choice, however, the possible conclusions which can be drawn from such cases and interpretations either for theory or for the practical economic policy are more or less the same:

a) *theoretically* the coincidence of a formal equivalence of exchange with the exchange of unequal amounts of individual labour, embodied in the products produced with unequal productivity of labour, or the coincidence of formally equal exchange of the latter with non-equivalence, and
b) *practically* the need and importance of increasing the level of labour productivity not only in the export sectors of the less developed countries but also in

their economy as a whole and of participating thereby more efficiently and successfully in international trade rather than delinking from it.

Another interpretation of the Marxian price theory for the world economy and the international exchange relations is based upon the application of his concept of "prices of production". Accordingly the world market prices (at least in those industries which are subject to international capital mobility) tend to fluctuate around "international prices of production" as the centre of price formation. This means, just like within national economies, that due to the equalization of profit rates those sectors of the world economy producing with a higher "organic composition of capital" (with relatively more materialized labour embodied in the means of production, and less "live labour" which is supposed to be the source of "new value", thus also of profits, in other words the relatively "capital-intensive" sectors) are sharing a part of the new value actually produced in the sectors of a "low organic composition of capital", i.e. in the relatively labour-intensive" sectors.

Insofar as the international distribution of the branches of production (and services) with different "organic composition of capital" is such as concentrating the relatively capital-intensive ("high organic composition") branches in one and the relatively labour-intensive ("low organic composition") branches of economy in another group of countries, while capital is freely moving among them, thereby inducing a tendency of profit rate equalization *via* the formation, as price centre, of "international prices of production", a further conclusion can be drawn both for theory and practice. Namely, that the countries with "low organic composition" branches of economy, i.e. with labour-intensive branches of production, cannot realize the total value they produced, while their partners are (at least) compensated for "high organic composition of capital" (or, in view of the more rapid technological development following there from, are over-compensated rather), as a hidden value transfer takes place through price formation in favour of the latter.

All this means theoretically that the equality of capitals of different "organic composition" implies non-equivalence of exchange while equivalence in the exchange relations excludes the equality of capitals. What follows, practically, for economic policy is that a lasting specialization on branches of production with typically "low organic composition of capital" is unfavourable even if or just because free mobility of capital is ensured, while specialization on more capital-intensive, "high organic composition" branches brings about, also through profit rate equalization, additional advantage.

It is to be recalled, however, that the Marxian concept of "organic composition of capital" refers not only to the "technical composition" but also to the "value composition of capital" (the cost ratios), which may actually counterbalance or intensify the former advantage of capital-intensive branches. Another remark versus the generalization of the concept may be induced by the recognition, still in accordance with Marx, of the role of the turnover rate of capital causing also different individual profit rates in a given period, which may also have a possible counteracting or reinforcing effect in the process of international equalization of profit rates.

A further implication, or rather distortion, of the Marxian "law of value" in international trade is related to the obstacles to international labour mobility which prevent the wage levels, more precisely the relative wage costs (in Marxian terminology: the "rates of surplus value" or "rates of exploitation", i.e. the ratios of "surplus value", representing the capitalist's share, and "variable capital", representing as wages the workers' share, in the new value) from equalization. If capital mobility is also constrained internationally, the differences of wage levels can be manifested also in differences in the national profit rates, in which case the low wage country may, in principle, realize higher returns to capital and gain larger accumulation sources or enjoy *ceteris paribus* a more competitive position in the world market. If, however, capital is more mobile than labour (as in reality, particularly in the international economy), then the tendency of the equalization of profit rates is accompanied by lasting inequalities in the national wage levels. Due to the consequently "abnormal", distorted price formation in the world market (different from that in national markets), this makes it possible for the producers and consumers of the high wage countries to share or fully appropriate the benefits from the low wage costs in the partner countries without suffering the disadvantages and unfavourable effects of the latter on the domestic market and social welfare.

As such cases are in the focus of those "new left" theories over-simplifying the problem of equality or inequality of international exchange, we shall return to their theoretical implications. For the practical policy the conclusion suggests that a low level of wages which may be temporarily favourable for domestic accumulation and international competitiveness, and also attractive (if not accompanied by a similarly low productivity) for foreign investors, can be a great disadvantage if it is a lasting phenomenon, not only for the development of the domestic market and social welfare but also in international trade.

As according to *Marx* the operation of the "law of value" normally leads, by competition, to increasing differentiation of the producers and to a growing concentration and centralization of capital, i.e. to the rise of monopolistic organizations, thus also internationally the replacement of free competition by monopolistic or oligopolistic one and the rise of *monopoly prices* as deviations not only from "values" but also from "prices of production" may represent a further implication of the Marxian theory for international economics.

Insofar as the international distribution among countries of the more or less monopolized and the non-monopolized branches of production (and services) is lastingly and markedly unequal, a part of the new value actually produced in the countries of non-monopolized production is (according to the logic of the Marxian economics) regularly transferred from the latter to countries with monopolized branches of economy. This transfer is supposed also to take place through the mechanism of international price formation, since (apart from other, counteracting conditions) non-monopolized, "under priced" products are exchanged for monopolized, "overpriced" ones. The resulting divergence of profit rates, however, may remain hidden or counterbalanced if the benefits or the burdens of such an exchange are shared by the workers *via* higher or lower wage level, respectively, in the countries concerned.

While monopolization as a tendency follows (according to Marx) from the differentiating effects of even a "perfect" operation of the market with equivalent exchange and "pure" competition, a special case of monopoly is registered in the Marxian *rent* theory, namely the monopoly over limited natural resources such as land. Capital mobility meets, in this case, almost absolute barriers, at least in respect of opportunities to expand, by new investments, the production extensively. As a consequence, and also due to the fact that the capitalist entrepreneurs (if different from the landowners) have to pay rent, the price formation of the products in such branches of economy (namely in agriculture, mining, etc.) may necessarily differ from the formation of "prices of production".

*Marx* assumed that, on the one hand, the "organic composition of capital" in such branches of economy is lower than the average, which implies that the surplus value (new value minus wages) actually produced here exceeds the average profit, and, on the other, that the barriers of capital mobility, preventing the formation of "prices of production"[169], make possible the realization of the total surplus value in the market price, while the entrepreneurs as tenants competing with each other by tender, have to put up with an average profit, and pay the difference as "absolute rent" to the landlords. In addition, as a consequence of differences among the various lands in fertility, in market distance and other conditions, a "differential rent" may also arise and be charged in all those lands or for all those additional investments, the yield of which surpasses that of the marginal (the poorest but still necessarily cultivated) land.

The international implication of the Marxian rent theory suggests a distinction of such cases in the international price formation, which as being linked with a monopoly over non-renewable scarce natural resources involve a rent component. Since, however, the regular realization of both the "absolute" and even the "differential rents" in the actual exchange presupposes a corresponding market equilibrium between demand and supply, thus the disturbances in the latter, the differences among products in supply and demand elasticities and the differences also among the trading partners in bargaining power, etc., make questionable the possibility for many countries to appropriate indeed such rents, not to mention the case when they have to pay a sort of monopolistic rent in the price of products involving a technological (instead of natural resource) monopoly.

All the above variants of the operation of or deviations from the Marxian "law of value", as interpreted on the level of international exchange, point not only to the relative and contradictory meaning of "equal exchange", if any, but also to the diversity and possible combinations or interactions of inequalities in the exchange relations. Even if the "law of value" is not violated by a forced, non-economic deviation of the applied prices in a given transaction from those prevailing in the market, a full equality of the partners and "just prices" for all can never characterize the exchange process. It is not the function of the market to make justice and equality socially or internationally.

---

[169] *Marx* noted (repr. 1966): "A surplus-profit may also arise if certain spheres of production are in a position to evade the conversion of the values of their commodities into prices of production, and thus the reduction of their profits to the average profit." He mentioned the case of "ground-rent". (p. 199)

## 3.6. On international trade, division of labour and capital export

*Marx* practically accepted the Classical views on the development-promoting role of international trade and division of labour in the development of nations as well as the world. While making several critical comments on some of the over-simplifying or naive assumptions of the Classical economists (particularly in regard to "equal partners" as opposed by the historical reality), and also pointing (like Smith) to the distorting effect of excessive specialization on the worker, but also on those nations doomed to remain primary producers only, he did not elabourate an alternative theory of trade and specialization[170].

Although *Marx* explained the tendency of the rate of profits to fall not by the same reasons as the Classical economists (who blamed primarily the diminishing returns to agriculture for it), he also attributed a counteracting effect versus this tendency also to international trade. Unlike the Classical economists, he connected this tendency as an effect, with that of the increase in capital-intensity (in his terminology: the growth of the "organic composition of capital") as a cause, which implies a relative fall within total capital invested, of wages paid to labour, i.e. the original source of profits. Since, however, not only the wage costs can be diminished by *foreign trade,* namely by the import of cheaper consumer goods (as also stressed by the Classicals), but also the costs of some capital goods, particularly by imported raw materials, and, as Marx emphasized, additional profits can also be earned in trade (by achieving higher prices abroad than at home), the rate of profits can be increased, both by a decrease in the denominator of the ratio, i.e. in total capital costs, and by an increase in the numerical, i.e. in the total profits earned.

*Marx* wrote (repr. 1966): "Since foreign trade partly cheapens the elements of constant capital, and partly the necessities of life for which the variable capital is exchanged, it tends to raise the rate of profit by increasing the rate of surplus-value and lowering the value of constant capital. It generally acts in this direction by permitting an expansion of the scale of production." (p. 237)

Without questioning the Classical views that participation in international trade and division of labour contributes to the economic development of the countries concerned, to the progress of their productive forces in general, Marx, on the one hand, focussed the attention, in this respect, too, to the effects on the social relations, namely to which *social class* would benefit at all or more from foreign

[170] Many of his followers believe, referring to his original plan on future volumes of his "Capital", that he simply had no time to write a chapter on international trade and the world economy, in general. This may be a realistic explanation, indeed, but in view of his presentation of capitalism in an abstract model, which can equally apply (if at all) to a national and the world economy, and also in the light of his statement about the world market as being the "natural sphere of operation of capital", this distinctive central force of capitalism, one may wonder whether the reason had been something else or what difference such a chapter could have made.

trade.[171] This appears quite clearly not only in the above-discussed effect of trade on the profit rate, but also in Marx's investigation of the role and profit-source of merchant capital. On the other hand, as follows from the application of his price theory to international trade, the possible various inequalities (behind even an "equivalent exchange") in, and income redistributions through, the price formation in the world market suggest the extension of his concept of exploitation also to international trade.

As regards the gains from trade, he believed that they are mostly (if not exclusively) reaped by the capitalists, though in regard to international exploitation he had already referred to that the rich, industrial nations could benefit more from the international division of labour they had imposed upon some less-developed, poor nations (particularly their colonies) which became exploited by the former[172]. However, and contrary to the views of some of his followers and other radical scholars, he never considered "exploitation", whether it meant that of the workers, or that of some nations, as blocking, excluding their development and benefits. (What Joan Robinson said about "exploitation", namely that only the position of the worker who is not exploited, as not employed, by the capitalist is worse than that of the exploited, i.e. employed one, seems to fairly correspond to Marx's view.)

The same approach seems to characterize the Marxian interpretation of the effects of *international capital flows*, as well.

While the Classical economists did not pay much attention to the phenomenon of capital export (which is quite understandable because that time it was not yet so important, large-scale and determining factor in international economic relations, as later), Marx already extended his investigation to it, as by the mid-19th century the increasing separation of the ownership of capital and its operation in the form of, and owing to the spread of the joint-stock companies[173] started to open a new phase in the historical development of the world economy, with international capital mobility playing the decisive role.

*Marx,* who clearly distinguished, in general, between *working capital* (implying the direct use, the investment and control of capital by the owner who receives the primary return to the invested capital, the *original income,* namely profit) and *loan capital* (offered for use to a borrower who pays, hopefully from profit, an interest

[171] *Marx* pointed (repr. 1966): "The favored country recovers more labor in exchange for less labor, although this difference, this excess is pocketed, as in any exchange between labor and capital, by a certain class." (p. 238)

[172] Referring to the extra benefits of the industrial metropolitan countries from both trade with, and investments in, their colonies, *Marx* noted (repr. 1966): "Since the rate of profit is higher, therefore, because it is generally higher in a colonial country, it may, provided natural conditions are favorable, go hand in hand with low commodity prices." (p. 239)

[173] "In stock companies the function is divorced from capital ownership, hence also labor is entirely divorced from ownership of means of production and surplus-labor." *Marx, K.* (repr. 1966), p. 437.

to the owner of the money lent), considered the international flow of working capital much more important than international lending and borrowing (even if the creditor–debtor relations do also represent inequalities and opportunities for exploitation as well as creation of market[174]) because thereby lasting internationalised ownership relations are created, and the "capital–labour" antagonism appears on international level, too.

As regards the *motive* of capital export, Marx, though basically approaching this question from the point of view of the rate of profit, by no means reduced it to the possibility of achieving a higher profit rate in a foreign economy. Instead, he explicitly or implicitly pointed to *manifold* motives, related to the possibility of improving the "realization of total capital", i.e. the aggregate rate of return to total ("social") capital, an *aggregate profit rate*. Thus, besides a possible higher profit rate of the exported part of capital, the export of "idle" capital (even if without earning a higher rate of profit abroad) can also motivate capital export, moreover the search for better markets or for opportunities to sell unsold products may also induce the export of working capital by which markets can be created or maintained abroad.

The export of capital actually appears in the Marxian concept as a means of temporarily overcoming the problem of "excess capital" and "excess supply of commodities" at home, which all necessarily follow from the capitalistic mode of production aiming the acquisition of profit.

*Marx* emphasized (repr. 1966): "Since the aim of capital is not to minister to certain wants, but to produce profit, and since it accomplishes this purpose by methods which adapt the mass of production to the scale of production, not vice versa, a rift must continually ensue between the limited dimensions of consumption under capitalism and a production which forever tends to exceed this immanent barrier. Furthermore, capital consists of commodities, and therefore, over-production of capital implies over-production of commodities." Thus: "If capital is sent abroad, this is not because it absolutely could not be applied at home, but because it can be employed at a higher rate of profit in a foreign country. But such capital is absolute excess capital for the employed labouring population and for the home country in general. It exists as such alongside the relative over-population, and this is an illustration of how both of them exist side by side, and mutually influence one another." He added: "How could there otherwise be a shortage of demand for the very commodities which the mass of the people lack, and how would it be possible for this demand to be sought abroad, in foreign markets, to pay the labourers at home the average amount of necessities of life?" (p. 256)

As it can be seen, the motives of capital export include, at least, the aim of reducing the problem of excessive capital and excessive supply of products, which obviously refers to the case of disequilibrium in the market economy concerned,

---

[174] In regard to the effect of providing loans in the form of golden money, namely "precious metal" as "directly loanable money-capital", to a foreign country or colony, *Marx* noted (repr. 1966): "In the long run, such a shipment of precious metal to India must have the effect of increasing the Indian demand for English commodities, because it indirectly increases the consuming power of India for European goods." (p. 577)

particularly to the case of recession. However, if applying the Marxian concept of a "social process of reproduction" one may conclude that practically all segments, all "links" of the vertical "chain" of production (from the exploitation of natural resources and production of raw materials, through the various levels of processing, to the final product and its marketing, to its transfer to the final consumer and even its further servicing, etc.) including all the related other services[175], do provide potential opportunities for economizing on capital costs and thereby improving the aggregate rate of profit.

The Marxian view on the general motives of capital export, and particularly the approach following from the Marxian concept, is practically an antecedent of the modern eclectic theory of foreign direct investments[176] which goes much further and gives much more realistic explanation in this field, than the rather narrow and over-simplifying concept of Neo-Classical school.

As to the results, consequences or effects of international capital mobility, *Marx* emphasized, besides its progressive internationalising effect, both its role in promoting economic development in the capital-importing countries, namely by giving an impetus to modernization in less developed countries, by spreading capitalistic relations there, and to their productive forces, as well, and the role it plays in establishing international exploitation relations between foreign capital and local labour, between capital-exporting and capital-importing countries.

## 3.7. On disequilibria and crises

As regards Marx's concept on *equilibrium* in a market economy, it was partly formulated in a negative sense, namely by means of explaining the regular trend of disequilibria and cyclical crises of the economic system of capitalism, i.e. by exploring those processes and conditions preventing the state of economic equilibrium from being lasting or perfect, and partly in a positive way, by outlining in his "reproduction schemes" the basic conditions of a dynamic equilibrium between the main sectors of the economy.

His explanation of the tendency, as a natural concomitant of the capitalist market economy, of disequilibrium and cyclical fluctuation leading to regular crises, is partly related to his concept of the "fundamental contradictions" of capitalism, such as:

1. the "antagonism between labour and capital", namely between those having but their own labour power (the physical and intellectual ability to work) to sell, i.e. the working class, and those owning also capital (accumulated means of production), i.e. the capitalist class, who can employ the former to work for them and thereby share the new value produced by the employed workers;

[175] Such as communication, transport, banking, insurance, etc.

[176] See *Dunning, J. H.* (1993).

2. the contradiction between increasingly collective, "socialized" production and individual, private appropriation of the product, which means the dual tendency of an increase in the size of producing units and in their interlinkages, and of a decrease in the number of those in dominant position, controlling the production process, receiving the major part of the new value and deciding on the use of the surplus;
3. the contradiction between the profit-driven expansion of production and the income-constrained consumption of masses, which follow from the tendency of income distribution to shift in favour of the capitalists, resulting in a declining share of the working masses in national income (i.e. from the "relative pauperisation" of the working class even in case of increasing real wages);
4. the contradiction between the more and more efficiently, highly organized nature (i.e. the increasingly well-organized management) of the production process "within the gates" and the "anarchy" of the market outside.

These contradictions regularly cause not only partial "overproduction", i.e. disequilibrium in single product markets, but from time to time also a general "overproduction" crisis, and disequilibria in factor markets as well, namely over-supply or rather under-demand in the labour market (manifested in large-scale unemployment), and also in the capital-market because of over-saving or under-investment (manifested in "idle capital" and under-utilised capacities).

As *Marx* summarized the basic anomaly of the system (repr. 1966): "The conditions of direct exploitation, and those of realising it, are not identical. They diverge not only in place and time, but also logically. The first are only limited by the productive power of society, the latter by the proportional relation of the various branches of production and the consumer power of society. But this last-named is not determined either by the absolute productive power, or by the absolute consumer power, but by the consumer power based on antagonistic conditions of distribution, which reduce the consumption of the bulk of society to a minimum varying within more or less narrow limits." (p. 244) "On the other hand, too many means of labour and necessities of life are produced at times to permit of their serving as means for the exploitation of labourers at a certain rate of profit. Too many commodities are produced to permit of a realisation and conversion into new capital of the value and surplus-value contained in them under the conditions of distribution and consumption peculiar to capitalist production, i.e., too many to permit of the consummation of this process without constantly recurring explosions." (p. 258)

The cyclical fluctuations and regular crises follow, according to Marx, also from the inability of the capitalist market economy to keep those basic *proportions* in its growth between the main sectors of the economy, making up the necessary conditions for its dynamic equilibrium, which were outlined by Marx in his famous "reproduction schemes"[177].

These schemes, which can be considered as the follow-ups of Quesnay's "tableaux économiques" and as the precedents of Leontief's "input-output tables",

[177] See *Marx, K.* (repr. 1967), Vol. II. Part III.

present a two-sector model of the economy, consisting of the consumer goods producing and the capital goods producing sectors which produce also for each other, thereby mutually providing market for the products of each other by means of their input-output linkages and income generation. By this simple model Marx revealed, in mathematical terms, the conditions of a lasting equilibrium, namely those mutual proportionalities required in the rate of growth and accumulation of both sectors being interlinked.

While the Marxian concept about fluctuations and crises appears as an antecedent of the Keynesian theory of business cycle and imperfect equilibrium (though approached from a different angle, focussing on somewhat different problems[178] of a spontaneously operating market economy, and leading to quite a different conclusion[179]), the "reproduction schemes", apart from certain difficulties (inducing so many debates in literature[180]) in the transformation of these schemes from "value" categories to "prices of production" categories without changing substantial assumptions, represent an important, though over-simplified, method of analysing the equilibrium conditions in the process of development and thus also a useful tool in development policy as well.

Since the development of national economies can proceed more rapidly or slowly, also depending on their position in, and on the equilibrium conditions of the *world economy*, the above concepts of Marx can also be taken into account in regard to the latter. The more so as here again it is possible to interpret, *mutatis mutandis*, the Marxian theses on the level of the world economy. E.g. those "fundamental contradictions" attributed by Marx to the system, can be considered accordingly.

For example:

1. the "antagonism" between labour and capital can internationally be interpreted as a conflict between domestic labour and foreign capital or vice versa;
2. the contradiction between increasingly "socialized" production and private appropriation as a contradiction between an increasingly transnationalized production and the national framework of institutionalised control and distribution;

---

178 While in the Marxian explanation a greater emphasis is put on the regularly arising contradiction between the profit-driven growth of production and the insufficient purchasing power of the masses of consumers, i.e. between (mass) production and (mass) consumption, which leads to regularly reappearing over-production and drop of the rate of profits, *Keynes* stressed the problem of a temporary but regular incongruence between the intention to save and actual investment (or between actual saving and the intention to invest), which follows from fluctuations of the "marginal efficiency of capital", i.e. from changes in the current expectations regarding the future yields of investment, heavily influenced by the actual spending of present incomes (thus, by the propensity to consume), and causing thereby fluctuations in the level of investment and employment, thus also of income (on which saving depends).

179 While *Marx* believed in the necessity of replacing, by revolution, the capitalist system of the economy by a new one, *Keynes* urged to reform it only.

180 About such difficulties and debates see *Szentes, T.* (1985).

3. the contradiction between profit-motivated ever-expanding production and the income-constrained consumption of masses as a contradiction between the expansion of export production encouraged by national policies and the obstacles, set by the poverty and/or balance-of-payments problems of many nations and by State-created artificial barriers, to the inadequate growth of effective demand internationally;
4. the contradiction between the highly organized nature of production "within the gates" and the "anarchy" of the market outside, as an incongruence, internationally, between the institutionalised system of national economies with certain, direct or indirect State-regulations, or the well-organized system of production, distribution and marketing within transnational companies on world level and the lack of adequate institutions with efficient mechanism to regulate the world economy.

Although such an application of the Marxian theses to the world economy may provide some additional insights to the problematic of *international inequalities and disequilibria* of the world economy, hardly any concrete practice-oriented conclusion can be drawn from it (except a possible but not new conclusion about the need to eliminate the State-created barriers of the realization of effective demand internationally).

More relevant and practice-oriented conclusions may follow from the "reproduction schemes" both for national economic policy and concerning the international economy. The relevance of such an approach to the structural conditions of equilibrium in the world-wide division of labour can hardly be doubted, particularly in the case of the relatively also simple pattern of division of labour, which has developed through centuries and mostly survived until recently, between two sectors of the world economy, namely the primary producing underdeveloped countries and the developed industrial ones.

It follows from the logic of the "reproduction schemes" that disequilibrium is inevitable if the growth rates of the two sectors substantially differ and are out of proportion to each other for some reason, e.g. because of markedly unequal conditions and opportunities of development in the two sectors. Since the primary producing branches of economy cannot provide such facilities as manufacturing industries do for the improvement of the quality of labour, for technological development, for internal and external economies, for the expansion, through input-output linkages, of the domestic market, etc., the primary producing sector of the world economy is *ceteris paribus* doomed to lag behind the industrial sector to an increasing extent. This makes it impossible for the two sectors to present mutually proportional markets for each other, even apart from protectionism or other obstacles. The tendency of cumulative indebtedness of the primary producing developing countries and the need for a regular and growing transfer of development resources to the latter in the form of financial aid and "technical assistance" (even if an opposite transfer *via* capital flight, brain drain or losses caused by the deterioration of the terms of trade did not occur) show the point.

## 3.8. On the anomalies and prospects of capitalism

By presenting a thorough analysis (a kind of "diagnosis") of the contemporary capitalism, though in a rather abstract model with illustrative cases only, i.e. in its "pure" form, Marx produced a sharp critique on the capitalist system of the economy which, in his view,

1. tends to increase social and international *inequalities* (even if the income distribution does not necessarily follow the rule of a "zero-sum-game"),
2. brings about, in a cyclical motion, regular crises as sharp manifestations of *disequilibria* (even if such economic crises restore, at least temporarily and at high social costs, equilibrium),
3. causes growing *alienation* of the members of society and also nations from each other, by making their relations "impersonalised", formed as relations to "things", as exchange- and monetary relations, and by commercialising human labour, sex, culture, religion, etc.,
4. and increases exploitation of the majority by a smaller and smaller minority.

It follows that according to *Marx* the capitalist market economy (whether it is a national or the world economy) can by no means operate in a harmonious way, based on or bringing about equally beneficial relations between equal partners. Nor can it ensure a lasting and dynamic equilibrium, however more developed or however more rapidly developing it can be than all the other previous systems of the economy.

Nevertheless, despite this sharp critique and the conclusion about a necessary anti-capitalist revolution, Marx considered capitalism not only as a *historically inevitable* stage in the development process of human society, but also as a far more developed system than any previous one, bringing ahead social development. Contrary to the belief of the Classical economist, he believed that it represents only a certain stage in the historical process of social development but not the final and highest one. And unlike some of his followers and other radical scholars criticizing capitalism, he did not qualify the capitalist system as a historical error or unnecessary roundabout of social development[181].

Moreover, while sharply condemning *colonialism* for its cruelty, humiliating effects and for the sheer force the colonizing capitalist states were using, he did attribute a certain positive role to it as a "tool of history" which breaks up rigid, traditional and stagnant precapitalistic systems and forces them to transform, to develop a capitalist mode of production[182].

[181] See e.g. *Wallerstein's* concept, which will be discussed later.

[182] "The question is, can mankind fulfill its destiny without a fundamental revolution in the social state of Asia? If not, whatever may have been the crimes of England, she was the unconscious tool of history in bringing about the revolution." *Marx, K* (1853), pp. 93–94.

*Marx*, who was primarily interested in investigating the roots of domination, oppression, alienation and exploitation both within and among countries and in finding out the way of social development towards an ideal system, believed that before capitalism fully unfolds (all over the world) and reaches (at least in the most advanced capitalist countries) its highest possible level of development, there would be no chance for a better, post-capitalist system to arise because the latter cannot be given birth but by a revolution.

While in respect of the assumed causes of dominance and exploitation a certain analogy may indeed appear between the case of a national system of capitalism and the world system, if applying the Marxian explanation to both, i.e. regarding the *deprivation*, by capitalism, of certain social classes and also of countries of the basic means of production or of development resources, respectively, an obvious contradiction can be found in the suggested recipe. Unlike a proletarian revolution within a country, which (if we disregard both the external environment and the internal social costs) can be, indeed, supposed to undermine and transform the system as a whole, by paralyzing the operation of its economy and by seizing the State power, a world revolution of the poor, "proletarian" nations can hardly be assumed to have the same chance, as being the action of the economically and militarily weakest countries of the world system. As regards a world revolution of the proletariat of all the countries, including the advanced ones, it contradicts the very concept of "proletarian nations" exploited by the rich ones. Not to mention that on the world level there is no central State power (at least for the time being), which could be seized and used for system transformation.

Here again, the very problem of the *confusion* regarding the primary level of analysis of capitalism (whether on the level of countries or of the world as a whole) seems to be the reason of such a contradiction.

*Another contradiction* or inconsistency appears in the Marxian theory also in respect of the ways and means of system transformation. Though Marx distinguished capitalism as a system based upon "economic force", i.e. upon the economic need of otherwise free workers to perform (if they can) wage labour for the capitalists, in contrast to all the precapitalist class societies in which the ruling classes were using sheer, non-economic force in the appropriation of surplus, he and his followers actually visualized and recommended a sheer, non-economic violence, instead of an economic counter-force ("countervailing power"), as the only ways of changing the system.

In other words, and strangely enough, while stressing the ability of capitalism to operate without sheer, non-economic force as a distinctive feature of this system versus other social systems of economy, Marx did assume sheer force, namely a revolutionary action to be a precondition for not only (and historically correctly) the rise of this system (including the process of "primitive" or "primary" accumulation of capital, depriving the producers of their means of production, mainly land) in the pioneering countries which were the first in developing it, but also of its spread in the most backward parts of the world (in the form of colonialism) and of its replacement by a new system, namely "socialism".

The role of sheer, non-economic force was also incorporated in the concept of "imperialist capitalism" of Marxists, particularly in *Lenin's* theory of imperialism[183] as the final stage of capitalism.

Although *Lenin* did not share the views of some other Marxists who interpreted imperialism and colonialism as simply a violent aggressive policy leading to colonial wars and military occupation of foreign territories, he nevertheless included among the five basic characteristics of the "imperialist", monopoly-capitalist stage he distinguished from those of "classical capitalism", also such characteristics as colonialism itself, the "territorial division among imperialist States of the world". At the same time, and in contradiction to the above, his all theory (or rather a sketch only) placed capital export into the centre of the operation of the modern system of international capitalism.

*Capital export* (as the third characteristic in his theory, actually linking the first two, nation-based characteristics, namely the concentration and centralisation of capital and the rise of a financial oligarchy from the coalescence of bank and industrial capital in the advanced countries, with the fourth one, namely the division of the world economy among international monopolies into spheres of interest) has played, no doubt, a decisive role in shaping the production relations (in Marxian sense, i.e. the relations of ownership, of division of labour, and of income distribution) internationally. This is particularly true in the case of the export of "working capital", i.e. investments in foreign economies, creating ownership and control positions there.

The "Marxist-Leninist" school did not only remain stuck with some original inconsistencies of the Marxian theory but definitely (and manipulatively) moved towards dogmatic over-simplifications and away from reality. Foreign capital, particularly that of the transnational corporations, was considered by it as the "evil" to be exorcised, and the modern world system of market economies was assessed as the manifestation only of "imperialist interests" and domination. Consequently the spread of capitalism by means of foreign penetration into less developed countries was interpreted by its representatives (just like by some extreme, radical, mostly nationalist scholars) as only and exclusively negative, harmful, development hindering factor in history. On the contrary, a sort of "orthodox Marxism" over-emphasized the other side of the same phenomenon, namely its positive, favourable role in developing the economies concerned, and consider imperialism as the "pioneer of capitalism"[184].

[183] *Lenin, V. I.* (1967).

[184] See it later.

## 3.9. On social systems as stages of historical development

The Marxian theory on *social systems*, social formations reflects a concept of unilinear development and a determinist perception of history. According to this theory human societies necessarily develop through the following stages as different "social formations"[185] (determined by their "mode of production"):

1. *primitive communism*, based upon common ownership and low productivity, in which production (gathering, fishing and hunting or primitive agriculture) is mostly a collective action without regularly resulting an appropriable surplus, and distribution is also common;
2. *slavery*, based upon the ownership of slaves, the acquisition of them by wars or other forms of violence, and the appropriation, by force, of their product, which, because of a somewhat higher total productivity of masses of cheap slaves, involves a regular surplus providing the source for the wealth of the slave-owner class and their state power;
3. *feudalism*, based upon the landlords' ownership of land and "serfdom", i.e. the personal subordination of agricultural producers to (but without being owned, as slaves, by) the landlords, and their life bound to the landlords' land, in which the "serfs" are obliged to perform a certain amount of labour directly in the landlords' economy and are also forced to deliver (not only the landlords but also to the Church and the King) a certain amount of product, more or less equal to the surplus produced regularly by them (as having improved techniques, accumulated experiences and better incentives than slaves) on that part of the landlords' land they are allowed to use;
4. *capitalism*, based upon the private ownership of the main means of production as capital, and the personal freedom of labourers, in which the latter are economically forced to sell their labour power to the owners of capital and induced, stimulated (more than the "serfs" were) to produce, with improving technology, skill and increasing productivity, surplus for them;
5. *communism* and its early, "transitional" variant: *socialism*, based upon common, collective (so-called "socialized") ownership of the main means of production, i.e. elimination of their private ownership and of the private appropriation of the surplus, in which economic activities are collectively organized

[185] *Marx* nevertheless referred to certain historical exceptions, too, which involved some roundabouts in development or mixture of the basic formations, such as the "Asiatic mode of production", which was considered by him as the most important deviation from the main (European) stream of social development and as characterizing huge Asian empires had to be investigated in more details. This mode of production, which has caused many debates among Marxists, the "horizontally" communistic social relations (particularly in the form of common land ownership of the producers) were somehow combined with the "vertical" relations of dominance and exploitation, imposed upon the latter, in which the appropriation and redistribution of the products was carried out by a state power.

in a planned and transparent way, alienation gradually disappears, and so does (via and after "socialism") the State[186] and the market[187], while the social activity of the individuals and the distribution of the product among them follow the principle of "each according to his/her ability" and "each according to his/her performance" (in socialism) or "each according to his/her needs" (in communism), respectively.

The Marxian thesis about this last "stage" of social development, which was obviously a politically motivated, ideological vision only about a future, alternative system versus the contemporary, rejected one, involved many utopian elements. Since it was not elabourated in details, it could easily be used and manipulatively modified later in communist ideology. This is one of the reasons why the so-called "existing socialism" in the former "socialist" countries were linked, even in the public opinion, with the Marxian vision, despite some obvious contradictions between the two, and why the official ideology in those countries, namely "Marxism–Leninism" could use it to legitimise the system, to provide apologetical justification to its changing policy.

## 3.10. Concluding remarks

The Marxian theory with its holistic and critical approach focussed the investigation of social (and world) development on its inherent contradictions which push the latter ahead, and on those unequal relations (even if dressed in formal equalities) determining the position of different classes or nations, which must not only undergo regular transformation, as enforced by and also enabling a further development of the productive forces, but also finally need to be liquidated for the sake of an ideal, just and socially equal system to arise.

In view of the above, the Marxian approach and theses may be of interest and useful particularly for those in development studies, who also wish to reveal the anomalies and undesired consequences of the development process.

As regards Marx's vision about a future ideal society, it obviously belongs to the world of utopian thoughts and dreams, but has also been used as a misleading ideology. His predictions concerning the future of capitalism with ever-sharpening contradictions and the eruption of a world revolution of the proletariat of all countries, have proved totally wrong. Since his time, as a matter of fact, capitalism

186 This is the famous concept about the "withering away of the state".

187 While in the transitional period of "socialism" a state-controlled market for consumer goods and a "quasi-market" (without independent actors and choices) for capital goods may still exist, but the labor force is assumed to cease to be a real commodity, in a communist society all markets disappear, which means that the products lose their "exchange value", there is no need for money, and production implies the production of "use values" only, directly oriented toward human needs.

has changed a lot (at least in the advanced countries), and those revolutions (in less developed countries) aiming at a new, post-capitalist system have all failed.

It seems that Marx who gave an excellent critical analysis of the 19th century capitalism but a false prediction about its future, behaved like a physician who carefully analyses the nature of a sickness "in abstracto", i.e. produces a "diagnosis" about it in itself, abstracted from the patient's living and reacting organism, and thus predicts death as the final outcome of the sickness accordingly, without trusting even those medicines he prescribed to the patient.

Although Marx did address his theory to the working classes, he missed to take into account how those "countervailing forces" (and not only revolutionary forces) arising from them and in the society in general, would bring about substantial changes in advancing capitalism.

## 4. Neo-Classical economics

The Neo-Classical stream of economics, which had also its roots (like the Marxian economic theory) in Classical economics[188], followed and reinforced the liberal principles of the latter, while rejected its labour theory of value, and replaced it by the concept of marginalism (by the subjective interpretation of value as "marginal utility" of the goods for the consumer, influencing the demand of the latter, and by the theory of marginal productivity as a micro-economic concept of cost determination and as a macroeconomic one of factor price and income determination). Neo-Classical economics combined the Classicals' production-oriented, cost and supply determining "objective" approach to the market price formation with the subjective, consumption-oriented, consumers' needs and demand determining approach[189].

As *Alfred Marshall* noted (1930): "We might as reasonably dispute whether it is the upper or the under blade of a pair of scissors that cuts a piece of paper, as whether value is governed by utility or cost of production." (p. 348)

Since its birth (more than a century ago) the Neo-Classical stream of economic theory has grown to a huge "body" which includes great many, often very diverse

---

188 It is to be noted here that *Keynes*, as he admitted, included in the "classical school" also "the followers of Ricardo, those, that is to say, who adopted and perfected the theory of the Ricardian economics, including (for example) J. S. Mill, Marshall, Edgeworth and Prof. Pigou." *Keynes, J. M.* (1936), p. 3. fn.1.

189 *Marshall* noted: "The book (*Principles*) was written to express one idea; & one only. That idea is that whereas Ricardo & Co. maintain that value is determined by Cost of production, & Malthus, McLeod, Jevons & (in a measure) the Austrians that it is determined by utility, each was right in what he affirmed but wrong in what he denied. They none of them paid, I think, sufficient attention to the element of *Time*..." – In Marshall's letter to N. G. Pierson, quoted by *Rostow, W. W.* (1990), p. 161.

theoretical concepts and methods, and has been developed by numerous scholars (unlike the Classical theory which was only by a few)[190]. Owing to the great diversity, to the rise of newer and newer branches of this Neo-Classical stream of economics and also to the fact that its famous authors often belonged to different "schools"[191], which some other, alternative theoretical streams have also originated from (such as the Keynesian economics and the Post-Keynesian Reformist theory of international economics, etc.), it is very difficult, if not impossible, to describe it as a homogenous "body" by equally characteristic common features. Even those characteristics appearing at first sight or attributed to it (particularly in standard textbooks) as the most common and typical, may turn to be *questionable* or, at least, over-generated, if reading some less frequently quoted text in the publications of its original authors.

For example, *R. Grabowski* and *M. P. Shields* (1996) point to the shorter time horizon and efficiency-orientation of the Neo-Classicals, as compared to the Classical views: "In the late 1980s marginalism began displacing Ricardian classical economics as the dominant mode of thought. The marginalists replaced the classical concern with a very long-run supply price with a concern over resource allocation and efficiency within a shorter, static framework." (p. 22)

Although those *short-term assumptions* considered to be more or less typical in Neo-Classical theories are usually attributed to *Alfred Marshall*, perhaps the greatest representative of Neo-Classical economics, too, he actually noted (repr. 1930) that "markets vary with regard to the period of time which is allowed to the forces of demand and supply to bring themselves into equilibrium with one another, as well as with regard to the area over which they extend." He also added that "this element of Time requires more careful attention just now than does that of Space". (p. 330)

Another remark of him (1930) points to the very shortcoming of the *static framework* of analysis: "...economic problems are imperfectly presented when they are treated as problems of static equilibrium, and not of organic growth. For though the static treatment alone can give us definiteness and precision of thought, and is therefore a necessary introduction to more philosophic treatment of society as an organism, it is yet only an introduction. The statical theory of equilibrium is only an introduction to economic studies; and it is barely even an introduction to the study of the progress and development of industries, which show a tendency to increasing return. Its limitations are so constantly overlooked, especially by those who approach it from an abstract point of view that there is a danger in throwing it into definite form at all." (p. 461)

---

[190] For a detailed investigation of the Neo-Classical economics see *Mátyás, A.* (1979).

[191] Such as, first of all, the *Austrian School* (not only with Carl Menger, Friedrich von Wieser, and Eugen von Böhm-Bawerk, who developed the concept of "marginal utility", but also, later on, with Joseph A. Schumpeter, and Friedrich von Hayek); the *Lausanne School* (with Leon Walras and Wilfred Pareto, the authors of the concepts of "general equilibrium" and the "Pareto-optimum", but partly also with the Russian Wassily Leontief); the *Stockholm School* (not only with Gustav Cassel and Bertil Ohlin, but also with Knut Wicksell and Gunnar Myrdal); the *Cambridge School* (not only with Arthur Pigou, but also with Johm Maynard Keynes and Joan Robinson).

Marshall (repr. 1930) clearly distinguished between "short-period" and "long-period" in economic analysis: "...the shorter the period which we are considering, the greater must be the share of our attention which is given to the influence of demand on value; and the longer the period the more important will be the influence of cost of production on value." (p. 349)

According to his notes (1930), in short periods the "supply of specialized skill and ability, of suitable machinery and other material capital, and of the appropriate industrial organization has not time to be fully adapted to demand...", but in long periods "all investments of capital and effort in providing the material plant and the organization of a business, and in acquiring trade knowledge and specialized ability, have time to be adjusted to the incomes which are expected to be earned by them: and the estimates of those incomes therefore directly govern supply, and are the true long-period normal supply price of the commodities produced." (pp. 376–377) "In a stationary state then the plain rule would be that cost of production governs value. ...But nothing of this is true in the world in which we live. Here every economic force is constantly changing its action, under the influence of other forces... In this world therefore every plain and simple doctrine as to the relations between cost of production, demand and value is necessary false". (pp. 367–368)

Despite his distinction, for analytical reasons, between "short" and "long" periods, Marshall made it clear that (repr. 1930) "the element of Time, which is the centre of the chief difficulty of almost every economic problem, is itself absolutely continuous. Nature knows no absolute partition of time into long periods and short;" (p. vii).

While Neo-Classical economics is often praised for its well-developed, *sophisticated analytical tools,* the same Marshall admitted (repr. 1930) the imperfections of analytical methods.

He emphasized that the "...main concern of economics is thus with human beings who are impelled, for good and evil, to change and progress. Fragmentary statical hypotheses are used as temporary auxiliarities to dynamical – or rather biological – concepts..." (p. XV)

In the first edition of his book (1890) he noted that there had always been a temptation "to gratify... the student's desire for logical precision, and the popular liking for dogmas that have the air of being profound and are yet easily handled. But great mischief seems to have been done by yielding to this temptation, and drawing broad artificial lines of division where Nature has made none. The more simple and absolute an economic doctrine is, the greater will be the confusion which it brings into attempts to apply economic doctrines to practice...". (repr. 1930, p. IX)

And in regard to *the use of mathematics*, for which Neo-Classical economics is also frequently praised, Marshall warned us to be cautious:

"The chief use of pure mathematics in economic questions seems to be in helping a person to write down quickly, shortly and exactly, some of his thoughts for his own use: and to make sure that he has enough, and only enough, premises for his conclusions (i.e. that his equations are neither more nor less in number than his unknowns). ...yet it seems doubtful whether any one spends his time well in reading lengthy translations of economic doctrines into mathematics, that have not been made by himself." (repr. 1930, pp. X–XI)

As regards the use of *abstract theoretical models*, he noted (1890): "...theory however, especially when aided by diagrams, helps to give definiteness to our ideas; and in its elementary stages it does not diverge from the actual facts of life so far as to prevent its giving a fairly trustworthy picture of the chief methods of action of the strongest and most persistent group of economic forces. It is only when pushed to its more remote and intricate logical consequences, especially those connected with multiple positions of equilibrium, that it slips away from the conditions of real life, and soon ceases to be of much service in dealing with practical problems." (p. 425)

A one-sided, *purely economistic* emphasis on allocative efficiency (versus social equality and distributive efficiency), an excessive or primary concern about *physical capital* as the most important factor of production and the principle of *selfish individualism* are also often attributed to Neo-Classical economics. But Marshall made quite opposite remarks (1890):

"It is sometimes said that economists regard it as 'natural' or 'normal', and in some sense even right, that man should be governed only by selfish motives; this opinion may however be dismissed at once as a popular error, which finds no support in the teaching or practice of the best economists. ...When the older economists spoke of the 'economic man' as governed by selfish, or by self-regarding motives, they did not express their meaning exactly." (p. 78)

He emphasized that "...We look at the individual, not as a 'psychological atom' but as a member of a social group" (p. 70), and that "a full discussion of a free trade policy must take account of many considerations that are not strictly economic". (p. 61)

According to him "...ethical forces are among those of which the economist has to take account. Attempts have indeed been made to construct an abstract science with regard to the actions of an 'economic man', who is under no ethical influences and who pursues pecuniary gain warily and energetically, but mechanically and selfishly. But they have not been successful, nor even thoroughly carried out." (p. vi)

Marshall also rejected (1890) the assumption about such an "economic man" whose way of thinking, intentions and actions are independent of his class position and unchanged in time.

"The normal willingness to save, the normal willingness to undergo a certain exertion for a certain pecuniary reward, or the normal alertness to seek the best markets in which to buy and sell, or to search out the most advantageous occupation for oneself or for one's children – all these and similar phrases must be relative to the members of a particular class at a given place and time..." (p. vii)

According to Marshall (1890), "The older economists took too little account of the fact that human faculties are as important a means of production as any other kind of capital; and we may conclude, in opposition to them, that any change in the distribution of wealth which gives more to the wage receivers and less to the capitalists is likely, other things being equal, to hasten the increase of material production, and that it will not perceptibly retard the storing-up of material wealth." (p. 295)

He criticized the Classical scholars for regarding "labour simply as a commodity without throwing themselves into the point of view of the workman; without allowing for his human passions, his instincts and habits, his sympathies, his class jealousies and class adhesiveness, his want of knowledge and of the opportunities for free and vigorous action. They therefore attributed to the forces of supply and demand a much more mechanical and regular action than they actually have..." "...their most vital fault was that they did not see how liable to change are the habits and institutions of industry. In particular they did not see that the poverty of the poor is the chief cause of that weakness and inefficiency which are the causes of their poverty; they had not the faith that modern economists have in the possibility of a vast improvement in the condition of the working classes." (pp. 62–63)

Marshall pointed (1890) to the cumulative nature of inequalities:

"It is...certain that manual labourers as a class are at a disadvantage in bargaining; and that the disadvantage wherever it exists is likely to be cumulative in its effects." (pp. 597–598)" The worse fed are the children of one generation, the less will they earn when they grow up, and the less will be their power of providing adequately for the material wants of their children; and so on;... And conversely any change that awards to the workers of one generation better earnings, together with better opportunities of developing their best qualities, will increase the material and moral advantages which they have the power to offer to their children..." "The advantages which those born in one of the higher grades of society have over those born in a lower, consist in a great measure of the better introductions and the better start in life which they receive from their parents. ...Not to speak of those who inherit a share in an existing business, or capital with which to start one of their own, they generally owe some of their success to the business or professional introduction which they receive from relatives or from friends of the family." (p. 591)

He also stressed (1890) that "...the study of the causes of poverty is the study of the causes of the degradation of a large part of mankind." (p. 3) He added: "...we are setting ourselves seriously to inquire whether it is necessary that there should be any so called 'lower classes' at all: that is whether there need be large numbers of people doomed from their birth to hard work in order to provide for others the requisites of a refined and cultured life; while they themselves are prevented by their poverty and toil from having any share or part in that life." (p. 3)

As regards *individualism and selfishness*, Marshall expressed his hope (1890) that "gradually we may attain to an order of social life, in which the common good overrules individual caprice." (p. 47)

He also praised Bentham for his uncompromising stand for social equality, for declaring "that any one man's happiness was as important as any other's, and the aim of all action should be to increase the sum total of happiness" and for admitting that "other things being equal this sum total would be the greater, the more equally wealth was distributed". (p. 58)

Marshall raised seriously the question: Are the opportunities of real life to be confined to a few? He believed that the same sum of money measures a greater pleasure for the poor than the rich, by which he practically justified the case of progressive taxation. He also pointed to the importance of real human needs.

He stated (1930) "that every increase in the wealth of the working classes adds to the fullness and nobility of human life; because it is used chiefly in the satisfaction of real wants"; and that: "The world would go much better if everyone would buy fewer and simpler things...preferring to buy a few things made well by highly paid labour rather than many made badly by low paid labour." (p. 113) Marshall concluded that there is no justification for extreme poverty side by side with great wealth. (pp. 136–137) He also noted (1930): "If human nature could be ideally transformed private property would be unnecessary and harmless." (p. 721)

Although Neo-Classical economics has turned, indeed, the attention to the operation rather than development of the market economy, to its micro- and macro-economic phenomena and processes, i.e. to pragmatic investigations of the market economy, its demand and supply determinants, consumer's behaviour, and the economy of firms, entrepreneurial choices, allocative efficiency, etc., it nevertheless has also enriched the literature on development since its very beginning. Along with its numerous results in praxeology and methodology (which can hardly be neglected in development economics either), it has also elabourated a number of new theses, approaches or models, which are obviously related to *development economics*. Such are, among many others,

- the re-formulated production function with the assumption of an unlimited substitution between labour and capital, and a greater role played by the latter; and the related
- new "models" (also in sophisticated mathematical formulas) of economic growth, in which "factor endowments", i.e. the relative abundance or scarcity of factors of production, and their growth, efficiency and combination are determinant;
- new price and incomes theory (Marshall, Böhm-Bawerk, Enter, etc.);
- the concept of "general equilibrium" as distinguished from partial equilibrium (Walras);
- the concept and method of "opportunity costs" as a new approach to making a choice between different products or export industries or even development alternatives in general;
- the methods of analysing the behaviour of demand and supply also in international markets (Marshallian "reciprocal demand/supply curves") and methods of calculating elasticities;
- new thoughts on consumers' attitude, market fragmentation and product differentiation, "conspicuous consumption", "inferior" and "superior goods" (Giffen, Engel);
- the concept of consumer's surplus (Marshall);
- new theses about monopoly and market imperfections (Marshall, Chamberlin, Robinson);
- the concept of "economic welfare" (Pigou);
- new approaches to technological progress, choice of technologies;
- the introduction of the time factor in economic analysis;
- the new concepts on the "basis" for international trade and specialization (e.g. the Heckscher–Ohlin theorem);
- the new ("elasticity") approach to an international equilibrium mechanism (an exchange-rate mechanism) or a "balance-of-payment adjustment" policy under specified (Marshall–Lerner) conditions;
- the thesis about the "natural" tendency (desirable direction) of international factor mobility, particularly capital flows, namely from relatively capital-rich (more advanced) to capital-poor (less developed) countries;
- the idea about international equalization of factor costs, incomes and productivities (thus also of development levels) assumed to follow from an internationally rational, and mutually beneficial specialization (Heckscher–Ohlin–Samuelson thesis) or from free international factor mobility, i.e. under some desirable conditions; and so on.

## 4.1. Neo-Classical views on the sources and determinants of economic growth

As regards the development or the growth of the economy and its major determinants, sources and motive forces, Neo-Classical economics has emphasized the role of factor endowments and the related marginal productivity of each factor of production[192].

Though in the short-run *factor endowments* are taken for granted, the growth in labour, as resulting from population growth, and the growth, particularly in capital, owing to increased savings, are also taken into account in the Neo-Classical concept and model of economic growth.

Neo-Classical economics makes a clear distinction between average efficiency or productivity of the factors of production and their *marginal productivity*. The latter means the ratio between the last (marginal) increment in the output and the last (marginal) unit of the factor in question which is used as an additional input in production, while other factor(s) of production are kept constant. Since under the circumstances of a given, unchanged technological level, the "disproportionate use of any agent of production" results in diminishing return[193], marginal productivity normally tends to decline. Thus the greater the number of units of a factor of production that a firm can employ (depending, of course, on the firm's budget and the market price of the factor of production) or that a country de facto possesses, the smaller its marginal productivity can be.

Since the factor prices and the incomes of the owners of the factors of production are normally, i.e. under equilibrium conditions, determined, according to Neo-Classical economics, by their marginal productivity[194], respectively, it means that the price and income of labour in relatively labour-abundant countries tend to be lower than in the relatively capital-rich countries where the price of and the returns to capital is made cheaper by the lower marginal productivity of capital. The implications of such a price and income theory are, of course, manifold, and may suggest not only new principles of specialization, but also different development paths for countries having different factor endowments. (See later!) One should never forget, however, what *premises* and assumed conditions make the basis (and limitations) of this concept, nor the fact that not only corrections but also alternative views can also be found in Neo-Classical literature itself.

---

[192] *Marshall* (1930) actually pointed to that "though there is a sharp line of division between man himself and the appliances which he uses; and though the supply of, and the demand for, human efforts and sacrifices have peculiarities of their own, which do not attach to the supply of, and the demand for, material goods; yet, after all, these material goods are themselves generally the result of human efforts and sacrifices. The theories of the values of labor, and of the things made by it, cannot be separated". (p. viii)

[193] *Marshall, A.* (1930), p. 407.

[194] "...the wages of every class of labor tend to be equal to the net product due to the additional labor of the marginal laborer of that class." *Marshall, A.* (1930), p. 518.

In view of that (a) the germs of the concept of "marginal productivity" had already appeared in the Classical as well as in the Marxian economics (at least in respect of agriculture and "differential rent"), and that (b) the Neo-Classical scholars also take into account, among the determinants of the growth of national income, the fertility of land (even if attributing less importance to it) and the average productivity of labour, one may conclude that the re-formulation by Neo-Classsicals of the aggregate production function implies a refinement and perhaps a certain shift in emphasis, rather than a profound revision of the earlier concepts.

As regards the average efficiency of the factors of production even under their given quantity, the Neo-Classical economists, despite their usual assumption of "homogeneous" and perfectly substitutive units of the factors of production in the models of rational choices by firms as well as in the models of international specialization, do also refer to the possible change in technology and in the quality of labour, as well as to some other circumstances, including institutional conditions.

Accordingly, the level of *economic development* of a country and its rate of growth depend not only on its given natural resources and available labour force as well as accumulated capital, i.e. on factor endowments and the related marginal productivity of these factors, but also on the changes in the efficiency of these factors of production, determined by technological development, education, income distribution, social security, etc.

*Marshall* noted (1890): "Accumulated wealth may be regarded as the result of labour and waiting, though not necessarily the labour of its present owners." "...the fruits of that production were the results of waiting for fruits of labour which this waiting made more effective...". "...on the whole it is perhaps best to say that there are three factors of production, land, labour, and the sacrifice involved in waiting." (pp. 613–614)

In summing up the major *sources of development* he stated: "...gross real income of a country depends on (i) the number and average efficiency of the workers in it, (ii) the amount of its accumulated wealth, (iii) the extent, richness and convenience of situation of its natural resources, (iv) the state of the arts of production, (v) the state of public security and the assurance to industry and capital of the fruits of their labour and abstinence...". He also added: "The rates of increase of the number and efficiency of the working population of a country depend, broadly speaking, on (i) the number and efficiency of the population already existing, (ii) the gross real income that there is to be distributed among the different classes of the nation, (iii) the evenness of the distribution of that income (for an increase of income of a less wealthy class at the expense of an equal aggregate loss to a more wealthy class generally promotes the increase of the number and efficiency of the population, providing it is obtained without injury to public security), (iv) on the strength of the family affections in so far as they incline people to lead a domestic life and to incur trouble and expense on bringing up their children, and (v) their willingness to sacrifice present and immediate enjoyment for more distant enjoyment (this counting in two ways, leading them on the one hand to delay marriage so as to retain a high Standard of Comfort, and, on the other to think highly of the advantages of a good education). In addition, the growth of the efficiency of the population depends on the magnitude of the reward that the existing state of the arts of production can be obtained by industrial ability."[195]

[195] Quoted in *Whitaker, J. K.* ed. (1975), pp. 309–312.

Marshall already emphasized the great importance of investments in *education* and "industrial training". He stated (repr. 1930): "No change would conduce so much to a rapid increase of material wealth as an improvement in our schools. ...the wisdom of expanding public and private funds on education is not to be measured by its direct fruits alone. It will be profitable as a mere investment, to give the masses of the people much greater opportunities than they can generally avail themselves of." (pp. 212 and 216)

Despite, however, the explicit or implicit involvement of *the technological* factor, the actual level of technology (the "state of arts of production") in the growth equation as one of the variables determining the "efficiency" of the worker population, *technological development* is mostly treated as an exogenous factor in Neo-Classical economics.

*M. P. Todaro* (1997) notes: "...neoclassical theory credits the bulk of economic growth to an exogenous or completely independent process of technological progress. ...this approach has at least two insurmountable drawbacks. First, using the neoclassical framework, it is impossible to analyse the determinants of technological advance because it is completely independent of the decisions of economic agents. And second, the theory fails to explain large differences in residuals across countries with similar technologies..." (p. 91)

In most of the neo-classical models of growth a primary role is actually attributed to *savings,* to a higher rate of capital formation, which determines the rate of investments. Consequently, those who save by sacrificing present consumption for future[196] and invest more, are the most important agents of development[197]. And since an unlimited substitution between labour and capital is assumed, labour is supposed to be fully employed at any level of capital stock. The growth of labour force depends on population growth. Investments and savings are assumed to equal (because of the automatic equalizing mechanism of the capital market with a flexibly changing interest rate), and investments simply mean an increase in the capital stock. The total output (or income) is distributed between total consumption and aggregate investments a part of which is needed for maintaining the capital/labour ratio as the labour force grows, and its other part can be used to increase the capital/labour ratio. Thus in the so-called "fundamental equation" of neo-classical growth theory the "growth in the capital to labour ratio is determined by the differences between the amount of investment per worker that actually occurs and the amount required to keep the capital to labour ratio constant as the population growth... Growth in per capita income can be achieved either by increased savings or reduced rates of population growth."[198]

---

[196] "The postponement of gratification which is generally involved in the accumulation of wealth, has been called abstinence but perhaps it is better described simply as waiting." "...the accumulation of wealth is generally the result of a postponement of enjoyment, or of a *waiting* for it." *Marshall, A.* (1890), pp. 289–290.

[197] "The power to save depends on an excess of income over necessary expenditure; and this is greatest among the wealthy." *Marshall, A.* (1890), p. 294.

[198] *Grabowski, R.–M. P. Shields* (1996), pp. 34, 36.

*Marshall* also stressed the primary importance of savings: "...with the growth of openings for the investment of capital there is a constant increase in that surplus of production over the necessaries of life, which gives the power to save." (p. 288) "The total net income available for saving is the excess of this gross income over what is required to provide the necessaries of life... The extent to which a country makes use of the power of saving which this net income gives, or in other words the rate of growth of its wealth, depends on (i) the amount of this net income, (ii) the willingness of its inhabitants to sacrifice present enjoyment for future, (iii) the strength of family affections among them (since it is not a man's own future enjoyment but that of his family which is generally the chief motive of his saving) and (iv) the rate of interest on capital, which affords a premium to saving..."[199].

## 4.2. On equilibrium and allocative efficiency in a market economy

While keeping its basic presumption of automatic equilibrium mechanisms in a "normally" operating market economy, the Neo-Classical scholars have not only refined by further details but in certain respects have also modified the classical concept of equilibrium.

In the Neo-Classical economics a clear distinction is made between *partial* and *general equilibrium.* The former refers to equilibrium between demand and supply in the "partial markets" (the separate markets of individual products and services, and also of the factors of production, capital, labour and land). In the partial equilibrium analysis (of Marshall, Hicks and Samuelson) it is assumed that the markets for individual products can smoothly operate and reach demand–supply equilibrium in isolation from the rest of the economy, from other markets. In the individual markets two motive forces are functioning: the interest of the producers to maximize profits within the constraints of their available funds, their budget (i.e. capital) and the interest of the consumers to maximize their pleasure, i.e. the consumption of utilities, within the constraint of their income.

The term *general equilibrium* implies an overall equilibrium in the entire economy, i.e. simultaneously in all the partial markets. It is assumed (by Walras and his followers) that a competitive, spontaneously operating market economy is able to harmonize the divergent interests of consumers and producers simultaneously in all the partial markets, and generate such equilibrium prices (responding flexibly to changes in demand and supply) as clearing all the markets.

Despite a certain diversity of views among Neo-Classical scholars (particularly in respect of the relevance of the described ideal model of the market economy to the actual reality), as a more or less typically neo-classical concept is registered in literature the above (Walrasian) theorem according to which a spontaneously operating market economy tends always to be in general equilibrium and also to ensure an optimum allocation of resources. This theorem is based upon the assumption (already manifested in Classical economics) about the reversibility of

[199] Quoted by *Rostow, W. W.* (1990), p. 165.

any changes, which disturb equilibrium, i.e. an automatic self-correcting mechanism that always restores, without State interventions, the equilibrium in the national economy. Such a reversibility results from the interaction in all the partial markets between changes in demand and/or supply and a perfectly flexible market price, which both demand and supply depend on, and, on macro-level, from the interrelations among the partial markets.

The self-regulating mechanism of the labour market, however, is based now, according to the neoclassical economics, on the marginal productivity of labour determining both the supply and the demand of labour (instead of a subsistence minimum and demographic rules as according to the Classics), and the equilibrium of the capital market is ensured automatically by the natural rate of interest determined by the marginal productivity of capital, regulating both the demand (for investments) and the supply (from savings) of this factor of production.

Since the marginal productivity of factors equally determines, on the one hand, their role as cost components in price formation, and, on the other, the reward to the owners of factors of production (as postulated in *Euler's theorem*), the *harmony* formulated thereby of prices, costs and rewards, i.e. in price formation and income distribution, has remained one of the pillars of the general equilibrium system. The social background of income distribution has been practically neglected. The rewards to labour and capital are now determined in theory apparently in the same way, by identical principles, in contrast to Ricardo's distribution theory which still prompted the question of why incomes of the owners of factors of production are determined by different laws (in one case: by the physiological needs of subsistence, and in the other case: by economic conditions).

The assumed perfect substitution and mobility of the factors of production, together with the assumption of perfect factor markets, reflecting the increased role of technology and the relatively decreased significance of natural endowments and indicating at the same time the developed state of commodity production, have become an increasingly general premise of the self-restoring and optimum equilibrium system.

Insofar as the spontaneously operating competitive market (without both State interventions and market imperfections) gives, by changes in prices, appropriate signals about demand and supply to both producers and consumers who are all "price-takers" (and none of them can be "price-maker"), and the latter follow the principle of rationality to gain maximum returns to capital (savings and investments) and maximum satisfaction (of needs), respectively, the market economy tends to ensure a "Pareto-optimal" allocation of resources which means that "production and distribution cannot be reorganized to increase the utility of one or more individuals without decreasing the utility of others"[200]. Such an optimal resource allocation presupposes competitive markets and that the price (reflect-

[200] *Gregory, P. R.–Stuart, R. C.* (1989), p. 47, fn. 8.

ing the marginal utility of consumption) of each commodity equals to its marginal cost of production, which actually reflects the social opportunity cost of producing the last unit of output.

Here again it is to be noted that the deviations from competitive markets, i.e. "market imperfections", and fluctuations and business cycles with phases of depression have by no means been overlooked by Neo-Classical scholars. *Marshall*, for example, devoted considerable attention to the problems of business cycle, outlining its main phases, looking for its causes, moreover presenting such thoughts about its mechanism as, in a sense, preceding the Keynesian concepts[201].

Neo-Classical scholars pay even more attention, of course, nowadays to the problems of disequilibria in partial markets and/or in the economy as a whole,.

Why, nevertheless, Neo-Classical economics has been quite generally attributed the concept of the market economy being normally in "perfect" and general equilibrium coupled with optimal allocation of resources is probably because of a certain gap or only an inorganic connection between its well-elabourated, primarily micro-economic analysis and a rather neglected, secondary macro-economic theory. The same applies to the relationship between neo-classical macroeconomics and international economics.

## 4.3. On international equilibrium, terms of trade and "balance-of-payments adjustment"

In Classical economics, as we have seen, an automatic equilibrium mechanism was assumed also in the international economy, without, however, an assumed international equilibrium price (a kind of "natural price", "value" or price centre, determined, like in a national economy and in consonance with the labour theory of value, by the amount of total labour inputs). Neo-Classical economics has maintained, with some modification, the concept of international equilibrium, but made also efforts to determine, in accordance with its general price theory, an international equilibrium price and terms of trade. Such an attempt is manifested in the concept of the Marshallian "reciprocal demand/supply curves" (often called also as "offer curves").

The simple application to international economic relations of the demand and supply analysis of the partial equilibrium theory and of the theses of the general equilibrium theory appeared to be impermissible to *Marshall*. He elabourated therefore a special theory[202] regarding the international economy. Marshall's concept of "reciprocal demands" (of "reciprocal demand/supply curves"), the basic idea of which had already been included in Mill's theory, was also based on the

[201] For more details see *Rostow, W. W.* (1990), p. 175.

[202] See: *Marshall, A.* (1923).

assumption that prices are determined in a double way: on the side of the demand by the consumers' subjective evaluation of the utility of goods, i.e. by the marginal utility of the latter, and on the side of the supply by the objective costs of production, shaped by the "law of diminishing return", i.e. by marginal productivity.

The "reciprocal demand/supply curves" express, in the usual "two-country, two-product model", the changes in those relative quantities of the two products the two countries are mutually wishing to exchange with each other or still ready to accept in exchange. Since in both countries the increase in the production of own product (which is partly or fully exported) implies decreasing marginal productivity, i.e. increasing costs, while the increase in the available supply of the imported product implies decreasing marginal utility for the domestic consumers, consequently both countries are willing to export more own product in exchange for less imported product at the beginning of developing international trade relations between each other, and less and less when their exports and imports grow. Correspondingly, the demand and supply curves of both countries gradually turn towards each other, expressing the above change in their desired ratio of exchange, until they finally intersect, thereby determining the point of an equilibrium in international price formation, representing an equilibrium terms of trade (as relative prices and quantities).

While the Marshallian curves excellently reflect the behaviour of both demand and supply as assumed by Neo-Classical economics, and also paved the way for the analysis of, and elabouration of new methods to calculate, the *elasticity* of demand and supply also in international economics, the Marshallian attempt to determine an international equilibrium price or terms of trade has hardly proved successful. Apart from the usual simplified reduction of international economic relations to the "two-country, two-product" model, the Marshallian curves are either drawn in a "vacuum" (as was practically done by Marshall who separated international economics from national economics) or on the tautological assumption of already given (but objectively not determined) prices and incomes on which the demand and supply of both countries depend. A third alternative (as observed in many textbooks), hardly better than the former two, is the derivation of the international reciprocal curves from those domestic "offer curves" assumed already to exist within the two national economies before their trade, in which case, however, the very effects of the evolving international trade on the domestic conditions of the partner national economies, i.e. on changes in their domestic "offer curves" are left out of consideration.

Demand analysis and the accurate methods of calculating various demand (and supply) elasticities are obviously very important issues not only in conventional micro- and macro-economics but also for both international and development economics.

No doubt, the differences between products in demand and supply elasticities (i.e. in the ratios of the percentage change in the quantity of demand or supply to that in price) play an important role in shaping the terms of trade. Different consumption patterns and consumers' preferences do also influence the latter. A country with an export product which is preferred both by the domestic and the foreign consumers is in a more advantageous position in respect of the equilibrium terms of trade, since the latter are determined, according to Marshall, by the intersection of the reciprocal demand curves. (The elasticity of reciprocal demand shows the ratio of the percentage change in the quantity of imports or exports to that of the relative export or import prices.)

The analysis of *demand elasticities* in international trade is, however, not only a useful tool to be applied but it has also to face considerable difficulties, which suggest a careful application. The behaviour of demand in international trade may be heavily influenced by various tariff and non-tariff barriers set by the governments, and may also differ according to the specificities of the products themselves (even apart from those of the so-called "inferior" or "Giffen goods" which suffer a decrease in demand when their price declines or the consumers' income rises, and vice versa). The demand for several products, mainly those exported by the primary producing developing countries, appears quite elastic when prices increase or incomes decline, while their demand proves to be fairly inelastic under opposite changes in prices or incomes. In contrast to the latter, certain primary products, such as particularly crude oil, may enjoy, within, of course, some time limits, the advantage of elastic demand in the case of price decline and income rise, as well as that of inelastic demand in the case of price increase and income fall.

The changes in *the terms of trade* in the international economy may reflect, of course, not only differences among products in demand elasticities, but also changes in their production conditions and other variables. Neo-Classical scholars do also refer to the latter, including the differences, already noted by the Classical economists, between the cases of increasing and decreasing returns in the production of various products, and also the differences in external economies.

*Alfred Marshall*, while sharing the worry (although for different reason[203]) with the Classicals about the Law of Diminishing Return, pointed (1890) to the "role of man" in counteracting this Law: "Thus then while the part which Nature plays in production conforms to the Law of Diminishing Return, the part which man plays conforms to the Law of Increasing Return". (p. 379)

As regards the *automatism of international economic equilibrium*, the Neo-Classical economics (unlike the Classical[204]) has placed the changes in the

[203] "The diminishing return from disproportionate use of any agent of production is akin to, but distinct from, Diminishing Return of land in general to more intensive cultivation, however appropriate." *Marshall, A.* (repr. 1930), p. 407.

[204] The Classics, as we have seen, assumed that the equilibrium of the international economy, i.e. between the mutual demand and supply of the trading partners as manifested in their balance of trade, is ensured by a free and adequate flow of golden money between them, which takes place in a direction always opposite to that of the product flows, and perfectly corresponds to the transaction demand for money, i.e. to the total value of the exchanged products to be paid.

*exchange rates* of the national currencies (instead of direct price changes measured in the same money) into the centre of the equilibrium mechanism, elabourating thereby the concept of an *automatic exchange rate mechanism.*

Assuming as a precondition that the currencies are fully convertible and the currency market is an ideal, perfect one in which the exchange rates depend merely and exclusively on the demand for and the supply of the currencies concerned (like in a "freely floating" exchange-rate regime), thus flexibly and spontaneously responding to the rise of deficits or sufficits in the balance of trade of the partner countries, Neo-classical theory concludes that equilibrium is automatically restored by an appropriate change in the exchange rates. Accordingly a new equilibrium rate of exchange will result from an automatic appreciation of the currency (due to the increased demand for it) of the country with an active balance of trade and from a corresponding depreciation of the currency of the deficit country. Since such changes in the exchange rates make the imports from the former more expensive while the exports of the latter cheaper, the country, which had an export surplus before, is going to lose it while its partner can eliminate its trade deficit by increasing exports.

The neo-classical concept of an automatic international equilibrium mechanism is, thus, based primarily upon the assumption of the existence of an "ideal" exchange rate system in which (as the *"monetary approach" to exchange rate determination suggests*) the change of the perfectly responsive, flexible (in modern terminology: "freely floating") exchange rate only and exclusively depends on changes in the demand for and in the supply of the currencies concerned. Such an exchange rate system, however, has never come into existence. The neo-classical concept also assumes, of course, a perfectly free trade among countries, and flexible responses in the product markets as well, i.e. within the domestic market of all the partner economies concerned, which in reality may also be hindered (particularly by tariff and non-tariff barriers).

The above mechanism, however, is related only to international trade, thus leaving international capital flows out of investigation, despite the increasingly decisive role of the latter in shaping international economic relations, including also trade. Despite such a limitation of this concept, the suggested "recipe" for economic policy, which follows from it, is called *balance-of-payments adjustment* policy. It refers to the case when the automatic exchange-rate mechanism does not work because of the lack of the required conditions, namely of an "ideal" currency market with freely floating exchange rates. In such a case it is the monetary authority, the government or the central bank which must act and do exactly the same what a spontaneous currency market would do: devaluation (as a substitute for automatic depreciation) of the currency of the deficit country, and revaluation (as a substitute for automatic appreciation) of the sufficit country. The logic behind this recipe is the same as behind the above-outlined exchange-rate mechanism: the country with a devalued currency is supposed to be able to export more and import less than before, while the other country with a revalued currency just the opposite.

Such an exchange-rate policy aiming at the improvement of the balance of payments by devaluation is also called "elasticity approach" to balance-of-payments adjustment, because the attached "Marshall–Lerner condition" (which is often forgotten by those suggesting or applying it) clearly refers to those minimal conditions under which it may be (if at all) successful: the sum of the elasticities of the demand abroad for the exported products and of the demand at home for the imported products must be more than 1. Under these conditions the balance of trade of the country applying the policy of devaluation can improve indeed.

But even apart from the fact that export-competitiveness cannot be reduced merely to price-competitiveness, and imports may also depend on other than price factors only, such a concept (which seems to support the quite general belief that a deficit in the balance of trade is always a sign of an overvalued currency and that devaluation is in general a natural and efficient means of improving the balance of payments) simply neglects the frequent cases of various structural, institutional and even cultural obstacles to export growth and the case of import dependence, moreover the possible import-intensity of exports. It also disregards the non-trade-related items of the balance of payments, and the diverse effects of devaluation on the latter, including services, repatriation of factor incomes, unilateral transfers of money, and, particularly, international capital flows (direct and portfolio investments, as well as loans) registered in the capital account of the balance of payments. It also overlooks the international debtor–creditor relations and their consequences in trade and monetary relations. Nevertheless such a balance-of-payments adjustment policy has become one of the characteristic "conditionalitites" applied by the international monetary institutions vis-à-vis the heavily (though for different reasons) indebted developing countries.

## 4.4. On international trade and specialization

As regards international specialization and division of labour, it is the differences between countries in "factor endowments", in their relative abundance or scarcity of the factors of production (instead of differences, caused mainly by natural conditions, in their production functions), which have become the "base" of trade in the most well-known neo-classical theorem, namely that of Bertil Ohlin and Eli F. Heckscher[205].

The *Heckscher–Ohlin theorem* on specialization states that countries which differ in relative factor abundance and consequently in respect of the relative factor prices within their national economy, will tend to specialize, when entering into trade relations with each other, in the production of those products requiring as inputs relatively more of the relatively abundant, thus relatively cheaper factor,

[212] See *Ohlin, B.* (1933) and *Heckscher, E. F.* (1919).

i.e. the factor in which they have comparative advantage. Thus, if in a country labour is abundant relative to capital, the production for export of the relatively "labour-intensive products will increase because the production costs of the latter are lower than in the relatively capital abundant partner country where labour is relatively scarce and labour-intensive products are more expensive. The basis of this theorem (just like of other neo-classical theses) is the *marginal productivity* concept as a macro-economic price and income theory, which establishes an assumed simple cause–effect relationship between the relative abundance or scarcity of the factors of production and the level of their cost/price and incomes.

The *relative abundance or scarcity of a factor of production* in a country is either determined by comparing the ratios of its *quantity* to the quantity of the other factor of production (i.e. the $K/L$ or $L/K$ ratios) in the two countries or by comparing the ratios of its *price* (or income) to the price (or income) of the other factor of production (i.e. the $i/w$ or $w/i$ ratios) in the two countries (where $K$ stand for capital, $L$ for labour, $i$ for interest annd $w$ for wage).

The *relative labour- or capital-intensity* of the production of a commodity, as related to another one, is determined by comparing their labour/capital or capital/labour ratios of inputs. Insofar as these ratios are calculated in factor prices, instead of physical units, changes in factor intensities may follow from factor price changes, too.

If specialization of the partner countries proceeds according to the above principle, it necessarily implies, at least under the conditions of perfect equilibrium and factor mobility within both countries, and without any international factor flows, that in the domestic factor markets the *relative demand* shifts in favour of the relatively abundant factor in both countries (the relative demand for which increases more than its relative supply arising from the declining branch of economy), thereby leading to a new, higher equilibrium price at the expense of a lower price of the relatively scarce factor. As a result of such changes in the domestic factor markets, specialization and trade, if following the H–O theorem, may bring about not only a higher level of welfare for all the countries participating in it, but also an *international equalization* of the factor prices and incomes, thereby also of the national income levels of the countries.

Thus the *Heckscher–Ohlin theory* actually involves two basic theses:

(a) the so-called *H–O theorem* concerning the assumed rational pattern of international trade and specialization according to differences between countries in their relative factor endowments, and

(b) the thesis about the international equalization of factor prices and incomes, which, in view of its explicit formulation by Samuelson, is usually called as the *"Heckscher–Ohlin–Samuelson theorem"*[206].

---

[206] See also *Samuelson, P. A.* (1948). *Ohlin* (1933) has related the international equalization of factor prices also to the international and interregional factor mobility (Ch. 2) In *Haberler's* view (1964) the tendency of international equalization extending also to the prices of products and services may naturally follow from a free flow of products, services and factors of production in the international economy.

Since the same conclusion on international equalization of factor prices and incomes is also drawn, as we shall see, from the neo-classical thesis on international factor mobility, a "third" thesis is linked with the above two, namely about the *mutual substitution of partial markets,* i.e. the substitution, internationally, of product markets for factor markets, that of trade flows for factor flows or vice versa.

The H–O theorem has extended the Ricardian "two countries–two commodities" model to a model of "two countries – two commodities – two factors". But many of the old *presumptions* and simplifications have remained unaltered. Such as: the premise of a perfect equilibrium within the national economy of the partner countries, i.e. the exclusion of the case of unemployment and under-utilised capacities which, of course, affect the factor prices; consequently the neglect also of business cycles; the assumption of perfect, competitive markets and free international trade, i.e. the exclusion from the model, of any monopolies as well as State interventions, tariff and non-tariff barriers; the assumption of a perfect mobility of the factors of production inside the countries and of their total immobility across the border, internationally; the presumption about "homogeneous" and perfectly substitutive units of both factors of production, i.e. the neglect of any difference in the quality of labour and in the applied technology; the exclusion from the model also of the case of increasing returns, "internal" and also "external economies", as well as technological development; a neglect of consumers' habits and differences between countries in consumption patterns, etc.

Insofar as in the H–O model the factors of production are assumed to be "homogeneous units" which can perfectly be substitute for each other, their qualitative differences and the actual impact of technological development on their mix, their input combination, are completely left out of consideration. Consequently, "labour intensity" and "capital intensity" appear as two alternatives excluding each other, with quantitative variations only in their degree, despite the results of modern technological development which bring about a combination, on a higher level, of the intensive use of both capital and labour (in the original sense of the word), by linking expensive, sophisticated techniques, capital-intensive technologies with high "labour intensity" not only in the sense of the faster tempo of work but also and mainly in terms of the qualification, of the "skill intensity" of labour[207].

What follows from the above simplifications in the H–O theory is that the very effect of the choice of specialization in the international division of labour, of the choice of (capital- or labour-intensive) industries and products, on the opportunities to improve the quality and productivity of labour and to develop modern technologies, i.e. on the *future development* of the productive forces of the national economy, is neglected, just as well as in the Ricardian concept. Since the comparative costs both in the Ricardian sense and as factor-price proportions in the sense

[207] See *Yeats, A. J.* (1985).

of the H–O theorem, do change along the development of productive forces, primarily depending exactly on qualitative improvement of labour, it is by no means sufficient for a rational choice of specialization to take, from the point of view of a national economy, only the given, momentary pattern of comparative costs into account, thus seeking for "static comparative advantages", without assessing the *future* consequences of the alternative choices in terms of "dynamic comparative advantages", i.e. estimating the differences in development opportunities opened thereby.

### 4.4.1. The Leontief paradox

Several scholars have also tested the relevance of the Heckscher–Ohlin theory empirically. The most well known test was done by Wassily Leontief (1953).

*Leontief* has investigated the labour- and capital-intensity of the US exports and imports for a year (namely 1947) to test whether the export and import structure of this capital-rich country corresponds, indeed, to the rules formulated in the H–O theorem, i.e. whether the US was exporting mostly capital-intensive products and importing mainly labour-intensive ones, in accordance with the H–O theorem. The result of his investigation has so surprisingly contradicted the latter that the economic literature has named it *Leontief paradox*. (This paradox can, as a matter of fact, easily be explained if some of the simplifying abstractions of the H–O theorem are released: if e.g. the fact of tariffs imposed on labour-intensive products, i.e. the protection of labour-intensive US industries, which can even logically follow from the H–O–S thesis, is taken into account; if a "third" factor of production, which has no place in the H–O model, is not neglected in qualifying some of the export products, namely the natural-resource-intensive goods, such as wheat; and if, particularly, the difference in the quality of labour behind "labour-intensity" is also considered, i.e. the high skill-intensity or "human capital intensity" of many US export products.)

### 4.4.2. Other concepts on the "basis" for international trade

Though the Heckscher–Ohlin model represents the most well-known and elabourated theory of trade and specialization in Neo-Classical economics, it has been complemented by a few other concepts which aim at overcoming one or another simplifications of the latter or focus on neglected aspects.

A certain revision or extension of the H–O theorem, such as in the concept of *technological gap* and in the *product cycle* model of R. Vernon (1966), may be considered, no doubt, as a concept of "dynamic comparative advantages". At least insofar as the former takes technological development and its unevenness into account, while the latter points to the shift of comparative advantages during the product-life-cycle from the innovative advanced nation with high R + D capacities and qualified labour, which temporarily enjoys technological monopoly when the new products or production processes are introduced, to less developed nations when the product cycle reaches the stage of standardized mass production with cheaper and less educated labour. Thereby a correlation is revealed between, on the one hand, the investments in "human capital" expenditures, i.e. on education, training, research and development activities, and, on the other, the comparative advantages in trade. The question, however, of what a different opportunity the various products may provide for (and what requirements they set on) technological development, innovations, R + D activities and the improvement of labour quality, etc. is still left open. Five other variants of the "basis" for international trade appear in the theorems of:

a) the concept of *technological gap* and of
b) *product (life) cycle,* the theorems of:
c) *international trade based on internal economies*, which suggests specialization in the case of economies of scale in production, even if no considerable differences appear in factor endowments between countries,
d) *trade based on external economies*[208], which, unlike the Classical theory and the Heckscher–Ohlin theorem, takes into account the costs of infrastructure (transport, communication, etc.) in international trade and the possibility of economizing on these costs,
e) *trade based on differences in "tastes",* i.e. in consumption patterns between countries, which, in view of diminishing returns and increasing opportunity costs, suggests international division of labour in the case of differences in consumers' preferences between countries, even if no substantial differences in their factor endowments and opportunity costs, or in technological levels may provide comparative advantages for them, nor can they achieve considerable economies of scale in the fields of production and the attached infrastructure, and (as a further variant of this concept):
f) *trade based on product differentiation*, which takes into account differences in consumers' preferences not only between but also within countries, and suggests an intra-industry division of labour between them in which export-production is oriented towards the "majority tastes" in one country (normally the home country's) which correspond to the "minority tastes" of another (normally foreign) country.

[208] "We may divide the economies arising from an increase in the scale of production of any kind of goods, into two classes – firstly, those dependent on the general development of the industry; and, secondly, those dependent on the resources of the individual houses of business engaged in it, on their organization and the efficiency of their management. We may call the former *external economies*, and the latter *internal economies*." *Marshall, A.* (1930), p. 266.

These concepts of international trade and specialization are also important contributions to both international and development economics, even if they overlook, or just take for granted, several decisive conditions in reality, and miss to answer or at least to raise important questions. Such as, for example, why countries are lagging behind in the development of technology and "human capital"; and how the gap in technological development would be perpetuated if the related concept is realized in longer-run; or why the costs of trade infrastructure are disproportionate for less developed economies forced to participate in long-distance, oversees trade; or how consumers' habits and preferences are shaped by demonstration effects radiating from the most advanced countries, etc.

## 4.5. On international factor mobility

The Neo-Classical economics which has devoted, as we have seen, a particular attention to the factor endowments of the countries as determining the marginal productivity and relative prices of their factors of production, has revised and corrected accordingly the Classical theory of international economics also in respect of international factor mobility.

Though the possibilities of exporting capital was not excluded by Ricardo either, for him it appeared as more or less necessarily coupled with the emigration of the owner of capital, too, and (in view of the conditions in his time quite understandably) did not seem to be an important phenomenon in the shaping of international economic relations. Since that time, however, the export of capital, particularly in the form of investment capital, the owners of which remain in their home country has become not only a large-scale, widespread and more or less typical practice but also a decisive phenomenon in the world economy which involves now international *ownership relations* and, besides commodity markets, also capital markets. Thus modern economics cannot leave it out of consideration any more.

The neo-classical views on international factor flows are based on the same logic and theoretical concept (namely that of marginal productivity) as outlined above in regard to the H–O theorem. Assuming that the factor endowments of the individual countries differ and that the factor prices as well as the incomes of the owners of the factors of production are determined by the relative factor abundance or scarcity, the Neo-Classical school formulates its thesis about the *natural direction* of international factor flows. According to it, if nothing prevents the factors from moving freely across country frontiers, both capital and labour tend to flow out of the countries relatively rich in the factor concerned, to countries, which are relatively poor in it. This is because in the latter the marginal productivity of the factor in question is higher, and consequently its price and reward are also higher, as being determined by the latter (at least under perfect competition and perfect equilibrium in the countries concerned). Another thesis, which logically follows from the latter, has also been formulated in Neo-Classical economics, namely about the *result* of such a "natural" direction of international factor flows. It states the same tendency *of international equalization* of factor prices and incomes, as also involved in the H–O–S theorem. But unlike the latter, this thesis explains equalization by international factor mobility, which results in a gradual reduction of the international differences in relative factor endowments. In other words, the international equalization of factor prices and incomes follows from that of factor endowments itself. Accordingly, if capital tends to move from the capital-rich (developed) countries to the capital-poor (underdeveloped) ones, while labour moves in an opposite direction, such an international factor mobility almost automatically reduces the international inequalities in factor endowments as well as marginal productivities and factor incomes, thus also national income levels. Though the well-known obstacles to labour mobility (even within countries, but particularly internationally) obviously contradict the above assumption, the application of the (already mentioned) thesis about the "mutual substitution of partial markets" suggests that the same result follows from international capital mobility alone, even without labour mobility.

Thus the assumed natural flow of capital from areas with a lower marginal productivity (where capital is relatively abundant) towards areas with a higher marginal productivity of capital and hence the assumed tendency of an international equalization of marginal productivities, factor incomes and also development levels, appear in the reformulated equilibrium theory.

The new assumptions can be fitted (and thus also graphically represented) in the above-mentioned mechanisms of the general equilibrium system. If, on the basis of (or expressed by) the otherwise indentically sloped production-function curve, the marginal productivity of capital, owing to the abundance of capital relative to labour, is lower in one country than in the other where the opposite situation prevails, then this also finds expression in the divergence of the equilibrium interest rates and real wage levels, i.e. in the already mentioned mechanisms of capital market and labour market. True, here it is not the subsistence minimum as a basis of equilibrium in the labour market that determines the real wage level, but the apparently objective amount of the "marginal product" of labour. Nevertheless the equalization of demand and supply both in the labour and the capital market (and all these at full employment and capacity utilization, that is at the level of maximum output corresponding to factor endowment) appears in these theorems just as in the earlier ones to be a natural self-regulating movement of the system – as a result of the interrelatedness of partial equilibrium conditions. Owing to the capital (or possibly labour) flows between two countries, induced by different relative factor incomes, the quantities and proportions of the available factors of production, i.e. the very factor endowments, are changing, which brings about a shift in their equilibrium factor prices/incomes towards an internationally equalized level, since a corresponding shift towards equalized marginal productivities of the factors of production also follows from international factor mobility.

The fallacy about the effect of the international flows of capital and of its tendency towards capital-short underdeveloped countries on ensuring equilibrium and an optimal utilization of resources and maximum welfare has become the theoretical basis of the "diffusion" concept[209].

Since the realization of an optimal system of international exchange and division of labour is also ensured, according to such theoretical assumptions, by the spontaneous movement and international flows of the production factor (capital), a national economic approach, which was still predominant in Ricardo, may become superfluous. The pragmatic world of the *micro-approach*, of rational decisions on enterprise level can increasingly be incorporated also into the theory of international economic relations to make it possible for factor endowments (divorced from all the historical background, among others from the consequences of an already established specialization), for entrepreneurial rationality (independent of national and class affiliation), for costs and benefits (without appropriate time dimensions) and demand elasticities (with no reference to their origin and social conditions) to become the subject matter of international economics, too.

Insofar as the process of economic integration makes headway (particularly if among more or less equally developed and dimensionally not very different national economies), such a change in approach, such a shift in favour of microeconomic approach to the issue of international factor mobility with a relatively symmetrical pattern, appears quite natural and practically useful. Since, however, on the level of the world economy the process of integration and the flows of the factors of production hardly show yet an all-embracing and symmetrical pattern, respectively, and in general the separation by State borders of national economies operating under State influence still has many implications, thus the macro-economic consequences, the positive or negative effects on the individual national economies (and societies) of international factor mobility (and also its obstacles, as in the case of labour) cannot be left out of consideration, or replaced merely by micro-economic analyses.

The above neo-classical theses on the direction and motivations of international factor flows seem to represent a step backward rather than forward, particularly in the theory of capital export and foreign capital investments, as compared to Marx's approach and the Marxian views on the complexity of the possible reasons of capital exports. According to the neo-classical assumption it is the higher return to capital in a foreign (relatively capital-poor) country, which motivates, induces the owner or user of capital to export it. In reality, however, this is not the only, not even a necessary condition for capital export (as already recognized by Marx). The neo-classical emphasis only on such a motivation likely follows from the more or less generalized premise of perfect equilibrium (thus from the neglect of prob-

[209] Its essence lies in the assumption that the underdevelopment of the developing countries could easily be overcome in such a way that an increasing volume of capital, technology and entrepreneurial skill would be transferred to them from the developed countries. For a critique of this oversimplified view see *Szentes, T.* (1971).

lems of possible overproduction and idle capital) and from the underestimation of the importance of ownership relations (for controlling resources and processes). In addition, the lack of a consistent distinction between profit-seeking and interest-seeking capital exports may also cause some confusions, since a higher factor price abroad, i.e. a higher rate of interest, which can be, indeed, a strong incentive for the export of loan capital and for some variants of foreign portfolio investments (such as bonds), may work as a disincentive for those companies making direct investments abroad which wish to borrow capital there.

As regards the domestic effects of international capital flows, it follows from the neo-classical concept, suggesting a complete freedom of factor flows and attributing an internationally equalizing effect to the latter, that the inflow of a production factor from another country affects quite unequally the owners of different factors of production in the host country, as it decreases the relative shortage of the same factor, thereby reducing its relative price as well as the relative income level of its owners.

But apart from this, the international flow of capital (and also labour, insofar as it is also mobile internationally, within much narrower limits, of course) obviously exerts manifold and divergent effects, both favourable and unfavourable ones (depending on its asymmetrical pattern, actual forms and terms) on the capital- (or labour-) exporting and importing countries alike. (Such as the effects on the available development resources, on investment and finance, on employment and "human capital", on the balance of trade and of payments, on the pattern of international economic relations, on their direction, on the access to foreign markets, technologies, management and marketing skill, on research and development capacities, on domestic market and competition, on migration, on structural decisions and the relative degree of national "sovereignty" over the economy, on the ways and level of participation in the increasingly globalised and interdependent world economy, etc.).

In view of the above, *no generalization* is admissible and no universal recipe can be prescribed for economic policy. Instead, a careful analysis of the concrete terms and conditions, of both the *potential advantages and potential disadvantages* is needed for which economic theories, including the neo-classical one, may supply important view-points and applicable methods only.

All those politically and ideologically biased over-simplifications appearing so often in the literature or the political phraseology, which, on the one side, emphasize only the favourable effects of foreign capital import and praise the activity of the transnational corporations as "angels" distributing benefits only in the world economy, or those, on the other side, which stress exclusively the harmful effects and accuse foreign capital for its exploiting nature and wish to exorcize as "devils" of the world the TNCs from the host countries, all such views are alien from science and dangerous to practice.

## 4.6. On stages and systems of the economy

Most of the representatives of Neo-Classical economics share the belief that the market economy of capitalism is, indeed, the best possible system and thus the final stage of historical development, which may, at best, be improved further by welfare measures or corrected by eliminating the "market imperfections". The previous historical process of development leading to the rise of such a system is mostly regarded as a unilinear one involving the same stages or systems for all the countries, which had started with the savage society and passed the stage of still primitive agricultural systems to be followed by those combining agriculture and handicraft industries and finally by the stage of modern factories, trade and services in a capitalistic market economy.

*Alfred Marshall*, for example, also referred (1879) to the egalitarian savage system as the earliest stage in historical development, which was followed by the emergence of agricultural systems, including slavery and serfdom, and then, thanks to the development of division of labour within society and to the appearance of the train, the steamship, the printing press, and telegraph, as well as modern factories, the industrial stage with increased mobility of labour and capital as manifested in the capitalist market economy[210].

Although Marshall sympathized with the aims of the collectivist movements and did not exclude the necessity of transformation of the prevailing system, while stressing also the role of the State in improving the life conditions of the working class[211], he had serious doubt about *socialism*. He admitted (1907) that the "world under free enterprise will fall far short of the finest ideals until economic chivalry is developed. But until it is developed, every great step in the direction of collectivism is a grave menace to the maintenance even of our present moderate rate of progress...". However, he was "convinced that, so soon as collectivist control had spread so far as to narrow considerably the field left for free enterprise, the pressure of bureaucratic methods would impair not only the springs of material wealth, but also many of those higher qualities of human nature, the strengthening of which should be the chief aim of social endeavour...Under collectivism there would be no appeal from the all-pervading bureaucratic discipline." (pp. 323–346)[212] Thus, instead of a socialistic transformation he predicted or hoped a gradual improvement of the system without short cuts.

But as to the *prospects* of the future development of the latter as the assumed last and most advanced stage in history, the neo-classical logic may suggest a final outcome which is very similar to the classical vision of a "stationary state", i.e. an exhaustion of development resources, a "zero-growth".

*M. Todaro* (1997) summarizes the final conclusion drawn from neo-classical development theory as follows: "In the absence of external 'shocks' or technological change, all economies will converge to zero growth. Hence rising per capita GNP is considered a temporary phenomenon resulting from a change in technology or a short-term equilibrating process in which an economy approaches its long-run equilibrium." (p. 91)

---

[210] Quoted by *Rostow, W. W.* (1990), p. 185.

[211] "Thus the State seems to be required to contribute generously and even lavishly to that side of the well-being of the poorer working class which they cannot easily provide for themselves..." *Marshall, A.* (1930), p. 718.

[212] Quoted by *Rostow, W. W.* (1990), pp. 192–193.

### 4.7. Concluding remarks

Neo-Classical economics has become the core and major, decisive component of what is called (with a misleading term) *mainstream economics,* embodied in standard textbooks and taught all over the world nowadays. On the one hand, it has extended the scope of development issues and economic analysis to a much larger area and far deeper details than any other stream of economics, and has also produced a number of refined analytical methods, sophisticated mathematical apparatus, as well as a great variety of theoretical concepts complementing or correcting each other (only a few of which were included in the above survey). On the other hand, it has become mostly identified (contrary to some controversial views) with its textbook-interpreted conventional variant applying a narrow economistic approach, short time-horizon, one-sided or fragmented viewpoint, over-formalized mathematical expressions, and seems to get imprisoned in those over-simplifying premises following from the perception of the capitalist market economy as an ideal system existing and operating harmoniously also in reality. It is also to be noted, however, that many of those "students" of the Neo-Classical economics realizing the gap between theory and reality, have often produced a sharper critique on the prevailing reality than some of the radicals attacking Neo-Classical theory.

## 5. Other streams: the "historical school" and institutionalism

Besides the Neo-Classical and the Marxian theory, some other theoretical streams, such as the *German historical school* and *institutionalism*, had also raised such issues of national or world development and economic systems already in the 19th and early 20th century, as still relevant to the economics of development and comparative systems today. Moreover, the historical pattern of development described by some representatives of the *historical school,* or the opposite concept, as shared by the advocates of "institutionalism", which stressed the specificities of each nation's development, caused by the "nations' diverging psychology, habit, moral, traditions and institutions (Schmoller), seem to represent the precedents not only of the later "stage theories" (such as Gras's, Clark's, Aron's or Rostow's) and of the later variants of institutionalism (e.g. Galbraith's) or the "new institutionalism (Coase), respectively, but besides the concepts of development sociology (as from Weber's and Boeke's to more recent ones), also of some post-second-world-war theories of development or underdevelopment.

## 5.1. The "historical School"

The *German historical school,* both its earlier and later branches[213], attacked those presumptions behind the theses of Classical and Neo-Classical economics, which imply an abstraction from the non-economic motivations of human beings as well as from the non-economic factors in economic development, and which lead to the idea of definable "laws" governing social activities and development of nations.

*Wilhelm Roscher* (repr. 1900), while conceiving of the system or "order" of the economy as similar to a biological organism which is born, develops and dies away, expressed his belief in learning from the historical experiences of the past, i.e. in studying the earlier events and their consequences, which might demonstrate analogies with the present ones. Though thereby he implicitly assumed some general regularity in history, he also rejected the applicability of the method of abstraction in social sciences. Like *Bruno Hildebrand* who outlined the general model of historical development of the economy as proceeding from the natural or barter stage to monetary and credit stages[214], Roscher has also distinguished (1843) certain stages. He investigated how the relative economic importance of the three factors of production: nature, labour and capital changed in the process of historical development. According to the predominance of each of these factors, he distinguished three periods in social development: the first, in which the rule of nature was decisive, the second, in which the role of human labour became prominent, and the third, the most developed period, in which capital is the dominant factor. Denied that selfishness would govern the economic life and that the economic actors behaved according to their self-interest. Instead, he emphasized the existence of a common social consciousness, which prevents income distribution from being subject to a class struggle.

According to *Karl Bücher*[215] the historical development involved three stages of economic growth: (1) the stage of independent domestic, or household economy, characterized by production for self-consumption, i.e. "subsistence economy" without exchange, (2) the stage of the urbanized, town economy, which already carried out but a limited exchange of products by supplying directly, without intermediaries, the consumers, and (3) the stage of the national economy in which production is oriented to exchange in the market, and there are intermediaries between producers and consumers, who are, in most cases, unknown to each other. This historical process with the transitions from one stage to the next one, has been motivated and induced, however, by certain political and social needs or changes (such as the defence of the community, as in the case of the transition from the first to the second stage, and the rise of the nation state in the transition to a national economy).

---

[213] For a critical review of these schools see also *Mátyás, A.* (1979).

[214] See *Grabowski, R.–Shields, M. P.* (1996), p. 14.

[215] See *Grabowski, R.–Shields, M. P.* (1996), p. 14.

*Friedrich List* (1841), whose name is mainly known as the author of the concept of "infant industries", and who may be considered as standing closer to the institutionalists (insofar as stressing the role of the government in national development, in promoting industrialization and protecting the "infant industries"), but not very far from Classics (as applying the above concept of necessary state interventions and protectionism only to a temporary and exceptional case, namely to that of a relatively less developed country), defined five *stages* of historical development: (1) savage, (2) pastoral, (3) agricultural, (4) manufacturing–agricultural, and (5) manufacturing–agricultural–commercial stages. Since, in his view, it is the temperate zone only, which is appropriate for the rise of manufacturing industries, the other nations should remain agricultural producers and develop a free international trade with the industrialized nations. An exemption of such a general rule (which is very similar, indeed, to the Classical principles) is the case of those countries in the temperate zone, which are lagging temporarily behind the more advanced countries in industrialization, and thus badly need import tariffs. According to List, industrialization is accompanied by changes in institutions and social culture, a shift away from despotism and tradition-governed behaviour, which characterized the former stage, towards individual freedom, political liberty, entrepreneurship, and innovative propensities.

A later representative of the *historical school, K. Knies* (1930) went further in placing the non-material factors into the focus of historical analysis. He went stressed that regularities, "laws of motion" can be observed only in the material world, in respect of material phenomena, which do not change in their effects. Thus, in the economy where non-material factors, such as changing spiritual, cultural ones, are also playing important or even decisive role, no "laws" or regularities exist at all. His conclusion is close to that of *G. Schmoller* (1923) who also doubted the possibility of formulating general "laws", in view of the great many diverse phenomena, causes and effects, factors and conditions in the economy, which would require multidisciplinary analysis to take also the cultural, moral, sociological variables into account which differ and vary from country to country and from time to time.

Thus, it follows from the logic and argumentation of the *German historical school,* that instead of a deductive method and abstraction, it is the inductive method only that should be applied in economics as a social science.

*R. Stolzmann* (1896) criticized the contemporary economists for disregarding the social side and framework of the economy, which stem from those legal and institutional relations, power structures and patterns of social cooperation, going through changes in history, which are created, shaped and modified by human beings of free will, and, unlike the purely economic phenomena rooted in the material reality and expressing the relations between Man and Nature, are not subject to causality.

*R. Stammler* (1906) also emphasized the socio-legal aspect of the economy, namely the importance of the legal order of society, which governs the cooperation among people in economic activities, and its role in determining the order of economy and its categories. In view of the free will and purposeful activity of human beings, Stammler also denied the relevance of cause-effect relations to the human society, thus the existence of determined regularities, and "laws" of causality in economic development.

## 5.2. Institutionalism

The *American school of institutionalism* expressed very similar views also reflecting the historical conditions of a country (in this case the United States) in the time of its increased efforts to catch up with the most developed ones, which prescribe, as a rule, a greater role of the State, its legal and institutional order, than after a successful "take off" indeed.

The most famous representative of this school, *Thorstein Veblen* conceived of the historical development of society as that of institutions, which undergo changes because people always need to adjust themselves to the ever-changing conditions in their struggle for survival. Since, however, present institutions are the products of the past, they can never meet the social requirements of the present.

With regard to the economic institutions of modern societies where the aim of economic activities is not restricted any more to the acquisition of subsistence goods (like in the pre-capitalistic societies), nor are the owners of capital necessarily the same persons as the entrepreneurial-managers (like in the early periods of capitalism), *Veblen* distinguished between the institutions of "industry" and those of "business", thereby also between those engaged in the former and those in the latter. While in modern industry it is the collective spirit and interest, honesty, diligence, professional skill, creative activity and hard work etc., which govern and characterize human behaviour, in business life the drive for profit and accumulated wealth, the unproductive, speculation-oriented activity to earn profit in banking and finance, and, in general, the selfish attitudes are the dominant features. Since most of the businessmen, even if involved in industry, follow primarily their own selfish profit-interest, they may not only promote but also considerably hinder industrial development, if being able to earn profit by speculation in the money market, i.e. without increasing the production and developing technology. Moreover, they can benefit even from the disturbances in the operation of the economy, from disequilibria. In Veblen's view, business cycles are also caused by the prevailing institutional order in which the profit-motivated business interests are dominating over the interests of industry and production, and the psychological expectations of speculating businessmen may lead to crises.

In view of the effects of institutional factors on the consumers' behaviour *Veblen* denied the conventional assumption about consumer's sovereignty. He pointed to the role of a conspicuous consumption demonstrating the financial position of the individual in modern business life, which, however irrational it may be, turns out to be "profitable". This also proves that the consumer's behaviour depends on social status in the given institutional order of society.

*Veblen* considered the dominance of business as temporary, transitional only, because it either leads to aggressive nationalism or, hopefully, to an industrial society in which the leadership of the unproductive elements of financial business is replaced by that of engineers and other active, professional and creative agents of society.

Such and other concepts of the *German historical* and the *institutional schools* have not only broadened the scope of topics involved in development research but have also pointed thereby to some of the weaknesses of the neo-classical approach, and often criticized, in one way or another, the contemporary reality, too.

## 6. The Keynesian economics

For John Maynard Keynes and his followers it has become obvious in the light of the regular crises, particularly of the Great Crisis in 1929, that the operation of the market economy is not so smooth and harmonious as assumed in the abstract, idealized models, but instead it "normally" involves a cyclical motion with varying levels of disequilibria (or "imperfect equilibrium") and that the socio-political consequences of the deep crises or recessions with large-scale unemployment, social distress and international conflicts in trade and finance, by paving the way for Fascism or Communism and leading to world wars, may endanger the prospects, moreover the very survival of this system.

As *J. M. Keynes* stated (1936): "Our criticism of the accepted classical theory of economics has consisted not so much in finding logical flaws in its analysis as in pointing out that its tacit assumptions are seldom or never satisfied, with the result that it cannot solve the economic problems of the actual world. But if our central controls succeed in establishing an aggregate volume of output corresponding to full employment as nearly as is practicable, the classical theory comes into its own again from this point onwards. If we suppose the volume of output to be given, *i.e.* to be determined by forces outside the classical scheme of thought, then there is no objection to be raised against the classical analysis of the manner in which private self-interest will determine what in particular is produced, in what proportions the factors of production will be combined to produce it, and how the value of the final product will be distributed between them." (pp. 378–379)

The "Keynesian revolution" in the history of economic theories implies, as a matter of fact, a radical breaking with some of the fundamental premises, basic assumptions of the Classical and Neo- Classical paradigms, rather than with their theoretical principles. The *Keynesian theory*, while questioning the very premises, the basic preconditions behind the conventional Classical and Neo-Classical theories[216], has presented a *new approach* to

[216] For a detailed investigation of the Keynesian school of economics *see Mátyás, A.* (1979).

**New approach of the Keynesian theory**

- the relationship between economic development and equilibrium;
- the problem of equilibrium, both within and among national economies (distinguishing between "perfect" and "imperfect" equilibrium),
- the conditions of an automatic equilibrium mechanism in the national and also in the international economy ("income mechanism") and consequently
- the policy of "balance-of-payments adjustment";
- the cause-effect relation between changes in export and in national income, as well as between the latter and imports (export multiplier and marginal import propensity); and this has pointed to
- the cyclical operation of the market economy (whether national or world economy) if not regulated by indirect interventions;
- the consequences of "demand constraints" on investment, national income and employment level, i.e. on "imperfect" equilibrium;
- the role of psychological factors, expectations and speculation in the operation and development of the economy;
- the role of money, the monetary and fiscal policy in the equilibrium and development process;
- the required activity of the State in the economy, etc.

## 6.1. The Keynesian views on economic growth and equilibrium

The most substantial change which can be attributed to Keynes in theory (besides the revision of the views on money functions and the application again of a "flow approach", instead of the "stock approach" to the concept of national income, reintroducing thereby the discredited concept of circulation with a *macro-approach*, is concerning the *equilibrium*, its assumed mechanism and "normal" level, both within and between national economies.

*Keynes* emphasized (1936): "So long as we limit ourselves to the study of the individual industry or firm on the assumption that the aggregate quantity of employed resources is constant, and, provisionally, that the conditions of other industries or firms are unchanged, it is true that we are not concerned with the significant characteristics of money. But as soon as we pass to the problem of what determines output and employment as a whole, we require the complete theory of a Monetary Economy." (p. 293)

He added: "The absurd, though almost universal, idea that an act of individual saving is just as good for effective demand as an act of individual consumption, has been fostered by the fallacy, much more specious than the conclusion derived from it, that an increased desire to hold wealth, being much the same thing as an increased desire to hold investments, must, by increasing the demand for investments, provide a stimulus to their production; so that current investment is promoted by individual saving to the same extent as present consumption is diminished." "If, therefore, an act of saving does nothing to improve prospective yield, it does nothing to stimulate investment." (pp. 211–212)

With regard to the *main sources of development,* Keynes did not reject the Classical (in his terms: "pre-classical") concept about the primacy of human labour as the only "productive factor".

He wrote (1936): "I sympathise, therefore, with the pre-classical doctrine that everything is *produced* by *labour,* aided by what used to be called art and is now called technique, by natural resources which are free or cost a rent according to their scarcity or abundance, and by the results of past labour, embodied in assets, which also command a price according to their scarcity or abundance. It is preferable to regard labour, including, of course, the personal services of the entrepreneur and his assistants, as the sole factor of production, operating in a given environment of technique, natural resources, capital equipment and effective demand. This partly explains why we have been able to take the unit of labour as the sole physical unit which we require in our economic system, apart from units of money and of time."

He also noted: "It is much preferable to speak of capital as having a yield over the course of its life in excess of its original cost, than as being *productive.*" (pp. 213–214)

He also stressed (1936) the differences in quality between labour units, and identified (like Marx) one hour of skilled labour with several hours of an unskilled labour:

"...the quantity of employment can be sufficiently defined for our purpose by taking an hour's employment of ordinary labour as our unit and weighting an hour's employment of special labour in proportion to its remuneration; *i.e.* an hour of special labour remunerated at double ordinary rates will count as two units." (p. 41)

Contrary to the Classical and Neo-Classical assumptions[217] about a "perfect" equilibrium always ensured or restored by an automatic mechanism of the unregulated, spontaneous market in the national economies (as well as in the international economy), which implies the possible maximum level of national income and employment, with a full utilization of all the available factors of production, the Keynesian concept is based upon the assumption that the equilibrium which results from the spontaneous operation of the market is "normally" an *imperfect* one with under-utilised capacities and unemployment[218]. While, accordingly, "perfect" equilibrium means an exception only[219], it is the very changes, the cycli-

[217] "The classical theory assumes...that the aggregate demand price (or proceeds) always accomodates itself to the aggregate supply price" *Keynes, J. M.* (1936), p. 26.

[218] As Keynes concluded from his analysis (1936): "...the system could be in equilibrium with less than full employment." He stressed: "...the evidence indicates that full, or even approximately full, employment is of rare and short-lived occurence." (pp. 249–250 and 243)

[219] *Keynes* noted (1936): "...the postulates of the classical theory are applicable to a special case only and not to the general case, the situation which it assumes being a limited point of the possible positions of equilibrium. Moreover, the characteristics of the special case assumed by the classical theory happen not to be those of the economic society in which we actually live, with the result that its teaching is misleading and disastrous if we attempt to apply it to the facts of experience..." "The effective demand associated with full employment is a special case..." (p. 3 and 28)

cal fluctuations in the level of the national income (thus also of unemployment) which can restore equilibrium (an "imperfect" one) between aggregate demand and aggregate supply in the national economies.

In this context, *Keynes* pointed (1936) to "the possible complications, which will in fact influence events:

1. Effective demand will not change in exact proportion to the quantity of money.
2. Since resources are not homogeneous, there will be diminishing, and not constant, returns as employment gradually increases.
3. Since resources are not interchangeable, some commodities will reach a condition of inelastic supply whilst there are still unemployed resources available for the production of other commodities.
4. The wage-unit will tend to rise, before full employment has been reached.
5. The remunerations of the factors entering into marginal cost will not all change in the same proportion." (p. 296)

Refusing the *quantity theory of money* and taking, besides the transaction demand for money (i.e. the demand for money as a medium of exchange), also a "speculation demand" for money and, in general, the so-called *liquidity preference*[220] (i.e. the demand for money as a liquid means of preserving value) into account, and detaching the assumed determinants of the demand and supply of money, as well as the determinants of the demand and supply in the factor markets, the Keynesian theory has completely revised all parts and the entire system of equilibrium mechanism. It has given up the Classical and Neo-Classical assumption about a flexible interaction between demand, supply and the price in the product as well as factor markets, namely the assumption according to which both demand and supply always depend on the *same* variable: the price; and thus changes in demand and supply alike respond elastically to changes in the prices which, in turn, also flexibly respond to any changes in demand or supply.

For *Keynes,* the prices, in general, are not so flexible (particularly the price of labour, as expressed in nominal wages, which appear to be quite rigid[221] because

[220] In Keynes' words (1936): "...an individual's liquidity preference is given by a schedule of the amounts of his resources, valued in terms of money or of wage-units, which he will wish to retain in the form of money..." "The three divisions of liquidity-preference...may be defined as depending on (i) the transactions-motive, *i.e.* the need of cash for the current transaction of personal and business exchanges; (ii) the precautionary-motive, *i.e.* the desire for security as to the future cash equivalent of a certain proportion of total resources; and (iii) the speculative-motive, *i.e.* the object of securing profit from knowing better than the market what the future will bring forth." (p. 166 and 170)

[221] In Keynes' words: "...relatively *sticky* in terms of money". He noted (1936): "...there is a presumption in favor of real wages being more stable than money-wages. But this could only be the case if there were a presumption in favor of stability of employment." "In actual experience the wage-unit does not change continuously in terms of money in response to every small change in effective demand; but discontinuously. These points of discontinuity are determined by the psychology of the workers and by the policies of employers and trade unions." (pp. 238–239 and 301)

of the trade unions), and, what are more important, changes in the demand and changes in the supply are not determined (only) by the same factor, the price. Keynes also expressed (1936) doubts about the concept of *marginal productivity* determining factor prices:

> "There are at least three ambiguities to clear up. There is, to begin with, the ambiguity whether we are concerned with the increment of physical product per unit of time due to the employment of one more physical unit of capital, or with the increment of value due to the employment of one more value unit of capital. The former involves difficulties as to the definition of the physical unit of capital, which I believe to be both insoluble and unnecessary." "The ordinary theory of distribution, where it is assumed that capital is getting *now* its marginal productivity (in some sense or other), is only valid in a stationary state." (pp. 138–139) He added: "...Marshall was well aware that we are involved in a circular argument if we try to determine along these lines what the rate of interest actually is." "But was he not wrong that the marginal productivity theory of wages is equally circular?" (p. 140)

In the *product markets* the effective demand depends also on the "propensity to consume" (the inverse of the "propensity to save"), which is also a function of incomes. In the *labour market* the price of labour, i.e. wage, is not changing flexibly (particularly downward, because of the trade unions), and the demand for labour does not depend merely on the wage level but also on other considerations of the employers, including future profit expectations, (while labour supply depends on, besides wages, population growth, too).

In the *capital market* the price of capital, i.e. *the rate of interest* can hardly ensure equilibrium between the demand for capital, i.e. investment decisions, and the supply of capital, i.e. savings, in the market, because the former depend also on the *marginal efficiency of capital,* while savings primarily depend on income level, and not only on interest rate.

*Keynes* noted (1936) that despite the tradition of the classical scholars who "regarded the rate of interest as the factor which brings the demand for investment and the willingness to save into equilibrium with one another", "...the rate of interest may perhaps have an influence (though perhaps not of the kind which they suppose) on the amount saved *out of a given income*." (p. 175 and 178)

> "The classical theory of the rate of interest seems to suppose that, if the demand curve for capital shifts or if the curve relating the rate of interest to the amounts saved out of a given income shifts or if both these curves shift, the new rate of interest will be given by the point of intersection of the new positions of the two curves. But this is a nonsense theory. For the assumption that income is constant is inconsistent with the assumption that these two curves can shift independently of one another. If either of them shift, then, in general, income will change; with the result that the whole schematics based on the assumption of a given income breaks down." (p. 179)
>
> "Thus, even if it is the case that a rise in the rate of interest would cause the community to save more *out of a given income*, we can be quite sure that a rise in the rate of interest ... will decrease the actual aggregate of savings... The rise in the rate of interest might induce us to save more, if our incomes were unchanged. But if the higher rate of interest retards investment, our incomes will not, and cannot, be unchanged. They must necessarily fall, until the declining capacity to save has sufficiently offset the stimulus to save given by the higher rate of interest." (p. 111)

Instead of the rate of interest, it is only the changes in the level of national income (and employment), which can restore equilibrium.

"...if the rate of interest is given as well as the demand curve for capital and the influence of the rate of interest on the readiness to save out of a given levels of income, the level of income must be the factor which brings the amount saved to equality with the amount invested." (p. 179)

The *marginal efficiency of capital*[222] reflects, besides the present rate of interest and the costs of investment goods also the expectations on the future returns[223].

*Keynes* stated (1936): "The relation between the prospective yield of a capital asset and its supply price or replacement cost, *i.e.* the relation between the prospective yield of one more unit of that type of capital and the cost of producing that unit, furnishes us with the *marginal efficiency of capital* of that type. More precisely, I define the marginal efficiency of capital as being equal to that rate of discount which would make the present value of the series of annuities given by the returns expected from the capital-asset during its life just equal to its supply price." "...the marginal efficiency of capital is here defined in terms of the *expectation* of yield and of the *current* supply of the capital-asset. It depends on the rate of return expected to be obtainable on money if it were invested in a *newly* produced asset". (pp. 135–136)

In Keynes' opinion savings primarily depend on income level, and not only on interest rate. Interest is determined, on the one hand, by the demands for money (not only the *"transactions demand"* but also the *"speculative demand"* for money) and, on the other, by an independent supply of money provided by the banking system.

In the analysis of the *business cycle* (trade cycle)[224] and the relationship between the growth of the economy and its equilibrium conditions, i.e. a "dynamic equilibrium", *Keynes* practically divided the economic processes into two types: (a) those which generate incomes, i.e. which the growth in national income depends on, and (b) those which as "leakages" absorbing a part of the generated incomes prevent the latter from creating additional demand which would lead to further income generation.

Incomes are obviously created primarily in the process of production. But incomes arise also in the process of *investments* and, if the economy is "open" in the sense of trading with other countries, also in the *export* production. Unlike the

---

222 "The schedule of the marginal efficiency of capital is of fundamental importance because it is mainly through this factor (much more than through the rate of interest) that the expectation of the future influences the present." "The schedule of the marginal efficiency of capital may be said to govern the terms of which loanable funds are demanded for the purpose of new investment; whilst the rate of interest governs the terms on which funds are being currently supplied." Thus, "the marginal efficiency of capital depends on the relation between the supply price of a capital-asset and its prospective yield.*" Keynes, J. M.* (1936), p. 145, 147 and 165.

223 "It follows that the inducement to invest depends partly on the investment demand-schedule and partly on the rate of interest.*" Keynes, J. M.* (1936), p. 137.

224 "The Trade Cycle is best regarded, ...as being occasioned by a cyclical change in the marginal efficiency of capital..." *Keynes, J. M.* (1936), p. 313.

production for domestic market, which may imply, in principal, the simultaneous appearance of incomes (as potential demand) and the products (as potential supply) resulting therefrom, in the case of both investments and export production there is necessarily a gap either in time (in the case of investments) or in space (in the case of exports) between the creation of incomes and the appearance of the products in the market. Though also in the case of production for domestic market an equilibrium requires equation between effective demand for the products and their actual supply (which as a natural tendency, assumed only in "Say's dogma", is, of course, questionable), *Keynes* focussed on the problem of what happens to those incomes generated in investments (and export production). Since (besides spending on consumption) it is savings (and imports) which can absorb such incomes, in a "closed" economy equilibrium basically depends on whether investments and savings are (also) equal, more precisely: whether the intended investments are equal to actual savings, or the intended savings are equal to actual investments (while in an "open" economy equilibrium requires also an equation between exports and imports).

Keynes also shared the view that savings tend to be equal to investments, at least in the final analysis[225].

He stressed (1936) that "...the old-fashioned view that saving always involves investment, though incomplete and misleading, is formally sounder than the new-fangled view that there can be saving without investment or investment without 'genuine' saving. The error lies in proceeding to the plausible inference that, when an individual saves, he will increase aggregate investment by an equal amount. It is true, that, when an individual saves he increases his own wealth. But the conclusion that he also increases aggregate wealth fails to allow for the possibility that an act of individual saving may react on someone else's saving and hence on someone else's wealth." "...Every such attempt to save more by reducing consumption will so effect incomes that the attempt necessarily defeats itself. It is, of course, just as impossible for the community as a whole to save *less* than the amount of current investment, since the attempt to do so will necessarily raise incomes to a level at which the sums which individuals choose to save add up to a figure exactly equal to the amount of investment." (pp. 83–84) Consequently: "Saving and Investment are the determinates of the system, not the determinants." (p. 183)

He pointed to that "...a rise in the rate of interest will have the effect of reducing the amount actually saved. For aggregate saving is governed by aggregate investment; a rise in the rate of interest ... will diminish investment; hence a rise in the rate of interest must have the effect of reducing incomes to a level at which saving is decreased in the same measure as investment."

According to him: "The traditional analysis has been aware that saving depends on income but it has overlooked the fact that income depends on investment, in such fashion that, when investment changes, income must necessarily change in just that degree which is necessary to make the change in saving equal to the change in investment." (pp. 110–111 and 184)

---

225 *W. W. Rostow* notes (1990) that Keynes has actually made a step backward in "The General Theory..." as compared to his earlier work, "A Treatise on Money", because the logical conclusion in the latter was: "Saving and investment are...unlikely be equal. The difference between them drives the economic system into expansion (if investment exceeds saving) or contraction (vice versa), but each process is inherently limited." (p. 272)

In his views, as already noted, it is, however, the change in *national income*, which restores equilibrium between savings and investments. As discrepancy may appear between the intended amounts of saving and those of investments, there is a time lag in the process which *via* the changes in the national income (and employment level) can restore (imperfect) equilibrium. If the intended savings exceed investments, the level of national income (and employment) decreases since the latter depends on the income generating effect of expenditures, i.e. on the non-saved part of incomes, which are actually spent on consumption and investments. However, on a lower level of national income savings will decrease (as the "propensity to save", the ratio of savings and income is smaller, while the *propensity to consume* is greater), and expenditures will grow, inducing further expansion of production and investments. Thereby the national income can move out from the state of "deflation" (in Keynesian sense of the word, i.e. a deficiency of effective demand, rather than a shortage of money) and reach a higher level of equilibrium with a greater national income (and employment).

The opposite occurs if the intended savings lag behind investments and the economy is in the state of a Keynesian "inflation" where national income (and employment) increases because of the income (and employment) generating effect of new investments. The income effect of investments as expressed in the Keynesian *multiplier* (i.e. the ratio of the increase in national income, as a consequence, and the increment of investment, as a cause[226]) results in a higher level of national income on which the "propensity to consume" drops and saving increases. This necessarily leads to a decline in the income (and employment) level in the national economy as long as again savings will equal investments.

In his words (1936):

"The ratio…between an increment of investment and the corresponding increment of aggregate income, both measured in wage-units, is given by the investment multiplier." *Investment multiplier = K,* which "tells us that, when there is an increment of aggregate investment, income will increase by an amount which is *k* times the increment of investment." (p. 115 and 248)

As an analogy with the Keynesian investment multiplier, the operation of an *export multiplier* is to be taken into account in view of the similar income effects of export production (generating incomes in the national economy concerned, with-

[226] It is to be noted that Keynes, "sympathizing…with the pre-classical doctrine that everything is *produced by labor*" (i.e. with the classical and Marxian "labor theory of value") in the sense that labor is "aided by what used to be called art and is now called technique, by natural resources which are free or cost a rent according to their scarcity or abundance, and by the results of past labor, embodied in assets", concluded that it is "preferable to regard labor, including, of course, the personal services of the entrepreneur and his assistants, as the sole factor of production, operating in a given environment of technique, natural resources, capital equipment and effective demand." And he added: "This partly explains why we have been able to take the unit of labor as the sole physical unit which we require in our economic system, apart from units of money and of time." *Keynes,* J. M. (1936), pp. 213–214.

out supplying the product in the market of the latter), which can be balanced *ceteris paribus* by the opposite effects of imports only. Any increment in the export production ($\Delta X$) results in an increment of money incomes ($\Delta Y$) which, if savings are disregarded, are spent either on domestic ($C$) or imported goods ($M$), depending on the marginal propensity to consume ($c$) or the marginal propensity to import (m), i.e. on the ratios of changes in consumption or imports changes in incomes, respectively. That part of incremental incomes spent on domestic products ( $[1\text{-}m] \times \Delta X$), however, generates again further, additional incomes, and so on: $[1\text{-}m] \times \Delta X + [1\text{-}m^2] \times \Delta X + \ldots$, etc. This process resulting in a total increment in incomes which is equal to the sum of such a descending geometric series, goes as long as all the additional incomes are absorbed by imports, i.e. $\Delta M$ equals $\Delta X$, which means that $m \times \Delta Y = \Delta X$. It follows that the export multiplier ($\Delta Y/\Delta X$) is the reciprocal of the marginal propensity to import ($m$).

While exports, like investments, have an "inflationary" effect, imports exert, like savings, a "deflationary" one. Thus an equilibrium in such an open economy with exports and imports, prescribes an equation not only (as in the case of a closed economy) between, on the one hand, the money incomes generated in the production of consumer goods ($\underline{C}$) as well as by investments in the capital goods production ($\underline{I}$), and, on the other, the expenditures spent on domestic products for consumption ($\underline{C}$) as well as the unspent incomes, i.e. savings ($\underline{S}$), but also an equation between all the money incomes, including those generated by export production ($\underline{X}$), and all the savings and expenditures, including those spent on imports.

The above conditions of equilibrium can be expressed by the following mathematical formula:

$(C +) I + X = (C +) S + M$, in which

"C" represents both the incomes created and the products produced in the process of production for domestic market, which, for the sake of simplicity, are assumed to be equal,

"I" marks investments,
"X" exports,
"S" savings, and
"M" imports.

Since that part of the incomes generated by investments and export production, which as neither saved, nor spent on imports, appears as additional demand for domestic products in the market (over and beyond the demand resulting from the incomes created in the production of domestic products), it may induce the growth of production and investments, thereby generating some further incomes and increasing both the level of national income and employment. (It means that both investments and export production have a "multiplying" effect on national income, as expressed in the Keynesian *multiplier* of investment and of export.) Since, however, the changes in both savings and imports depend on the changes in national income (as expressed in the Keynesian terms of the *marginal propensity* to save and to import), the increase in national income which results from increased investments and/or increased exports automatically leads to increased savings and/or increased imports.

Thus instead of the flexible responses of product and factor prices (interest and wages) it is the fluctuations of the *national income* (and level of employment), which play the role of restoring equilibrium (on varying, thus mostly "imperfect" level).

As can be seen, a revised concept of automatic equilibrium mechanism appears here, based upon the very fluctuations of the national income, which is therefore called as *"income equilibrium mechanism"*. What radically distinguishes this Keynesian concept of automatic equilibrium mechanism from the Classical and Neo-Classical ones is that the restored equilibrium, except in extreme case, cannot be perfect and the cyclical changes in national income imply a series of imperfect equilibria, i.e. varieties of lower than maximum output and lower than full employment and capacity utilization.

The *cyclical motion of the economy* implies changes in the level of (imperfect) equilibrium, i.e. fluctuations in the level of employment[227]. Crisis erupts when the marginal efficiency of capital suddenly collapses and liquidity-preference sharply increases[228].

*Keynes* points (1936) to that "...the dismay and uncertainty as to the future which accompanies a collapse in the marginal efficiency of capital naturally precipitates a sharp increase in liquidity-preference – and hence a rise in the rate of interest. Thus the fact that a collapse in the marginal efficiency of capital tends to be associated with a rise in the rate of interest may seriously aggravate the decline in investment. But the essence of the situation is to be found, nevertheless, in the collapse in the marginal efficiency of capital..." (p. 316)

To the worsening of the business conditions unfavourable *psychological factors* do also contribute. As he wrote: "...it is not so easy to revive the marginal efficiency of capital, determined, as it is, by the uncontrollable and disobedient psychology of the business world. It is the return of confidence, to speak in ordinary language, which is so insusceptible to control in an economy of individualistic capitalism. This is the aspect of the slump which bankers and business men have been right in emphasising, and which the economists who have put their faith in a 'purely monetary' remedy have underestimated." (p. 317)

---

227 "*Any* fluctuation in investment not offset by a corresponding change in the propensity to consume will, of course, result in a fluctuation in employment." *Keynes, J. M.* (1936), p. 314.

228 *Keynes* notes (1936): "...a more typical, and often the predominant, explanation of the crisis is, not primarily a rise in the rate of interest, but a sudden collapse in the marginal efficiency of capital. The later stages of the boom are characterised by optimistic expectations as to the future yield of capital-goods sufficiently strong to offset their growing abundance and their rising costs of production and, probably, a rise in the rate of interest also." For "...the marginal efficiency of capital depends, not only on the existing abundance or scarcity of capital-goods and the current cost of production of capital-goods, but also on current expectations as to the future yield of capital-goods." (p. 315)

Thus, according to *Keynes* (1936) the business cycle (in his term: the "trade cycle") is obviously connected with the changes in the profit expectations of the investing entrepreneurs, i.e., particularly, with the cyclical fluctuations of the *marginal efficiency of capital.* Crisis is primarily caused, in his view, by a sudden collapse in the marginal efficiency of capital. While the optimistic expectations as to the future yield of investments lead to both "commodity inflation", i.e. to the rise of prices, and "income inflation", i.e. the rise of production costs, and to a situation in which investments tend to exceed savings for a while, later on, when profit expectations tend to fall as a result of the over-supply of the consumer goods which "can no longer be sold at the previously ruling price"[229], and the entrepreneurs suffer increasing losses, the "marginal efficiency of capital" radically declines[230], and the business cycle turns downward, implying a new phase in which savings exceed investments.

The *psychological factors*, as it appeared, play an important role in the Keynesian concept of equilibrium and growth. Among the "ultimate independent variables" determining the growth in national income and employment (including "the wage-unit as determined by the bargains reached between employers and employed, and...the quantity of money as determined by the action of the central bank) *Keynes* (1936) mentioned "three fundamental psychological factors, namely, the psychological propensity to consume[231], the psychological attitude to liquidity and the psychological expectation of future yield from capital assets". (pp. 246–247)

A change in the *expectations* concerning the future profits may suddenly cause a drop in investments, first in the given sector and then, because of interlinkages among the various sectors of the economy, in all the other sectors as well.

*Keynes* (1936) added that "a decline in investment primarily caused by a reversal of expectations about the expected rate of return over cost (i.e., the collapse of the marginal efficiency of capital)" is aggravated by "a sharp rise in liquidity preference – and hence a rise in the rate of interest"[232], which "renders the slump so intractable".

His conclusion was: "In conditions of *laissez-faire* the avoidance of wide fluctuations in employment may, therefore, prove impossible without a far-reaching change in the psychology of investment markets such as there is no reason to expect. [Thus]...the duty of ordering the current volume of investment cannot safely be left in private hands." (p. 317 and 320)

---

229 "...even where the primary phase [of the cycle – T. S.] is caused by an increased production of capital goods, the secondary phase brings with it the seeds of a reaction, which will germinate as soon as the increased supply of consumption goods is ready for the market. Thus, sooner or later, consumption goods will be coming on to the market which can no longer be sold at the previously ruling price; so that the downward price phase of the Cycle now commences." *Keynes, J. M.* (1930), p. 289.

230 In addition, as Keynes noted (1936), "a serious fall in the marginal efficiency of capital also tends to affect adversely the propensity to consume." (p. 319)

231 The *marginal propensity to consume* (as already stated) is a ratio of change in consumption to change in income. See *Keynes, J. M.* (1936), p. 115.

232 "Thus the fact that a collapse in the marginal efficiency of capital tends to be associated with a rise in the rate of interest may seriously aggravate the decline in investment." *Keynes, J. M.* (1936), p. 316.

Besides the psychological factors, *Keynes* (1930) referred to other reasons of the business cycle, such as *innovations* and the behaviour of the *banking system* and the rate of interest. Investments tend to have great fluctuations also because of "the innovations made from time to time by the relatively small number of exceptionally energetic business men", which lead to a wave of investments exceeding savings. While it would be the responsibility of the banking system to keep saving and investment at equality, the market rate of interest tends systematically to lag behind the natural rate, and if it does not decrease as fast as the natural rate, the result can be a "prolonged tendency for investment to fall behind saving". (pp. 195–210[233])

As regards intersectoral linkages, *Keynes* (like Marx) emphasized particularly those between the consumer goods producing and the capital goods producing sectors. He paid special attention to the operation of the *accelerator* which implies that an increase in the demand for consumer goods encouraging investments and thereby a proportionate increase in consumer goods production induces such an increase in investments also in the capital goods producing sector as leading finally to a more than proportionate increase in consumer goods production. Such an accelerator works also in the opposite direction, and thus reinforces the tendency of fluctuations.

## 6.2. On the economic role of the State

Since large-scale unemployment is a very undesired phenomenon not only economically, as reducing the aggregate performance of the economy and its growth rate, but also socially, as depriving many people of their means of existence, and politically, as causing social unrest and working for extreme radical political forces, the Keynesian *conclusion* is that the governments must act in order to overcome it. In other words, the market economy cannot be left to operate spontaneously because its "invisible hand" can ensure, indeed, neither the maximum economic efficiency nor social justice and equity.

*Keynes* admitted (1936): "I expect to see the State, which is in a position to calculate the marginal efficiency of capital-goods on long views and on the basis of the general social advantage, taking an ever greater responsibility for directly organising investment; since it seems likely that the fluctuations in the market estimation of the marginal efficiency of different types of capital, calculated on the principles I have described above, will be too great to be offset by any practicable changes in the rate of interest." (p. 164)

"The State will have to exercise a guiding influence on the propensity to consume partly through its scheme of taxation, partly by fixing the rate of interest, and partly, perhaps, in other ways. Further more, it seems unlikely that the influence of banking policy on the rate of interest will be sufficient by

[233] Quoted by *W. W. Rostow* (1990), pp. 274, 277.

itself to determine an optimum rate of investment. I conceive, therefore, that a somewhat comprehensive socialisation of investment will prove the only means of securing an approximation to full employment".

"The central controls necessary to ensure full employment will, of course, involve a large extension of the traditional functions of government. Furthermore, the modern classical theory has itself called attention to various conditions in which the free play of economic forces may need to be curbed or guided." (pp. 378–380)

Thus, it is Keynes' conviction that the *State* must intervene (but, of course, not by means of commands and direct instructions as in the "socialist planned economies"[234]), and regulate, by *anti-cyclical measures*, by various monetary and particularly fiscal policies, the operation of the market economy.

The Keynesian "recipe" for indirect government interventions in the market economy is logically based upon the consideration of *demand-constraints*[235] caused by over-saving and liquidity preference, i.e. the high propensity to save of the richer people and/or their refraining from spending their incomes on consumption or investments.

*Keynes* noted (1936): "The destruction of the inducement to invest by an excessive liquidity-preference was the outstanding evil, the prime impediment to the growth of wealth, in the ancient and medieval worlds." In his views, "the primary evil is a propensity to save in conditions of full employment more than the equivalent of the capital which is required, thus preventing full employment except when there is a mistake of foresight." (p. 351 and 368) Keynes agrees with Hobson and Mummery that "in the normal state of modern industrial Communities, consumption limits production and not production consumption." (p. 368)

Consequently, the government should directly or indirectly encourage investments and spending, by such measures of the fiscal policy as e.g. financing from the central budget public works[236], welfare programs (for education, public health, social security, etc.) or other, "unproductive" expenditures (including, perhaps, military ones) and also some purchases from or support to (e.g. in research and training) private companies, and/or redistributing incomes[237] *via* progressive taxation

---

[234] "The authoritarian state systems of to-day seem to solve the problem of unemployment at the expense of efficiency and of freedom. It is certain that the world will not much longer tolerate the unemployment which, apart from brief intervals of excitement, is associated – and, in my opinion, inevitably associated – with present-day capitalistic individualism. But it may be possible by a right analysis of the problem to cure the disease whilst preserving efficiency and freedom." *Keynes, J. M.* (1936), p. 381.

[235] "If the propensity to consume and the rate of new investment result in a deficient effective demand, the actual level of employment will fall short of the supply of labor potentially available at the existing real wage..." *Keynes, J. M.* (1936), p. 30.

[236] "...public works even of doubtful utility may pay for themselves over and over again at a time of severe uneployment" *Keynes, J. M.* (1936), p. 127.

[237] "...measures for the redistribution of incomes in a way likely to raise the propensity to consume may prove positively favorable to the growth of capital." "...in contemporary conditions the growth of wealth, so far from being dependent on the abstinence of the rich, as is commonly supposed, is more likely to be impeded by it." *Keynes, J. M.* (1936), p. 373.

in favour of the poorer people with lower saving propensity, etc. which may all lead to increased effective demand in the market, and also by such measures of monetary policy as influencing the rate of interest to decrease, making thereby money "cheap" and encouraging investors to borrow, while inducing the propensity to consume to increase.

"Thus the remedy for the boom is not a higher rate of interest but a lower rate of interest." "The remedy would lie in various measures designed to increase the propensity to consume by the redistribution of incomes or otherwise; so that a given level of employment would require a smaller volume of current investment to support it." "Whilst aiming at a socially controlled rate of investment with a view to a progressive decline in the marginal efficiency of capital, I should support at the same time all sorts of policies for increasing the propensity to consume." *Keynes, J. M.* (1936), (p. 322 and pp. 324–325)

"The expectation of a fall in the value of money stimulates investment, and hence employment generally, because it raises the schedule of the marginal efficiency of capital, *i.e.* the investment demand-schedule..." *Keynes, J. M.* (1936), pp. 141–142.

Though such a fiscal and monetary policy necessarily creates a deficit in the central budget which is financed by inflationary emission and credit creation (leading to a "deficit-financing" type of inflation), the resulting increase in national income is supposed, or at least hoped, to cause a growth also in the revenues of the central budget, thereby eliminating the former deficits. As long as this really occurs, inflation may not only support economic growth (in the demand-constrained economies) but can also remain temporary and be kept within narrow limits.

It follows that the *growth of the national income* depends, on the one hand, on how much incomes are generated in the processes of production (for domestic and also foreign markets) and investments, both induced by the propensity to consume, while the latter determined by the marginal efficiency of capital, and, on the other, on how much of the generated incomes are absorbed by savings (depending on the level of incomes and influenced by the rate of interest) and imports, or, instead, actually spent in the domestic market, thereby inducing, *via* additional effective demand, an increase in production and investments.

*Keynes* noted (1936): "Our present object is to discover what determines at any time the national income of a given economic system and (which is almost the same thing) the amount of its employment; which means in a study so complex as economics, in which we cannot hope to make completely accurate generalisations, the factors whose changes *mainly* determine our *quaesitum.* Our final task might be to select those variables which can be deliberately controlled or managed by central authority in the kind of system in which we actually live." "Our independent variables are, in the first instance, the propensity to consume, the schedule of the marginal efficiency of capital and the rate of interest, though, as we have already seen, these are capable of further analysis. Our dependent variables are the volume of employment and the national income (or national dividend) measured in wage-units." (p. 247 and 245)

In the *growth models* of the Keynesian school, the growth of the economy thus basically depends, in general, on the rate of investments and the capital/output ratio. In view of the regular imperfection of equilibrium, however, particularly in the case of large-scale unemployment, government actions (spending) are needed to overcome the constraints manifested in insufficient aggregate demand.

In the *Harrod-Domar model* saving is proportional to income, capital depreciation and technological changes are (for simplification) neglected, the growth of the labour force is an exogenous variable and supposed to be constant, and aggregate output depends on the labour to output and the capital to output ratios. Insofar as the latter are fixed, output is determined by the quantity of labour or the available quantity of capital. It follows, for practical purposes, that once an aggregate capital/output ratio is determined, and the expected rate of population growth is known, it is possible to calculate how much capital is needed (from domestic savings or from abroad) to achieve a certain rate of growth in per capita income.

## 6.3. On international economic equilibrium

It may follow from the modified criteria of equilibrium that "the inflationary impulses from investment and exports have finally to be restrained by deflationary purchasing power absorptions S and M"[238], and that a "saving deficit" (I–S) can be counterbalanced by a deficit on the balance of trade (M–X), or vice versa, while savings surplus (S–I) corresponds to an export surplus (X–M), or the other way around (if incomes from consumption goods production and consumption expenditures on domestic products correspond to each other, i.e. C = C).

Since a deficit in the balance of trade and payments of a country is caused, accordingly, by a wave of investments coupled with low savings, i.e. from an "inflationary" state of the economy, neither the Neo-Classical mechanism of flexible exchange rates, nor the policy of devaluation (following the same logic) may help. Instead "deflation" is needed, in the sense of a reduction of investments and the increase in savings.

Insofar as a changing and imperfect equilibrium is the more or less "normal" state of the national economies with a spontaneous market system, which enter international relations with each other, the Classical-Neo-Classical mechanism of automatic equilibrium does not operate internationally either.

The reason why nevertheless the Keynesian school has not elabourated a completely new concept of *international* equilibrium is probably linked, besides its focus on national equilibrium, with the belief, shared by many followers of Keynes, that if the Keynesian recipe of economic policy is generally applied by the governments of all the countries concerned, then there is no need for a new theorem. In other words, if an indirect regulation by the State (*via* "open market oper-

---

[238] See *Pen, J.* (1965), p. 94.

ations", fiscal and monetary policies decreasing the rate of interest, encouraging investments by "cheap money", creating additional demand and employment by public expenditures and public works, and by a redistribution of incomes by taxation in favour of the poorer strata of society whose propensity to save is smaller, etc.) ensures full employment and an almost perfect equilibrium in the national economy of all the partner countries, then the conventional theses on equilibrium may stand which need no revision in international economics. However, the logic of the Keynesian theory undermines the basic premises of the Classical and Neo-Classical concepts of international economics anyway.

Nevertheless, even according to the Keynesian theory a certain *automatism* can be assumed to work in the international economy, which may restore equilibrium. Insofar as taking the conventional two-country model, in which two countries are only trading with each other, if one of them achieves an active balance of trade, which corresponds to a trade deficit for the other, then the increase in the national income of the former, resulting from her export growth, will increase her propensity to import, while the decrease in the national income in the latter, caused by increased "leakage" (import) leads to reduction of her imports. In this way both the export surplus of the first country and the trade deficit of the second may automatically disappear. This is an "income equilibrium mechanism of the international economy".

Though one may conclude (as many do) that the Keynesian concept has replaced only the Classical-Neo-Classical price and exchange-rate adjustment mechanism by a more or less also automatic adjustment mechanism of the balance of payments, such a conclusion may be questioned, at least insofar as the already mentioned complexity of interdependencies among the trading partners is taken into account, together with the widely divergent state and income levels of the individual countries.

It would be extremely naive and unrealistic to assume that such an income adjustment mechanism can properly work in *all* the partner countries and the resulting changes in the national economies concerned, and in the pattern of their exports and imports, perfectly correspond to and proportionally counterbalance each other. This assumption is also illogical in the light of the great varieties among countries (their different levels of economic development, different cultures, traditions, structural or institutional rigidities and economic policies, etc.) in respect of import dependence and the average propensity to import, of the actual export capacities and the elasticity of export, of the commodity structure of trade and the pattern of trade relations (by destiny and origin of trade flows), etc., not to mention the various effects of international capital mobility which may also counteract the required adjustment.

It may happen, e.g., as it often does, that the income generating effect of exports (or investments) does not lead, even apart from the possible State interventions such as import restrictions and tariffs, to the required (counterbalancing) increase in import (or saving) but instead leads to a further expansion of exports and export-oriented investments, as a result of foreign investment capital inflow into the country or the opening of new export markets, etc. Another exception, but a more frequent and general one, appears when despite the decrease in the income level of a country, imports are not reduced, simply because of the heavy reliance of the country concerned on imported goods for subsistence or production, such as food or technologies, respectively, not to mention the consequences in import demands, of the demonstration effects of consumption habits abroad or the "putting-out system" (spare-parts producing or assembly workshops in foreign subsidiaries) of transnational companies, with a regular transfer of input elements across the borders.

But even if the income effect of increased exports (or investments) always led indeed, without any obstacles, to the required increase in imports, it is still more than doubtful that the actual direction of import increment would be adequate, i.e. the additional demand for import would orientate to the countries with trade deficit. (While most of the deficit-countries belong to the less-developed countries, the import demands of the developed countries, including those with a regular trade surplus, are increasingly concentrated on the export products of each other, because of the shifts in the structure of their production and consumption, not to mention the unfolding process of integration among them).

What logically follows from the above-outlined automatic international equilibrium mechanism is another quasi-Keynesian "recipe", which instead of being addressed to the problem of low-level equilibrium and large-scale unemployment, as caused by demand-constraints, is aimed at the elimination or reduction of the deficit in the balance of trade or the improvement of the balance of payments. Since it is also based upon the "income effects", just like the assumed automatic income equilibrium mechanism, it is called *income adjustment of the balance of payments* or *balance-of-payments adjustment by income effects.*

The logical consideration behind the policy of "balance-of-payments adjustment" by means of reducing investments is the following: while an increase in export obviously depends on the behaviour of foreign markets which can hardly be influenced by the government of the deficit country, investments can be encouraged or discouraged by the latter.

It is worth noting that besides such a state intervention *Keynes* (1930) who otherwise was very much in favour of free international trade as well as capital flows, suggested, if necessary for overcoming disequilibria and the concomitant unemployment, the remedy of applying "differential terms for home investment relatively to foreign investment, and even, perhaps, ...differential terms for home-produced goods relatively to foreign-produced goods". (p. 189)[239]

While the Keynesian policies aimed at approaching a perfect or a higher-level equilibrium and overcoming large-scale unemployment are obviously addressed to the advanced market economies, as can be relevant only to demand-con-

[239] Quoted by *W. W. Rostow* (1990), p. 276.

strained (and not to supply-constrained) economies being in recession or imperfect equilibrium, the above "balance-of-payments adjustment" policy, by suggesting reduction in investments, is not only counteracting the demand-creating anti-cyclical policies even in the advanced countries (thus should not be applied in phases of recession) but is also obviously counterproductive, moreover harmful in the case of all those (mostly underdeveloped) economies suffering a more or less permanent, structural-type mass unemployment, and facing the primary task of development and catching-up with the more developed ones.

A similar, related concept of "balance-of-payments adjustment" is formulated in S. *Alexander's* (1959) "absorption approach", which involves certain elements of the Keynesian "recipe". This concept of Alexander states that since the national income depends on both consumption and investment as well as (in an "open economy") on the active balance of trade, i.e. $Y = C + I + [X - M]$, thus a balance-of-payments adjustment via an active balance of trade can be achieved by a reduction of both consumption and investments (if national income cannot be increased). $[X - M = Y - C - I]$. In other words, a *restrictive* economic policy is recommended (or rather prescribed, e.g. by IMF) to those countries suffering deficit in their balance of payments.

Needless to emphasize that such a "recipe", if applied in less developed and poor countries where a drop in investments retards development and a reduction in consumption may aggravate mass poverty, can cause more harm than success.

## 6.4. On interdependencies in the world economy

As an implication of the above concepts of international equilibrium, the Keynesian theory points to the complex interdependencies in the international economy, thereby also questioning the over-simplified Neo-Classical concept of equilibrium. Since the export of each country depends, among other conditions, of course, on the national income level (determining the propensity to import) of the partner countries, while the import of each country depends on her own national income, and so on her own export production, too, (which by its income effects also contribute to the growth of national income), thus the cyclical changes, caused by "inflation" or "deflation" in the national income (and employment) of the partner countries are heavily interacting and influence not only the foreign trade but also the very state ("inflationary" or "deflationary") of the domestic economy in the countries concerned. In view of such interdependencies no illusions should be attached to the actual scope and effectiveness of a national policy of balance-of-payments adjustment. It also follows from the above that the cyclical movements of the partner national economies, if more or less synchronized, may result an international "trade cycle", in which the "deflationary" state of the economy of some countries reduces the income generation process also in others and vice versa, leading to oversupply of exports and marketing problems. Or the "inflationary" effect of over-investment and over-spending in a group of countries induce similar processes in others, causing trade deficits and balance-of-payments problems elsewhere, too.

## 6.5. Implications of the Keynesian theory with regard to international specialization and factor flows

The new Keynesian concept of equilibrium makes the validity of the Classical-Neoclassical *principles of specialization* also questionable. While Keynes was very much in favour of free international trade and shared the concept of benefits from international division of labour[240], he criticized the prevailing order of international trade for involving regular conflicts between countries, which intend to shift, by means of trade, the burden of unemployment to others.

*Keynes* noted (1936): "...under the system of domestic *laissez-faire* and an international gold standard such as was orthodox in the latter half of the nineteenth century, there was no means open to a government whereby to mitigate economic distress at home except through the competitive struggle for markets." International trade "is...a desperate expedient to maintain employment at home by forcing sales on foreign markets and restricting purchases, which, if successful, will merely shift the problem of unemployment to the neighbour which is worsted in the struggle". "But if nations can learn to provide themselves with full employment by their domestic policy (and, we must add, if they can also attain equilibrium in the trend of their population), there need be no important economic forces calculated to set the interest of one country against that of its neighbours. There would still be room for the international division of labour and for international lending in appropriate conditions. But there would no longer be a pressing motive why one country need force its wares on another or repulse the offerings of its neighbour...". In such a case international trade could be "a willing and unimpeded exchange of goods and services in conditions of mutual advantage." (pp. 382–383)

Insofar as the partner economies in the international trade are not necessarily and automatically in the state of perfect equilibrium, but, instead, they operate on different and changing level of imperfect equilibrium, there is of course no reason any more to assume the existence of such an automatic equilibrium mechanism internationally either, as based upon the flexible adjustment of prices and money flows or the exchange rates to changes in demand and supply, ensuring always an equilibrium at a full use of all factors of production.

The principle of specialization according to comparative advantages based on relative productivities or relative factor endowments in the partner countries presupposes, of course, a full utilisation of all factors of production, i.e. a perfect equilibrium both within and between the national economies, since imperfect

240 "There are strong presumptions of a general character against trade restrictions unless they can be justified in special grounds. The advantages of of the international division of labor are real and substantial, even though the classical school greatly overstressed them." *Keynes, J. M.* (1936), p. 338.

equilibria modify the real costs of production and the prices of the under-utilised factor of production. If, in addition, there are cyclical fluctuations in the level of national income and equilibrium of the partner economies (which are not even synchronized or compensating each other necessarily), then the very calculation of comparative costs and relative factor prices becomes subject to the cycles of the individual countries and their relationship, perhaps to an international trade cycle.

There may be other disturbing factors, too, which can also divert investments from those export branches promising comparative advantages. Such as the Keynesian "liquidity preference" and "speculative demand for money", as well as the assumed dependence of investments on the "marginal efficiency of capital" reflecting expectations on future profits (instead of a present marginal productivity determined by the given factor endowment).

The same approach to the spontaneous operation of the market economy and its equilibrium in the Keynesian theory necessarily questions also the validity of the Neo-Classical concept of *international* resource flows, *capital and labour mobility*, too.

An imperfect equilibrium with under-utilised capital resources makes, of course, the relative cost of capital differ from its cost under perfect equilibrium (and invalidate also the conclusions, if drawn from the calculation of the relative factor prices, on the relative capital abundance or scarcity of the country concerned). Thus, capital may appear paradoxically as an abundant factor even in capital-poor countries and may tend to utilize the more remunerative investment opportunities abroad, in the otherwise capital-rich countries. It would be naive to assume that in a recession both labour and capital become under-utilised exactly in proportion to their relative scarcity and abundance, respectively, under perfect equilibrium, i.e. no changes occur in their relative prices, and that the same applies also to the economy of the partner countries. A desynchronised recession or recovery of the economy in the partner countries may induce both labour and capital to move from countries where the rewards of both decreased because of the recession, to those in a recovery with increasing rewards.

The *cyclical fluctuations*, also in the economy of foreign countries, imply of course changes in the actual motivations of capital export. Insofar as investment decisions are function of the "marginal efficiency of capital", the choice among the alternative uses of the available capital, including its export and investment abroad, depends also on the expectations concerning the future profits and interests both at home and abroad.

The "speculative demand for money", which detaches, anyway, the actual savings from the available investment funds, thereby also modifying the measure of the relative abundance or scarcity of capital, may also directly affect and alter the motives of capital export, for in an open economy it reflects the expectations on the future changes not only in the domestic rate of interest but also in the rates of interest in other countries, and because the very object of this speculative demand may be foreign currencies as well. The "perverse flow of capital"[241] and particularly the syndrome of "capital flight" from typically capital-short, underdeveloped countries clearly point to such deviations of reality from the Neo-Classical assumptions and to the relevance of some implications of the Keynesian theory or approach.

## 6.6. An anti-cyclical policy on the world level?

In view of the marked disequilibria and cyclical fluctuations in the contemporary world economy with regular oversupplies and demand shortages the Keynesian "recipe" of an anti-cyclical economic policy and an intervention of the central authorities generating additional demand by public expenditures and by a redistribution of incomes in favour of the poorer strata with lower saving propensity, which is aimed at an increase in employment and income level, may also appear relevant internationally. No doubt, a redistribution of world incomes (or income increments) in favour of the poor nations and the resulting increase in their effective demand would, *ceteris paribus*, give such an impulse to the expansion of world trade that the economy of the rich, developed countries could also benefit therefrom.

The international application of the Keynesian "recipe" would require the operation, also on the world level, of a Welfare State, which, however, does not exist (at least yet). But even apart from the difficulties, following from the absence of such a world State, in the implementation of a demand generating economic policy with income redistribution and public expenditures, it is to be noted that one of the main reasons why the Keynesian theory has been heavily criticized, in general, is precisely those practical conclusions of it and its recommendations for economic policy which an increased role of the State follows from.

## 6.7. Neoliberal critiques

The neoliberal critique of the Keynesian theory points to the large-scale social costs of State bureaucracy and to the danger of biased, irrational decisions of the latter (the so-called "government imperfections") which may cause greater losses in the economy than those following from the cyclical under utilisation of resources.

Another reason of critique is that the Keynesian "recipe" of generating effective demand by public expenditures outside the spheres of production may suggest not only such socially useful investments by the State, as in education, public health and other welfare spheres, or such public works creating additional employment which develop the transport and communication infrastructure, but also the growth of military expenditures, investments in the military sector and the

[241] See *Balogh, T.* (1963).

increase in the size of the army, i.e. socially or internationally harmful and dangerous way of overcoming the demand constraint and reducing unemployment.

The Keynesian model is often criticized also for its reliance on such aggregate macro-economic indicators and psychological variables, as for example the propensity to import or the "marginal efficiency of capital" and the various expectations, which either blur important differences within the society or cannot be properly measured and quantified.

The most important critical argument against the Keynesian concept, or more precisely against its general application, however, refers to the fact that it was elabourated for and reflects the problem of the demand-constrained economies only, and thus can hardly be relevant in the case of those (less developed) national economies being in a "Hayek situation"[242] (where resource constraints increase competition for the available factors of production) or belong to the Kornai-type "shortage economies"[243] (which suffer a regular supply-constraint).

## 6.8. Concluding remarks

While the Neo-Classical theories, assuming a more or less harmonious operation of the market economy, paid, in general, more attention to the micro-economic phenomena of the latter and its particular details, the Keynesian school shifted attention (back) to macro- and international economics which involve also some basic issues of development economics and system analysis.

It also questioned the illusions about "laissez-faire" economics[244] and rejecting the "pseudo-mathematical methods" pointed to the very complexity of reality[245].

---

[242] See *F. A. Hayek* (1931).

[243] See *J. Kornai* (1980).

[244] "The celebrated *optimism* of traditional economic theory, which has led to economists being looked upon as Candides, who, having left this world for the cultivation of their gardens, teach that all is for the best in the best of all possible worlds provided we will let well alone, is also to be traced, I think, to their having neglected to take account of the drag on prosperity which can be exercised by an insufficiency of effective demand. " *Keynes, J. M.* (1936), p. 33.

[245] "We are merely reminding ourselves that human decisions affecting the future, whether personal or political or economic, cannot depend on strict mathematical expectation, since the basis for making such calculations does not exist". "It is a great fault of symbolic pseudo-mathematical methods of formalising a system of economic analysis, ...that they expressly assume strict independence between the factors involved and lose all their cogency and authority if this hypothesis is disallowed; whereas, in ordinary discourse, where we are not blindly manipulating but know all the time what we are doing and what the words mean, we can keep 'at the back of our heads' the necessary reserves and qualifications and the adjustments which we shall have to make later on, in a way in which we cannot keep complicated partial differentials 'at the back' of several pages of algebra which assume that they all vanish. Too large a proportion of recent 'mathematical' economics are mere concoctions, as imprecise as the initial assumptions they rest on, which allow the author to lose sight of the complexities and interdependencies of the real world in a maze of pretentious and unhelpful symbols." *Keynes, J. M.* (1936), pp. 162–163 and 297–298.

It predicted the "euthanasia of the renter" and called for reforms (instead of revolution)[246] to reduce "large disparities" in income levels.

The above survey of the theoretical concepts of the major "schools" of economics before the second world war has not only demonstrated their genuine concern in development issues, in general, and the related questions of comparative systems or "stages", as well as in the operation of the world economy, but also revealed both the linkages and the differences between their viewes. While the former prove the organic development of economic theory, in whith new theses (and methods) are build upon the application or rejection of old ones, the latter reflect the changes in historical conditions and shifts in interest.

Differences among the already disussed "schools" appeared particularly:

- in the *approach* (whether economistic or interdisciplinary, whether "stock", "flow" or "relation" approach);
- in the perception or emphasis regarding the *nature* of "development" (whether economic or socio-political, harmonious or conflict-generating, unilinear or specific, endless or limited, self-sustaining or State-promoted);
- in the judgement of the basic *source(s), most decisive factors, motive forces* of development (which factor of production, activity or industry, what interests, etc. bring it ahead);
- in the appraisal of the role of *market* spontaneity and/or *State* interventions, and the *socio-political* and *institutional* (system-related) factors in the development process;
- in the assessment of the *results and prospects* of development (whether accompanied by equality and justice or inequality and dominance, perhaps exploitation; whether bringing about benefits for all, or only for some classes, nations; and whether involving a tendency of ever-lasting progress or leading to standstill or decay, break and transformation);
- in the views on the contemporary and the previous *economic systems* or "stages" of economic development;
- in the concept of the relationship between the development process and the *equilibrium* or disequilibria of the economy;
- in the consideration of the *international* conditions and effects of development;
- in the views on the role and "basis" of *international trade,* on the "laws" of specialization and division of labour, on the distribution of benefits from trade;
- in the concept of international *equilibrium mechanism* and the "recipe" for *balance of payments adjustment;*
- in the consideration of *international resource flows,* factor mobility and the views on *capital export,* its direction, motivations and expected results:

246 "...the euthanasia of the rentier, of the functionless investor, will be nothing sudden, merely a gradual but prolonged continuance of what we have seen recently in Great Britain, and will need no revolution." *Keynes, J. M.* (1936), p. 376.

- in the assumption of a harmonious or disharmonious operation of the world economy with *equalising or disequalising* tendencies; thus also
- in the expectation concerning the future state of humankind, the prospects of social and international development.

The list of those essential development issues (and theses of international economics) involved in the above-discussed theories of various schools of economics is, of course, far from being complete. It can be completed by great many others, which were also treated in the theories in question. Their survey should also be extended to other theoretical schools, particularly those arising after the Second World War or more recently (such as the "Post-Keynesian Reformist" school of international economics, the "new left" theory of "trade imperialism" and Neo-Marxism, the neoliberal Monetarism or the new American political economy and neo-institutionalism, etc.). While some of them, as being directly related to the post-war "economics of development" (and of "comparative systems"), as well as international economics, will be discussed later in this study, the above survey seems fairly sufficient to prove that the problem area of development (and economic system) was, indeed, an *organic part* of economic theories (and social sciences in general) throughout their history, even before the appearance of "development economics" (and "economics of comparative systems") as special field(s) of studies.

Thus what has actually happened after the Second World War in thes field of development studies was the *separation* only (rather than the birth) of "development economics" (and "economics of comparative systems") from the body of economics in general and interntional economics in particular. Under those historical circumstances already mentioned, "development economics" became "a distinct branch of economics...with its distinctive analytic and methodological identity" as "the economics of contemporary poor, underdeveloped, Third World nations"[247].

Such a separation as well as the above definition of "development economics" seems to reflect fairly well both an aversion from "mainstream" economics (or at least doubts about its applicability in underdeveloped countries) and those ideological effects stemming mainly from the former cold-war conditions. Those scholars or "development agents" of international organizations, dealing with development problems of less developed countries or elabourating development program for them, had to realize (much more easily, of course, in these countries than elsewhere) the irrelevance of many of the basic assumptions, premises behind some theses or recommended policies of the "mainstream" economics of the West, while rejecting also the so-called "Marxism–Leninism" (a politically manipulated and distorted version of the Marxian political economy) which became as an

[247] *Todaro, M. P.* (1997), p. 7.

opposite "mainstream" the official ideology, imposed by force upon social sciences, in the Soviet bloc. Intentions within the "South" to remain outside the East-West conflict and the two military blocs, have also reinforced the aversion from both Western and Eastern "mainstreams", while the representative of the latter did also the best to prove (if not the applicability of their own, then at least) the inapplicability of the opposite stream of economic theories (or rather ideologies).

Paradoxically, however, the above perception of "development economics" perfectly corresponded to the conventional view, rooted deeply in Western "mainstream" theories and expressed in the Rostowian "stages theory", according to which the development of national economies cannot be harmfully affected by international forces or conditions, and the advanced capitalist market economies, having passed the critical stage of economic development, namely "take off", are already in the stages characterized by "self-sustained growth" which do not require profound, far-reaching "structural and institutional changes" any more. It could also fit the former assumption, propagated by "Marxist–Leninists", that the "socialist countries" had already sold the problems of modernization and catching-up successfully and represented, therefore, an alternative road of development.

# IV. Economics of World Economy, National Development and Economic Systems after the Second World War

## 1. Development economics as a special field of study: its rise, evolution and decline or rebirth

1. In the first stage of the short history of development economics, roughly from the late 1940s to the mid-1960s[248], two, diametrically opposite theoretical streams appeared within this field of studies or in connection with the latter. They may be confronted as "internalists" versus "externalists" (if their difference in the explanation of underdevelopment is stressed), or as "neoclassicals" vs. "structuralists" (if their link with "mainstream" Neo-Classical economics or with the Latin American school of "structuralism" is considered), or as "universalists" vs. "particularists/exceptionalists" (if the acceptance of rejection of a unilinear process of development is the criterion of distinction), or as "flat-earthers" vs. "round-earthers" (according to belief in harmony, in mutual interests or an emphasis on conflicts and struggle), etc.[249]

This first stage was still more or less characterized by the dominance of an economistic "developmentalism" as following from the conventional "internalist", "neoclassical", "universalist" and "blue" views mentioned above. These theoretical concepts (as we shall see) tried to explain the economic backwardness or "underdevelopment" of the less developed countries (called later euphemistically as "developing countries") by various unfavourable internal conditions, growth inhibiting or limiting factors, such as demographic explosion, capital shortage, and narrow market (Viner), poor quality of labour and traditional social behaviour (Hoselitz), etc. or by a "vicious circle" of poverty (Nurkse, Gill), by a "quasi-stable equilibrium" of low per capita income (Leibenstein). Most of them assumed that underdevelopment of the developing countries represents a natural, aboriginally "traditional" stage of the same unilinear and universal path of economic development as had been passed earlier by the developed nations (Rostow) which may help, assist the developing countries and show them the way of development. Such views which that time heavily influenced the UN concepts of "development assistance" aiming at a "diffusion" of more capital, skill and entrepreneurial spirit from the developed to the developing countries, have gained a theoretical support

[248] See *Meier, G. M. and Seers, D.* eds. (1984).

[249] See *Little, I. M. D.* (1982) and *Streeten, P.* (1985).

in Rostow's theory of the stages of economic growth and a methodological instrument in the widely applied "subtraction approach"[250] which compared an idealized abstract model of the advanced capitalist countries with a negatively "idealized" abstract model of a typical underdeveloped one, and as a result what appeared to be a "plus" on the former side, became a factor explaining the higher level of development, and what appeared as a "minus" on the latter, served to explain underdevelopment.

One can argue, of course, that whenever we *compare* different phenomena, things or persons, we normally apply such a subtraction (or contrast) approach. What makes, however, such an approach unacceptable, unrealistic and unscientific in the case of defining (moreover explaining) the (still originally backward, self-reproducing, or "quasi-stable equilibrium") system of underdevelopment of the developing countries as distinctive from the system of the advanced countries (or the former system of "socialism" from that of capitalism) is not only the comparison of idealized (thus also ideologised) entities but also and primarily the very assumption that what are thereby compared are completely separable entities, independent of each other. This assumption (whether explicit or implicit only) contradicting their historical development within the global system of extending and deepening interdependencies, means that "the intellectual question" is taken out of both the historical and the global context, i.e. out of the very reality.

Opposite views which questioned the concept of a "uniform modernization path" following the "ideal-type of Western capitalist development", and attributed "underdevelopment" to external rather than internal causes, appeared first only sporadically in literature (except that in the "East" where the official ideology called "Marxism–Leninism" did present an over-simplified critique of colonial imperialism and oppressive world capitalism), but they gained later a growing share in it. They were manifested in several publications of separate individual authors only, who pointed to the role played in the "political economy of backwardness" by the internationally exploitive nature of monopoly capitalism (Baran), to the "backwash effects" of international trade (Myrdal), to the transfer of benefits of increased productivity from the primary producing countries to the industrial ones, the drain of stimuli to development by the latter and to the regular deterioration of the terms of trade of developing countries (Prebish, Singer), to the "dualism" (Boeke) and the consequent "unlimited supply of labour" (Lewis) and "segregation" (Myrdal) or to "internal colonialism" (Casanova) caused by the penetration of foreign capitalism and culture, to the limited applicability of the "economics of the special case", i.e. of the few developed countries (Seers), etc. They also denied the "original", or intact, genuinely precapitalistic nature of societies in the Third World, thus also the assumed "feudalism" in Latin America (Frank).

[250] See *Frank, A.G.* (1967).

2. The second stage (from about the mid-1960s to the mid- or late 1970s) brought about not only an increased popularity of the latter, critical views and a more or less temporary defeat of the unilinear concept of development and "internalism", but for a while also a certain integration or association of all the critical views on the prevailing world order of international inequalities and dominance relations in a broad theoretical stream embracing almost all those schools and theorists (except the official "Marxism–Leninism" of the East) which and who denied or questioned the harmonious operation of the world market, the mutual benefits and comparative advantages from international trade and specialization, the conventional views of modernization.

In this period the "externalist" theories became quite dominant (if not in the conventional "economics of development" then, as often distinguished from the latter) in the multi- or interdisciplinary field of social science called "development studies". Their old and new or renewed views have been disseminated worldwide and seemed to form a more or less coherent set of interrelated theoretical conceptss. Such as the theorem of dependence (stemming from the "old" Latin-American "dependencia school", and manifested in the writings of Prebisch, Cardoso, Furtado, Marini, Sunkel, Santos, etc.), the theses about international dominance relations and unequal partners (Balogh, Perroux), the concept of "structural violence" (Galtung), the Neo-Marxist theses on international exploitation and uneven development of the capitalist world economy (Amin, Bettelheim, Brown, Cardoso, Mandel, Palloix, Seidman), the concept of "backwash effects" of international trade and primary product specialization (Myrdal, Singer), the "new left" theory of "trade imperialism" and unequal exchange (Emmanuel), the various theses on socio-economic disintegration, functional dualism and marginalisation in the economy, on the dualism in labour market, technology and culture of the developing societies penetrated by foreign capitalism (Sachs, Lewis, Furtado, Quijano), the concept of "alternative development" (Nerfin) and the views on special (non-Soviet) ways of socialism to overcome underdevelopment (e.g. Saul, Arrighi, Benachenhou, Rweyemamu, Seidman, Shivji), the concept of the "basic needs oriented development strategy" (Emmerij) and ideas of reforming the international economic order (Tinbergen).

The relative unity of this group of theoretical streams was quite manifest, indeed, versus the Neo-Classical economics and conventional modernization concepts, but it has blurred to a great extent over the differences in views between its less or more radical representatives, the liberal-humanitarian, social democratic reformists, Neo-Marxists and radical New-Left theorists.

A departure and breaking away from the conventional theories has brought, indeed, many scholars into or close to the above "camp". This was evidenced also by those views of a "revised internalism" recognizing the unfavourable international conditions for and their adverse effects on the "late late-comers", but attributing the latter primarily internal anomalies or weaknesses (e.g. Meier, Myint, Viner) or explaining the unfavourable external circumstances by the imperfections of the market and the harmful behaviour of the TNCs (e.g. Helleiner. Hirschman). At the same time, within the "school of dependencia" a "revised externalism" has also appeared, namely in the concept of "lumpen-development" (Frank) or in analyses of the dialectical interrelationship between external and internal factors (e.g. Cardoso, Sunkel, Szentes[251]), i.e. the idea of negative interactions of the presumably decisive external and the historically derivative internal conditions.

The above phenomena and particularly the evolving debates (often very heated ones) within both "camps" on theoretical or pragmatic issues, such as the debate on "unequal exchange" (Emmanuel, Bettelheim, O. Brown, S. Amin, Sau, Dandekar, de-Kadt, Anderson, Raffer, Szentes[252], etc.) or on capitalist and "social imperialism", on TNCs, or on a New International Economic Order etc., and also the split in both camps between "globalists" and "nationalists", in general, have already marked the beginning of the dissolution of the former "unity" of the two opposite theoretical streams and also the decreasing relevance of the former distinction between "internalists" and "externalists".

3. The third phase, from about the mid- or late 1970s to the early 1990s, reflecting the effects of the world-economic crisis and the various responses to it, has resulted not only a further and increasingly manifested differentiation in both camps, but also the forging ahead of the "world-system approach" (Wallerstein, Hopkins, Frank) and a "new structuralism" (Chenery), on the one hand, and a kind of "counter-revolution of development economics" (Lal, Bauer, Warren, Smith, etc.).

Another result of this phase was (as already noted) the extension of development research also to the advanced countries of the West. This is marked by the recognition of development problems even of a country like Britain (Seers) and by studies on the European periphery, Eastern and Southern Europe (e.g. Berend and Ránki), as well as by the birth of new concepts such as "maldevelopment" or "overdevelopment" of the North (Guha) representing the other side of the coin, and by the claim to differentiate also within the North and study accordingly its varying development history (Senghaas).

This third phase has witnessed a certain weakening and almost a defeat (at least temporarily) of the critical, "externalist" schools, both reformists and radicals, not only and much less in theory, but also and far more considerably in practice.

The theoretical "counter-revolution" in development economics, obviously induced or influenced by the "Monetarist counterrevolution" or rather by the new government "philosophy" of economic policy ("Reaganomics") and by the spread of restrictive adjustment policies as well as by the obvious failure of the "development policy" of several corrupt governments in the Third World, has made a coun-

[251] See *Szentes, T.* (1971).
[252] See *Szentes, T.* (1985).

terattack primarily against the "dependencia school". Strangely enough (?) this counterattack coming from neoliberal "internalists" (Lal, Bauer, etc.) has more or less coincided and harmonized, as we shall see, with another counterattack which came from orthodox Marxists (Warren and Smith). Any way, unlike the "monetarist counter-revolution", these attacks representing a "counter-revolution in development economics" had no specially new or considerable effect on theoretical development.

However, the increase of influence, in practice, of neo-conservative or neo-liberal views, monetarist policies and internal or international neo-classicism, and the widely accepted or forced policies of the balance-of-payments "adjustment" prescribed by the credit "conditionalities" of IMF, the new ideal and misinterpreted model of a NICs-type modernization and the fading away of the former hopes attached to NIEO and (non-Soviet type) "socialist orientation" in the Third World are clear proofs of a decline or even a "crisis" of those views and policies accusing or approaching critically the international economic relations and seeking for alternatives versus the prevailing world order.

While the lasting nature of this (counter-)trend in practice and policies is, indeed, very questionable in view of the actual aggravation of the problems that the "neoliberal" or restrictive "monetarist" policy has been unable to solve (such as the debt crisis, the unemployment problem and the widening development gap), the collapse and transformation of the "socialist" systems in the "East" gave a new impetus to it, at least temporarily.

4. The collapse of the communist regimes and the fading-away (not of the State and the market, as Marx visualized, but instead) of "real" or "existing socialism" has produced a new challenge to development economics (too) and has broadened both the "geography" and the "subjects" of the field of development economics, opening thereby a new stage in its history.

The new changes in reality have led, on the one hand, to new polemies and further differentiation of views in development economics, and, on the other, despite "counter-revolutions", to a strengthening of the tendency of certain convergence, at the expense of those extremist variants of both "internalism" and "externalism" which were more influential in the former periods.

Such a *tendency of convergence* and towards a sort of synthesis, a kind of "constructive eclecticism" can already be illustrated e.g. by the 1991 Development Report of the World Bank and the response to it, prepared for the "group of 24" and published by UNCTAD (1992)[253]. The difference between them, even if the

[253] Another manifestation of the rise of a "constructive eclecticism" can be found in the latest editions of Gerald Meier's famous book *"Leading Issues in Economic Development"* which (just like the former editions) include selected readings as well as his own Notes and Comments, the former reflecting the variety of views, indeed, while the latter summarize them in an eclectic way, by pointing to those common conclusions derived from them. Such an "eclectic approach" – as he states – "best serves the student's needs". See *Meier, G. M.* (1995), p. V.

former obviously represents the "internalist" rather than "externalist" stand, while the latter vice versa, seems often to manifest in emphasis rather than in substance.

It is perhaps the main result and also message of the "short" history of development economics that reality is much more complex than perceived, and the levels of its analysis are more than usually applied by any particular theory, which all suggest, indeed, learning from all, without fully accepting any, of the theories.

## 2. Conventional theories of national development, economic "backwardness" and systems as stages of growth

After having outlined the brief history of the development of "development economics" as a special field of study, separated from economics in general, let us see more details of those theories explaining the international "development gap", i.e. the underdevelopment of the developing countries versus the development of the advanced ones, by various internal factors and circumstances or their unique form of motion, thereby representing the conventional views of economistic developmentalism which seemed to dominate this field of study in the *first stage* of its history! (Most of the references will therefore go back to the 1950s and 1950s.)

### 2.1. Underdevelopment as the aggregate of certain internal factors and circumstances which have been limiting or hindering development

The very first, and perhaps the most typical and popular variant of the "internalist" theories has been the one which explains underdevelopment by means of a summary of certain "typical" features, factors and circumstances hindering or limiting the process of development. As already mentioned, the "typical" features, development-limiting factors have usually been specified by simply comparing the idealized abstract model of the advanced capitalist countries with a negatively "idealized" abstract model of the underdeveloped ones, and what, as a result of such a comparison, appears as a "plus" or "minus" for the latter, constitutes the aggregate of various deficiencies, shortages or obstacles hindering development, which defines and explains their underdevelopment. This "subtraction approach" or "ideal typical index approach" (as it is called by A. G. Frank[254]), or "gap approach" has become so popular, indeed, that it has been applied even by those such as e.g. Leibenstein (1957), who going beyond a summarized description and specification of the development-limiting factors, has described "underdevelop-

[254] *Frank, A.G.* (1967).

ment" as a peculiar qualitative "form of motion" or, more exactly, as a "system" and not just a relative phenomenon. In other words, this approach has often served as a departure point also for theories concentrating on the relationships between the various development-hindering factors[255]. On the other hand, it has also offered some support for those "historical" concepts[256] interpreting underdevelopment as an original and natural state, a general but earlier stage of development from which the historical process of socio-economic development naturally leads towards higher stages, finally to the ideal type of the advanced societies. It has also been utilized in those theories, which, in compliance with or independently of the already mentioned "historical" approaches, concentrate on the sociological and psychological differences between advanced, and underdeveloped countries and identifies the state of underdevelopment with a closed, stagnant, traditional society.

Thus the "subtraction approach" has been used to explain underdevelopment by such a mere comparison, thereby constructing a theoretical concept in itself, or it has served as an introduction to other, more complex interpretations.

Let us examine it first as an independent theory, as a separate interpretation of underdevelopment. It exists in a great number of varieties. It seems that the number of factors considered characteristic or determinant might be added to at will. This is, of course, only the natural result of lifting them out of the real historical context[257] and basic causal relationships[258]. On the other hand, and as a consequence, the characteristics (or limiting factors) of a different number and nature often include very superficial phenomena, or such as would require further explanation. Many of the enumerated characteristics would not prove to be generally common in the underdeveloped world if the latter were classified by qualitative criteria.

---

[255] See later the critique of the concepts of the "vicious circle", and the "quasi-stable equilibrium system".

[256] Such as *Rostow's* theory of the historical "stages of economic growth", which will be discussed later.

[257] *H. Leibenstein* (1957) – though admitting that the explanation of differences in per capita income is as much a historical problem as an analytical one – believed that "in view of the framework of ignorance" (concerning the economic history of each of the countries under consideration) "within which we are forced to work, it would certainly be convenient if we could frame our problem in such a way as to take the intellectual question out of its historical context". (p. 3)

[258] *Benjamin Higgins* (1959) noted: "It is easy enough to list distinguishing characteristics of underdeveloped countries. Unfortunately, our hopes of isolating causal relationships in this way have not been fulfilled. For each of the characteristics has a hen-and-egg nature that makes it virtually impossible to separate causes from effects." (p. 23)

*H. Leibenstein* (1957), whose list is perhaps the most comprehensive, enumerated the following characteristics of the underdeveloped countries as limiting or hindering their development (pp. 40–41):

**1. Economic**

**a) General**

1. A very high proportion of the population in agriculture, usually some 70 to 90 percent.
2. "Absolute over-population" in agriculture, that is, it would be possible to reduce the number of workers in agriculture and still obtain the same total output.
3. Evidence of considerable "disguised unemployment" and lack of employment opportunities outside agriculture.
4. Very little capital per head.
5. Low income per head and, as a consequence, existence near the "subsistence" level.
6. Practically zero savings for the large mass of the people.
7. Whatever savings do exist is usually achieved by a landholding class whose values are not conducive to investment in industry or commerce.
8. The primary industries, that is, agriculture, forestry, and mining, are usually the residual employment categories.
9. The output in agriculture is made up mostly of cereals and primary raw materials, with relatively low output of protein foods. The reason for this is the conversion ratio between cereals and meat products; that is, if one acre of cereals produces a certain number of calories, it would take between five to seven acres to produce the same number of calories if meat products were produced.
10. Major proportion of expenditures on food and necessities.
11. Export of foodstuffs and raw materials.
12. Low volume of trade per capita.
13. Poor credit facilities and poor marketing facilities.
14. Poor housing.

**b) Basic characteristics in agriculture**

1. Although there is low capitalization on the land, there is simultaneously an uneconomic use of whatever capital exists due to the small size of holdings and the existence of exceedingly small plots.
2. The level of agrarian techniques is exceedingly low, and tools and equipment are limited and primitive in nature.
3. Even where there are big landowners as, for instance, in certain parts of India, the openings for modernized agricultural production for sale are limited by difficulties of transport and the absence of an efficient demand in the local market. It is significant that in many backward countries a modernized type of agriculture is confined to production for sale in foreign markets.
4. There is an inability of the small landholders and peasants to weather even a short-term crisis, and, as a consequence, attempts are made to get the highest possible yields from the soil, which leads to soil depletion.
5. There is a widespread prevalence of high indebtedness relative to assets and income.
6. The methods of production for the domestic market are generally old-fashioned and inefficient, leaving little surplus for marketing. This is usually true irrespective of whether or not the cultivator owns the land, has tenancy rights, or is a sharecropper.
7. A most pervasive aspect is a feeling of land hunger due to the exceedingly small size of holdings and small diversified plots. The reason for this is that holdings are continually subdivided as the population on the land increases.

**2. Demographic**

1. High fertility rates, usually above 40 per thousand.
2. High mortality rates and low expectation of life at birth.
3. Inadequate nutrition and dietary deficiencies.
4. Rudimentary hygiene, public health, and sanitation.
5. Rural overcrowding.

**3. Cultural and Political**

1. Rudimentary education and usually a high degree of illiteracy among most of the people.
2. Extensive prevalence of child labour.
3. General weakness or absence of the middle class.
4. Inferiority of women's status and position.
5. Traditionally determined behaviour for the bulk of the populace.

**4. Technological and Miscellaneous**

1. Low yields per acre.
2. No training facilities or inadequate facilities for the training of technicians, engineers, etc.
3. Inadequate and crude communication and transportation facilities, especially in the rural areas.
4. Crude technology.

*Leibenstein* tried to create a logical order in the multitude of characteristics by dividing them into two main categories: into "income-determining" characteristics (e.g. capital per head, credit facilities, entrepreneurial ability, technical knowledge), and "income-determined" characteristics (e.g. standard of living, indebtedness, housing, nutrition, etc.). He further distinguished those characteristics, which cannot be explained "in terms of our simple production, consumption, and savings functions". In spite of this, however, the system of his characteristics has remained basically arbitrary, unordered, heterogeneous[259], and even contradictory.

Many of the characteristics are already in themselves inexactly formulated and difficult to define (e.g. "poor", "crude", "rudimentary", "exceedingly low", "very little") or they are just overemphasized and exaggerated (e.g. "rural overcrowding", "lack of employment opportunities outside agriculture"). Many characteristics cannot be accepted as general for all or even the majority of the underdeveloped countries. What meaning can be attached e.g. to the afore-mentioned "rural overcrowding" in a number of sparsely populated regions of Africa, the Near East or Latin America?! The interpretation of the terms "absolute overpopulation" and "disguised unemployment" is also debatable on theoretical grounds[260], and in practice these problems are too complex to be just simply stated.

There are several indices among the characteristics whose relative size and trend of change rather than their absolute size, low or high value, must be regarded as crucial. It is true, the high mortality rate is really characteristic and tragic, and therefore demands further effective measures, yet – as Leibenstein himself pointed out later (pp. 56–57 and 190–191) – it is the divergence of the mortality and fertility rates that constitutes the acute problem, and indeed, to a certain extent, the obstacle to any further decrease in the mortality rate. The low volume of trade per capita is still more or less typical of the underdeveloped countries, but at the same time, the comparatively high volume of foreign trade per

[259] As *B. Higgins* (1959) remarked: "Leibenstein's 'characteristics' are of three different kinds: statistical facts, general observations, and conclusions from analysis." (p. 13)

[260] See *Haberler, G.* (1957), and *Nurkse, R.* (1957).

capita in relation to the volume of per capita national income is contradictory and requires explanation.

Similarly, the contradictions inherent in the real essence of underdevelopment are conspicuous even among Leibenstein's characteristics, making the combined list itself contradictory. Thus, no conventional production, consumption and savings functions can explain the contradiction between the "low volume of trade per capita" and the "major proportion of expenditures on food and necessities" on the one hand, and the "export of foodstuffs and raw materials" on the other. Nor do they explain why the "low capitalization on the land", the "uneconomic use of capital", the "existence of exceedingly small plots", "little surplus for marketing", and at the same time "a modernized type of agriculture confined to production for sale in foreign markets" are characteristic of underdevelopment. To explain these obvious and striking contradictions it is not sufficient "to take the intellectual question out of its historical context".

Less detailed but similarly mixed and heterogeneous lists of underdevelopment characteristics have also been given e.g. by A. Sauvy and E. Gannagé.

*Sauvy* (1956) attributed the following characteristics to underdevelopment: (1) high mortality rate and short life expectancy; (2) high fertility without birth control; (3) poor nutrition; (4) high proportion of illiteracy; (5) lack of full employment owing to insufficient capital supply; (6) strong predominance of agriculture and fishery over the processing industries; (7) low social status of women and child labour; (8) insufficient development of the middle classes; (9) authoritarian political regimes; (10) lack of democratic institutions (pp. 241–242). Thus Sauvy mentioned first the high death and high birth rate among the characteristics of underdeveloped countries. Originally, this was, indeed, characteristic of the traditional, more exactly, precapitalist societies. Today, however, the nature and relations of the traditional societies can no longer explain the divergence of the two rates. As far as Sauvy's other characteristics are concerned, they reveal the justifiable endeavour to account for underdevelopment not only by economic but also social, cultural and political factors, but there is already a certain amount of confusion about the nature and relationships of these factors. Thus factors 3 and 4 and even 7 can be easily explained (just as 1 and 2) on the basis of traditional social relations, while the problems concerning employment and capital supply (5) as well as the structure of the economy (6) – the latter is characterized rather inaccurately without specifying what kind of agriculture is meant by it – already indicate capitalist *commodity-production* relations. Criteria 9 and 10 reflect, at first glance, the peculiarities of traditional societies, but the Arab or Asian feudal relations and the traditional communal system of certain Tropical-African tribes cannot be evaluated on the same basis. On the other hand, the lack of democratic institutions may be a characteristic of modern regimes too, and it is not clear either to what extent any evaluation is possible merely on the basis of the formal existence or non-existence of certain institutions. Thus it seems that Sauvy's criteria, even covering as they do mostly surface phenomena, contain very heterogeneous elements and can hardly be included in a uniform system of causal relationships.

*E. Gannagé* (1962), too, put a demographic factor, high birth rate, first among the criteria of underdevelopment. Its consequence, high population growth, is, in his opinion, one of the main obstacles to development. His system of criteria is similar to Sauvy's in that it also involves both economic and social factors, and these factors are the elements of highly different rank and nature of different causal relationships. His further criteria were: (2) predominance of agriculture and mining; (3) capital shortage; (4) unbalanced and rigid social structure; (5) insistence on traditions; (6) passive attitude of the population towards necessary changes. Here again certain factors (e.g. 1, 5, and 6) refer to traditional societies, others (e.g. 2 and 3) to capitalist ones. But Gannagé also shed some light on relationships investigating the coming into existence of opposite poles, the emergence of a dual structure, various vicious circles (to be discussed later), and also certain international relations.

Instead of presenting here further lists of characteristics produced by other authors, let us investigate one by one only those few characteristic features considered, in general, to be the most important which have most frequently been mentioned in the related theoretical literature explaining underdevelopment.

The authors would, perhaps, protest against such an isolation of characteristics from each other, saying that the latter provide an explanation for underdevelopment only together or in conjunction with others. But the lists of factors – as we have seen – are rather arbitrary and can be lengthened or shortened at will. If the factors are related at all and are not combined at random, there must be some connection between them. If this relationship is causal, i.e. where one factor determines the other, then it is fully justified to examine them one by one and ask to what extent they can be considered as causes or effects. If, however, the relationship among them is circularly mutual, as supposed by most authors[261], then in the following we shall treat it as a separate concept.

### 2.1.1. Unfavourable natural conditions, scarcity or underutilization of natural resources

One of the unfavourable conditions setting obstacles to development, which has often appeared in the literature explaining underdevelopment by internal factors, is natural endowment.

For example, *Jacob Viner* (1953) considered the low level of productivity in the developing countries as being caused (besides the poor quality of the working population in respect of culture and education, health and nutrition) by the unfavourable natural endowments (poor-quality soil, virgin forests, lack of mineral resources, and waterpower, unfavourable climatic and precipitation conditions, poor transport facilities, unfavourable geographical situation with respect to its opportunities for profitable foreign trade, etc.).

No doubt, great many developing countries suffer, indeed, the scarcity of natural resources, the unfavourable climatic conditions, the disadvantage of geographical position, etc.

However, as a matter of fact, the natural conditions and resources of all the developing countries can hardly be regarded as unfavourable in general. (There are several countries in Africa, Latin America and Asia, which are very rich in some mineral resources, and the world reserves in a few minerals are heavily concentrated in the South[262]. And as the case of Switzerland or Japan may show, the *lack*

[261] "If A, B and C are obstacles that are related in such a way that there is no way of overcoming them one by one, since all of them change as anyone of them is tampered with, there is no way of determining that one is much more important than the others." *Leibenstein, H.* (1957), p. 55.

[262] The share of the "South" (i.e. the group of developing countries) in the known world resources of tin is about 71 per cent, of zinc 65 per cent, of copper 50 per cent, of nickel 49 per cent, of bauxite 48 per cent, and of iron ore 30 per cent. See: *Hveem, H.* (1977), pp. 222–225.

*of mineral resources* is not a fatal obstacle to development, anyway. Some of the developing countries do have very high *water power potential*[263], and, though the climatic conditions are, indeed, unfavourable in a number of countries, they are definitely favourable in some others[264].

The *geographical location* may, of course, be of primary importance in transport, communication and foreign trade. The backwardness of transport and communication, and/or the high cost of their development, as well as the great distance from international trade routes, are indeed considerable obstacles to development. On the other hand, the very development of the transport and communication system depends on the pattern and tempo of economic development more than natural conditions today. Therefore, an underdeveloped transport and communication system is a concomitant symptom rather than a determining factor of underdevelopment. In most of the developing countries the sporadic, uneven development of the transport and communication system with a distorted pattern reflects fairly well the historical fact that they have been intensively involved in long distance (overseas) trade with the metropolitan countries for a long time. It was the ("colonial") pattern of international division of labour which has shaped their transport and communication system and for which their geographical position could matter at all. Thus the importance of the latter can hardly be assessed without considering the external conditions such as international trade, and their changes.

*Gerald Meier* and *Robert Baldwin* (1957) also pointed to the state of natural resources as one of the factors causing underdevelopment (pp. 291–303). But, as *Meier* himself noted in another publication (1958), however popular it is to refer to the lack of resources, and however evident it is that the possibilities of development are highly restricted where natural resources are lacking, in 1870 very few countries could have been said to be poor in them. "The present phenomenon of a low amount of resources per head is the result of either the exhaustion of resources or such a rapid growth in population that overpopulation now puts pressure on the available resources." (p. 56) Thus, *Meier* pointed out that the abundance or shortage of natural resources is a *relative* phenomenon only and that the position of the developing countries today is more unfavourable in respect of natural resources than it was in 1870.

The fact that the *natural resources* that had existed earlier were "exhausted" soon and turned out to be scarce due to a rapid growth of population might prove that they had been considerably limited in an absolute sense, too. If resources did not represent a bottleneck earlier (but only since they became exhausted and scarce in relation to the number of population), the question ought to be answered why they did not promote development efficiently when and where they were still available in abundance. It is hardly enough to refer to the exhaustion of natural

[263] For example, Africa's water power potential amounts to about 40–50 per cent of the potential hydraulic power of the entire world.

[264] In Latin America there are immense areas of virgin land which could yield three crops annually if they were cultivated.

resources without also posing the question: *by whom and for what purposes* the resources were exploited. Did the national economy of the countries benefit from the exhaustion of their resources or not? And was the exploitation of the resources justified at that time and to such an extent from the point of view of the development of the countries concerned? It is obvious that what is needed here too, is a genuinely *historical* answer and not a type of explanation based on demographic trends or the "natural" exhaustion of resources.

It should also be noted that as regards the scarcity or abundance of natural resources it is not quite realistic to speak of the "drying up" of resources because *geological explorations* can never be regarded as finished (they are, in fact, still in a rather the initial stage in many developing countries), and because science and technology are continuously developing[265].

There is, however, one natural-geographical endowment which seems to be a more or less common feature, indeed, namely that "almost all the newly developing countries are tropical countries", as was noted by *Jan Tinbergen* (1963). In this respect reference is often made partly to the unfavourable psychological effect of the *hot climate*, which "does not encourage hard work and makes a primitive way of life bearable in many respects" and partly to the *poor quality of the tropical soil* which prevents any considerable agrarian, and thereby also industrial development.

The fact that *physical work* under tropical conditions is more difficult is a well-known fact. It is also self-evident that the lack of that system of work involving regularly repeated and constant efforts, which is objectively required by agriculture in the temperate zone, and the objectively greater possibility of a mere reliance on the mercy of Nature in the tropical zones, may, indeed, retard development[266]. At a certain stage of the development of productive forces, natural conditions have an increased importance in social development. There is no doubt that such circumstances may still play a decisive role in determining the life conditions and economic development of certain tribes inhabiting the depths of the forests. But, on the other hand – as Tinbergen (1963) also noted – it was just in the tropical belt that the great ancient cultures had developed, while primitive tribes of that time had lived in the temperate zone. Thus, even if in a certain period some zones are more favourable to socio-economic development than others, this does not preclude the possibility of the opposite in another period. And as to the more recent historical period, it was exactly in the countries of the "South" (particularly in the colonies) where the most "sweating" methods of exploitation were (and in many places still are) applied, such as a long working day, low wages, various penalties, poor mechanization, hard manual work, etc.[267]

[265] The book *of J. Barnett and C. Morse* (1963) set this problem in its proper perspective.

[266] *Marx* did also take into account such circumstances when he called the temperate zone the natural fatherland of capital.

[267] For further details see among others: *Woddis, J.* (1961); *UN* (1958); *Hunton, W. A.* (1956); *Fanon, F.* (1961); etc.

A realistic assessment of the *quality of tropical soil* still needs considerable scientific work and research[268]. It seems to be sure, however, that the transplantation of some crops to tropical soil has proved unsuccessful, and certain methods of cultivation used in the temperate zone (e.g. deep ploughing) may be definitely harmful in the tropics. It is also an established fact that the qualitative deterioration of the tropical soil (mechanical disintegration and erosion) may be very rapid if it is not protected against the sun which "would burn away the organic matter and kill the micro-organisms" and the heavy rainfall which "would crush the structure of the soil, seal off the underlying soil from the air, and leach out the minerals or carry them so far into the earth that the plant roots cannot reach them"[269].

No doubt, the great dependence on weather, a high degree of exposure to frequent *natural disasters* (flood, drought), the uncertainty of the marketable surplus and the progressing erosion, etc., are, indeed, serious constraints on agricultural development. However, such phenomena (even if less frequently and less intensively appearing) have not been unknown in Europe either, and the solution for mitigating their harmful effects has proved to be primarily a social and technical question, i.e. a function of economic development itself. In addition, the considerable share of the developing countries in the world production of a great number of agricultural products[270] must warn us not to make too general and far-reaching conclusions about their natural endowments and soil quality. The difficulties in marketing these products call our attention rather to the fact that the problems of the development of agriculture are not primarily connected with the natural conditions. It is even less admissible to link up economic development as a whole with the blessings of soil and climate.

As *B. Higgins* noted (1959): "The soil and climate of Japan did not suddenly change in the latter part of the nineteenth century when its transformation to an industrialized country began." (p. 273)

According to *H. Leibenstein* (1957), the low agricultural yields of underdeveloped countries can be explained, in principle, by three factors: "(1) some of the capital found in advanced agricultural countries may not be of a kind for which we can substitute labour; (2) advanced countries may utilize superior agricultural techniques; and (3) on the average, the quality of the cultivated land may be superior in the advanced countries."

As far as the former two points are concerned, they are obviously the functions of economic development, and not the other way round. About the third factor Leibenstein stated the following: "Certainly, persistently low yields cannot be ascribed to climatic characteristics since these are often more favourable to high yields in the underdeveloped countries than in the developed ones. But the

[268] "Little is known about how best to exploit and improve tropical soils." *Kamarck, A. M.* (1967), p. 92.

[269] *Kamarck, A. M.* (1967), p. 93.

[270] For example, in the late 1970s the percentage share of the developing countries in the total export of *coffee* was 91 per cent (Brazil and Colombia supplied 35 per cent), of *tea* 86 per cent (India and Sri Lanka 59 per cent), of *cocoa* 83 per cent (Ghana, Nigeria and Brazil more than 50 per cent), of *spices* 88 per cent, of *sugar* 75 per cent (Cuba alone nearly 30 per cent), of *rubber* 61 per cent (Malaysia, Singapore and Indonesia about 50 per cent) and *of cotton* 53 per cent (Egypt and the Sudan supplied about 17 per cent). See *UNCTAD* (1979), pp. 266–285.

average quality of the land may be inferior for two reasons. First, because incomes are low, the margin of cultivation is carried much further in the direction of poorer land... But, second, and more to the point, there may be an inherent dynamic process in the utilization of the land that keeps yields low." And this is because, as a result of certain "counter forces", "an improvement in the quality of the land generates a more intensive utilization of that land". "Increased current yields imply improved nutrition, a diminution of periodic starvation, and consequent diminished mortality rates, resulting in an increased population and necessary further subdivision of holdings..."; "...there is now little room for quality-maintenance measures that imply a diminution in the current yield." (pp. 48–51)

This explanation is in perfect consonance with Leibenstein's "quasi-stable equilibrium" idea[271], and it is completely devoid of any historical context. The fact that the acceleration of population growth in the developing countries was *de facto* not a consequence of improved soil and higher yields is so evident that there is no need to prove it. But the further subdivision of holdings is a fairly general phenomenon, and so is the gradual disuse of the traditional quality-maintenance measures. Is it possible not to see behind such phenomena the spreading of the big monocultural plantations and the growing of export crops[272]?

The question of natural resources is dealt with by several scholars, including *H. Myint*, not as an absolute or relative plenty or poverty, but as the measure of the utilization of potentials (which theoretically may mean the utilization of mineral resources as well as soil potentials)[273]. Myint (1958) referred to the "underdevelopment of natural resources" (in connection with "backward people") as one of the determinants of underdevelopment (pp. 93–96).

The term "underdeveloped resources" is meant, in fact, the under utilization of potential resources or the non-optimum allocation of the given resources to possible uses, i.e. "a species of deviation from the productive optimum". Thus the concept "unfavourable natural endowments" has been replaced by the concept "under utilization of existing natural resources" (available perhaps in abundance) in explaining underdevelopment.

This is, no doubt, more realistic than the generalizing assumption about unfavourable natural endowments though it does not reveal more about the roots, the deep-lying causes of underdevelopment, either. Here, too, quite a number of questions remain unanswered: What is the yardstick by which the inadequate utilization of potential resources can be measured? What are the causes of "under-utilization"? Why did even those colonial countries in which a part of the

---

[271] See later!

[272] Instances of and references to the harmful effects of *monocultural plantation farming* (depletion of land, increased sensitivity to plant diseases and insects) and its drawbacks, as opposed to traditional cultivation methods, can be found in a great number of books, official reports and studies published in the 1940s and 1950s. (See e.g.: *Batten, T. R.* (1947); *Woddis, J.* (1961); *Brown, K.* (1959); UN (1958*); Higgins, B.* (1959), and so on...

[273] *Jacob Viner* (1958), too, stressed the utilization of potentials when he defined the concept of underdeveloped countries by declaring that an underdeveloped country is one "which has good *potential prospects* for using more capital or more labor or *more available natural resources* to support its present population on a higher level of living or if its per capita income level is already fairly high to support a larger population on a not lower level of living". (p. 12)

resources was exploited intensively (as according to Meier, perhaps even exhaustively) not achieve a higher level of development, i.e. the phase of "self-sustained growth"?

## 2.1.2. "Demographic explosion" and "overpopulation"

The high rate of population growth is one of those phenomena most frequently and commonly referred to as an obstacle to development in the various studies on "underdevelopment".

It was included, as we have seen, in *Leibenstein's* combined lists, and ranked first among *Sauvy's* and *Gannagé's* characteristics, too. Most of the scholars explaining underdevelopment by (partly or exclusively) internal conditions have pointed to "population pressure" and the unfavourable age composition of the population (namely: the high proportion of dependents within the latter), which result from the rapid growth of population caused by the divergence of the mortality and fertility rates[274]. Owing to the application of modern medical science and the extension of public health services, mortality tends to decrease at a quicker rate than the opportunities of productive employment increase, while the birth rate does not decline proportionally. Thus population growth has been considered unfavourable because of the problem of employment, i.e. in relative sense, and also in view of the supply of basic necessities.

"Population pressure" – as according to *Meier and Baldwin* (1957) – may manifest itself in three ways: (a) latent unemployment in agriculture ("rural underemployment"); (b) high proportion of dependents per adult due to the high birth rate; (c) rapid population growth due to the drop in the mortality rate together with a high birth rate. In their view, "population pressure" is responsible for the fact that the labour force is an "abundant factor" in the developing countries. (pp. 281–290) Since its supply tends to exceed the demand, the expansion of any sector of the economy (e.g. the export sector) cannot bring about an increase in real wages[275].

The rate of population growth did really increase considerably and quite suddenly in the post-second-world-war period, first and most markedly in Asia, and later on in Africa, too, where it is still remarkable. Thus a kind of "population explosion" occurred which spread from the most densely populated areas of the world. The rapid increase in population and especially the number and proportion of young dependents have further deteriorated the economic indices (per capita income, consumption and production) of the countries concerned. It requires increased efforts to attain a higher level of development, and brings about serious

[274] See among many others: *Viner, J.* (1953), p. 118; *Meier, G. M. and Baldwin, R.* (1957), pp. 281–290; *Perroux, P.* (1966).

[275] A similar concept appeared (as we shall see) in the famous model of *Arthur Lewis* (1958), pp. 400–449.

bottlenecks in the spheres of food supply, public education, health and social services, and also heavily aggravates the employment problem[276].

Thus there is no reason to deny the importance of population growth. However, the "space"[277] and time aspects of the phenomenon "demographic explosion", the causes of its incidence and particularly its causal relationship with underdevelopment require a more thorough investigation. On the one hand, the perspective side of the problem of population growth is quite different in the densely populated countries[278] (particularly in those with poor natural resources) from that in the sparsely populated countries[279]. A rapid population growth does not necessarily prevent, but in the long run (i.e. apart from the temporary problem of age distribution), might, in fact, promote the development of the sparsely populated countries. One should not forget that population growth means the increase in the number of potential labour force which, if efficiently used, is the primary source of any development.

On the other hand, the phenomenon itself, namely the rise in the rate of population growth, must be accounted for. It is not enough to recognize the diverging trends of the two rates[280] and explain the fall of the mortality rate by improved health service and protection against epidemics. The core of the question is whether or not such a divergence of the two rates is a natural demographic symptom in a certain stage of social development.

If the answer is an affirmative one[281], then this divergence ought to be discovered also in the history of the already developed countries. Then it raises further

[276] For illustration: in 1977, the total labor force of the developing countries numbered about 800 million. Of these about 40 million were unemployed and about 300 million were underemployed.

[277] Referring to statistical data *Benjamin Higgins* (1959) emphasized that the underdeveloped countries in general could not be said to be "densely populated". He also doubted that high population growth rate could be a distinguishing characteristic of underdevelopment since "rates of population growth show a similarly wide range". (pp. 16–18)

[278] It is true that nearly 50 per cent of the total population of the underdeveloped world (in 1977, 1 billion out of 2093 million) has been concentrated in five countries (India, Bangladesh, Pakistan, Indonesia and Nigeria), and most of these countries (or several big regions of them) are very densely populated, indeed. However, this fact can hardly justify to qualify all the developing countries, including the very sparsely populated ones, in a uniform way, as suffering "population pressure". It seems that underdevelopment theories in general were strongly biased in the 1950s and 1960s, due to their concentration on the economic problems of the overpopulated Asian countries mainly. This was in many respects understandable, of course, but it has often led to faulty generalizations.

[279] It is worth mentioning that not long before "demographic explosion" reached also Africa, its "underpopulation" had been considered as a serious obstacle to economic development. The 1951 Africa report of the UNO ascribed the economic backwardness and poverty of the people of the African countries mainly to underpopulation. See *UN* (1951).

[280] See *Leibenstein, H.* (1957), pp. 56–57, and 190–191.

[281] *Fritz Baade* (1964) pointed out that the already developed countries had also passed through a demographic phase in which the mortality rate began to drop when the birth rate remained virtually unchanged. But it has not prevented economic development; in fact, the two processes, namely the growth of the population and the growth of the economy had coincided until, at a certain stage of economic development, the birth rate, too, began to decrease.

questions: why has it not caused or maintained economic underdevelopment in the case of the latter, why has it not prevented their development?

If, however, the divergence of the two demographic rates is not a universal and natural phenomenon (or, even if only its order of magnitude differs substantially from that in the past, namely in the case of the already developed countries), then how can we account for this more or less new phenomenon?

And if the decline of the mortality rate in the past of the already developed countries was mainly due to economic development itself while in the case of the developing countries it is attributable to improved health services, i.e. to a factor more or less independent of economic development, then a new question arises again: Why has economic development in the developing countries tended to lag behind the development of sanitary services and population growth? It appears that the high population growth does not account for underdevelopment, and indeed the latter must be explained first to account for the development of the demographic situation.

Thus, *Viner's* remark (1953) that high population growth involves danger only when employment opportunities do not expand at the same time (p. 118), is tantamount to saying that a high rate of population growth hinders economic development only if the latter comes up against obstacles in any case, i.e. under the conditions of an already existing state of underdevelopment.

The connection – in fact the inverse relationship – between the rates of economic and population growth has been clearly demonstrated by *Simon Kuznets* (1958). Pointing out (1966) the difference and dissimilar conditions between the demographic patterns of the already developed countries *prior* to their industrial development and of the developing countries, he drew the conclusion that the present higher birth rate of the developing countries is the consequence of their *own* lower level of development, while the fall in the death rate is the result of the economic development, technological and medical progress achieved by *other*, i.e. by advanced countries. The developing countries cannot resort to emigration which was formerly available to the European countries, and so they have to pay the penalty for "being late", for lagging behind in development.

Whether it is really just a matter of "being late", of "lagging behind", is a question we shall have to discuss later, but even this explanation may have made clear the role of a foreign, external element in the development of population growth.

According to *Ragnar Nurkse* (1957), "the population explosion in Asia, due largely to the fall in death-rates, reflects the uneven impact of Western civilization". This, in his interpretation, means that while mortality has decreased due to the adoption of advanced medical techniques – in the consequence of which population has doubled – technology, capital supply and the size of cultivable land too have remained much the same.

Though *H. Myint* (1958) also pointed to the relationship of overpopulation and underdevelopment, which "mutually aggravate each other in a vicious circle", he added that the concept of "overpopulation" is not the answer to the problem. Incidentally, it may be the main cause of backwardness, but there are a number of underdeveloped countries, which are not under the pressure of overpopulation or became overpopulated only at a later time. (p. 107)

*Gerald M. Meier* (1958) also remarked in an earlier publication that "overpopulation is synonymous with underdevelopment" but "not the answer" to it, and that "the problems of increasing capital per head and raising per capita real income are common to all backward economies, whether overpopulated or not". (p. 57)

In *Leibenstein's* view (1957) the "demographic characteristics of economic backwardness present a dual problem": on the one hand, "they help to explain", and on the other "their existence and persistence have to be explained". On the analogy of induced and autonomous investments he distinguished "induced changes in population explainable by changes in per capita income" and "autonomous effects" which are independent of the changes in income and consumption. (Such as chemical, bacteriological, medical and public health discoveries by which the central government can decrease the mortality rate without a simultaneous increase in per capita income. (pp. 55–57)

Though *Malthus* is still very often (and quite incorrectly) referred to, the problem of "overpopulation" – as might be seen from the above – appeared as a much more complex and relative problem[282] in underdevelopment theories. The *relative* character of "overpopulation" has been strongly emphasized, and stress was laid rather on the available technology, modernized production methods and the capital supply.

*Colin Clark* (1953), for example, when dealing with the problems of population growth and living standards, strongly attacked Malthus. In his view the "law of diminishing returns can only be said to be, in any sense of the word, a law if two further conditions are fulfilled: first, that the inhabitants of the more densely settled area do not use any different farming methods from those of the less densely settled area, and secondly, that they do not employ any more capital per head. These two further conditions make the law of very limited application indeed. For the use of improved farming methods and greater quantities of capital per man are precisely the steps taken by progressive countries when they find their population increasing and their area of agricultural land limited".[283] By classifying 26 countries with respect to the relationship between the intensiveness of cultivation and agricultural output per person engaged in cultivation, he proved that there was little relation, if any, between density of settlement and average product per head. In Denmark e.g. per capita yield was five times that of Turkey with an identical population density. In Denmark, ten men (working) per square kilometre of land supplied 200 people. If "population pressure" was measured by this ratio, i.e. on the standard of Danish agriculture, only Belgium, the Netherlands, Japan and probably Switzerland (none of them is a backward country) could qualify as "overcrowded"; the countries in Latin America, Africa and the Middle East, and even India, Bangladesh and Indonesia could not be regarded as such. Thus it is obvious that low agricultural output (just as underdevelopment itself) was not caused by overpopulation.

It would, of course, be wrong to underestimate the consequences of rapid population growth and unfavourable age distribution that is the grave problems of "population pressure" especially in relation to densely populated countries. No doubt, this factor can really be a major obstacle, ceteris paribus, to development. However, underdevelopment, whether interpreted as a complex socio-economic product or as a mere relative difference, a "lagging behind", cannot be traced back simply to demographic conditions. The popularity of those views attributing a decisive or primary role to "population explosion" in perpetuating underdevelopment has declined, any way, since the reduction of birth rates has started to moderate the growth of population in the most densely populated countries of Asia[284].

[282] *A. A. Dawson* (1962) contrasted "the continuous growth of population in the traditional sector" with "the slow or arrested growth of the modern sector". (pp. 37, 43)

[283] See *Clark, C.* (1953) in: *Agarwala, A. N.* and *Singh, S. P.* eds. (1958), pp. 35–36.

[284] In the late 1980s the annual rate of population growth was only 1.3% in China, 2.2 in India, 2.1 in Indonesia, and 2.8 in Bangladesh, respectively, while several "low income" African countries still witnessed a rate above 3% (e.g. Kenya 3.8, Zambia 3.7, Ghana 3.4, Niger, Tanzania and Togo 3.5, Malawi 3.4, Nigeria and Rwanda 3.3, Benin, Liberia and Uganda 3.2, Sudan and Zaire 3.1 per cent a year). In other words, "population explosion" has started to shift away from Asia where (particularly in China and Indonesia) economic performance has also improved, and has been affecting more those African countries where in the period from the mid-1960s to the mid-1980s the average annual growth rate of per capita GNP has either declined as in most cases or remained very low. See the data in *World Bank* (1990).

### 2.1.3. Poor quality of labour

One of the most striking differences revealed by a comparison between the economy of the developing countries and that of the advanced countries is in the level of *labour productivity*. It is beyond doubt that low labour productivity is one of the most general and principal obstacles to development as it sets narrow "absolute" limits to surplus production and capital accumulation[285]. (Within the "absolute" limits, however, the possibility of actual accumulation depends on the income distribution relations and the use of incomes[286].) It also stands to reason that labour productivity also depends (though not exclusively[287]) on the physical and intellectual capacity of the worker.

In view of the latter the poor *physical and intellectual capacity* of the labour force, i.e. the poor quality of the working population has often been presented as the main reason, the principal cause of underdevelopment and poverty. Accordingly, the underdeveloped countries are poor because they do not produce enough, due to the low efficiency of labour of their working population[288].

As many others, *J. Viner* (1958) also noted, in connection with low labour productivity, the poor quality of the working population as a limiting factor of economic development. This poor quality comprises, in Viner's view, not only the poor quality and unfavourable composition of industrial and agricultural labour, but also the lack or insufficiency of the entrepreneurial and managerial elite and of engineers and technicians. Differences in this field, when compared with the advanced countries, are attributable, in his opinion, to historical (!) and cultural factors, to environment, quality of health, nutrition and education, as well as to the quality of the leadership provided by government and the social elite. He also added that where there is a traditional agriculture there is often a strong resistance to technical education, and to any change in the working processes. (p. 17)

The poor physical and intellectual quality and unfavourable composition of labour, and the shortage of skills, etc., though evidently great obstacles to development, are *consequences* and indicators rather than causes of the underdeveloped state of the economy of the developing countries. It is obvious enough that the

---

[285] *Celso Furtado* (1958) noted: "The main obstacles in the path of development... are encountered at the lowest levels of productivity." "When productivity is very low, the satisfaction of elementary needs absorbs a high proportion of productive capacity..." "When productivity is at such a low level, it is difficult to start a process of capital accumulation within the economy." (pp. 318–319.)

[286] As we shall see, several scholars (such as Lewis, Prebisch, Myrdal, etc.) have not only noted the fact of the low level of labor productivity in the underdeveloped economies, but they have also investigated certain mechanisms by which the benefits from even the rise in labor productivity are (according to their views) transferred from the latter to the advanced countries.

[287] The technological level, the "capital supply" of labor force, is, of course, another important determinant of the level of labor productivity (though not independent of the intellectual quality of labor). Labor productivity also depends on the actual pattern of organization, division and management of labor.

[288] See e.g. *P. de Briey* (1955), p. 123; and *O. Brown* (1946), p. 15.

"physical quality" of the labour force primarily depends on the nutrition and health conditions as well as some other components of the living standard in general, while the "intellectual quality" referring to skill, education, literacy and the accumulated experiences of the labourers, develops along with the development of the educational system and of the intra-society division of labour, and depends also on the employment and career prospects as well as on the incentives (not only for the workers to become educated, trained, to acquire skill but also for the employers to provide in-service or other training facilities). All these conditions normally reflect the state of the economy, its structure, mechanism, development level and income distribution as well as the sociological-cultural relations and government policies.

Consequently, when assessing the present quality of the labour force it is first a historical question which has to be answered: How has the physical and intellectual quality of labour has (hardly) developed in the course of economic (under)development shaped by external forces or influences, i.e. in the context of the type of economy and the related sociological pattern of behaviour which have evolved, and also under the impact of government policies in the past? Only after having revealed the historical roots of the problem can we properly analyse the present situation, the major obstacles, within the societies concerned, to the improvement of the quality and performance of labour, can point to some traditionally unfavourable social conditions or even may blame the inappropriate government policies in several cases.

We cannot simply refer (like Viner) to the historical factor in general, or the leadership qualities of governments and the social elite, particularly with regard to the past centuries. We must also ask: what concrete historical factors did prevent the physical[289] and intellectual quality of the working population from improving? And what governments are to be blamed?

Thus the poor quality of the working population cannot stand on its own as the explanation of underdevelopment. It requires concrete investigation, partly as to its own history, partly as to the causal relationships of which it is itself a part and, consequently, as to its sociological implications. (We shall come across this factor again in the chain of interdependent limiting factors as the element of a particular concept (e.g. the vicious circle theory), and again in the theory of a "stagnant, traditional society".[290])

[289] Numerous references and ample evidence can be found in several historical or empirical studies and official reports about the fact that the physical capacity of the African labor force has been determined by the poor nutrition conditions which had definitely deteriorated with the rise and development of the "colonial economy". See e.g. *J. de Castro* (1952), pp. 179–180, 191; *Doney, A. and Feldheim, P.* (1956), pp. 680–681; and the "Sierra Leone Review of Present Knowledge of Human Nutrition" (Freetown, 1938.) or the "Summary of Information Regarding Nutrition in the Colonial Empire" (Cmd. 6051, London, 1939), or the WHO report (by J. A. Munoz), all quoted *by J. Woddis* (1961), pp. 165–167.

[290] See it later!

The popularity, nevertheless, of this concept about the poor quality of labour was due to the support it gave, by overemphasizing the shortage of educated personnel, managerial elite and technicians, to the policy of a lasting reliance on the increasingly great number of Western experts and of long-run dependences on "technical assistance". This concept, together with that of "capital shortage", seems also to be in perfect compliance with the "subtraction approach", since accordingly the course of development of the developing countries is visualized in such a way that "the West diffuses knowledge skills, organization, values, technology and capital to a poor nation, until over time, its society, culture and personnel become variants of that which made the Atlantic community economically successful"[291].

## 2.1.4. Capital shortage, insufficient savings and capital formation

Capital shortage is usually considered to be one of the most characteristic features of underdevelopment, the more so as it also apparently provides a suitable explanation for the low level of productivity, the acute problem of unemployment, and, in general, underemployment, as well as for the underutilization of the natural-resource potential. In addition, the general demand of the developing countries for increased international financial assistance, their growing budget and balance-of-payments deficits, as well as the rather frequent phenomenon of usurious local credit rates, still further corroborate the assumption that the basic cause – and also the remedy[292] – of underdevelopment must be sought along this line. Therefore, of all limiting factors of development, capital shortage has been rated of especial importance by most authors. Some of them, however, have emphasized the relativeness of capital shortage, in view of the limited opportunities for profitable investments in the underdeveloped economies.

It has already been mentioned that *Sauvy*, too, referred to the insufficiency of capital stock, in connection with unemployment. *Gannage* pointed out the low volume of per capita capital *in production*. In *Viner's* view (1958), capital shortage belongs to the second category of obstacles to development (it comes after the quality of natural resources and working population), and he added that capital shortage should not be measured by the rate of interest. A high rate of interest may be due to economically different causes: high investment risks, high marginal productivity of capital, etc. The measure of capital supply should be related to the available *opportunities for profitable investments*, and it is more appropriate to apply as an index number the amount of capital per capita *in use* within the country than the amount of capital per head *owned* within the country. (pp. 17–18)

---

[291] *Nash, M.* (1963), p. 5. Quoted by *Frank, A.G.* (1967).

[292] *M. Todaro* noted (1997) that in accordance with the traditional neo-classical (and new growth) theory analysis, "foreign private investment (as well as foreign aid) is typically seen as a way of filling in gaps between the domestically available supplies of savings, foreign exchange, government revenue, annd human capital skills and the desired level of these resources necessary to achiece growth and development targets." (p. 538)

This remark of Viner's, touching upon a highly essential problem, needs to be commented upon. It might be really justified to measure the degree of capital supply of a given fiscal year or of a development program extending over several years by the amount of capital actually used or available. But from the point of view of the present and future position of the country in question, it is far from being immaterial to what extent it can rely on its own resources, too, and to what extent the relative stock of foreign capital assets, compared to that of the national ones and/or that of the country's assets abroad, increases within the country, i.e. to what extent the latter becomes, and remains for long, unilaterally dependent on foreign financial powers. Nor is it justifiable in the search for a correct and historical explanation of underdevelopment, to overlook differences in the origin of the capital in use, the differences between foreign and national capital, since it is precisely the activity and predominance of foreign capital that in most cases have shaped the structure of the economy and its external relations, the position of the country concerned in the worldwide division of labour, and thereby brought about – deliberately or spontaneously – such conditions or induced such socio-economic processes in the past as those determining, producing or reproducing the state of "underdevelopment".

As regards the relative interpretation of insufficient capital supply – i.e. capital shortage related to profitable investment opportunities – the question arises first of all whether "profitability" is measured on a micro-economic level, from the entrepreneur's point of view, or on a macro-economic level, from the long-term aspect of the national economy. Secondly, however correct such a relative interpretation of capital shortage may be, it hardly offers a general characteristic (even less general than population pressure) of underdevelopment.

True, in a number of developing countries (mainly in Tropical Africa) the increase in capital inflow has really been restricted by a limited absorbing capacity. Consequently, in some countries capital abundance rather than capital shortage can be observed in terms of concrete opportunities for profitable investments (of course in an even more relative sense!).

For example, *I. M. D. Little* (1964) firmly pointed out that in Tropical Africa it is not capital shortage in general, but rather the lack of skilled labour, the economic fragmentation of the continent and the lack of information on opportunities for profitable capital investment that are the main obstacles to development. Accordingly, man and not money is the limiting factor. *Arthur Lewis* (1958) did not share this view, as considering the shortage of skilled labour as a "very temporary bottleneck" only. He noted, "If the capital is available for development, the capitalists or their government will soon provide the facilities for training more skilled people". Thus according to him: "The real bottlenecks to expansion are, therefore, capital and natural resources." (p. 406)

*S. P. Schatz* (1967), on the basis of the results of surveys and his research carried out in Nigeria, called attention to the false appearance of capital shortage: "Frequently the belief that a capital shortage is the effective or operating impediment to indigenous private investment is mistaken,...it is an illusion created by a large false demand for capital, ...what really exists is not an immediate shortage of capital at all, but a shortage of viable projects." (p. 93)

Thus it seems justified to say that not only the emergence and chronic character of capital shortage need explanation, but the limitations of investment possibilities, too.

*Paul Baran* (1958) has actually considered capital insufficiency and the deficiency of investment opportunities as two aspects of one and the same problem.

(pp. 75–92) According to *Ragnar Nurkse* the lack of investment incentives rather than the insufficiency of savings constitutes the basic problem. The inducement to invest, however, is limited by the size of the market. Nurkse made this relationship a circular[293] and thereby an undetermined one, when defining the expansion of the market as a function of the "reductions in any cost of production", i.e. of the rise of the "level of productivity," which, in turn, depends on the use of capital in production. Insofar as capital shortage is considered as (not only a cause but also) a consequence of the narrow market, the explanation of underdevelopment actually shifts to another development-hindering factor, namely the *limitedness of the domestic market* (or, market imperfections in general). Though Nurkse put the latter and capital shortage into an interdependent relationship, *Celso Furtado* (1958) criticised him for exaggerating the importance of the size of the market. Furtado emphasized that the investment incentive may also come from the direction of the external market. By this, however, he only widened the question.

Insofar as the limitedness of profitable investment opportunities is explained by the *narrowness of the domestic market*, the logic of the explanation of underdevelopment by various internal conditions goes only further, to another development-limiting factor. However, the basic problem behind the limitedness of the market – whether domestic or foreign – is the very problem of the pattern of *division of labour.*

The size of the domestic market depends not only on the level of national income, and it is not even the rise in productivity simply and thereby the reduction of production costs which determine the expansion of the market. The latter provides only the possibility for an expansion, namely by means of increasing the marketable surplus. But marketable surpluses build up in vain if there is no adequate organic (input–output) connection among the individual productive sectors, if the system of complementary sectors producing for each other has hardly developed. (In addition, the development of the division of labour is the main motive force of the rise in productivity itself!) Thus the question of the *economic structure* will inevitably arise, the question about input–output linkages within the entire economy of the countries concerned, more concretely: the question about how and why those "enclave sectors" isolated from and inhibiting the internal division of labour have come into being which still characterize most of the developing countries, and why these *export-oriented enclaves* have proved to be increasingly unable to find a proportionally expanding external market either. The last part of the question refers to the pattern of international division of labour and the changes in it, i.e. an obviously external condition.

Thus the problem of capital shortage (and, for that matter, the market problem, too) needs explanation, rather than being an explanation itself. And as it is a complex problem it can be explained only in its complexity.

[293] See it later!

The actual capital supply is, of course, the sum of available foreign and national capital. As regards the former, the question of how much foreign capital comes from outside or is reinvested in the country concerned, goes far beyond the (already discussed) problem of profitable investment opportunities and also the question of the government policy concerning foreign capital investments[294]. It merges into the problems of the pattern of international capital flows and the changes in it. That is to say it becomes part of a problem the understanding of which requires the analysis of processes taking place also in the advanced countries and the world economy as a whole. It raises, in addition, the question of direct and indirect effects of foreign capital on the formation of incomes, the direction and nature of investments, the level and pattern of employment, the structure of economy, the structure of foreign trade, the balance of payments and, in general, foreign economic relations, etc.

As regards the formation and supply of "national" capital, it raises the questions about the *surplus producing capacity*[295] of the various sectors of the economy, the pattern of *income distribution and use of incomes*, aggregate savings and the potential sources of accumulation, the pattern of consumption, the conditions of entry and competition in the market, i.e. market imperfections, the actual government policies ("government imperfections") and the pattern of incentives, etc.

Thus, investigations must be made as to how and to what extent surplus is produced (what the productivity of social labour is, and how the national labour force is used and allocated among the various economic sectors and activities, i.e. what the structure of the national economy is like), who appropriate the surplus (what "class structure" of society has developed), and what conditions impede the conversion of the surplus into productive investments, or its investment within the country (repatriation and remittance of profits). And, in case the value produced is realized outside the country, on the world market, it is also to be investigated how this affects (just as the purchases made in the world market) the real value of economic surplus. Consequently, the criteria of underdevelopment must also be sought in this direction of analysis.

As to the proportions and *pattern of consumption*, it would hardly suffice to refer to the high marginal propensity to consume in the developing countries and to the elasticity of demand for basic consumer goods, in general. No doubt, a quantitative comparison between the advanced and the developing countries on this basis would perfectly correspond to the "subtraction approach" and it would even simplify the problem of development along the line of a sort of "orthodox

[294] This has considerably varied, by the way, from country to country, and also from time to time.

[295] To quote *Celso Furtado* (1958): "Capital, as is well known, is nothing else but work carried out in the past, the product of which was not consumed." In other words, we are faced, first of all, with the problem of *surplus*. (p. 317) The issue of "surplus" (namely "surplus product" or "surplus value") has traditionally been in the focus also of the Marxist literature, and has been thoroughly investigated in respect of the underdeveloped economies by *Paul Baran* (1960).

Keynesianism". But certain qualitative features pointing to deeper relationships are evident enough to rid this sort of orthodoxy[296] of its credit. More and more scholars have been pointing to the fact that the proportions and pattern of consumption are partly determined by the economic and social structure of the countries concerned and partly, moreover increasingly by external conditions and influences, particularly be the "demonstration effects".

Hence, capital shortage as a characteristic assumed to be general and as an explanation for underdevelopment has turned out to be very superficial and deficient. Its validity is not only impaired by the wide differences among the individual countries and is rendered unreliable by the problems of profitable investment opportunities and capital-absorptive capacity, but it also raises such further problems as the pattern of international capital flows, the trends in the world market, structural problems connected with the productivity of social labour and the pattern of consumption, the relations of income distribution and surplus "appropriation", etc. – all problems that must be considered far more fundamental and determining.

Despite all these, a particular importance and priority are attributed to capital shortage by two types of views. The one has emphasized its significance in order to fight for the free inflow of private investment capital from the advanced countries. The other is intended to support the "comfort policy" of relying exclusively on foreign aid, a policy which has become official particularly in those developing countries where the political elite wish to divert attention from the necessity of internal social transformation and radical economic reforms.

The above criticism of the explanation of underdevelopment by capital is, of course, not aimed at underestimating the seriousness of *financial bottlenecks* (both the "savings-gap" and the "foreign-exchange-gap") of the developing countries, their acute balance-of-payments problems and need for international aid.

### 2.1.5. Narrow domestic market and market imperfections

As we have seen, the market problem, namely the small size and imperfections of the domestic market, is often mentioned in relation to the shortage of capital or the limited opportunities for profitable investments in an underdeveloped economy. In addition, the narrowness of the domestic market, i.e. the insufficiency of effective demand inside the domestic economy can also be presented as a cause of the disproportionate export-orientation of commodity production, while the various market imperfections (including perhaps the more or less monopolistic position of foreign capital, the operation of state trading organizations, marketing

[296] For a criticism of the application of Keynesianism to underdeveloped economies see e.g. *Rao, V. K. R. V.* (1964), Ch. 2.

boards, the use of administered or transfer prices, the fragmentation of market, etc.) may explain the lack of appropriate competition, thereby also the weakness of incentives for technical progress, innovation and skill-orientation. Insofar as the effective demand within the domestic market depends, of course, on the level of incomes, it may also reinforce the quantitative approach to the classification of countries, namely the use of per capita GNP to measure the level of economic development.

In view of the above, the narrowness and imperfections of the market in the developing countries, as opposed to the assumed large and more or less perfect market of the advanced countries appears as another development-limiting factor, another unfavourable internal condition hindering economic development. However, despite all the obvious deficiencies of the market within the developing countries, and also the undeniable consequences of the latter, they can hardly explain underdevelopment, nor the advanced state of development can simply be associated with large and perfect markets. The expansion of the domestic market (as already noted) depends not only on the income level but also and primarily on the *input–output linkages* between the various sectors (producing and servicing units) of the economy, i.e. on the very structure of the latter. As regards market imperfections, they do not simply reflect the poor conditions of communication and information, the backward legal system and institutions, etc., but also and again the structure of the economy and its biased integration in the world economy, as well as the tendency of concentration of economic power in fewer hands in the latter, i.e. not only in the developing countries but also in the advanced ones.

Consequently, the market problem does also need a historical explanation and both a politeconomical and a structural analysis.

### 2.1.6. State imperfections, irresponsible governments, "soft states"

In the early stage of the development of "development economics" the conventional theories explaining underdevelopment by exclusively or primarily internal conditions have rarely referred to the government policies or the weakness of the state as another development-hindering factor – perhaps because in the case of the former colonies it could have been a blame on the metropolitan states, the colonial administration of the developed countries, i.e. a clear reference to an external factor. (Exceptions were mainly made in relation to the Latin American countries, the failure of which in industrial modernization was often attributed primarily to the mistaken government policies.)

Later on, however, in the light of unsuccessful "development decades", of the abortive attempts to catch up with the more advanced countries and the failure also of the development assistance programs of international organizations causing "aid fatigue" in the advanced countries, *either* the weakness of the state power, the inability of "soft states" to carry out the necessary process of modernization, to plan and implement rational development programs, and ensure a greater equity and also equilibrium in the economy has been put to the fore in explaining (if not the origin, then the perpetuance of) underdevelopment[297], *or* (particularly since the late 1970s, and under the impact of the "counterrevolution" in development economics) the accusation of the government policies of the developing countries, the blaming them for irresponsible measures, adverse interventions in the economy, and the resulting spread of corruption, rent-seeking activities, squandering, etc. have been presented as a major development-hindering (or -distorting) factor.

No doubt can be raised about the importance of the role of the state in the development process, whether it is positive or negative. "Soft states" can hardly act as efficient agents of development, while the dictatorial regimes (such as those many juntas in the "South" or as the former Soviet-type regimes) inevitably distort and bring to a blind alley the development of the economy (not to mention the related socio-political consequences). "State imperfections" and government failures are not less serious hindrances, indeed, as "market imperfections"[298]. Corrupt governments with their clientele and client–patronage–system may cause enormous losses and wastages for the economy and society.

However, like in the case of market imperfections, here again questions arise: How such regimes have developed? Why "soft" and/or corrupt regimes and dictatorships have emerged and survived? What actually explains these undoubtedly important phenomena? Such questions as requiring a historical answer and a complex structural analysis bring us again to the historical course and to the investigation of the world system as a whole.

## 2.2. Underdevelopment as a specific form of motion: a "vicious circle" or a "quasi-stable equilibrium"

Since (as we have seen) the various internal development-inhibiting or -limiting factors which are also linked with each other, cannot offer, either separately or in their simple aggregate, a satisfactory explanation of underdevelopment, some of the scholars have presented a specific model representing the system of underdevelopment in which the mutual cause–effect relationship of the development-inhibiting or -limiting factors involves such a circular motion as regularly returning to its starting point, thereby making any actual progress impossible. Two variants of this model can be distinguished: (a) the "vicious circle of poverty or underdevelopment", and (b) the "quasi-stable equilibrium system".

[297] See e.g. *Myrdal, G.* (1968).

[298] See a list of the problems of government interventions in *Todaro, M.* (1997), p. 593.

## 2.2.1. The "vicious circle of underdevelopment"

The substitution of interdependencies for causal relationships has never found such an independent theoretical manifestation, and pure tautology has never reached such a high pedestal as in the vicious circle theorem. The explanation of underdevelopment by itself means, of course, – at least seemingly – an escape from the necessity of historical analysis. If, by inserting a few interdependent factors, the direct relationship of underdevelopment to itself can be made indirect, even the appearance of an obvious tautology can be avoided. And the question of the causes of the individual inhibiting and limiting factors can be evaded by reference to another factor, and so on, until we come back to where we started from.

Though it would be possible to set up a number of circular relationships and interdependencies of any advanced country and any historical period, they have become popular and widespread particularly in the various development theories so that underdevelopment seems to be, at least in economic literature, the separate world – an independent system of the various vicious circles.

Underdevelopment in these theories is no longer the simple aggregate of individual deficiencies or obstacles, but an interdependent system of their relationships. The explanation of a characteristic deficiency or obstacle is provided by another, and that, in turn, is explained by a third and so on, or vice versa.

By way of example, let us pose the question: what is the cause of capital shortage as one of the obstacles to development?

It is the insufficiency of domestic capital accumulation, which, in turn, results from the low rate of savings. And the latter is low because per capita national income is low, which again cannot grow quickly because of capital shortage.

In poor countries – as was stated e.g. by *J. Viner* (1953) – the inner accumulation of capital is low. The source of saving is income, and if income per capita is low, the annual rate of saving per capita is low, too. (p. 105)

*Gerald Meier* and *Robert E. Baldwin* have also stressed that economic backwardness is due to the fact that "...total output is low and after consumption needs are fulfilled, little remains as a surplus for capital accumulation. Because of the low level of real income...the flow of saving is small. The low level of real income is, in turn, primarily due to the lack of an adequate capital stock and secondarily to market imperfections. And the low level of capital stock is, in turn, a result of the low level of real income". (p. 319)

What is the cause of poverty of the underdeveloped countries? "A country is poor because it is poor", noted *Ragnar Nurkse* (1958), but added: "This seems a trite proposition, but it does express the circular relationships that afflict both the demand and the supply side of the problem of capital formation in economically backward areas... The inducement to invest is limited by the size of the market... The general level of productivity determines the size of the market. Capacity to buy means capacity to produce. In its turn, the level of productivity depends – not entirely by any means, but largely – on the use of capital in production. But the use of capital is inhibited, to start with, by the small size of the market." (p. 256)

*E. Gannagé* (1962), also outlined some vicious circles, which, however, did not prevent him from referring to factors that go beyond those "magic" circles. He proposed as a vicious circle the relationship between economic development and the rate of population growth and pointed out the circular connection of the following factors: low standard of living – surplus-absorbing consumption – insufficient capital formation – low standard of living.

In his textbook for universities *Richard T. Gill* (1963) described the vicious circle theory as one of the general theories of modern economics. He contrasted the vicious circle of poverty with self-sustained growth and attributed the gap between the advanced and the underdeveloped countries to these two motions of different character and deviating from each other. "Because it is poor, the country does not develop; because it does not develop, it remains poor." (pp. 28–30) But besides this general statement he also illustrated various concrete and more detailed vicious circles. For example the following is the one concerning capital accumulation:

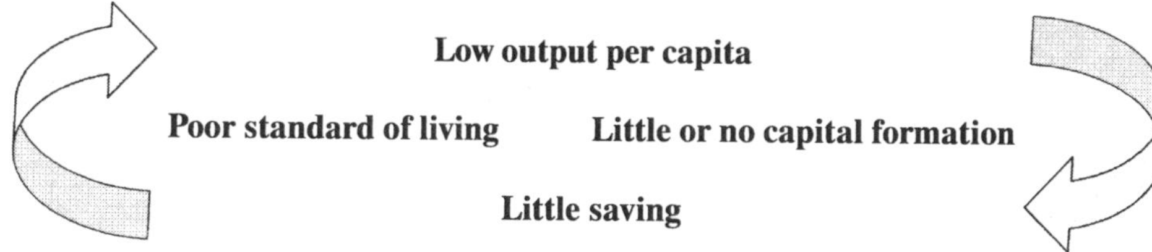


Gills has noted that this example is, of course, hypothetical and rather oversimplified, and that, in reality, even in quite poor countries, there are typically some important potential sources of saving and investment. Even in the poorest countries it would be possible to make savings and productive investments from the money spent on ceremonies, celebrations and luxuries. But savings for such purposes are not made not only because of the hindering effect of social attitudes and institutions, but mainly because the market is restricted, because of the vicious circle of a limited market. "Large-scale industry requires a big market. But in a poor country the extent of the market is bound to be small. It will remain small, moreover, until large-scale industry is somehow established."

These and similar circular relationships and "magic" circles could be drawn up in any number, and they really crop up with the followers of the most different schools[299]. As simplified schemes of the results of some partial analyses these vicious circles undoubtedly reflect actually existing mutual relationships and dialectic contradictions. It is beyond doubt, e.g. that a low national income also limits the volume of accumulation, which, in turn, restricts the growth of national income by means of productive investments. Similarly, a chain of interrelations does indeed exist in many other cases, too. But these chains are never complete. Very often important factors are disregarded and the missing links make the continuity of the chain very doubtful.

[299] See e.g. *Buchanan, N. S.* (1946), *Singer, H. W.* (1949), *Enke, S.–Salera, V.* (1951), *Hirschman, A. G.* (1958), etc.

As regards e.g. the relationship between savings and national income, *Arthur Lewis* (1958) correctly noted "there is no clear evidence that the proportion of the national income saved increases with national income per head". (p. 417) Arguing with Nurkse, he pointed to that savings are small not because the people are poor but because the capitalist (or state-capitalist) sector is so small, because the share of capitalist profits in the national income is low. Thus he emphasized the importance of the distribution of national income. Of course, from the increase in the share of capitalist profits, it does not follow automatically that savings will grow and even less that there will be an increase in those productive investments which are of particular importance for the whole national economy. All this points to the role played by the *distribution and utilization of national income*, i.e. factors, which are not involved in the vicious circles outlined above.

*Richard Gill* (1963) pointed to the manner of spending incomes and, in this context, to certain negative features of society (that have already been mentioned earlier). If this only means that another hindering factor has to be included in the vicious circle, which is not only the cause but also the consequence of one of the links, then this interrelation has also to be demonstrated in the figure, which most probably will disclose newer gaps and contradictions in it. If, however, the cause of this hindering factor is outside the circle, then just this very fundamental cause must be sought for because, maybe, it determines the whole circular motion.

However, not only can the inaccuracy and deficiency of the chain of relationships be demonstrated – in the case of all vicious circles as well as in the case just discussed – but what is more important is that any factor of the vicious circle can change without the preceding factor being changed, or it can remain unchanged even after the preceding one has changed. Thus the vicious circle, despite the seemingly dialectical character of mutual relationships, is in fact metaphysical and mechanical. *No process* in reality, apart from processes under artificial labouratory conditions, can be repeated or repeats itself unchanged in time, especially not the processes of social motion. If there is any circular cause–effect relationship – and such certainly exists – it can only move spirally upwards or downwards, and, therefore, has a starting point, too (just like a spiral spring but unlike a ring)[300].

[300] *Gunnar Myrdal* (1957) – to whose views we shall return later – transcended the static concept of the vicious circle and investigated the interrelation between the factors that promote and those which hinder development in a dialectic way, and described a cumulative, ascending or descending *spiral* motion: "If either of the two factors should change, this is bound to bring a change in the other factor, too, and start a cumulative process of mutual interaction in which the change in one factor would continuously be supported by the reaction of the other factor and so on in a circular way..." (pp. 16–19) The great progress Myrdal made seems to be vitiated by his statement – which, by the way, reveals the influence of the vicious circle idea – that it is absolutely useless to look for any basic, primary cause, "as everything is cause to everything else in an interlocking circular manner". To illustrate the ascending spiral motion, Myrdal gave the following example: "Quite obviously a circular relationship between less proverty, more food, improved health and higher working capacity would sustain a cumulative process upwards." (p. 12)

If it has a starting point, then it is this starting point, i.e. the fundamental cause of the circular relationship: the *historical* root of underdevelopment, which must be explored.

Despite their realistic appearance, the main weakness of the vicious circle theories is that they reveal neither the historical circumstances out of which the assumed "magic" circle originated, nor the underlying socio-economic relations and the fundamental, determinant causes.

In trying to explain the vicious circle by itself, the authors of this idea see it as a natural, given phenomenon. But, if that is the case, the question is to be answered: How have the already developed countries succeed in getting over this "natural" phenomenon, how have they managed to break out of the vicious circle of poverty? Thus, even if the historical question of how the vicious circle came into operation is missed, the other, nonetheless historical question of how it was broken must be answered, any way. The question about the possible breaking out of the vicious circle has usually been answered in two alternative ways:

The *first* answer, which is more consistent with the logic of the concept of vicious circle, presupposes the help of an external, exogenous factor, and some sort of a *Deus ex machina.* Such can be the inflow of foreign capital, or technical assistance, the import of skills, knowledge and innovations, and, in general, the full opening up of the economy towards the outside world.

The assumption of the unambiguously positive, favourable effects of foreign capital inflow, of technology transfer and of free international trade is in full consonance with the *conventional theory of international economics.* This theory includes, as we have seen, (a) the Classical concept of free flows between autonomous national economies, of commodities and money establishing or re-establishing equilibrium in the partners' trade, and the theorem of comparative advantages guiding the specialization of partners and equally shared by them; and, besides the revised, Neo-Classical theses of international equilibrium mechanism and of comparative advantages, also (b) the Neo-Classical theorem of international factor mobility, which suggests a natural tendency of international capital flow towards the less developed countries with capital shortage, equalizing thereby the factor endowments, factor costs, and incomes, thereby also the very level of development among nations.

Though in full harmony with the "diffusionist approach" mentioned earlier, this assumption may be invalidated or even contradicted, *first* of all, by some of the adverse consequences of the "diffusion" of capital, technology, consumption habits, experts, etc. of the developed countries and/or by the unfavourable effects of the world market[301]. *Secondly,* it raises the question of why this diffusion and outward orientation have not resulted so far in breaking the vicious circle of underde-

[301] Even the authors adopting the vicious circle idea have often admitted these adverse effects and consequences.

velopment by many of the developing countries[302]. *Thirdly,* to regard the diffusion of the superior values and assets of the already advanced countries as the prerequisite for breaking the "natural" vicious circle leads to such a historical and logical absurdity which *ad infinitum* presupposes the existence of a more developed environment, or does not offer any explanation for those very countries which first broke the vicious circle[303].

According to the *other* answer the breaking of the vicious circle could and can occur by means of a cumulative growth[304] of certain internal factors, or the change of social propensities, independent of the economy, *via* the emergence of the entrepreneurial class. This answer, however, makes it clear that the vicious circle is *de facto* not vicious but cumulative, and does not determine underdevelopment, does not involve a blockade of development.

### 2.2.2. The "quasi-stable equilibrium system"

"If the circle is truly vicious, there would appear to be no way out... But this, of course, does not explain how countries that were once poor are no longer poor, or are not as poor as they were," – noted (1957) *H. Leibenstein* (pp. 95–96) In his view the vicious circle idea has been worked out somewhat carelessly "in technical economic terms". Though he derived his theory from the vicious circle idea, and acknowledged as his own only its more exact elabouration and the explanation of how the vicious circle can be broken, he actually substituted a dynamic approach for a static and mechanical one.

Backwardness, in his view, is a self-reproducing state, equilibrium without development, which is re-established through and by permanent changes: through the play of promoting and counteracting forces. "The state of backwardness, as viewed from a day-to-day basis, represents fluctuations of the variables around a low income per capita equilibrium... Periodic stimulants and shocks result in a dance of the values of the actual variables around the equilibrium state. In this way the persistence of general economic backwardness is explained, although the explanation allows for small variations from time to time." (Ibidem.)

While the advanced countries are characterized by the disequilibria system (in which there is a continuous secular growth), the underdeveloped countries are distinguished by the characteristics of a "quasi-stable subsistence equilibrium system,

[302] The most frequent answer to this question has referred to the "*resistance* to this diffusion" resulting from the traditional behaviour of the actors in the countries concerned, from the primitive conditions, backward social attitudes and unfavorable propensities of the people there. *Myrdal* (1968) also referred to thc resistance: "Certainly the main resistance to change in the social system stems from attitudes and institutions." (pp. 1873)

[303] A similar contradiction can be found with *Rostow* (as we shall see it in his theory later).

[304] See e.g. *Leibenstein's* concept about a "critical minimum effort".

in which the absolute magnitudes of some of the variables, such as capital and labour force, expand constantly, whereas the relation between the expanding variables is such that their interaction with the other variables in the system manifests itself in a tendency of the resulting per capita income to approach or fluctuate near and about a subsistence level". (p. 186) The complete stationary state (in which "there is no expansion") is merely a less likely extreme case of this system.

Thus the system is in constant movement; it is dynamic. Unlike the idea of vicious circles, here the quantitative change in the value of the individual variables, or even its constant growth does not contradict the fact that the system returns to its original state, and – or more exactly because – among these factors, there are dialectic contradictions instead of harmonious interdependencies.

The system works, in brief, in the following way: The equilibrium proper is around the subsistence-level value of per capita national income. If this equilibrium is disturbed "the forces or influences that tend to raise per capita income set in motion, directly or indirectly, forces that have the effect of depressing per capita income" (p. 16). Thus, as a result of the direct or indirect effect of an increase in national income (higher living standard, better nutrition, and improved public health, respectively), the mortality rate drops (with the birth rate rising or remaining unchanged), and thus the increased population growth reduces per capita national income. Or likewise, higher agricultural yields improve nutrition, decreasing periodical starvation and, consequently, mortality rates, too, but the increased population growth resulting from it leads in turn to a further subdivision of holdings, which restricts quality-maintenance measures and results in lower yields. Or, the improvement of the quality of soil leads to its more intensive exploitation and eventually to the deterioration of soil fertility. Another example: investments outside agriculture create additional employment opportunities, which, in turn, induce a more rapid growth of population and labour force.

Since in the state of disturbed equilibrium "the effects of the income-depressing forces are greater than the effects of the income-raising forces", the system returns to the low, underdeveloped equilibrium income.

As we see, it is the national income per capita which is put in the centre of Leibenstein's theory, as well as the equilibrium outlined by him. In this respect his theory is in full harmony with the theories that link up underdevelopment with a certain level of per capita national income. It is also in compliance with the vicious circle idea, in that this level, and with it the whole system, remains unchanged. But this stability reproduces itself through permanent changes, and this is where the new feature in Leibenstein's theory comes in. And the variable, which restores this stability, the quasi-equilibrium, is connected, in one way or another, with population growth. This is the reason why Leibenstein paid special attention to demographic problems.

The linking up of the problems and laws of economic development with population growth is as old as economics itself. This close symbiosis had its heyday, as is well known, at the time of classical economics. Though working on a different basis and arriving at different conclusions, *Malthus* made the idea the central concept of his theory, a theory concerning the advanced countries of his time. *Smith* and *Ricardo* regarded natural population growth as a factor determining the return of wages to the "natural price of labour", a factor, which immediately reacts to the rise in real wages when the expansion of production, through the increase in the demand for labour, sends up the market price of labour[305]. But while *Malthus* assumed a population growth greater (moving at the rate of geometrical progression) than economic growth (moving in food production at the rate of arithmetical progression), and conceived of it as a quasi-natural fatality (that are mostly "relieved" by epidemics, wars, natural catastrophes, or can be avoided only by increased self-restraint, higher educational level and living standard of the workers), and while Smith and Ricardo believed in the self-regulating, more or less harmonious and progressive movement of economic development and population growth,[306] Leibenstein, by connecting the economic factors (incomes, yields) and the demographic ones (population growth) demonstrated an equilibrium without development. Though he did not regard population growth as an exclusive[307] and such a direct consequence of the improvement in the economic factor, as Smith[308] and Ricardo did, yet the crucial point on which his hypothesis was built is the same and is similarly false.

The time dimension of the economic and demographic factors – as follows from their very nature – is necessarily different, and their coincidence is a mere chance. As it was a naive assumption of Ricardo and Smith to consider the expansion of production, i.e. economic development as dependent directly on the absolute increase in population (to interpret it as a dependent variable)[309], nonetheless it is naive and unscientific to assume as a natural matter of course that the interrelated

---

[305] "The liberal reward of labor, as it is the effect of increasing wealth, so it is the cause of increasing population," wrote *Adam Smith* (repr. 1776). See: Smith, A. (1961), p. 90.

[306] Apart from the fall in profit rate, which *Ricardo* attributed not to the absolute natural limits of food production but to the rise in ground rent. And though, in his view, this rise in ground rent results from the growing food demand of the increased population, with the consequence that society is obliged to cultivate lands of increasingly inferior quality so that the law of diminishing returns comes more and more into force, in the last analysis, it is the existence of the parasitical landowner class — i.e. a social factor – which he defined as the final cause of the fall in profit rate, since this class benefits, on the one hand, from this process accompanied by a steady rise in differential rent, and, on the other, it prevents through legislation (in the England of Ricardo's time) a liberal foreign trade policy, i.e. the import of cheap food.

[307] In addition to the inducing factors, Leibenstein distinguished in his population theory, as we have seen, autonomous, exogenous factors, too.

[308] "...The demand for men, like that for any other commodity, necessarily regulates the production of men..." – wrote *Adam Smith*. See: *Smith, A.* (repr. 1961), p. 89.

[309] It is worthwhile quoting here a critical remark of *Marx* (repr. 1964) concerning the "dogma of the economists": "... that would indeed be a beautiful law, which pretends to make the action of capital dependent on the absolute variation of the population, instead of regulating the demand and supply of labor by the alternate expansion and contraction of capital. (p. 637)

movements of the economic and demographic factors in the whole "South", i.e. in all the developing countries, exactly coincide in time and quantity, that is, correspond to each other's size and time-dimension, and so by counteracting each other they determine economic stagnation.

What sort of method is it to suppose, on the one hand, that the rise in agricultural yields induces more rapid population growth and leads inevitably, through more intensive exploitation of land and further subdivision of holdings, to a drop in yields, and to disregard, on the other hand, those new opportunities for a further rise in agricultural yields which arise from creating or increasing surplus, particularly when the former is a long-run process while the latter can materialize in the short run?! Would it not be far more reasonable to examine what happens "in the meantime" to the surplus, who gets hold of it, what it is used for, in other words, to analyse the actual social relations of production, and from a historical viewpoint?!

And what sort of explanation is it for the persistent phenomenon of unemployment to say that the expansion of employment opportunities induces a further population increment, which, in turn, will offset the former?! How long would it take the labour supply to become overabundant in this way? Is it not more realistic to examine[310] how the army of unemployed is filled up from those latent sources which already exist and to analyse the causes of the outflow of labour from one sector to another and the incapability of the latter to keep pace in absorbing more and more?! That is to say, to analyse the character, the growth problems and the relation to each other of the individual sectors of economy!

Is it acceptable at all, to take a per capita index (national income per head) as the determinant of a system, of a recurring equilibrium, as the key factor that *via* its self-reproduction reproduces the whole system as well? Where is that absolutely homogeneous society, without classes and stratification, in which the proportions of the distribution and utilization of incomes are determined solely by the ratios of production and population growth?! Is it permissible to simply average out the figures of income and population growth for such heterogeneous and different societies?!

Finally, the same question has to be answered as in the case of the vicious circle: How is it possible to break out of this circular movement which, although not static, but dynamic, is nonetheless recurring? While the necessity of an external force would follow – in a logical and consistent way – from the vicious circle idea, Leibenstein postulates the necessity of a certain *critical minimum of internal efforts*: "There is some crucial level of per capita income, and a related level of per capita income growth, above which the economy ceases to be of the equilibrium type and changes into the non-equilibrium type...a certain minimum per capita income level has to be achieved in order for the economy to generate sustained growth from within."(p. 187)

[310] As *Arthur Lewis* did.

This thesis is based partly on a tautological hypothesis, and partly on a simple statistical observation (or a logical inference). The former states that while "at low per capita income levels the income-depressing forces are more significant than the income-raising ones...", "at high per capita income levels the reverse may be true". (Ibidem.) The latter asserts that there is, or at least must be, an absolute limit, a maximum to the rate of population growth[311].

The changes, within certain magnitudes, in the two factors of the per capita income index neutralize each other. If, however, one of the two factors has an absolute limit, a maximum value, while the other has none, then in case the latter grows in whatever way beyond the limit of the former, the value of the index changes. And, subsequently, will there be a sustained growth in the value of the index? Most probably – according to Leibenstein. The advanced countries are in a state of sustained growth, in the system of progressing disequilibria, and the magnitude of their per capita national income is much greater than that of the underdeveloped countries.

Thus, if the state of development of the advanced countries is characterized by sustained growth and the per capita income of these countries is much higher, then – according to Leibenstein – the underdeveloped countries, in order to attain sustained growth, must achieve a per capita income above a certain level.

The question is, *first of all,* how they can achieve this, if, by the time an underdeveloped economy attains this income level, the self-compensating factors are in operation resulting in equilibrium at a lower level. Leibenstein answered this question by stating that though "an increase in stocks that implies increased income per head" generally results "in roughly compensating increases in other stocks which, in turn, imply decreasing incomes per head", however, "*certain* stocks and forces appear to be *cumulative* in nature" (p. 36 – my italics: T. Sz.), that is, the former mechanism does not always come into operation. (That is why the equilibrium is only a "quasi"-equilibrium!) It would be justified to ask: what, then, was the whole idea good for? In other words, the investigation of the roots of underdevelopment should be continued (or even started) outside the equilibrium system, concentrating on the problem why "certain stocks and forces" could not grow sufficiently to ensure an escape from a low level equilibrium!

*Secondly,* the question must be raised: What is the magnitude of the "critical minimum effort" that makes sustained growth possible? Is it sufficient to achieve an income growth exceeding the maximum rate of population growth of about 3 per cent? Leibenstein did not dare go so far as to state this, because it is quite easy to find refuting examples. He only noted: "*Whatever* we may mean by it, it is clear that the critical minimum effort is *something* that either directly or indirectly has a magnitude of *some sort*, part of which can *usually* be stated in terms of money value." (p. 105 – my italics: T. Sz.) Moreover, he added: "It is probably impossible

[311] According to Leibenstein, it is around 3 per cent.

to define the critical minimum effort in such a way that we always, under all conceivable circumstances, mean exactly the same thing by it." (Ibidem.)

Consequently, we cannot know what the magnitude of the critical minimum effort is, neither what this effort means at all. We only know that it must exist even if it is not the same under all conceivable circumstances and even if its magnitude is indefinable. That it does or did exist can be inferred from the fact that it resulted in sustained growth[312]. Is it a logical explanation from which we can learn why the developing countries are underdeveloped and how they can overcome underdevelopment?!

Thus, as we have seen, despite its dynamic approach and vivid mathematical demonstration Leibenstein's theory is of no avail. There is a penalty to be paid for an abstraction from concrete social relations and historical development, for taking the intellectual question out of its historical context"! No realistic theoretical explanation for underdevelopment and development can do without social analysis and historical interpretation.

## 2.3. A sociological explanation of underdevelopment: the idea of a stagnant traditional society

Two main variants of sociological explanation of underdevelopment have emerged and can be distinguished – even if these two types tended to coalesce in the concept of some scholars. The first has looked at the society of the developing countries as a more or less homogeneous, stagnant, and *traditional*, backward society, while the second has emphasized its heterogeneous, dual or even plural nature.

The investigation of the sociological characteristics of underdeveloped countries and the integration of these characteristics into the various underdevelopment or development theories has become so popular since the late 1950s that one can hardly find any authors, in fact, who failed to point out, in one way or another, some of the unfavourable phenomena of society and their effects in the developing countries.

As *G. M. Meier* noted (1958): "Although a commonplace, it is nevertheless necessary to recognize at the outset that the socio-economic environment within a country may or may not be conducive to development. Certain religious and social attitudes are more favourable to development than are others." (p. 55) In the same place *Meier* pointed to the unfavourable socio-political factors in connection with market imperfections, the ignorance of market conditions, the lack of technical know-how, and the immobile nature of the labour force. He always stressed the need to take the social structure and institutions, the religious and moral set of values of the developing countries into account when analyzing the problems of their underdevelopment.

---

[312] As also *Rostow's* take-off can only be inferred in a similar way-despite its seemingly quantitatively determined character. (See it later!)

*J. Viner* also emphasized the importance of the socio-political factors. According to *E. Gannagé* the rigid social structure and the low degree of responsiveness of society belong to the typical features of 'underdevelopment".

*H. Myint* (1958) who interpreted the concept of the "backwardness of people" in a broader sense, pointed to the unbalanced relationship between society and changed economic environment, maladjustment of society and its members, the existence of a "plural society" and, in general, the significance of the exogenous non-economic factors. He made a distinction between the economics of "underdeveloped resources" and of "backward people", i.e. between the economic and social sides of underdevelopment, by considering the former as the economics of stagnation or relatively slow rates of growth in total or per capita national income and productivity, while the latter as the economics of social maladjustment and discontent. (p. 119) In another study (1963) he emphasized the importance of the social peculiarities of the underdeveloped countries, and the need for taking them into consideration adequately.

*Francois Perroux* (1966) identified the brakes and obstacles to development primarily in social institutions, in the way of thinking and habits of society, i.e. in the social relations and the socio-psychological features of the population, including the system of large estates, the lack or insufficiency of propensity to innovate, the poor labour discipline, and the absence of entrepreneurship, as defined by Schumpeter, etc. For the promotion of development he stressed the importance of certain exogenous, non-economic changes, such as in the institutional structure, in social mentality, and habits. Thus Perroux opposed thereby the purely economic explanation of underdevelopment and "economistic developmentalism", i.e. the development policy, which focuses merely on the per-capita GNP level, and growth.

A number of other well-known scholars could be added to those mentioned above, authors who in different contexts have touched upon the social implications of "economic underdevelopment". This goes to show that factors like social environment, the responsiveness, propensities, customs, habits and institutions of society all rank fairly high in the various underdevelopment theories. However, the "sociology of backwardness" has developed mostly as a theory separate from development economics, being concerned with economic theories only at certain marginal points, while the latter include social phenomena only as exogenous factors in the interpretation of underdevelopment, by referring to the results of the "bordering discipline". This rigid dichotomy in the research on economic and social phenomena was obviously the result of the conventional isolation of the various social sciences from each other in the past[313]. The demand frequently made in economic literature, for a sociological approach, and, for the necessary and useful cooperation of economics and sociology, as well as the inclusion of sociological factors in the list of criteria defining underdevelopment, were no doubt signs of the turning away to a certain extent from "pure economics" (at least as regards the developing countries) already in the early stages of the history of development economics. This was, however, still a long way from accepting a real political economy[314] which, instead of the Robinson-problem of the "distribution and utilization

[313] This is clearly demonstrated by the isolation of "political science", sociology and "pure" economics.

[314] Today *a real* political economy must differ not only from the German historical school and institutionalism but also from orthodox Marxism and the new, "neo-classical political economy" and neo-classical institutionalism as well. It cannot be merely "state- (and institutions-) centered" or merely "class- (and interest groups-) centered, nor can it be based simply on the assumed rationality of "public choices".

of scarce resources", puts the emphasis on the analysis of the social process of reproduction, the social relations of production and distribution both on "national" and global level, and examines underdevelopment as a complex socio-economic formation in the context of the world system. The sociology of underdevelopment has usually disregarded the economic determinants, or regarded them as secondary, while in the economics of underdevelopment sociological factors have appeared as exogenous and unexplainable[315].

When *Meier* and *Baldwin* (just like many others) referred (1957) to the "backwardness of people" as distinct from the economic phenomenon of underdevelopment, they were in fact depicting a *traditional society*, which "has been relatively unsuccessful in solving the economic problem of man's conquest of his superior environment". This failure – according to their views – manifests itself in low labour efficiency, factor immobility, limited specialization in occupations and in trade, lack of entrepreneurship, economic ignorance, lack of individualism, rigid and stratified, caste-like structure of society, and especially in the institutions and in the religious and moral values, etc. (p. 293)

The usual definition (such as above) of the "backwardness of people" is the obvious outcome of a comparison with an idealized model of the advanced capitalist societies, i.e. a product of the "subtraction approach". The lack of capitalistic entrepreneurship is regarded as the main characteristic of backward societies inhibiting development. Many of those scholars who conceive underdevelopment as of an original and stationary state, "invert the problem and ask for the reasons for development rather than for those for underdevelopment"[316] Since, in their view, the development of advanced countries is due to the special qualities of entrepreneurs and "growth agents" who, with a dynamic outlook, constantly tend to disturb the stationary equilibrium by means of innovations[317], underdevelopment merely means that the idealized entrepreneurial qualities have not yet developed.

In accordance with the "subtraction approach", in the relevant literature there is a long list of qualities, propensities, motivations and incentives that (in contrast to the advanced countries) are missing in the underdeveloped, "backward" society of the developing countries and should be created as an absolute precondition for their development.

*Leibenstein* (1957) enumerated the following as desirable attitudes: (1) Western "market" incentives, that is, a strong profit incentive..., (2) a willingness to accept entrepreneurial risks, (3) an eager-

[315] *Celso Furtado* noted (1958) that economic development itself is determined by sociological factors not explainable in terms of economics: "The theory of economic development in its general form does not fall within the categories of economic analysis... Economic analysis cannot say why any society starts developing and to what social agents this process is due." (p. 316)

[316] *Tinbergen, J.* (1963), p. 86.

[317] *J. A. Schumpeter* (1951a) distinguished five types of innovations: new goods, new methods of production, new markets, new sources of raw material and new forms of organization.

ness to be trained for industrial and "dirty" jobs..., (4) an eagerness to engage in and promote scientific and technical progress. (p. 109) While, in his view, developed countries are characterized by *"positive-sum incentives"*, i.e. "those that lead to activities that yield increases in national income" and by such "growth contributing activities" as "the creation of entrepreneurship, the expansion of productive skills, and the increase in productive knowledge", the "backward societies" are marked by *"zero-sum activities* directed toward the maintenance of existing economic privileges through the inhibition and curtailment of potentially expanding economic opportunities; the conservative activities of both organized and unorganised labour directed against change; the resistance to new knowledge and ideas; increases in essentially non-productive conspicuous public or private consumption, etc". (pp. 188–189)

*Jan Tinbergen* (1963) was obviously endeavouring not to fashion the list of desirable attitudes exclusively on the model of the Western capitalist entrepreneur –, which was presumably in line with his view about the convergence of the development of East and West that time. He maintained that, at the very least, those who play leading roles in society should "(1) be interested in material wealth, (II) be interested in the future, (III) be willing to take risks, (IV) be interested in technology, (V) show persistency, (VI) be able to work hard, (VII) be able to cooperate with many people, (VIII) be open to new ideas, (IX) be able to make logical analyses of complex phenomena". (p. 68)

Though "social behaviour, attitudes and propensities", the "social value system", etc., have been attributed a central role in the historical process of economic development or growth by W. W. Rostow (1960a) and Raymond Aron (1962), too, and their importance have also been emphasized by N. S. Buchanan and H. S. Ellis (1955) as well as by A. Gershenkron (1955) among many others, a specific sociological or socio-psychological theory of economic development and underdevelopment has been represented, indeed, rather by the works of *Bert F. Hoselitz* (1953, 1960, 1963, 1964), *Everett E. Hagen* (1957a, 1962), *David McClelland* (1961a, 1964), and *John H. Kunkel* (1965).

Let us see now – without going into the details of these theories and examining the differences between them or discussing other, similar concepts and their theoretical antecedents[318] – what picture these theories have actually drawn of the system of underdevelopment (versus that of development).

*Hoselitz* contrasted the differing nature of social roles and behaviours in the advanced and the underdeveloped countries. By making use of *Talcott Parsons'* pattern variables (1951), he described the society of the advanced countries as being characterized by "universalism, achievement orientation and functional specificity", and attributed the opposite characteristics: "particularism, ascription and functional diffuseness" to the "backward society" of the developing countries. It follows that the latter are underdeveloped because (a) in their society *particularism* prevails instead of universalism, particular interests direct the movement and

[318] For example, *Max Weber's* theory.

processes of society; (b) recruitment and reward are determined by *ascription* rather than by achievement and thus achievement motivation is missing in social activities; (c) the social roles are characterized by *functional diffuseness* rather than by functional specificity.

As far as the validity of such a general comparison is concerned, it will suffice to refer to its criticism by *A. G. Frank* (1967)[319]. As regards the particularism-universalism contrast, Frank pointed out that, on the one hand, particularism can be found also in developed capitalist countries where, in fact, particular private interest are the governing factors, and can be discovered even behind the universalist slogans exported to the developing countries (e.g. "freedom", "democracy", "economic liberalism of free trade", "free elections", etc.). On the other hand, the developing countries have also shown – along with false, imported universalism – the signs of true universalism (such as anticolonial movements, militant nationalism, etc.).

To refute the statement that the social, economic and political roles in underdeveloped countries are distributed almost exclusively in terms of ascriptive norms, *Frank* mentioned the example of the political leadership produced by the Latin-American coups and that of the emerging African "national" bourgeoisie, and in general the example of those who, having "commercial and financial ties to the developed metropolis", take up top roles. At the same time, he mentioned as a striking example of the very ascriptive distribution of roles in advanced countries the position of the Negroes in America (that time).

Frank also rejected that statement of Hoselitz according to which the roles in the developing countries are functionally diffuse rather than specific, in contrast to those in the developed countries. He pointed to that the roles in the lower strata of the underdeveloped societies are really diffuse in that the same person may "practice many professions at a time (such as farmer, trader, peddler, artisan, odd jobber, thief, etc.)," and such are also the top roles where monopoly control is exercised. But, on the other hand, the same role diffuseness can also be observed in the military–industrial complex of the upper leadership of the USA, while "a whole series of intermediate roles in underdeveloped societies occupied by such members of the middle classes as military officers, government bureaucrats, junior executives, administrators, policemen, and others, are functionally quite specific". (p. 30)

Frank summed up his criticism by saying that Hoselitz, when "confining his attention to the arithmetic sum of social roles in general" forgot "about the social, political and economic structure of a particular society under study"; Hoselitz assumed that even if underdevelopment is connected with a certain structure of social system, "the system's structure can be changed simply by changing some of its parts" – which is "contrary to all empirical reality". (pp. 33–34)

[319] For another criticism of Hoselitz see *Mátyás, A.* (1963), pp. 60–62.

*McClelland*[320] also disregarded (as a matter of fact to an even greater extent than Hoselitz) the problem of the social system as a whole and its structure, and discovered the roots of underdevelopment (or, in reverse, development) in the differences of individual psychological motivations. *Hagen*'s approach seems similar, when in analysing underdevelopment, characterized by him as "peasant society"[321], he put emphasis on the different nature of basic motivations and on inter-personal relationships. While Hoselitz' arguments allow one at least to draw the conclusion that the breaking out of underdevelopment requires certain changes in social roles and that – although not the whole structure – at least some parts of the social system must also be changed, all that follows from McClelland's arguments, however, is the necessity to change the psychological motivations of individuals only[322].

McClelland accepted the view that the prime mover of economic and social development is entrepreneurial behaviour, i.e. "pioneering service", the "vigorous activities of a number of individuals who behave in an entrepreneurial fashion". However, he characterized entrepreneurial behaviour not by the profit motive but by the so-called "*n*-Achievement" (a variable for measuring achievement motivation, a factor also used by Hoselitz). What seemed "new" in his theory was perhaps the greater degree of psychological mystification. Otherwise his line of thought was composed of rather old elements: it is not the way of action for profit, which makes the capitalist entrepreneur (and which may undoubtedly include actions objectively promoting the development of social productive forces such as innovations, rationalization, etc.), but, instead, it is the inner psychological motives of the "need for achievement", "desiring to do well" and "competing with a standard of excellence". It is these psychological motives that induce individuals to bring in innovations, starting a "pioneering service" for society, and taking risks in the hope of greater results, in other words, to behaving as entrepreneur[323]. (Profit is, of course, the product of this idealized activity. Its role in entrepreneurial motivation is no longer the aim but rather "a means of measuring how well one has done one's job".)

McClelland presented these motives as "autonomous forces within individuals",

[320] The theories represented by McClelland and Hagen are called by *Manning Nash* (1963) "smaller scale hypotheses" and by *Benjamin Higgins* (1959) "partial theories" – expressing thereby their extraordinarily narrow, limited character. (p. 294) The "small-scale" character, the concentration on merely partial social changes finds a telling expression in *J. H. Kunkel's* conclusion (1965): "Since usually only a few aspects of the societal environment can be altered, present efforts to create behavioural prerequisites must begin on a small scale." (p. 277)

[321] At the same time, *Hagen* conceived of peasant society as a dual society. (See in the following subchapter.)

[322] "McClelland is quite explicit in telling his readers that not the social structure as Weber had it, nor even assignment of and reward in social roles based on achievement (as in Hoselitz's view), but only a high degree of individual motivation or need for achievement is the alpha and omega of economic development and cultural change," – wrote *A. G. Frank* (1967), pp. 64–65.

[323] "...Certain motive combinations predispose individuals to act like the successful business entrepreneurs..." – wrote *McClelland* (1957), p. 6.

but admitted to a certain extent that they are dependent variables, when e.g. he noted that the motives of individuals can be changed by "persuasion", "by education", "by early character training", and when he pointed out that the average n-Achievement varies with children from different "class backgrounds"[324].

Accordingly, the rapid development in advanced countries is due to the fact that the entrepreneur's motivational complex (especially the n-Achievement) has developed in a number of persons, while this motivational complex has been in short supply in underdeveloped countries. Differences in the average level of certain motives such as n-Achievement, predict differences in the rate of economic growth.

*Hagen*, with a somewhat wider outlook, described the "peasant society" of the underdeveloped countries in the following way: social mobility through economic success is of a low degree, the middle classes are undeveloped; the physical sciences are backward; the production techniques are primitive. In the sphere of individual motivations, which play such a prominent role in development, rather unfavourable motives prevail, such as: (a) high need-conformity (need to conform, placing high value on conformity), (b) high need-dependency (need to feel inferior to someone), and (c) high need-affiliation (need to please friends). Contrary to these, the advanced capitalist societies are characterized by: (a) high n-Achievement, 0 high need-dominance (need to be a leader) and (c) high need autonomy (need to be independent of others). The former motivations hamper technological progress.

Though individual motivations also appear autonomous in Hagen's list, it turns out nevertheless that "high need-achievement, aggression and dominance may exist among the elite of a peasant society", too. Thus one can draw the conclusion that the difference between advanced and developing countries shows itself less in the mere existence or absence of these motivations than perhaps in the measure of their incidence or intensity. When Hagen pointed to the role in the changes that may be played by such factors as social tension among the elite, subordination, imposition of change through physical force such as colonial rule[325], external

[324] *McClelland* also mentioned the fact that it is the middle classes rather than the upper classes, i.e., only the "relatively elite group" that strives upwards, which show a high n-Achievement. *Hagen* elaborated this point further into the "law of the subordinated group", and as McClelland referred to the role of the Jews and Protestants, he mentioned the role of Scots in England and of the low-caste samurais in Japan, etc.

[325] Even *Rostow* and some other authors, too, refer to such an effect of colonialism (and also racial discrimination) eliciting this positive reaction. (See later.) Sometimes the naive reader may even be led to believe that colonialism had a doubly positive effect: in addition to the overpraised transplantation of modern technology and methods of production even its much critized, anti-human, oppressive and humiliating activity had a beneficial role in awakening or setting into motion some positive psychological motivations. It is curious enough that some "purist revolutionaries" often used very similar arguments, though with a contrary aim in view, when they said that war, oppression and exploitation (the greater the better) – in spite of the sacrifices involved – were favorable just because they evoked the revolutionary spirit, while peace, democratic reforms or improving standards of living were unfavorable as they endangered it. Such "apostles" of revolution forgot "only" one thing; why and for whom a revolution may be needed (when it is unavoidable). Such views could also be found in *Franz Fanon's* "violence dialectics" (1961).

threat to the nation, etc., it appears that what he was talking about really is rather only the setting into motion or the expansion of the latent positive forces already in existence. If, however, this is the case, then the small-scale analysis and the examination of individual psychological motivations will not suffice, and the exploration of the entire social environment is called for.

What can finally be said about the sociological and psychological theories of underdevelopment or development and, in general, about the role of social behaviour, customs, propensities, ideas and individual psychological motivations in socio-economic development?

Two distinct hypotheses can be found in the centre or, more exactly, at the basis of both the sociological and the "small-scale" psychological interpretations:

1. There exist social and individual *qualities, which* are either *generally favourable or generally unfavourable* to economic development. Sociological theories of development tend to emphasize the former, while psychological interpretations usually emphasize the latter. However, insofar as social environment, social behaviour, customs, ideas and roles, and the rise of an entrepreneurial class, etc., are independent of the economic system, the sociological pattern itself is in the last resort a function of the pattern of individual psychological motivations. Consequently, the sociological qualities seem merely to be an aggregate of individual qualities and so the sociological variant of the development theory is based on the psychological variant. (It is, by the way, not difficult to discover a certain analogy between the starting points of hypothesis No. 1 and of the psychological aptitude tests. As certain adequate or non-adequate qualities, promoting or hindering factors and motivations exist and can be specified for the various activities and professions, in the same way certain favourable or unfavourable qualities must exist and be specified also for economic development *in general*.)

2. If the international distribution of these generally favourable or generally unfavourable social and individual qualities is such that the *generally favourable qualities* are concentrated in the *developed* and the *generally unfavourable qualities* in the *underdeveloped countries*, then this provides the evidence that economic development is attributable to the generally favourable individual qualities (or their social aggregate), and economic underdevelopment to the generally unfavourable social and individual qualities. Consequently, the *conditio sine qua non* and determining factor for a society to overcome underdevelopment is a change in the psychological qualities of its individuals.

Nevertheless, the question is raised how and on what basis the generally favourable or unfavourable qualities can be specified. The implicit answer is: on the basis of a distinction between those qualities possessed by the developed and the underdeveloped countries. The tautology is evident: economic development is resulting from the favourable social behaviour or its individual psychological components; and those social behaviours can be defined as favourable which have *de facto* resulted in economic development. The advanced countries are advanced because they possess those favourable qualities, which *ex definitione* belong to them, and the developing countries are underdeveloped because they do not possess those favourable qualities, which *ex definitione* are not possessed by them[326].

This tautology is, of course, less evident if a given quality, which is at work in a concrete socio-economic context, is made abstract and idealized, that is, if it is deprived of its *concrete* content. That is one of the reasons why it is important to substitute the general achievement motivation for the profit motive in the entrepreneur psychology as is suggested by McClelland, and that is the reason for applying such "ideal pattern variables" as Parsons' and Hoselitz's universalism, achievement orientation and functional specificity. In this way even the contradiction inherent in the tautology can be resolved, the contradiction namely that the concrete psychological qualities observed in certain societies appeared as qualities *generally* favourable or unfavourable to economic development. If these qualities lose their concrete content and become abstract and idealized, they can already be dealt with, even without the former tautological proof, as generally favourable or unfavourable qualities, independently of space and time, from the point of view of an abstract economic development, similarly independent of space and time. This sort of idealization, however, raises serious doubts as soon as it is confronted with empirical reality. Not only the distribution of Hoselitz's variables prove to be inconsistent with the distribution of development and underdevelopment, as correctly pointed out by A. G. Frank, but it turns out that even the idealized entrepreneurial behaviour is far from being an unambiguous development-promoting factor, in that the profit motive, which determines its content, not only stimulates but may often stifle the idealized achievement motivation and innovation propensity (when, e.g., profit hunger leads to the use of means like speculation, monopoly prices, monopolization or freezing of patents, deliberate quality deterioration, under utilization of capacity, restrictive business practice, let alone arms trade and outright destruction by war).

Can we draw the conclusion from these insufficiencies and contradictions of the sociological–psychological interpretations that there exists no connection or only an inverse one between economic development, on the one hand, and social environment and behaviour, on the other? Not in the least! It would be totally wrong to deny that social and individual consciousness, habits, behaviours, propensities, ideas and institutions or even individual psychological qualities play an important part in economic and social development either by furthering or hampering it.

The question that arises, however, is how ideas are born and become effective,

---

326 *Benjamin Higgins* (1959) pointed to the same tautological element in *Schumpeter's* development theory: "Schumpeter's theory of economic growth has a large element of tautology in it, making it difficult to test empirically... Economic growth occurs when the social climate is conducive to the appearance of a sufficient flow of New Men, but the only real way to test whether the social climate is appropriate, is to see whether the New Men are in fact appearing; that is, whether there is economic growth. If vigorous economic growth appears, the social climate is appropriate; when there is no vigorous economic growth, the social climate is by definition inimical to it." (pp. 141–142)

how a favourable social environment and an appropriate social behaviour are created, how the individual qualities needed for "pioneering service" develop[327]?

It does not help if we refer to such general factors as Hagen's "law of subordinated group", and "social tensions among the elite", to some pressure or other which may threaten the structure of social relationships within the society, or to external factors like attacks and dangers. These may have a stimulating or constraining effect in a given situation and context. They do not determine, however, the content of social behaviour itself, the substance of the emerging idea, or the direction of pioneering service. In the course of history they have frequently recurred and in different historical periods helped to give birth to different ideas, propensities and behaviours under different socio-economic conditions.

Moreover, the same sort of behaviour, habit, propensity or psychological motivation, the same type of personality or the same idea, etc. may be found in different historical contexts, amidst different socio-economic relations. While they may be effective or even dominant in one case, they may fail to be so in the other; and, what is more, they may prove to be favourable now and unfavourable then, depending on the situation[328].

In other words, apart from cases bordering on the absurd, there are no *generally* favourable or generally unfavourable behaviours, development-promoting or -hampering ideas, customs, individual qualities and motivations. Their role, impact and value depend on whether they express a "social need" in a given situation. It is indeed the latter that gives rise or priority to the adequate ideas and behaviours embodying it. However, the content of this "social need" is constantly changing and is determined, in the last analysis, by the actual conditions of society, primarily by its "social relations of production" (but in a broader and more up-to-date sense of the word, than in the Marxian interpretation which over-emphasized the material side of social life and involved a narrow perception of "production"). Ideas, institutions, customs and individual qualities of the members of society develop and change primarily under the impact of their *social relations*, which are also influenced by them. "Social roles" cannot manifest themselves in general but

---

327 *Celso Furtado* (1958) also raised this question in connection with Schumpeter's entrepreneurial class : "And what factors make for the existence of such a class in our society? Why do certain individuals have that social function? Indeed, the problem of economic development is but one aspect of the general problem of social change in our society, and cannot be fully understood unless we give it a historical content." (p. 315)

328 Many scholars (like *Max Weber*) attached a particular importance to the *puritan abstinence* e.g., so much so that they put down the rapid rise of early capitalism in some European countries and in North America either to Puritanism as such, or to its reflection in religion (Protestantism in the first place). They ignore the fact that though Puritanism prevailed in the early Middle Ages, too, it did not produce comparable results. In fact, its direction was altogether different. The squandering age of the Renaissance had to come with capitalistic development in its wake for Puritanism to acquire a new meaning, this time that of serving capitalistic development. Individualism and collectivism had different roles and meant different things in different periods and under different conditions.

rather in the context of social relations, and, instead of being independent variables, are determined by these relations.

Thus, instead of an investigation of purely sociological phenomena isolated from such social relations, and instead of a micro-analysis of the individual psychological motivations, it is, in the first place, the above-mentioned "social relations of production" in a broader sense, including (*a*) the relations of ownership and also control over resources, such as the "means of production", i.e. "physical capital" as well as over other development resources and forms of "capital" as accumulated and monopolized assets, such as "knowledge capital", R & D capacities, information and social contacts, political power ("political capital"), etc., (*b*) the relations of income distribution, and (*c*) the allocation of "roles" in the social organization and division of labour, that must be analysed in order to get a right answer to the question about the place and role of the above-mentioned sociological and psychological factors, and to assess their favourable or unfavourable nature.

Consequently, no pattern of sociological and psychological variables can determine economic development or underdevelopment *in general*. It can, at best, promote or check it under certain concrete conditions. Since the pattern itself is determined, in the last analysis, by processes taking place in the socio-economic system and in the interactions between Nature and society, between also economic and technological progress, it cannot be the simple ultimate determinant of economic development itself.

These thoughts may appear to the reader as perhaps too philosophical rather than directly concerned with the explanation of economic underdevelopment. But if it were true that economic development is simply determined in the last analysis by individual psychological motivations[329], furthermore, if we were to assume that the given way of thinking and the predominant propensities of society are absolutely *independent variables*, then it would follow from such assumption that some nations live in more advanced economy only because they have more favourable psychological characteristics, better propensities or a more developed way of thinking to begin with, or could take possession of these qualities by their *superior* mind. Such a train of thought may easily lead to the conclusion that economic underdevelopment is due to the inferior intellect, consciousness and propensities of certain peoples. And here we are, within an age of racial ideology declaring the inferiority of certain peoples. That is why the explanation of economic development of societies by "propensities" and "motivations" is so utterly wrong. That is why it is also wrong to reverse the cause–effect relationships. If the development of society is abstracted from the natural geographical environment and, especially, from the changing social relations, then either it proves to be completely inexplicable why in one place and in a given historical period the productive forces devel-

[329] According to *Raymond Aron* (1962), the determining factor of growth is the attitude of economic subjects, i.e. certain manner of living and way of thinking of people. (p. 192)

op more rapidly than in another place or period, and why the propensities, customs and institutions are different; or everything must be ascribed eventually to some given capacities of intellect and consciousness, which is bound to end in differentiating between superior and inferior peoples, i.e. in racial ideology.

The sociological and psychological theories have, as a rule, one more serious shortcoming. Concentrating on the *ideal* pattern variables they forget about the real pattern variables, the heterogeneous character of behaviours, propensities, motivations, social roles and institutions within the developing countries. They generalize certain customs and institutions which were, let us assume, really characteristic of the traditional sector of society, and apply them to the whole society of the developing countries, i.e. they regard these societies in their entirety as "traditional" (precapitalist) societies[330].

This deficiency deprives the theories under discussion of validity, even if they regard sociological–psychological factors not as final determinants but only as interdependent variables. The invalidity of the assumption of a homogeneous traditional society has been demonstrated by the capitalist elements actually present in the economy and society for long time in these countries, i.e. by the fact of a socio-economic "dualism". That the basic assumption is false can also often be inferred logically from the way some scholars assess unfavourable social reactions, behaviours and the backwardness of people. When e.g., they have referred to the insufficient knowledge of the peasants of the market, they necessarily, and correctly, presupposed that *de facto* there has been some sort of market. When they speak of the maladjustment of individuals to modern economic relations, they presuppose, of course, the *de facto* existence of such relations. When they have pointed to the immobility of the labour force as an unfavourable condition from the aspect of wage employment, they implicitly referred to the existence of wage labour at least in a part of the economy. This means that they have assessed traditional customs, reactions and behaviour in their relation to another (modern) socio-economic element. Then it is neither sufficient nor correct just to compare these customs and behaviours or institutions to their "modern" counterparts and explain them in isolation as if they were independent of the latter.

Summing up our conclusions: (1) The sociological–psychological variables are not independent variables and can by no means be regarded as final determinants of economic development or underdevelopment. (2) Their place, role and effect can all be evaluated only in the context of the given socio-economic system. Consequently, the socio-economic system and especially the social relations of production and distribution in their complexity must be given priority in the analysis. (3) The analysis of the socio-economic system, as well as of the sociological–psy-

[330] "The folk characteristics which were studied by Robert Redfield, and which Hoselitz seems to associate with the pattern variables of underdeveloped society, do not characterize any whole society existing today..." – wrote *A.G. Frank* (1967), p. 32.

chological factors themselves, reveals the presence of a "dual" system in the underdeveloped economy of the developing countries, the co-existence of modern, alien, imported elements with those of the old traditional societies.

Let us see how such a "dualism" has been reflected in certain development theories!

## 2.4. The concept of "dualism"

Instead of the false picture of a "homogeneous", stagnant and traditional society[331], those scholars describing the society of the developing countries as a "dualistic" one undoubtedly provide a more realistic concept. Though in most of the theoretical explanations of underdevelopment reference is made, in one way or another, to the existence of two heterogeneous sectors of the economy and society[332], namely a "traditional" sector (with a subsistence economy) and a "modern" sector (with a commodity-producing capitalistic economy), the concept of "dualism" has appeared as a specific theory of underdevelopment only in those views putting the phenomenon of "dualism" into the centre of analysis and deriving therefrom all the specific problems and laws of motion of underdevelopment.

As such a separate theory, it seems to have two main variants: (a) the theory of *sociological dualism* (which is – as mentioned above – another sociological explanation of underdevelopment) and (b) the theory of *technological dualism*. While the latter has gained increasing influence in the literature of development economics because of and along with the problems of unemployment and the choice of techniques coming to the forefront, the theory of sociological dualism has been exposed to more attacks from various sides.

Sociological dualism cannot in fact exist without economic dualism, and vice versa, and whether the one or the other is justly criticized is usually due not to their different character but rather to their identical or similar shortcomings.

---

[331] Or, perhaps, even together with it, e.g. in *Hagen's* theory. Hagen (1957b) described the traditional "peasant society" itself as a dual society. The two poles of dualism: a number of agricultural villages with little migration into or out of each village, on the one hand, and the centre where the elite live, on the other. Contrary to the general interpretation of dualism according to which one pole of the dual structure of society, the "modern sector" is in organic contact with foreign countries, Hagen interpreted the "dual" society as an essentially traditional society which has little contact with the outside world. Thus *Higgins* (1959) had every reason to write, while disregarding Hagen's own terminology, that: "From the analytical point of view the main weakness of Hagen's statement of his thesis is his failure to take account of the dualistic character of most underdeveloped countries." (p. 320)

[332] See, among others, e.g. *Boeke, J. H.* (1953a and b), (1954), *Higgins*, B. (1959), (1964), *Ellsworth, P. T.* (1962), *Ellis, H. S.* (1962), *Lutz, V. C.* (1958), *Elkan, W.* (1963), *Hirschman, A. O.* (1957), *Leibenstein, H.* (1960), *Arrighi, G.* (1967), *Sachs, I.* (1964), *Dasgupta, S.* (1964), *Lewis, A.* (1958), *Eckaus, R. S.* (1965), *Dawson, A. A.* (1962).

## 2.4.1. The idea of "sociological dualism"

The pioneer of the idea of sociological dualism was *J. H. Boeke's*. His theory was given a stormy reception by Western economists, not because of its analysis but rather on account of the unpleasant conclusions that would be drawn from it. Boeke based his work on his experiences in Indonesia and presented it as a theory of "Eastern societies".

His theses may be summed up as follows (1953): "Social dualism is the clashing of an imported social system with an indigenous social system of another style. Most frequently the imported social system is high capitalism." Unlike temporary social dualism which, e.g., comes into being "when a late-capitalistic social system is gradually superseded by a socialistic system" (at times by the most violent disturbance, war or revolution), and in which the "society maintains its homogeneous character", a dual social system is a *lasting* formation and always the result of the penetration of an imported, foreign social system. The penetration by Western capitalist societies into Eastern pre-capitalistic agrarian societies has resulted in "a form of disintegration". Since the two societies are diametrically opposed in character, and "neither of them becomes general and characteristic for that society as a whole", therefore, "as a rule, one policy for the whole country is not possible...and what is more beneficial for one section of society may be harmful for the other".

The radically different character of the two societies manifests itself in many ways. The pre-capitalistic sector can be characterized by the "limited needs" (in contrast with the "unlimited needs" of a Western society), by the backward-sloping supply curves of effort and risk-taking, by the almost complete absence of profit-seeking (with the exception of speculative profits), by the "aversion to capital" (i.e. by "conscious dislike of investing capital"), lack of business qualities, lack of organization and of discipline, by "fatalism and resignation", lack of mobility of labour, absenteeism of regular labourers, by export being "the great objective", etc. – while the capitalistic sector has the opposite characteristics.

As disintegration has caused only disturbances and upset the normal living conditions of pre-capitalistic society, *Boeke* (1953b) concluded that the penetration of Western capitalism had been useless and fruitless. The efforts aimed at the rapid capitalization of Eastern society, at achieving considerable technological progress and a radical change of social reactions have likewise been in vain[333]. They could even enhance the retrogression and decay of this society. "The contrast is too all-inclusive, it goes too deep. We shall have to accept dualism as an irretrievable fact." (p. 289) And as for economics he expressed the view (1953a) that Western economics is totally inapplicable to Eastern economies: "...every social system has

[333] "There is no question of the Eastern producer adapting himself to the Western example technologically, economically and socially." *Boeke, J. H.* (1953a), p. 103.

its own economic theory" and "therefore, the economic theory of a dualistic, heterogeneous society is itself dualistic". (p. 5)

Boeke's theory has been criticized mainly because of this "defeatism". According to *Higgins*, Boeke has generalized certain experiences, which were limited in time and space, and his theory has only reflected the Indonesian failure of the Dutch "ethical policy". Higgins denied, on the one hand, that the characteristics considered by Boeke as typical were really characteristic of the Eastern societies[334] in general, and pointed out, on the other, that "many of the specific characteristics of the 'Eastern' society described by Dr. Boeke seem to be attributable to Western societies as well"[335].

Higgins' final conclusion (1959) is that there is no reason to suppose that the Western social theory is inapplicable to dual societies. "If dualism is not primarily the product of a clash of two irreconcilable cultures, its existence is not in itself a barrier to the application of Western social theory to underdeveloped areas. Sectoral differences are a challenge to economic theorists, but one that can be met." (p. 288) Instead of socio-cultural dualism, Higgins pointed to the sectoral dualism of *economy*. He admitted (1964) that "some degree of 'dualism' certainly exists in underdeveloped areas" and that "it is possible to discern two major sectors: one which is largely native, in which levels of techniques, and levels of economic and social welfare are relatively low; and another, usually under Western leadership and influence, in which techniques are advanced, and average levels of economic and social welfare are relatively high". (p. 61) The former is "confined mainly to peasant agriculture and handicrafts or very small industry, and the trading activities associated with them"; the latter "consisting of plantations, mines, petroleum fields and refineries, large-scale industries, and the transport and trading activities associated with these operations". In this way the explanation of

[334] Thus he emphasized (1959), in contrast to the "limited needs", the fact of the high marginal propensity to consume and the high marginal propensity to import, and pointed to the rise of new needs and through them the applicability of economic incentives. With reference to *Lewis, A.* (1955), *Bauer, P. T.* (1957), and *Bauer, P. T. – Yamey, B. S.* (1957), he tried to prove – in disagreement with Boeke – that economic responsiveness may be intensive among the peasant population. The assumption of the immobility of labor contradicts, in his view, the fact of large-scale migration. Moreover, "it may be questioned whether occupational mobility is not greater in underdeveloped areas, where trade unionism is far less widespread than it is in the advanced countries". (pp. 281–292)

[335] "Some degree of *dualism* exists in virtually every economy" – according to Higgins (1959). Not only Italy but also the USA and Canada "have areas in which techniques lag behind...standards of economic and social welfare are correspondingly low". "The preference for *speculative profits* over long-term investment in productive enterprise appears *wherever* chronic inflation exists or threatens." Western society is not free either from the reluctance of investors to accept risks or illiquidity. Absenteeism is not unknown to it either. As regards the supply curves of effort and risk-taking, they are "normally backward-sloping, in a *static* world... In dynamic societies the *illusion* of upward-sloping supply curves has been created by continuous *shifts* to the right of both demand curves and supply curves, in response to population growth, resource discoveries, and technological progress". (pp. 285–287)

dualism must be sought – according to him (1959) – not in the nature of society, as Boeke believed, but "dualism is more readily explained in economic and technological terms". (p. 281)

### 2.4.2. The idea of "technological dualism"

With Higgins and also other economists the theory of *technological dualism* appears to be the opposite of the idea of Boeke's sociological dualism rather than its complement. Making use of Higgins', Meier's and Eckhaus'[336] descriptions, the theory may be summed up in brief as follows:

"Technological unemployment" is attributable to "technological dualism" which means the use of different production functions in the advanced and the traditional sectors. Productive employment opportunities are limited, not because of the lack of effective demand, but because of constraints on resources and technology in the two sectors.

In the traditional sector the products can be made with a wide range of techniques and alternative combinations of labour and capital (improved land), i.e. this sector has variable technical coefficients of production. Labour is the relatively abundant factor, so the techniques of production are labour-intensive. In the modern, industrial sector they are capital-intensive. Moreover, they are characterized in fact either by relatively fixed technical coefficients (fixed proportions in which factors of production must be combined), or are assumed by entrepreneurs to be so[337]. The former, traditional sector produces as a rule necessities (foodstuffs or handicraft products) for domestic consumption. The latter, the industrial sector usually produces industrial raw materials for export purposes.

The industrial sector was initially developed by an inflow of foreign capital. As foreign enterprises operated under efficient management with modern production techniques, output in this sector expanded. Industrialization, however, generates population explosion. The rate of population increase in some cases considerably exceeded the rate at which capital was accumulated in the advanced sector. Since the production process in this sector was capital-intensive, and fixed technical coefficients were used (or assumed), this sector did not have the capacity to create employment opportunities at a sufficiently fast rate to absorb the greater labour force.

Far from bringing a shift of population from the rural to the industrial sector, industrialization may even have brought a relative decline in the proportion of

[336] See *Higgins, B.* (1959), pp. 325–344; *Meier, G. M.* ed. (1964), pp. 68–71; *Eckhaus, R. S.* (1965), etc.

[337] In accordance with the model of *R. Solow*, the assumption of initially fixed technical coefficients may also be omitted. "The industrial sector, which starts with a relatively high ratio of capital to labor, would move toward an equilibrium expansion path with a high ratio of capital to labor, even if technical coefficients were not fixed." *Higgins, B.* (1959), p. 335.

total employment in the latter sector. Entry into the traditional sector was then the only alternative open to surplus labour. As the labour supply increased in the traditional sector, land eventually became relatively scarce and labour increasingly became the relatively abundant factor. Since technical coefficients were variable, the production process became even more labour-intensive. Finally, the point was reached where all available land was cultivated by highly labour-intensive techniques and the marginal productivity of labour fell to zero, or even below, and disguised unemployment appeared. Under these conditions there was no incentive in the traditional sector to move along the production function toward higher capital-labour ratios, no incentive to introduce labour-saving innovations, no incentive to increase efforts, in order to achieve an increase of output per man.

This "structural" or "technological" unemployment is aggravated if technological progress takes a form favouring the capital-intensive sector, and if wages are kept artificially high by trade-union activity or government policy.

As a result of technological dualism, a strange situation arises which is contradictory to "orthodox theory" that labour does not flow from the rural sector where its marginal productivity is close to zero into the industrial sector because the supply of capital to this sector is limited[338] and technical coefficients are fixed. On the other hand, capital does not flow to the rural sector either where the marginal productivity of capital ought to be higher (since the ratio of labour to capital is higher). The supply of domestic capital is not directed toward improving techniques, because, although the elasticity of the substitution of labour for capital may be high, the elasticity of the substitution of capital for land is low. It may well be then that the marginal productivity of both labour and capital is close to zero in the rural sector.

Thus the theory of technological dualism serves to explain one of the most acute problems of underdeveloped countries, namely the problem of open and disguised unemployment. On the basis of the undoubtedly evident fact of population explosion and the phenomenon of different production functions in the two sectors, it explains why the abundant labour force is not absorbed and how it becomes abundant.

Though the theory reveals numerous important relationships, it is nevertheless open to criticism on several counts.

Although *Meier* (1964) accepted it as an answer to the question "why factor endowment and the differences in production functions have resulted historically in the rise of underemployment of labour in the traditional sector", he raised doubts about "its empirical relevancy". (p. 71)[339]

[338] The reason for this – according to *Higgins* (1959) – is that "each investment project in an underdeveloped country competes against projects the world over in the international capital market". (pp. 341–342)

[339] It is not completely clear, of course, how something can be true historically and at the same time irrelevant empirically.

He also questioned whether the modern sector really works with "fixed coefficients", whether the techniques – even if a capital-intensive one were initially imported – have not been adjusted to the abundant labour supply, and whether technical progress is actually labour-saving in the advanced sector, etc. However, by raising these equally "technological" questions, his criticism has not gone much farther. The question of the choice of techniques is far from being a simply technological question, and is not a question of factor endowment either, just as the "dualism" in the underdeveloped economy of the developing countries is not identical with the technological dualism of the various production functions.

The *main shortcoming* of the theorem of technological dualism is, however, that by concentrating on the technological problems of the economy, it disregards the basic differences between the two sectors in the type of economy, in their mode of production and social relations of production. Though its authors may have noted the pre-capitalistic character of the traditional sector and the capitalistic nature of the modern sector, moreover, Higgins referred even to certain difficulties arising from the foreign origin and outward orientation of the modern sector[340], all this appeared as of secondary importance only, instead of being the very basis of analysis. Yet without this veritable basis the starting assumptions and the conclusions, too, are most unreliable. The theory also offers a narrow and mechanical interpretation of the relation between the two sectors, which again is the source of further weaknesses.

As far as the population explosion is concerned, the statements on its causes, extent and effect are highly debatable. The contention that "industrialization generates a population explosion"[341], is not only an insufficient explanation but on the whole it is hardly one at all. (An appropriate real and sound industrialization usually has the opposite effect.) And when the extent and effect of the population explosion are discussed, it is impossible not to take into account the sparsely populated countries[342] and the time-lag between the actual rise in the number of births and the resulting expansion of labour supply (even if continuity seemingly makes it disappear). Owing to the inaccurate interpretation of the population

340 "The industrial and rural sectors are not parts of the same 'economy' in the ordinary sense. Geographically, the plantations, mines, and oil fields are in the same country, but economically they may be more closely tied to the metropolitan country providing the capital, technical knowledge, and managerial skill than to the underdeveloped country in which the operation is located." "The demand from the *world* market prevailed in the political as well as the economic sense; achieving the optimal allocation of resources from the standpoint of the European entrepreneurs and administrators meant an increasing conflict of that goal with the maintenance of full employment in the rural sector of underdeveloped countries." *Higgins, B.* (1959), pp. 333, 343.

341 *Higgins, B.* (1959), p. 328.

342 *G. Meier* (1964) noted: "It is interesting to note that the originators of the idea (Nurkse and Rosenstein-Rodan) are careful to point out that conditions in the sparsely populated countries of Latin America are not the ones where one would expect disguised chronic unemployment." (p. 78, in footnote.)

explosion and the mutual relationship between the two sectors, the labour flow as described by the theory is to some extent just the reverse of the actual one: industrialization brings about a higher population growth in the modern sector, and as this increased population cannot be absorbed because of the technology applied, it "has to seek a livelihood in the other sector"[343], thereby flooding the labour force in the traditional sector, too. In reality, it is the traditional sector, however, which has become the source of a rapid population growth and the expansion of labour supply, and labour force drifts – under the impact of various factors[344] – rather to the modern sector where, owing to several conditions, it cannot be absorbed either.

*Arthur Lewis* (1958) based his theory exactly on this real process of opposite direction and regarded the traditional sector as the basis of the unlimited supply of unskilled labour force for the capitalist sector. In Lewis' view, the main source of the abundance of labour is disguised unemployment in rural areas, with the high rate of population growth coming into play only indirectly through the latter.

With regard to Lewis' supposition, of course, just the same question may be raised as to the assumption involved in the theory of technological dualism: Can the marginal productivity of labour be regarded, indeed, as zero[345] (or close to zero) in the traditional sector or, in other words, can the labour force be drained away from it without an appreciable drop in the aggregate product of the working combination of the factors of production? A number of reports and studies have given evidence to the contrary[346], while *Ragnar Nurkse* examined the question in the context of land use, the problem of the actual ownership relations[347]. A further objection can be raised: Is it true that yields cannot be increased in the traditional sector any more by increased human labour-investments? Economists concentrating on practical possibilities rather than on abstract theoretical models would question this assumption – at least in respect of the majority of the developing countries.

It would likewise be justified to doubt the statement that in the rural sector as a whole labour-intensive cultivation is carried on in the strict sense of the word (and not only with regard to the proportion of the factors of production), i.e. the possibilities of increasing the "intensity" (in the sense not only of the tempo of work but also of the rational division and organization of labour) are already fully exhausted. As regards capital investment, it is not only such general questions are to be raised

[343] *Higgins, B.* (1959), p. 329.

[344] For more details see *Szentes, T.* (1964).

[345] It is usually regarded as the criterion for disguised unemployment.

[346] See, for example, *UN* (1953), p. 67; *Elkan, W.* (1959), p. 188. etc. – These papers have pointed out the harmful effect of labor outflow and migration on the agricultural yields of the traditional economy.

[347] *Nurske* (1957) noted: "To that extent that the labor surplus is absorbed – and concealed – through fragmentation (of the individual holdings), it cannot be withdrawn without bad effects on output unless the fragmentation is reversed and the holdings are consolidated." (p. 2)

as concerning the lack of incentives and the obstacles to the inflow of capital from outside, namely from the advanced sector, but also the concrete problems of marketing and actual market relations as well as the formation, distribution and utilization of the economic surplus, and its conversion into productive investments.

A great number of further questions may also be raised to the theory of technological dualism outlined above. Such as:

(a) In respect of the traditional sector: Why did the process of fragmentation of holdings start and what has prevented the type of land use that is burdened by fragmentation from changing? Why did a "continuous shift to the right of both demand curves and supply curves of effort and risk-taking, in response to population growth, resource discoveries, and technological progress" not take place? Why do the incentives to increase efforts, the levels of technique and man-hour productivity not operate, or why did they not operate before the population explosion made itself felt? Why did such subsidiary occupations and employment opportunities not develop in the rural areas so as to have absorbed the labour surplus? And so on...

(b) As regards the modern, capitalist sector: Why does industrialization, allegedly proceeding on the path of a capital-intensive technique, preclude the adequate expansion of employment opportunities? This is not natural at all, as capital-intensive technique, when leading to a more rapid expansion of surplus and increased reinvestments may have after all a favourable impact on the expansion of employment opportunities – *via* the higher rate of growth. If, however, this does not take place, the questions have to be asked: What prevents the increased reinvestment of the surplus; what happens to the surplus; why has industrialization not become everywhere cumulative? And is industrialization really capital-intensive in general and in the strict sense of the word (not only in regard to the proportion of labour force employed or especially in regard to the limited capacity of absorbing unskilled labour)?! And is it true in general that the contradiction of surplus labour and capital-intensive techniques constitute the crucial point of development? Can we speak of labour surplus in general, or, only of the surplus of unskilled labour in most cases? Why are there no market incentives of sufficient intensity to raise the output of the modern sector? And so on...

It is obviously impossible to answer these questions from the limited point of view of technical coefficients of production. To provide the appropriate answers, it is indispensable to analyse the very mode of production, the social relations of production and distribution, and the whole structure of economy and society.

To explain the fragmentation of holdings, it is necessary to recall how it has started, i.e. to consider the consequences of the mass alienation of lands in many of these countries in the past, and to take into account the present land tenure system. The lack of incentives is closely connected with the insufficiency of internal market relations and the existence of subsistence economies. Capital formation is hindered not only by the "marginal productivity of labour and capital being close to zero" owing to land scarcity, but also by the unproductive utilization of the actual surplus. Not only could the labour-absorbing capacity of the traditional sector not expand sufficiently, but it has also dropped owing to the deterioration of its conditions of operation, which was caused precisely by the penetration of the "modern" mode of production. Besides land alienation it was also of importance that "a number of handicraft industries were ruined by competition from cheaper machine-made goods... imported from abroad"[348]. Consequently, the growth of the modern sector *per se* has created underemployment and reduced the level of income in the traditional sector.

And if the labour-absorbing capacity of the modern sector could not grow sufficiently, then it is attributable not necessarily to the higher rate of population growth but rather to the obstacles of development in this sector: to the specific deviating factors of capital accumulation and reinvestment, i.e. partly to profit repatriation and mostly to luxurious (mainly import) consumption, as well as to the structural diseases of the sector, such as its exclusively outward orientation and primary producing nature[349]. Much more decisive than the allegedly fixed technical coefficients of the modern sector is the internal structure of the sector itself. Its generally capital-intensive character is debatable in any case as some of its typical branches (such as the export-oriented monocultures) were based on the abundant supply of cheap unskilled labour (or even on the forced labour of indigenous people in the past) and have not forged ahead on the road of mechanization.

It is to be noted, however, that in the last few decades, along with the rise and growth of manufacturing industries in most of the developing countries (including, since independence, the former colonies, too), a certain bias can be observed, indeed, in favour of capital-intensive techniques. But this is not characteristic of all the branches of the modern sector and results from a number of specific factors[350] rather than from the competition on the world market (or from the belief "that technical coefficients are fixed"). And as regards the input-output linkages of the modern sector which are much more important than the choice of technique from the point of view of its dynamism and effects on the growth and employment facilities of the national economy as a whole, unfortunately both the old ("colonial"-type) primary producing branches of the modern sector and in most cases its new, industrial branches fail to generate but sporadically only such linkages, and show also a bias against capital–goods production, particularly against technology development.

Instead of raising further questions and doubts about the narrow concept of technological dualism, let us summarize the critical assessment of the theories of sociological and technological dualism!

---

[348] See: *ILO* (1961), reprinted in *Meier, G. M.* (1964), pp. 71–74.

[349] The above-mentioned *ILO* report (1964) has laid emphasis just on these circumstances when explaining the slow growth and limited absorbing capacity of the modern sector: "A large part of the export earnings returned to the capital exporting countries in the form of withdrawal of profits and other incomes." "...the investment activities hitherto undertaken in the modern sector in a number of less developed countries did not produce on the domestic economy any significant 'linkage' effect...", "the linkage effect mostly leaked abroad." (pp. 71–72)

[350] See e.g. *Arrighi, G.* (1973).

The very fact that the phenomena and problems of "dualism" have been put into the focus of analysis in these theoretical concepts, has undoubtedly contributed to a better understanding of the real nature and mechanism of underdevelopment. Instead of those superficial, quantitative characteristics, and lists of development-hindering factors presented in the most conventional theories of underdevelopment, the idea of dualism has called attention to structural diseases, to certain peculiarities of the operation of the underdeveloped system, and, in general, to the need for a much more complex analysis.

The two main variants of the theory of dualism discussed above contain, however, such fundamental weaknesses as making difficult or even impossible to understand the phenomenon of dualism itself. The one-sided analysis of this complex socio-economic phenomenon, either from an exclusively sociological–cultural or from an exclusively economic–technological point of view doom both variants to failure. Owing to the separation of the *economic and social* sides of dualism, sociological dualism becomes unexplainable, while economic dualism is simplified to technological dualism and the latter to the problem of technical coefficients and the asymmetry of production functions.

This simplification, in particular, and the overemphasis on the *technological* nature of dualism, in general, are, of course, highly relevant to the final conclusions drawn for economic policy. In this way the issue of social conflicts will be taken off the agenda. (True, in the theory of sociological dualism they appear in a false presentation: as conflicts between different forms of social consciousness, behaviours and cultures.) Technological dualism manifests itself in the last analysis in a vicious circle which – like other vicious circles – can be broken by large-scale foreign aid, by the "infusion" of capital and technical assistance. In this way the qualitative problems are reduced to *quantitative* ones (namely to the questions of the comparative ratios of population growth and of the formation or inflow of capital needed to absorb labour). Consequently, the "efforts to produce a take-off into sustained growth in underdeveloped countries through vigorous development programs supported by technical and capital assistance from the West"[351] seem to provide the key to the solution. Moreover, if the differences between underdeveloped and advanced economies are "of degree rather than of kind"[352], then the conventional, "mainstream" economics seems (despite Boeke's view) equally applicable both to the former and the latter.

As we have seen, Higgins' criticism of Boeke's sociological dualism was made just in favour of these very final conclusions. That is, against Boeke's pessimistic conclusions and in defence of the policy of the diffusion of Western capital, technology and institutions as well as in defence of the "mainstream" theories. While *Boeke* stressed the resistance of the "Eastern" society against which the application of any technical, outside means whatsoever "makes the problem more insolu-

[351] *Higgins, B.* (1959), p. 281.

[352] Reference to *Bauer, P. T.–Yamey, B. S.* (1957) in Higgins, B. (1959), p. 293.

ble than ever", *Higgins* presented the way of overcoming underdevelopment as a process in which transplanted Western capitalism (in the form of the modern sector) supported by further transplantations of capital and technical assistance would gradually diffuse into the precapitalist, indigenous sector. While Boeke called for a separate theory, for new paradigms, Higgins seems to have assessed the "mainstream" economics as providing a proper tool not only for understanding the phenomenon but also for guiding the transformation process.

In spite of these different conclusions, both theories have a *common* and basic assumption. Namely, they assume the traditional social or economic sector as something *given* in its original state, against which the penetration and spread of the modern capitalistic sector will be ineffective (as in Boeke's view) or – given above a certain order of magnitude – effective (as in Higgins' view). Insofar as the question of the *survival* of the traditional sector is raised at all, they seem to explain it merely by the inner essence of the sector itself or by its resistance to the modern sector. Neither variant examines how the survival and conservation in a distorted form of the traditional sector and thereby dualism as a whole follow from the *specific nature* and limits of operation of that particular "modern" sector established in most of the developing countries, which has become one but the determining part of "dualism". Neither variant analyses dualism as a whole, as the product of a specific historical development, in which the determining element was, in most cases, the transplanted product of another, *external* development. Neither variant regards dualism as a *particular unity*, the two parts of which not only differ from or contradict one another, or simply react to one another, but in which the differences, contradictions and effects on one another of the two sectors are determined by the specific character of one sector (i.e. "modern"), and in which *functional relations* have developed between the two sectors. It is the organic relationship between the whole and its parts, and the contradictory interactions between the determining and the determined poles that has not been grasped.

This is what *Andre Gunder Frank* (1967) had in mind when he wrote about these theories: "They do not deal with, and even deny the existence of, the structure of the whole system through which the parts are related – that is, the structure which determines the duality of wealth and poverty, of one culture and another and so on... If they see and deal with any structure at all it is at best the structures of the parts."

While the two variants of dualism under discussion concentrated on how different the parts (the two sectors) are – in sociocultural or technological terms –, and how one of them can be (or cannot be) transformed, Frank stressed that the task proper is "to study what relates the parts to each other in order to be able to explain why they are different or dual" and "to change the relationships that produce these differences: that is, ...the structure of the *entire* social system which gives rise to the relations and, therefore, to the differences of the 'dual' society". (p. 61)

We could completely agree with *Frank* if, in the critique of these variants of the concept of dualism, he had not gone so far as to deny the internal problem of dualism itself by merging it into the "dualism" of the entire capitalist *world system*, into the contradiction of the centre and the periphery.[353] Thus he seemed to have underestimated (or even denied) the problem of dualism and contradictions[354] within the socio-economic system of underdevelopment, and thereby the task of changing this system, of carrying out a transformation also *within* the latter. It is only the "dualism" of and contradiction between the metropolitan centres and the underdeveloped peripheries in the world economy, which Frank (1967) was concerned with when stressing the task, or the sequence of tasks, that "in order for the underdeveloped parts of the world to develop, the structure of the world social system must change". (p. 63) However, as both the logic suggests and those successful cases of overcoming underdevelopment within the same world economic system may prove, the "parts" may change within some limits even if the "whole" remains more or less unchanged, and thus the task of transforming the "local" system of underdevelopment is not less important than that concerning the world system as a whole. In other words, the *dual* task, namely a progressive national policy aimed at the internal transformation of the local system and structure, on the one hand, and a struggle for structural and institutional changes in the international economy, for a new policy of international cooperation promoting (instead of inhibiting) the progressive local changes, on the other, seems more realistic than the slogan of "world revolution" which can easily be manipulated by the ruling elites as an excuse for not tackling the task of transforming the local system.

## 2.5. The theory of the "stages of growth": Rostow's historical explanation

As it has turned out from the above survey on the various concepts explaining underdevelopment by one or another internal condition, individual development-hindering factors or their interconnections in a vicious circle, a *historical* investigation can hardly be avoided for the understanding of the rise, survival or repeated form of motion of the latter (whether considered specific in the case of the developing countries or general in a certain phase of historical development of all countries).

It would be perhaps an overstatement to declare that the demand for a historical approach to socio-economic phenomena has arisen simply from the insufficiency of

[353] According to *A. G. Frank* (1967): "The supposed structural duality is contrary to both historical and contemporary reality: the entire social fabric of the underdeveloped countries has long since been penetrated and transformed by, and integrated into, the world embracing system of which it is an integral part." (p. 60)

[354] *Frank* ignored the fact that there are also other interpretations of the dualism within underdeveloped countries than those criticized by him, and that several scholars pointed out the fact of dualism. See e.g. *Ignacy Sachs* two-sector model (1964). Strangely enough, Frank referred to *Jack Woddis'* work (1961) for support of his general denial of dualism, in spite of the fact that it was exactly Woddis who gave an excellent analysis of the dualism of the reserves and the capitalist plantations within African agriculture in the past, revealing thereby the position of Africans migrating between the traditional and "modern" sectors.

the theories of economic underdevelopment outlined in the preceding chapters. The historical approach had, of course, considerable precedents earlier, too, (as in the German "historical school"). This demand has also followed from the fact of the former co-existence of different socio-economic systems, of the so-called "real (or existing) socialism" and capitalism, which called for an explanation and prediction as to their future development that time. But this very explanation and prediction seemed also to depend on how the question about the prospects of the newly independent countries of the "third" world is answered.

In addition, insofar as the anticolonialist struggle (lasting decades or even centuries) of many of the developing countries induced their leaders to see colonialism as fully responsible for their underdevelopment and to identify colonialism with capitalism[355], it seemed increasingly important to extend a historical explanation to the phenomena of economic underdevelopment and include the developing countries in the general historical pattern of socio-economic development by relating their present state to the past of the advanced countries and their future to the present state of the latter, i.e. by outlining a *unilinear* process of development.

The historical explanation of socio-economic development as well as underdevelopment has been presented by the *theories of the stages of economic growth*. Among these theories we shall discuss that of *W. W. Rostow*[356], partly because it is probably the best known and most popular, and partly because there is no substantial difference between the various theories as far as their basic concept is concerned. Rostow's theory was not specifically aimed at dealing with "economic underdevelopment", but it has not only exercised considerable influence on underdevelopment theories, but appeared also as historically underlining and reinforcing the conventional views explaining the differences in the level of development merely by internal conditions.

Rostow purposefully opposed his historical explanation to that of Marxism[357]. He actually presented the state and development of all possible societies of the past and present as a certain stage or part of a single, uniform development process. In other words, he offered a comprehensive historical explanation, just as Marxism did. However, unlike Marxism, he classified in the highest stage of this process not socialism or communism, but the ideal of developed capitalism.

*Rostov* distinguished (1960a) five main stages:

The *traditional society*. It is characterized by a lack of systematic understanding

355 Here we do not wish to discuss the question of how the historical responsibility of colonialism has been oversimplified by "Marxism–Leninism" and restricted to the past and how "colonialism" has often been interpreted in a formal sense.

356 For the theories on a unilinear process of historical development and its stages of growth see – among others – also: *Aron, R.* (1962), *Gras, N. S. B.* (1930), *Hoselitz, B. F.* (1960a), *Fay, C. R.* (1940), *Giersch, H.* (1955), etc.

357 This is emphasized, among other ways, by the sub-title of his book: "A Non-Communist Manifesto". *Rostow, W. W.* (1960a).

of the physical environment, which, in turn, hinders the development of technology and productivity. A minimum 75 per cent of the working population is engaged in food production, and national income, apart from consumption, is wasted mostly on unproductive ends. The army and civil servants of a hierarchical structure where political power is concentrated in the hands of the landowners or is embodied in a central authority support the society.

The transitional stage: the *preconditions for the take-off.* Rostow characterizes (1958) this stage by radical changes in three non-industrial sectors, i.e. transport, agriculture and foreign trade. The latter manifests itself in the expansion of imports financed by the more effective exploitation and exports of natural resources or capital imports. The development of transport and communications is often connected with the marketing of raw materials "in which other nations have an economic interest", and is often "financed by foreign capital" (p. 158) Society is characterized by the gradual development of a new mentality, the rise of the propensity to accept new techniques and the emergence and "freedom to operate" of a new class of businessmen. The new mentality, the idea of economic progress usually comes from outside, and spreads within and through the social elite.

The *take-off* stage. This is the crucial stage of growth, a relatively short (one to two decades long) interval in which, under the influence of a "particular sharp stimulus" the rate of investment increases to such an extent that real output per capita rises and the initial increase carries with it radical changes in production techniques. This stage, which in practice involves the industrial revolution, is characterized by a rapid expansion of a small group of sectors (leading sectors), and by such a minimum rate of productive investments over 10 per cent of annual national income which is achieved not only once but has been kept up permanently by society. The take-off witnesses a definitive social, political and cultural victory of those who would modernize the economy over those who would either cling to the traditional society or seek other goals.

*Drive to maturity.* Typical of this stage are the spread of growth from the leading sectors to the other sectors and the wider application of modern technology. The structure and quality of the labour force experience a change, shifting towards the urban and skilled categories. Higher consumption demands development. The new labour force makes itself felt in the political life, too. The character of industrial leadership also changes and professional managers (the "nameless comfortable cautious committee-men") with a wider outlook and knowledge come to the force. Society begins to seek objectives, which include but transcend the application of modern technology to resources. The extension of industrialization ceases to be acceptable as an overriding goal.

The stage of *high mass consumption.* This stage can be reached by a technically and technologically *mature* society after having attained a certain level of national income if it is able to resist the attractions of world power and chooses the alternative of increased private consumption including automobiles, durable consumer goods, family homes with gardens in suburbs, etc.

In Rostow's view, after a brief and superficial flirtation with the attractions of world power at the turn of the century, the United States opted whole-heartedly for this alternative of mass consumption in the twenties and has continued to be in this stage ever since that time. Moreover, while Western Europe and Japan were entering the era of high mass consumption and the Soviet Union was "dallying on its fringes" in the 1960s, the USA already exceeded it to a certain extent insofar that "the march of compound interest" was bringing its society "close to the point where the pursuit of food, shelter, clothing, as well as durable consumer goods and public and private services, may no longer dominate" its life. New horizons opened up beyond high mass consumption and society was turning its focus towards new, superior objectives[358]. By referring to the unexpected increase in the birth rate and the increase in the proportion of large families in the US, Rostow believed his statement being proven.

In his view, the "socialist" countries did also represent one or another stage or variant of the general development process, which means that Rostow did not consider the "socialist" system as a historical absurdity or error, a wilding to be weeded, but a specific case only which – like other specific cases – eventually leads on the same path of historical development of nations to such higher stages of growth represented by the capitalist system of the most developed nations[359]. Though this seems to be a more realistic approach, particularly today, i.e. *ex post*, after the collapse and transformation of this system, nevertheless it has blurred the real nature of this system and also the substantial differences between "systems" in general, because of the classification of countries according to their achieved level of economic growth, i.e. in a simple scheme built on differences between the present development levels of their productive forces.

Despite the obvious effort to acknowledge historical specificities and to outline historical development in its complexity by taking into account cultural, sociological, political and other factors as well, *Rostow* – like Raymond Aron, Colin Clark[360] and several others – concentrated so much on the growth of productive forces, or on certain general manifestations and prerequisites of this growth, that

---

358 In view of the superpower position and policy of the US on the one hand, and in the light of the successive Presidential messages on poverty and life insecurity even in this rich and strong country on the other, such a statement about the restrain from "world power" attraction and about a progress going even further than mass consumption, could hardly be convincing, but sounded rather irrealistic or at least too optimistic (particularly in the time of its publication).

359 In this context *Richard Gill* criticized Marx who was greatly mistaken, when differentiating the "stages" in social development according to changes brought about by class struggle in the control over the means of production (more precisely: according to changes in the ownership relations), and did not prove a good prophet in that he did not foresee either the considerable improvement in the living standards of the Western countries, or the circumstances of subsequent socialist revolutions.

Although it goes beyond the scope of this study, let it be noted in passing that this sort of refutation of Marx, and the assessing of Western capitalism of the present as the highest imaginable and possible stage of human development in general as well as the interpretations of economic underdevelopment outlined so far, derive from an obvious failure to understand the real historical development of the world, i.e. from an approach that intends to analyse the development of individual countries in themselves as if global interdependencies in a world capitalist system had not been existing and developing since quite a long time.

360 For example, *Colin Clark* (1957) distinguished three stages in the general process of growth according to changes in the sectoral structure: (1) In a backward society *agriculture* is the dominant sector. (2) In a developing society the proportion and importance of the *processing industry* increase in relation to agriculture. (3) In a developed society the relative importance of the *"tertiary" industries*, i.e. services, grows. Clark's theory of stages reminds us of *Friedrich List's* classification of economic stages.

he willy-nilly presented a unilinear development process the concept of which seemed to perfectly correspond to the conventional approach of "economistic developmentalism" and those related theoretical concepts explaining the international "development gap" merely by different *internal* conditions. Yet, Rostow's theory cannot be regarded by any means as a one-sidedly technical–economic approach.

In compliance with the traditions of the old "historical school", Rostow, as well, investigated the growth of productive forces from the aspect of *social* development. By illustrating the historical changes in this growth, he presented – like *W. Roscher* – one society, namely advanced capitalism, as the highest stage of social evolution. Of course, by the very nature of the matter, it does not suffice to investigate only the self-movement of productive forces. The real point to be brought out is that the social environment determines the development of productive forces and that the most favourable environment is capitalist society, as it ensures the highest level of growth.

Thus according to *Rostow* social environment, i.e. "social relations" (as interpreted by him), determine and are not determined by the evolution of productive forces whilst, on the other hand, he put societies into an order and specified the "stages" of historical development according to the level of productive forces.

This is apparently acceptable and convincing as the development of productive forces really depends on social relations, and, inversely, the superiority of a society is to be proven and demonstrated, among others, also by a higher development level of productive forces.

However, Rostow deprived social relations of their economic roots and substance and considered them as economically indeterminate[361] in an absolute sense, explaining them in the last analysis *in se*. He disregarded e.g. ownership relations, one of the important and determining elements of social relations (blurring thereby a basic difference between societies) and investigated instead the changes in social attitudes, the "propensities" of society[362]. Thus, no matter how strongly he stressed (1958) the importance of social and political factors and their effect on economic development and no matter how much he emphasized that the realization of the preconditions for take-off "requires a major change in political and social structure and, even, in effective cultural values" (p. 157.), – he did not

[361] "This structure is not economically determinist." *Rostow, W. W.* (1960b), p. 53.

[362] *Rostow* (1960b) distinguished six fundamental propensities: (1) propensity to develop basic sciences; (2) propensity to apply science to economic ends; (3) propensity to accept innovations; (4) propensity to seek material advance; (5) propensity to consume; (6) propensity to have children.

According to *Raymond Aron* (1962) these propensities determining economic growth can be reduced to three factors: (1) the capacity for innovations (including theoretical knowledge, the readiness and incentive to apply it: the wish to achieve material improvement); (2) propensity to consume, which is related to the propensity to invest and thus appears, in fact, to have merged with the problem of capital; and finally (3) the demographic factor. (pp. 200–201)

reveal how, on what basis this change takes place in the political and social structure, and in the scale of cultural values. He did not make it clear why the propensities vary from society to society, and even from one class or social stratum to the other within the same society. It seems that e.g. a capitalist businessman always thinks as a businessman not because he is a capitalist but the other way round: he became a capitalist only because he began to think as a businessman. And a wage earner, a peasant or even a nomadic tribal herdsman has not yet learnt to think in a business-like way, because his propensities to consume, to innovate, etc., are different.

Thus Rostow intended to define the various stages of economic growth by certain economic and social characteristics. However, the economic characteristics appear oversimplified and restricted to quantitative indices or the simple description of the state of productive forces, while the social characteristics are narrowed down to the attitudes, propensities of society or the actual places and roles of individuals, endowed with certain propensities, in society's organization.

As regards the *former*, it is scarcely possible to distinguish objectively between the different stages and societies on the basis of the *quantitative* evolution of productive forces. Unlike the qualitative differences such as in ownership, control, division of labour and distribution relations (i.e. the social relations of the economy) – which provide an objective basis for marking out the individual socio-economic systems or "stages" – distinctions made on the basis only of the development level of productive forces are arbitrary and artificial.

As to the *latter*, if we conceive of the social propensities as variables completely independent of the social relations of the economy, their very nature and the cause of their change become inexplicable. Since these social propensities, whose nature and change seem to be due to some accident or *Deus ex Machina* (or perhaps some sort of predestination?) constitute the motive forces of growth in Rostow's theory, the sequence of stages remains, as a matter of fact, scientifically undetermined (or just fatalistic?).

Consequently, the individual "stages" do not constitute an organic and qualitative unity either historically or logically; they can hardly be regarded as scientifically defined and the interrelationship between the individual stages is indeterminate, too.

This theory of five stages is practically a theory of the industrial revolution interpreted in a particular way, in which the first two stages are seen as being preparatory to the industrial revolution, and the last two as its result, i.e. self-sustained growth.[363] The fact of the industrial revolution, of the "take-off", however, can

363 "... the sequence of economic development is taken to consist of three periods: a long period, when the preconditions for take-off are established; the take-off itself, defined within two or three decades; and a long period when growth becomes normal and relatively automatic." *Rostow, W. W.* (1958), p. 157.

only be inferred from its result, from sustained growth.[364] Thus the "take-off" has only seemingly a positive definition.

Though according to Rostow "the take-off is defined as requiring all three of the following related conditions: (a) a rise in the rate of productive investment from 5 per cent or less to over 10 per cent of the national income; (b) the development of one or more substantial manufacturing sectors, with a high rate of growth; (c) the existence or quick emergence of a political, social and institutional framework which exploits the impulse to expansion (p. 164), it turns out that the rate of productive investment cannot alone ensure the take-off (p. 170), and – as *S. Kuznets* noted – a "high rate of growth" of the manufacturing sectors can only be considered as defined, "once 'high' is explained", and the passage concerning the "political, social and institutional framework"..."defines these social phenomena as a complex that produces the effect Professor Rostow wishes to explain; and then he treats this definition as if it were a meaningful identification".[365]

*Rostow* (1958) himself declared that his "definition is also designed to rule out from the take-off the quite substantial economic progress which can occur in an economy before a truly self-reinforcing growth process gets under way". (p. 165)

But as the take-off cannot be unambiguously defined, so it is also impossible to define self-sustained growth either. As *Kuznets* observed: "The concept (and stage) of 'self-sustained' growth is a misleading oversimplification. No growth is purely self-sustaining or purely self-limiting."[366]

The inaccurate and sloppy nature of Rostow's definitions has been pointed out by several of his critics. *Simon Kuznets* emphasized that any division of growth into "stages" sets the minimum requirement that "a given stage must display empirically testable characteristics...; ...the characteristics of a given stage must be distinctive...; ...the analytical relation to the preceding stage...and...to the succeeding stage must be indicated". But Rostow's classification does not meet this requirement. The characteristics of the individual stages are far from being distinctive. "Yet much of what Professor Rostow would attribute to the take-off has already occurred in the precondition stage." "The line of division between the take-off and the following stage of self-sustained growth or drive to maturity is also blurred... ; ...given the distinctiveness only in the statistical level of the rate of productive investment, there is no solid ground upon which to discuss Professor Rostow's view of the analytical relation between the take-off stage and the preceding and succeeding stages."[367]

In connection with the preconditions for the take-off, *H. J. Habakukk* (1961) pointed out: "In many cases the increase of agricultural output and the creation of overhead social capital are not conditions whose pre-existence explains the acceleration of growth; they are part of the acceleration which needs to be explained." Also the definition of the maturity stage is inaccurate in saying that "a society has

[364] This has been pointed out by *H. J. Habakukk* (1961): "The take-offs can only be confidently identified retrospectively; one can only tell if growth is going to be self-sustaining if in fact it has been sustained for a long period."

[365] *Kuznets, S.* (1960), reprinted in: *Meier, G. M.* (1964), p. 28.

[366] Op. cit., p. 33.

[367] Op. cit., pp. 25–33.

effectively applied the range of modern technology to the bulk of its resources", as "the bulk of a country's resources has no clear meaning independent of the level of technology".[368]

*A. K. Cairncross* (1961) also pointed to the inaccuracy of the definition of the various stages and the overlapping of their characteristics. He raised the question: "If the various stages overlap, what is then the meaning of a 'stage'?"[369] He also criticized the tautological character of the definition of "take-off": "a definition in these terms tells us nothing about the factors at work since we can only deduce their existence from the fact of take-off, never the likelihood of take-off from the ascertained fact of their existence."[370]

*Francois Perroux* (1961) also criticized in general the classification of the stages of development on the basis of quantitative changes in productive forces. In economic history, he emphasized, the stages of development differ from those periods of growth characterized by the percentual acceleration or slowing down of the growth of production. (p. 162)

Besides the faulty interpretation of the relationship of economy and society, the essence of social development and the superficial or sometimes even tautological definition of the arbitrary stages, there is still a very important and fundamental *methodological* error in Rostow's theory. He outlined the imagined process of social development in such a way that he actually placed societies existing side by side in *space* one after the other in *time* (or one before the other), as representing different "stages" of a general process of growth (not according to their inner substance and historical content, but simply on the basis of the given level of their productive forces), while their interdependent relationship, the mutual determination of their development since the emergence of the capitalist world economy, finds scarcely any appreciation in the analysis, and if it does, then with some prejudice.

There exist the present-day societies, each with its peculiar, variegated face, with its different socio-economic set-up, historical past and natural-geographic environment and, above all, with their interrelationships different in measure and direction. But, despite all these differences and interrelationships the societies can, indeed, be classified at discretion in certain categories according to economic indices representing the levels of their productive forces. Thus, irrespective of all differences between them, some countries may be put into the highest, some into the lowest, and many others into the intermediate groups. And then comes the logical "salto mortale": the individual features of the societies already classified reappear, but this time no longer as the indicators – mostly very superficial – of a certain phase of their own specific development, but as characteristics of a certain stage of *general* historical development. If a society classified among the highest group has such and such characteristic features, then every society that reaches this stage, owing to the development of its productive forces, will assume the same features. Moreover, in order to reach this higher stage on the strength of its pro-

[368] *Habakukk, H. J.* (1961), reprinted in *Meier, G. M.* ed. (1964), p. 37.

[369] *Cairncross,* A. K. (1961), reprinted in: *Meier, G. M.* (1964), pp. 33–36.

[370] For other reviews and critiques of Rostow's doctrine see also: *Checkland, S. G.* (1960), *North, D. C.* (1958), *Schackle, G. L. S.* (1962), *Higgins, B.* (1959), *Ohlin, G.* (1961), *Baran, P.–Hobsbawm, E.* (1961), *Frank, A. G.* (1967), *Mátyás, A.* (1963), etc.

ductive forces, it must develop the same characteristics. Thus, from groups classified by a very narrow and one-sided criterion, *Rostow* formed historical "stages": a society in a lower group corresponds to the earlier "stage" of growth of a society in a higher group, while a society in a higher group is but a stage to be reached by a lower-ranking society in the further course of its development. After that all that remains to be done is to illustrate this process by historical analogies to point out a few phenomena which seem to be really similar in the past of the more developed and the present of the less developed, developing countries – and the logical "somersault" appears justified and acceptable.

By this method the development of the former colonial areas can be treated as "one of the variants" only of the general case and allotted to a specific stage of growth.

Of course, all this is not presented by *Rostow* in such an over-simplified and open, clear way. The individual "stages" are shown to be far more complex and varied, the historical illustrations given are far more numerous (and the number of "or"-s is too many) with the result that it is not very easy to find out at first sight the rather ahistorical nature of this historical approach.

The picture Rostow drew of the societies in the pre-take-off stage seem, indeed, to resemble, in one way or another, most of the contemporary developing countries.[371] Moreover, *some of the characteristics* of the transitional stage[372] are such that they are far more – or even exclusively – typical of most of the underdeveloped, developing countries in the mid-twentieth century than of any earlier historical period in the development of the now advanced countries. Such as particularly: the simultaneous growth of agricultural, i.e. primary production and foreign trade along with the development of the related infrastructure, the resulting growth and heavy dependence on the export of primary products to countries which process them, the inflow of foreign capital and also of new, modern ideas, entrepreneurial spirit and habits, etc. which stimulate modernization, etc. Whether the above characteristics can be found also in the past of the already developed nations or not, they obviously *presuppose* an already existing more advanced external environment, that is the existence of more developed countries.

If the preconditions for the "take-off" include, in general, such features, and thus the presumption of an external environment with already developed coun-

---

[371] In a former study *Rostow* (1958) classified *four types of underdeveloped countries* on the basis of their economic indices: *(a)* pre-take-off economies (where the apparent savings and investment rates, including limited net capital imports, probably come to under 5 per cent of net national product), *(b)* economies attempting take-off (where these rates have risen over 5 per cent of net national) product), *(c)* growing economies (where these rates have reached 10 percent or over), and *(d)* enclave economies (where the rates have reached 10 percent or over, but the domestic preconditions for sustained growth have not been achieved). Thus the majority of the developing countries have been classified into the "transitional" stage. (p. 170)

[372] It is to be noted, however, that *Rostow* outlined these characteristics far less definitely and he also mentioned a number of other characteristics, together with various historical examples. Nevertheless the critique is reasonable even if the overall picture drawn by him is not quite clear.

tries which had passed the "take-off" is applied *ad infinitum*, even for the latter countries, then in the end at least one of the countries had to be an *exception* to the outlined process of general development, which had no recourse to a more developed environment in her transitional stage and whose transition from the traditional stage had to be induced by other factors than those considered typical ones.

*Rostow* (1960) seems to have followed, indeed, this train of thought and considered Great Britain, even within Western Europe, to be such a special, exceptional case. Great Britain was the first country to outgrow the traditional stage under the influence of a number of mixed factors such as – according to him – the gradual evolution of modern science and the modern scientific attitude (due, among others, to the impetus given by the discovery of new countries and continents), the settling of political and religious issues, increased social mobility, the role of non-conformists in the process of industrial innovation, on the one hand, and the widening of the external market, the upswing of foreign trade, the increased specialization of production and the extension to trade and colonies of the old dynastic competition for control over European territories, on the other.

As far as the first group of factors is concerned (progress in scientific thinking, and in social, political and religious fields), the same question must obviously be raised as in the case of "propensities": What determined this change and progress? What real and objective processes were involved? For if this question remains unanswered, we are bound to come to the conclusion that the British people were endowed with specific and superior intellectual qualities differing from those of other peoples. If, however, we consider the factors of the second group as determinant (those that helped Britain to move out of the traditional stage), then the question arises first: How did Britain manage at all, to reach historically (and of course above all economically) the stage of being able to penetrate into external markets, foreign territories and colonies? Then, secondly, it necessarily becomes clear at once that international trade and the "mutual relations" between nations that promoted Britain's (and Western Europe's) take-off were by no means *equally* advantageous for all parties. If this is the case, then the causes of the economic underdevelopment of other countries, particularly of the colonies, must be looked for and revealed in this context!

It inevitably leads to a logical deadlock if it is assumed that the rise out of the traditional stage had been furthered by the widening of international economic relations in the case of Britain (and Western Europe) only, while for the other participants of these relations the precondition for their rise has been that Britain (and Western Europe) had already reached the take-off stage, unless those international economic relations developing between them are by no means considered equal and mutually favourable![373]

[373] *Rostow* actually made a remark that Britain's take-off set in motion a series of positive and negative demonstration effects which progressively unhinged other traditional societies.

Apart, however, from the details, it is obviously an extremely great shortcoming of a theory of historical development if it makes an exception to the law of the general process of development exactly in the case of the very country, which first started and reached a higher stage on the road of development!

As regards *contemporary underdevelopment*, i.e. the actual state of conditions in the developing countries, including the many excolonies, Rostow seems to have considered it as a natural stage of growth which every country (except Britain) had or has to undergo. Hence the distorted foreign trade pattern and one-sided dependence appeared for him not as the harmful consequences of international forces, moreover even colonialism itself could be assessed in the last analysis as only favourable. The import of foreign capital and its dominant role in financing, the switching over to primary production and export, etc. – all seem, accordingly, to belong to the normal preparatory process of the take-off stage. The penetration of the ideas of more developed societies into the traditional ones represents a basically "positive demonstration effect" and is likewise an important component of the preparation for take-off.[374] True, Rostow noted (1960b) that colonization also had its "negative demonstration effect", imposing the will of the more developed society on the less developed one by the use of sheer military force, but even the latter may be considered beneficial in the end for "without the affront to human and national dignity caused by the intrusion of more advanced powers, the rate of modernization of traditional societies over the past century and a half would have been much slower than, in fact, it has been...". (p. 315)

Rostow's "historical" explanation (together with some other, similar concepts about underdevelopment) could actually provide a theoretical justification for the use of the terms "economically backward" or "underdeveloped" countries. Namely in the sense, that if what these countries have to pass through – though belatedly, owing to several internal factors – is the *same* natural and general stage of economic growth that the more developed countries had also passed through earlier, then their present state is simply backwardness indeed in the strict sense of the word. And if this is true, colonialism and other external forces can by no means be made at all responsible for that state. On the contrary, they appear as only accelerators of progress. If, for example, a traditional society, even after having been colonized, passes through the same stages of growth (only with a certain time lag) as the colonizing one, and if the former colony finds itself even after the collapse of colonialism in a stage identical with that which the former colonizing country had also passed through in its earlier development, then it seems to be clear that colo-

374 *Frank* noted (1967): "Characteristic of Rostow's second stage is the penetration of underdeveloped countries by influences created abroad – mostly in the developed countries – and diffused to the underdeveloped ones, where they destroy traditionalism and simultaneously create the preconditions that will lead to the subsequent take-off in the third stage". "Yet these same metropolitan conditions and influences...have not brought about economic development or even led to a take-off into development in a single one of the '75 countries'." (p. 39)

nialism, itself, whatever negative effect it might display, did not fundamentally change the direction and process of development. It did not force the two poles to develop farther away from each other, but rather brought them nearer up to each other.

The interpretation of the present state of "backwardness" or "underdevelopment" as an original, primitive state, or as one of the natural transitional stages of the normal evolution from the original primitive state toward maturity, has appeared explicitly or implicitly as the basic idea of most of the conventional theories of underdevelopment.[375] This interpretation has, on the one hand, gained its proper explicit, theoretical treatment in Rostow's theory, but, on the other, a logical denial as well.

"It is explicit in Rostow, as it is implicit in Hoselitz, that underdevelopment is the original stage of what are supposedly traditional societies – that there were no stages prior to the present stage of underdevelopment" – noted *A. G. Frank* (1967). "It is further explicit in Rostow that the now developed societies were once underdeveloped. But all this is quite contrary to fact. This entire approach to economic development and cultural change attributes a history to the developed countries but denies all history to the underdeveloped ones." (p. 37)

Consequently, this "historical" interpretation of underdevelopment is, in fact, ahistorical, denying history to the majority of the world's countries and peoples. But it is also ahistorical from another important point of view: it simply disregards the historical fact, which by the way is truly reflected by the most typical and specific characteristics of underdeveloped countries[376], that "the economic and political expansion of Europe since the fifteenth century has come to incorporate the now underdeveloped countries into a single stream of world history, which has given rise simultaneously to the present development of some countries and the present underdevelopment of others". [377]

The theoretical view which has considered "the characteristics of development and underdevelopment as *sui generis* to the country concerned"[378], had been rather widespread in the literature of the 1950s and was often shared even by some of those who criticized Rostow for his method of periodisation, for the economic and non-economic criteria of his classification, for the obvious oversimplifications, contradictions, tautologies or the far from precise terminology and definitions.

---

375 In opposition to the conventional theories of underdevelopment *Celso Furtado* (1964) stressed that: "underdevelopment is not a necessary stage in the process of formation of the modern capitalistic economies. It is a special process due to the penetration of modern capitalistic enterprises into archaic structures. The phenomenon of underdevelopment occurs in a number of forms and in various stages." (p. 138)

376 *C. Furtado* (1964) pointed to one of the most typical characteristics by saying: "The displacement of the European economic frontier almost always resulted in the formation of hybrid economies in which a capitalist nucleus, so to speak, existed in a state of 'peaceful coexistence' with an archaic structure...it would be incorrect to conclude that the hybrid economies we have been discussing have behaved in all circumstances as if they were pre-capitalistic structures." (pp. 133, 133)

377 *Frank, A. G.* (1967), p. 37.

378 *Frank, A. G.* (1967), pp. 43–44.

Most of the scholars dealing with the problems of underdevelopment or the "international development gap" have accepted without reservation the separation and isolated interpretation of development and underdevelopment, looking at both as comparable but basically independent "states of affair". The difference in their views was mainly shown in the extent to which they conceived of underdevelopment of the developing countries as being identical with the former state the already developed countries found themselves in some time ago.

According e.g. to *Leibenstein* (1957): "the broad characteristics of backward economies today are not different from what they were in advanced economies in a former period". (p. 102) *Simon Kuznets* (1958), on the other hand, when analysing the state of advanced countries prior to industrialization and comparing it with the mid-twentieth century state of the underdeveloped countries, came to the conclusion that the latter are in a far worse situation, both in respect of their income levels and also their demographic conditions (because of the time lag) than the now advanced countries were in earlier periods. "Both the absolute and relative economic position, as well as the general cast of the immediately antecedent history of the now developed countries in their pre-industrial phase were cardinally different from the economic position and the immediate historical heritage of the underdeveloped countries of today." (p. 151)

It is because of the demonstration effect that *Ragnar Nurkse* (1953) found a considerable difference between the present position of the underdeveloped and an earlier state of the advanced countries. The former, seeing the higher consumption levels that exist in the latter, tend to save a smaller percentage of their real per capita income than the now advanced countries did several decades or centuries ago when they had the same real income. *Celso Furtado* agreed in that with Nurske but he, on the whole, opposed to seeing analogies.[379] When referring to Kuznets and Gerschenkron, *G. M. Meier* (1964) also emphasized, in contradiction to Rostow's analogy, the relatively more unfavourable position of the underdeveloped countries of today. Though he did not consider this analogy out of place, he maintained that "there are also differences – by way of different kinds of problems now confronting poor countries, and in the manner in which some problems, although similar in kind to those of the past, are now expressed in different degrees of intensity and complexity". (p. 43)

What really matters, however, is not the measure of comparability, neither the degree of identity. What is questionable is the sort of approach itself "in all its variations" which ignores that the historical and structural reality of the present underdeveloped countries "is the product of the very same historical process and systemic structure as is the development of the now developed countries".[380]

---

379 *Celso Furtado* (1958) noted: "The absence of basic information and the resultant ignorance of the real economic facts have given rise, among economists in the underdeveloped countries, to the habit of reasoning by analogy, in the mistaken belief that, up to a certain point, economic phenomena are the same everywhere." (p. 309)

380 *Frank, A. G.* (1967), p. 44. *Frank* mentioned specifically the case of the so-called *tabula rasa* countries, i.e. those Latin-American countries which "had no population at all before they were incorporated into the developing mercantilist and capitalist system", and consequently had never experienced Rostow's first stage, but entered world history by stepping right into Rostow's second stage. And "the relationship between the mercantilist and capitalist metropolis and these colonies succeeded in implanting the social, political, and economic structure they now have: that is, the structure of underdevelopment". (pp. 38, 40)

In the case of those theories explaining "underdevelopment" by various development-inhibiting factors or their vicious circles, *either* – as we have seen – the question arises why these limiting factors were not at work in the earlier periods of the now advanced countries, *or* if they were, another logical question has to be posed, namely why and how these countries managed to break out of the vicious circles. Both alternative questions require a historical answer. Rostow's answer was to try to find in the history of the now developed countries the stage that corresponds to the present state of underdevelopment. It turns out, however, that he did not succeed even at the expense of a logical "salto mortale", and was compelled to make the very first country (Britain) that started along the path of growth, exempt from the analogy.

It has also turned out, as evidenced by Kuznets' calculations, that even the most superficial economic indices and phenomena reveal a substantial difference between the contemporary state of underdevelopment in the developing countries and the supposedly analogous state of the economy in earlier periods of the now advanced countries. Therefore, it is obviously impossible to explain this difference merely by the autonomous and isolated self-evolution of the societies of these countries. (Except for those who are ready to resort to the ideology of "superior" and "inferior races" by accepting some original, predestination differences in intellectual capacities between peoples.) Even if we assumed that the autonomous self-evolution of societies would proceed roughly in the same direction and *via* the same principal stages, and that the delay, lagging behind, loss of tempo could simply be explained by local, internal conditions, nevertheless, if, as it turns out, the direction and an essential stage of development are different, we cannot disregard an obviously and necessarily *external* cause which partly or mostly accounts for this difference. Hence, the present state of "underdevelopment" must be, at least partly, the result of an "external" factor.

This "external" factor, the system of "international" economic relations (and colonialism itself) did not play only the positive role that Rostow finally assumed, namely that it unhinged the traditional societies by its demonstration effects. Economic colonialism and the penetration of external forces and effects have also *diverted* the course of development, brought about a different kind of "state" and widened the international development gap.[381] On the basis of what has been said it is rather obvious that economic underdevelopment can neither be satisfactorily explained by merely internal factors nor can it be seen as a natural stage in the general process of growth.

Since Rostow had to make an exemption in the case of Britain and explain the first "take-off" by other conditions, including favourable effects and benefits from

[381] *Kuznets* (1958) noted: "Not only have the relative differences among the developed and underdeveloped countries, judged by per capita income persisted over the last century, but the disparity has increased." (p. 145)

international trade with the still less developed countries (instead of primary exports to and capital inflow from more advanced, industrial nations), it is hardly surprising that his historical explanation appeared not only as an outstanding manifestation of the conventional theories explaining underdevelopment by internal factors only, but has also provided an impetus (both by the critiques it provoked and the above strange exemption) to the *opposite* stream of development theories.

## 3. Critical theories, with reformist ideas, of international and development economics: the post-Keynesian reformist school

The concept of underdevelopment as an original stage or as a natural stage of transition to "take off", explicable in itself, leads to an obvious contradiction with both empirical reality and historical facts. The peculiar features of the socio-economic structure of the developing countries (as we shall see in more details later) still bear witness to the fact that this very structure has been determined by a historical development in which external forces have (also) played, directly or indirectly, a prominent part. But even apart from the legacy of the past, empirical facts and recent experiences of the development policy of many developing countries since independence have also made quite evident that even the most successful "critical minimum (or maximum?) effort" could fail because of counteracting forces and deteriorating conditions of the international economy. In view of all these the external, international factors (not only those with a supposedly positive but also those with a negative effect) have been increasingly taken into consideration in the course of development of development economics, while the recognition of a widening international "development gap" and the growing concern about the worsening position of the developing countries in the world economy with the resulting disequilibria, have given birth to more or less new theoretical streams in international economics as well, such as the *Post-Keynesian Reformist school* of international economics as well as some *New–Left* and *Neo-Marxist theories.*

Insofar as these theoretical streams have all paid primary attention to the problems of the economically less-developed part, the so-called "periphery" of the world economy, i.e. of the developing countries, their critical theses on the nature, operation and trends of the world economy, particularly on international trade, and their investigation of the role and effects of colonialism, imperialist policies and penetration of foreign companies as determining the development path of the periphery, have actually appeared not only as opposite views versus the conventional theories of international economics but also as theories of development economics in opposition to those conventional views explaining "underdevelopment" by internal conditions only. In such a way and along with the separation of development economics from economics in general after the Second World War, international and development economics have partly been interwoven, at least in regard to certain streams of both.

The above-mentioned reformist theoretical stream has been unfolding since the Second World War only, even if it is partly rooted in the Keynesian critical approach to the spontaneously operating market economy and partly in the Latin American "structuralism" and "school of dependencia"[382]. By extending the Keynesian critique of the conventional theories to those of international economics, and rejecting the naive views about a harmonious operation of the world economy, i.e. all the liberal theses of the Classical and/or Neo-Classical economics on international trade, specialization, capital flows, automatic equilibrium mechanisms with "reversible" processes, and spontaneous equalization tendencies, etc., it has not only produced a sharp critique of the prevailing international economic order, and suggested reforms and Keynesian-type regulations in it, but has also presented an explanation of "underdevelopment" as a product of international forces.

## 3.1. The critical views and theses of Raul Prebisch

One of the most outstanding figures and pioneers of both the Latin American school of "dependencia" and the Post-Keynesian Reformist theory of international economics is Raul Prebisch.

Prebisch found the main reasons of "underdevelopment" of the developing countries, the major obstacles to their economic development in their unfavourable position in the international economy, particularly in their deteriorating terms of trade and increasing indebtedness.[383]

[382] The *Latin American school of "dependencia"*, stemming mainly from the earlier, inter-war stream of Latin American "structuralism", includes, indeed, a few Marxist or Neo-Marxist scholars, too (such as O. Sunkel, F. H. Cardoso, S. Michelena, A. Quijano, T. Dos Santos, O. Braun, etc.), while the dependent position of the developing countries has also been emphasized and the concept of "unequal exchange" is also shared by many other scholars with quite different theoretical background (such as R. Prebisch, C. Furtado, G. Myrdal, A. Lewis, H. Singer, T. Balogh, A. Hirschman, P. Streeten, A. Emmanuel, S. Amin. etc.). Nevertheless *nothing* can justify, except a general aversion to all the critical views on "liberalism" and contemporary world economy, to mix up the substantially *reformist* critiques on the international economy and the *radical* ones. Nor can it be justified to label all those scholars questioning the harmonious operation of the market economy or not believing (like Pangloss in Voltaire's "Candide") to live in the best possible world, as the "prophets" of the so-called "dependency school or as the representative supporters of "dirigisme" (the "Dirigiste Dogma"). Such an over-simplified classification of views is presented by *Deepak Lal* (1983) despite his declared agreement on "the disadvantage of...attempts at an ideological classification of economic theories". (p. 2)

[383] See *Prebisch, R.* (1950), (1959), (1962), (1964), (1972), etc.

He attributed the regular deterioration of the (net barter) *terms of trade* partly to the pattern of the international division of labour and the internal structure of the countries participating in it, and to the changes that have taken place in this structure mainly as a result of scientific and technological development, and partly to the purposeful trade and customs policy of the developed countries.

He pointed out that the developing countries had developed as "the periphery of the world economic system" with the function of providing cheap foodstuffs and raw materials for the centre. In his view such an international division of labour cannot ensure the conventionally assumed benefits from international trade for all the participants, the realization of comparative advantages. The benefits from technological progress are also very unevenly distributed in the world economy. Not even the benefits of increased productivity in primary production can be enjoyed by the developing countries as they are transferred, via price changes, from the periphery to the industrial centre of the world economy.

Prebisch – like Gunnar Myrdal, Hans Singer and Arthur Lewis but in a somewhat different model – described how a specific *mechanism of income drain* through international trade is operating. In his model the benefits of increased productivity in the export sectors of the developing countries are systematically transferred to the developed countries importing the primary products of the latter. The reason for this is that in the world market the price ratios (relative prices) of the various products do not adjust themselves to the ratios of labour productivities in those economies producing them. If all prices dropped in accordance with and in proportion to the rise in productivity, which, owing to the natural-resource constraints limiting the latter in primary production more than in manufacturing, it would imply a faster and greater decrease in the relative prices of manufactured products. In this case – according to Prebisch – the countries of the world could equally share the benefits from technological progress resulting productivity growth. The discrepancy between changes in productivity and price ratios, however, is substantial and due to the fact that the *income* as well as *price elasticity of demand* for various products or product groups is very different.

Prebisch emphasized that to a great disadvantage of the developing countries the demand for the primary products exported by them was, in general, *inelastic*, i.e. demand does not increase proportionally with the rise of income in the importing countries and/or with the fall of prices, and as a consequence a rather regular tendency of oversupply of primary products has caused deterioration of the terms of trade of the primary exporting developing countries.

It is to be noted, however, that a fall in relative prices, i.e. a deterioration of the net barter terms of trade does not necessarily follow from inelastic demand at all. Inelasticity of demand can, as a matter of fact, be just favourable for the exporters when the prices of their products are increased (as the case of petroleum exporting countries has shown in the time of the "oil-price explosion") or when the income level of the importers declines.

Prebisch, like Singer, Furtado and others, also pointed to other reasons of the unfavourable position of the developing countries in the world economy. Such as the *demonstration effects*, which increase the demand for imported industrial products and may force the developing countries to maintain and expand further the given production of primary products and increase the volume of their export even at declining prices.

Another reason is the need to maintain and expand employment, which makes it necessary to create or sustain marginal sectors with a labour productivity much lower than in the export sector, thereby causing *technological heterogeneity*. The latter may also account for the transfer abroad of real incomes corresponding to productivity differences, while the intention to improve the price competitiveness of exports leads (among other considerations) to currency devaluation, and consequently to a deterioration of the terms of trade and a fall in the wage level measured in terms of foreign currency.

In explaining the international divergences between productivity, price and income ratios, Prebisch also referred to differences in the *bargaining power* of the owners of the factors of production between developed and less-developed countries, namely to the strength of the trade unions in the former and the weakness of the labour organizations in the developing countries[384]. While in the developed countries, i.e. in the "centre", well-organized labour can regularly achieve an increase in real wages or successfully resist to wage cuts, and, in general, the incomes of the owners of the factors production tend to increase relatively more than their productivity, in the developing countries, i.e. in the periphery the increase in income is less than that in productivity, the wage level may not rise even when productivity increases. Instead, a higher productivity in the export sector of the developing countries tends to result in an increased output and thereby an oversupply of those primary products in the world market, which are exported by many developing countries competing with each other. The consequence is the deterioration of their net barter terms of trade (with an unchanged or also worsening factoral terms of trade) causing enormous losses for them. All this is unavoidable under the circumstances of an unrestricted play of the market forces, i.e. under the spontaneous, unregulated operation of the market[385].

---

384 *Prebisch* noted: "The characteristic lack of organization among the workers employed in primary production prevents them from obtaining wage increases comparable to those of the industrial countries." Quoted by *B. Higgins* (1959), pp. 367–368.

385 "... it is not possible to arrive at the optimum solution of this problem if market forces are left unrestricted. The classical mechanism of the free play of market forces, either in its original form of wage adjustments or in its contemporary version of price adjustments through exchange rate movements, does not bring about that optimum solution. On the contrary, the periphery transfers to the outer world a greater part of the fruits of increased productivity than if the market forces had been contained at a certain point, either through customs protection or some other form of interference in the process." *Prebisch, R.* (1959), quoted by *B. Higgins* (1959), pp. 255–256.

The mechanism of income transfer itself can briefly be described this: Given a "country A which is prevailingly industrial and a country B which is prevailingly primary", and granted that the "income elasticity of demand for industrial products is higher than for primary commodities", and, further, that "B is unable or unwilling to send to A manpower which would increase the latter's rate of industrialization", then B "has no other way out than to decrease the proportion of manpower in primary activities in favour of industry". As in B "manpower is transferred from primary occupations with a favourable productivity ratio to industrial occupations with an unfavourable ratio...consequently, the pressure of the surplus manpower will force employment down on the productivity ratio curve from 1.00 to say 0.80, with the wage ratio falling correspondingly at the new equilibrium point... Export prices will fall, transferring income to country A".[386]

Prebisch's concept makes it completely clear that contemporary "economic underdevelopment" has been closely connected with a specific development of world economy. Consequently, no explanation or solution can be found by investigating exclusively or even primarily the internal conditions of development. His interpretation is at the same time a clear answer to all the conventional theories, which, by referring to the thesis of comparative advantages, try to prove the mutually advantageous character of the existing international division of labour between the developed and the developing countries.

Prebisch also questioned the validity of the neo-classical theses on international factor flows and the assumed benefits from foreign direct investments for the recipient countries in all cases. According to him foreign capital "does not fulfil its function", fails to expand the domestic resources of investment, and to help in relieving, by export expansion and reduction of the import coefficient, the "external bottleneck" manifested in trade deficit[387]. His critique of the activity of foreign companies seems, however, reduced to the problem of a certain period of development, a "too early" point of time[388] (namely the time of the incidence of profit repatriation in excess of net capital inflow, and the time when national capital is not strong enough yet to compete the foreign giants).

It is by no means accidental that Prebisch's ideas have become theoretical arguments supporting the claim of the developing countries for a new international economic order in the 1970s.

By explaining, however, the mechanism of indirect income transfer and partly also the deterioration of the terms of trade by a general law of income elasticity of demand[389] (Engel's law) and by "technological disparity", Prebisch made not only

[386] *Prebisch, R.* (1959), quoted by *B. Higgins* (1959), pp. 261–262.

[387] *Prebisch, R.* (1972), p. 61.

[388] "The only trouble is that the Latin American countries have gradually approached and have actually reached it [namely the stage of remitting funds abroad in excess of the net capital inflow – T. Sz.] abnormally far ahead of the proper time." *Prebisch, R.* (1972), p. 13.

[389] "In the last instance, the pressure upon export prices and the corresponding tendency upwards deterioration in the terms of trade in the peripheral process of growth subject to the unrestricted play of market forces is the result of disparities in *income elasticity of demand* and the uneven form in which technical progress has spread into the world economy." *Prebisch, R.* (1959), quoted by *B. Higgins* (1959), p. 261. (My italics. – T. S.)

his concept vulnerable[390] but also weakened his criticism of the prevailing order of the world economy.

Prebisch formulated (in much the same way in this respect as *Samir Amin*) the deviation of international income distribution (and of "just prices") from productivity ratios as international differences in relative wage levels, which implies the implicit (or explicit) assumption of an international equalization of capital incomes, of the formation of an internationally average rate of profits. Whether this assumption is justified or not, two substantial questions arise: *First*, should the relative wage-level differences be regarded merely as a manifestation and consequence of international inequalities, or, instead, as the determining cause of the latter? *Second*, and besides the problem of international comparability of labour productivities and the related wage levels, are the aggregate macroeconomic (i.e. "national") productivity and income levels of a given country to be compared to those of others, or is it

- only the direct incomes of workers of the productive sphere related to their productivity, or
- the relative wages in the export branches, or
- only the productivity and wage levels of workers producing identical products,

which should be compared internationally?

If the international price and income ratios deviate from the productivity ratios because within the developing countries (in contrast to the technological homogeneity of the developed ones) *technological disparity* is the typical case which is due to the use, motivated by the over-supply of labour, of primitive technology in certain sectors of the economy, then it follows that the actual cause of the regular trade losses of the developing countries is to be looked for not in the better bargaining position of labour in the developed countries but rather in the distorted domestic structure of economy in the developing ones or perhaps in the international origin of the structural distortion of their economy.

---

[390] For example, *Gottfried Haberler* (1957) rejected the "Prebisch–Singer thesis" on the secular deterioration of the terms of trade for the developing countries, because in his view the Engel's law "cannot bear the heavy burden which is placed on it by the theory under view". For it does not follow from Engel's law that a rising income leads in every case to a relative decline in demand for every kind of food and for industrial raw materials. Haberler also doubted that income transfer would take place as a result of the monopolistic behaviour of trade unions and oligopolies in the developed industrial countries, increasing the gap between the prices of industrial commodities and primary products in favor of the former. See also in *Higgins, B.* (1959), pp. 373–374. It is to be added that the laws of the elasticity of demand prove not only inadequate to explain changes in terms of trade in the world market but also manifest themselves in a quite specific, often contradictory way in the case of some typical export products of the developing countries. For example, unlike basic foodstuffs, quoted in textbooks as characteristic instances of inelastic demand, several food exports of tropical countries are relatively luxury products (though not belonging to the "superior goods") whose price elasticity of demand, affected by the world-market shares and supply elasticities of other products, may vary in accordance to the direction of price changes. See also *Helleiner, G. K.* (1972).

If, however, the price and income proportions deviate from the productivity ratios because (as *Arghiri Emmanuel* assumed) the working class of the developed countries taking advantage of its stronger bargaining position, gains higher and regularly increasing wages, which in turn causes rising prices of the products of the developed countries and deterioration of the terms of trade for other countries, then it is logically superfluous to add it a reference to technological conditions or demand elasticities. *Prebisch* however, treated the wage differences sometimes as a cause, sometimes as a consequence.

In his view technological disparity prevents the rise of relative wages in the developing countries, whereas in the developed ones, under the circumstances of technological homogeneity, wage struggles prevent prices from falling in proportion to the increase in productivity. Therefore, what is behind the diverging prices in the world market is the divergent changes in wage levels, which in turn are influenced, by changes in productivity. Though wages are supposed to be affected by productivity through prices only, Prebisch in fact presupposes that prices are determined prior to wages.

Nevertheless Prebisch's theory, despite some inconsistencies, is one of the first and most outstanding critical revisions of the conventional theories of international economics as well as development economics.

## 3.2. Singer's critique of international specialization and technology transfer

Hans W. Singer's views on the unfavourable position of the non-industrialized countries in international trade appeared as roughly identical with those of Prebisch. It was rather in the emphasis he placed on the aspects investigated and the conclusions he made that they differed from the latter.

Singer investigated first of all the *international distribution of gains* from trade, specialization and technological progress.

In criticizing the prevailing international division of labour as being unfavourable for the developing countries[391], and also assessing the effects of foreign direct investments, he was quite definite in his earlier works[392], too.

He also pointed out (1964) that the benefits from technological progress were very unevenly distributed in world economy. While the advanced industrialized

[391] *Singer* noted (1964) that "the present structure of comparative advantages and endowments is not such that it should be considered as a permanent basis for a future international division of labor". (p. 172)

[392] See, first of all, *Singer, H. W.* (1964). It is to be noted that later on Singer revised his thesis by putting emphasis on the general weakness of the underdeveloped economy of the developing countries and on the harmful effects of the transfer of *inappropriate technologies* rather than on the type of specialization. For more details and a critique see *Szentes, T.* (1985).

countries "have had the best of two worlds, both as consumers of primary commodities and as producers of manufactured articles, whereas the underdeveloped countries had the worst of both worlds, as consumers of manufactures and as producers of raw materials". (p. 167)

The overspecialization of the developing countries in primary exports is, in his views, too, a factor that has retarded their development. Not only the deterioration of the terms of trade but also their fluctuation is harmful for these countries. The income losses resulting from a fall in primary products deprive them of capital badly needed for industrialization, while the rise in prices, though enabling them, in principle, to finance the import of capital goods necessary for industrialization, in fact diminishes the stimulus to industrialization and structural changes and induces, instead, the growth of import of consumer goods and luxuries.

Singer also pointed (1964) to the harmful, structure-distorting effects of foreign investments and to their *enclave* character. These investments "never became a part of the internal economic structure of those underdeveloped countries themselves, except in the purely geographical and physical sense... Economically they were really an outpost of the economies of the more developed investing countries". (p. 163) The flow of foreign investment capital into these countries, designed to make them the suppliers of primary products for the industrialized countries, has proved not only unable to ensure the expected advantages of investment and trade but also explicitly harmful.

"The specialization of underdeveloped countries on export of food and raw materials to industrialized countries, largely as a result of investment by the latter, has been unfortunate for the underdeveloped countries for two reasons: (1) it removed most of the secondary and cumulative effects of investment from the country in which the investment took place to the investing country; and (2) it diverted the underdeveloped countries into types of activities offering less scope for technical progress, internal and external economies taken by themselves."[393]

On the other hand, "the capital-exporting countries have received their repayment many times over in the following five forms: (1) possibility of building up exports of manufactures and thus transferring their population from low-productivity occupations to high-productivity occupations; (2) enjoyment of the internal economies of expanded manufacturing industries; (3) enjoyment of the general dynamic impulse radiating from industries on a progressive society; (4) enjoyment of the fruits of technical progress in primary production as main consumers of primary commodities; (5) enjoyment of a contribution from foreign consumers of manufactured articles."[394]

From all this Singer inferred the necessity and utmost importance of industrialization for the peripheral (developing) countries. A certain *revision* of his views

[393] *Singer, H. W.* (1964), p. 165.

[394] *Singer, H. W.* (1964), pp. 165, 168.

and a more radical character of critique in his later works[395] are presumably the result of his recognition that not all sorts of industrialization can ensure a way out of underdevelopment and dependence. The rather peculiar kind of industrialization which means only a "geographical shift" in the location of certain manufacturing plants, but not real development, results mostly in such import-substituting production whose social marginal productivity may be – according to him – zero or negative, and which further sharpens the problem of unemployment. In addition, from the point of view of the terms of trade, these new, simple manufactured products produced now in some developing countries share many of the characteristics, which Singer, like many others, attributed earlier to primary products only.

Consequently, Singer no longer remained satisfied with approaching the problem from the angle of different products and their characteristics. Instead of a distinction between primary products and manufactured goods, he came to approach the problem of inequalities in international economic relations on the basis of *different types of countries.* He stressed that *whatever* relationship, trade or other relations should be involved; it is always the investing developed country, which is the chief gainer of benefits.[396] The bargaining and business position of the developed and the developing countries is always unequal, and this fact has a bearing upon *all* their relations. The developed countries possess a more developed technology and a monopoly over technological development. They monopolize to a great extent even the channels of information needed for business negotiations.

When Singer moved from an investigation according to types of products to an analysis according to types of countries, he continued to emphasize, in compliance with his earlier views, that economists tended to become "slaves of the geographers" by accepting the fictions of country A and country B, beloved of the theory of economic advantages in textbooks. But it is in the context of the worldwide activity of transnational corporations that he increasingly emphasized the need for a *global approach*. In this connection he mentioned that "international" transfers within these corporations more and more supersede the real market operations, and that they have at their disposal wide possibilities of concealed income drains, since their centralized system of decision-making is assuming increasingly international dimensions.

However, Singer seems to have defined the ultimate source of the troubles in the "nature of modern technology". The development of the latter is concentrated

[395] See e.g. *Singer, H. W.* (1971).

[396] One may conclude therefrom that the great dependence on foreign trade and the harmful effects of the fluctuations in the terms of trade are the more or less general and natural consequences of underdevelopment, of a low national income, rather than resulting from a certain type of development distorted by external forces. *Singer* himself stated (1964): "Foreign trade tends to be proportionately most important when incomes are lowest... ...fluctuations in the volume and value of foreign trade tend to be proportionately more violent...and therefore *a fortiori* also more important in relation to national income." (p. 161)

in the developed countries and serves the solution of their own problems by methods appropriate to their circumstances and factor endowments". The transfer of "modern" (capital-intensive, raw-material- and labour-saving or substituting) technology may have a harmful effect on the recipient developing countries.

No doubt, the radical critique of the quality and inadequate nature of transferred technology calls attention to an acute problem which has a great importance, especially in the light of increasing (open) unemployment in most of these countries. However, this critique in itself, i.e. without a consideration of the sectoral orientation of foreign direct investments, without the discovery of the deeper socio-economic causes of both technological and sectoral preferences, as well as without the examination of the fundamental questions of ownership, control and of the "social orientation" of product, remains largely unfounded and may even lead to some false conclusions. Such as, for example, that modern capital-intensive technology from the developed countries has to be rejected in every respect and everywhere *in toto*, and the developing countries should instead change over to the general application of simpler, labour-intensive, capital-saving technology (incidentally originated also mostly from the developed countries). Or it may lead to the apparently correct and "revolutionary" conclusion that the developing countries should evolve a completely new technology of their own, independently of the achievements attained by science and technology in the developed countries. Both conclusions suggest a discontinuation of the transfer of technology from the developed countries, a sort of *technological delinking*.

## 3.3. The "backwash effect" of trade and cumulative disequalisation in Myrdal's theory

Gunnar Myrdal, the Swedish Nobel-laureate professor, sharing the Keynesian critical views on the spontaneity of the market economy, also pointed to the *dependent* position of the underdeveloped regions in the world economy, and explained underdevelopment of the developing countries in the context of the latter, as the consequence of colonization and/or the unequal relations of the international economy.

It sounded like an answer to the theories that looked for analogous "stages" of economic growth and perceived "underdevelopment" as an aboriginal state of backward societies or as a normal and universally experienced historical transition only from one stage to another, when Myrdal declared: "The now highly developed countries were able to develop as small islands in the large ocean of underdeveloped peoples, they could exploit them as sources of raw materials and markets for cheap industrial goods and could for this purpose even keep them under colonial domination."[397]

[397] Quoted from *Myrdal's* "Indian Economic Planning in its Broader Setting" by Ignacy Sachs. *Sachs, I.* (1964), p. 26.

Myrdal very unambiguously rejected the conventional belief in the mutually shared benefits from trade and in the export sector being always the "engine of growth". He emphasized the economic disadvantage that results, in general, for a dependent country from its relations with the metropolitan country, the adverse impact of the economic policy of the colonizing powers on the development of their colonies, the disequalising operation of the world economy, and the possible "backwash effects" of trade on economic development in the case of those dependent countries suffering regular deterioration of the terms of trade. His theoretical concept (1965) centred on the *cumulative* process, which he described as the general law of the motion of social systems.[398] If the cumulative process is not kept under control, it increases the inequalities in society and the economy. This cumulative process is primarily due to the free play of market forces. In his view the play of the forces in the market normally tends to increase, rather than to decrease, the inequalities between regions.

The increase of inequalities and the *backwash effects* of trade can only be compensated by the *spread effect,* or by the purposeful intervention and regulation on the part of the State. In a poor country, however, "the free play of the market forces will work more powerfully to create regional inequalities and to widen those which already exist", since the centrifugal force of economic expansion, the "spread effect", is weak.[399] In other words, the spontaneous motion of the international market economy generates cumulative, irreversible and disequalising effects just as well as by that of the economy of countries, particularly the less developed ones where neither an efficient state regulation nor strong spread effects can counteract them.

According to Myrdal (1965): "That there is a tendency inherent in the free play of market forces to create regional inequalities, and that this tendency becomes the more dominant the poorer a country is are two of the most important laws of economic underdevelopment and development under laissez faire." (p. 34)

It is worth noting that by this statement, referring only to the conditions of "laisser faire" and without clarifying which socio-economic system's laws are reflected by the spontaneity of the market, Myrdal may give the impression that the above "laws" had been working in all the backward societies since the very beginnings or have already ceased to operate in those developed economies under

[398] *Myrdal* stated (1965): "...in the normal case there is no such tendency towards automatic self-stabilization in the social system. The system is by itself not moving towards any sort of balance between forces, but is constantly on the move away from such a situation. In the normal case a change does not call forth countervailing changes but, instead, supporting changes, which move the system in the same direction as the first change but much further." (p. 13)

[399] "...the higher the level of economic development that a country has already attained, the stronger the spread effects will usually be. For a high average level of development is accompanied by improved transportation and communication higher levels of education, and a more dynamic communion of ideas and values-all of which tends to strengthen the forces for the centrifugal of economic expansion or to remove the obstacles for its operation." *Myrdal, G.* (1965), p. 34.

state control and regulation. It seems that the weakest point of his analysis is here, the point from which it would be easy to return by logical inference to the interpretation of underdevelopment *per se*, to its explanation by a new, specific sort of vicious circle.

If such a cumulative process, deriving from the free play of market forces and bringing about inequalities, was already at work in all backward countries prior to colonialism and penetration of foreign capital, then underdevelopment can hardly be attributed to the latter. Moreover, it may also follow, that the less developed a society was and the farther back we go in history, the more intensive this process was. Hence one may conclude that what can be witnessed on the level of international economy in regard to the increase of inequalities between individual countries seems to be only the secondary manifestation of what takes place primarily within the individual countries.[400] Both underdevelopment and its liquidation may thus appear to be natural phenomena: if the building up of inequalities in a single country is a natural process, independent of the social system, then the rise and growth of international inequalities is just as natural and independent. If it is natural that the poorer and the less developed a single country, the greater the inequalities in its society and economy, then the same is just as natural in the case of the whole world society as well. And finally: just as the inequalities fade out at a higher level of the development of a single country, so can the relative backwardness of the poor countries of the world fade out, too. But if this is true, then it is not the specific laws of the economy of the metropolitan countries which – by expanding their sphere of action over the world economy – penetrated into the backward countries from outside, leaving their mark on the whole socio-economic development of the latter, but rather some inherent, natural laws being in force in all the single backward countries, too, which rose to an international level. In other words, underdevelopment can be put down to basically internal causes, not to external ones related to colonialism.

As a matter of fact, *Myrdal* did not return to such conventional views explaining underdevelopment out of the context of the world economy. Instead, he specified (1965) the various factors of the cumulative process responsible for the inequalities that arise: "Colonialism meant primarily not only a strengthening of all the forces in markets which anyhow were working towards internal and international inequalities. It built itself into, and gave an extra impetus and a peculiar character to, the circular causation of the cumulative process." (p. 60) In addition to such a spontaneous effect, the purposeful policy of the colonial powers was also responsible for the arising pattern of production[401] in the underdeveloped countries since they "took special measures to hamper the growth of indigenous industry". "A metropolitan country had, of course, an interest in using the dependent country as a market for the products of its own manufacturing industry... Likewise, the

[400] In *Myrdal's* view (1965): "The discussion of the problem of regional inequalities within individual countries is relevant to the...analysis of international inequalities." He even noted: "Basically the weak spread effects as between countries are thus for the larger part only a reflection of the weak spread effects within the underdeveloped countries themselves caused by their low level of development attained." (pp. 50, 55)

[401] One may add that this pattern itself may spontaneously limit the strengthening of the "spread effects" since the rural sector does not produce the raw materials for the expanding industrial sector, nor does the expanding industrial sector demand the products (foodstuffs) of the rural sector.

metropolitan country had a clear and obvious interest in procuring primary goods from its dependent territory...thereby exploiting in its own interest local natural resources and indigenous cheap labour... A metropolitan country had also a self-evident interest in monopolizing the dependent country as far as possible for its own business interest, both as an export and an import market."[402] Thus Myrdal pointed to two characteristic features of the contemporary developing countries: their *dependence and exploitation*. He also noted that capital exports were directed to the foreign-controlled economic "enclaves" producing mainly primary products for export. These "enclaves" were isolated from the surrounding economy like alien bodies and tied directly to the economy of the metropolitan country.

As a result of the outward linkage and foreign control of the enclave sectors and owing to the appropriation and repatriation of profits by foreign companies, the net effect was to arrest the process of economic growth short of the point at which new demand in the non-agricultural sector and in particular demand for manufactured products of domestic industries would have been generated.

Thus, such an economic structure with enclaves provides the explanation of the narrowness of domestic market and the limited capacity of capital accumulation. It also explains, together with the "cheap labour policy" of the colonial powers and foreign companies, the labour problems of these countries. The economic relations of the enclave sectors with the indigenous population were restricted to the employment of unskilled labour only. The racial and cultural differences and the extremely low level of wages and living conditions have brought about as a natural consequence strict *segregation* even within the enclaves themselves.

So Myrdal also called attention to the *distortions* of the economic and social structure and ascribed the weakness of the "spread effect" and the resulting great intensity of the cumulative process increasing inequalities in underdeveloped countries, to this segregation, i.e. in the last instance to those distortions which, under colonial rule and as a result of the activity of foreign capital, took place in the economic and social structure of the developing countries. "Segregation is one of the main reasons" – according to him (1965) – "why the spread of expansionary momentum was extremely weak or altogether absent". Thus he corroborates – even if, in our view, at the cost of some inconsistencies – his stand that under colonialism a persistent tendency was at work, which could "not result in much economic development". (pp. 57–58)

Myrdal pointed out that the type of *specialization* of the developing countries, namely in the export of a few primary products, has not been able to lead to a more balanced economic growth extending over their economy as a whole and to a progressive process of development also starting in other sectors. Instead, it has served as a basis for "abortive development". Such a specialization has made their

402 *Myrdal, G.* (1965), p. 60.

economy extremely vulnerable to changes in the world market and has also resulted in one-sided orientation in trade relations. The latter has manifested in a sort of "enforced bilateralism" linking their economy directly with far-away metropolitan countries. Even their infrastructure, their transport and communication networks were built in accordance with such an "enforced bilateralism". The general deterioration and vigorous fluctuations in their terms of trade, which are also due to a low supply elasticity of primary products in their economy, cause serious losses for them.

## 3.4. The Lewis-thesis and the model of an economic system with unlimited supply of labour

Arthur Lewis, another Nobel-laureate representative of the new school of international economics, also recognized the unequal distribution of benefits from international trade between the developed and the developing countries[403] but approached the problem of the international transfer of incomes from an aspect which is related to the specific structure of the underdeveloped economy of the developing countries. Instead of sharing Prebisch's concept about a low income elasticity of demand for primary products in general and the Prebisch-Singer thesis of a regular deterioration of the terms of trade of the developing countries[404], he presented a model in which the mechanism of the transfer of benefits from the increase in productivity in the "modern" export sector of these countries is based on the unlimited supply of labour provided by their "traditional" rural sector. Insofar as labour supply is unlimited, and the marginal productivity of labour is negligible or even zero, the price of labour is adjusted to a subsistence minimum, because the income level determines the wage level of the "modern" sector, more precisely by the subsistence conditions of the "traditional" sector. Since productivity in the "traditional" sector consisting mostly of subsistence economies is low (while the rate of population growth is high), the subsistence level remains also low, thus exerting a downward pressure also upon the wage level in the "modern" sector.

With a certain simplification and in brief one might say that this model of an economy with "unlimited supply of labour" implies the following mechanism of income distribution and international exchange relations: Given a few developed countries with industrialized economy and a number of

403 In his view (1958), too: "Practically all the benefit of increasing efficiency in export industries goes to the foreign consumer". (p. 449)

404 After having worked out a statistical relationship between the prices of raw materials and the volume of manufacturing production, and another for prices of foodstuffs as a function of manufacturing production and the volume of food production, he made estimates on the improvement of the prices of primary products. See *Lewis, W. A.* (1952).

developing countries with underdeveloped, "dual" economy, which export each other industrial goods and primary products, respectively, but also producing foodstuffs for their own domestic consumption (not for exchange), the terms of trade for them cannot be determined simply by the different productivity levels of their respective export sectors (nor by the productivity levels of the "marginal industries" needed to absorb their surplus labour, as assumed by Prebisch) but by the very differences in the productivity of labour engaged in producing food in these countries. In other words, the low productivity in the agricultural food production of the developing countries, i.e. mostly in the subsistence economies of their "traditional" sector, predetermines a real outward transfer of income, a draining of benefits from any increase in productivity in their export sector, no matter what the technological level of the export sector is and whether the demand in the importing countries is elastic or not. This is so because in an underdeveloped, "dual" economy such as in the developing countries, irrespective of a rising productivity level in the export sector, the wage level of workers employed in the latter is always determined by the invariably low productivity level of the subsistence economies which supplies labour (with a nearly zero marginal productivity) in unlimited number to the "modern" export sector employing it at subsistence wage level.

If, as it is mostly assumed, the rates of profit are internationally equalized by the free flows of capital, which reduces the profit rate in the export sector to an average only, then the benefits from any increase in productivity in the export sector of the developing countries can be mostly or fully enjoyed by the importing countries, by their consumers.

From the assumption, however, that an increase in productivity in the export sector does not result in a rise of real wages does not follow that the consumers of the developed countries appropriate all the benefits. Even if we disregard the monopolistic obstacles to an international equalization of the profit rates and accept the assumption of a perfect mobility and competition of capital internationally, even then what follows is merely an equal(ized) but not a constant level of profit rates. In the case of an unchanged level (or a negligible increase only) of the real wages an increase in productivity in the export sector tends, first of all, to increase profits (first directly and, depending on market conditions, more or less proportionately the profits in the same sector only, as long as the profit rates are equalized, and then indirectly, by the resulting increase in the average rate of profits, everywhere). What may prevent (even in a longer run) an increase in productivity in the export sector from resulting in a rise either in the wage level or in the profit rate in the same sector cannot be but a particular structure of market and international division of labour and/or monopolistic conditions of international capital flows. Therefore, the latter should not be neglected even in the very mechanism of the Lewisian model.

From the logic of the model of the economies with unlimited supply of labour and its consequences it might appear (and in fact such conclusions have often been drawn) that it is, in the last analysis, the developing countries themselves that are responsible for the income transfer through international trade as everything hinges on the low productivity of their traditional sector. But Arthur Lewis clearly indicated (1958) the concrete historical context and reasons: "The fact that the wage level in the capitalist sector depends upon earnings in the subsistence sector is sometimes of immense political importance, since its effect is that capitalists have a direct interest in holding down the productivity of the subsistence workers... This is one of the worst features of imperialism. The imperialists invest capital and hire workers, it is to their advantage to keep wages low... In actual fact the record of every imperial power in Africa in modern times is one of impoverishing the subsistence economy, either by taking away the people's land, or by demanding forced labour in the capitalist sector, or by imposing taxes to drive people to work for capitalist employers." (pp. 409–410)

In explaining the international income transfer and increasing inequalities, Lewis also pointed to the *structural* problem of the developing countries, but (unlike Prebisch and some other scholars) not merely or primarily to the biased pattern of production with a certain type of export specialization. Instead, it is the *dual structure of the economy*, a sectoral dualism, i.e. the coexistence of the "traditional" sector of subsistence economies and the "modern" sector of export-oriented economies, which has been in the focus of his analysis. Thus Lewis placed the emphasis on the question: what socio-economic structure has come about and how in the developing countries as a result of the operation of the international economy, and how this structure has been linked with the development of the structure of the latter.

In supposing, however, an unlimited supply of labour from the "traditional" sector and a limited absorbing capacity of the "modern" sector, Lewis seems to have failed to take into account the shortage of skilled labour and the pressure of trade unions in the newly independent countries (which in several cases may have forced the governments and employers to pay higher wages even if without productivity increase). Lewis also presupposed an unlimited substitutability and mobility of labour (i.e. consisting of homogeneous units) which appears as an oversimplification even in the past case of the typical colonial sectors (plantations and mines) operated indeed by cheap unskilled labour and with low capital intensity, not to mention the more recent cases, namely of those manufacturing industries operating mainly with capital-intensive technology and demanding skilled labour, and in the light of the disintegration of the labour market.

It is clear enough that the conclusion, which can be drawn from the model of Lewis, is the necessity of *industrialization*. The mechanism described in it can only be brought to a stop if the expansion of the industrial sector in the developing countries is rapid enough to reduce overpopulation in the rural sector, raising thereby the man-hour productivity in that sector.

What can also be inferred from it is the requirement (in the shorter run) of technological development in the agrarian sector and thereby a gradual transformation of the dualistic economy. Unfortunately, however, Lewis left the question unanswered: what sort of industrialization and what way of integrating the dualistic economy may lead to the end of the income transfer described in his model.

This model is of course a simplified one. The mechanism of the relationship between the two sectors is far more complex, owing to the migrant labour system, than it is as actually presented in the model. This is also true for the role and operation of the modern sector. The income transfer is linked up with other factors, too, and the framework of the whole mechanism has much deeper roots than are suggested by the model. Despite all this, Lewis' model is a very valuable contribution as it throws light on many new aspects of the mechanism of dual economies and the international division of labour.

## 3.5. Balogh's thesis of unequal partners in the international economy

Sir Thomas Balogh, in opposition to the Marshallian concept and in agreement with Myrdal, stressed (1953) that the international economy is characterized by *irreversible* processes rather than spontaneous movements along some given, independent demand and supply curves or adjustments bringing about reversed motion along them. In his views those general doctrines and mathematical formulas derived from conventional analysis are mostly tautologies empty of empirical content. The demand and supply curves cannot be regarded as being independent of one another, and it is inadmissible to abstract from the income effects and particularly from the international distribution of incomes.

Balogh's main thesis is that in the international economy the partners are *not equal*, and thus the key question of analysis is: *Who is reaping the gain?* He pointed to that abstracting from the one-sided dominance of the stronger partner, and in general from the nature of the forces acting between nations of unequal strength is the weakness not only of the neoclassical but also of the Keynesian theory.

Differences in technological and economic development are closely related, according to Balogh, to national (state) boundaries. In international economic relations the partners are not micro-units competing atomistically (and perfectly) but national units competing oligopolistically, acting with due regard to the policy of each other. These national units show no similarity in their development, and even within these national entities the productive units are undergoing a rather discrepant development. In the industrialized countries large-scale units are predominant and prices are "administered". In the rest of the world primitive agriculture and handicraft have remained characteristic, with some enclaves of modern economies.

Trade between unequal partners has not a harmonizing or equalizing but a cumulatively disequalizing effect both on the international distribution of incomes as well as development resources and on the growth rates of national economies. Total world income may increase along with the steady growth of poverty in the poor areas. International trade tends to enhance the comparative growth of development resources of the stronger countries and their comparative advantages. Moreover, those comparative advantages based upon natural or factor endowments, which have been conventionally assumed to govern trade, are increasingly replaced by advantages derived from capital accumulation and technological progress.

Chronic unemployment, ignored in the neo-classical model, invalidates the "law of comparative costs" in that it reduces the marginal cost of social production to almost zero. Unemployment also affects the rate of capital accumulation and thereby again the changes in comparative costs. Consequently, as emphasized by Balogh, neither open nor disguised unemployment can be left out of consideration in the analysis of international trade and division of labour.

The different and cumulatively diverging patterns of factor endowments and factor incomes lead to increasing inequalities and further shifts in comparative advantages, too. Thus not only the rise of the division of labour between industrialized and primary-producing countries but also its further continuous changes takes place at the disadvantage of the latter. Such changes are initiated by the strong, rich, industrialized countries and are imposed by them upon the weak, poor, underdeveloped ones. In this way the latter are repeatedly forced to readjust their production pattern again and again to the changed conditions of international trade, which causes them not only a loss of output related to the former demand pattern but also a regularly suffered waste of human resources as well as a total loss of some capital goods not amortized yet, which were also adjusted to it. Consequently the benefits from trade and international division of labour are offset (or might be even more than offset) by losses arising from regular changes in the pattern of trade.

It follows, according to Balogh that *disequilibria* in the international economy cannot be looked upon simply as a consequence of some accidental, autonomous changes or monetary imbalances. It is, instead, of structural nature, behind which the interactions of the components of the international system as a whole should be revealed.

Contrary to Ohlin's and Samuelson's theses, the H–O–S theorem and the thesis about the natural direction of capital flows also resulting in factor price equalization, Balogh presented his thesis of a "perverse" mechanism, of an opposite direction of capital flows (namely towards the already developed capital-rich countries) leading to further increase in inequalities. In its explanation he referred to the internationally very uneven *technological progress*, which increases the marginal productivity of the factors of production. While in the developed countries the result is a higher level of factor prices and incomes, in the poor, technologically also less developed countries, owing not only to lower marginal productivities but also to unfavourable changes in their relative export prices, factor incomes remain unchanged or rather decline. Thus the relative scarcity of capital does not necessarily imply a higher marginal productivity and higher return to capital. Another reason of the above-mentioned "perverse" mechanism is the higher *risk* in the poor countries, which may follow (among other conditions) from those recurrent losses in capital and labour resources caused by the necessary readjustments to new changes in the pattern of trade, and which can also divert foreign capital investments away from these countries.

In Balogh's view the disequalizing and harmful effects of international trade and division of labour on the internal development of the poor, weaker countries are manifested also in the shifts in the pattern of income distribution within these countries in favour of the landowners (in the increase in land rents) as well as in the rise of conspicuous luxury of a small elite, which also reduces the investment capacities.

In the last resort, however, Balogh seems to have attributed the structural inequalities and disequilibria of the international economy to the pattern of technological progress, while the weaker position in the unequal relationship of partners mostly to the smaller size of those "national units"[405] in question. The perception of the economies of the dependent periphery as real "national units" appears, anyway, to contradict his very concept.

### 3.6. Furtado's concept of a dependent subsystem with "cultural dualism"

Celso Furtado has also dissociated from the conventional, mostly neoclassical views[406] when stressing that such assumptions as about the rational allocation of resources by market forces or about "sovereign" consumers and producers, and the assumed possibility to draw reciprocal demand and supply curves as independent from each other, etc. are totally unrealistic and inapplicable in the case of a *global* economic system which is, as in reality, characterized by the relations of dependence and dominance. The "optimum" (as assumed by neoclassical economists) for the allocation of resources in the underdeveloped economy of the developing countries is necessarily derived from the pattern of income distribution, which in turn is determined by the dependence process resulting in a persistent structural heterogeneity.

In Furtado's view (1971), it is inappropriate to regard the relations between the parts, i.e. the subsystems, of the global world-economic system as "international relations" in a conventional sense because the actual behaviour of the subsystems cannot be fully understood out of the context of the structure and functioning of the entire global system. (p. 1) Thus the theory of "underdevelopment" should essentially be a "theory of dependence". It can only be the lack of knowledge concerning the structure and functioning of the global system, which may prevent us from defining the "laws of dependence".

Since foreign companies have played a prominent role in the emergence, maintenance and intensification of economic dependence, Furtado critically investigated the impact particularly of the US companies, mainly vertically integrated super corporations and horizontal conglomerates, on the Latin American economies. He pointed to the exploitive nature and disintegrating effect of their activities which thereby set obstacles to a normal evolution of national capitalism. He emphasized that the reduction of the operation of the local entrepreneurs to that of subordinate, dependent ones has interrupted the process of the unfolding of a national capitalist class. In view of the contradiction between the reality of dependence relations and the ideas concerning the national economy as a unit of analysis, Furtado raised the question of whether it is reasonable at all and to what

[405] He noted (1963): "It is their smallness which is one – important – cause of their poverty." (p. 31)
[406] See e.g. *Furtado, C.* (1970), (1971), (1973), etc.

extent possible to apply the concept of "national economy" in the analysis of such economies.

While sharing Prebisch's, Singer's and others' view that the increase in average labour productivity in the export sector of the developing countries could not lead to an increase also in the wage level, Furtado pointed to that it had resulted instead in a rise in the income level of a narrow elite (including landowners, urban professional and bureaucratic strata) within these countries and a change in its lifestyle. This change, which, owing to the demonstration effects, is manifested in the inflow of consumer habits and foreign cultures from the developed countries and in their copying, has been determining the consumption and production patterns and the very path of development of these countries. A *cultural dualism* has developed, with a gap between the traditional cultures, lifestyle and consumption pattern, on the one hand, and the imported ones, on the other, which tends to be projected into the structure of the production system. As a consequence import substitution has evolved in the fields of manufacturing locally more or less the same products, which were previously imported to meet the demand of the ruling elite. And as the required quality of the products prescribes the same technology to adopt, the high capital intensity of the import-substituting industries prevents the diffusion of technological development to reach also the marginalized segments of the dependent economy. The high and rising capital coefficient does not correspond, anyway, to the actual factor endowments. It contributes to the diversion of productive investments away from the production of goods, which meet the basic needs of the masses of population. This explains why and how an increased rate of economic growth may have caused a lowering, even in absolute terms, of the living standard of the latter.

According to Furtado (1971), "dualism" is originally a socio-cultural phenomenon, which from the economic point of view appears as a discontinuity in the "surface" of demand. (p. 9) The link between the "periphery" and the "centre" of the global system, i.e. between the underdeveloped dependent subsystem of the developing countries and the dominant developed subsystem of the developed ones materializes primarily through a social "enclave": the local elite, which has become an integral part of the latter. Dependence of the periphery follows from the "modernization" process, i.e. from the adoption, by the local ruling elite, of an imported, more sophisticated pattern of consumption under cultural domination. This imported pattern of consumption leads to the import also of inappropriate technologies, which causes aggravating disequilibria in the allocation and use of the factors of production (manifested particularly in growing unemployment), and deepens the gap in income distribution and consumption level between the elite and the masses, between the urban minority and the rural majority.

*Furtado* also pointed to the increasing replacement of the market by internal transactions of the big multinational companies (namely by transfers between their own subsidiaries operated in different countries) and to the fact that the economic growth of the dependent subsystem is but a result of the activities of the latter, which control the diffusion of new technologies. Since these companies are the main actors of the "international" economy, of the global system, and their decision centre is outside the dependent subsystem, i.e. the economy of the developing countries, the development of the latter appears as "international" in a sense, as an expansion of multinational activities.

## 3.7. Perroux on dominance and dependence

Francois Perroux, the famous French scholar, may also be considered as one of the representatives of the theoretical stream[407] which rejected the conventional theories on the international economy[408]. He also paid primary attention to the phenomena of dominance in the world economy, to the dependent position of the less developed countries[409]. His critique of the Classical, Neo-Classical and even Keynesian views was motivated by the conviction that power relations, structural inequalities and asymmetric effects can by no means be disregarded, nor can those irreversible and cumulative processes observed in reality can simply be abstracted from in economic analysis.

*Perroux* (1979) stressed that the phenomena of external influence, dominance and domination could find no place in the conventional models of international trade, whether of the Ricardo–Hume or the Heckscher–Ohlin type. "The feature common to such models is that they are statically constructed, with perfect competition assumed, production factors supposedly homogeneous, technology being given and constant, and the substitutability of products supposedly faultless." As regards the Keynesian theory of macro-economic equilibrium and growth, Perroux pointed to its neglect also of "structures, historical dynamism and structural inequalities", as well as of "the phenomena blocking development and the economic handicaps of the developing countries". (pp. 25, 28–29, 54)

Perroux perceived the power relations not simply as relations between small and large countries but as being linked with dimensions determined by structural characteristics, i.e. as relations of unequal structures with different functions. He pointed out that the dominant economy exercises a determining impact on the dependent economies by the volume of investments exported and by the volume of products imported by it. The developed nation is able to impose its decision on

407 In view of Perroux's numerous publications, it is, of course, impossible to assess here all the valuable contributions he has made to the development of economics in general. As in the case of other famous scholars, we have to restrict our survey to a few important points only in his works.

408 See e.g. *Perroux F.* (1964), (1969), (1975), (1978).

409 *Perroux* (1979) actually distinguished between "influence" (as manifested e.g. in copied consumption pattern), "dominance" (which manifests itself in great inequalities in respect of possessing technological know how's and financial means), and "domination" (exerted by monopolistic market powers). (p. 53)

the less developed dependent economies by virtue of the effect of the nature of its activities, its economic dimension and bargaining power. The inequality of structures is the consequence of the active and often very deliberate policy and operation of the dominant partners.

Perroux stressed also the role of foreign capital investments in forming the dimensions and international power relations in general, and in forming or rather deforming the structure of the dependent countries, in "extroverting" their development, in creating a dualism of the enclave-type modern and the archaic sector in their economy, and in exposing them to a "process of decapitalization" (via regular income losses). He also pointed to the dangers involved in the activity of transnational companies rooted in the economy of rich, powerful nations.[410]

As a crucial requirement of the reforms in the international economy he suggested (1979) to replace "the logic of the economy of the market" by "the logic of the economy of solidarity". (p. 37)

## 3.8. Hirschman's critique of foreign direct investments

Even though Albert Hirschman's association with the Post-Keynesian Reformist school of international economics (marked primarily by Prebisch, Singer, Lewis and Myrdal) seems rather marginal, his critical approach to some of the most typical theses or premises of Neo-Classical economics, such as about the harmonious operation of international trade[411] and about the equalizing effect of international capital flows, appears to provide a sufficient justification for classifying him (and of course many other economists not mentioned here) as one of the followers of this critical stream. Owing to his early works on the problems of the underdeveloped economies (1945) and development strategy (1958), he has been considered, anyway, as one of the "pioneers" of development economics. He has also contributed to the critical analysis of the role of foreign direct investments in the underdeveloped economy of developing countries. He pointed to the link between the biased specialization of the latter and foreign direct investments.

In his views foreign capital investments may bring about not only the danger of economic exploitation and political influence but other, more concealed, harmful side effects as well. In a certain stage of economic development such as the one characterizing Latin America (where a national entrepreneurial stratum has already appeared but not gained sufficient strength yet to compete) these harmful side-effects, which are manifested in the oppression of local entrepreneurial qualities, in the ousting of many domestic producers from the local market and in the

[410] See *Perroux, F.* (1975) and (1978).

[411] Already in one of his early works (1945) *Hirschman* pointed to the role of power relations in international trade.

paralysing of the qualitative improvement of domestic factors of production, tend to outweigh the benefits from the inflow of foreign investment capital. As a consequence, conflicts of interest, clashes and tensions arise between the recipient and the capital exporting countries. When writing his study on such questions (1964) Hirschman primarily and concretely referred to the worsened relationship between US and some Latin American countries which that time seemed to result from the sensitive reaction of Latin American nationalism to the activity of US corporations.

As a solution for this problem Hirschman presented his idea of "divestment". In order to release such tensions Hirschman called on foreign (US) capital to "divest". Accordingly, a policy of a selective and gradual winding up of foreign private investments, which, in his views, would correspond also the interest of the USA, could be implemented by means of an international financial body monitoring that all the equity capital of foreign companies would, indeed, be gradually passed into national ownership. The deadline of such a divestment would also be fixed, by restricting foreign ownership to an agreed period of time, i.e. by defining its termination, or by setting a reasonable income ceiling for foreign companies. As it appears, Hirschman was seeking a peaceful compromise, a solution not only in the interest of the development of national capital in the developing countries concerned, but also in defence of the reputation of the USA and US companies as well. Such a concept, however well it reflected the political atmosphere that time, was not only obviously naive (namely in respect of its expectation regarding the response of the companies to it) but was also tinged with a kind of romanticism by the belief in the possibility to return to an era of international economy prior to international capital flows or perhaps to a kind of "harmony" that had prevailed before[412] in it.

Though Hirschman mostly reduced his critique to the "package" character of foreign capital investments[413] and to a certain transitional stage of economic development in which their unfavourable effects are stronger than the favourable ones, his views and new concepts seemed to have enriched the critical stream of theories in question.

## 3.9. Concluding remarks

Though obviously several other great names may be mentioned among those having revised, in one way or another, the conventional views on economic development (or underdevelopment as explained by internal conditions) and its interna-

[412] *Hirschman* admitted that he tried to recall the important mechanism of a smooth, gradual and peaceful divestment, which went lost in the transition from joint ventures to private investments.

[413] *A. K. Cairncross* (1962) also shared the opinion that from the point of view of the host countries the most unfavorable feature of the foreign-owned companies arising from the inflow of investment capital, is their capability to eliminate all bottlenecks at the same time.

tional context, i.e. concerning international economics, too, the above-discussed scholars represent fairly well a new theoretical stream both in development and international economics. As we have seen, when explaining contemporary underdevelopment by the unfavourable position of the developing countries in the international economy, by those harmful effects and losses regularly suffered by them in it, they have actually rejected or at least in regard to certain cases have questioned all the earlier theses on international trade, specialization, factor flows, foreign capital investments, etc. and on the assumed reversible processes ensuring automatic equilibrium, which had been shared by almost all the "schools" of economics before, and been replaced by others.

1. While national development had been traditionally (from Adam Smith through Marx to Rostow) assumed to go through identical "stages" of economic growth or the same "socio-economic formations", i.e. following a *unilinear path*, the above-discussed "school" has clearly pointed to the *divergence* in the path of economic development between the already developed, dominant countries and those being dependent on them.

2. While practically all the previous "schools" shared the view that *participation in international trade* and division of labour, specialization and export production bring about benefits, additional incomes and promote economic development in the case of all countries, the new "school" has not only denied the relevance of "comparative advantages" in the contemporary pattern of trade and their realization by the developing countries, but has also presented theses about the *backwash effect of trade*, disequalising specialization, regular deterioration of terms of trade, and transfer of benefits from primary exporting to industrial countries, etc.

3. While some kind of *automatic equilibrium mechanism* with a reversible nature of processes (whether resulting in perfect or only imperfect equilibrium, and at what social price) was assumed to operate in a spontaneously operating market economy by almost all the previous "schools" (including even the Marxian and the Keynesian), the Post-Keynesian Reformist theories have looked upon those processes disturbing equilibrium as basically irreversible, i.e. as leading to *cumulative disequilibria*.

4. While according to neoclassical economics the *"natural" direction* of international capital flows is from the relatively capital-rich, more developed countries to the capital-scarce underdeveloped ones, the new "school has pointed to an opposite, *"abnormal"* tendency.

5. While "mainstream" economics attributes foreign direct investments a generally *beneficial effect* for the host countries as helping them to release financial, trade, foreign exchange "gaps" or other (managerial, technological, etc.) bottlenecks, the new "school" has questioned the general validity of such assumptions and pointed to certain *adverse* effects of them, at least in some (transitional) cases.

6. While in the "mainstream" economics a harmonious operation of the international economy is assumed with *equal partners* and with the tendency of *equalization of income levels* (as following from trade and specialization, formulated in the

H–O–S thesis, or from the natural direction of international factor flows), the new "school" has emphasized that the partners are *unequal* in the international economy which involves dominance relations and cumulatively *disequalising* tendencies.

7. While the representatives of "mainstream" economics are more or less satisfied with the prevailing *international economic order*, its general rules and institutions, those of the new school have urged *reforms* in it in favour of the less-developed countries.

8. While almost all the representatives of the previous "schools" (including even those suggesting temporary exemption of the general rule of liberalism in the case of "infant industries" or economies) have advocated internationally free trade and factor mobility, and thus "mainstream" economics is unambiguously in favour of "open economy", i.e. of an unrestricted openness of all the national economies towards each other and the world economy, the new school has come up with the idea of "delinking", i.e. an economic policy for the developing countries to isolate themselves economically from the advanced part of the world, at least in case and as long as no appropriate reforms are implemented in the international order.

9. Finally and consequently, in opposition to those liberal views of the Classical and Neo-Classical economics advocating the spontaneous operation of the *market with its* "invisible hand" and without any state intervention, the representatives of the Post-Keynesian Reformist school have emphasized the need for regulating the operation of the market both on national and international level, and thus also the *role of the State* in the economy, the responsibility of governments for development, particularly in the case of developing countries which have to overcome economic underdevelopment and dependency[414].

## 4. Radical (new-left and neo-Marxist) views on the world economy, uneven development and economic systems

Marxism has, of course, always been critical versus the capitalist system of market economy and therefore also those theories describing it as the best and final variant of socio-economic systems. However, the followers of Marx have presented quite divergent views not only about the assumed final stages of capitalism and the ways of its projected "collapse" and transformation[415], but also on the effects of its worldwide expansion by means of colonialism and/or capital export. While many of them, even apart from the representatives of the so-called Marxism-Leninism,

[414] It is to be noted here that all this does not mean at all the acceptance by them of what *Deepak Lal* (1983) has called the "*Dirigiste Dogma*". (See it later!)

[415] Such as e.g. the concept of a gradual evolution, or that of a self-defeat, a sort of destruction by full accomplishment, or of a revolutionary action.

have emphasized the negative role only of colonialism, imperialism and foreign capital investments, namely in creating international relations of dependence and exploitation, thereby "blocking" the development of the dependent areas[416], some others have stressed also or only their positive role, namely in promoting the rise of national capitalism[417] and the expansion of the world capitalist system which necessarily precede and pave the way for a socialist transformation.

Anyway, the concept of dependence and foreign exploitation has got a not less important and deep root in Marxist theories than in the Post-Keynesian Reformist School. (This may be the reason why several Marxists are often grouped also into the "Latin American school of dependencia".) Since those Marxists radically attacking the prevailing world system and explaining the underdevelopment of the developing countries as the historical product of the latter, who have also criticised the so-called "existing socialism" in the Soviet bloc, thereby breaking with its official ideology ("Marxism–Leninism") too, have distinguished themselves or became labelled as "Neo-Marxists", it seems reasonable or at least practical to discuss their views under such a name.

Marxist traditions, as a rule, prescribe the belief in the worldwide solidarity of working classes, a belief which, as a matter of fact, has been shared both by communist and social-democratic parties, i.e. these two streams of the "old Left". When in the 1960s quite a number of Western intellectuals and particularly student politicians, as being disappointed not only by the so-called "existing socialism" but also by the policy of the "old Left" as a whole, explicitly and jointly turned against the latter, and expressed new, radical ideas, they appeared as representatives of a "New Left" which has questioned, among others, also the idea or the relevance of the international worker solidarity. In view of this, those radical theories of international and development economics sharing the critique of Marxism in regard to the prevailing world system and particularly the views of Neo-Marxists concerning international exploitation by trade relations and the resulting underdevelopment, who, unlike the latter, have obviously doubted and explicitly rejected the concept of international workers solidarity, seem to represent "new left" theories. Thus, in the following they will be discussed under this name.

## 4.1. Gunder Frank's radical views on the world system

When *Paul Streeten* (1985) confronted two theoretical streams of "development economics" according to his "Litmus test", namely according to their opposite answers to the question: "if the advanced countries were to sink under the sea tomorrow, would the developing countries (after a period of adjustment) be better or worse off" (pp. 239–240), he nominated *Andre Gunder Frank* as the primary representative of the "school" which rejects the "mutual interest" thesis and regards "underdevelop-

[416] See e.g. *Rodney, W.* (1974).
[417] See e.g. *Warren, B.* (1980).

ment" of the developing countries as a consequence of their dependent relationship with the developed ones. Though among the representatives of the "school" Streeten enumerated Prebisch, Singer, Myrdal, Hirschman, Perroux and Furtado together with such radical scholars as Samir Amin, Johan Galtung, etc., that is missed to distinguish between reformist and radical ones, Gunder Frank seems, indeed, to have marked by his provocative writings already in the 1960s[418] perhaps the most spectacular break and division line between conventional and critical views in general, and, also to represent a certain "link" (if by no means between reformists and radicals, then) at least between the "Latin American school of dependencia" (including both reformists and radicals) and all those other theoretical streams criticizing the global system of capitalism and explaining "underdevelopment" as the product of the latter.

Frank, the "renegade from Chicago economics"[419], actually turned against not only those conventional theories he had to study before and confront with reality, but also and increasingly all the reformist views which expressed a belief in the possibility of making better the existing global system of capitalism or even in the opportunity of developing an alternative system in its parts. Paradoxically, this No.1 representative of the "school of dependencia" went so far with his radicalism as criticizing the theory of dependence, too, and the concept of "delinking" as well. Though in general his critical remarks mostly contain very realistic and relevant considerations (moreover, very often such new concepts as being rejected from him but later accepted as others'[420]), it is likely due to his negative and rather pessimistic attitude (his "catastrophism"[421]) that he has remained or felt to be a "lonely warrior".

*Frank* raised first serious doubts about the conventional perceptions of economic "efficiency", social or international "equity" and economic "development" in general (by posing the questions: "efficiency" from whose point of view?; "equity" among unequals?!; "economic development" for whom?), but finally also redefined the concept of "development" by denying the appropriateness of the conventional unit of analysis, namely the "nation", or the country, and by interpreting it as a process taking place only at world level, if at all, without final or even intermediary "stages".

Accordingly, "if 'development' has any operational sense at all, it is not in reference to a country or (often non) nation state. Instead, the only meaningful development is of the world economy and society at one level and for much smaller social groups or individuals at another level." Furthermore: "there is only world development. ...development is a process, and not a state or stage. ...by this definition, no country, nation state, economy, or people would be developed". ...notions of 'national development' are the result of a myopic illusion. ...any discreet national or other sub-global development is now even more impossible than before. No independent national state development is possible at all."[422]

While the questions concerning the social content and direction of development are absolutely relevant (and coming to the fore again, at least in rhetoric, at inter-

---

418 See e.g. *Frank, A. G.* (1963), (1966) and (1967).

419 In his autobiographical essay (1991) he himself recalls this label received from a colleague, who refers to his Ph.D. studies (including a course of Milton Friedman) at the University of Chicago, this centre of neoliberal "mainstream" economics.

420 Such as, for example, the concept of "human capital", "total productivity", or even the "world-system approach".

421 *Frank, A. G.* (1991), p. 26.

422 *Frank, A. G.* (1991), pp. 10, 54–55, 58.

national organizations and to some extent even in "mainstream" literature, too), and a global approach in comparative studies of development has not only been appropriate since long time ago, but in view of accelerating globalisation has become an imperative necessity nowadays, all these do not justify the negation of the process of development taking also place within any country surrounded by existing state borders, which even if primarily determined by global forces or by no means independent of the global process, is distinguishable from and comparable with that of other countries. It is one thing to question the "independence" of "national state development" in an interdependent, increasingly globalized world, and it is to be another thing to deny its very existence. Frank, like Wallerstein in this respect, seems to suggest an absolute and exclusive application of the *world-system approach.*

One of the first attacks of Frank (1963) against conventional views was addressed to the myth of "feudalism" in Latin America, which was also related to the refusal of the concept of "dualism", i.e. of the coexistence of two distinctive sectors in the economy and society in the developing countries. However convincing and illuminating his argumentation against the former was indeed, in the light, particularly, of the export-orientation of the private plantations operated by "feudal" employment methods, his denial of "dualism" (like that of Amin's) can be verified but with regard to one variant only of its possible interpretations. Namely to the one, introduced by *Boeke* and spread in literature, which has presented the two sectors, a "modern" and a genuinely "traditional" one, as simply existing side by side without forming a functionally intertwined system of a disintegrated economy. What he described as "internal colonialism" is actually the very picture of an economy consisting of a dominant, relatively modern, outward-oriented, capital-centred sector and another, subordinated, more backward and exploited one, i.e. a disintegrated, "dualistic" economy with a certain functional relationship between the two sectors. The very fact that under the impact of the dominant "modern" sector the "traditional" one cannot remain of course intact and operate like before the rise or penetration from outside of the former, implies "only" that *no* genuine traditional societies and economies have survived, but does not mean the complete disappearance and absorption of the quasi-"traditional" sector in an integrated unit.

In his view (1991) the mere existence of "separate sectors in a 'dual' economy or society" (p. 19) does not specify whether they are isolated from each other or functionally interlinked! Frank, like Amin, attacked the word, instead of a content. His term "internal colonialism", insofar as it refers to an external force in the rise of such a disintegrated system, may mislead even more than the term "dualism", because apart from external force it may have resulted, as it did in several cases, from an internal choice and policy (in Frank's words: of a kind of "lumpen-development"[423])

[423] *Frank, A. G.* (1972).

of the domestic ruling stratum. However, Frank really assumed and has not changed this view even later (1991) that "capitalism inevitably takes some colonial/imperial form" (p. 25), which means a form of non-economic violence, i.e. sheer force – contrary to the *par excellence* capitalist method of appropriation of the surplus through the market, and to the historical collapse of colonial empires. If this "colonial/imperial form" includes, as it appears in Frank's writings, "neocolonialism" as a basically economic method of domination over *de jure* independent countries, then the role in the choice or maintenance of peripheral development (in the "development of underdevelopment") of the internal ruling class can hardly be underestimated by referring to external forces.

Insofar as Frank defines (1991) "the development of underdevelopment... within a single world capitalist system" exclusively "as a result of dependence" (p. 24), he practically seems to exclude the case when such a "development of underdevelopment" as well as dependence itself have followed from a free choice of the local ruling stratum which responded to new challenges and opportunities by developing an export-oriented primary producing enclave sector of the economy, employing (as a "second edition of serfdom", as in the independent countries of the 17–18th century Eastern Europe, or "of slavery" as in the post-independent countries in Latin America and before the Civil War even in the USA, respectively) not freed or only semi-proletarian labour force: serfs, slaves or migrant workers coming from the half-destroyed, half-preserved "traditional" sector.

Frank fully rejected (1991) the conventional views in development and international economics which equate *development* with measurable[424] economic growth, the "social" aspect of growth with "modernization" modelled on the Western societies, its "political" aspect with "freedom" of Western style (pp. 14–15), the global system of the capitalist *world economy* with the aggregate of independent national economies cooperating with each other, and the various parts, segments or sub-systems of the world economy with separate units representing different, comparable *economic systems*.

With regard to "development economics", which at the end of the Second World War "came into their own" with a "new development thinking" arising as "the child of neo-imperialism and neo-colonialism" (op. cit., p. 14), Frank primarily attacked (1967a) those sociological explanations of "underdevelopment" blaming the obsolete patterns of attitudes and motivations in the "backward", alleged to be aboriginal traditional societies[425] and also the "stages" theory of W. W. Rostow which by presenting foreign penetration as a necessary or favourable condi-

[424] In his autobiography (1991) he referred to the motto engraved on the cornerstone of the University of Chicago: "Science is Measurement", as symbolizing this conventional approach.

[425] We have already referred to his critique on the concepts of Everett E. Hagen, David McClelland and Bert F. Hoselitz.

tion for "take off" in the underdeveloped countries[426], strongly supported the "diffusionist approach", i.e. the idea that "the West diffuses knowledge, skills, organization, values, technology and capital to a poor nation, until, overtime, its society, culture and personnel become variants of that which made the Atlantic cummunity economically successful".

But as having observed or assumed quite a similar approach in all the main theories of development economics he criticized (1991) not only the development theory derived from Neo-Classical and Monetarist economics or conventional sociological and historical schools, but also the Keynesian and (Post-Keynesian) "structuralist", Latin American theories as well as the "orthodox Marxist" concepts because "they all shared the view that underdevelopment was original or traditional". (pp. 22–23) Though, as he admits (1991), in the 1960s and early 1970s he "still welcomed any proposed reforms, but considered them insufficient", and together with R. M. Marini, T. dos Santos and others shared the views, quite similar to those of Prebisch, Myrdal and other reformists, of the "school of dependencia", later on he questioned the "usefulness of dependence theory", at least "for political reason", and the assumed possibility of reforming the prevailing international economic order or implementing in reality such naive concepts as "Basic Needs" or "Growth with Distribution". (pp. 45–46) Moreover, in view of the global crisis of the world economy in the 1970s (leading to deepening debt crisis) and the response to it by monetarist and neoclassical "supply side reactionary theory", Frank moved on, *beyond the theory of dependence,* to the concept of "accumulation in the world system" (1978a and 1978b) reflecting a new development thinking, and suggesting an analysis of the world crisis of capital accumulation. He declared (1991) not only liberal, Keynesian and structural development theories to be in crisis but also "neo-liberalism, post-Keynesianism, and neo-structuralism" having become "totally irrelevant and bankrupt for development policy" (pp. 48–49).

In view of the failure of those developing countries following the policy of "gradual de-linking and self-reliance along the 'non-capitalist road'" in the 1950s and 1960s, of the "blind alley" where "socialist orientation" has led several countries, and first of the increasing "reincorporation of the socialist countries in the capitalist world economy" and then, finally, of the crisis and collapse of "existing socialism", Frank also revised his views about *socialism, delinking and development.*

[426] *Frank* (1991) noted: "characteristic of Rostow's second stage is the penetration of underdeveloped countries by influences created abroad – mostly in the developed countries – and diffused to the underdeveloped ones, where they destroy traditionalism and simultaneously create the preconditions that will lead to the subsequent take-off in the third stage". And: "Yet these same metropolitan conditions and influences...have not brought about economic development or even led to a take-off into development in a single one of the '75 countries'". (p. 315)

He wrote (1988), already before the collapse of the "socialist systems" in Eastern Europe: "...the socialist countries have failed to establish a division of labour and market as a viable to the world capitalist one..." "...really existing socialism offers scant realistic hopes *alternative* for any real alternative solution to Third World problems today. The socialist economies offer the Third World no alternative escape". (pp. 324, 327)

Finally, after so many disappointments, Frank came to the almost nihilist, pessimistic conclusion that all the previously assumed alternative roads of development, including "socialism" and "de-linking", all the suggested models are inadequate, all hopes to make progress towards equity in economic development are in fact illusions.

By referring to that the "political crisis of military and authoritarian rule in the Third World and the crisis of socialism (and Marxism) in the East increasingly opened peoples' eyes", he stated (1991) that "none of the now available 'models' of development are adequate for the present, let alone for the future. ...This inadequacy characterizes the magic of the world and domestic market, Western top down political democracy, eastern to down economic democracy, and recent attempts at self-reliant national state de-linking. However hopes are illusory for a capitalist new international economic order, or for the non-existent and ever less available alternative socialist division of labour / international economic order. Nor does anything else on the horizon offer most of the population in much of this Third World any chance or hope for equity or efficiency in economic development." He also stressed that in the contemporary world economy "de-linking is impossible...contrary to my own previous view". (pp. 58, 61–62)

However, in search for an *alternative,* Frank redefined the concept of development, not only in the already mentioned sense of regarding it as a "process" on a world level, but also in respect of replacing the concept of the "man made development" by that of a "progressive change in the whole gender structure of society itself", of shifting the "emphasis from social factors in or for economic development to social and economic development, especially for women and their children", and for "the ethnic, national, linguistic, racial, social, sectoral, age, vocational and other minorities" which are all subject to inequity. Contrary to his pessimism, *Frank* welcomes (1991) the "new" social movements of participatory civil democracy, such as the "growing peace and human rights movements..., with notable women's leadership and participation" which are "important (today and tomorrow perhaps the most important) agents of social transformation", making increasing contribution to a real development, and "redefine democracy from traditional state political and economic democracy to civil democracy in civil society". (pp. 62–67) This is a new concept what he calls "alternative self-development" and also a new approach to system-transformation as well.

What he, as an auto-critique, designated as the weakness of dependence theory, namely that "dependence theory...never answered the question of how to eliminate real dependence and how to pursue the chimera of non- or in-dependent growth", seems to apply to this new concept of "alternative self-development, too, which is based on the social movements of civil society, unless those new opportunities and challenges opening the room for an increasing role of such civil movements and also mobilizing them, are also revealed, which may result perhaps from new information and communication technologies and from the growing pressure of the desperate poor.

On the other hand, the new emphasis Frank put on the need to avoid the danger of an "involuntary de-linking" and marginalisation (which may result in a "new dualism", namely "between those who do and those who cannot participate in a world wide division of labour"[427]), and also the threats of nuclear war and environmental degradation, and also on the need for participatory democracy and respect of human rights everywhere, definitely mark a turn in Frank's views away from the excessively radical or pessimistic conclusions towards more realistic and somehow less pessimistic ones.

## 4.2. Emmanuel's theory of "trade imperialism"

The concept of an unequal exchange between the developing and the developed countries, which, as we have seen, appeared in the writings of Prebisch, Myrdal, Singer, Lewis and others, too, has gained perhaps the most sophisticated theoretical explanation in the famous and widely debated[428] book of Arghiri Emmanuel (1972a).

Emmanuel, rejecting Lenin's perception of imperialism[429] as a "myth of investment imperialism", elabourated his own theory of what he called "trade imperialism" which implies a permanent practice of unequal exchange in international trade, and in which the relations of dominance and exploitation are just as well manifested as the causes of underdevelopment are rooted.

By identifying the export of capital with the transfer of money in general, with a transfer of purchasing power, moreover, with the export of "unpaid goods"[430], and

[427] This is quite the opposite to Frank's earlier conclusion about de-linking as an alternative, and also to the rejection of "dualism". Frank distinguishes this "new dualism" from the one he has been rejecting by that in the case of the former "the separation comes *after* the contact", while the latter implies the assumption of the separate existence of sectors "before 'modernization' would join them". Needless to repeat that such an interpretation of the "old" concept of dualism is but one of the variants only. But Frank's perception of the "new dualism" and of its distinctive nature refers to "involuntary de-linking" only, moreover to separation after the contact became useless (in Franks' words: "the lemon is discarded after squeezing it dry"), instead of a dual system with separate but functionally interlinked sectors. *Frank, A. G.* (1991), p. 59.

[428] Among the many scholars who responded to Emmanuel's theorem of unequal exchange, the following may be mentioned, for example: Bettelheim, C. (1972), *Amin, S.* (1973), *Saigal, J. C.* (1973), *Anderson, J. O.* (1976), *Braun, O.* (1977), *Diouf, M.* (1977), *Bacha, E. L.* (1978), *Sau, R.* (1978), *Bose, A.* (1979), *Dandekar, V. M.* (1980), *Sau, R.* (1978), *Bose, A.* (1979), *Evans, D.* (1984), (1984), *Szentes, T.* (1985), *Raffer, K.* (1987).

[429] See it in: *Lenin, V. I.* (1967).

[430] Such a perception of capital export (which seems to recall a kind of physiocratic approach) can hardly be correct even in the case of loan capital, since such a lending of purchasing power results not only in payments of debt service but in most cases also in well-paid, if not over-paid exports of goods.

mixing up, when comparing the inward and outward capital flows, all the outflows of money from the developing countries (whether they are repatriated incomes of foreign capital invested earlier, or real capital exports), thereby also neglecting the structural effects of earlier investments, Emmanuel come to the conclusion: first, that the net balance of capital flows was showing a regular plus for the developed and a minus for the developing countries, which means that the benefits from foreign investments were mostly enjoyed by the developed host countries; and second, that foreign investments has not been playing a significant role in the economy of the developing countries, unfortunately for them[431]. In his view (1972b), the export of investment capital to the underdeveloped economies has not hindered their development, just the contrary, "it is the interruption of these exports and the reversal of the flows that is detrimental to the underdeveloped countries." (p. 56) Emmanuel attributed the inflow of foreign investment capital to the less-developed economies an internationally equalizing effect on development and income levels[432] and found a certain correlation, supported by some international statistics, between the amount of imported capital and per capita GDP, from which he concluded (1976) that "either there is no causal link between foreign capital and underdevelopment" or it is an opposite relationship, in the sense that underdevelopment is due just to the absence of foreign capital. (p. 760)

It is to be noted that it is one thing to say that foreign capital may promote development in the host countries, and that the export of capital may exert, to a certain extent, an impeding effect on the development of the capital exporter, and quite a different thing to interpret this development-promoting, respectively development-slowing effect in an absolute sense, and to infer therefrom the tendency of levelling up. But Emmanuel's over-simplifying statement appears as an anti-thesis of the vulgar concept of "imperialism" and domination of foreign capital which sees only and exclusively a negative phenomenon in the inflow of foreign capital and looks upon underdevelopment as an absolute lack or blockage of development caused by the latter. Such a vulgar view is of course easy to refute, just like those vulgar critiques on the transnational companies considering them as the "evils" of the world economy to be "exorcized". A refusal, however, of such views does not necessarily mean the acceptance of an opposite over-simplification.[433]

---

[431] To prove it, *Emmanuel* presented data on the ratio of foreign capital assets to national income. Such a ratio, however, can hardly show the structural effects and the real controlling power of foreign companies in the economies concerned as not indicating what positions they actually have in which sectors of the economy, nor revealing the intertwining of foreign and national capitals.

[432] In this context *Emmanuel* referred (1972b), in agreement, to Lenin according to whom the export of capital accelerates the development of capitalism in capital-importing countries, while it may, to a certain extent, tend to arrest development in capital-exporting ones. (note 29)

[433] Perhaps this was somehow overlooked by *Robert Cox* (1979) when stating that my views on the "multis", i.e. the TNCs did not substantially differ from Emmanuel's, simply because I had not joined the "exorcists". See Szentes, T. (1981).

Though Emmanuel admitted (1972b) that the allocation of foreign capital investments is not necessarily the best, the most favourable one for the national economy of the developing countries from the point of view of their specialization, but if it is so then it is due to the peculiar structure of their economy and the narrowness of their domestic market. (pp. 56–57) The question of how the peculiar structure of economy and the obstacles to the expansion of the domestic market may have followed from the "allocation of foreign capital" is left unanswered as it does not fit into his interpretation of causality, nor into his concept divorcing market relations from production relations.

Owing to an economistic approach to the issue of foreign capital investments and international capital flows in general, Emmanuel's concept makes completely disappear the historical turning-point, manifested in the large-scale separation of capital ownership from the functioning of capital (by the spread of joint stock companies) making capital export a decisive factor shaping the pattern of international economic relations as well as the economic structure of the recipient countries[434].

In Emmanuels' view (1972a) "second imperialism (i.e. the one after 1875 – T. Sz.) does not seem to have differed at all from the first one [i.e. mercantile colonialism – T. S.] except that instead of sending one's customers to settle in conquered countries one now tried to turn the existing population into customers". (p. 186)

Emmanuel flatly rejected all the criticism levelled against the multinational companies. That some of the critiques are really devoid of a realistic approach and conjure up the atmosphere of some ritual ceremonies of exorcism, hardly justifies his view which completely excludes from his analysis the problem of the consequences of absentee ownership, of a possible foreign control over the national economy, etc. Thereby his view seems to conflict even with his own national–economic approach in the analysis of unequal exchange. He also rejected the charge of "enclave investments" by reasoning that if something is assumed to be an enclave, then it cannot be considered harmful to its environment, or if a harmful effect is attributed to a foreign investment then it cannot be accused of being an enclave. He also denied (1976) that the usual charge put forward against the multinational companies' price formation, namely their transfer pricing with under- or over-invoicing practices, can be justified, and recalled *Marx* who emphasized that "exploitation is not cheating but the inevitable effect of the mechanics of the system" (p. 768) The question of how this practice of price formation has stemmed from the very mechanism of the system and the fact that "cheating",

[434] The same approach seems to have influenced (among others) *Immanuel Wallerstein* (1977), too, who conceives of "the circuit of capital as a chain of economic activities" only, thereby excluding, or making secondary, the question of ownership relations materialized in capital investments, and neglects the problem of the "nationality" of capital assets by stating that "individual capitalist firms are juridically quartered in particular states", with the conclusion that "there is no good reason to believe that such chains were more likely to cross state boundaries after 1870 than before." (p. 8)

though not covering or explaining "exploitation", does not deny it either, remain outside Emmanuel's line of thought. In his defence of the multinational companies he went (1976) so far as to deny (disregarding any related surveys and the lessons drawn from case studies) that as far as the balance of power between these companies and the local government is concerned, the latter is in a stronger position, and "there had never been a case where an MNC had won conflict against a sovereign government of any sort of size". (note 34, p. 772)

As regards *trade imperialism,* Emmanuel distinguished two forms of "unequal exchange": one which he called the "primary" and "apparent" form of "non-equivalence" arises, in his opinion, when the "rates of surplus value"[435] are internationally equal and the "organic compositions of capital"[436] are different. This form is the consequence, internationally, of the transformation of "values"[437] into "prices of production"[438] (similar to that stemming from such a transformation inside the national economies).

The other, which he called "non-equivalence in the strict sense", arises from international differences in wage rates, more precisely from the lasting divergence between the rates of surplus value owing to the international immobility of labour, along with the international equalization of the rates of profit under the circumstances of international capital mobility.

Emmanuel found a difference not only of degree but also of quality between these two forms. Though admitting that the former, the first form of unequal exchange is also accompanied by a transfer of "surplus value", yet he did not define it as a real variant of internationally unequal exchange simply because it has taken place within the national economies, too. Thus, according to him, no country can complain about a phenomenon in the international economy if the same appears also inside its own economy. Moreover, while differences in the "organic composition of capital" stem from the specific technical features of the different branches of production, and are inevitable even under perfect competition, differences in wage rates result from imperfect competition and the limited mobility of labour in the international economy. Hence, the differences in the "organic composition of capital" are due to objective circumstances of production, the disparity in wage rates is the consequence of *institutional* factors. These two cases have to be distinguished, according to Emmanuel (1972a), also from the

435 That is the ratio of wages to "surplus value" (which is the difference between the total "new value" produced by labor and that part of it received by the latter in the form of wage).

436 The "organic composition of capital" refers to the proportion of "constant capital" (i.e. the costs of raw material, energy, machinery, etc. produced in an earlier process of production) and "variable capital" (representing the cost of labor which creates "new value" in the given production process).

437 In a Marxian sense: the "socially necessary amount of labor needed for the reproduction" of the products in question.

438 In Marxian sense: the sum of "constant" plus "variable capital" plus "average profit" (instead of the actually created "surplus value").

point of view of the optimization of the international division of labour and the terms of trade, because an international division of labour conditioned by international differences in wage rates is necessarily sub-optimal as "there is no necessary correspondence between the natural and objective advantages of each country and a location of branches of production that is determined by differences in wages". (p. 164) And the long-term deterioration of the terms of trade can hardly be accounted for by differences in the "organic composition of capital" because in that case the country with a lower "organic composition of capital" will receive less only in terms of "value" and not in terms of the quantity of "use values", while in the case of wage-level differences the country with lower wage level will receive less in "use values", too.

Thus, in Emmanuel's view, international differences in the "organic composition of capital"[439] do not play a direct and substantial role in the inequality of international exchange. (Their role can be indirect only, insofar as they influence economic and social development, thereby the development of the wage rates.) In the final analysis, the ultimate cause, according to Emmanuel, of the inequalities of international exchange (and even of the unequal development of countries in the world economy) is the international disparity of wages.

The empirical fact of international differences in wage rates, and particularly such problems as resulting from the phenomenon of "run-away industries" or from the competition of low wage-cost products in the world market and the evidence of the protectionist behaviour of certain Western trade unions have induced, as a matter of fact, several other scholars, too, to assign a specific role to wage differences in the analysis of international economic relations. But it was Emmanuel who went as far as to build the price theory as a whole upon wage rate as an "independent variable".

The basic idea underlying Emmanuel's theory is that the possibility of unequal exchange is created and maintained by the international immobility of labour, which means that unequal exchange would hardly exist if the international mobility of capital was supplemented by the free and unlimited international mobility of labour, too. (Such a view is quite consonant with the assumptions of the Neo-Classical economics.)

As we have seen, the representatives of the Post-Keynesian Reformist "school" have expressed quite an opposite view by emphasizing that the spontaneous operation of the market with the free flows of products and factors of production in the international economy does not necessarily lead to equalization, and that the direction of factor flows does not necessarily coincide with the "natural" direction assumed by the Neo-Classical theory.

[439] *Emmanuel* revised (1972a) *Marx* even in the interpretation of the "organic composition of capital" by applying a combined coefficient *K* (namely the sum of "constant" and "variable capital" weighted by their respective turnover rates), in which "the distinction between past labor and new labor, constant capital consumed and variable capital, here ceases to be significant", and thus the result of surplus-value production too loses its relation with its source proper". (p. 58)

Emmanuel's assumption contradicts also the Marxian concept, even if the differences in the "organic composition of capital" are disregarded (and thereby also the international redistribution of the "surplus values" according to the equalization of profit rates), because the formal "equivalence" in international exchange, i.e. equivalence in the Marxian terms of the "socially" (in this case "globally") necessary amount of "universal human labour" implies, given differences in labour quality and productivity in individual nations, the exchange of different amounts of individual (national) labour.

In explaining his theory of unequal exchange Emmanuel produced, on the one hand, a certain *price theory* which seems to be based on the Marxian category of the "price of production" but cut from its background of labour-value theory, and, on the other, a peculiar *wage theory*, which seems also linked with a Marxian concept, but substantially differing in content from the latter.

Despite the reference to the Marxian "law of value" and the use of Marxian terminology, Emmanuel defined *prices* in the last analysis as the sum of incomes of the owners of factors of production.

*Emmanuel* gave up completely the Marxian postulate of deriving the prices of production as the centre of market price formation from values as a more abstract category, and of keeping their sum equal in the analysis of the "transformation" of the latter to the former. He interpreted such a theoretical transformation as a historical replacement of value by price of production marking a new, different system of price formation, and thereby cutting the link between these two abstract categories defined the price of production as determined by its "components": the factor incomes. In other words, he did not only substitute wage, i.e. income of the labourer or wage cost, for the performance of a certain amount of labour socially needed in reproduction, but also attributed a role, along with labour, to other factors of production, such as particularly capital, too, in price formation. According to him the common denominator, "the intermediate common property which enables us to quantify the sum of the factors" is the "claim" of the owners of factors of production to have a share in the incomes resulting from production.

The determination of prices and of incomes on a subjective basis, and the subjective evaluation by the owners of the factors of production of their own sacrifice have been quite old ideas, compared with which the technical term "claim" appeared only new.

But Emmanuel obviously wished (1972a) to distinguish his theory from such concepts and to reconcile it with some "objective" interpretation of the price formation. He thought to resolve the problem which follows from the indeterminacy, on a subjective basis, of prices or price proportions, and from the mutual irreducibility of the factors of production (concretely: labour and capital), by stating that the price-of-production formula is constructed not in terms of labour and capital as irreducible things in themselves but "in wages actually paid (variable capital) and profit, things that are perfectly reducible to one another, as shares in a given entity, the economic product of society". (p. 400) Since these two shares (of course, within the given sum) are inversely proportional to each other, there is an inevitable antagonism between the two classes. This implies that the "class conflict" is confined merely to the domain of income distribution, just like in Ricardo's view, and contrary to the Marxian concept of "class antagonism" rooted basically in the social relations of production. Emmanuel has also presented a Ricardian assumption about the possibility of changes, necessarily in opposite direction only (like in a zero-sum game) in wages and profits, as a thesis of Marx's wage and profit theory[440], despite the fact that in analysing the dynamics of reproduction and the process of capital accumulation, *Marx* pointed to the possibility (moreover, probability) of a parallel growth of the real wages and real profits, along with an assumed regular shift in favour of the latter.

---

[440] According to *Emmanuel* (1972a): "if wages are not 'given', if they do not constitute an independent variable, then the problem of defining value on an objectivist basis is insoluble." (p. 403)

According to *Emmanuel* (1972a) "exchange value is...the sum of the workers' wages, plus the profit on the means of labour, plus the profit on wages". (p. 16) These components, in the last analysis, are nothing but the expressions of the "claims" of the owners of the factors of production to a part of the social product.[441] The Marxian concept of "socially necessary labour" is, in his opinion, not valid without this "claim" as a common denominator because the reduction of complex and concrete labour units to simple and abstract labour units and their quantification is possible only by "a 'claim' to an undifferentiated, quantifiable, and thereby abstract share of the social product". (pp. 323–330)

The determination of shares on the basis of "claims" and the perception of total social value or aggregate total price as a sum of "claims" imply not only renouncing any objective determinacy but also a conceptual contradiction in Emmanuel's theory.

The "claim" of the capitalist entrepreneur would be formed according to his/her capital inputs, i.e. the individual cost level, but under the conditions of competition would be realized only according to the social average. And since the "claims" of the capitalists *vis-à-vis* the "claims" of the workers as "claims" of different classes, established on quite different grounds, cannot be deduced from the process of exchange but only from the social relations of production, Emmanuel identified the latter with the "relations between claims on the social product". The private ownership over the means of production is, in his views, nothing else but a "claim on the product of someone else's labour", more exactly, the most developed "legal" form, which is "merely the capitalization of a primary and pre-existent claim to income". The other, earlier forms of this claim (such as e.g. taxes) led to "the idea of the first kind of private ownership". Consequently, "it is not the appropriation of the means of production that is the cause, and the rewarding of the factors that is the effect...but the existence of the factors as claims that leads to the idea of appropriation, as the legal form assumed by the rewarding of the factor". Exploitation "begins not with the creation of surplus value but with its *appropriation*", which is *"a matter of exchange,* not of production... Between the capitalist and the worker *it begins with the contract for the purchase of labour power...* After the contract comes the act of production... During this act nothing happens by way of exploitation...The exploitation engendered by the preliminary contract of employment is in suspension, kept on ice... Finally comes the phase of circulation and the exchange of product, in the course of which not only the 'subject', the agent of exploitation change, since the surplus value produced is partly transferred from one 'subject' to another...but also the volume of exploitation changes, since the total amount of surplus value is modified by the prices at which the workers' consumer goods will be sold. (Op. cit., pp. 324, 327–328)

Hence, at the beginning there were the "claims" which must be conceived of as *a priori* given factors of production. The formal development and the creation of the most developed legal form of these "claims" engender private ownership as the "claim to someone else's labour". The appropriation of alien labour begins on the market, where the worker sells his labour power, and is determined by the market where prices are formed. Why a capitalist has a "claim" to others' labour and why the worker has none, and how this "claim" of the capitalist has taken a "legal form" in the private ownership over means of production, remains unanswered in such a logic, moreover cannot be answered at all with such an approach. For, accordingly, capitalists had to exist before capitalist ownership itself came into existence, and, even before workers deprived of means of production existed at all. The ahistorical approach of Emmanuel turns, in such a way, his logic upside down.

---

[441] "A factor is an established claim to a primary share in the product." Op. cit. p. 32.

Since he identified the factors determining prices as "claims" on part of social product, it logically follows to regard both indirect taxes[442] and land rents[443] as price-forming elements, as components of prices, just as profits and wages. Moreover, since the feature common to all these "factors" can only be their "extra economic", *institutional* origin, their root in some sort of *monopoly*, therefore every monopoly can be, in Emmanuel's view, conceived of, in the last analysis, as a price-forming component element.[444]

Emmanuel regarded the main deviation of his own price theory from the Neo-Classical ones in that in his concept, quite inconsistently, the rate of reward of the principal factor of production, namely *labour*, i.e. its wage, is an "independent variable", while the Neo-Classical concepts treat factor prices just as the prices of other commodities, i.e. as "dependent variables", determined, on the one hand, by consumer demand, and, on the other, by the marginal productivity of the factors of production. No doubt, the indication of an "independent variable" held to be an ultimate determinant, as against the interdependent components of prices and versus the neo-Classical concept of prices and incomes being mutually determined by each other, appears as a view considerably differing from the latter and seeking, indeed, causal relationship. A statement that labour as a commodity is of a peculiar nature different from other commodities, and as an "independent variable" differs also from other factors of production, may, indeed, be a distinctive feature versus Neo-Classical concepts, but obviously contradicts the concept of prices determined by factor incomes (and "claims") as components.

Thus, Emmanuel not remains consistent even with his own concept. On the one hand, and in consonance with the above concept of wage being the "independent variable" he interpreted profit (like Ricardo) as a residue, i.e. a dependent variable, which as a part, inversely proportional to the share of wages, of the joint product valued at an already existing price, remains after the deduction of the wage cost in the income distribution process, while, on the other hand, defined the formation of prices as a dependent variable, i.e. as being determined by wages, profits and other factor incomes alike, which therefore are all supposed to be independent variables.

Confusing the natural-material aspect of the process of reproduction in the economy with its social aspect, *Emmanuel* looked upon capital as a physical element (factor) of production only, and conceptualised profit as a result of the natural time factor of production. According to him (1972a) social total costs of production include not only labour, present and past, and goods offered by nature freely though in limited quantities, but also "something that corresponds to capital: the employment of accumulation

---

[442] As he wrote (1972a): "Indirect taxes fulfill the conditions of my definition of a factor, since they undeniably constitute an established claim to a primary [?!] share in the economic product of society." (p. 228)

[443] He also stated (1972a): "Absolute rent depends solely on the monopoly of landownership... and does not result from prices but, on the contrary, modifies them... Absolute rent...is undeniably a factor in prices." (pp. 216–217, 222)

[444] In his view (1972a) "Every monopoly, whether agricultural or industrial, engenders a twofold rent, absolute and differential... A monopoly is not obliged to regulate its prices by the price of production or the value of the least productive enterprise in the branch." (p. 222) This means that any monopoly takes part in price formation by the amount of rent "claimed" by it, independently of the "price of production" or "value".

funds..., that is, time". What distinguishes a capitalist society from any other society is "the *appropriation* of this factor by a certain social group, the owners of the means of production". (pp. 412–413 and 399–400) Accordingly, appropriation in a capitalist society is possible only in regard to the time factor, and it does not mean the appropriation of the product of labour.

*Emmanuel* categorically rejected the idea that "total social product is the product of human labour" (not only in the sense that the production of use values, i.e. the physical process of production, always presupposes, in addition to human live labour, other factors of production, too, but also as regards "exchange values" which cannot be reduced to one single, common standard of measurement independent of subjective human evaluation). In his opinion, the idea that the product belongs to the worker, is merely an ethical but not a scientific proposition.

Emmanuel seems to have identified (1972a) the specific nature of labour as a commodity (unlike Marx) not in that the "consumption" of its "use value" in the process of production is a source of "new value" (and if exceeding its own value, the source of surplus value), but that labour "is the only commodity the production of which necessitates *only* raw materials", "only use values" (but no direct labour), and this "is intimately and closely bound up with a certain quantity of use values, a certain basket of goods". (p. 108)

In explaining (1972a) why wages behave as an "independent variable", Emmanuel in his *wage theory* declared the "determination of wages by prices" an "absurd" assumption (pp. 64–65), and instead, in agreement with Marx who defined wages as determined by the "value of labour power", he also stressed the role, besides the "biological factors" also of the sociological, "moral and historical factors" in the determination of wages. But, unlike Marx, he divorced these "historical and moral elements" to such an extent from those objective conditions of the reproduction of labour power determined by the development of the productive forces, i.e. from the changing costs of its reproduction and from the changing social needs of the working class as well as from the changes in the quality of labour, conditioned and required also by the development of the productive forces, that finally all what has remained of the "moral and historical factors" seems to be reduced to some "moral constraints upon the labour market" only which have changed during history. Accordingly, the economic struggle of the workers for higher wages is so much abstracted from the very mechanism of the operation of a capitalist market economy (from what Marx called the "capitalist mode of production" with the process of surplus-value production) and thus from the development of its productive forces (labour productivity and technology development), too, that it is simply reduced to the manifestation of an *institutional force* (of a monopolistic nature) "preventing the free play of the market". In other words, the determination of the "value of labour power" is traced back, in this way, to two "extra economic factors": the ethical, moral factor which originates in the "psychological constitution" of man, and the institutional factor which is represented by the trade unions.

Though Emmanuel did not deny (1972a) that an increase in labour productivity is a means to increase surplus value insofar as it decreases the "necessary time" to be spent on the production of goods needed to reproduce labour power, benefiting thereby all capitalists, but at the same time he categorically declared that (apart from the political consequences of the demonstration effect on the behaviour of the trade unions) the development of the productive forces had in itself absolutely no effect on the value of labour power. (pp. 335 and 418–419)

Emmanuel seems to have completely ignored the relationship, both on social and firm level, between the rise in the productivity of labour and the changes in wage rates. Since, however, the latter depend on the price level of those goods (and services) needed for the reproduction of labour power, and a change in labour productivity in those branches of economy producing such goods (and services) normally brings about changes in their prices, too, wages cannot be indifferent to changes in labour productivities on social, i.e. macro-economic level. (In other words, the increase in productivity in branches in which the means of the "necessary" consumption of the workers are produced, brings about a decline, *ceteris paribus*, in the "value" of labour power, without necessarily causing a fall in the consumption of workers.) As regards firm level, since a capitalist entrepreneur who by means of increased labour productivity can press the cost of own products (or services) below the average cost level of the branch of economy concerned, may gain "extra profit" (until, of course, as a result of other entrepreneurs following this example the average cost also falls to the same or even a lower level), the method of applying wage incentives to increase productivity, i.e. of paying higher than average wages for more efficient work, can establish an even more direct relationship, on microeconomic, i.e. on firm level, between changes in wages and changes in labour productivity. Insofar as competition itself compels other entrepreneurs to apply the same method, this relationship on microlevel may also lead to or reinforce that on macrolevel.

If, in spite of all these Emmanuel denied any effect of the development of the productive forces on wages, then we can only infer there from that either (a) he rejected the Marxian "law of value" *in toto,* i.e. in relation to both the "value" of labour power and the price formation of commodities, or, at least, (b) he divorced the process of the production of "surplus value" from that shaping the level of wages and profits. As a matter of fact, he seems to have done both.

As a conclusion from his above-described price theory (in which the "prices of production", though they are, as sums, equally formed by their components, namely the factor incomes or rather the "claims on a part of social product", depend primarily on wages as the "independent variable") and as a conclusion also from his wage theory (according to which it is the institutional power which primarily determines the wage level and its changes), Emmanuel explained "unequal international exchange" by the growing international wage differences between developed and underdeveloped countries, on the one hand, and by the resulting divergences in changes of the prices of their products, on the other. He therefore traced back (1972a), in the final analysis, the international exploitation by "unequal exchange" to one single factor: the "monopoly position of the working class" of the developed countries, to that "quasi-rent", that wage differential which results from the monopolistic power of their organized labour, the trade unions, under the conditions of international immobility of labour: "Wages are the cause and external exploitation the effect"... "the initiative is held, consciously or unconsciously, by the working class; it is their demands that become the driving force of the world economic antagonism, and international workers' solidarity becomes an historical misconcept." (pp. 421 and 189)

What follows, in this logic and according to Emmanuel, is that the *workers* of the developed countries have been (by their organized wage struggle) not only the real cause of unequal exchange[445], but they are, in fact, also the only real *beneficiaries* of

[445] *K. Raffer* (1987) noted that "Emmanuel's assumption..., that wages are independent variables has an unpleasant result: Northern workers cannot reduce wages in the South. Otherwise *not wages* but *only Northern wages* would be an independent variable." (p. 36)

that, while all the consumers , i.e. the entire society of the developing countries appear to be the losers of unequal exchange. It also follows that the fundamental contradiction of "world capitalism" is between the working class of the rich, developed countries and the society as a whole of the poor, developing ones. (The capitalists of the former can hardly gain from unequal exchange, because of the equalization of profit rates, and also because wage increases may reduce their profits.)

Emmanuel actually identified the *degree* of international exploitation (by unequal exchange) with the actual difference between the wage level in the developed and that in the underdeveloped countries[446]. This means, indeed, that differences in their labour productivity have no role at all in wage differences. In order to prove that the higher wage level in the advanced countries has nothing to do with their higher labour productivity (but it results merely from the strength of organized labour), Emmanuel presented an argument according to which it is the underdeveloped countries rather than the developed ones, which have a higher productivity in their export sectors. Even apart from the fact that a comparison of labour productivities in the export sectors only, instead of that of the social (average macro-economic) productivity levels, may not only be misleading, but (insofar as specific products are involved) also meaningless or depending on the prices, such a statement should seriously be doubted. Emmanuel obviously ignored also the quantitative difference in the "value-creating" capacity between qualitatively different, namely complex or simple, skilled or unskilled labour. He considered the possibility of differences only in the intensity of work as manifested also internationally, but without associating such differences with technological development, either.

Emmanuel did not only deny that wage increases might have been caused also by productivity increases in the developed countries and thus by their development of productive forces, but came to a diametrically opposite conclusion as regards cause–effect relationship. While, in his view, the *underdevelopment* of the developing countries is the historical product of "trade imperialism", i.e. of unequal exchange caused by the lasting and growing international wage differences, the very *development of the advanced countries* is also the historical product not only of the regular benefits from this unequal exchange but also of its basic, final cause, namely the rise of wages[447] induced by an institutional factor. Accordingly, the historical turning

[446] The conclusion that the higher wage level of the working class in the developed countries is on the whole the result of unequal international exchange necessarily involves a tautology since unequal exchange itself has already been described as the outcome of the increase, a sort of "take off" of wages.

[447] *Kunnibert Raffer* (1987) pointed to an "important function of wages in Emmanuel's approach" which "lies in the correlation between high wages and development." It means that wages "act 'directly – that is by mere operation of the law of value – upon economic factors, by determining the necessity for an intensification of the organic composition of capital and by encouraging investment through the expansion of market' (Emmanuel, 1972b, p. 124, stressed in original)." *Raffer* added: "Emmanuel is in fact quite a strong Keynesian as far as effective demand is concerned." (p. 37)

point for economic development has been the "take-off" of wages, i.e. their departure from a (Ricardian) subsistence minimum level, owing to the rise, for some reasons, of new demands and "claims" of the working class and its organized trade unions.

Though Emmanuel referred to an "interaction" of the changes in wages and economic development, yet he invariably ascribed a development-promoting effect to wage rises[448], flatly denied that the latter resulted from economic development. In his views, once a country through some historical accident, e.g. "additional needs" caused by a harsher climate, had passed the "take-off" of wages and got ahead in development, it has made other countries pay for its higher wage level through unequal exchange. From that point onward the impoverishment of one country becomes an increasing function of the enrichment of the former, and vice versa. In the country benefiting from unequal exchange new forms of consumption spread everywhere and create fresh needs. This is accompanied by the expansion of the market, which attracts foreign capital speeding up development. In other words, *uneven development* between the "centre" and the "periphery" of the world economy is not the cause but the effect of the unequal exchange between them[449], which arises from the divergent trends of the changes in wage level.

The role of *capital* in uneven development and international "exploitation" is confined in Emmanuel's theory to that, as a result of its international mobility, the rates of profits are internationally equalized.[450] If labour were also mobile internationally, the international disparity of wages could also disappear.

Though Emmanuel pointed to the *specific nature of the products* exported by the

---

[448] According to *Emmanuel* (1972a): while "the development of the forces of production can never go very far in a capitalist country unless institutional factors cause wages to take off from the subsistence level, ...there is not a single example where high wages have not led to economic development". Moreover, "even when, for one reason or another, economic development precedes an increase in wages, this increase takes place only *after* an institutional factor has intervened". (p. 128)

[449] The "same cause", wrote *Emmanuel* (1972a), "that is, the disparity between wage levels that produces unequal exchange and thereby, indirectly, a certain unevenness of development through the draining off of part of the surplus value available for accumulation, also produces, directly and independently of this draining-off process, uneven development itself, as a whole...". (p. 372)

[450] This means that for *Emmanuel* the nature and origin of foreign capital, the complexity of motivations of capital export, the pattern of capital flows and their effect on the international allocation of resources, on the patterns of international division of labor, ownership and control relations, and on the very structure of production of the recipient countries, etc. do not matter at all. Thus, he also left out of consideration the differences between capital inflows coupled with the immigration of the owners and those with owners' absenteeism, i.e. FDIs manifesting the separation of the ownership and the operation of capital. As a matter of fact, Emmanuel made exactly that factor appear neutral, which has been primarily forming the world economy and its asymmetric structure since the late 19th century. As regards the motivations of capital export. Emmanuel simplified them to one, namely to find marketing facilities. Accordingly, capital tends always to move towards high-wage countries where the domestic market is more extensive.

developing countries, i.e. to the specialization of the "periphery" in branches of production different from those of the "centre", he did not attach it any significance either from the point of view of the terms of trade in the world market or of national development. In his view, it would be useless for the low-wage developing countries to change over to the production of those products by the export of which the rich developed countries enjoy the benefits of unequal exchange, since the latter would always be in a position to give up their earlier specialization and to specialize in manufacturing such new products as would save them from the competition of low-wage countries. Moreover, instead of aspiring to the higher vertical links of production, they might return even to those branches of production, which the low-wage countries have already given up.[451] It is therefore absolutely indifferent *per se* whether a high-wage country specializes in growing bananas, roses, etc. or in producing machineries[452]. Owing to the limited mobility of labour and to the lack of competition of the export products of the developed high-wage countries and those of the low-wage developing countries, their national wage levels permanently diverge from one another, irrespective of their levels of labour productivity. Their different production structures and the non-competitive, specific character of their export products[453], too, result from the disparity of wage levels.

As regards *development policy*, the logical conclusion which can be drawn from such a train of thought by the low-wage developing countries is *either* to increase the wage rates in order to achieve (?!) higher export prices *or* to cut the trade relations with, i.e. to delink from the developed countries in order to avoid unequal exchange. However humanitarian and democratic the former alternative might at first sight appear, the illusion it creates[454] (the more so as the economic precondi-

[451] In his view (1972a), a rich, high-wage country, like Britain, "whatever she makes and whatever she sells, she must realize the advantage that comes to her from unequal exchange and that corresponds to the difference...in wages". (pp. 145–146)

[452] According to *Emmanuel* (1972a) the "capacity to absorb technical progress is fundamentally the same in the primary sector as in the others". Moreover, "...if exchange is assumed to be equal, it is hard to see why a country that produced nothing but roses...should not be as highly developed and as happy as any other". (pp. 139, 148 360–362)

[453] Among others, it seems a conspicuous weakness of Emmanuel's theory that thus the very phenomenon of unequal exchange is confined merely to the exchange of non-competitive, specific products.

[454] *Samir Amin* (1973) called the idea of an "artificial" increase in wages "naive", and rejected the "myth" that "development" could be ensured in that way. (pp. 66–67) *Emmanuel* was also aware of the difficulty to raise immediately the wage level in underdeveloped countries. Therefore he recommended (1972a) for the meantime two other solutions to reduce foreign exploitation by trade: the taxation of exports that would pass that part of the surplus value which was formerly transferred abroad into the hands of the State, and diversification with import substitution, both leading in the direction of autarky. (pp. 267–268) Needless to say that taxing the export may have a counterproductive effect, and that import substitution *per se* can hardly be a lasting solution.

tions of wage increase, namely productivity growth is left out of consideration) is so obvious that Emmanuel seems to have preferred the latter, i.e. a policy of *delinking*[455] (at least as long as the wage level of the developing countries does not catch up with that of the developed ones, or a revolt of the South, of the developing countries does not force the North, the group of developed countries to change the terms of trade).

## 4.3. An alternative variant: Braun's concept of unequal exchange

Oscar Braun did not only make critical comments on Emmanuel's theory[456] in the wide international debate on it, but also presented (1977) an alternative variant of the concept of unequal exchange. The latter, however, shows a similar approach and theoretically a sort of eclectic nature[457].

Braun rejected the idea that prices are determined by incomes (primarily by wages as "independent variables") and also the view on a world capitalist system in which international exploitation by trade is caused by the wage struggle of the workers' organizations of the developed countries. At the same time he also assumed a cause–effect, function-like relationship between prices and wages, but in an opposite direction (opposite to what Emmanuel assumed), namely by regarding *prices* as "independent variables" which determine incomes.

Such a reversal of the assumed causal relationship follows, perhaps, from the consideration of the fact that in the contemporary world market most of the prices are indeed manipulated, "administered", dictated or heavily influenced by transnational companies and the strongest States. Braun pointed to that the "imperialist" countries through the manipulation of import duties and other trade restrictions can determine the price at which dependent countries sell their products. In other words, it is primarily the "imperialist" trade policy, which

455 As *Emmanuel*, himself, concluded (1972a): "The choice is thus between unequal exchange and autarky." (p. 146) Nevertheless, *Kunibert Raffer* doubted (1987) that Emmanuel really suggested a policy of delinking: "The solution Emmanuel proposes is not a de-linking of the South which some authors wrongly assume (cf. Samuelson, 1976, p. 107; Jungfer, 1982, p. 14, who thinks this to be the necessary conclusion of the 'doctrine of Unequal Exchange), but a retention of 'excess surplus value' (Emmanuel, p. 233) in the periphery." In Raffer's view, "Emmanuel...mainly recommends the use of 'other factors', i.e. rent or indirect taxes on exports." (p. 45)

456 According to *Braun* (1977) Emmanuel's theory "fails to explain why there is no massive flow of capital to dependent countries for the manufacture at economic costs of commodities for export to world markets" (i.e. why capital does not make use of the advantages of low wage costs), and also to answer the question "why the ruling classes of the dependent countries do not deliberately increase wages or export prices". (p. 51)

457 *Braun* (1977) admitted to have attempted "to embody some of the conceptual and methodological tools developed by the economists of the so-called 'Cambridge School' in the classical and modern Marxist theory of imperialism". (p. X)

is responsible for the losses regularly suffered by the dependent developing countries[458].

The departure point in Braun's explanation of unequal exchange seems to be his observation that the dependent developing countries are compelled to import certain *specific* products, mostly means of production, which they are not in a position to produce locally. To finance their imports they have to produce and export more of their own commodities when the prices of the latter are relatively falling. The deterioration of their terms of trade implies a reduction of incomes and their balance of payments develops a *"structural deficit"* which, as a consequence of trade barriers, becomes the main obstacle to their economic development.[459]

When dealing with the problem of the *wage level* and the *over-supply of labour*, *Braun* explained (1977) "the constant reproduction of the reserve army" of unemployed labour by the slow development of productive forces and "the slow growth of the exports", leaving thereby the distorted structure of the economy out of consideration, and rejecting the idea of dualism. In his view, "full employment requires a minimum availability of foreign exchange... If the total available foreign currency is inferior to this minimum *quantum*, the level of income must be reduced, and consequently the level of employment. ...The natural growth rate in the supply of labour power is, to a large extent, determined autonomously by the population growth rate." (p. 56)

The serious problem of *foreign-exchange shortage* and (ceteris paribus) the growth-inhibiting effect of the limited import capacity can, of course, hardly be questioned. But to place the balance-of-payments deficit (and the balance-of-trade deficit which, according to Braun, determines the former in a linear way) and thus the inadequacy of export earnings caused by trade restrictions in the very centre of the mechanism explaining the entire system of underdevelopment with

[458] This concept of "trade imperialism", strangely enough, involves somehow the Classical-Neoclassical illusion of liberalism, namely by assuming that without trade barriers applied by the developed countries and in the case of perfectly free international trade exchange were equal and no "exploitation" could take place. *Braun* (1977) even explicitly stated that "This potential exploitation [namely the one through unequal exchange – T. Sz.] becomes a reality thanks to restrictions on trade." (p. 63)

[459] While, on the one hand, *Braun* (1977) defined the "main barrier" to the development of dependent countries (i.e. the ultimate cause of underdevelopment) in the "structural deficit" of the balance of payments (caused, in his view, by *trade restrictions*) "preventing them from breaking off their relations of dependence with the capitalist centers", while elsewhere, on the other hand, he pointed out that "the restrictions on trade as well as the general problems which the dependent countries must face to increase their exports may be explained by the *unequal development of their productive forces* and by the *social relations of production* which the unequal development has given rise to". (pp. 69 and 75) [My italics – T. Sz.] If what is involved here only a demonstration of the dialectical cause-effect relationship, the reaction of the effects, we should have no objection to such statements. But what would be needed in such a case is first to clarify the relation of historical causality (with specifying the historical time and space) and the politico-economic content and the place of the decisive link within the present-day complexity of the cause–effect relations. Or else we inevitably get involved in a vicious circle of tautology.

chronic unemployment and international exploitation, is, indeed, a misleading simplification. That unemployment can exist even in the case of a lasting balance-of-payments surplus has been evidenced by a number of concrete cases in reality.

Unlike Emmanuel, Braun undoubtedly stressed the specificity of the products exchanged between developed and developing countries, thereby the unequal *structure* of international division of labour, too. This specificity appears, according to him, on the side of the imports of the developing countries, which is the consequence of the incapability of the latter to produce capital goods, i.e. of the monopoly position of the developed countries over certain industries. "Economic dependence" thus primarily implies the inability of countries to produce autonomously the capital goods they need, since some of the latter or other countries monopolize their certain input elements.

If, however, as a result of such a dependence the developing countries cannot, indeed, reduce their imports, while the developed ones are able to do so, then the question arises why the former produce products for which they have to rely on imports, or why they do not change over to the local production of the capital goods they need. *Braun* actually attributed the forcing need for import to such circumstances, on the one hand, as existing also in other, developed countries, too (e.g. the lack of certain raw materials, the high cost of production making uneconomic some of the industries, etc.), and, on the other, to such phenomena (e.g. the shortage of skilled labour or the lack of adequately qualified specialists, the insufficient supply of investment capital or weak investment incentives, the availability only through import of the required technological know-how's, the heavy bias of the elite consumption for imported luxuries, etc.) as being consequences rather than causes of economic underdevelopment.

While Braun wished to explain the system of "imperialist exploitation" as a whole, he practically interpreted unequal exchange so narrowly (by reducing it to the case of trade restrictions and balance-of-payments deficit, and by assuming the specificity of imports only) that his concept fails to include even other forms of unequal exchange.[460]

The elimination of the labour theory of value, the neglect of the increase in labour productivity and the concentration on the phenomena of "circulation", i.e. on trade relations only, instead of analysing the social relations of production in general and the asymmetrical international relations of capital ownership, etc. inevitably bring Braun's theory close to Emmanuel's despite all the critique Braun addressed to the latter.

Though Braun rejected the concept making the working class of the developed countries responsible for "imperialism" and "exploitation", the logic of his train of

[460] Though *Braun* (1977) actually mentioned (p. 97) some other forms of international exploitation (such as a direct extraction of surplus value by repatriation of profit and interest), but in the final analysis he practically reduced the mechanism of international exploitation and also uneven development to unequal exchange (in his own interpretation).

thought, his assumptions and statements concerning the relations between "variables" may lead, in the last analysis, to the same conclusion.

By taking the tendency of the equalization of profit rates for granted and assuming also equal "organic compositions of capital", *Braun* also regarded the international wage differences as corresponding to the deviations in the "rates of exploitation" in which differences in labour productivity and labour qualities (therefore what Marx called "relative" method of surplus-value production, too) have no role to play. Insofar as the differences in "prices of production" are assumed by Braun to correspond to real-wage differences (and to differences in the "rates of exploitation" inversely proportionate to the latter), his concept, like Emmanuel's, also seems to involve the belief (even if he originally attributed these differences to "imperialist" trade policies) that the *degree* of "exploitation" of the peripheral, dependent countries can simply be measured by the actual differences in real wages.[461]

Braun also tried to prove the basic role of exploitation by unequal exchange in the survival of "imperialism" and in the development of its "centre", i.e. the developed countries by a rather tautological reasoning. Having attributed the existing wage and income differences entirely to unequal exchange, he predicted a drastic fall in the income level of the developed countries and a collapse of the system of "imperialism" in case unequal exchange is terminated.

His final conclusion was (1977): "the imperialist system could not maintain its present capitalist structures without trade, because of the difficulties of substituting the imports of products from the dependent countries, without unequal exchange – that is to say, without the perpetuation of the present wage differentials and of the poverty of the dependent countries." (p. 48)

But who has ever asserted that the "imperialist system" could exist without trade?! The necessity of international trade is one thing, and the question of substitutability of imports from the developing countries is another. In addition, Braun obviously made also a logical mistake: after having related the inequality of exchange to the specificity of the products *imported* by the developing countries, he explained the necessity of unequal exchange for the developed countries by the specific character of the products *exported* by the developing ones. As regards the inevitable collapse of the system of "imperialism" in the case of an end of unequal exchange, he simply declared (1977) as an explanation that "equalization of wages could create massive transfers of income towards the dependent countries as a consequence of the relative rise in their export prices, which would certainly upset the internal structure of domination of the imperialist countries." (p. 48)

One could pose the question: is it indeed the equalization of wages, i.e. wage increases in the developing countries, which promises a way of eliminating "imperialism", so simply?! Braun explicitly rejected the concept making the working class of the developed countries responsible for "imperialism" and "exploitation".

[461] *Braun* (1977) assumed that the relative prices express "unequal exchange in the real sense of the term" in such a way that the ratio indicating how many times "the relative prices of the commodities exported by the imperialist country" are higher "than they would have been if wages were equal" expresses exactly the degree of exploitation by unequal exchange. (p. 87)

But, as a matter of fact, however different from Emmanuel's is the conclusion that he wished to arrive at in respect of the front lines of international conflict, however vigorously he emphasized (1977) that "it cannot be deduced from the theory of unequal exchange that the contradiction between social classes is today superseded by the contradiction between imperialist and dependent nations" (pp. 50 and 111), and however strongly he rejected the thesis concerning the exploitation of the dependent nations by the working classes of the imperialist countries, the logic of his analysis has also led, involuntarily, to the same conclusion. Though *Braun* strongly criticized Emmanuel's theory of unequal exchange and replaced it by another, alternative variant, he seems to have failed to get rid of those analytical errors and simplifications involved in that theory.

## 4.4. Wallerstein's "world-system approach"

Immanuel Wallerstein, one of those very few social scientists whose name is just as well known among historians as among economists, sociologists or political scientists and particularly among those engaged in development studies, waged a war against not only the fragmentation of social science into separate disciplines such as history, economics, sociology, political science, etc., but also the conventional approach characterizing the mainstreams in the above disciplines, namely the one taking the individual "national" economies, societies or states, i.e. the country level, as the primary unit or level of analysis. As opposed to the latter he advocates a "world-system approach".

As a matter of fact, the application of such an approach, i.e. choosing the global system, the world economy or society or its political–institutional order as a unit of analysis, does not mean something new which had no precedence before Wallerstein (and T. Hopkins)[462] proposed it in the analysis of the world economy and of the development–underdevelopment dichotomy in the latter. Even apart from the Marxian model of capitalism (if applied, perhaps originally but inconsistently, to the global system of capitalism), and from those, quite numerous Marxist theoretical works since the beginning or the 20th century, having pointed, at least in view of colonial empires, imperialist wars and expanding capital exports, to that capitalism had become a "worldwide system", the "Latin American school of dependency" and particularly the early writings of *Andre Gunder Frank* (1967a), (1967b), etc. have already marked a certain frontline between those interpreting "pre-capitalism" and "underdevelopment" in the Third World as aboriginal phenomena and those explaining these phenomena in the context of the world system. Nevertheless Wallerstein's claim for a world-system approach seems to have gone much further in the sense of suggesting the world-economy as the only appropriate unit of analysis of the system of capitalism, and insofar as conceiving of the national economies as merely fictitious phenomena.

Within this subchapter it is of course impossible (and would be just as hopeless as in some other cases, too, such as Amin's case) to give a comprehensive critical

[462] *Hopkins, T. K.–Wallerstein, I.* (1977).

presentation of Wallerstein's theoretical works which are not only very rich in ideas but also extremely numerous. Therefore we have to restrict our survey to some of the most substantial elements only of his concept, which are more closely related to our subjects.

Wallerstein, while accepting the holistic approach of Marxism[463], i.e. the method of analysing the social reality as a whole, criticized Marx for his Eurocentric "stage theory" of development. According to him a society should not be analysed in abstract terms nor should it be identified with a "nation", with a politico-cultural unit surrounded by state boundaries. The identification of society with a community within state boundaries is an erroneous approach which is typical of all development theories, in general, (including most of the contemporary Marxist literature) and of the "development concept" what he calls "developmentalism" as a whole. However, he described the latter in such a way that it is eventually reduced to and becomes identical with the economistic concept of unilinear development and those conventional theories explaining underdevelopment by internal conditions only. Consequently, all views that do not fully share Wallerstein's variant of the "world-system approach" as an alternative to "developmentalism" are to be considered as inappropriate, conventional ones. He drew the division line simply between those believing that "the world...consists of a number of related but basically autonomous 'societies', each moving upward along an essentially similar path of development"[464] and those taking, like him, the world-system as being always the primary, moreover rather absolute and exclusive unit of analysis.

The *unit of analysis* must be chosen, according to him, on the basis of the measurable social reality of interdependent productive activities, i.e. on an "effective social division of labour", in other words, on an "economy" which includes exchange relations[465]. This emphasis placed on the *division of labour* as an essential (though not exclusive!) content of the "economy" and its role played in social stratification and conflicts of interest seems quite justified. However, specialization and the resulting relations of division of labour within a system are by no means the only components, which may make as lasting relations a system organic, and a division of labour may be accompanied by distribution without exchange, too.

[463] Referring to *G. Lukács* (1968) who pointed out that "it is not the primacy of economic motives in historical explanation that constitutes the decisive difference between Marxism and bourgeois thought, but the point of view of totality" (p. 27), *Wallerstein* (1972) also stressed the need "to analyse the social whole". (p. 1)

[464] And on this path of development those societies having started earlier are assumed to be "showing the way to the late-starters". *Hopkins, T. K.–Wallerstein, I.* (1977), pp. 111–112.

[465] Accordingly, economic actors belonging to the same division of labour operate (consciously or unconsciously) on the assumption that "the totality of their essential needs – of sustenance, protection, and pleasure – will be met over a reasonable time-span by a combination of their own productive activities and exchange in some form". *Wallerstein, I.* (1972), p. 9. and (1978a), p. 2.

While the above reduction of the complexity of social production relations only to one (however important) form of the latter makes the definition of a system too partial, the coupling of the division of labour with exchange is an historically erroneous generalization. As a consequence, not only the "national" economies engaged (to whatever degree) in regular exchange with one another on the basis of a division of labour, may, despite all the cohesive mechanisms and centripetal forces working within them, disappear (or should not be considered) as "systems", but also those socio-economic systems operating without exchange relations, carrying out direct distribution or redistribution of goods among producers or including predominantly subsistence economies.

*Wallerstein* himself refers to, and calls as "mini-systems" (entities that have within them a "complete division of labour, and a single cultural framework") those primitive agricultural, or hunting and gathering societies within which there already existed a certain division of labour (at least according to sex and age or already also according to the main spheres of activities), demonstrating the social substance of human existence, and the inevitably social implications of production. The exchange, however, among the community's producers was by no means a condition for the operation of these "systems".

Even less meaningful application can Wallerstein's own definition (1972) have to the variant of the "world systems", of the social systems of later historical ages held by him to be the only possible ones, which was characterized as a unit with "a single division of labour and multiple cultural systems", i.e. the so-called "world-empires". For they are assumed to be "basically redistributive in economic form", and even though a certain economic exchange existed there, too, (primarily in the form of long-distance trade), it was "not fundamentally determinative" and not a mediator of an internal division of labour (p. 4)

The definition of the "system" merely by the scope of division of labour (and exchange), without taking into account the social relations, in their broader sense, of production, thus, first of all, the social relations of ownership (and control) over the means of production, leave completely indeterminate the allocation of roles in the social division of labour itself. In this case the latter can only be explained by repeated coercion in all cases, by already existing differences in power to be taken for granted. Wallerstein, in fact, reduced the substance of the conflict of interest among "economic actors" to exchange relations.

Despite the obvious existence of intra-society division of labour coupled with exchange, however, the formation of national economy and national society has not taken place, according to Wallerstein, even in the centre of the world economy. The different ethnic, religious and other communities have not been integrated into national society in the developed capitalist countries, either. Thus he regards (1972) "national society" as a misidentified, in fact a never existing entity, a false concept which stems from equating the existing, visible and functioning states and certain ethnic communities and which gives rise to non-problems such as the comparison of the development of individual "national societies" and their grouping into different "stages" of development. Classes, ethnic groups, or "status-groups" and "ethno-nations" are, in his view, phenomena of the world-economy. "National development" does not really exist. The illusion of the development of national societies through stages and of the co-existence of different social systems, or of the historical sequence of systems is the result, according to him, of the fact that the individual states are falsely described as either feudal, or capitalist, or socialist societies. In real fact, however, social systems can and should only be interpreted as "totalities", and since totalities have historically existed only either as "mini-systems", or "world systems", to speak of capitalist national societies or of socialist societies would be as void of meaning as to speak of "feudal" societies in the periphery. (pp. 3, 4, 17 and 25)

True, the concept of *"nation"* necessarily refers to other nations (since a nation can exist only in relation to, and distinguished from, other nations), and thus national development means development not only in terms of own past but also in terms of that of other nations, i.e. placed in a broader context. This, however, does not mean that a social system within a "national" framework, i.e. within state frontiers, cannot represent a (relative) "totatility" and thus should not be regarded as "system", nor can we conclude there from that the term "national economy" and the measuring of its development in relation to the development of other national economies is meaningless. (It is to be noted that in this respect Wallerstein himself seems inconsistent.[466])

While defining an "effective social division of labour" combined with exchange as the *caracteristica specifica* of any real "system", Wallerstein emphasized that the limits of the latter cannot be determined merely by the scope of exchange relations. Therefore he distinguished between the "external arena" of a system and the "periphery" as its organic part. The criterion, however, of this distinction is whether the commodities exchanged are "essential for daily use" as in the case of the periphery, or "preciosities" as in the case of trade with the "external arenas". Despite this distinction, and partly because of its rather vague and questionable criterion, the definition of the "system" has remained inaccurate and partial, as already noted.

Differences between the individual social formations or their combinations, moreover the disparities even between systems of the same social formation manifest themselves, among other things, in whether their normal operation and reproduction presuppose, and to what extent, external relations and expansion, or whether they are of a "closed" character. In other words, to what extent the societies in question are expansive or more or less isolated. Wallerstein's distinction

[466] A certain inconsistency appears when *Wallerstein* speaks elsewhere (1974) about the rise of the British "national economy", of "the existence of a single world-economy of uneven national development", of the significance of foreign trade from the point of view of "national economies", etc. (pp. 263, 271, 290, etc.)

between "world-systems" and "mini-systems" seems to be designed to express this undoubtedly real difference.

The spatial dimensions of social formations, however, hardly provide the basis for an unambiguous categorization. Though the social system of slavery presupposes, indeed, by its very nature regular expansion and repeated warfare for the acquisition of slave labour, while the social formation of feudalism (and what Marx called the "Asiatic mode of production") are operative even as more or less closed, self-sufficient systems, yet from this does not follow, either logically or, and mainly, historically, that no feudal- (or "Asiatic"-) type of systems of an expansionary character could evolve, and if they could (as in reality), then only as accidental exceptions. Moreover, even the primitive tribal societies, or the so-called "mini-systems" characterized by Wallerstein as a "reciprocal mode of production" may have been very different according to the extent to which they were more or less expansive systems (as e.g. the nomadic pastoral societies) or rather "closed" ones (as predominantly the agricultural communities).

As regards capitalism, its worldwide expansion and the relations it has maintained from the very beginning with areas outside the centre of its evolvement as well as its operation creating a really world economic system and a worldwide division of labour are just one side and typical aspect of its development as a "system". The other side, and a no less important and no less essential aspect, of the development and even of the very existence of this system is its rise and operation also within "national" framework, giving thereby birth to modern nations, bringing forth national economies and markets, "nation states" or nationalist aspirations to create such. This is how a contradictory interaction between "national" and "international" development, namely the contradictory tendencies of developing (or suppressing) national societies, economies and states, on the one hand, and of international, worldwide expansion aimed at drawing on extra-national resources and of growing internationalisation, globalisation, on the other, become the law of motion and development of capitalism.

Instead of the latter, Wallerstein's *schema of historical development* involves a process from the "mini-systems" through the "capitalist world-economy" to the "socialist world government". Though the spatial dimensions of the systems are of secondary or even "accidental" nature, or derived characteristics, in Wallerstein's schema (1976) seem to play a significant role.

Accordingly, the *"mini-systems"*, assumed to be the earliest in history and based on reciprocity, were replaced by the so-called "world-systems" not as a result of their own development, but, being communities small in physical dimension, they appeared to be historically short-lived (at least, separately, one by one) because they were technologically primitive and less resistant to natural calamity and conquests, or because their internal division of labour had disrupted for some other accidental reason. (pp. 343–352) The evolvement of the "world-systems", at least of their first form: the *"world-empires"*, was made possible by the "rationality" of administration. And though in these systems, in opposition to the reciprocity-based mode of production, already a class (of state administration) came into being which no longer produced, merely appropriated, namely by force, material goods, yet – according to Wallerstein – this redistribute-tributary mode of production also had, like the earlier one, the characteristic that maximal production and the development of technology were just as non-desirable in it as in the "mini-systems".

Though there did occur some expansion of production and advance of technology, but not following from and promoting the development of the system, but rather accidentally and for offsetting the decline of material production. Hence, the development of the productive forces, the accumulation of human production experiences, the discovery of new products and technologies, the formation of the various branches of material production, the unfolding of the social division of labour had no significant role to play in the development of the "mini-systems" and "world-empires", in the transition from the "reciprocity-based mode of production" to the "tributary–tributary mode of production". Consequently, this transition appears be a rather accidental and even reversible phenomenon. The "world-empires" are characterized by a cyclical pattern of expansion and contraction, and Wallerstein to attributes their decline and collapse that beyond a certain point the bureaucratic costs of appropriation and redistribution exceed what as surplus can be appropriated.

The evolvement of the capitalist mode of production, i.e. the rise of a new variant of "world-systems", namely the capitalist "world-economy", also appears in Wallerstein's presentation (1976) as a kind of historical accident (moreover, as an ill-fated one[467]) rather than the natural product and necessary "stage" of a general development of society. As a result of the decline of feudal Europe (which is explained by rising "real wages" caused by demographic disasters, by a fall in the real income of the ruling strata, and by peasant revolts and warfare) "a sort of creative leap of imagination on the part of the ruling strata" resulted, according to him, in the experimentation of a new, alternative mode of surplus appropriation, namely the appropriation of the surplus via the market, which led to geographical expansion, to the economic specialization of territories, to the rise of the "absolutist state" and to the creation of a world capitalist economy. (p. 350)

As it appears, Wallerstein regards feudalism as a variant only among other "mini-systems" or "world-empires", without pointing to its advantages or disadvantages with regard to the transition to capitalism and revealing its specificities compared to those of other variants. The demographic disasters and the assumed "real wage" rises (implying also the assumption of the existence of a wage-earning class) seem just as accidental phenomena as the peasant revolts or as such phenomena as may have occurred anywhere else without having led to capitalism.

[467] "Capitalism has been more exploitative…and destructive of life and land, for the vast majority of persons located within the boundaries of the world-economy, than any previous mode of production in world history." *Wallerstein, I.* (1978a), p. 11.

Hence the historical turning point seems to have been made by the "creative leap of imagination" of the European ruling strata. Such an explanation, without revealing the roots of transformation in the development of productive forces, in the changes in material conditions as well, is reflecting a somewhat idealistic viewpoint, and presents the rise of capitalism not as a sign of historical progress but as a (rather unfortunate) product of accident[468].

Wallerstein does not attribute any significant role in the rise of the capitalist system to *proletarianization.* This is because, in his view, the distinction made in literature between wage-worker, on the one hand, and self-employed artisan, peasant cultivator, petty merchant, "serf", "slave" or the "rent-payer" or "crop-sharing" tenant, on the other, is "heavily juridical in nature" and misleading. Though also distinguishing them, he denied that the "coerced" forms of labour (and the flows of goods and services in kind) could be called traditional, feudal or precapitalist as against the "capitalist" forms of "free" labour (and monetary flows)[469]. He regards the distinction between them as being based merely on their different "judicial positions" because of failing to pay attention behind the latter to their essential difference in respect of ownership, control and use of the means of production and resources.[470]

According to Wallerstein, the process of "primitive" (or "primary") capital accumulation (which in the Marxian analysis of history appeared as the "departure point" and precondition for the rise of capitalism) is a "secular" trend of the capitalist mode of production, which as a permanent process regularly repeats itself for centuries, i.e. a process which is hardly distinguishable from that of capital accumulation taking place on the basis of an already existing capitalist mode of production. Since such a constant process, belonging to the normal operation of the system, is going on throughout history until proletarianisation is completed[471], it cannot be, of course, a yardstick either, which qualitatively distinguishes the capitalist development of the centre and the periphery. Thus Wallerstein fails to underline the historical role of the *forceful* deprivation of producers of their

[468] According to *Wallerstein (*1977) "the progressive character of capitalism is a historically meaningless issue". (p. 9) It is to be noted, however, that in his historical monograph (1974), Wallerstein presented not only a more realistic appraisal when stating that "for all its cruelties...it is better that the world capitalist economy...was born than that it had not been" (p. 357), but also set the birth of capitalism in the complexity of changes in social, economic and political relations, duly emphasizing the role of such objective factors as the development of agricultural commodity production and trade, the modification of class relations, etc., as well as the effect of geographical circumstances.

[469] *Hopkins, T. K.–Wallerstein, I.* (1977), p. 139.

[470] According to *Wallerstein* (1978b), it is also entirely irrelevant to the actual size of the market whether all laborers are wageworkers or slaves. (p. 4)

[471] Here again we find a view similar to that of *Rosa Luxemburg,* according to which the normal operation of the capitalist economy presupposes the existence of not yet proletarianized producers and pre-capitalistic sectors of the economy. What follows from this view is the role of proletarianisation, namely its completion, in the demise, rather than in the rise, of capitalism.

means of production (such as land), of the primary appropriation of these means by non-economic coercion, which was a precondition for, and the overture to, the transition to indirect (capitalist) surplus appropriation via the market, i.e. an appropriation without non-economic violence. He also fails to underline the substantial difference, i.e. not only in terms of the degree but also in terms of quality, between capitalization in the centre and that in the periphery, between the fulfilment of "primitive capital accumulation" in the former leading to the unfolding of national capitalism, and the semi-fulfilment of primitive accumulation in the latter resulting in a disintegrated structure of economy and society, a "peripheral" type of capitalism only, mixed with semi-traditional elements.

It is to be noted that if the "primitive" accumulation of capital were really an evolutionary process taking place gradually both in the centre and the periphery, only with a time lag in the latter, and if we ignored not only the difference between those entering into exchange relations with capital, namely those selling a product and those selling their labour power, but also the difference between "national" and foreign capital, then we would have no reason indeed to question the concept of "stages of growth", reduced to quantitative differences only, of the conventional theories which have been fully rejected by Wallerstein.

Though Wallerstein emphasized that "the world-system...does not first exist and then move to develop..., but its development is its existence"[472], the formation of this system seems, in his presentation, to be a single and, in a sense, an accidental event, as an emergence in an almost ready form already in the 16th century, rather than the result of a development process preparing it. As regards the movement of the system, it is characterized by its expansion in space and by a cyclical pattern in time only, instead of a development of it as an organic system.

Thus instead of the "development perspective" which is related to progress in time, Wallerstein suggests a "world-system perspective" which refers to the *spatial* unit of analysis, and though these two are not necessarily excluding each other, he practically reduces the analysis of the "spatio-temporal whole" to the cyclically changing scope of commodity relations.

He distinguishes the capitalist world-economy from the previous "mini-systems" and "world-empires" (whether the latter imply their "feudal" form maintaining, along with the "political unity of the economy", an "extreme decentralization of administration", or their genuine imperial form ensuring a relatively high centralization) by defining the world-economy as including a single global division of labour (within which a multiplicity of cultures is located) without, however, a single overall political system. Due to the lack of a single global political system, surplus, by necessity, can only be distributed via the market.

Wallerstein's perception of "commodification" blurs the substantial difference in nature between the commodification of labour power and that of products and

[472] *Hopkins, T. K.–Wallerstein, I.* (1977), p. 124.

other factors of production, and role of the former in the rise and operation of the system.

The "basic contradiction" of capitalism in his interpretation appears as a conflict between the actors of the *market*[473]. Insofar, of course, as the social relationship between labour and capital is conceived of as a market exchange relation only between the owners of these two commodities, or a quantitative ratio between the two "factors of production"[474], then the role of labour in the production of "surplus value" appears to be simplified to the quantitative ratio of live labour, while the role of capital in the "appropriation of surplus value" appears to be reduced to a market force, to the bargaining power.

The capitalist world-economy involves several other contradictions among which the contradiction between economy and politics is, according to Wallerstein, of the most general nature. Due to the worldwide integration of the economy by exchange and the simultaneous formation of strong nation-states in the centre versus weak states in the periphery, i.e. the lack of an integrated world-political system, a twofold conflict relationship (with two specific contradictions) has evolved: (a) between the "core" and the "periphery", i.e. the economic central areas and the peripheral territories, and (b) between the dominant states and the states subordinated to them.

The division of labour within the world-system of capitalism implies that the various geographical areas "are specialized in specific productive tasks", and, though their "nature" varies overtime, it always remains true that "these tasks do not receive the same economic rewards". Hence, complementarity goes along with inequality. Whatever the products involved – according to Wallerstein, too – "the core has always specialized in comparatively highly mechanized, high-profit, high-wage, highly-skilled activities" in contrast to the periphery, which has specialized in the opposite varieties[475]. This "spatial hierarchy" of economic specialization gives rise to the exploitation of the producers of the periphery by the core, to what is called "unequal exchange". Thus, in Wallerstein's view, unequal exchange "is based on an economic specialization in tasks"[476].

As regards the question of *what* determined the distribution of the roles in the world division of labour, and what induced or compelled the peripheral countries to accept "activities" causing their unfavourable position, Wallerstein seems to have

---

473 Wallerstein, like *Karl Polányi* and his followers, as well as several "new left" opponents of capitalism, seems also inclined to identify capitalism simply with market economy and regard its "abnormality" as that of the market in general.

474 Such a view seems to result merely from inconsistency since elsewhere Wallerstein pointed (1976) to one of the "basic dichotomies", namely to the substantial difference between the two classes with respect to decisions on the production of goods, owing to "property rights, accumulated capital, control over technology, etc.". (p. 350)

475 *Hopkins, T. K.–Wallerstein, I.* (1977), p. 127–128.

476 *Wallerstein, I.* (1976), pp. 350–351, and (1978b), p. 6.

answered it by referring to coercion, to the different strength of the states[477], while, on the other hand, "differences in the strength of the state-machineries" have been traced back by him (1972) to the "structural role a country plays in the world economy". (p. 15) This sounds rather tautological.

Anyway, to explain the unequal division of labour, the divergent specialization of countries or groups of countries by coercion in general is hardly satisfactory even if the application of force was the main reason in many cases, even if the production structure and pattern of foreign trade of the developing countries were in most cases undoubtedly influenced by the policy of colonial administrations or of puppet governments serving foreign interests, and also by trade agreements imposed on them by foreign big powers. Though external force did play a significant role, indeed, in shaping the international division of labour, it was by no means the only, exclusive, and in itself (i.e. without local forces) determining factor. It should not be forgotten that, on the one hand, quite a number of countries have practically started as politically independent states or only after the end of colonial rule to specialize in production typical of the periphery, while, on the other, quite a few countries have managed to rise to the "core" even if before they had been under the control of foreign states and/or specialized on typical peripheral products. What has determined in reality whether a country developed as a periphery and remained in such a position in the world economy, is the very failure in accomplishing the process of "primitive capital accumulation" (capitalization and "proletarianisation") as a precondition for the rise of an integrated national economy, almost no matter whether obstacles to it was set by foreign or domestic forces. The abortive variant of this process, with the resulting partial capitalization and semi-proletarianisation, with a disintegrated structure of the economy involving, besides a "modern" also a "traditional", pre-capitalistic sector, has always been the characteristic feature of peripheral capitalism, whether the "abortion" of national capitalism was caused by sheer external force, by the influence of foreign powers or by the choice of a peripheral adjustment policy of the domestic ruling class.

Though Wallerstein did not take a stand for any concrete variant of the theory of "unequal exchange" (for the concept of Emmanuel, Amin, Braun or others), he also regards it as a central, decisive phenomenon that "continually reproduces the basic core–periphery division of labour", no matter what specific products the latter implies. This seems to contradict the assumed link between the "strength" of the states and the "structural role", even if Wallerstein often regards the latter as "not essential" or defines the division of labour as between "integrated production processes" instead of "specific products". Anyway, he seems to agree with those attaching no importance to the specificity of products in unequal exchange.

While presenting the world capitalist system as a bipolar system, Wallerstein has also distinguished, along with the "core" (i.e. the centre) and the periphery of the world-economy, a so-called "semi-periphery", to which he attributes a special role in the operation of the system.

As a matter of fact, to any bipolar system, to any social dichotomy, to any system with a contradictory pair of two basic sectors, or social classes presupposing each

---

[477] *Wallerstein* noted (1972): "Once we get a difference in the strength of the state-machineries, we get the operation of 'unequal exchange', which is enforced by strong states on weak ones, by core states on peripheral areas". (p. 13)

other also belong, as of necessity, other, "intermediate" or transitory elements, sectors, classes or strata. Their existence does not deny the functioning of the bipolar system, on the contrary, the formation of such elements constitutes an important part of the history of its rise, changes and decline. Nonetheless, when the substance, the *caracteristica specifica*, the basic relations and laws of motion of the system are analysed, an abstraction from these intermediary and transitory elements is not only justifiable but also necessary at the beginning, even if a more complete and concrete picture of the system with its complexity cannot be gained, indeed, unless this abstraction is gradually dismantled later.

Wallerstein, while regarding the dichotomy of the "core" and the "periphery" as the basic, central and decisive relationship characterizing the world-economic system, and the "semi-periphery" as a phenomenon "derivative" from it[478], eventually converted the semi-periphery into a "third" and "structurally distinct" category (which has got a political role in the smooth operation of the system, namely the role of a kind of buffer due to which "the upper stratum is not faced with the *unified* opposition of all the others because the *middle* stratum is both exploited and exploiter", and also in the breakdown of the system, owing to the increasing costs of its "cooption" into the ranks of the privileged)[479]. However, the structural specificity of this "third category" has not been defined but by a mixture only of the characteristics that are typical of the "core" and the "periphery". The "semi-periphery" is in fact the product of the movement between the two poles. Hence it has no determinacy of its own, independent of them. Thus it is necessary to distinguish the direction and the (historically changing!) conditions of this movement, i.e. the cases of rising from the periphery position and of the falling from the "core" status, and to define their qualitative criteria in the given historical period, instead of merely registering the intermediate position distinguished, at most in quantitative terms, from the "core" or the periphery position and without revealing the direction of movement.

If the *caracteristica specifica* of the successful capitalist development of the centre, of the so-called "core" (i.e. the accomplishment of the process of primitive capital accumulation and the unfolding of an internally integrated national capitalism) gets blurred as against that of peripheral capitalism (i.e. the abortion of primitive capital accumulation and the disintegrated nature of the economy without a national market), then the rise of the semi-periphery to the centre also appears to be merely a kind of relative and gradual step. Similarly, the rise from a periphery to a semi-periphery status seems to be only a matter of time, i.e. the result of a certain quantitative evolution. Accordingly such movements are presented as a game of musical chairs within the world system, a form of "circulation of privilege" only.

The redistributions of the "core" and "periphery" positions and particularly the cases of rise of the "semi-periphery" are, according to Wallerstein, linked with the

---

478 *Hopkins, T. K.–Wallerstein, I.* (1977), p. 116.

479 *Wallerstein, I.* (1972), pp. 6–7 and 25.

long-term fluctuations of the world-economy and its recurrent crises, which affect the structure of employment and the wage-level differences.

However, the "circulation of privilege" within the centre, i.e. the shifts of the leadership among the developed countries, represents only one variant of "uneven development" of the world economy, which is quite different from that producing the "international development gap", i.e. polarizing countries into the centre or the periphery. The assumption of a general and cyclical redistribution of positions necessarily reduces these two substantially different types of uneven development to a single one, which is simply related to technological innovations and wage cost advantages. But insofar as the loss of leadership is caused (besides technological innovations of the rivals) by the rise in wages, which, after the proletarianisation process has been completed(!), follows – according to Wallerstein, too – from the struggle of organized workers, the resulting "circulation of privilege" can hardly apply to the periphery. In the "circulation of privilege" the acquisition of the hegemony is attributed by Wallerstein to the advantage of the "late-comers" (by their ability to introduce the newest technology) while the loss of leadership, of a hegemonic position to the rising wage costs caused by the organized labour movement as well as the intentions to pacify the latter, resulting in worsened competitiveness. Yet the question arises why the peripheral countries cannot also enjoy the advantage of the "late-comers" (especially the advantage of competitiveness following from the lower wage-cost level).

Wallerstein himself noted that the "mechanism of capitalist development...applies essentially only to the core areas with fully proletarianized populations, where all means of production are capital".[480] This statement of him, which points to the cumulative, irreversible process of the unequal development of the centre and the periphery, and thereby to the decisive role played in it by the relatively completed process of proletarianisation and capitalization and its abortion, respectively, obviously contradicts the proposition that "primitive" capital accumulation is a steadily spreading process belonging to the very operation of the system and tending to bring proletarianisation to completion in all parts of the world.

Wallerstein, like many others, when interpreting the worldwide *accumulation of capital* has often mixed up processes of different politico-economic content. The historically decisive process of primitive capital accumulation is partly identified in general with the capital accumulation process effected in the periphery and/or at the expense of the latter[481], and, as already noted, it is presented by him not as a process creating only the very conditions for the rise and full unfolding of the cap-

[480] *Hopkins, T. K.–Wallerstein, I.* (1977), p. 137.

[481] *Samir Amin* (1974a) distinguished and defined primitive accumulation in opposition to the accumulation process typical of a "completely auto centric capitalism" characterized by expanded reproduction, by the growth of productive capacity attainable through the saving and reinvestment of profit gained from invested capital. In the case of primitive accumulation the return on capital cannot stem from earlier capital investments but from "the exploitation of non-capitalist sectors". (p. 382)

italist mode of production but as an organic and permanent part of its normal operation. True, a certain (though not the only) element of the latter may be appropriation of the surplus by unequal exchange. But since proletarianisation is regarded by him as a gradual, evaluative process leading to its completion, as a primarily market-expanding process, a general spread of commodification, thus the picture drawn by him about accumulation taking place in, and at the cost of the periphery remains vague, and misleading. It does not show as a distinctive feature the recurrent abortion of primitive capital accumulation (the accomplishment of which could lead to the unfolding of the capitalist system of a real national economy) and the reproduction of the semi-proletarian masses of the labour force. Nor does it point distinctly to the fact that a normal accumulation process in the expanded capitalist reproduction is also taking place, within certain limits, even in the periphery, i.e. to the growth of (foreign or domestic) capital ownership through profit reinvestments. The former feature expresses the *peripheral* character of capitalism (fraught with precapitalist elements subordinated to capital) while the latter manifests the *capitalist* character of the periphery (not only as part of the world capitalist system but as such also in itself).

The identification of the peripheral process of accumulation with the "primitive" one and its reduction to unequal exchange conducted with non-capitalist producers may actually conjure up the vision of the presumably still really "traditional", "precapitalist" societies in the South[482], which cannot be juggled away even by the terminological alteration, the qualification of precapitalistic small commodity producers as proletarians. What may also follow from the above is the fallacious conclusion that capitalism not only turns to its own advantage, but also always presupposes the existence of pre-capitalistic sectors.

As a consequence of not paying due attention to the national affiliation of capital ownership, to the production relations between labour and foreign capital, to the asymmetrical, moreover hierarchic relationship between different "national" capitals, that is to the social relations of ownership, in general (and on the world scale, in particular), and also because of assuming that the world economy is integrated by exchange (and division of labour), Wallerstein can hardly explain why capital has not yet created a *world-state*, and what keeps the "nation-states" in existence despite the globalism of capital. (As presenting exchange (based on a division of labour) as a central category and *caracteristica specifica* of capitalism, which alone ensures the capitalist unity of the world-system and makes all the

[482] If the (worldwide) process of capital accumulation manifests itself in relation to the peripheral countries as "primitive accumulation", which is defined as the appropriation of surplus from non-capitalist producers through the market, and the content of the centre-periphery relationship is made up by unequal exchange, then the totality of the economy and society of the periphery might logically be conceived of as a precapitalist socio-economic system connected with capitalism only externally (exploited from outside). This false vision is hardly mitigated by references to certain internal effects of this merely "external" relationship on the ("internally") non-capitalist traditional society.

non-capitalist elements, sectors or local modes of production the integral parts of world capitalism, he assigned the latter a substantially capitalist content or function.)

As regards the *prospects* of world development, Wallerstein (1978c) identified the post-capitalist system as a *"socialist world government"*, i.e. as a third variant of world-systems (following the first two, namely "world-empires" and "world-economy"), which – in contrast to the anarchic and disequalising system of the market – would implement "socialist planning". Since such a planning is possible only at the world level (pp. 4–5) and not at the level of states, because the latter are always and necessarily planning ultimately for the firms and not for the economy as a whole. Hence the withering-away of nation-states is implicitly assumed to be a requisite even for a socialist transition.

Wallerstein also stressed that the aim of socialist production is consumption (and not profit-making) and thus its governing principle is the primacy of "use values" (and not exchange values). Such a separation of the two sides of commodity production, namely of "use value" and "exchange value", and distinguishing according to the dominance of the former or the latter socialism from capitalism, is rather misleading. First of all, because capitalism is not simply an exchange system, a market economy and even less an economy that can get over the requirements and problems posed by "use value", i.e. the fact that the value generated in a profit-motivated production process must ultimately be realized also in consumption. Secondly, because in the presumed process of constructing a socialist system the elimination of "exchange value", i.e. of commodity production, by some political decision can hardly be counted as a realistic possibility. (Such a decision, if taken within single countries, would presuppose a complete isolation, but if made, by a *Deus ex machina,* valid for the world as a whole, would require the organization overnight of a new, worldwide form of product supply without commodity exchange, if such is possible at all in view of the dimensions.) Anyway, Wallerstein has left unexplained *how* the present world capitalist economy would be transformed to a "world socialist state". His views (somehow idealistic) on "socialism" which necessarily begins with a world government, and his reduction of the centre–periphery relationship to a mere gradual one as well as his thesis of the circulation of these roles in the world-economy seem to suggest an immediate change of the system as a whole as the only possibility of transformation. Apart from the naïveté of the assumption that some sudden emergence of a "socialist world government" may overnight put an end to the inequality of the parts of the world economy, the possibility and necessity of actions on the level of the latter to "change the world" are left out of serious consideration. At the same time Wallerstein's concept was an obvious critique of all those views believing in the idea of "socialism in single countries" and simply overlooking the problem and dilemma of how to reconcile, if possible at all, the socialist aim, principles, internal institutions and mechanism with the predominant "rules of the game" in the world economy.

## 4.5. A Neo-Marxist theory: Samir Amin's views on trade and imperialism

In his several books[483] Samir Amin has presented a comprehensive theory on the capitalist world system, its historically uneven development, dependence and exploitation relations, and analysed, in many details, the socio-economic system of countries belonging to the "periphery" of the world economy. He also attributed the rise and reproduction of "underdevelopment" to those external forces and international effects stemming from the capitalist nature of the world system and concluded from his analysis on a global conflict between the imperialist forces of the capitalist centre and the peoples of the periphery of world capitalism, recommending the latter both a unified struggle against the former, and a policy of delinking from it, an inward-looking, "self-reliant" national policy towards a kind of "socialism" (different both from the former Stalinian type and the East-European "reform-socialism"). type).

Amin opposed all those concepts trying to explain underdevelopment, uneven development in the world economy, "imperialism", exploitation, dominance and "unequal exchange" by taking such phenomena out of the context of the "mode of production" as a whole, of the dialectical relationship between the latter and the class struggle, of the objective economic laws and historical materialism, i.e. without applying a Marxian approach. Thus he rejected not only the views which divorce the "surface phenomena" of trade, i.e. exchange, the circulation and distribution relations from the process and relations of production, but also the economistic approach in general as well as "politicism", this political-science counterpart of economism, which perceives the socio-political relations of the economy as purely political or institutional ones.

Amin (1973) criticized *Emmanuel* because the latter "remains on the surface of phenomena" in that he "entirely separates exchange from the production process" and divorces the wage level from the level of development of the productive forces by treating the former as "independent variable". (p. 44) He disagreed with *Braun*, too, who placed such surface phenomena as the restrictive trade policies applied by imperialism, however important they may be, in the centre of his analysis, and failed to go beyond the "phenomenal issue" of what to consider "independent variable".[484]

In compliance with the Marxian concept and logic of analysis, *Amin* (1978) pointed out not only the difference but also the interrelationship between "value" *and* "price of production", and stressed that the former is not "a nebulous, metaphysical, incalculable category" but a real and calculable one, though "not immediately apparent". In contrast to price, value "is independent of income distribution between wages and profits". The quantity of abstract social labour expressed in value is the only "common denominator" which "makes it possible to relate all the economic quantities (prices and incomes)", and equally "characterizes a given phase" and "the change from one phase" to another in the progress of the productive forces", or, to put it differently, it is the "true standard" which "makes it

[483] See e.g. *Amin, S.* (1973), (1976), etc.

[484] In another work (1976), Amin qualified as "pointless" the question of "which is the cause and which is the effect: the international prices, or the inequality in wage levels". (p. 151)

possible to define precisely and objectively" and "to measure from one phase to another" the development of the productive forces. Any other "standard" is necessarily "tautological" and "elastic", which "varies with what it measures". (pp. 74, 84–85, 87, 89, 96–98) The correspondence, however, between values and prices does indeed mean that the values created in the production process can be redistributed differently. According to Amin: "This effective redistribution (the prices) is the synthesis of multiple determination" of which fundamental is "the structure of the productive system (including the rate of exploitation of labour)". Another determination is "the competition of capital" which leads to the equalization of the profit rates (thereby to the rise of the "prices of production), and a third one is the historical circumstances influencing the choice of the actual currency "which determine only the factor of proportionality". Consequently, and contrary to Emmanuel's concept, the "prices of production" originate in the synthesis, first, of the "law of value" and, second, of the law of the "competition of capital". (pp. 5 and 87)[485]

In contrast to Sraffa and in agreement with Marx, *Amin* (1978) stressed the primary role of "live labour" and considered labour productivity as the proper measure of the development of productive forces which can only be expressed in the category of "value" independent of income distribution. (p. 28) In his view (1978), the course of capitalist expanded reproduction presupposes as a requirement that the *value of labour power* rises as the productive forces develop because "the value of labour power is not independent of the level of development of the productive forces". It is exactly this requirement that the "historical element" determining the value of labour power is manifested, though "this objective necessity ...constantly clashes with the true inherent tendency of capitalism which is opposite to it". But if wages are formed not according to this requirement, "equilibrium is not possible unless there develops simultaneously a third sector of consumption which does not produce surplus value". (p. 21)

Though it clearly follows from Amin's train of thought that the higher wage level in the developed countries must be related to the higher development level of their productive forces, too, the relationship, as described by Amin, between the value of labour power and the development of productive forces seems over-simplified (even if reference is made to counteractions).

Even apart from the questionable presumption about the need for a "third sector of consumption" as a prerequisite of equilibrium (which was already expressed by *Rosa Luxemburg* who predicted that the solution of the "realization problem" requires the integration of newer and newer "virgin territories" and the extensive spread of proletarianisation among independent producers, without which the system would collapse), it is worth mentioning that, on the one hand, the development of productive forces may induce also an opposite tendency, namely of declining value of labour power, and, on the other, the increase in the latter may follow not only, as a "necessity", from the required conditions of realization but also directly from the process of development. As regards the first remark about the opposite tendency, it refers to that the increase in labour productivity in the branches of economy producing the necessary goods and services for the reproduction of labour power tends to reduce its value (according to Marx, who derived from it the "relative" method of surplus production). As to the second remark, it simply warns to that the very process of development of the productive forces necessarily

[485] *Amin* (1978) rejected *Sraffa's* model, too, which "directly defines the production price of every commodity as the sum of the value of inputs consumed, of the distributed wage and of a profit in proportion to the capital advanced, and which expresses the interdependence of all the relative prices" as well as the inverse relationship between wages and profits. Amin pointed to that the "standard" Sraffa applied is (in contrast to value) not independent of distribution, and that Sraffa's model is not suitable for "the analysis of the conditions of dynamic equilibrium". (pp. 14–15, 17, 29, 92 and 95) Without discussing here Sraffa's concept, it is to be noted that he focused on the effect the changes in the distribution relations exert on the "prices of production", and that the pattern of the latter varies with such changes does also follow from the logic of Marx. As *Antal Mátyás* (1979) noted: "If we express the technical composition of capital not in terms of value but in terms of production price, the composition of capital expressed in prices of production will change with the order of distribution." (p. 123)

involves an improvement in the average quality of labour, a process of unskilled labour increasingly becoming skilled labour, which means not only an increase in the (education, training and other) costs of the reproduction of labour power but also its growing "value-creating" ability. Though Amin (1976) noted that the "ultramodern industries" accord "a much bigger place to highly skilled labour" (p. 189), he seems to have missed to conclude therefrom.

While emphasizing the role of the State in the international class struggle and the importance of a self-reliant, inward-looking national policy of development for the developing countries, *Amin* (1973) seems to share the view according to which the *world system* as a whole is the primary unit of the analysis of capitalism. He explicitly argues against the perception of the "world system as the juxtaposition of national systems". (pp. 30 and 21)

In his view, the *unity* of the world capitalist system is *par excellence* manifested in the "pre-eminence of international value", in the "commercial alienation" of labour and in the universality of the reduction of labour power to commodity. But "unity" has never been identical with "homogeneity", he noted. The contemporary world capitalist system includes quite different social formations and heterogeneous segments, such as in the centre and in the periphery of the world economy. In view of this and of the still *national character of institutions,* the world capitalist system cannot be homogeneous though it forms one single unit[486].

Amin defined this *unity* of the world system by its *worldwide trade relations,* and directly concluded from the latter on the primarily global, world-character of all commodity production. Such a perception of the unity of the world system, however, which is actually reduced to its integration by exchange only, is quite the same as, or at least leads logically back to, the interpretation of the world system as a "juxtaposition of national economies" interlinked merely by trade relations, even if reference is made to the dominance of international capital (but without its historical and politico-economic analysis, and without a clear distinction between commodities and labour power as a commodity). Not to mention that integration by exchange is, owing to the limited proportions of international trade with commodities, necessarily partial only, and the premise of the primarily international, global (world) character of all commodities (even if the scope of "non-tradable goods" has been narrowing) is such an argument of verification which itself needs to be verified, if it is not simply tautological. It seemed surprising why *Amin,* who in his works has actually revealed also those decisive forces having shaped the fundamental relations (which are much more important than exchange relations) between the centre and the periphery of the world economy (such as "the decisive role played by foreign capital in the periphery", "forcing upon the periphery the kinds of production that the centre needs", and "the appropriation by this capital of the principal means of produc-

[486] Contradicting to some extent to his concept, *Amin* in a later paper (1993) stated that: "...The repeated attempts in the history of capitalism to build world unity still remain a reactionary utopia which has only been realized for very short periods, because it inevitably tends to intensify the revolt by the majority of the world's peoples who are its victims." (p. 134)

tion", i.e. "foreign ownership of capital", or its "monopoly of the supply of specific types of equipment", etc.[487]), was seeking the unity of the system and the cause of its *inequality in international exchange*. (True, more recently, perhaps because of the criticism he received, Amin has somehow revised his concept[488].)

It is not less surprising that Amin, when explaining (1973) *underdevelopment* of the periphery by external forces, defined, in general, the *"peripheral mode of production"* as consisting "in the simultaneity of a modern technology (hence of a high-level productivity) and of low wages within the framework of capitalist social organization". (pp. 84 and 86–88). This definition contradicts his own analysis of the rise and development of "peripheral capitalism" insofar as it sheds light on the role of the penetration of foreign monopoly capital, on the structural distortion and the "extroversion" of the economy, on the concomitant disintegration, the "incomplete" character of proletarianisation, i.e. of "primitive capital accumulation", and so on. It also conflicts with his statement (though made in another context, but with a claim to general validity) that (1976) rejects the simplification of the critique of a social system of that of technology *per se.* (p. 384)

Apart from that the above definition obviously presents "the specific mode of production" of the periphery as of a rather *recent origin* since in the case of typical colonial investments[489] one can hardly speak of the influx of modern technology, Amin's reference to the "technological dependence" of the local bourgeoisie, just as the assumption that the modern technology is introduced by foreign capital, presupposes direct capital inflow (and the local activity of foreign capital or the subordination of local capital to the latter) as a *primary* dependence relationship. To resolve the contradictions mentioned above, Amin realistically referred to changes since the time of earlier colonial-type investments[490]. However, the complex and lasting system of economic dependence (more precisely: asymmetrical interdependences) cannot be reduced to a single, however important form, namely *technological dependence*, which is, as Amin himself admits, of rather recent origin, coming to the fore, together with other forms, in the wave of industrialization.

---

[487] *Amin, S.* (1976), pp. 248, 181, 251.

[488] "The law of globalized value – the foundation of the global system – is at the very origin of world polarization (contrast: centres/peripheries). Capitalism as a world system cannot be reduced to the capitalist mode of production, as the capitalist mode of production assumes an integrated three-dimensional market (goods, capital and labor)." *Amin, S.* (1993), p. 132.

[489] *Amin* was, of course, quite aware of the fact that the earlier investments of "colonial-type" of foreign capital were directed towards the primary producing branches of the "peripheral" economies, which had been operated with unskilled labor and can hardly be characterized by "modern technology". In view of this he noted (1993): "In the beginning, analysis had put the emphasis quite naturally on the industry/no-industry contrast". (p. 133)

[490] *Amin* (1976) pointed to that the "direct form of appropriation tends to become pointless as soon as the time arrives when, through technology, central capital is in a position to dominate the industries of the Third World and draw substantial profits from them without even having to finance their installation". So "technological dependence will gradually tend to replace domination through direct appropriation". (pp. 154 and 251)

According to Amin (1993): "The industrialization of the periphery does not put an end to capitalist polarization, but it does move the centre of gravity of the forces giving rise to the phenomenon to the control of technology, international finance, and of course the media (and through them political control), armaments (the monopoly of the means of genocide), of the discourse on the environment. In this context, peripheral industrialization can become a sort of modern putting-out system, controlled by the financial and technological centres. The newly industrializing countries of the South (and of the East?) are already the very core of tomorrow's periphery." (p. 133)

Though some of these changes, including industrialization, are not of the most recent origin at all, while the development of new information and communication technologies which brings about even more substantial shifts are neglected in the above statement, it seems to reflect a more balanced view, except perhaps the over-generalization about "peripheral industrialization" as "a sort of modern putting-out system" characteristic of all the cases, including the South-East Asian NICs as well as perhaps all the former "socialist" countries.

Anyway, the actual rise, the production relations and the reproduction of the "peripheral mode of production" can hardly be disclosed by a description, in a direct interrelationship, of the quality of technology and of the formation of the wage level. Amin seems to have underestimated also the role that the *spontaneous mechanism* based on the established distorted socio-economic structure has played not only in promoting proletarianisation but also in preventing it from becoming complete.

In his reasoning with regard to the mechanism of "unequal exchange" and imperialist exploitation, *Amin* made the following basic presumptions:

a) international mobility of all commodities and the "pre-eminence of world values", i.e. the assumption that all the products of the capitalist mode of production are internationalised, (global) world commodities,
b) international mobility of capital, consequently the international equalization of the rates of profit,
c) the internationally immobile nature of labour, the restricted, limited international flow of labour power,
d) the international implication of the determination of the value of labour power, its formation on the world level, and the requirement of equilibrium on the level of the world system between the value of labour power and the level of the development of productive forces,
e) the indifference of the "specific" character of the commodities exported by the periphery, and the indifferent nature of use values, in general, from the point of view of unequal exchange.

(a) With regard to the first presumption, namely about the international mobility of all commodities and the pre-eminence of their world-values, it seems, in such a general formula, to involve the premise of a perfectly free international trade, a "perfect" world market, moreover, of a complete absorption of all the spheres of local ("national") production by the commodity production for the world market, i.e. the disappearance of any division line between production for export and that for domestic consumption in all the countries.

What follows therefrom is a complete disinterest, among other things, in the differences in the "organic composition of capital" (and in the turnover rate of capital, too) between the export sectors and other branches of the economy, and also in respect of the price-modifying effect of the trade policies and government interventions. However, insofar as production for export (for the "world market") and production for the national market, or for the self-consumption of the subsistence economies (a still quite typical phenomenon in the developing countries) are separated from one another, even if there may be some inter-sectoral input-output linkages between them and they all may participate in the reproduction of labour power, and insofar as the "organic composition" and turnover rate of capital operating in the export sectors deviate from the average, such an indifference can hardly be justified for a Marxist.

How can anyway products be considered as "international", "world commodities", which are produced in more or less subsistence economies with some pre-capitalist mode of production, not primarily for the market, and become, if at all, marketable commodities by no means regularly?! Inter-sectoral linkages are, particularly in the developing countries with (as Amin calls it:) "extroverted" development and disintegrated structure of economy, far from being so comprehensive as to make it possible for the production of *all* commodities to be conceived of as the result of the production of all the other commodities, that is to say, that in the input of the export products all the other sectors are participating. It is hard to accept the argument about even an indirectly "world-commodity" character of the products of the subsistence economies and the indirect participation of the latter in the world capitalist commodity production, which is based on their assumed role in the reproduction of the labour power of workers employed in the export sectors or on the import origin of some of the wage goods.

Despite all the above doubts about it, the "pre-eminence of world values" according to Amin, "provides the essence, the content of the statement on, and constitutes the precondition for the unity of the world system". However, when qualifying even the "apparently precapitalist zones" in which "products, only partially marketed, are obtained in the context of various peasant modes" (of production), as components, as constituting parts of the world system, Amin himself made questionable the "international character" of all commodities and the "pre-eminence of world values". In view of this Amin admitted that the "world capitalist system...cannot be seen as the capitalist mode of production on a world scale"[491].

[491] *Amin, S.* (1978), pp. 52, 55 and 62, as well as (1976), pp. 104, 118 and 147.

In a more recent paper of him (1993) *Amin*, though repeating substantially the same concept about the base of the unity of the world system (namely that "the law of *globalized value*" is "the foundation of the global system" which "is the very origin of world polarization" between the centres and the peripheries), explained the existence, without a "capitalist mode of production on a world scale", of a world capitalist system in a different way, by placing the issue into a different, undoubtedly realistic context, which, however, hardly resolves the contradiction. He noted: "Capitalism as a world system cannot be reduced to the capitalist mode of production, as the capitalist mode of production assumes an integrated three-dimensional market (goods, capital and labour). This integration, effected in the context of the history of the formation of central bourgeois nation states, was never extended to world capitalism. The world market is exclusively two-dimensional in its growth, progressively integrating exchanges of products and the flow of capital – to the exclusion of labour, for which the market remains compartmentalized. This very fact is enough to bring about unavoidable polarization." (p. 132)

It is, indeed, important to recognize and also stress that unlike the developed market economies, the capitalist "world market" has not been fully integrated yet, and, particularly, does not involve an integrated market for labour. This fact has got great many implications, and undoubtedly plays a significant role in the lasting survival or even deepening of the "international development gap". However, on the one hand, we can hardly speak about a fully and perfectly integrated world market of the products and services either (in view of the still applied various tariff and non-tariff barriers, open and disguised restrictions of trade), nor can we consider even the most extensively integrated market for capital as totally free of "compartmentalization". On the other hand, as *Amin* himself also noted, but without pointing to those changes forced by the growing pressure of "the march from the South" (i.e. the masses of refugees and others trying to immigrate to the North) which can already be observed and particularly expected in the future, there exists labour migration internationally, too, the growth of which, together with the spread of the arising facilities of long-distance employment created by new communication technologies, may gradually develop or expand an international market of labour, too.

But even apart from the above, it is one thing to emphasize, realistically, the lack of an integrated labour market on a world scale and its consequences in the operation of the world economy, including the lasting survival of international wage differences, and it is another thing to explain polarization by this fact. The labour market has not been integrated *within* the developed "centre", either, (except and until the rise of such regional integration as the European "common market" or "economic union"), and despite it "polarization" among the developed countries is hardly a characteristic phenomenon. But polarization between the developed group of countries and the underdeveloped group of developing ones does also follow from the very *structure* of the international division of labour (both of the "colonial pattern", namely between industrial and primary producing countries, and the new one between those producing, developing and exporting new technologies and know–how's, and those relying on their imports only). Moreover, according to Marx, polarization inevitably follows from the operation of the "law of value", from an "equivalent exchange" in the market (whether the labour market is integrated or not), since "equivalence" involves deviations from the average, thus remunerating more those producers with a higher than average productivity and penalizing all the others with lower productivity, thereby differentiating them also in progress.

Anyway, if the mode of production is not globalized yet on a world scale, the concept of "world values" must necessarily be meaningless for a Marxist, since it is to be assumed that the export products of the individual countries enter into the process of world-market price formation *not* at their "individual" (national) "values" but at their "individual" (national) "prices of production", more precisely: they would enter at the latter, provided there existed no monopolistic price diversion, state intervention, export taxes, subsidies, etc.

In other words, the "world value" of a product appears not only as an abstract but also as a totally unrealistic category. It can reflect *neither* its "national value" representing the total inputs which are as an average "socially", i.e. "nationally", within the given country, necessary for its reproduction, simply because the product enters the foreign market at a "price of production" instead of "value", *nor* can it express the average of total inputs which from the point of view of the world society as a whole appears "socially necessary" for its reproduction, because the average of its "national prices of production" hardly equals an assumed average "world value".

(b) As to the (more realistic) presumption about *international capital mobility*, it is to be noted again, first, that in reality this mobility has not been yet all-comprehensive and fully unlimited, either (not only on account of the monopoly character of a significant part of internationally mobile capital, but also due to various government restrictions or measures regulating capital flows), and, second, that the character, location and positional power of internationally mobile capitals are largely different (in favour of capital of the developed countries and at the expense of the developing countries the weaker, less concentrated capital with much less manoeuvring capability is suited to gain only secondary positions). Consequently, the international equalization of profit rates, too, is necessarily partial (limited to the spheres of free capital flows) and imperfect (implying mainly equalization between relatively equal partners), thus allowing for differences in profit rates between capitals belonging to the "centre" and those of the "periphery". Unlike Emmanuel, Amin does not denil the important role of the international capital flows, particularly FDIs, in the mechanism of "imperialist exploitation", even if he also defined unequal exchange as the main channel of exploitation.

(c) The assumption about the international immobility of labour and its mobility within the national economies has already been commented above. Since the mobility of labour is not perfect within the national economies, either, nor is it perfectly lacking on the international scene, and certain changes are taking place and expected in the future, one has to be more careful with generalization and static approach.

(d) Amin's thesis that equilibrium between the value of labour power and the level of development of the productive forces is established at the level of the world system is extremely doubtful. First, because it is linked with, and based upon, the concept of the "pre-eminence of world values". Second, because an equilibrium on the world level between the value of labour power and the development of productive forces presupposes, indeed, that the differences in the national wage levels compensate each other, which inevitably leads to an explanation of the income distribution between the various segments of the world working class by a "game theory" (that Amin strongly criticized[492]), more precisely as a "zero-sum-game" in which the working class of the periphery is confronted with that of the centre, and the more the latter gets, the less the former receives.

Amin's concept of the "universality of the reduction of labour to commodity" on a world level unambiguously suggests a primarily (or exclusively) international, more precisely global, "world" nature of the social relations of production, which integrate the system as a unity. But Amin could hardly prove this "universality". The phenomenon of labour becoming commodity can hardly be interpreted so broadly as also to imply the subordination of small commodity producers to and their exploitation by capital as a worker-capitalist relationship.

Amin, from the fact that the small-commodity peasant producers of the periphery are *de facto* dominated by capital and from his assumption that the price of their products is determined by the "law of value…not in its simple form"[493], reached (1973) the conclusion that the peasant small-commodity producer "sells in fact not his product but his *labour power*". (p. 24) The condition, however, at least according to *Marx*, of labour becoming commodity is its deprivation of the means of production. A small commodity producer working on his own land, even if he is, in the supply of other means of production, dependent on the capitalist who buys his commodity, is not in a *socially* identical position with that of a wage worker. (Economically, in respect of the income level, his situation may, of course, be similar or even worse.)

As a consequence of the confusion of the exploitation by capital with its *par excellence* capitalist form, and of the conditions of selling an ordinary commodity with those of selling labour as a commodity, even that specific feature of the "peripheral mode of production" gets lost which can be formulated as the abortion of the process of "primitive accumulation of capital", its incomplete nature (stressed also by Amin[494]).

---

492 See *Amin, S.* (1978), p. 47.

493 This is, by the way, nowhere and at no time the case, since the "small-commodity mode of production" as an independent mode of production has never existed.

494 *Amin* pointed to the remnants of the pre-capitalist mode of production, to the "incomplete, specific character of the phenomena of proletarianisation" and to "impoverishment without proletarianisation of the peasants". Amin, S. (1973), pp. 46, 56–57, 65 and 89, as well as (1976), pp. 333 and 194.

(e) Since Amin denied the role in unequal exchange, of the "specific" nature of the products exported and/or those imported by the periphery, thereby underestimating the unequal structure of international division of labour, he also got into a difficult position when answering the question why the periphery is compelled to enter into unequal exchange at all if it could produce any products at lower wage costs or why the capital of the centre does not transfer all the industries to the periphery where it could have any product produced more cheaply. Amin's answer to this question (1973), namely that "if all industries were to emigrate to the Third World, ...their production would find no outlet in the developed world" (pp. 53–56) is hardly convincing. Braun's (1973) comment (though serving an opposite approach only) sounds correct: "if the countries engaged in trade can produce the entire range of existing goods, then all of them are autonomous and hence there can be no unequal exchange". There is no reason "why it (the low-wage country) should import products which it can produce more cheaply at home" (p. 6).

Amin (1973) actually defined *unequal exchange* in such a way that, "irrespective of the mode of production of the parties taking part in exchange", and also of the "use value" of their products (pp. 53, 58–59, 62), it is supposed to be valid for all cases in which differences in wages in the production of the goods exchanged exceed the differences in labour productivity.

This definition does not include any reference to the unequal structure of international division of labour and to the role of international capital flows in shaping the latter, nor to the related specific character of the export products of the developing countries, moreover it is explicitly indifferent vis-à-vis the "use value" of products. It points only to the *relative international wage differences*, i.e. differences in wage levels greater than those in labour productivities[495].

Though Amin (1976), unlike Emmanuel, did not deny the role of foreign capital investments in the mechanism of imperialist exploitation, moreover he emphasized that "only ownership of capital makes exploitation possible" (p. 196), yet it is exactly the role of this ownership which disappears from the context underlying his definition. He also regarded (1973) unequal exchange as the *main* channel and manifestation of international exploitation, and reduced the complex motivations of the export of investment capital to the "searching of higher profit rate" attainable by the "simultaneity of modern technology and lower wages" in the periphery. (p. 83)

In his more recent paper (1993) Amin seems to have revised his view on the primary importance of unequal exchange and its role in polarization, by writing: "Actually, unequal exchange – involving products embodying efforts for which the remuneration is more unequal than the difference of productivity suggests – is but the tip of the iceberg. Four polarization mechanisms operate outside any exchange: (a) capital flight from the peripheries to the centres; (b) selective migration of work-

[495] It is worth mentioning that, in another context, this concept of "relative international wage differences" may actually give an excellent (though not complete and not exclusive) explanation for the policy of the transnational companies transferring industrial plants with modern technology.

ers in the same direction (even though such migration, precisely because it is selective, excludes the formation of a world labour market); (c) control by the centres of access to the natural resources of the entire Earth; (d) the various monopoly positions held by the companies of the centre in the world division of labour." (p. 133)

The linking of imperialist exploitation to wage differences seems to have compelled Amin, too, to put the beginning of it (which followed the three centuries of previous mercantilist plundering and of a general scramble for gold) to the time when the European wage level began to rise, and thereby to suggest, *nolens volens*, the implicit conclusion that the Western working class was at least the initiator of international exploitation.

Since, however, *Amin* was insisting on a Marxist class approach, he flatly refused all those views accusing the Western working class, its wage struggle, for the exploitation of the periphery, and called a "myth" the view that the Western working class automatically draws benefits from the transfer of surplus value. He has also rejected the conclusion, which can be drawn from such views and myth, namely that the basic conflict of interest appears between the working class of the "North" and that of the "South".

In order to resolve the contradiction between his explicit statements and the logical conclusions following implicitly from his own interpretation, too, of unequal exchange, he (1976) designated the rise of monopolies at the centre as the final cause of international exploitation, by making the Western *monopolies* responsible both for the rise in prices and for having "created the conditions needed...for wages at the centre to rise with the rise in productivity". (pp. 91, 144, 181)

The contradiction, however, does not disappear in this way, but merely shifts somewhere else. For if it is the monopolies which cause the rise in the export prices of the centre, then the role of relative wage differences appears to be superfluous in shaping the terms of trade. (Not to mention that to assume a *de facto* equalization of profit rates under monopolistic conditions is not only superfluous but also contradictory.)

*Amin* seems to have attributed an (at least "potentially") *equal productivity* to labour in the periphery as in the centre (though the former is performed, as a rule, under conditions of technical supply much inferior to that in the developed countries and of a much more unfavourable organization of production). He in fact assumed an equal value-generating capacity of both. Since the lower productivity of the countries of the periphery, particularly in their traditional peasant economies, can hardly be doubted, Amin look their "potential productivity" into account, i.e. the productivity which these economies could be supposed to attain if they were supplied with modern technology. By doing so, however, he had to interpret all differences (irrespective of their origin and content) as the manifestation, or the cause and evidence of *unequal exchange* while explaining differences in the development of productive forces only from their technological aspect, i.e. ignoring the problem of the quality and skill content of labour.

The assumption, however, that general and abstract human labour (i.e. abstracted from its concrete kinds) has a *qualitatively* identical value-creating capacity, does not justify to mix up, as Amin has done, like Emmanuel, the qualitatively identical value-creating capacity with the capacity to produce *quantitatively* equal value, too, and to disregard the difference that exists between complex and simple, between skilled and unskilled labour in respect of the quantitative measure of value generating. Nor can it justify the belief that an unskilled labourer or an uneducated peasant may easily reach the same level of productivity as a well-educated, skilled worker, once he is simply equipped with the same technology (without having already acquired the necessary knowledge, skill and experience, i.e. before having undergone a substantial change in his labour quality).

As a consequence of the above simplifications and premises, Amin seems to be inclined, despite his own concept, to ascertain the inequality of exchange on the basis of *absolute* rather than relative international wage differences[496], i.e. to forget about actual differences in productivity. And, like Emmanuel, he appears to determine the *measure* of "international exploitation" by differences in the level of real wages or in the level of consumption between developed and developing countries (and also to pay particular attention to the deterioration of the terms of trade of the latter).

As regards the deterioration of the *net barter terms of trade*, it is to be noted here again, that it may constitute just one of the possible losses suffered in the international economy,

(1) which does not necessarily mean "exploitation" (in the sense of an objective relationship determined by, and reproduced outside the exchange process between the exploiter and the exploited),

(2) which, at best, may indicate merely a *change* in the degree of "exploitation" and not its actual degree or existence,

(3) which can also occur, and has actually occurred, on the part of the economies of the "centre", too, in the course of the history of the cyclical motion of the world market.

Though *Amin* considered the *double factoral terms of trade* as the proper indicator of unequal exchange, since it includes the changes in labour productivities, too, its regular deterioration for the developing countries (even if proved as a general tendency) may signal their unjust regular losses from international trade only in case their productivity increases faster than in the developed countries (and this difference in the changes of relative productivities is always counteracted, overcompensated by the changes in relative prices, i.e. by the deterioration of the net barter terms of trade).

Despite his own critique on the theoretical roots of Emmanuel's and partly of Braun's interpretation of unequal exchange, *Amin* also captured the inequalities between the centre and the periphery of the world economy primarily in income distribution relations. As regards *development policy* or, in more general terms, the *prospects of a new world* without exploitation, dominance and inequalities, Amin expressed his belief not only in the possibility of an *alternative* path of development for the periphery, namely an "introverted" (instead of "extroverted"), "self-reliant" (instead of dependent) and people-oriented (instead of elite-favouring) development, but also in the international class struggle between the proletariat of the world and the bourgeoisie of the centre, in which the spearhead of the revolutionary forces on the world scale is the "super exploited" proletariat of the periphery, and which leads to *a socialist transformation* of the world system.

---

[496] He wrote (1973): "The only necessary condition for a case of international unequal exchange is evidently the possibility to compare real wages, which implies that wage goods should be international commodities." (pp. 18–19 and 63)

In view of the proletariat of the centre benefiting "from the growth of its real wage more or less parallel to that of labour productivity" and of the proletariat as well as the peasantry of the periphery subjected to super-exploitation mainly by unequal exchange, Amin (1978) defined the principal antagonism of the world system as "between the peoples of the periphery (the proletariat and exploited peasantry) and imperialist capital" (pp. 61, 64 and 99), shifting the centre of revolutionary forces towards the periphery.

As having been, since long time ago, fully disappointed by Soviet-type "socialism" (what he called "capitalism without capitalists", a "state-run mode of production") and also by its reformed variants ("producing the same products, in the same way and for the satisfaction of the same needs" as in capitalism, moreover preparing its return), Amin (1974b) has visualized an ideal variant of *"socialism"* which has to fully realize perfectly new social relations and produce not only with different aim (to meet real human needs), with different orientation (towards "use value" only) and for different consumers (the working masses) but also different products in a different way, i.e. a variant which *in toto* denies capitalism. Though in a less naive but not in a less idealistic way than many radical leftist intellectuals, Amin seems also inclined to consider and reject capitalism in its entirety merely as an abortive product of history, neglecting its achievements in the development of productive forces and democracy.

In view of that "the *total* realization of new production relations" cannot be achieved an overnight, particularly on a world scale, and as Amin does not share the belief in a near chance for a successful world revolution, he practically recommends the policy of "self-reliance", preferably in a collective way, and "delinking".

The idea of "self-reliance", which was already the famous slogan of the first government of the independent India and also of the Tanzanian leadership after the "Arusha Declaration", etc. has been interpreted in various ways. One of the variants calls for "self-help" only, i.e. besides the claim for international assistance it suggests concentrated domestic efforts only within the countries concerned. Another variant, as manifested in the above-mentioned Indian and Tanzanian perception, urges a reduction of dependence on foreign powers and international relations, while an extreme version suggests a full "economic independence" even at the price of cutting off all economic relations with the developed countries, i.e. isolation. Its "collective" variant, i.e. "self-reliance" of the South as a whole, may also mean either a realistic call for promoting primarily ECDC (economic cooperation among developing countries) or a collective delinking from the North, with the illusion of a lasting unity of interests within the South and its societies, and without a due attention both to the given structures and the difficulties, if not the impossibility, of such a delinking.

In view of the accelerated and far-reaching process of *globalisation* Amin (1993) outlined three, theoretically possible options: "(a) Take up the challenge of capitalist globalisation as it is, while trying to better the national position by joining in the game of international competition; (b) Act to change the world system in a direction favourable to a "better" (and even "fair") globalized development; (c) Stand aloof from such a world system ('delinking')." (p. 132)

Though such options do not necessarily exclude each other, Amin, in agreement with the Report of the South Commission (1990) that "there are no pipe dreams about mitigating the harmful effects of capitalist globalisation and in particular, for South–South co-operation", unambiguously suggests the last option alone. In his view (1993): "In any event, globalisation – with or without regionalisation – is unacceptable to the peoples of the periphery". (p. 136)

With regard to the changes since the collapse of the Soviet Union, Amin noted (1993): "...The 'new world order'..., following quickly upon the beginning of the Soviet break-up, is ...a new empire of chaos, of the utmost instability, due to be afflicted by violent contradictions, renewal of inter-centre rivalries and upheavals in the peripheries in the South and tomorrow in the East. In these circumstances, ...it is the evolution of this competition [between Europe, Japan and the United States – T. S.] that will determine the structure of globalisation or its possible partial negation by the construction of regional groupings and/or by the delinking of regions in the periphery. ...one can see how – in the context of transnationalization – regional sub-poles crystallize around each of those three major poles". (p. 135)

This seems to reflect reality fairly well but without taking those new changes stemming from the technological revolutions, particularly in communication and information, into account, and involves an excessive extrapolation of what has been observed in a few years only. True, Amin added: "It is premature...to speak of reorganization within transnationalisation. The peripheries remain largely open to competition of the rival poles within their commercial and also financial markets". (p. 135)

In rejecting the arguments about the necessary participation in the process of globalisation, and in order to underline the need for *delinking* as an escape from the latter, Amin (1993) produced a new concept of development: "Development should, by definition, be different in nature so as to overcome polarization. The development concept is in essence a concept critical of capitalism." (p. 136)

"The argument that no society can escape the permanent challenge of (capitalist) globalisation, that development is nothing other than development within this system, and that no autonomous development is possible outside it, is tied to the reality of the facts alone – that is, that this is how capitalist development works – but immediately forswears the idea that it may be possible to 'change the world'. Because the two have to be kept distinct, I suggest that the two concepts of capitalist expansion and development should not be mixed up even if in current usage they are frequently confused. Capitalist expansion is by nature polarizing." (p. 136)

Amin dissociates himself from the "development ideology that prevailed after the Second World War" because it "did not make this distinction clear". He explains the failure of all those attempts to overcome "underdevelopment" while remaining within the world capitalist system by the acceptance of the argument mentioned above. Strangely enough, despite the policy of isolation and autarky of the former "socialist" countries, particularly before those few, partial and inconsistent reforms taking place in East-Central Europe, he connects their failure, too, just like that of the developing countries in general, with the "staying within the world capitalist system"[497].

[497] He wrote (1993): "For some – the national bourgeoisies of the Third World of the Bandung era (1955–1975) – the objective of development was 'to catch up', while staying in the world system, through appropriate state policies (nationalization, industrialization, etc). For others, the 'socialist' states, this same objective ('to catch up', which implies evident similarities) was mixed up with some shreds of the contradictory objective of building 'another society'." (p. 136)

Though it is true, that contrary to the ideological declarations of the leadership of the former "socialist" countries about "breaking out of the world capitalist system" and about the rise and existence of another, "socialist system of world economy", these countries had never been able to escape from the former and establish the latter, nevertheless their failure of development (of really "catching up") is due to a great extent to the very policy of delinking[498]. Moreover, their complete failure in developing towards a true socialist system in a democratic way, has also been linked with the policy of isolation which as coupled with hostility between these countries and the outside world had almost inevitably to induce militarisation and lead to the institutionalisation of a party-state dictatorship. It is another question, of course, how an original, at least partly socialistic endeavour, and the declared aim of socialist development (which was used as a demagogy only for legitimising the system), had been completely replaced in practice by the nationalistic aim of "catching up" with the advanced capitalist countries. And it is also another issue whether a real socialist transformation is possible at all in local dimensions, within single countries or even their blocs, either with or without delinking, as long as the global system works in an opposite direction.

As a consequence of the "development crisis" both in the South and the East, an *ideological crisis* has emerged which, according to Amin, gives birth to new false ideas, such as the denial of the possibility of "national" development in a globalized world and the illusion about a "social democratic" solution on a world level[499]. Though *Amin* is unable to suggest a better alternative, he opposes the latter simply by assuming a never changing attitude, almost a sort of conspiracy and concerted action of the Western powers (without or independently of the responses within their society) aiming at the maintenance of the "status quo" and thereby blocking the development of the periphery.

In *Amin*'s view, "...the peoples of the periphery are blocked by the objectives of the Western powers, for these are preoccupied exclusively with the maintenance of the *status quo* of which they are the beneficiaries. The postulate affirming the identity of capitalism and democracy, which is the underlying theme in the orchestration of the North's interventions in the South, is a deceitful trick... Endless examples could be given to show that this new 'humanist and universalist' discourse is not credible." (p. 137)

---

[498] On this issue see my former article: *Szentes, T.* (1986).

[499] *Amin* noted (1993): "...The failure of the 'development', incapable of reducing the gap, led to an ideological crisis. In its place a series of new initiatives appeared... Democracy, in this spirit, was advanced as the condition for development and no longer as its delayed product." "...At the same time the idea was put forward that interdependence at all levels...is such that only 'world development' is henceforth conceivable (national development is described as a myth); that this development, founded on political democracy and the market, could be 'something else' (and better) than that known up to now in the history of capitalist expansion. Put otherwise, social-democracy could become the solution to the problems on a world level as it has been for the Western countries." (p. 137)

As it appears, *Amin* himself becomes to some extent the victim of the old idea of "third-worldism" (also manifested in some "new left" concepts) insofar as sharing the assumption that the North as well as the South are, in the final analysis, homogeneous units, each with one single interest, always and everywhere conflicting with each other, and that the South[500] alone may or should "change the world". Thereby Amin seems also questioning the prospect of progressive changes in attitude and also in interest, particularly under the pressure of the public opinion and/or the aggravation of global problems, leading to new dialogues and constructive compromises. This follows perhaps from that Amin rejects capitalism *in toto* and denies that it could ever promote development at all. Moreover, he qualifies it as a "criminal" system doomed to "suicide"[501]. This presentation of capitalism as a "criminal" and "suicidal" system is not only ahistorical (quite contrary to Marx's perception, and particularly to the changes since Marx's time) but also indistinctive (regarding the many variants of the system). It is *willy-nilly* just as a false, purely ideological perception of "capitalism" (supposed to be a given, single, unchangeable, all-embracing entity) as its opposite appraisal, which apologetically presents it, in general, or any of its present variants within countries or its prevailing world system as the "best of all the possible worlds", as the final stage of human development. Reality does not know such opposite extremes only, and a realistic option cannot be found accordingly, either.

Amin himself, contrary to his exaggerating critique of capitalism, cannot (1993) suggest but a reconciliation of "self-reliance" with "general interdependence" and a mutual, reciprocal adjustment of both the North and the South, which presupposes, of course, *compromises* and on-going dialogue. He finally interprets the very concept of "delinking", too, accordingly, thereby giving it a more moderate but also ambiguous content:

> "...'General interdependence' and the legitimate concern for self-reliance must be reconciled, the logic of mutual and reciprocal adjustment must replace the logic of unilateral adjustment on the part of the weakest in the pursuit of expansion for the exclusive benefit of the strongest. This is precisely my definition of delinking: the submission of external relationships to the needs of internal development. This concept is therefore exactly the opposite of the concept of unilateral adjustment advanced today in theory and practice." (p. 138)

---

[500] *Amin* (1993) believes that the bargaining power of the South, which temporararily decreased because of technological revolution, will be increased in the future by a growing scarcity of mineral resources again: "...True, the revolution of technology, on the one hand, and the quantity of mineral resources of the North American and Australian continents, on the other, have diminished for the time being the importance of the contributions of the Third World. But this does not mean that the Third World is now marginal. ...There is every chance of an all-out race for raw materials once again. This is all the more likely as these resources may very well become scarce, not only because of the exponential cancer of waste in Western consumption, but also because of new industrialization in the peripheries." (p. 133)

[501] He wrote (1993): "... the uncontrollable exponential growth that follows from the logic of the capitalist mode of production is, as was rediscovered by ecologists, suicidal. Capitalism both as a mode of production and as a world system is therefore simultaneously suicidal and criminal..." (p. 136)

This shows, anyway, that Amin had to realize that globalisation can hardly be stopped, delinking as isolation is not possible, and there must be a way without isolation, by means of interest reconciliation "to change the world" for better.

## 5. "Counter-revolutions" versus reformist and radical views

### 5.1. The "monetarist counter-revolution" against the "Keynesian revolution" in economics

If it was the marked manifestation of disequilibria in the economies of the developed countries and the Great Crisis of 1929 which induced the "Keynesian revolution" in economics, while the drastic deterioration of the terms of trade of the developing countries from the mid-1950s and their cumulative indebtedness manifesting the disequilibria also in the world economy were obviously giving an impulse to the formation of the Post-Keynesian Reformist school, then it is more than likely that the "monetarist counter-revolution" have been linked with the grave problem of accelerated inflation in the late 1960s and early 1970s, and with the disturbances caused by growing budget and/or balance-of-payments deficits, in the mechanism of the Welfare State as well as in the system of indirect State interventions regulating the market economy in the developed countries. The lost efficiency of the Keynesian methods of regulation paved the way for *neo-liberalism* suggesting a return, by deregulation, privatisation and liberalization, to a spontaneous market economy.

Though Neo-liberalism and Monetarism have come to the fore hand in hand, their inner logic is not only substantially different but to some extent also contradictory. While Neo-liberalism opposes, in principle, all kinds of interventions in the spontaneous operation of the market economy, and advocates a full deregulation, indeed, Monetarism refuses certain types of regulation only and suggests the substitution of a monetarist policy, i.e. a regulation of the economic process by means of money supply, for the Keynesian fiscal policies and all those interventions based upon budget expenditures, central income redistribution, and the State sector. Neo-liberalism is more or less identical with or very close to the Neo-Classical economics, while Monetarism, besides its liberal principles and also Neo-Classical components, seems to reflect a certain Mercantilist approach and involve also some elements of the attacked Keynesian theory, too.

*Milton Friedman*, who is considered to be the "father" of modern Monetarism, presents the issue of economic equilibrium as a monetary equilibrium, i.e. equilibrium between the supply of and the demand for money, and attributes the money supply, i.e. the available *quantity of money* a decisive role in determining economic processes. According to him, under normal conditions in a free market economy, i.e. without disturbing interventions of the State, a slow, gradual (and almost predictable) increase in the supply of money, which corresponds to a "golden rule" of emission to be kept by the central bank, tends to lead to a growth of demand in the markets for commodities, consumer and capital goods, bonds, securities and other assets. This is because of the psychological response of the people, consumers and producers alike, who (as feeling to be better off though only their nominal incomes increased, or having high inflation "expectations") is inclined to spend more, thereby causing an increase in effective demand. The latter induces, by rising prices, a growth in production and investment, the result of which will be finally, through a cyclical process[502] and time lag, an increase also in the demand for money. In such a way the demand for money adjusts itself to the increased supply of money after some time during which national income also increases.

The ratio of the increment of national income to that of money supply is expressed by the so-called "money multiplier", which thus shows by how much national income changes due to a unit change in the quantity of money, or more precisely: how much national income should change then in order to reach again a monetary equilibrium in the economy. (The multiplier effect of an increase by one unit of the money supply is attributed to its spread effect in the banking system, which follows, like the case of the investment multiplier, a declining geometrical series.)

Thus, instead of the rate of interest it is the quantity of money through which a monetarist policy can influence the economy. A permanent but slow and small increase in money supply can promote *economic growth* without resulting in lasting disequilibria. However, an unexpected sudden and large increase in the quantity of money seriously disturbs equilibrium and deviates the actual rate of unemployment from its "natural rate". Under these conditions a deflationary policy is needed, and insofar as increased savings have to be encouraged to absorb the excess supply of money, an income redistribution (e.g. by regressive tax rates and a reduction of taxes on profits and other capital incomes) in favour of the rich rather than the poor may be recommendable[503] in view of the higher saving propensity of the richer strata.

The Monetarist concept, though still reflecting the Classical views on (a neutral) money and their quantity theory of money, and also accepting the Neo-Classical price mechanism of "cleaning the market" and leading automatically to equilibrium, seems to make use of certain elements of the Keynesian economics, too. For example, when applying the concept of "multiplier" (in the sense of attributing a certain growth stimulating effect to an appropriately increased money supply), when taking psychological "expectations" into account, when

[502] See e.g. *Friedman, M.* (1969), and for a detailed critical summarization of Friedman's monetarist theory: *Mátyás, A.* (1979) and (1999).

[503] It is to be noted that otherwise and in general, *Friedman* did also advocate, for humanitarian reasons, financial support to the poor (as a "negative tax").

looking at money as a real asset which may function not only in the exchange process, and when recognizing the cyclical motion of the economy (though explaining it differently and rejecting the Keynesian recipe for anti-cyclical policy).

As regards the *international economy*, the Monetarist theory, while also assuming an automatic tendency, in the long run, towards *equilibrium*, i.e. the existence of a self-correcting mechanism with reversible processes, derives the growth of the actual deficits or sufficits in the balance of international payments from the excess in the domestic money supply over the demand for money or from the excess in money demand over the domestic money supply, respectively.

With a certain simplification the Monetarist concept can be summed up as follows: Insofar as the monetary authorities do not satisfy the excess demand for money by increased emission, it will be met by an inflow of money from abroad, thus resulting a surplus in the balance of payments, while in the opposite case the excess quantity of money tends to flow out of the country, thereby causing a deficit (or a growth in the latter). The same is the result if the excess demand for money implies a reduction of expenditures on goods and services, i.e. a decline in effective demand for the latter, within the country, which encourages their exports, or, on the contrary, if the excess supply of money leads, because of increased domestic prices, to increased import of goods and services. Since, however, under a flexible ("freely floating") exchange rate system, i.e. under the conditions of an ideal currency market with exchange rates determined only by changes in supply and demand of the currencies, the excess money supply which causes deficit (or its growth) in the balance of payments of the country concerned, results automatically in a depreciation of its currency, while an excess demand for money in the partner country, thus causing a surplus in its balance of payments, will make its currency automatically appreciated, the temporary disequilibria are almost immediately corrected without any intervention. Such an automatic equilibrium mechanism seems similar to the classical "price-specie-flow" mechanism and its neoclassical version based upon exchange rates adjustment, but unlike the latter does not necessarily imply differences and changes in the price levels of the partner countries.

As according to this theory the deficit or the surplus in the balance of payments is merely or primarily a monetary phenomenon, following from an excess in the supply of or the demand for money, the mechanism of self-correction is also a monetary process, namely the outflow of excess money or the inflow of money from abroad, which may finally eliminate disequilibria also under fixed exchange rates. (The policy of devaluation may have the same temporary effect in the case of the deficit country, but only if the resulting increase in the demand for money is not counterbalanced by an increased domestic supply of money.)

No inflation may occur (or last long) if the money supply keeps pace with the growth of the economy and its demand for money. This applies both to the individual countries and the world economy as a whole. Since, however, the rates of economic growth (GDP) of the countries in the world widely differ, the demand for money tends to grow faster in those countries with a higher rate of GDP growth, while the slowly growing economies tend to have an excess supply of money. The former may thus enjoy an inflow of money and a surplus in the balance of payments, while the latter face a (growing) deficit in their balance. (While the Keynesian theory assumed that a fast growth of the economy and incomes, generated by investments, might result in a trade deficit, since import depends on income, the monetarist concept attributes the growth of the GDP a favourable effect on the balance of payments.) Those countries whose money supply growth is above the world average, as a consequence of their GDP growth rate remaining below the world average, actually export their inflation to other countries, thereby disturbing the monetary equilibrium in the latter, too.

What follows is that equilibrium both within countries and internationally is disturbed, as a rule, by an irresponsible policy of the monetary authorities in the countries where the policy of money emission (and credit creation) does not follow the "golden rule" and creates excess money supply, which the demand for money is unable to adjust itself. Since such an irresponsible policy is most often aimed at *deficit financing,* i.e. to finance by emission the growing deficit in the central budget (which may stem from Keynesian-motivated or welfare expenditures), the Monetarists pay particular attention to the central budget and fiscal policy, and suggest a strictly balanced budget or, if necessary, a radical cut of expenditures.

The Monetarist theory has certainly influenced not only the government policy of many countries in the 1980s but also the conditionality policy of the international monetary institutions. No doubt, the corresponding restrictive monetary and fiscal policy has proved relatively successful in cutting drastically the rate of inflation and in improving the balance of payments, but in most cases either at the expense of other countries or of keeping unemployment at a still high level, and destroying the "social safety nets" of several welfare states by drastic reductions in the budget of social security, education, public health, and other social services.

The main shortcoming of this theory follows exactly from its bias for monetary phenomena, from paying primary attention to the monetary side of economic processes. It is to be noted, however, that those, particularly politicians, making use of the monetarist theory for legitimising, under the label of "stabilization" and balance-of-payments adjustment, an excessively restrictive economic policy, often in a form of "shock therapy", which radically cuts the welfare expenditures in the budget (rather than the costs of state bureaucracy and its fringe benefits), are simply ignoring that modern Monetarism does not completely neglect the real economy and its growth. Since a disequilibria between the supply of money and the demand for it can be overcome not only by a reduction of the former but also by an increase in the latter, which normally results from the growth of production and investment, the Monetarist school (at least its logic) hardly suggests an exclusively monetary solution to the problem of disequilibria, an absolute priority to monetary (and fiscal) restrictions at the expense of economic growth.

## 5.2. "Orthodox counter-revolutions" in development economics: a Neo-Classical and a Marxist one

Along with, and partly influenced by the so-called "monetarist counter-revolution" the credit and influence of those theoretical schools or individual views[504] blaming the prevailing international economic order for its "exploitive" nature, for "unequal exchange" and "immiserizing growth" and suggesting a policy of delinking with self-reliance and increased role of the State, have drastically declined, and a sort of "counter-revolution" has taken place in international and development economics, too.

The "counter-revolution" in international economics seems to have been well-manifested in the "Washington consensus"[505] which, in view of the Monetarists' concern about the over-supply of money typically caused by deficit-financing (of a Keynesian type of fiscal policy), has urged the governments to exercise fiscal discipline, and in consonance with the neoliberal "mainstream" economics has recommended liberalization of trade and financial markets, devaluation to make exchange rates competitive, privatisation of state companies, deregulation and tax reforms, removal of discrimination versus, and of the barriers to entry of foreign firms, the safeguarding of property rights, the diminution of the role of the State in the economy (restricting it to public security, environment protection, etc.) and an "outward-orientation", "openness" of the economy. Such a consensus appearing as a "one world consensus", i.e. as universally valid for all the countries of the world became the major guideline of the conditionality policy of the IMF and the World Bank.

According to *Michael Todaro* (1997) the "neoclassical counterrevolution", i.e. the "neoclassical challenge to the prevailing development orthodoxy can be divided into three component approaches: the free-market approach, the public-choice (or 'new political economy') approach, and the 'market-friendly' approach." (p. 87) While the "free-market" approach suggests that "markets alone are efficient", the public-choice theory (or "new political economy") goes even further to argue that "the governments can do nothing right" (since "public officials use their positions to extract bribes from rent-seeking citizens", and "states use their power to confiscate private property from individuals", causing thereby "misallocation of resources" and "reduction in individual freedoms").

These two "component approaches" seem, indeed, to represent the "counterrevolution" in question, as both correspond to the conventional Neo-Classical principles of liberalism and market-spon-

[504] *Deepak Lal* (1983) quotes, with full agreement, *Phyllis Deane* who stated that the "disadvantage of most attempts at an ideological classification of economic theories...is that they tend to reveal more about the political and intellectual bias of the compiler and his mentors than about the methodological qualities of the economic doctrines thus labeled." (p. 2) *Deane* seems to be right, indeed, insofar as the "political bias" is concerned, but hardly with regard to the "intellectual bias" (which does not necessarily follow from a politically motivated ideological stand), nor is it acceptable to put the emphasis on "methodological" qualities only, neglecting thereby the qualities in substance, in the relevance of the content and approach.

[505] See *Williamson, J.* (1997) and *Waelbroeck, J.* (1998).

taneity. Though in Todaro's view the "neoclassical counterrevolution" is also marked by the third variant, namely the "market-friendly approach" which has been manifested in the World Development Reports of the World Bank in the 1990s, it appears to indicate ("by accepting the notion that market failures are more widespread in developing countries") a move towards eclecticism rather than back to conventional myth of the market.

Almost parallel with the regained dominance of the liberal concepts in international economics and of the belief in "monoeconomics", in the universal validity of the Neo-Classical – Monetarist "mainstream economics", a certain "counter-revolution" appeared in (or rather against) development economics as well, which has primarily (though not exclusively) manifested itself in two, opposite variants, namely in an orthodox Neo-Classical and in an orthodox Marxist attack.

Though former is represented by several scholars, such as, among others, Peter Bauer, Ian Little, Bela Balassa, Jagdish Bhagwati, etc., in the following we shall discuss in details *Deepak's* arguments only, as they were addressed to the critical theories more directly than others.

According to *M. Todaro* (1997) "the central argument of the neoclassical counterrevolution is that underdevelopment results from poor resource allocation due to incorrect pricing policies and too much state intervention by overly active Third World governments", and "by permitting competitive free markets to flourish, privatising state-owned enterprises, promoting free trade and export expansion, welcoming investors from developed countries, and eliminating the plethora of government regulations and price distortions in factor, product, and financial markets, both economic efficiency and economic growth will be stimulated." (pp. 86–87) While such recipes did perfectly fit the "Washington consensus" concerning the policies to be followed by all countries of the world, the above-mentioned "central argument" is nothing but an old, ahistorical explanation of the phenomenon called "underdevelopment", taking it out of the context of the world economy and even of the structural, institutional and sociological legacies of the past.

*Jean Waelbroeck* (1998) summarizes the tenets of the "Washington consensus" as follows:

"– Governments should exercise fiscal discipline, obviating the need for an inflation tax.
- Public expenditure priorities should be shifted from politically sensitive areas to neglected fields with high-income returns and the potential to improve income distribution.
- Tax reform should broaden the tax base and reduce marginal rates. Ways should be found to tax flight capital.
- Financial markets should be partially liberalized.
- Exchange rates should be kept competitive.
- Import quotas should be replaced by tariffs.
- Barriers impeding the entry of foreign firms should be removed; foreign and domestic firms should compete on equal terms.
- State enterprises should be privatized.
- Governments should remove regulations that are not justified by such criteria as safety, environment protection, or prudential supervision on financial institutions.
- Property rights should be safeguarded." (p. 140)

### 5.2.1. Lal's attempt to denounce development economics

In his argumentation Lal has, indeed, fairly well utilized the vulnerability caused by exaggerations, one-sidedness or inconsistencies, of the reformist and radical theories which reject the myth of a harmoniously operating market economy and call for corrections or transformation. Despite the enormous differences in views of the latter, particularly in respect of the desired nature, role and sphere of activity of the State, Lal (1983) focussed his attack on the so-called "Dirigiste Dogma" and all those (from Keynes, through Willy Brandt[506], to Samir Amin) having fed it by sharing the "belief that the price mechanism, or the working of a market economy, needs to be supplanted (and not merely supplemented) by various forms of direct government control, both national and international, to promote economic development" (p. 5) and also questioning the relevance of "orthodox economics".

Lal criticized Keynes and the Keynesian heritage for having provided, by its critique of "orthodox economics" and its "concentration on macro-economics", the "analytical and empirical bases for development economics"[507]. (p. 7)

In Lal's opinion, the Keynesian theory, by suggesting "an implicit or explicit rejection of the primary role assigned by orthodox economics to changes in relative prices in mediating imbalances" (p. 8), i.e. neglecting "the role of the price mechanism", and by concentrating on macro-economics, i.e. "thinking in terms of aggregates of different commodities'", has led, through the works of Tinbergen and Leontief, "to a particular type of applied economics research in both developed and developing countries which can be termed 'mathematical planning'" and to the "input-output analysis", respectively. This has resulted in the practice of "development planning" which "seemingly acquired a hard scientific and quantifiable character". (p. 9) Following the "Leontief input–output system", which "building as it did on the Soviet practice of 'material balance planning', ignored relative price changes", the "typical development plan first laid down a desired rate of growth of aggregate consumption. Then the quantities of different commodities required in fix proportions, ...were derived from an input–output table for the economy. Since such plans were presented in terms of desired quantities of production of various goods, their implementation most often entailed direct controls on production...". (pp. 9–10)

While accepting *Hirschman's* criteria (1981) of classification of the various schools of economics according to accepting or rejecting (a) "mono-economics", i.e. the relevance of the same economics also for developing countries, and (b)

[506] According to *Lal* one of the most influential expression of the "Dirigiste Dogma" was the famous *Brandt Commission's* Reports (the "North–South – A Programme for Survival" in 1980, and the "Common Crisis – North–South: Co-operation for World Recovery" in 1983).

[507] Though *Lal* (1983) attributes such a decisive role in shaping "development economics" to the Keynesian theory, he refers to *V.K. R. V Rao* who among others denied its relevance for the developing countries which, "unlike developed ones, did not face unemployment of both men and machines". Apart from this, practically all those scholars attacked by Lal as representing "development economics" (p. 8), including even those few in the "post-Keynesian reformist school" who were really Keynesians, either criticized the Keynesian economics, and also questioned its applicability, or gone much further than Keynes in the analysis of the world economy.

"the mutual-benefit claim", i.e. the assumption of mutual benefits resulting from international economic relations, *Lal*, contrary to Hirschman, categorized "development economics" as a whole, despite its great many variants, into the same group as Neo-Marxists belong to, which rejects both. The only difference, according to him, is that Neo-Marxists, unlike "development economists", wish "to smash the whole world capitalist system".

It seems quite obvious that for Lal what really matters is whether one shares the belief in one single stream of economic theories, namely the conventional "mainstream" economics (particularly the so-called "welfare economics") and its general validity, universal applicability, rather than any other difference between theoretical schools of economics in general or between the variants of development economics in particular. In the light of such an insistence on one particular theory of economics, such an almost religious belief in its universal and exclusive applicability, one would question who is making indeed an ideological classification with a political bias?!

It is also worth mentioning that, as we have seen, "developmentalism" and "development economics", interpreted, of course, in a different way, namely implying exactly those conventional explanations of "underdevelopment" following from "mainstream" economics, have been fully rejected by Neo-Marxists, too, who are the major target of Lal's critique.

Lal regards *welfare economics* that "branch of economic theory which provides the logic to assess the desirability of alternative economic policies". (p. 10) But he adds that "far from being an apologia for the *laissez-faire* doctrine, as many suppose, modern welfare economics provides the precise reasons why, even in the absence of distributional considerations, a real-world *laissez-faire* economy is not likely to be Pareto-efficient – because (a) it is unlikely to be perfectly competitive, and (b) it will certainly lack universal markets." (p. 14) Lal wishing to defend the belief in a spontaneous market mechanism, without, as he strangely thinks, "arguing for *laissez faire*" (p. 6), calls it "absurd...to jump to the conclusion that, because *laissez faire* may be inefficient and inequitable, any form of government intervention thereby entails a welfare improvement". (p. 14) Apart from the lack of clarification of what distinguishes, in his view, the argumentation for "laissez faire" from a general rejection of the role of government intervention in the economy, it is to be noted that if the very form, content and direction of the latter are not specified, the attack against the concept which assumes that "*any* form of government intervention" is "dirigisme" obviously misses the target since nobody has ever stated it!

If there is, at all, any distinction made by Lal between the acceptance of "laissez faire" in general and the rejection of a particular government policy, it seems to refer to the *policy of foreign trade and international capital flows*.

He primarily criticizes "development economists" for suggesting "inward-looking" instead of "outward-looking" policy, import-substitution or autarky instead of "export-orientation", and protectionist trade policy. As simply neglecting the fact that for very long time most of the developing countries had been specialized exactly in an export-oriented primary production, which obviously points to that not any export-orientation may lead to success, he blames the "terms-of-trade myth" (p. 21) and the trade pessimism created by the Prebisch–Singer thesis (and reinforced by the "two-gap" models of development in McKinnon's study and the article of Chenery and Strout[508]) for suggesting an import-substituting industrialization, trade and exchange controls and/or foreign aid, respectively, as a panacea.

Lal (1983) refers, with agreement, to the empirical and historical studies of Ian Little, Tibor Scitovsky, Maurice Scott, Béla Balassa, Jagdish Bhagwati, Anne Krueger and others, which made a "final attack on the protectionist aspects of the *Dirigiste Dogma*", and "provided an impressive empirical validation of the theoretical case against protection and for the view that, even though *laissez faire* may not be justifiable, free trade remains the best policy for developing (and developed) countries." (pp. 27–28) Lal enumerates and, by the case of India, also illustrates the disadvantages of protectionism.

As regards the "effective rates of protection which determine the relative profitability of producing different goods", they result, according to him, in such a "pattern of resource allocation" as "often been based on no economic rationale", and insofar as "the structure of effective protection" implies a relative cheapening of capital goods, producers have "an incentive to choose relatively more capital-intensive methods of production at the expense of employing more labour". The application of the so-called "indigenous availability criterion" may lead to "a complete insulation of domestic production from foreign competitive pressures which, coupled with an overall excess of demand in the economy" implies that the domestic producers have "little incentive to reduce costs". The use of "import entitlement for exporters in the form of import licenses" whose premium provides the exporter with a subsidy, it may create "a host of new distortions in the export sector". And insofar as these entitlements are "tied to the import content of exports", they subsidize "import-intensive exports rather than those with a high domestic value-added". (pp. 29–31)

The great many disadvantages of protectionism, which are all well known from standard textbooks, including those few repeated by Lal, can hardly be doubted in general. Even those, like Friedrich List and others, who, in view of the uneven competitiveness of the products of a more and a less developed country, suggested a temporary protection of the so-called "infant industry", would not have questioned them. How can one simply disregard the enormous gap in efficiency, determined primarily by technologies and qualities of labour, between developed and developing countries?! How can one deny the right of the latter to follow the past (if not also the present) example of the developed countries, i.e. to promote also by temporary protection versus oppressive foreign competition, the development of those industries having at the present, i.e. according to a *static* approach, perhaps no (given) comparative advantage, but promising, indeed, (created) competitive advantages in the future, i.e. in a dynamic sense?!

[508] See *McKinnon, R. I.* (1964) and *Chenery, H.–Strout, A. M.* (1966).

Lal's conclusion (from the Indian case) is that the trade control system may engender incalculable "inefficiency, waste, and corruption", and, in general, that the "obstacles to the growth of developing countries' exports are largely internal, not external; economic agents in these countries have reacted to the distorting incentives created by protectionist regimes of trade control much in the way that standard economic theory predicts; planners have often shown a lack of foresight which would have swiftly bankrupted a private agent!". (p. 32) One may agree with such a critique of the actual policy of many governments and of the short-sightedness of planners, indeed. However, the general statement about the internal rather than external obstacles to the export growth of the South, besides contradicting to some extent Lal's correct attack on the North's protectionism[509], ignores the structural consequences of the century-old specialization (whether imposed from outside or chosen "freely") of the latter on primary production, and also the changes, since the second world war and more recently, in the production and consumption patterns of the North, which all represent directly or indirectly "external" obstacles indeed. His statement seems to serve only one purpose: to underline the old dogma which by taking the problem of the rise or survival of "underdevelopment" of the majority of countries out of the context of world development, defines it as the consequence of internal factors only.

Lal, in order to support his conclusion and oppose the "new trade pessimism" (of the 1980s), criticizes the "demand-oriented theory of development" which regards foreign trade as the "engine of growth" and exports as "driven by external demand". It is to be noted, by the way, that the concept of foreign trade being an "engine of growth" is one of the most typical propositions of the Neo-Classical, "mainstream" economics in general, i.e. exactly of that "orthodox economics" Lal wishes to defend! It seems strange to accept the latter, on the one hand, in general, but to reject its thesis, on the other, if applied to a particular case. Lal opposes the "engine-of-growth models" as applied to the developing countries not only because they "assume that the supply of developing countries' exports is perfectly elastic so that export volumes will be solely determined by developed countries' expenditure on these goods", but also because they cannot explain why developing countries' manufactured exports have been able to grow faster than developed

[509] *Lal* (1983) noted that "protectionism poses a more serious threat to Southern prosperity than the mere slowing down of Northern growth since they pinpoint both the real dangers to Third World development in the external environment and the unrealism of the major assumption behind Lewis-type views." He suggests the North "the replacement of inefficient lines of production by cheaper imports" which "apart from the obvious gains it confers on consumers, allows the release of resources for more efficient and productive uses" in accordance with the "emerging comparative advantage". He accuses the "protectionist lobbies" in developed countries, criticizes the application of import quotas which inflict on the well-being of both workers and consumers, and qualifies "the 'voluntary' export restraints increasingly imposed by the developed world" as "particularly biased against those countries which are just about to climb a particular rung of the ladder". (pp. 36–39)

countries' incomes". Here again, where reference is obviously made to the success in industrial growth and export of a few "newly industrialized countries", the historical changes, which, having taken place since World War II and more recently (in technologies and structures of production, consumption, investments, capital flows, "gravitation centre", etc.) in the world economy, are completely neglected, no matter how these changes have been facilitating the catching-up of a few, while hindering it for most of the developing countries.

Lal also rejects the "Myrdal-Balogh type of argument about the inimical effects of trade as a 'zero-sum game'", and the concept of unequal exchange, including the one (based also on "Lewis's second model" and all the one-factor models) which equates commodity (net barter) and double factoral terms of trade, and "suggests that a productivity gain which reduces the prices of Southern exports would not lead to any Southern gain". Lal notes that even if an increase in labour productivity in e.g. coffee production results, by lowering the relative price of coffee, in a deterioration of both commodity and factorial terms of trade of a developing country, the latter would still enjoy a "consumption gain", if this country "also consumes coffee it produces and exports". (Can one blame the people of developing countries for not consuming coffee enough or for producing products for export, which they do not consume themselves?! Even if it is a mere assumption used for an argument, the presumed freedom of choice of producers and consumers alike, may fit the standard textbooks' naivety fairly well, but by no means reality.) Lal accepts neither the assumption about the "unlimited supplies of labour available at fixed real wage for export production in the South" (which, indeed, and as already noted, is an excessive simplification even though it points to a disintegrated structure of economy with a certain function of the "traditional" sector), nor the assumption "that the South does not produce the capital goods it requires for domestic capital formation and growth and can only acquire them from the North by trading its primary commodity exports". (Op. cit., pp. 33–34 and 41–43) As to the latter, the proceeding industrialization in most of the developing countries, which is also linked with the already mentioned historical changes in structures, can hardly prove the general ability of these countries to produce whatever capital goods they need, not to mention the technologies, know-how's and "intellectual properties".

In the argumentation against "dependency theories" Lal refers not only to those Marxists (like B. Warren and S. Smith) attacking Amin and other advocators of the concepts of self-reliance and delinking as an escape from dependence and exploitation, but also to *I. M. D. Little* who drew the conclusion from studying the case of the "four little dragons" (Hong Kong, Singapore, Taiwan and South Korea) that: "their success is almost entirely due to good policies and the ability of the people", to "a marked change of policy from import substitution to export promotion", and that the major lesson from the success of South Korea is "that the labour-intensive, export-oriented policies, which *amounted to almost free-trade conditions for exporters,* were the primary cause of an extremely rapid and labour-intensive industrialisation"[510]. In defence of Little's conclusion versus *Amartya Sen's* comment, who cited instances of government intervention in Korea, Lal, stressing the distinction between "laissez faire" and free trade, considers it Sen's mistake to identify these two, and allows an argument that "success has been achieved *despite* intervention".

Lal also refused the concept of "foreign-exchange bottleneck" and "the argument that *external capital inflows* are required to ease this bottleneck" and/or "to supplement domestic saving which was assumed to be too low and not easily raised to yield rates of investment and of growth of national income considered sufficiently high". The above concept and argument, which support both the claim of developing countries for foreign aid and capital inflows (justified by Post-Keynesian Reformist views) and the "diffusionist approach" (stemming from conventional explanations, by internal causes, of underdevelopment, and intensively attacked by Frank and other radicals of the "school of dependencia"), are refused by him. In his view, "there is no such bottleneck – except of a country's own making", and "the role of foreign capital inflows has been much exaggerated". He doubts that "poor countries would not be able to raise their rate of saving". (pp. 52–53) In this way Lal, in fact, argues against the *capital shortage* theorem as well as against the related concept of the "vicious circle of poverty"[511], but, strangely enough, for defending his explanation of underdevelopment reduced also to internal factors.

Noting that foreign aid "has been criticized from both the Left and the Right for retarding development", Lal makes a good point, namely that "it would be strange if so much evil could flow from so little", but questions even the moral base of the "right to aid" since "there is no international society, nor even a commonly-accepted moral standard amongst the different peoples of the world", and the "poverty which concerns Western taxpayers is that of poor people, not poor nations, and giving money to the latter may have no or little effect on the former". (pp. 54–55) However lacking such a "commonly-accepted moral standard" may be, and however much the very perception, if it exists at all, of "human rights" may differ in various cultures, such an argument willy-nilly justifies the most cynical, selfish attitude (often camouflaged as "aid fatigue") of the rich in developed countries, and questions not only the case of human community but also the community of some basic interest. (It is by no means the European culture and the Christian religion or the Western labour movement alone which have been teaching human or international solidarity, but in one

[510] Reference to *Little, I. M. D.* (1982), in op. cit., p. 45.

[511] In another place of his study (1983), *Lal* explicitly attacks the concept of the "vicious circles" for paving the way for "dirigiste arguments". He writes: "One of the major assertions of development economists in the 1950s, obsessed with so-called 'vicious circles' of poverty, was that the fruits of 'capitalist growth', with its reliance on the price mechanism, would not 'trickle down' or spread to the poor. Various *dirigiste* arguments were then advocated to bring the poor into a gross process which would otherwise by-pass them." (p. 90)

way or another all the historical religions and traditional cultures prescribe it. And aid to the poor may serve, as experienced within Western societies, common interest, either by expanding the market and/or preserving peace.)

Instead of financial aid (including "soft" concessional loans), Lal suggests *portfolio lending* from richer to poorer countries, and points to the significance of the restoration of a private portfolio capital market to which developing countries have access, and which "provides LDCs with a relatively apolitical market for both their reserve placements and their borrowings". He believed (more or less the same time when the Mexican debt crisis erupted) that the fear about "the danger that simultaneous defaults by some of the larger Third World and East European countries could lead to the collapse of the whole Western banking system", or the fear "that developing countries have reached the limits of their ability to service their mounting debt" are also "grossly exaggerated". (pp. 61–62) While questioning the "justification for the IMF duplicating its role", namely by providing concessional loans to developing countries to remove the distortions in their economies, i.e. development assistance[512], which belongs to the competence and mandate of the World Bank, Lal stresses the need and justification for conditionalities[513].

As regards *foreign direct investments*, Lal follows the conventional, Neo-Classical approach which does not emphasize the substantial difference between foreign loans and financial aid on the one hand, and FDIs on the other, in nature, termination, structural effects, etc. of the relations established by them. Thus, he mitigates the role and effects of FDIs, too, just like those of aid: "The malign as well as the benign effects attributed to DFI are completely disproportionate both to its past and likely future role in Third World development".

Contrary to the critical views on "colonial-type" of FDIs, he considers them as having promoted development: "Historically, DFI has been important in the development of natural (mainly mineral) resources and public utilities in the Third World." Without taking into account those changes in the orientation and investment policy of foreign companies, particularly the leading new TNCs, resulting from changes in technologies, production and consumption structures and patterns of business interest, Lal blames "economic nationalism" and "the desire of host countries to acquire all the rents from the exploitation of their natural resources" for having steadily blocked these traditional avenues for foreign investment. (p. 57)

---

512 *Lal* (1980) points to a counterproductive effect of IMF's concessional lending for structural adjustment as development aid: "By confusing development aid with the remedies required for a financial crisis (precipitated by inappropriate macro-economic policies), concessional IMF lending would reduce the incentive for countries to avoid getting into a crisis in the first place". (p. 68)

513 *Lal* notes (1983): "The conditionality of IMF stabilization programmes is of major importance both in helping establish sound macro-economic policies in countries and in warning others against unsound policies which might land them in the arms of the IMF". (p. 67)

Lal disagrees with those[514] attributing "inimical effects" to capital inflows on domestic savings and thereby on economic growth, or on the balance of payments of the developing countries. He notes that "no evidence was provided that foreign capital inflows reduce domestic investment", and that the problem of balance of payments, "if there is one, is with the government's fiscal and monetary policies, and not with DFI"[515]. He also refuses the criticisms which attribute harmful social effects to FDIs, namely in respect of income distribution and consumption pattern, or concerning the quality of the goods, the "inappropriate" nature of the products produced or the technologies applied by foreign investors. Such criticisms are, in Lal's view, stemming from tautological or schizophrenic argumentations. But he adds, what reflects a more balanced approach, that if "the deleterious effects of DFI are exaggerated by its opponents, so are its beneficial effects by its proponents". (p. 60) Lal rejects the idea about controlling transnational companies simply on the same ground that "there is nothing in DFI generically harmful to the economic health of developing countries". (p. 82)

In opposition to those calling for urgent reforms of the international economic order and still keeping the idea about a New International Economic Order, Lal expresses his belief in the post-war liberal international economic order.

> "The best service the West can give the Third World in to ensure that *this* economic order is not eroded by refusing to surrender to the blandishments of either the Southern *dirigistes* of the New International Economic Order or the Northern advocates of the 'new protectionism". (p. 69)

In his final conclusions, while repeating his attacks against "the quest for a new 'unorthodox' economics, of special application to the Third World", which, in his view, was underlying much of development economics and based on the appraisal of "the orthodox neo-classical model" as unrealistic and irrelevant, Lal accuses the proponents of "dirigisme" also because "behind at least part of the *dirigiste* case is a paternalistic attitude born of a distrust of, if not contempt for, the ordinary, poor, uneducated masses of the Third World". (p. 104.) Though such an attitude is far more characteristic of the representatives of the conventional than the critical (dependence) theories of "underdevelopment", and "dirigisme" is not necessarily suggested by all those calling for reforms, this critique of the paternalistic attitude is justified, just as well as the refusal of the assumptions about "irrational" behaviour (even in strictly economic sense) of people in developing

---

[514] E.g. *Griffin, K.–Enos, J.* (1970), and *Weiskopf, T. E.* (1972).

[515] According to *Lal* (1983): "...Even if domestic output rises as a result of DFI – which is a good thing – a government can, through fiscal and monetary means, raise domestic expenditure by even more and thus engineer a balance-of-payments deficit – a bad thing!" (p. 58) Who could deny such a possibility or its realization in many cases? But does it prove or reveal anything from the complexity of the various effects of FDIs on the balance of payments, which *in principio* can potentially be favorable and unfavorable alike, in reality can be assessed *in concreto* only.

countries[516]. Lal insists on his belief in orthodox Neo-Classical economics and its message: "get the prices right" (i.e. in the price mechanism), but at the same time accepts what *Keynes* (1926) wrote about the role of the State[517], and finally seems inclined to be in favour, in general, of a "middle course between *laissez-faire* and the Dirigiste Dogma", which, however, in his view, is blocked by ideologies[518].

Apart from the obviously ideological, almost religious belief in one particular school of economics (the Neo-Classical) and from the not less obvious contradiction between an unlimited trust in the price mechanism of the market and the acceptance of what Keynes suggested the State to do (exactly because the market mechanism is unable to do, namely to work for "perfect equilibrium"), Lal's final conclusions seem to mark a more balanced approach. Even his inconsistencies (e.g. his criticism of "development economics" in general, including the conventional theories of underdevelopment, too, such as the capital shortage theorem, the concept of "vicious circles", etc., and his distinction between "laissez-faire" and free trade) appear in a sense as a sign, within "counter-revolution", of a search for compromise.

### 5.2.2. An orthodox Marxist attack against dependence theories

Marxism, as already noted, has never been or remained a homogeneous stream of social science theory. Marx's views have not only been revised, as natural, by his followers in the last century and a half, but has always been interpreted quite differently, moreover, they were not fully consistent in his original works, either. This may explain not only the ideological and political split between social democrats and communists, but also the variety of theoretical views on the development of capitalism after Marx's death, on imperialism and colonial system, on "monopoly capitalism" and its prospects, on "bourgeois democracy" and methods of exploitation, on "proletarian revolution" and birth of socialism, on the nature, operation and future of "existing socialism", on the world capitalist system and its uneven development, on globalisation, on the transnational companies, on international

[516] "It is easy to suppose that these half-starved, wretched and ignorant masses could not possibly conform, either as producers or consumers, to the behavioural assumption of orthodox neo-classical economics that 'people would act *economically*; when the opportunity of an advantage was presented to them they would take it'. ...There is by now a vast body of empirical evidence from different cultures and climates which shows that uneducated peasants act economically as producers and consumers." Op. cit., pp. 104–105.

[517] "The most important *Agenda* of the State relate not to those activities which private individuals are already fulfilling, but to those functions which fall outside the sphere of the individual, to those decisions which are made by *no one* if the State does not make them. The important thing for governments is not to do things which individuals are doing already, and to do them a little better or a little worse; but to do those things which at present are not done at all." *Keynes, J. M.* (1926), pp. 46–47.

[518] *Lal* notes (1983): "In these deeply ideological times, it may be vain to hope to steer a middle course between *laissez-faire* and the *Dirigiste Dogma*." (p. 109)

trade and capital flows, as well as concerning the causes of "underdevelopment". All these issues are, of course, related to the question of the primary unit of analysis (and of action) what Marx has missed to clarify.

It is hardly surprising then that the radical views of those "Neo-Marxists" (and "New-Left" scholars) accusing the world imperialist system of capitalism with its all-embracing centre-periphery relationship, global accumulation, income drain, dominance and exploitation, etc. for the "development of underdevelopment", have been rejected (not only partly, selectively, as by the so-called "Marxism–Leninism", which vehemently refused the critiques on "existing socialism", but) almost completely by a few "orthodox" Marxists insisting on certain theses of Marx.

One of the most outstanding expressions of the counter-attack against the "dependence theory" of Neo-Marxists and others is *Bill Warren*'s book (1980). Warren recalled the Marxian view about the progressive historical role of capitalism as a necessary stage in economic and social development which is supposed to pave the way for socialism, i.e. for the transition to the advanced variant of a collectivist society, namely communism. And since "imperialism", including its cruel form: colonialism, serves the expansion and spread of the capitalist mode of production all over the world, Warren formulates his thesis about "imperialism being the pioneer of capitalism".

Warren noted (1980) that "the bulk of current Marxist analyses of and propaganda about imperialism actually reverse the views of the founders of Marxism, who held that the expansion of capitalism into pre-capitalist areas of the world was desirable and progressive... The theoretical fulcrum of this reversal of the Marxist view is the theory of the advent of a new and degenerate stage of capitalism (monopoly capitalism) that can no longer perform any positive social function, even in those societies Marx and Engels regarded as backward compared with the capitalist West during the nineteenth century and most of which, by the same criteria, are still backward today."(p. 3)

Contrary to this "reversal", Warren correctly refers to the fact that "the new, reactionary stage of capitalism turned out to have immeasurably greater economic vigour and capacity for technological innovation than its nineteenth century predecessor." (p. 4) It is to be noted, however, that the evidence of the economic vigour and capacity of technological innovation is by no means a proof also of the favourable effect of imperialism, particularly of colonialism on the development of the dominated countries.

Warren stresses that the "the role of capitalism in human progress", the "unique achievements of capitalism, both cultural and material, must not be overlooked", nor "the important connection between capitalism and parliamentary (bourgeois) democracy". He holds that the "Marxist analysis of imperialism was sacrificed to the requirements of bourgeois anti-imperialist propaganda, and indirectly, to the security requirements of the encircled Soviet state." (pp. 7–8)

Criticizing the theories of dependence and "neo-colonialism", Warren states that "empirical evidence suggests that the prospects for successful capitalist development in many underdeveloped countries are quite favourable", and even "direct colonialism, far from having retarded or distorted indigenous capitalist development that might otherwise have occurred, acted as a powerful engine of progressive social change". What follows as a conclusion is that "insofar as there are obstacles to this development, they originate not in current relationships between imperialism and the Third World, but in the internal contradictions of the Third World itself." (pp. 9–10)

All this sounds to be in full consonance with the most conventional explanations of "underdevelopment" (as an earlier, backward stage of development on its universal, linear path), which had been dominating the literature of development economics before the "school of dependencia" gained popularity. But Warren does not wish, of course, to join the conventional stream, and this may be the reason why he adds, quite inconsistently, to the above that: "one dimension of imperialism is the domination and exploitation of the non-communist world by a handful of major advanced capitalist countries" (despite of which "we are nevertheless in an era of declining imperialism and advancing capitalism." (p. 10)

Since socialism is "the system of organization of society appropriate to technologically advanced, large-scale machine industry", the historic function of industrial capitalism is "to build up to this level of development". (p. 25) This function of capitalism involves, in Warren's view, the building up of democracy, as well. Quoting (p. 27, footnote No. 36) the Marxist *Kautsky* (who stated: "Democracy is indispensable as a means of ripening the proletariat for the social revolution"), Warren concludes that "capitalism and democracy are...linked virtually as Siamese twins". (p. 28)

As regards colonialism and capitalist imperialism, Warren recalls Marx's famous and often debated statement about the historical mission of the British colonialism in India[519], namely its role in transforming the pre-capitalist society. Without making any distinction in time or between different cases, Warren declares, in general, that the "exogenous introduction of capitalism does not imply a static dualism or sterile compound of the newly-entered capitalist mode of production with precapitalist modes of production within the same polity, for the devastatingly superior productivity and cultural attributes of capitalism are bound in the end to subordinate all other modes of production and eventually eliminate them entirely." (pp. 39–40)

It is worth noting that those Neo-Marxists explaining "underdevelopment" as the product of foreign dominance and exploitation, who are so intensively attacked by Warren, do also reject the idea of a static "dualism" and stress the very subordination of all the other, pre-capitalist modes of production to the dominant capitalist one! The "only" difference is that they, unlike Warren, doubt the full elimination of such modes of production, i.e. a completed transformation.

[519] *Marx* wrote (1853): "...whatever may have been the crimes of England, she was the unconscious tool of history in bringing about the revolution".

Warren calls it a "strange paradox", that while "imperialism, conceived by Marx and Engels[520] as the historical process of capitalist expansion into the non-capitalist world, and regarded as progressive precisely because of their analysis of capitalism as the most advanced social system hitherto achieved, came to be regarded as the characteristic of capitalism that nullified its previously progressive features". (pp. 46–47) Though the source of this paradox is "a contradiction in Marxist thinking itself", it was *Lenin's* essay on imperialism in 1917[521], which is primarily responsible for it, since it "reversed Marxist doctrine on the progressive character of imperialist expansion" and declared the "historic mission of capitalism" as ended.

> Insofar as such a conclusion of Lenin was connected with his theses on monopolization supposed to lead to stagnation, and on capital exports manifesting international exploitation, Warren had to argue against both. In his view, Lenin's explanation of the "new imperialism" was "effectively the reverse of the truth. Imperialism, far from being the product of a senile, decaying capitalism compelled to invest abroad the capital it no longer had the 'vigour' to absorb at home, was on the contrary the product of young and vigorous capitalist economies newly emerging onto the international arena to challenge their rivals in *trade*. The expansion of trade rather than of foreign investment, was the logical conclusion of the accelerated industrialization of the nineteenth century, along with the mounting interdependence of national economies as the result of massive improvements in communications". (pp. 67–69)[522]

Like Emmanuel and other proponents of the "unequal exchange" who underestimate the role of international capital flows as compared to international trade, Warren also emphasizes the latter as the primary concern of capitalism: "Moreover, the rise of foreign capital flows was markedly more moderate than that of trade flows". To prove this, he also refers to "statistical evidence"[523], i.e. a quantitative comparison between the growth of international trade and of capital exports. Such an approach is particularly strange if applied by an orthodox Marxist, since it testifies the neglect of those lasting ownership and control relations established through FDIs, which can shape the very patterns of trade and determine, even by a relatively small increment, the growth of the latter.

Though *Warren* is obviously right when rejecting the assumption that capital export is primarily motivated by "excess capital", it is not quite fair vis-à-vis *Lenin's* theory of imperialism, (however biased and over-simplifying concept it

---

520 *Warren* notes (1980) that Marx and Engels in fact "did not use the term 'imperialism' as such". (p. 46 footnote 81)

521 See *Lenin, V. I.* (1948).

522 Warren cites *D. S. Landes* (1969) versus those "Marxist students of history" (p. 248) who fail to see such real facts.

523 In *Warren's* view (1980), "Lenin's assertion that the export of capital became more important than that of commodities for the capitalist countries in the imperialist epoch was incorrect, as the statistical evidence on trade and foreign investment shows." (p. 70)

was), to interpret it as deriving imperialism from the "excess of capital"[524]. Lenin qualified capital export as the third characteristics of "imperialism", which follows from the process of monopolization (fuelled by concentration and centralization of capital) and the appearance (due to the fusion of industrial and banking capital) of "finance capital" coupled with the rise of "finance oligarchy". Thus, accordingly, the rise of excess capital represented a partial or derived phenomenon only in the rise of imperialism (partially explaining its capital export and resulting, if at all, from the tendency of monopolization itself).

"Lenin's final point", namely "the supposed retardation of technical progress by monopoly capitalism" has undoubtedly been refuted by reality. Warren correctly argues (1980) that "it was precisely the 1890s that opened a new phase of technology", that "the years since 1914 have witnessed...a breathtaking number of technical innovations", and that "these achievements have been most striking since the Second World War". (pp. 77–78) These waves of "technological revolutions", particularly those taking place since the Second World War, have, indeed, clearly proved that modern (so-called "monopoly") capitalism in the advanced countries has by no means lost its vitality, and that competition, this driving force in technological progress, has not been eliminated by the process of monopolization[525]. What, however, Warren missed to take into account is the new (transnational) forms and dimensions of monopolization in the post-second-world-war era of technological progress, the new relationship between the latter and monopolistic competition, i.e. the changes which, though by no means verify Lenin's ideologised thesis about a declining, over-ripe and dying capitalism, have opened an obviously new "stage" in the development of capitalism both on "national" and world level.

Warren pointed (1980) to that in the first two decades of the twentieth century, when Marxist theories of imperialism were elabourated by Kautsky, Hilferding, Luxemburg, Bauer, Bukharin and Lenin, all the latter "shared the thesis that imperialism would develop the productive forces in backward areas, and in particular would promote modern industry", and it was only after 1928 (the 6th congress of the Communist International) that this view has been reversed[526].

Warren blames first of all *Lenin* for the "fusion of 'imperialism' with 'capitalism'" which as being motivated also by the need for defending the young Soviet state, has later led to the "fusion of world revolution and Soviet international

---

524 According to *Warren* (1980), "Lenin's theory" assumed that "imperialism was rooted primarily in an excess of capital in the imperialist countries seeking outlets abroad". (p. 69)

525 According to *Warren* (1980): "The reasons why Lenin's thesis that monopoly capitalism was parasitic and decadent is invalid are not difficult to enumerate. The rise of oligopolistic market structures – or monopolistic firms, as they are popularly called – has not reduced competition but on the contrary has intensified it." (p. 79)

526 "The resolutions of this congress formalized the surrender of the Marxist analysis of imperialism to the requirements of bourgeois anti-imperialists propaganda." (p. 107)

security requirements..., lending nationalism greater scope to influence Marxism", and to "the blurring of the distinction between bourgeois-democratic and socialist revolution in Third World countries". (p. 108–110)

"The 'world revolution' against imperialism – a fusion of the movement of the working class against its bourgeois rulers in the West and the revolt of the colonial and semi-colonial peoples against the major imperialist powers – turned out to be not a world revolution against capitalism *as such*, but rather (to the extent it was a world revolution at all) only a struggle against particular capitalist countries. More precisely, the struggle against imperialism, which Marxism expected would be synonymous with the struggle against capitalism, actually confused two quite distinct movements: the socialist working-class movement in the industrialized capitalist countries and the intrinsically bourgeois movement of Third World nationalism...". (pp. 4–5)

Despite the truth included in the above, it is to be noted that Warren (as a real orthodox) completely overlooked all the changes, which were taking place in the class structure, in the composition and political attitude of the wage- and salary-earners in the developed countries, and also in the nature and orientation of "Third World nationalism".

Warren seems to have actually revealed the real content of the so-called "socialist revolutions" when pointing not only to "the contradictory but real substance of the Soviet revolution, which itself fused a socialist and a national revolution", but also to "the state interests of the Soviet Union" (p. 105), to the above-mentioned "Soviet international security requirements" and particularly to *nationalism*, which actually became predominant.

*Warren* notes (1980) that insofar as "imperialism" was defined by Lenin as monopoly capitalism representing the present stage of capitalist development, and thus "the sins of imperialism are ascribed to mainly impersonal forces, such as the destructive effects of the world market or of exploitative foreign investment" (p. 126), such an approach could directly and logically lead to the "notion of neo-colonialism" (i.e. the "post-war version of Lenin's *Imperialism*, expressing the latter in the era after decolonisation), and to "the elabouration of a conspiratorial interpretation of the concept of the 'world market'". It is also this background against of which "the rise of the fiction of underdevelopment must be situated". (pp. 110, 112)

Having interpreted this "fiction" of underdevelopment, in general, as meaning no development at all, Warren easily refutes it by stating that "the term 'underdevelopment' actually corresponds to no objective process", and that, on the contrary, "a process of *development* has been taking place..., and ...this has been the direct result of the impact of the West, of imperialism". (p. 113)

In Warren's view "the notion that the world market is the source of inequality between the 'metropolis' and 'periphery'" implicitly attributes a permanently "sinister" role to the world market, and reflects the typical approach of the "petty-bourgeois left". In addition, "the idea that the world market is the root of international exploitation tends to dissolve any distinctive *imperialist* aspects of such exploitation" and "...blurs the demarcation between the negative effects of the growth of capitalism as an indigenous phenomenon and the negative effects of the impact of the advanced capitalist countries (imperialism)". (115–116) He points also to the resulting "theoretical difficulty...to explain how international economic relationships could be exploitative only of the less developed countries in a world of independent nation-states"[527].

Warren attacks (1980) also the assumption about "the non-existent secular deterioration of the terms of trade of the Third World" (p. 118, footnote 9), and rejects the "two interrelated assumptions", characterizing the Latin American school of dependency, namely "1) that the 'dependent' international division of labour is in some sense unnatural; its existence therefore implies that an alternative, 'normal' development has been displaced artificially; 2) that if this 'normal' development has not occurred, it is because peripheral economies have been externally conditioned and not because of their internal contradictions". (p. 119)

In defence of the progressive and beneficial role of colonialism Warren enumerates various data to prove that the health conditions, the supplies of consumer goods, educational facilities, general welfare, etc. had improved. He also disagrees with the view, attributed to "dependentistas" as well as Neo-Marxists, that imperialism, even its former, direct form, namely colonization has really tended to preserve "archaic or pre-capitalist modes of production". (pp. 152–156)

> Moreover, he simply attributes *Gunder Frank's* famous thesis simply to the attempt "to strike at the political roots of revisionist Communism" by arguing that the problem of underdevelopment arose not from imperialism's preservation of pre-war non-capitalist social structures (like feudalism), but from its transformation of all peripheral countries into capitalist societies". (p. 121)

Warren actually revealed the contradiction in views between those (if any among Neo-Marxists and "dependentistas") assuming the operation of real, "original" pre-capitalist modes of production, preserved by imperialism, and those (among the latter), like Frank, denying "dualism" and stressing the capitalist nature of the peripheral economy as a whole. He also pointed out a certain inconsistency in both views. For, as regards the former views, the very existence, not only in Latin America but in all developing countries, of a local bourgeoisie and the predominance of market-oriented commodity production, whether resulting from imperialist penetration or not, clearly deny the pre-capitalist nature of the economy as a whole, and allow the survival in destroyed pieces only of the traditional mode of production along with, and under the dominance of the capitalist one, i.e. in a functional "dualism". In this case it is hardly enough to refer to some political alliance between the traditional leaders, feudal or tribal chiefs or a "comprador bour-

527 *Warren* poses (1980) the related question: "Why, for example, was direct US investment in Europe not imperialist, whereas in Guatemala it was?" (p. 118)

geoisie" and the imperialist forces, but the functional relationship between the dominant mode of production and the remnants of the traditional one has to be analysed, which, however, has not remained unchanged at all. As regards the latter, the more typical views of Neo-Marxists and "dependentistas", which reject the concept of "dualism" and conceive of the peripheral mode of production as entirely capitalist (including the traditional, non-wage forms of employment), they are doomed, at least logically, to present underdevelopment as merely and exclusively the product of dependence resulting from sheer force, in the rise and survival of which no role is played by internal forces and the peculiar mode of production.

While pointing to contradictions or inconsistencies in the views of others, Warren (1980) simply denies the fact of distortions in the structure of the peripheral economies, and refutes all the main theses of the critical theories, including that on the "drain of surplus from the periphery to the centre", and "the creation of a self-reinforcing international division of labour whose effects are to generate further self-reinforcing structural imbalances in the colonial economy", as well as "the conservation of precapitalist modes of production". (p. 140)

He argues that "for such a drain to retard economic development it must be an *absolute drain*, not simply an unequal 'transaction' that nevertheless leaves both sides better off than before, or better off than they would otherwise have been" and that "it is essential for the thesis that the development of the productive forces has been blocked". (pp. 140–141) This is, indeed, a convincing argument but only versus the extreme variant of the explanation of underdevelopment by external forces, which blames the latter for preventing the dependent countries from any development and interprets "underdevelopment" as an absolute stagnation, as no development. No doubt, such an interpretation has been manifested in the "dependence" literature, but in the 1950s–1960s and early 1970s rather than later, and has never become characteristic of the "school of dependencia" or Neo-Marxism.

Warren refutes the assumption of an absolute drain of surplus even in the case when the outflow of profits exceeds the initial inflow of foreign investment capital, because "investment is generally value-creating, ...the value-added will have also increased wages, salaries, and government revenues". (pp. 141–142) Though this argument may theoretically be correct, it oversimplifies the problem just as much as the opposite argument, which equates any profit repatriation to an absolute loss for the country. The question of what have been the *sources* of the repatriated profits (to what extent the originally invested or reinvested foreign capital or those special allowances, privileges, monopolistic advantages ensured, under pressure and corruption, by the host government), and of how the repatriation of profits has been affecting the balance of payments, should also be answered but *in concreto*. Even less should such questions be left out of consideration as how, in what direction foreign capital investments do shape the structure of the economy, and how the very operation of foreign companies in the economy affects its pattern of trade and balance of payments, in general.

The distinction between absolute and relative *gains and losses* is, of course, very important. But depending, of course, on the interpretation of "underdevelopment" in the context of the centre-periphery relationship[528], one can easily conclude, if conceiving of it as a regularly slower development relative to others', that even in case a country enjoys absolute gains and suffers only relative losses, its underdevelopment may be maintained thereby. Warren actually referred to this case when saying: "it is possible for both partners to gain, although one more than the other". (p. 142) Strangely enough he failed to see the inequality of positions (for whatever reasons) of the partners in this case and the consequent possibility, or probability rather, of a growth of difference in their development, which is obviously related to their relationship. With regard to the *specialization* of the developing countries in primary production, which, as we have seen, is not considered by all proponents of unequal exchange as decisive or even important condition, Warren (1980) posed the question, first, of whether an alternative line of development to such an export-oriented primary production was possible or not, and, second, of whether such a specialization had really "erected serious impediments to diversification, especially along the lines of industrialization". (p. 143)

The answer to his first question may be affirmative, provided that we assume the necessity of export even before a domestic market arises, and not because, as Warren holds, the export of primary products is a "natural growth pole". By referring to the example of Australia, Canada, New Zeeland, and the United States, he denies that "primary commodity exports suffer inherent disadvantages as potential 'engines of growth', that there is any "inherent tendency for agricultural productivity to be lower than productivity in manufacturing" (p. 146) and that a development initiated by primary commodity exports should necessarily remain so based. What, however, he missed in the above arguments is to point to the substantial difference between the case of the exemplifying countries and most of the developing ones not only in the structure and mode of production of the economy as a whole, but also in the type of the primary products they produce for export[529].

His second question, while reducing the problem to that of "diversification" only, is related to the debate among historians and economists alike, on whether the export-oriented primary production can prepare (as one of the Rostowian "preconditions for take-off") industrialization or, on the contrary, may hinder it. But apart from the differences, in general, between the main variants of primary products (i.e., between basic food products consumed also within the country, and industrial raw materials inducing, at least potentially, their up-grading processing,

[528] Whether it is regarded as a lack of development, i.e. an absolute "blockage" in the development of the periphery, due to its unequal relations with the centre, or as a slower, relatively retarded and distorted type of development only, which implies a widening of the "international development gap" between two unevenly developing sides.

[529] Though *Warren* seems to have acknowledged the substantial differences existing between the characteristics and linkages of different staples, in the final analysis he disregards them and confirms (1980) that "there is nothing inherent in the economics or technology of primary production that prevents it from acting as a growth stimulus to a more diversified economy". (pp. 148, 152)

on the one hand, and the relatively "luxurious" and easily substituted food products or those raw materials increasingly replaced by synthetics, on the other), the follow-up depends, as history has proved, on the capitalist transformation of the entire economy and society, which requires not only an accumulation of capital, supported perhaps by primary exports, but also a change in the entire system of labour employment and land tenure. Certain types of primary-producing economies with the vested interests attached to them, may actually set obstacles to such a transformation and the required changes.

Warren recognized a certain shift in view of the dependentistas, the "dependency theorists", namely away from a rigid and static interpretation of dependency towards a more flexible and dynamic one which emphasizes the internalisation of the external forces, thereby the responsibility of internal political alliances, too, and conceives of dependence as a "conditioning situation" allowing but restricting development and alternative choices[530]. But instead of welcoming the revised, more moderate and realistic approach, Warren concluded that "the notion of 'the development of underdevelopment' is even less definable than that of underdevelopment itself", and tried to prove that "all the normal indicators of 'dependence' point to *increasingly* non-subordinate economic relations between poor and rich countries". (pp. 170–185) In doing so he did not only under-estimate the manifestations of all the non-symmetrical interdependencies (except, perhaps, the one related to the technological superiority of the West) and over-estimated the bargaining power and options of the governments in the poor countries (often facing transnational firms with a capital power far exceeding the GNP of the host countries) but also questioned that the LDCs are particularly trade or foreign-investment dependent at all.

*Warren* refers (1980) to *I. M. D. Little* who noted that "Third World countries are much less trade dependent than the developed countries", and their "foreign-owned assets per head" is also small. (p. 183) Trade dependence, however, can hardly be assessed merely on the basis of export and import coefficients, nor the dependence on FDIs can be estimated and compared to that of other countries simply in view of per capita foreign assets.

To refute completely the Neo-Marxist concept of "development of underdevelopment" which "postulates that underdevelopment is a *sui generis* state of distorted development caused by Western capitalism" and "that capitalism in Third World countries, being externally introduced (and generally forcibly imposed), has no healthy internal roots or vigorous dynamic of its own", Warren enumerated a number of "empirical data" proving, as he believed, "that substantial, accelerating, and even historically unprecedented improvements in the growth of productive capacity and the material welfare of the mass of the population had occurred in the Third World". (p. 189)

---

[530] Though such a shift or revised perception is particularly manifested in *Gunder Frank's* writings (such as his 1972 book "Lumpendevelopment") and also in *Samir Amin's* concept, Warren refers to *T. Dos Santos* and *F. H. Cardoso* only.

Warren denied the relevance of the concept of "growth without development", which implies the case when parallel with increasing GDP the quality of life worsens and income distribution become more unjust, and the "widespread belief that the rapid economic progress in the Third World since the Second World War has generally been associated with worsening aggregate inequality". (p. 200) Instead he suggested priority to economic growth over social equality since the latter results from, rather than leads to, a higher level of economic development[531]. He also found the reference to "marginalisation"[532] and the idea of "basic needs" orientation totally irrelevant, no matter how the number of people living below subsistence minimum had grown in the Third World according to all the official statistical data.

While accepting the view that the advance of modern manufacturing industries is crucial to the elimination of underdevelopment, Warren qualified "an initial development of mineral and cash crops before using the resources so gained for manufacturing progress" as "a rational strategy for many economies". (p. 244) At the same time he stressed (pp. 241, 244) that the underdeveloped world *as a whole* (?!) has not only made considerable progress in industrialization (so much that the difference between the developing and the developed countries in the share of manufacturing in GDP "is becoming rather small"), but had also oriented it towards consumption of lower- and middle-income people, instead of the wealthy elites. Warren concluded so partly because "the market for 'luxury goods' is too small to sustain profitable production" (which is exactly the reason why, according to the critical views, the growth of some industries has failed to promote development), and partly in view of the industrialization policy of a few countries, such as e.g. India and Tanzania in the 1960s and early 1970s, (which, however, was hardly characteristic of all the others and not even lasting). And if the "purchase of consumer durables by low-income households occurs at the expense of public and perhaps other forms of consumption", which may be regarded as a distortion of resource allocation consequent to Western influence, then in Warren's view there is nothing peculiar in it because "when did the poor ever know what was good for them?" (p. 249)

Finally, Warren, like Lal, accused the erroneous *government policies* for a failure, if any, in development, particularly the policy which, as having being influ-

[531] According to *Warren* (1980) "the move towards more equal income distribution is generally the by-product of high levels of economic achievement (and of growth-promoting measures) rather than the reverse", moreover "changing, probably rising, income differences are...likely to contribute to economic growth in various ways". Paradoxically, Warren accused the Neo-Classical "consumption-oriented" approach: "The view that growing inequality is detrimental to material welfare is rooted in neo-classical assumptions of declining marginal utility of consumption with given tastes (so that transference of income from the rich to the poor leads to an absolute rise in total utility). But such a static analysis can suggest no presumption of declining welfare with growing inequality in a growing economy, especially since tastes are changing rapidly and the situation is not a zero-sum game." (pp. 207–208)

[532] According to *Warren* the "apparent 'marginalisation' in urban area is actually a progressive phenomenon reflecting the fuller *integration* of the population into the economy as the market widens". (p. 252)

enced by "development economics", by "Western liberal-egalitarian ideals" as well as "by the Soviet example of development through rapid industrialization" and "by an anti-imperialist bent related to both Leninism and liberalism", has "favoured rapid industrialization primarily for the home market". (p. 254) Instead, and contrary to the ideas of the "liberal-populist school of development economics", the promotion of rural commercialisation could be, in his view, the proper policy, along with and under the realities of capitalist development.

As it has appeared from the above, there are great many common elements of both variants of orthodox counter-revolution (the Neo-Classical and the Marxist alike), despite their diametrically opposite theoretical backgrounds. While both addressed their criticism primarily to the "school of dependence", its reformist and radical, Post-Keynesian and Neo-Marxist representatives alike, strangely enough, Lal attacked some typically conventional concepts, too, (which were more or less based on "mainstream", mostly Neo-Classical economics), while Warren practically filtered out not only the critical elements but also all the social and human aspects from the Marxian theory, thereby coming closer to the most economistic variant of Neo-Classical economics and to the most vulgarised concept of unilinear development, far surpassing that of Rostow.

In the light of the above one may question: do we witness certain chaos of views caused by logical inconsistencies or mutual influences of opposite theories, or, instead, the signs of certain convergence resulting from polemics within each theoretical stream and/or from empirical refutal of naive ideas?

# 6. Economics of comparative systems: precedents, development stages, changing approaches and topics

## 6.1. Concepts of economic system and conventional approaches

In the former historical and critical survey of the theories of the main "schools" of economics, in general, and international as well as development economics, in particular, we have already met various concepts of economic systems, their assumed characteristics or desired features, their role and sequence in historical development.

Though, except perhaps Marxism[533], definitions of economic systems were hardly formulated in economic theories before the rise of the "economics of comparative systems" as a separate field of economics or social studies, economic systems were mainly distinguished according to which of the *factors* of production or which

[533] It is, of course, by no means surprising that a theory which criticizes the prevailing order of society needs a clear-cut distinction between the existing and the desired systems more than others, and that such a need may lead a formalized definition, but in the case of *Marx* it was obviously his historical philosophy and analysis, extended also to the earlier variants of systems, too, which also induced him to define "social formations".

of the various economic *activities or branches* were supposed to play the decisive role in the economy. And since accordingly a logical sequence of economic systems seemed to appear, theorists concluded therefrom to an assumed historical order of the related systems following each other in a *unilinear path* of development. Thus, "economic systems" were mostly conceived of as one or another "natural phase" in the general process of economic growth or socio-economic development. In other words, what is called today "economics of comparative systems" was mostly interpreted as that of *comparative "stages"* following each other in the historical course of development – in full consonance with a unilinear concept of development. In the conventional theories of development and/or underdevelopment this perception actually survived even after the Second World War. Moreover, as shown in the related chapter, it gained an outstanding expression in *Rostow's* historical theory which interprets the system of the most advanced countries as the highest "stage of economic growth" and inserts the "system" of the developing countries, as well as that of the former "socialist" ones, in the general pattern of historical sequence of "stages of growth", as each representing one or another "stage". (It actually means that Rostow does not consider the "socialist" system as a historical accident, roundabout or error but a specific manifestation only of one or another "stage".)

While, on the other side, those scholars interpreting capitalism as a global, world-system have either applied the general principle of the superior system following and replacing the inferior one, to the world-economy as a whole, or they consider the capitalist system as a historical error and long roundabout with a sort of "rotation" of roles within it[534], the above approach to define economic systems as subsequent stages of development has remained popular up to the present. (Moreover, the traditional method of distinguishing them according to the most characteristic sectors or activities is still influencing the interpretation of systems in conventional perception, as demonstrated by such terms as "industrial society" following the rural or agricultural one, or by the more recent concepts of "post-industrial" and "post-material society" or the newest concepts of "information society" and "knowledge-based" or "science-based society".)

Despite or along with such an influence of the *"stages approach"*, however, the "new" field of studies called "economics of comparative systems" which came into existence already before the second world war[535] but developed as a separate sub-

[534] See the subchapter on Wallerstein's theory.

[535] In view of the rise of a new system of economy with central planning and collective property relations in the Soviet Union, quite a number of Western scholars turned attention to (either in response to the Marxist–Leninist propaganda or because of a genuine interest in a "post-capitalist" non-market economy) to such questions as the compatibility of democracy, freedom and central planning or that of macro-economic efficiency, growth performance and collective ownership in the 1930s. See e.g. *Hayek, F. A.* ed. (1935), *Lange, O.* (1936), *Lippincott, B. E.* ed. (1938), etc. According to *Alexander Eckstein* (1971) "Comparative systems began to emerge as a distinct branch of economics with the crystallization of a new economic system in the Soviet Union". (p. 1)

discipline or multidisciplinary sphere of research in the era of the cold war and has become "institutionalised" accordingly, has somehow modified the above perception by stressing the *contrast* (instead of a historical linkage in a sequential order) between the system of "capitalism" and that of "socialism". This *"contrast approach"* has always been politically and ideologically motivated, and has become somehow reinforced, strangely perhaps, even by those critical theories (such as the theory of imperialism, dependence, unequal exchange, etc.) explaining underdevelopment by external/international forces of capitalism which have rejected the very concept of a unilinear process of development. However justified, by empirical facts as well as logically, the criticism of the concept of an assumed unilinear process of historical development has been, the application of the "contrast approach" in the analysis of different existing "systems" has actually resulted in not less misleading over-simplifications.

## 6.2. The system controversy in the precedents and in the short history of the "economics of comparative systems"

As we have seen in the former historical and critical survey of theories of the main "schools" of economics, in general, and international as well as development economics, in particular, the representatives of the *Classical and Neo-Classical economics* expressed their belief in (or their desire to have) a system, supposed to be the most efficient and developed one which is based on individual initiatives, private property and personal freedom. Such a system should involve a division of labour (both within and between countries) and a spontaneous operation of the market with its "invisible hand" which rationally allocates the available resources and ensures a just income distribution, social welfare as well as perfect equilibrium, and allows but a limited role only for the State (namely to defend the nation, to protect properties, to guarantee freedom and "fair" competition, to create an appropriate legal framework, to promote the development of infrastructure, education, health service, etc.). With regard to the future of such a system, some worries, if at all, were expressed by the representatives of the Classical "school" of economics only in view of the tendencies of over-population, and of the fall of profit rates caused by "diminishing returns" in primary production, which may lead to a general stagnancy, to a "stationary state" but of an already affluent, rich, highly developed society. For most of the representatives of the Neo-Classical economics it is only the rise of monopolies causing "market imperfections", the activity of trade unions disturbing the operation of the labour market, and the interventions of the State implying "government imperfections", which could give rise to worries about the future of the described or visualized ideal market economy.

It has also been noted that contrary to such concepts of the prevailing or desired system, *Marx* presented not only a critical view of the capitalist market economy but also placed it in the historical context of human development. He defined it as one of the "social formations", which was born from the womb of the previous one, and gives birth to the succeeding, more developed social formation – owing to the historically natural process pushed ahead by the interactions and increasing contradiction between the ever-growing productive forces and those social relations of production marking the substance of each social formation, and owing to the social "class struggle" expressing, and sharpening with, such a contradiction, which leads to social revolution and to the transformation thereby of the system. (According to the Marxian concept a "social formation" involves, on the one hand, a material fundament, the "economic base" which consists of the progressing productive forces and the given related social relations of production, and a certain pattern of political, sociological, institutional, legal, cultural and traditional features, the "superstructure".) For a long time the followers of Marx have all shared the same view about the advent of such a revolution resulting in a systemic transformation, and leading, through a socialist transition, to a communistic society. If they disagreed, as they did already before and even more after the First World War, it was concerning the question of whether the change of the system requires revolution or could occur as a gradual evolution; whether social revolution should be violent or could be peaceful; and whether it could be successful only as a "world revolution" starting in and extending to the most developed countries or even in less developed single ones.

It was only the inter-war period and particularly after the Second World War, that due to the split and increasing conflict between communists and social democrats the political philosophy of the latter turned away from the idea of breaking with capitalism and suggested the reforming of the system rather than replacing it by another one (particularly by a Soviet-type "socialism"). This reform idea has been supported fairly well by the *Keynesian* theory which, as we have seen, marked out the possible way of improving, both economically and socially, the capitalist market economy, namely by means of indirect state interventions, by making use of monetary and financial policies to regulate the economic processes, to bring the economy closer to a perfect equilibrium with full employment, and by welfare measures of the State to counteract the socially most unfavourable effects of the market economy, to diminish social conflicts.

Such a reformist policy, which had already manifested in the "New Deal" in the US before the Second World War and had its theoretical roots also in the "Stockholm school" of economics, were widely applied after the war in the Western countries and worked fairly well in the first two post-war decades. Moreover, partly because of the huge tasks of post-war reconstruction in Europe and of the post-colonial programs in the developing countries, partly under the influence of the Soviet-type central planning, some forms and degrees of *national planning* (medium- and long-term plans of development, fund-raising programm of investment, elabourated perspective aims of national development, indicative, informative government plans of economic development, tripartite interest-reconciling negotiations on development between the representatives of the government, of the employers and employees, national development program or sectoral projects to be supported by international aid, etc.) were also introduced in many countries, which all required an increased role of *the State* in the economy[536].

Since this was also accompanied for a while by the growth, due to government investments and/or nationalizations, of the public sector in most of the non-communist countries, too, including the developed market economies, while under détante the Soviet-type command system of economic management was to a more or less extent liberalized, allowing a somewhat greater role to be played, under control, by *the market* (prices and money) in some of the East- and Central-European "socialist" economies, the famous concept of "convergence" (advocated, among others, by Jan Tinbergen) has gained increasing popularity and influence. Together with the détante principle of "peaceful co-existence" of the two socio-economic systems, it seemed to replace the "contrast approach" in the economics of comparative systems by a search for similarities, common features, tendencies and reconcilable or joint interests.

The reformist ideas have been brought further and made related to the international economic relations, as we have seen, by the *Post-Keynesian Reformist school* of international economics, the representatives of which in the 1960s and 1970s urged reforms of the international economic order, the establishment, via compromise-seeking negotiations and UN resolutions, of a "New International Economic Order.

Though the "hard-liners" and cold-war politicians on both sides did strongly opposed both the idea of "convergence" and the need for a "New International Economic Order"[537], the former over-politicised, ideologically biased definitions of "comparative economic systems" have been increasingly replaced by more moderate and sophisticated ones, at least in the related social science literature, even if not so much for politicians[538] and by no means eliminating yet the over-simplifications involved in the "contrast approach".

---

536 As a result of the spread of "national planning", a wide theoretical debate was unfolding about alternative forms of planning such as "indicative" and "command" variants (the former being mostly considered as represented by France, the latter by the Soviet Union) and also on centralization versus decentralization, the alternative forms of "social control" over the economy, etc. See e.g. *Tinbergen, J.* (1964), *Ward, B.* (1967), *Millikan, M. F.* ed. (1967), *UN ECE* (1965), *Levine, H. S.* (1971), etc.

537 It seems enough to recall that e.g. *Patolitsev*, the that time Minister of Foreign Trade of the Soviet Union declared that the developing countries if wishing to have a new international economic order, had better join the "socialist world economy". Even the moderate and realist *Henry Kissinger*, the US State Secretary expressed his doubts about the need of reforming at all the post-second-world-war international economic order which, in his view, had worked fairly well as long as the petroleum-exporting countries did not cause disturbances in it.

538 For example, *Ronald Reagan* as the President of USA, simply and ignorantly identified all the countries, political regimes and movements, which appeared hostile to USA, with Marxism (thereby attributing a particular social science theory such a role as being able to form socio-economic or political systems alone) and wished to wage a general war against Marxism.

## 6.3. Development stages of the "economics of comparative systems": changes in concept, definition, approach and topics

Apart from the *pre-war* debates on the system of central planning[539], the "economics of comparative systems" seems to have developed through a *few stages* since the late 1940s, which reflect the changes in the East–West political relations and ideological confrontations fairly well, and somehow differ from each other not only in respect of the more or less manifest ideological bias but also of the focus of interest, of the dominant topics of research and debated questions, or even regarding the very definition of "economic systems", and their characteristics, classifications.

The *definition* of "economic systems" and the chosen criteria of their *classification* have shown, in fact, quite a variety and modification, reflecting the changes in approach and in attention of comparative system analysis during the last few decades. Parallel with changes in the definition and criteria of classification of "economic systems", and also reflected by the latter, the major topics in the focus of comparative systems analysis have also shifted and expanded.

*In the late 1940s and early 1950s,* i.e. in the period of a sharpening cold war between "East" and "West", when the "economics of comparative systems" arose as a separate and heavily ideologised disciplinary sphere of studies, it was only the very contrast between the capitalist system of market economy and the "socialist" (or communist) system of centrally planned economy, which was the main concern of those scholars dealing with comparative system analysis[540]. Mostly applying the "contrast approach" they described (depending on their ideological stand) one or the other "system" as having negative features only versus the positive characteristics of the opposite one. Thus they have also presented various lists of the system-specific characteristics in +/– "pairs" (in a very similar way to the early conventional theories of underdevelopment, without suggesting, however, a natural sequence of stages in evolution and a peaceful transformation from one to the other).

The *contrasting pairs* were mostly formulated in rather vulgar, propaganda-motivated, journalistic style, obviously and explicitly reflecting the sympathy or the antipathy vis-à-vis one or the other system, such as

---

539 The debates, as already noted, were focused on whether a "centrally planned economy", such as in the Soviet Union, was able to ensure rational and efficient resource allocation.

540 As *Alexander Eckstein* noted (1971): "The emphasis was on the grand 'isms', that is capitalism, socialism, communism, and fascism or variants of thereof. The field was strongly influenced by the traditional comparative government approach; many of the analytical categories were political and ideological rather than economic. At the same time, comparisons of economic systems tended to focus on their contrasts and polarities; they principally dwelt on differences in kind rather than on differences in degree, on discontinuities rather than on continuities. Finally, the approach was predominantly descriptive and institutional rather than theoretical or analytical." (p. 1) What, however, Eckstein missed to add to his criticism of the ideologised "contrast approach" is that the latter has also been ahistorical and completely neglecting the common global unit within which the interdependent parts were contrasted!

(a) in the pro-Western, *anti-Soviet* and anti-communist literature:
- democracy as characterising the Western system vs. dictatorship in the communist regimes,
- freedom vs. oppression of people,
- aggressive Soviet bloc vs. alliance of democracies to defend world peace,
- normally operating market economies with efficient allocation vs. an "abnormal" command system of the economy with wastages, and so on;

(b) in the pro-Soviet, *anti-Western*, communist literature:
- capitalism as unequal, exploitive, oppressive, alienating system vs. socialism as egalitarian, exploitation-free, liberalizing ad collectivising system,
- bourgeois dictatorship under a formal democracy vs. people's democracy under proletarian dictatorship,
- monopoly-capital-governed imperialism vs. the "peace camp",
- anarchic market vs. planned economy,
- regular crises vs. the "law of proportional, planned development",
- "pauperisation" of the working classes vs. regular improvement of the living standard of people,
- mass unemployment vs. full employment and job security, and so on...

In this early period of the short history of economics of comparative systems, i.e. in the cold war era (and a few decades before) the related debates in scientific publications were mainly concentrating on the advantages/disadvantages of the "centrally planned economy" as contrasted to a market economy, from the point of view of rational resource allocation, efficiency, employment, equilibrium, growth, social welfare, individual freedom, competition, etc., which were all linked in one way or another with the central issue, namely *ownership* (private or State). The latter perfectly corresponded to the over-simplified and ideologised concept which primarily distinguished "capitalism" from "socialism" according to the dominance of private or State ownership, and was well-manifested also in the Marxist–Leninist idea of the "transition from capitalism to socialism" implying the replacement of the private by "social", in fact State, ownership.

Later, *in the* (fluctuating) *period of détente* and with the rise, not only in Yugoslavia but in some other European "socialist" countries, too, (such as, particularly, Hungary and Poland), of what was called "reform socialism" (or, as often, "market-socialism"), the attention in the studies on comparative systems shifted to some extent away from the markedly ideological issues towards more specific ones (including those appearing to be common in both systems), such as bureaucratisation, macro-organizations (TNCs and STOs), consequences of industrialisation and technological progress, decentralisation and "mixed economy", variants of national planning, etc. In accordance with such a shift in attention, somewhat more moderate, balanced, and realistic features appeared in the descriptions of the opposite systems, *more sophisticated*, scientifically interpretable "pairs" of diverging *characteristics* were getting used in the related literature, such as in general:

- market economy vs. centrally planned economy,
- predominance of private ownership in capitalist market economies vs. predominance of public or state ownership in the socialist economies,
- priority of material/financial incentives vs. that of political/moral ones,
- market-coordinated allocation vs. plan coordination,
- demand-constrained economy vs. "shortage economy"[541],
- "hard" vs. "soft budget barriers",
- export-led economy vs. import-dependent, export-forced economy[542],
- oversupply of labour and a "normal rate of unemployment" vs. labour shortage and "unemployment within the gates",
- over-saving and under-investment vs. "investment hunger" and shortage of investable funds,
- profit- and exchange-orientation vs. project- and plan orientation,
- market prices vs. administered prices,
- market imperfections vs. government imperfections,
- business cycles vs. political cycles,
- allocative vs. distributive efficiency,
- autonomous civil society vs. social organizations functioning as "transmission belts",
- parliamentary democracy with opposition parties vs. "democratic centralism" with latent opposition within the ruling party,
- a welfare state based upon an advanced economy, ensuring high level social services vs. an "immature", paternalistic welfare state with free but poor quality social services,
- an institutionalised respect of all the "human rights" vs. infringement, or selective allowance of them, and so on…

*In the mid-1960s*, for example, *Gregory Grossmann* (1967) defined economic system as "the set of institutions that characterizes a given economy". The *Webster's International Dictionary*[543] gave a more complex definition, which stated that the economic system is "an aggregation or assemblage of objects united by some form of regular interaction or interdependence; a group of diverse units so combined by nature or art as to form an integral whole, and to function, operate or move in unison, and often in obedience to some form of control; an organic or organized whole".

*In the early 1970s* according to a definition of *Simon Kuznets* (1973), an economic system implies "long-term arrangements by which various units within a society are introduced to cooperate in production, distribution and the use of aggregate product – including means of control over productive factors, and freedom or constraint of individual units in the existing factor or good markets". (p. 249)

Though *Marxists* have traditionally classified the different socio-economic systems according to the dominant pattern of "social relations of ownership" over the main means of production, the related pattern of social division of labour, and income distribution relations as well as the political-institutional

[541] See *Kornai, J.* (1960).
[542] See *Pajestka, J.–Kulig, J.* (1979).
[543] Quoted by *Eckstein, A.* (1973), p. 3.

"superstructure", which all have shown a great variety in both the West and in the East, not to mention the Third World, the *Marxist–Leninist ideology* has practically grouped all the developed market economies into the category of "imperialist" countries, and distinguished among the developing countries according to their political, ideological or mainly military-bloc orientation (as between those, the so-called "socialist-oriented" countries, being allied with the Soviet bloc, and the rest). It differentiated the "socialist countries" according to their declared "stage", achieved by copying the Soviet model and acknowledged by the Soviet leadership, in the unilinear progress towards "developed socialism" and "communism". As more or less opposing the latter, *Neo-Marxists* have primarily distinguished between dominant, "core" or "centre" countries and dependent "peripheries" which are variants of the same capitalist system, or rather parts only of its global, world economy. But the latter have paid more attention to the nature and behaviour of the political elites in system analysis.

*During détante* the literature of comparative economic systems seems to have moved further away from predominantly ideological concepts, and tried to elabourate or combine more objective criteria for defining and classifying economic systems.

In this long period, which lasted until the sudden collapse of "existing socialism" in the East-Central and Eastern European countries and disintegration of the Soviet bloc, the progressing changes in the relations between countries having different socio-economic systems and the observed differentiation among the "socialist" countries, particularly between reformist and hard-liner ones, have already turned the attention to the *differences also within* the same "systems", between their different variants, and popularised the concept of "mixed economies" and for a while also the idea of "convergence", namely between socialism and capitalism. Such a shift in attention was reinforced by further events from about the late 1970s or early 1980s. Thus, and owing to the effects of the world economic crisis of the early 1970s (and to the different responses to it), to changes in the economic power relations among the developed countries, to accelerated differentiation in the Third World, to the declining performance of many "socialist" economies, etc., the approach in comparative systems analysis has become more selective (by distinguishing more variants within each system) and less static (by paying more attention to changes and tendencies).

At the eve of the collapse of the "socialist" systems in Europe, distinctions in the economics of comparative systems were mainly made

- still between (a) "market-socialism" and (b) "centrally-planned" (or "command") socialism, on the one hand, and
- already between (a) the US-type individualistic "market capitalism", (b) the (European) "social-market economy", and (c) the (Japanese or East Asian) "State-directed capitalism", on the other, as regards the two, still supposedly basic forms of economic system,
- while within the Third World between (a) the successful "NICs" ("newly industrialized countries"), (b) the "high-income developing countries" or "petroleum-exporting countries" (c) the "middle- and low-income developing developing countries" and (d) the "least developed" ones (and as a special category: the "heavily indebted developing countries", too).

At the same time the topic area of comparative systems studies has also enlarged, and attention has turned, besides the former, already enumerated issues, also to such questions as e.g.

- the social security models (likely because of the weakening of the "welfare states" in the West and the growing unemployment also in several "socialist" countries, coupled with rapidly aggravating disturbances in financing the free social services)
- the role of the State or the market not only in the economy but also in other "social sub-systems" (culture, education, public health, science, environment, etc.), and also
- such methodological issues as how to compare in a sophisticated way the actual economic performance of different economic systems or their variants (in general, the "economic outcomes in different economic settings") and how to measure the impact of the given economic system on the non-economic spheres of society, which all seemed to be common rather than specific problems of the different economic systems.

*Since the early 1990s*, with the collapse of "socialism" in Eastern and Central Europe, not only the idea of "convergence" has turned to be a misconcept or illusion but also "reform-socialism", i.e. the belief in the reformability of the former system and its becoming democratised "market socialism" with "human face". Moreover, comparative system-analysis has practically lost its former major topic: the contrast between "capitalism" as such and "existing socialism" in general, as two distinctive systems. Thus, the literature of the "economics of comparative systems" has shifted even more than before towards the comparisons of the sub-variants of the same system, namely the capitalist market economy, while qualifying the former "socialist" economies as simply being in "transition" only to the latter, and considering the economic system of the developing countries as merely underdeveloped or emerging market economies. After the collapse of the "existing socialism" in Europe, the approach in comparative studies of"systems" seems, nevertheless, to have become *divergent*: (1) more ideological, politics-oriented and over-simplifying again, manifested in a reinforced "contrast approach", on the one hand, and (2) more eclectic and research-oriented, on the other.

1. The *first* variant is mostly related to the fashion-wave of *neo-liberalism*, spreading also in the East, the followers of which interpreted the systemic change in the former "socialist" countries as a triumph of one system, namely capitalism[544], over the other, the "socialist" one.

For example, *Francis Fukuyama* (1991) did not only welcome the defeat of communism, manifested in the collapse of "existing socialism" in Europe and disintegration of the Soviet bloc, but conceives of these undoubtedly historical changes

[544] See, e.g. *Fukuyama, F.* (1991), *Reich, R. B.* (1991), etc.

as the "end of history" which was marked by ideological struggle, and as the final triumph of the most efficient economic system, namely that of free market, coupled with liberal democracy. Even apart from the very ideology involved in such a view, it is to be noted that Fukuyama obviously missed to recognize the common background in growing international inequalities, of the soviet-type systems and that of religious/nationalist fundamentalisms, which he considers temporary phenomena only, causing minor problems and tending soon to fade away.

Most of those sharing the view about a final victory of one particular system, namely "capitalism", look at the process of transformation in the former "socialist" countries as merely a "transition" from socialism to capitalism or from "centrally planned" to "market economy" (often accepting the self-identification of the former system with "socialism" and "central planning", and assuming a free choice of societies between systems, independently of the global system of the world, and also without questioning what type, which variant of "capitalism" such a simple transition would lead to).

An ideological, politics-oriented and over-simplifying concept with the predominantly "contrast approach", however, also been reinforced by the new wave of *nationalism*, mostly favoured by fundamentalist ideologies, which gained a strong impetus by the large-scale frustration, social disappointment, deteriorating life conditions in the beginning of systemic change and by the surfacing of many, unsolved but previously suppressed problems of nationality, ethnic, religious conflicts, inter-state border disputes, and by the disintegration of federative states in the former "socialist" part of the world, as well as by the increasingly worsened and desperate position of quite a number of developing countries.

2. The *second* variant, which corresponds to the general tendency in the recent development of social science theories, namely away from ideological biases and towards a more balanced viewpoint which allows drawing lessons, but critically, from all theories alike and from all empirical cases, too, seems to spread more and reach increasing application in the last few years.

The main topics investigated in the recent literature on comparative systems are to some extent chosen accordingly, i.e. as reflecting the above two different variants of approach. The *neo-liberal* simplification of the systemic change suggests a focus on privatisation (i.e. the opposite counterpart of "socialization"), its ways and means in the individual "transition economies", and liberalization in general, while stressing the "government imperfections" versus the views pointing to "market imperfections". *The nationalist-fundamentalist* ideology interprets the transition or return to capitalism as the consequence of a successful conspiracy of the leading capitalist powers forcing the societies in question to accept their dominance, which was supported by traitorousness of the local political elite aiming at the appropriation of accumulated state capital, thereby transforming into a real ownership-based bourgeoisie.

From the point of view of the prospects of comparative studies of systems it is the eclectic stream and the related research topics, which seem to be more important.

## 6.4. The major characteristics of comparative economic systems – as outlined by some representative studies

In the course of the short history of the economics of comparative systems, along with the above-outlined shifts in approach, interest and topic areas, and despite the obvious influence of ideologies, certain criteria of defining an "economic system" and a number of more or less substantial characteristics of its distinctive variants have been presented in the related literature. The set of such criteria and characteristics has not only extended to include newer and newer ones, but has also become increasingly mixed, eclectic indeed, as some of them originate from Neo-Classical, others from Marxian or Keynesian, or institutional and other theoretical concepts. Let us illustrate the above by a few cases!

### 6.4.1. Eckstein's review

Alexander Eckstein (1973) referred to five characteristic concepts (five "axes of comparison") in the literature classifying countries according to their economic systems: such as emphasising (1) the type of property relations, (2) the kinds of "economic freedom", (3) the character of incentive system, (4) the coordinating and resource-allocating mechanism, and (5) the locus and system of decision-making.

The first one (1), concerning *property relations*, which reflects a Marxian concept but, as being simplified and applied to modern times, also the "ismistic approach", is undoubtedly important but hardly sufficient criterion. The "property holding as a source of control and a source of claims upon the product or the income produced by it" or as "a custody over resources and man-made means of production" is a substantial determinant, but there are several specificities and complexities which make it difficult, if not misleading, to apply it as a decisive one. Such as (noted by Eckstein) the separation of ownership and control in some modern forms of organizations, the "complex criss-crossing of controls and claims" in the mixed companies, corporations, joint ventures, the great variety of ownership and control structures, the differences in degree between economic systems in respect of the latter, the wartime experiences of centralized control over private-ownership-based economies, too, etc.

As regards (2) "economic freedom", an obviously Classical-Neoclassical idea, which involves the freedom of "consumer choice", of "occupation" and of "enterprise", this criterion may also prove vague, even more than the former. The "freedom of consumer", depending on income and on supply, appeared to exist, within different limits only, in all the contemporary systems, (and, as Eckstein notes (p. 9), was more or less equally restricted in wartime by the system of rationing the consumer goods), but was increasingly fading away under the growing impact of demonstration effects. The "freedom of occupation" depends, among other conditions, on educational facilities (in respect of which some "socialist" countries did not lag behind) and on economic growth, while differences in the existence, operation and structure of the labour market appeared within the group of "socialist" countries rather than between the two systems, and also between developed and developing countries.

With regard (3) to the *incentives*, it is hardly correct to characterize the capitalist system, even its main agents, by material incentives only (as the managers of the big companies are motivated, besides income, by the aim of improving their prestige and the image of the company), while the so-called "moral" incentives in the former "socialist" countries were always accompanied by some fringe benefits, material advantages[545], if not by force, and along with reforms the open material incentives became the dominant ones.

In view of the modern corporate systems and the operation of transnational companies, it is also to be noted that (4) *the resource allocation and coordination mechanism* is hardly based only or even primarily on the market. (Not to mention that the assumed "plan mechanism" in the former "socialist" countries has never worked efficiently and alone.)

Finally, (5) as to the *decision-making*, its centralisation can hardly be considered as an exclusively "socialist" characteristic.

### 6.4.2. Views of Koopmans and Montias

Talling C. Koopmans and John M. Montias (1973), distinguishing between three contemporary economic systems, namely "capitalism", "socialism" and "communism", have outlined the major criteria for classification (with an institutional approach) in terms of organizational arrangements, such as (1) coordination of productive activities, (2) accumulation and utilisation of means of production, (3) research and development for new means and methods of production, (4) distribution of goods and services, (5) maintenance of aggregate stability, and (6) protection of individuals.

According to them the comparison of such different economic systems is to be extended to (a) their environment (resources, technology, external factors, impact of random events), (b) activity (defined by inputs and effects), (c) economic outcomes (which depend not only on the system but also on policy and environment factors), in terms of economic growth, efficiency, income distribution, stability, development objectives and continuation of national existence), and (d) norms, goals and preferences (such as high consumption, world power, national strength, efficiency, equity, stability, adjustment, etc.).

[545] *János Kornai* (1992) points to the "material benefit" (including higher pay, bonuses, benefits in kind, and privileged access to goods and services) which the leaders in the "socialist" system enjoyed. (p. 119)

Apart from mixing up not only "socialism" but also "communism" as economic systems with the declared (system-legitimising) aim of and the actual leadership of the political party being in state-power, respectively, *Koopmans and Montias* actually presented a set of various criteria for comparative analysis, which, on the one hand, can be applied to any comparison of countries, independently of their systems, and, on the other, can be complemented, indeed, by great many others. Since the identification of a distinct economic system is necessarily involves abstraction, one has to choose the major determinants only of what is supposed to make a system substantially different from another.

It is to be noted that *Koopmans and Montias* pointed to the *interactions* between different systems, too: "Since the boundaries between systems more or less coincide with boundaries between nations, interactions between non ruling entities in different systems cannot be discussed without at the same time considering interactions between governments pursuing political as well as economic objectives." (p. 75) Instead, however, of inferring there from that the contemporary "national" systems are but parts of an organic global system, they explain the interactions by "the transfer across state or system boundaries of goods, services..., contacts between members of organizations whose membership or range of activities extends across these boundaries, including all interactions such as direct investments, transfers of know how..., and other informational interactions..., informal contacts..., etc." (p. 76), i.e. by the various "flows" only. Here again we may witness the shortcoming of an approach, which neglects the lasting relations between the interdependent and interacting "entities" which make them parts of an organic system.

### 6.4.3. The concept of Gregory and Stuart

In the late 1980s, just before the system-transformation in Eastern Europe, P. R. Gregory and R. C. Stuart (1989) in their definition emphasised "organizational arrangements...used to allocate resources to achieve economic objectives". They qualified the economic system itself as an "important input to the economic process", along with the conventional inputs (land, labour and capital), but also added that social, geographical, political, cultural, ideological forces influence economic outcomes, too. In short, they defined economic system as "a set of mechanisms and institutions for decision-making and the implementation of decisions concerning production, income, and consumption within a given geographical area". (pp. 4–5)

They classified the main variants of "economic systems" on the basis of four major attributes: (1) organization of decision-making arrangements" (whether centralised or decentralised), (2) mechanism for the provision of information and coordination (whether by means of the market or the plan), (3) property rights: control and income (whether private or public or collective ownership rights, in respect of disposition of the object, right to use the products or services generated by the object, etc.) and (4) incentives (moral or material).

Accordingly they described:
- *capitalism* as having (1) a primarily decentralised decision-making arrangement, (2) a primarily market-mechanism for information and coordination, (3) primarily private ownership structure, and (4) primarily material incentive system;
- *market socialism* as characterised also by (1) a primarily decentralised decision-making arrangement, (2) a primarily market-mechanism for information and coordination, but unlike "capitalism" by (3) a predominantly State and/or collective ownership structure, and (4) by both material and moral incentives;
- *planned socialism* as, contrary to the above two, by (1) a primarily centralised-decision making system, (2) a mechanism for information and coordination which is primarily based upon the plan, (3) the predominance of State ownership, and (4) by moral and material incentive system. What seems to be new and less oversimplifying in their description of the above systems is the stress on the relativeness of each characteristic, the "primarily" and not exclusively appearing features.

### 6.4.4. Kornai's analysis of the "socialist system"

More recently, after the collapse of "socialism" János Kornai (1992) outlined the main characteristics of "socialism" in its so-called "classical" variant, as distinctive from the capitalist market economies, and also from "the revolutionary-transitional system (the transition from capitalism to socialism)" (p. 19) and its abortive "reform"-variant (the "reform system")[546] which introduced alien, incompatible elements to its mechanism.

In view of the inconsistencies (such as "the symbiosis between the bureaucracy and the private sector..., and the linking of the party-state's political power and state ownership with the market mechanism of coordination", etc.) experienced in the course of previous reforms in the former "socialist" countries, *Kornai* (1992) concluded: "The reform destroys the coherence of the classical system and proves incapable of establishing a new order in its place", since "each inconsistency breeds new conflicts...", and "the system undergoing the contortions of reform is inherently unstable", "the reform socialist system...is not lastingly viable". (pp. 571, 573–574)

Since in his opinion the "key to an understanding of the socialist system is to examine the *structure of power*" (p. 34)[547], he starts the investigation of the "anatomy of the classical system" with

1. the "the fundamental institution in the power structure": the Communist

[546] Kornai also distinguished, of course, the "system" which arose *after* the collapse of "socialism", namely the "post socialist system".

[547] *Kornai* notes: "Socialism comes into existence only when and where the Communist party is in power; power is a fundamental, ultimate value." (p. 87)

party as a "vanguard" party, and its organizational rule (heavy centralisation called "democratic centralism"), its dominance over the State and the so-called mass organizations, the cohesive forces of the party and state bureaucracies (such as ideology, power, prestige, privileges and coercion), i.e. "the totalitarian nature of power". (pp. 33–48)

His analysis of the "classical socialism" continues with the other characteristics of this system, all derived from (1) the *power structure,* namely in terms of

2. *ideology* (officially disseminated, supplying the sense of the "superiority of socialism", and basic promises for the future, and prescribing discipline, "willing sacrifice" and vigilance)[548],

3. *property* (the predominance of state-ownership as the highest form of "social property"[549], the secondary role of cooperative property as a transitional and lower form only, and the restricted, if still existing, private property)[550],

4. *coordination mechanism* (predominance of bureaucratic coordination[551],

5. *planning and direct bureaucratic control* (a top-down process of planning, decision-making and control, with "vertical bargaining", with "taut plans" and "lopsided quantity drive", etc.[552]),

6. *money and price* ("semi-monetized system", with a passive role of money in the public sector, controlled money flows, state-owned banking system, an excessive role of the central budget with "soft budget constraints", administrative prices, primary role of "non price signals", "weak price responsiveness", etc.),[553]

---

[548] Op. cit., ch. 4, pp. 49–61.

[549] "The property form of the state-owned firm occupies the 'commanding heights' of the socialist economy, the positions that allow the other, nonstate sectors of the economy to be dominated". (Op. cit., p. 71)

[550] "Socialism differs first and foremost from capitalism in having replaced private ownership with public ownership". (Op. cit., p. 87) This means that while "the primary attribute of the socialist system is that a Marxist-Leninist party exercises undivided power", now "a further characteristic can be added: the party is committed to eliminating private property". Kornai notes that further attributes will be added, for example, "the predominant role of bureaucratic coordination", etc. (pp. 89–90)

[551] *Kornai* (1992) distinguishes 5 types of coordination mechanisms: "(1) bureaucratic coordination, (2) market coordination, (3) self-governing coordination, (4) ethical coordination, and (5) family coordination". (p. 91) The first one, which is usually operating "in the army and the police, in the internal administrative apparatus of a large modern firm, and in the regulation of rail traffic", is characterized by "commands, discipline, being at the mercy of superiors, rewards and penalties, strictness, legal stipulations" – quite contrary to "market coordination" which is associated with "price, money, gain, profit, business". "Under the classical socialist system, bureaucratic coordination is the mechanism applied most widely and forcefully. The other main types exist, but they are repressed and to some extent atrophied, whereas bureaucratic coordination reproduces itself continually." (pp. 94–97)

[552] Op. cit., ch.7, pp. 110–130.

[553] Op. cit., ch. 8, pp. 131–159.

7. *investment and growth* ("expansion drive and investment hunger", centralized allocation with specific priorities[554], "priority products and investment projects", economic development at the expense of environment, dominance of extensive methods under a forced growth, drive for quantity at the expense of quality, investment tension and chronic shortage, fluctuations and investment cycles)[555],

8. *employment and wages* (full employment policy with low efficiency and chronic labour shortage, direct bureaucratic control of employment and wages)[556],

9. *shortage and inflation* (the general, frequent, intensive and lasting shortage phenomena, making characteristically the socialist economy a "shortage economy" with a "sellers' market"[557] and a "forced adjustment mechanism" of demand to supply, a curious "shortage equilibrium", a high propensity, caused by shortage, excess demand, biased short-term behaviour and long-term decisions of firms and of the managerial bureaucracy, to inflation, distorted relative prices, repressed inflation, low efficiency and technical backwardness)[558],

10. *consumption and distribution* (a basic economic security, manifested in full employment, free public education, public pension system, etc., but coupled with low material welfare and a "paternalistic tutelage of the population by the party and the state" (p. 315), with "constraints on the individual's freedom of choice", egalitarian principles in income distribution and equalisation tendencies, along with differentiation and special privileges of the party cadres)[559], and finally,

11. *external economic relations* (economic isolation complemented with scientific and cultural isolation, induced by the fear of a hostile political environment, strict control of foreign trade and foreign exchange transactions by state-monopolistic institutions, causing delayed adjustments, "import hunger" and "export aversion", propensity to indebtedness)[560].

*Kornai*, stressing the "affinity among the elements of the system", presents a scheme to show how they are interlinked and interacting (see figure on page 378).

*Kornai* has undoubtedly given the deepest insight into the details of the mechanism of the system, as can be seen only from inside and by those being familiar with both the ideology and the reality of "socialism". His excellent investigation of

---

554 Such as the priority of *domestic production* over imports, of the *production sphere* in general (i.e. of the production of material goods over services, and of "productive activities" over "nonproductive" ones), of *investment goods* (and thus the priority of "class-one production", the production of the means of production over the production of consumer goods), *of industry*, and within the latter of *heavy industry*, of the *arms industry*, and of *new installations* (over maintenance and renovation), and of *big installations* (with a "cult of scale" and gigantomania). Op. cit., pp. 171–176.

555 Op. cit., ch. 9, pp. 160–202.

556 Op. cit., ch. 10, pp. 203–227.

557 "Classical socialism never changes from a sellers' market regime to a buyers' market regime; it never ceases to be a shortage economy." (Op. cit., p. 253)

558 Op. cit., chs. 11–12, pp. 228–301.

559 Op. cit., ch. 13, pp. 302–332.

560 Op. cit., ch. 14, pp. 333–359.

the operation of the system is, however, based unfortunately on the same conventional approach as characterizing most of the literature, which is rather misleading with regard to the genesis and real nature of the system called "existing socialism". It is the application of the "national" (country) level of analysis as the primary one, which the "international" or "external" implications are derived from, and thus the application of the "contrast approach"[561], too, in other words the neglect of the existence of the global, organic system of the world with interdependencies, within which the "national" systems arise, develop, change or collapse. In the case

**Affinity among the elements of the system by Kornai (1992), p. 361.**

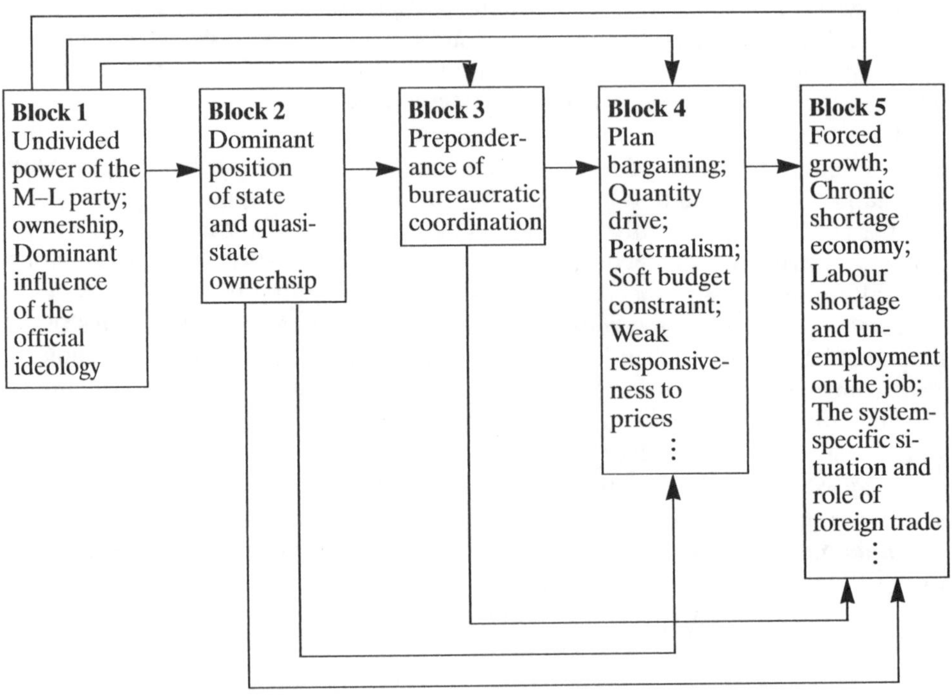


of the "socialist system" this approach and such neglect are unjustifiable even more than in other cases, since neither its birth nor its deviant development and final death can really be explained out of the context of international relations and the world economy.

[561] *Kornai* (1992) presents "system-to-system comparisons" which are very enlightening, indeed, as to the differences in "short-term behaviour of the firm" (p. 264) or the "shortage syndrome" (p. 291) and the "factors in material welfare" between "capitalism" and "classical socialism" (p. 310). However, such comparisons as made without considering the different positions in the world economy and the changes in the conditions as well as the interactions, correspond to the "contrast approach", indeed.

While in the analysis of "underdevelopment" *Leibenstein* (1957), as we have seen, took the "intellectual question out of its historical context" (p. 3), *Kornai* seems to have taken the question of how "classical socialism" came into existence, how and why it was inconsistently reformed, and why the "socialist systems" collapsed, *out of the global context*. For him the "external economic relations" of the system appeared to be derivative features only, which (as it logically follows from such an approach) are to be dealt with, as the last item, after the investigation of all the other characteristics. This perfectly corresponds to the conventional practice of dealing first with the "internal" aspects, and then the "external" ones, no matter whether the latter are more decisive or not. The use of the "contrast approach" does also fit this practice.

It is also to be noted that the identification of "socialism" with the system of those countries under Communist rule, which called themselves "socialist", can be opposed not only in view of the broader perception of socialism as an idea, or of the existence of Western socialist parties and welfare states (which Kornai himself mentions). Even apart from this and even if such an identification merely serves, as Kornai explicitly says, to avoid unnecessary debates on semantics and to dissociate the analysis from debates on what is to be considered "true" socialism, it may also blur the kinship (or, perhaps, a substantial identity) of the "classical system of socialism" with those few *other systems* already or still existing, or coming to arise in the future for quite the same reasons in a global context, which also oppose "Western capitalism", but make use of different label and are not ruled by a Communist party. Such as those nationalist-fundamentalist regimes without the leading role, or even a legal operation, of the Communist Party.

Whatever was originally the social nature of the Russian revolution and the arising Soviet power, the key to understanding of its unfolding nature is the turn (no doubt, under Communist rule) of the power for serving primarily *nationalistic* endeavour (to catch up with the advanced countries and to reach a world power status). The real nature of "classical socialism", i.e. its *militarised* order of society[562], followed from such a nationalistic endeavour coupled with a hostile confrontation with the dominant powers of the world. The soil for similar systems (including fascist ones) to arise was still given, and the applied social(istic) rhetoric should not mislead us!

[562] In certain parts of his book (1992) *Kornai* does also refer to such features of "socialism" as characterizing the *army*. For example, he notes, as we have seen, that bureaucratic mechanisms of coordination, which are predominant in "classical socialism", do also "operate in the army", and quotes A. Bek who described the Soviet economic cadres as behaving with "the highest soldierly virtue: to execute orders without questioning". (p. 94, and p. 121, footnote 21)

## 6.4.5. Schnitzer's concept of comparative systems

Like Kornai and many others after the "end of communism", Martin C. Schnitzer (1994) also investigated the origin and characteristic features of the "socialist" and "communist" systems, as compared to "capitalism", though in a less detailed way but outlining also the variants of both, and (what is more important) in view of the "same planet" and its future.

Schnitzer put the origin and development of the capitalist and also the socialist/communist economic systems into a historical context, but, unfortunately, without revealing their interactions in a globalised world system (despite pointing to "globalism" as a main current in the world today).

In comparing different economic systems *Schnitzer* focuses on the "differences in economic and political institutions". In his definition "capitalism is an economic-cultural system, organized economically around the institutions of private property and the production of goods for profit and based culturally on the idea that the individual is the centre of society. (p. 41)

Referring to the idea of "socialism" as an "antithesis of individualism" (p. 42), Schnitzer distinguishes between the various concepts of socialism[563], and briefly surveys (pp. 43–45) on the historical development of the idea of "socialism" (from Plato's "republic" or the idea of Thomas Aquinas the Saint who advocated private ownership together with common use of goods, and Thomas More's "Utopia" where everything is commonly owned and money does not exist, or from Owen's concept of "new harmony", Saint-Simon's socialist principle of work and distribution, and the "original state of goodness" visualised by such utopists, to the Marxian concept of withering away of the State, distribution according to needs, and economic planning, etc.).

The *communist systems* (called by themselves as "socialist") which prevailed until recently in Eastern Europe, were based – according to Schnitzer, too – on such general principles and institutions as: "economic planning", "state ownership of property", "concentration of power in the Communist Party", and the principle of "cooperation" implying that the interests of the individual are subordinate to those of society". (pp. 58–59) Investigating the major features of the former system under communist rule, Schnitzer describes its "economic institutions" in terms of:

1. *economic planning* (including physical and financial planning, long-term, medium and annual plans),
2. *public finance* (with a centralised budget, indirect taxation and direct share of the State in enterprise profits, and budget expenditures to support the economy, central allocation of investment funds, etc.),

563 *Schnitzer* notes (1994) that "it is necessary to differentiate between socialism as the concept is applied to the government of France and socialism used as a self-description of the countries controlled by communist parties... Socialism today has also come to be associated with the concept of a welfare state...". (pp. 41–42)

3. *organization of industry and agriculture* (in large units, industrial combines and State farms, cooperatives),
4. *political institutions* (the central party organs, the "nomenklatura", the control system, etc.)

He also added that in this system the private *property* was limited to consumer goods only, and the *price system*, being isolated from the world prices, could not play an appropriate role in the decisions on resource allocation and production.

In explaining the "collapse of communism" (pp. 160–161) Schnitzer emphasises that the Soviet bloc was lagging behind the Western nations in economic performance and technological development (due to its isolation in time of a complex, dynamic world[564], to inefficient planning, lack of market signals, waste of resources, weak incentives, etc.).

By outlining the problems of transformation and the "legacies of communism" (pp. 162–171), Schnitzer actually referred to other characteristics of the former system, too, such as *supply shortages*, inflationary tendency, *bureaucracy,* underdeveloped infrastructure, uncompetitive trade with state-monopolistic foreign trade organizations, environmental pollution, and so on.

Besides the above features as more or less general characteristics of the "communist systems", their varieties and the changes in their operation before collapse, do also appear in Schnitzer's book, in its chapters devoted to individual countries.

In the same way, the *system of capitalism* is also presented as it historically developed and appeared in different variants, instead of a static homogeneous system. Schnitzer defines (pp. 22–32) capitalism as an economic system, in general, by the following characteristics:

- *private property* (freedom and predominance of private ownership, but along with the existence of public properties),
- the *profit motive* (inducing cost reduction, increase in efficiency, measured by profitability),
- the role of the *price system* (in coordinating mechanism and in giving signals),
- *freedom of enterprise* (except if immoral or harmful activities follow therefrom),
- *competition* (stimulating innovations, leading to increased efficiency, to greater variety of consumer goods, and to equitable diffusion of real income, etc.),
- *individualism* (with the right to succeed or fail, with equal opportunities, and as a safeguard against the tyranny of the State),
- *consumer sovereignty* (reflecting the principle that production is the means but consumption is the end),

[564] *Schnitzer* (1994) noted: "The pace of international technological innovation is a driving force in the world economy… The communist world was pretty much isolated from the rest of the world, and its insularity cost is dearly." (p. 160)

- a protestant *work ethic* (inducing hard work, diligence, abstinence and saving),
- *limited government* (with the policy of "laisser faire" and the functions of government to be limited to defence, law and order, and only to "those functions that the individuals could not do for themselves"),
- *income distribution* based on "factor contributions" (with two types of incomes: "earned incomes" from wages, salaries and self-employment, including "entrepreneurial incomes" and "property incomes" from capital, natural resources and consumer durable goods).

With regard to the historical development of capitalism and its changes, *Schnitzer*, having distinguished the main stages (pp. 34–35), namely "mercantilism", "industrial revolution" and the rise of "finance capitalism" (with banks and corporations), points to the *modifications* of the system, due to a decline of individualism, to the rise of welfare state, to increased role of the government in education, in infrastructural development, to certain state monopolies (such as over alcohol and tobacco), to restrictions on competition (stemming from the operation of cartels, trusts, holding companies, trade unions, and from state subsidies as well as from restraints on foreign competition), and to the rise of a *mixed economic system* with state-guided capitalism. (pp. 36–37)

Along with the general features and historical modifications of the system of capitalism, Schnitzer also[565] distinguished (pp. 6–8):

(1) the US-type *free market capitalism* (with a relatively free market mechanism, smaller role of the State in the economy, involving legal regulations, such as anti-trust laws, consumer protection laws, etc., rather than redistribution, with a emphasis on the individual, on wealth and consumption, and on competition),
(2) the European-type *social market capitalism* (as developed in Germany and other European countries, with social welfare programs, tax-financed social security system, income redistribution, unemployment compensation, workers' representations in boards and ownership-sharing, state subsidies, and indicative planning, etc.), and
(3) the East-Asian-type *State-directed capitalism* (emerged in Japan and South-East Asian NICs, with a close relationship between the State and business, i.e. cooperation between the government and the companies, indicative planning based on consultations with the latter and a government industrial

565 *Schnitzer* disagrees with *Lester Thurow's* (1992) distinction between "individualistic capitalism" (such as existing in the United States and other Anglo-Saxon countries) and "communitarian capitalism" (assumed to characterize Europe and Japan), because the term "communitarian" has a number of connotations, and "communitarian capitalism is the result of different cultural and historical developments in Europe and Japan". (p. 6)

policy, a State support to industrial development, the operation of group-oriented forms of economic organizations, etc.)

No doubt, *Schnitzer's* concept of comparative systems reflects more of the historical context and seems to present thereby the different systems and their variants in a more realistic pattern. Unfortunately, however, he is also inclined to explain some of the features of the compared systems by referring to one or another theoretical thesis or assumption, such as the "labour theory of value" (sometimes misinterpreting it[566]) or the "marginal factor productivity" as supposed to determine income distribution, not to mention such assumptions as e.g. about the existence of a real "consumer sovereignty" in the era of business propaganda and demonstration effects, or that the consumer durable goods make a source of "property incomes", and that the work ethic has stemmed only from protestant culture.

Though referring, among the causes of the failure of the communist system, to the heavy burden of defence expenditures (p. 161) due to the arms race with the USA, Schnitzer does also take the changes in the systems out of their interrelations. Owing to the lack of an analysis of how the different economic systems are interrelated and interacting within the same global system of the world economy, the comparisons made by him, too, between e.g. the "centrally planned" and the "market institutional arrangements" (p. 166), also appear as the products of the "contrast approach".

## 7. Is a constructive eclecticism possible?

### 7.1. Signs of convergence in some general concepts of development issues

Though, as *Paul Streeten* noted (1985), "eclecticism and compromise are not attractive to scholars", and "two different scientific paradigms cannot coexist for long", in the last decade there seemed to appear certain obvious signs of a tendency towards an eclectic approach and paradigmatic synthesis in both the economics of development and comparative systems.

*Streeten* himself outlined (1985) the major lines (at least the desired ones) of such an eclecticism, by referring to (1) the "the transition of development economics from the 'economics of a special case', viz. Third World economies, to a new global economics of shared problems, but with a greater differentiation of approaches and analyses"; (2) "the need for an appropriate intellectual technology" which

[566] For example, he attributed *Marx* (instead of Ricardo or others) the concept of the determination of wages by "subsistence minimum", and misinterpreted, like many others, also the "labor theory of value".

"calls for a unification of the formal and informal intellectual sectors"; (3) "the need for multidisciplinarity work at the deepest level"; (4) "a selective policy..." which "is capable of producing a synthesis between those who advocate total linking to the international market system and those who advocate delinking"; (5) the strengthening of three, neglected dimensions: "the historical dimension, ...the global dimension" and "the dimension which Harvey Leibenstein called *Micro-Micro Theory*"; (6) the perception of the large-scale and small-scale activities "as alternatives"; and (7) "a combination of careful attention to detail with visions for alternative futures". (pp. 245–246)

The very fact that "development economics" has more or less lost its original meaning and limitedness (both geographically and in terms of topics) and can gain again (if surviving) a universal and global relevance while keeping its more or less interdisciplinary nature, necessarily brings about changes in views on several issues which were considered in a narrower context before. The actual development experiences of the past decades and the polemies, induced thereby, inside the various "schools", do also contribute to a certain revision of those confronting paradigms presented by opposite theoretical streams earlier, since no one-sided, ideologically motivated "recipe" for development policy (whether it suggested an unlimited market spontaneity or "state-socialism", full, unregulated openness or delinking) has been verified in practice.

While the collapse of "socialism" in the Soviet bloc countries seemed to justify the general supremacy of "capitalism" (no matter what form it takes under which conditions), the subsequent troubles, crises or grave difficulties coupled (as a result of unexpected pauperisation, loss of the former "social entitlements" and growth of inequalities) with socio-political discontent, and the rise of a "crude" or "wild" capitalism in some of the former "socialist" countries, etc. have dispelled many illusions about "the" system called capitalism. Not to mention what new problems it has produced for the international community. The end of the "bipolar world" and of the fear of Soviet danger has, perhaps, also contributed to the spread of a more moderate and balanced, less ideologically motivated viewpoint and the recognition of the great diversity of cases and problems both with regard to "systems" and "development".

Accelerating globalisation and its new challenges to the world society as a whole, are most likely to work also for more realistic approaches and against ideological narrow-minded concepts.

In the centuries old polemy between opposite streams of economic theory one of the central issue has concerned the role of the *State* and that of the *market*. We have already seen in the previous chapters how different answers to this question were given by or followed from one or another "school" of economics, and how it has gained a particular emphasis both in development economics (in view of the structural and institutional changes distinguishing development from economic growth) and in the economics of comparative systems (in view of the "contrast" between market economies and "centrally planned economies"). We have also seen how the "neo-classical counter-revolution" of development economics has attacked the "dirigiste dogma" which it attributed to all those criticising the prevailing world order and the myth of a harmoniously operating market. But we had also to note not only its relatively small effect but also the distinction (made by Lal) between the rejection of government interventions as "dirigisme" and the acceptance of "laissez faire".

As it has been increasingly recognised even among liberals and neo-classical economists that no perfect "laissez-faire" system exists, and that the economic actors can hardly receive (particularly in the less developed countries) appropriate information (as "signals") from the market, nor they have an equal access to it, the question about the relationship between the State and the market obviously needed a revision.

As a matter of fact, already in the mid-1970s *Joseph Stiglitz* (1974) pointed to the problem of information as causing obvious market failures as well as government failures: "Traditional economic theory has ignored the central problems associated with costly information. When due attention is paid to these information theoretic considerations, the basic propositions of neoclassical analysis no longer remain valid: market equilibrium may not exist, even when all the underlying preferences and production sets are 'well behaved'; when equilibrium exists, it is, in general, not Pareto efficient…". "…information problems may give rise to public (governmental) failures just as they give rise to market failures." [567]

Another important recognition of market failure has been related to the increasing public consciousness of the need to protect natural environment, which can hardly be left to the market[568].

One of those signs marking a tendency towards an eclectic approach appeared in the 1991 *World Development Report* of the World Bank (1991) and the reply to it in the Research Papers for the Group of Twenty-Four published by *UNCTAD* (1992), even if these two documents still reflect the controversy between those with a basically liberal, neo-classical orientation and those with a more or less structuralist, critical orientation.

The World Bank's Report (1991), having defined "the challenge of development" in the broadest sense[569] (far from the early economistic perception of development as a growth in per capita GDP), admits that "markets sometimes prove inadequate or fail altogether", and concludes accordingly: "It is not a question of state or market: each has a large and irreplaceable role". Thus the "central issue in development, and the principal theme of the Report, is the interaction between governments and markets" (p. 1). Instead of recommending an overall deregulation and full liberalisation (at least for the developing countries), the

[567] See it in: *Meier, G. M.* (1995), p. 101.

[568] As the *World Bank* (1991) states: "Government intervention to protect the environment is necessary for sustainable development." (p. 9)

[569] "The challenge of development, in the broadest sense, is to improve the quality of life. …Any notion of strictly economic progress must, at a minimum, look beyond growth in per capita incomes to the reduction of poverty and greater equity, to progress in education, health, and nutrition, and to the protection of the environment." *World Bank* (1991), p. 4.

World Bank advocates a *"market-friendly" approach* only, which involves an appropriate combination of market spontaneity and government interventions[570].

Though *Michael Todaro* (1997) regards this newly propagated "market-friendly approach" as a recent variant of the neo-classical counterrevolution in development economics, it means also a break (even if inconsistently) with the conventional views on the rational operation of a spontaneous market. As Todaro notes, it "recognizes that there are many imperfections in Third World product and factor markets and that governments do have a key role to play in facilitating the operations of markets through 'nonselective' (market-friendly) interventions", and accepts also "the notion that market failures are more widespread in developing countries in areas such as investment coordination and environment outcomes". Todaro adds: "In an environment of widespread institutional rigidity and severe socio-economic inequality, *both* markets and governments will typically fail". (pp. 88, 90) What makes, indeed, inconsistent the break with the conventional approach, unfortunately not only in the World Bank Report, but also in Todaro's view, is the implicit or explicit assumption that "market failures" appear in the less developed economies only.

Praising the remarkable achievements of the East Asian economies the *World Bank's Report* (1991) concludes that "these economies refute the case for thoroughgoing dirigisme as convincingly as they refute the case for laissez-faire". (p. 5) Thus, "the challenge to policy-makers is to exploit the complementarities between state and market". (p. 11) It regards privatisation not as an end itself, but "as a means to an end" only, i.e. "to use resources more efficiently". (p. 144) Apart from that there is no proven correlation between efficiency and type of ownership in general, and that the efficiency of modern companies depends more on management qualities, the above statements seem to mark a certain deviation from the conventional views, characterizing "comparative systems analysis", too, on the public sector and privatisation.

The Report takes a more intermediary stand also in respect of the internal/external forces of, or obstacles to, development. While stressing that "global integration in the flow of goods, services, capital, and labour also brings enormous benefits...and gives poor countries access to basic knowledge in medicine, science, and engineering", it notes that "increasing exposure to external influences undoubtedly puts the developing countries at risk." (p. 3) Without denying that "protection has stimulated growth in some instances" (p. 14), it argues, in general, for a full participation in the world economy and "outward-orientation", but completely neglects the historical fact that the type of "outward-orientation" characterising for long most of the developing countries specialised in primary exports has failed, for various reasons, to facilitate their "catching up" with the advanced countries. It refers only to the Prebisch–Singer thesis about the assumed regular deterioration (causing losses or declining benefits from trade) of the net barter terms of trade, which it flatly and easily rejects (p. 106), in view of the inherent

570 "When markets and governments have worked in harness, the results have been spectacular, but when they have worked in opposition, the results have been disastrous." *World Bank* (1991), p. 2.

ambiguity of the latter and the opportunity to counteract it by diversification and increased volume of trade (not to mention increased productivity). In other words, it leaves the structural effects of such a specialisation completely out of consideration, though at the same time it states that "development has almost always involved a shift in the sectoral composition of output" (p. 32).

While noting that "economic theory suggests that productivity and per capita incomes could converge across countries over time, assuming that the countries which are now developing get access to the new technology introduced by the industrial countries", the Report also admits that "most of the world had failed to make much progress" by 1945. (p. 13)

Though the Report points to the "external shocks" suffered by developing countries, it denies that the "effects of external factors...can account for *differences* in performance among individual countries", i.e. the association between differences in growth rates and the magnitude of external shocks". (p. 46)

Regarding the major determinants of development, the Report seemed to recall the classical concept (shared also by Marx) about growing productivity as the "engine of development", but it conceived of it as resulting from the contributions of both labour and capital (as according to a neo-classical perception), or as the "residual", the growth of "total factor productivity" resulting from technical change, improved quality and discipline of labour, etc. (in accordance with the "new growth theory")[571].

The Report points to that the success stories of a few countries "have two features in common: they invested in the education of men and women and in physical capital; and they achieved high productivity from these investments by giving markets, competition, and trade leading roles. New ideas, progress in technology, and pressures to achieve efficiency thus were nourished by their economies. The extent and efficiency of the state's involvement in the economy has been crucial. One lesson is that it is better for the state to focus on areas where it complements and supports the private sector...A second lesson is that the quality of government matters as much as the quantity." (p. 31)

According to the Report, "the key to global development has been the diffusion of technological progress". (p. 14) It also notes (p. 93) that "migration, transfers of skilled personnel, and returning workers from abroad all contribute to the diffusion of technology" (and that labour mobility is also "another avenue for reducing the disparity in incomes worldwide"). Nevertheless, it seems to support without any reservation the "greater protection of intellectual property" (p. 92), and does not even raise the problem of the obstacles, set even by the most democratic and liberal states, to the exercising of the right (as one of the human rights) to immigrate.

[571] Op. cit., pp. 42–43.

The Report sums up "the clearest lesson from work on development during the past thirty years" as follows: "...there is a premium on pragmatism and an open mind... In development, generalizations can be as rash as unbending commitments to theories." (p. 49) It is only strange (if not contradictory) that at the same time it attacks only "the early faith in the ability of the state to direct development" (p. 31) without equally criticising the old and renewed "faith in the ability of the market", too.

The reply to the Report in the *UNCTAD* document (1992) is mostly criticising its inconsistencies rather than its overall content or general approach.

For example, referring to that the Report "stresses throughout that development problems occur precisely because of strong distortions in product and factor markets", poses the rhetoric question: "How is it that departures from perfect competition so weakly affect econometrics but so strongly explain differences in development performance?" (p. 3)

It also points to that "not much evidence is presented" in the Report to verify such propositions as e.g. that "a strategy of import-substituting industrialization...may have grave long-term costs in terms of low efficiency and slow technical progress, i.e. low productivity growth", or "that external openness and competition are associated with high growth and productivity", or "that macroeconomic instability diminishes the return on investment and the growth of output". (p. 2)

The critique blames the Report for its "neoclassical philosophy" manifested in the assumption of an automatic market mechanism ensuring, by changes in interest rate, equilibrium between savings and investments, and for its neglect of how the very policy prescribed by IMF, and WB as well, (including, particularly, the removing of exchange controls) has contributed to capital flight from the developing countries. (pp. 8, 19)

It also accuses the Report for sharing the IMF concept and policy package of stabilisation and failing "to see aspects of imbalances created by the debt crisis" (p. 12), and, particularly, for ignoring "structural features linking the saving, external and fiscal gaps" and thereby understating "the complexity of stabilization, especially if stagnation is to be avoided". (p. 15) It disagrees with the (textbook-type) way of distinguishing between "stabilization and structural reform" and the suggested order of sequencing each other, with the division of labour between the IMF (dealing with stabilization) and the Bank (designing the policy package for growth).

In view of the various inconsistencies and simplifications, the critique in the UNCTAD document concludes finally that from the vague definitions and ambiguous statements of the Report about government interventions "to implement reforms in the face of sometimes trenchant political opposition" and "powerful interests", it is quite possible to "come back to an interventionist State".[572]

[572] "Doubts about its efficacy and possible autocratic nature (even in a market-friendly context) are conspicuously missing in the WDR. Partisans of democracy might find this to be a risky political stance." *UNCTAD* (1992), p. 26.

It seems quite *symptomatic* that even the critique of the "market-friendly approach" of the World Bank's Report is warning us of the danger of autocratic state interventionism!

Over and beyond the above controversy, there are *many other signs* of a certain motion in literature towards some eclecticism. In regard to the role of the State (and the market), it is remarkable that *"neo-structuralists"*, too, including one of the outstanding representatives of the Latin American "school of dependencia", namely *Osvaldo Sunkel*, together with Gustavo Zuleta, also noted (1990): "The neo-structuralists recognize many of these problems [of the governments – T. S.], and following a pragmatic approach and using the lessons of experience, are seeking to build a consensus as regards the new role of the State."[573] Such a "consensus" seems to represent a balanced and equally critical view concerning both the State and the market, by pointing not only to their functions but also to their possible failures.

*Joseph Stiglitz* noted (1989): "We need to recognize both the limits and strengths of markets, as well as the strengths, and limits, of government interventions aimed at correcting market failures." (p. 202) *Michael Todaro* (1997) repeats the same: "...governments can fail as well as markets". (p. 86) He also adds: "...successful development requires a skilful and judicious balancing of market pricing and promotion where markets can indeed exist and operate efficiently, along with intelligent and equity-oriented government intervention in areas where market forces would lead to undesirable economic and social outcomes." (p. 94)

According to *Colin I. Bradford* (1986): "The dichotomy between market forces and government intervention is not only overdrawn: it misconceives the fundamental dynamic at work. It is the *degree of consistency* between the two sectors – rather than the extent of implicit or explicit conflict – that has been important in the successful development cases. (p. 123)

*Gerald Meier* (1995) also concludes: "Developing countries need to avoid both market failure and government failure." (p. 514) "...development policy might be better devoted to improving and strengthening the market system than to supplanting the market with detailed administrative controls. Government interventions, however, may still be necessary to remedy the pervasiveness of 'new market failures'...and to make markets work more effectively". (p. 513)

Compromising views, reflecting also a sign of eclecticism, appear in respect of trade policies, too, and in the assessment of countries' *development performances* as resulting from domestic or external conditions, in general, as well as in regard to *comparative systems*. Moreover, there seem to be a certain attempt to incorporate some elements of the "old" political economy in the "new" one.

*Michael Todaro* (1997) writes: "In short, the current consensus leans toward an eclectic view that attempts to fit the relevant arguments of both free-trade and protectionist models to the specific economic, institutional, and political realities of diverse Third World nations at different stages of development." (p. 481)

He stresses the diversity and complexity of reality which excludes the applicability of universal doctrines and ideologies, but suggests, instead, learning from dif-

[573] Quoted by *Meier, G. M.* (1995), p. 533.

ferent approaches: "It is not simply an either/or question based on ideological leaning; rather it is a matter of assessing each individual country's situation on a case-by-case basis." (p. 90) "Each approach has its strengths and weaknesses... each of these approaches to understanding development has something to offer." (pp. 93, 95)

He adds: "Even more than other fields of economics, development economics has no universally accepted doctrine or paradigm. Instead, we have a continually evolving pattern of insights and understandings that together provide the basis for examining the possibilities of contemporary development of the diverse nations of Africa, Asia, and Latin America." (p. 94)

One may question, however, why all what he sums up as an eclectic conclusion is presented as relevant to the developing countries only?!

As regards the debate about the favourable or unfavourable effects of the *international environment* on the development process, *Paul Streeten* (1985) also believes in a possible compromise of views: "A reconciliation between the two perceptions (namely, that development can be speeded up by global economic integration and that underdevelopment is caused and perpetuated by it) is possible along the following lines. The advanced industrial countries emit a large number of impulses of two kinds: those that present opportunities for faster and better development than would otherwise have been possible, and those that present obstacles to development, that stunt growth." (p. 241)

On the *interactions* of domestic and external factors of development *Michael Todaro* notes (1997) that "the stages theory failed to take into account the crucial fact that contemporary Third World nations are part of a highly integrated and complex international system in which even the best and most intelligent development strategies can be nullified by external forces beyond the countries' control." (p. 75)

In accordance with the latter *Todaro* makes also a general conceptual point concerning "comparative systems", too: "economic systems ...must be viewed in a broader perspective than that postulated by traditional economics. They must be analysed within the context of the overall *social system* of a country and, indeed, within an international global context as well." (p. 12)

With regard to the "new political economy", *Gerald Meier* (1995) states: "Going beyond the limitations of formal rational choice models, a richer analysis might be achieved by incorporating some concepts of the old political economy, such as nationalism, power, ideology, class, and relationship between the state and society. Future research may provide a synthesis of the old and new political economy that will point up the possibilities of policy changes including more political variables and a more favourable view of the political process." (p. 584)

## 7.2. Dunning's eclectic theory of transnational investments

In view of the increasingly decisive role of the world-wide activity of the *transnatioal companies* in international economic relations, in the international trade of products and services and in the flows of capital and other resources in the last decades, more attention has been paid, in general, to the *motivations* of these companies' foreign direct investments and business policy in theoretical works as well. One of the best and most elabourated among them is that of John Dunning[581].

This new, "eclectic" theory[582], while breaking with the over-simplifying concept of Neo-Classical economics, which (as we have seen) practically reduces the reason of investing capital abroad to a higher return, resulting from relative capital shortage, in the foreign economy concerned, points (again) to other possible motivations and approaches the latter from the point of view of the overall interest, a sort of "global optimization" policy of multinational companies. By making use of the great variety of the earlier concepts on international capital mobility, FDIs, and the "multis" (TNCs), and concluding from an enormous empirical material, Dunning presents the most realistic picture of the *complexity* of FDI motivations and business strategy of the transnational firms.

In view of the corporate structure and multinational composition of the companies exporting and investing capital abroad, Dunning focusses on their overall performance and suggests accordingly a calculation of the *aggregate return* (profit rate) on total capital[583]. With regard to the profitability of a subsidiary, an affiliate firm aboad, its calculation should take into account, accordingly, not only the net income of the subsidiary firm only (and its ratio to the invested capital by the latter) but also the *effects* of its operation on other subsidiaries, i.e. the resulting changes in their total revenues, costs and investments.

Having outlined the alternative choices of the "multis", namely between the export of products, the sale of know hows, and FDIs, Dunning has logically grouped the various motivations of FDIs, and categorized them as according to different criteria.

One of his categorization has made a distinction between the aim (motivation): (1) to gain certain advantages, (2) to make use of and preserve the already gained advantages, and (3) to overcome certain disadvantages.

---

[581] See among his other writings particularly: Dunning, J. H. (1993).

[582] Its eclectic nature should not be interpreted in a negative sense. It represents a constructive eclecticism insofar as over and beyond or behind its originality, which follows from the systemic analysis and logic of elaboration, it reflects all the applicable results of the former theoretical concepts, including the Marxian and even the neo-classical ones, as well as, particularly, some more recent views.

[583] The calculation of such an aggregate rate of profit for the entire company, instead of a spot rate of return only, has logically followed from the Marxian approach, too.

Another, more widely used categorization of Dunning distinguishes between: (1) resource seeking[584], (2) market seeking[585], (3) efficiency seeking[586] and (4) strategy asset/capability seeking[587] motivations.

A further distinction between motivations is expressed by Dunning's famous "OLI paradigm", which refers to (1) ownership advantages, (2) location advantages, and (3) internalization advantages. Since *ownership* may ensure the most direct control over the operation of a foreign subsidiary, transnational companies drive for and make use of such an advantage whenever and wherever their business interest prescribe such a strong control over important resources or the quality of inputs and the final product, for the protection of copyright, brand names etc., as not available by other methods. The "location advantages" may include, of course, all those specific conditions of a given country or region, as distinctive from others', providing "comparative advantages" and "base" for international trade (such as considered in the classical and neo-classical trade theories), but also many other, objective or created circumstances (for example, the geographic position as related to the contemporary centre of gravity of the world economy, the "economic" and "cultural distance" from, in fact the closeness rather to the home base of the company, the hospitable, TNC-friendly atmosphere, "free trade zones", tax and other allowances, etc.). "Internalization" implies the organization, within the same company, of cross-border transfers of products and services among its subsidiaries located in different countries. Its great advantage follows not only from saving such transactions from market fluctuations and uncertainties, but also from making possible to use special, manipulated or even artificial prices, the so-called "transfer prices" in accountancy, and thus, by means of over-invoicing or under-invoicing the imports or exports, to reduce the local tax burden.

Contrary to the one-sided aproaches of both conventional liberalism and nationalist or ultra-leftist rethorics, Dunning's works do also point to the "double face" of the foreign capital investments, in general, and of the activities of the

---

584 "Resource seeking" may practically refer to all the possible resources (natural, labour, capital resources, including physical and human capital, technologies, know hows, managament, administration, organization and marketing skill, credit and loan facilities, etc.) which are needed for the operation of the company.

585 Though such a motivation appeared already in the Marxian concept, which also referred to the role of capital export in promoting the export of products, but it was limited to the marketing abroad of unsold, at home hardly marketable products only, i.e. to the case of a recession in the home economy. Dunning has qualified market-seeking a general motivation, which reflects, indeed, the contemporary practice fairly well.

586 "Efficiency seeking" obviously refers to the already mentioned overall performance, aggregate profit rate of the company, i.e. to how its aggregate productivity can be increased (by better technologies, improved quality of labour, economies of scale and scope, etc.) and its total costs be reduced (by economizing on their various components, including both "internal" and "external" costs).

587 This motivation refers not only to the aim of smashing and pushing out the rivals in competition, but also – if reasonable – to possible "strategic alliance" with them.

transnational companies, in particular. From his analysis it is clear enough that, on the one hand, transnational companies bring about "equalization" in income level or development resources neither within nor between countries (but may actually increase the "gaps"). But it also follows therefrom, on the other hand, that, as a result of their efficiency oriented and integrated business policy organizing and managing their cross-border activities in production and services, new opportunities (not only new dangers and challenges) open up for countries. This is because such firms when intending to capitalize on all the available local assets throughout their corporate system, are ready to locate or relocate their activities[588].

## 7.3. Porter's eclectic concept of the "national competitiveness"

The question of why some countries are more developed and enjoy a better position in the world economy than great many others, has been a central issue not only in development studies but also in international economics since the very beginning. With the end of the so-called "historical competition between capitalism and socialism", i.e. of the end of political and ideological confrontation between two military blocs, the economic competition among all the members of the same, single world-economic system, and, particularly, the competition between rivals within the developed centre of the world economy, could gain (again) primary attention. While "structural adjustment" has become the key word addressed to those countries intending to catch up with the more advanced ones, the task to increase "competitiveness" has appeared as an imperative for the latter. It has also turned out in general that in the contemporary world economy the actual position of countries, their competitiveness in trade, and even their potential rate of economic development as a whole, are determined not only by those advantages they possess as given, inherited "endowments", but also and increasingly by those they can construct, they can purposefully create.

In his extended study, which soon became a best-seller book (1990), Michael Porter has investigated the determinants of the competitiveness, of the "competitive advantage of nations".

[588] The fact of new opportunities opened by TNCs for the less-developed economies has been emphasized even by *UNCTAD*, which has always paid particular attention to the interest of developing countries: "The decision to locate any part of the value-added chain wherever it is best for a firm ...to convert global inputs into outputs for global markets means that FDI and trade flows are determined simultaneously. They are both immediate consequences of the same locational decision...Reduced obstacles to trade and FDI and the possibilities that they open up for TNCs to disperse production activities within integrated international production systems create new opportunities for countries. The challenge is to attract FDI and then to maximize the benefits associated with it in order to realize the opportunities arising from the new environment." – See UNCTAD (1996), *World Investment Report 1966*. UN. New York and Geneva. p. xxiv.

Porter, however, disagrees not only with those views defining the competitiveness of nations by rich natural resources or abundance of cheap labour, etc., i.e. by given endowments, but also those explaining it by other "macroeconomic" phenomena, such as depreciating currency, low rate of interest, or government policy in general, and even those referring to management practices[589], which all imply actions (though not necessarily correct ones, indeed) to "create" competitive advantages.

Though he accepts (1990) that "the only meaningful concept of competitiveness at the national level is national productivity", since "productivity is the prime determinant in the long run of a nation's standard of living" (p. 9), he actually refuses the concept of "national competitiveness"[590] and believes that competitiveness should be examined "at the level of particular industries" as that of individual firms. In other words, he considers competitiveness as a basically micro-economic issue[591].

In his view, the (ill-defined) question why a nation is more "competitive" internationally, i.e. more successful in the world economy, is in fact a question of "why firms based in a nation are able to compete successfully against foreign rivals in particular segments and industries." (p. 10). The "competitive advantage" of firms belonging to a certain nation manifests itself in its *lower cost level* and/or its *differentiated products* commanding "premium prices"[592]. But competitive advantage can be sustained by a firm over time only if it provides higher-quality products and services or produce "more efficiently", which all refer to "productivity growth."

---

589 *Porter* notes: "Some see national competitiveness as a macroeconomic phenomenon, driven by such variables as exchange rates, interest rates, and government deficits. But nations have enjoyed rapidly rising living standards despite budget deficits (Japan, Italy, and Korea), appreciating currencies (Germany and Switzerland), and high interest rates (Italy and Korea)." "Others argue that competitiveness is a function of cheap and abundant labor. Yet nations such as Germany, Switzerland, and Sweden have prospered despite high wages and long periods of labor shortage." "... Another view is that competitiveness depends on possessing beautiful natural resources. Recently, however, the most successful trading nations, among them Germany, Japan, Switzerland, Italy and Korea, have been countries with limited natural resources that must import most raw materials." "More recently, many have argued that competitiveness is most strongly influenced by government policy. ...Yet such a decisive role for government policy in competitiveness is not confirmed by a broader survey of experience..." "... A final popular explanation ...is differences in management practices, including labor-management relations...The problem with this explanation, however, is that different industries require different approaches to management." – Op. cit. (1990), pp. 3–5.

590 "We must abandon the whole notion of a 'competitive' nation as a term having much meaning for economic prosperity...". – Op. cit. p. 9.

591 "...we must focus not on the economy as a whole but on *specific industries and industry segments*. While efforts to explain aggregate productivity growth in entire economies have illuminated the importance of the quality of a nation's human resources and the need for improving technology, an examination at this level must by necessity focus on very broad and general determinants that are not sufficiently complete and operational to guide company strategy or public policy...". – Op. cit. p. 9.

592 "Lower cost is the ability of a firm to design, produce, and market a comparable product more efficiently than its competitors. ... Differentitation is the ability to provide unique and superior value to the buyer in terms of product quality, special features, or after-sale service... Differentiation allows a firm to command a premium price, which leads to superior profitability provided costs are comparable to those of competitors." – Op. cit. p. 38.

These points hardly contain anything new, which was not emphasized earlier in economic literature.

But Porter, fortunately, goes further, and brings the question closer to the issue of transnational (multinational) companies[593] and (despite his above-mentioned remarks) to certain macro-economic aspects and government policies related to the foreign companies, too[594]. He correctly notes that the *multinational companies* follow a global strategy "in which trade and foreign investment are integrated" and intend to choose as a *"home base"* those countries ("nations") where their "competitive advantages" can easily be created and sustained.

The "home base" is "the location of many of the most productive jobs, the core technologies, and the most advanced skills". When chosing the "home base" the companies take into account those differences "in national economic structures, values, cultures, institutions, and histories" which "contribute profoundly to competitive success" (p. 19).

Though "the nature of competition and the sources of competitive advantage differ widely among industries and even industry segments" (p. 69), for a multinational company which embraces an interdependent system or network of activities (a *"value chain"*[595]), connected by *linkages*, the competitive advantage may stem not only from the lower cost level and product differentiation, but also from "exploiting interrelationships by competing in related industries", i.e. from *"competitive scope"* which is important exactly because industries are segmented. (p. 38)

Finally, as regards the determinants of *"national advantage"* in global competition, i.e. the answer to the question why multinational firms chosing a country as "home base" can be more successful in certain segments of industry, Porter identifies four major determinants: (*1*) the "factor conditions" (particularly "the nation's position" in respect of "skilled labour" and infrastructure), (*2*) the actual "demand conditions" ("the nature of home demand for the industry's product or service"), (*3*) the presence and development of "related and supporting", supplying industries (which are also internationally competitive), and (*4*) the

593 "Multinationals that are the leading competitors in particular segments or industries are often based in only one or two nations. The important questions are *why and how* do multinationals from a particular nation develop unique skills and know-how in particular industries? Why do some multinationals from some nations sustain and build on these advantages and others do not?" – Op. cit. p. 18.

594 "Competitive advantage is created and sustained through a highly localized process. ... The role of the home nation seems to be as strong as or stronger than ever. While globalization of competition might appear to make the nation less important, instead it seems to make it more so." – Op. cit. p. 19.

595 "A firm's value chain is an interdependent system or network of activities, connected by *linkages*. Linkages occur when the way in which one activity is performed affects the cost or effectiveness of other activities. ...A company's value chain for competing in a particular industry is embedded in a large stream of activities that I term the *value system*." (Op. cit. 41–42). The "value system" includes not only the firm's own "value chain" but also that of the supplier, the intermediary and the buyer.

"strategy, structure, and rivalry" of firms ("the conditions in the nation governing how companies are created, organized, and managed, and the nature of domestic rivalry." (p. 71) In view of the interrelations and interactions between these four determinants, Porter illustrates (and names) their system as a *"national diamond"*[596].

What obviously follows is that in order to attract or give birth to such internationally competitive TNCs choosing the country as a "home base", the country itself and particularly its government can do a lot, by developing human capital, promoting the development of education, training, research and development capacities, technological progress, infrastructure, and the input-output linkages as well.

While in the past the economic policy recommended by the theories of international economics was to make use of the given "comparative advantages" in trade, today a *new paradigm*, following from such modern, eclectic theories as elabourated e.g. by Dunning and Porter, and reflecting the new conditions of the world economy, suggests a policy of *creating* "competitive advantages". Namely: by providing favourable conditions and attractive terms for the rise locally, and/or the inflow from abroad, of transnational firms which choose the country concerned as "home base" and can successfully operate in dynamic industries and services on international level.

## 8. Some final conclusions

As it appears, many of the traditional dilemmas of development (such as openness or delinking) are put into a new context, many of the old controversies (such as about the internal or external causes of development/underdevelopment) are resolved by compromising views and more complex approaches, many of the former one-sided, biased concepts (such as concerning "capitalism" and "socialism") have become more balanced, many of those alternatives assumed earlier to exclude each other (such as the functioning of the market and state interventions, etc.) are now regarded as complementaries. All these may raise the hope that ideologies tend to fade away, and the new century marks the "Eve of a *new Enlightment"*, the one, which totally expels all ideologies from social sciences.

Since, at the same time, owing mainly to improvement in global information services, public consciousness all over the world is getting increasingly aware of how much each nation and each human being is depending on all the others, there can arise also the hope for the recognition of our common destiny and the need for common efforts to overcome the international (as well as intra-society) devel-

[596] "Nations are most likely to succeed in industries or industry segments where the national 'diamond', a term I will use to refer to the determinants as a system, is the most favorable." – Op. cit. p. 72.

opment gap. It requires the establishment of a new system, both on country and global level, better than even the seemingly best today, which integrates without uniformising, takes care of all its members without paternalism, allocates resources and distributes incomes without commanding or disequalising, and ensures a sustainable development on this Earth.

It is worth quoting again *Todaro:* "As the realities of global interdependence slowly penetrate the political perceptions of developed-nation governments, and perhaps eventually their populaces as well, it may lead to the realization that their real long-run economic and political interests in fact lie with the achievement of broad-based development in Third World nations. Eliminating poverty, minimizing inequality, promoting environmentally sustainable development, and raising levels of living for the masses of LDC peoples may turn out to be in the most fundamental self-interest of developed nations. This is not because of any humanitarian ideals...but simply because in the long run, there can be no dual futures for humankind, one for the very rich and another for the very poor, without the proliferation of global or regional conflict." (p. 558)

* * *

# GLOSSARY

## Key terms, concepts and methods of general economics, applied in international and development economics

**"Accelerator"** = a concept (or "principle") which implies that an increase in the demand for consumer goods encouraging investments and thereby a proportionate increase in consumer goods production induces such an increase in investments also in the capital goods producing sector as leading finally to a more than proportionate increase in consumer goods production. Such an accelerator works also in the opposite direction, and thus reinforces the tendency of fluctuations in a spontaneously operating market economy.

**Autarky** = a more or less complete isolation of the national economy of a country from the world economy, i.e. the absence of its trade or other relations with other countries.

**Automatic equilibrium mechanism within national economy** = an ideal mechanism, visualiSed in classical as well as neo-classical economics, of a spontaneously operating market economy, which is supposed to involve a reversibility of the equilibrium-disturbing processes and is based on an assumed equilibrium-restoring interactions within the partial markets (in all the product as well as factor markets) where both demand and supply depend on the same, namely an always flexibly responding, i.e. perfectly elastic price, and also on the interconnections between these partial markets. It means that if demand exceeds supply, then the price will increase, thereby causing a reduction in demand and/or an increase in supply so much as restoring equilibrium. The opposite happens in the case of over-supply. In product markets it is the price of the product concerned, which should flexibly respond to any change in demand or supply, in the labour market it is the wage level, in capital market it is interest rate.

**Appreciation** = a spontaneous improvement of the exchange rate of a national currency, which means an increase in its relative value as compared to other currencies, i.e. a decrease in the domestic price of foreign currencies, under a (more or less) freely floating exchange rate system.

**Balance of (foreign) trade** = see under (B).

**Balance of (international) payments** = see under (B).

**Balance of payments adjustment policies** = see under (B).

**Capital** = an accumulated and exclusively owned resource (manifested in various assets, such as money; in means of production, i.e. "physical capital"; in accumulated knowledge, i.e. "knowledge capital"; in monopolized position in the access to information and in social contacts; in political power, i.e. "political capital", etc.) which is used to result in an increased income for its owner.

**Capital account** = see under (B).

**Capital-intensity** = the relative amount of capital, as compared to the number of labour units (or the size of the land) used in the production of a commodity, i.e. the capital-labour (K/L) ratio, the amount of capital per unit of labour (or the capital–land ratio, the amount of capital per unit of land).

**Capital-output ratio** = the amount of capital per unit of output, i.e. the number of capital units needed for the production of a certain output.

**Community indifference curve** = the curve showing an assumed equal level of subjective satisfaction provided to a community (a society) by various combinations of (only) two consumer goods.

**Competitive market** = a "perfect" market without any imperfections (i.e. without concentrated powers or monopolies on the side of the supply or the demand, and without State interventions), in which actors are atomistically dispersed, and all of them are "price-takers", i.e. none of them is "price-maker".

**"Constant capital"** = the term (introduced by Marx) to distinguish that part of total capital, which is invested in the means of production (raw materials, machinery, buildings, etc.), i.e. the products of labour performed in the past, from "variable capital", on the basis of the assumption that the value of the former is only transferred, without changes, to the final value of the product in the production process, while the latter undergoes a substantial change (leading to a "new value").

**Consumer surplus** = the assumed difference between the sum that the consumers are willing to pay for a certain good in the market and the sum they actually pay.

**Current account** = see under (B).

**Commodity** = a product produced for exchange, an article of trade.

**Cross (price) elasticity of demand** = the percentage change in the quantity of demand for a certain product ("x") divided by the percentage change in the price of another product ("y").

**Deficit financing** = the (rather irresponsible) policy of the government and/or the monetary authorities financing the deficit in the central budget by increased emission of money and other inflationary methods.

**Depreciation** = a spontaneous deterioration of the exchange rate of a national currency, which means a decrease in its relative value as compared to other currencies, i.e. an increase in the domestic price of foreign currencies, under a (more or less) freely floating exchange rate system.

**Devaluation** = a deliberate decrease, by an action of the monetary authority, in the relative value of the national currency, i.e. an increase in the domestic price of foreign currencies, under a peg exchange rate system.

**Diminishing returns** = decreasing increments in total output when input is increased and despite the equal measure of additional input.

**Dual nature of economic phenomena and processes** = the unity of two different aspects of all economic phenomena and processes, namely: a "real" (physical, technical) and a monetary one, which, as the "two sides of the same coin", cannot be isolated from each other. An example is the symbiosis in each commodity of a "use value", a "utility", i.e. its physically consumable/usable nature and an "exchange value", i.e. its ability of being exchanged for money or other commodities.

**Economies of scale** = increasing returns to scale, i.e. economizing on the costs by increasing the size of an activity, such as the volume of production when the costs increase less than proportionally with an increase in output.

**"Edgeworth box diagram"** = a box diagram which is constructed by means of combining two coordinate systems (both measuring the available quantities of the two factors of production, labour and capital, and expressing the same factor price proportions within the national economy), but one of which shows the isoquants of one of the two products, while the other coordinate system shows those of the other product, in such a way as turning the latter upside-down and placing it, from above, on the former. Thereby all the isoquant curves of both products and all the isocost lines of the two factors of production appear in a single coordinate system forming a "box", in which not only the optimum points of input combinations for the two products can be separately marked out (as in the case of the isoquants of one or the other product to which the lowest isocost is tangent), or only the optimum points of output combination can be illustrated (as in the case of the "transformation curves" leaving out of account the possible varieties of input combinations), but all those points showing both the optimum output and optimum input combinations (i.e. the common tangent points of the isoquants of the two products and the lowest isocost line.

**Effective demand** = demand coupled with purchasing power, appearing in the market.

**Elasticity of demand** = a more or less flexible responsiveness of demand to a change affecting it, such as, primarily, in the price of the product, service or factor of production demanded, and in the income level of those setting such a demand. Accordingly, the two basic variants of demand elasticity are: (a) price elasticity of demand and (b) income elasticity of demand. There are also other, composite variants. Demand elasticities are measured by the ratios of the change in demand to a change in its determinant. Demand is qualified "elastic" if the ratio is 1 or more than 1, i.e. if demand changes proportionally or more than proportionally to the change in the price, income or other determinants. In the calculation of demand elasticities, both the changes in the quantity of demand and in the conditions causing them are measured in percentage, and the former, as being the consequence, must be put into the numerator, i.e. above the line in the fraction, while the latter, as being the cause, into the denominator, i.e. below the line in the fraction.

**"Engel's Law"** = the observation and concept of Engel, according to which if incomes increase, the demand pattern of consumers tends to shift away from basic necessities, "inferior goods", towards durables.

**Equal exchange** = an exchange of goods or services which represent equal values or costs (as measured according to different theoretical concepts).
**Equity capital** = a share in the ownership of a joint-stock company.
**Euler's theorem** = a theoretical thesis which postulates that under the conditions of constant returns to scale the total output produced is equal to the sum of the marginal productivity of each factor of production times their amount used in production. It also follows therefrom that under perfect equilibrium the owners of each factor of production should receive an income determined by the marginal productivity of their factor.
**Exchange rate of currencies** = see under (B).
**Exchange value of a product** = its ability to be exchanged for another commodity or money, measured in the quantity of the latter which it can be exchanged for.
**Export multiplier** = see under (B).
**Export orientation** = see under (B).
**Export tariffs** = see under (B).
**External economies** = economizing on the costs of or enjoying benefits from "externalities" (such as from a developed infrastructure), i.e. a reduction, owing to economies of scale, of those costs to be paid for activities needed by a given producing unit but taking place outside in its sphere of production, or a reduction of the average cost of production of a given producing unit owing to the expansion of the entire industry or region it belongs to.
**"Factor endowments"** = the relative abundance or scarcity of factors of production in a given national economy. - See also under (B).
**Flow approach** = A view-point which focusses on the flow, movement, transfer, change of place or position of the objects of economy (goods, money, assets, manpower, etc.).
**Foreign direct investment (FDI)** = investment made by a foreign resident entity (foreign individual investor or "parent company") in a country, which results in a lasting relationship of ownership, control and interest between the investor and the host country. Unlike portfolio investment, it involves the purchase of real assets and a significant degree of influence of the investor on the management of the enterprise established by FDI. FDI may consist of "equity capital" and reinvestment of capital-income (i.e. the retained part of profit which is not "repatriated", remitted to the country of investor, nor distributed as dividends among the local share-holders or affiliates), moreover it may result also from intra-company loans or debt-transactions (i.e. borrowing or lending of investment funds between the parent company and its affiliate firms.
**Forms of international capital flows** = see under (B).
**General equilibrium** = an overall equilibrium in the entire economy, i.e. simultaneously, in all the partial markets between demand and supply.
**"Green-field investments"** = investments in a new area of economic activity where enterprises did not exist before in the country concerned.

**Gross domestic product (GDP)** = The total value of all final goods and services produced in a year within the country.

**Gross national product (GNP)** = gross domestic product plus the incomes received by the residents of the country from abroad, minus the incomes paid by them to foreigners.

**Harrod–Domar model** = see under (C).

**"Hayek situation"** = see under (C).

**Import substitution** = see under (B).

**Import tariffs** = see under (B).

**Income elasticity of demand** = the percentage change in the quantity of demand for a certain product ("x") divided by the percentage change in income.

**Income elasticity of import** = see under (B).

**"Inferior goods"** = the goods (mostly some basic necessities) the demand for which declines in absolute terms, when income increases or their price decreases, and the demand for them increases when income decline or prices go up.

**Internal economies** = economizing on the internal costs, owing to economies of scale within a given producing unit, a factory or farm, in the sphere of production. It implies a reduction of the average cost of production as the output of the given unit expands.

**International resource flows** = see under (B).

**Investment multiplier** = the ratio of the absolute change in national income to the absolute change in investment (expenditures), which manifests an assumed direct cause-effect relationship (in the Keynesian concept) between changes in investment and changes in national income (the latter being a function of the former).

**"Invisible hand" of the market** = the assumed favourable, ideal role of the spontaneously operating market, which ensures, without government interventions, a rational allocation of resources, an efficient coordination of economic activities and a just distribution of incomes in the economy. This concept of the economically rational and socially favourable operation of an unregulated, spontaneous market economy is attributed to Adam Smith who believing in the principles of liberalism postulated that if everybody follows self-interest (but without infringing the interest of the community) it promotes economic development and social welfare.

**Isocost lines** = the lines drawn in the coordinate system (the axes of which measure the quantity of the factors of production used as inputs) to mark the same total cost level of the various combinations of (only) the two factors of production (labour and capital), thereby their prevailing price proportions.

**Isoquant curves** = the curves drawn in the coordinate system (the axes of which measure the quantity of the factors of production used as inputs) to show the equal levels of output of one or another product, produced by various combinations of (only) the two factors of production (labour and capital). Thus along any particular curve the level of output is the same, but factor proportions are changing. The higher a curve the bigger the level of output. An optimum combination of the two factors of production is assumed to appear when the isoquant curve is tangent to the lowest "isocost line", or a given isocost line reaches the highest isocost curve.

**Labour-intensity** = either (a) the working tempo of labourer, i.e. the number of labour inputs per unit of time, or (b) the relative amount of labour, as compared to the number of capital units (or the size of the land) used in the production of a commodity, i.e. the labour/capital (L/K) ratio, the amount of labour per unit of capital (or the labour-land ratio, the amount of labour per unit of land).

**Labour productivity** = the ratio of the output to the number of labour units used to produce it, i.e. the amount of output per unit of labour input.

**Labour theory of value** = a concept, in general, of "natural prices", i.e. "values" as centres of market price formation, being determined by the quantity of human labour used in production (from which it could logically follow that incomes are also be determined by the labour actually performed). In its classical variant it is assumed that the cost of all the other factors of production (such as Nature and capital) contributing to the formation of "value" or "natural price", can be expressed in or traced back to labour (such as in its productivity influenced e.g. by land fertility or to labour performed in the past, respectively). The Marxian variant the "value" of a commodity is equal to that amount of labour "socially necessary for its reproduction".

**"Laissez faire, laissez aller"** = the first explicit expression of the principle of liberalism (as a precedent of Smith's concept about socially beneficial result of the activity of individuals following their own interest).

**"Law of diminishing returns"** = An assumed natural phenomenon in the process of production which appears at a certain level of output above which the increment in the latter is getting smaller and smaller along with an equal increase in input.

**"Liquidity preference"** = the preference of the individuals to keep their assets in the form of money, i.e. in liquid form, which can be used at any time at their discretion, either because of the transactions-motive, i.e. the need of cash for the current transaction of personal and business exchanges, or for a precautionary-motive, i.e. the desire for security as to the future cash equivalent of a certain proportion of total resources; or due to a speculative-motive.

**"Marginal efficiency of capital"** = a Keynesian term which expresses the relationship between the value, discounted by the rate of interest, of the expected future returns on the invested capital and the present supply prices of capital goods, i.e. it reflects, besides the present rate of interest (the supply price of the capital borrowed by the investor) and the costs of investment goods, hired labour, etc., also the expectations on the future returns on investment.

**Marginal productivity** = ratio between the last (marginal) increment in the output and the last (marginal) unit of the factor in question which is used as an additional input in production, while other factor(s) of production are kept constant. In view of an assumed diminishing return under the circumstances of a given, unchanged technological level, marginal productivity normally tends to decline. Thus the greater the number of units of a factor of production that a firm can employ (depending, of course, on the firm's budget and the market price of the factor of production) or that a country de facto possesses, the smaller its marginal productivity can be.

**Marginal productivity theory of prices and incomes** = a neo-classical concept of price formation and income distribution within a (closed) national economy, which suggests that the factor prices and the incomes of the owners of the factors of production are "normally", i.e. under perfect equilibrium conditions, determined by their marginal productivity, respectively. It means that the price and income of labour in relatively labour-abundant countries tend to be lower than in the relatively capital-rich countries where the price of and the returns to capital is made cheaper by the lower marginal productivity of capital.

**Marginal propensity to consume** = the ratio of an absolute change in the total (expenditures spent on) consumption to the change in income.

**Marginal propensity to save** = the ratio of an absolute change in total savings to the change in income, which manifests an assumed direct cause-effect relationship (in the Keynesian concept) between changes in income and changes in saving (the latter being a function of the former).

**Marginal propensity to import** = the ratio of an absolute change in the total (expenditures spent on) imports to the change in national income, which manifests an assumed direct cause-effect relationship (in the Keynesian concept) between changes in income and changes in import expenditures (the latter being a function of the former).

**Marginal rate of transformation (MRT)** = a ratio (or the absolute slope of the transformation curve) showing how much of one of the products is to be given up in order to gain one more unit of the other one by transforming the production structure, thereby releasing resources from the production of the sacrificed product for that of the other one.

If the direction of transformation, i.e. the shift in the composition of total output is from product "*y*" to product "*x*", i.e. "*y*" is sacrificed for "*x*", then $\mathbf{MRT}_{yx}$ = – delta *y* / delta *x*, which implies also their cost or price ratio, too, namely $\mathbf{P}_x / \mathbf{P}_y$. If the direction of transformation is the opposite, then, of course, $\mathbf{MRT}_{xy}$ = – delta *x* / delta *y*, which is equal to $\mathbf{P}_y / \mathbf{P}_x$.) Depending on constant, increasing or decreasing opportunity costs, the shape of the transformation curve can be linear, concave or convex.

**Marginal rate of substitution** = the ratio of the number of units of one of (only) the two consumer goods sacrificed by a community (the society of a country) to the number of extra units of the other consumer good gained thereby, i.e. the amount of the sacrificed consumer good given up in order to gain one more unit of the other consumer good, without any change in the level of total satisfaction of the community, i.e. with a shift only on the same "community indifference curve".

**"Market-friendly" approach** (of the State) = see under (C).

**Market failure** = the failure of the market, due to such "market imperfections" as monopolistic or oligopolistic structures, government interventions, various externalities, etc., to fulfil its assumed "normal" role in resource allocation, income distribution, and by giving signals to the producers and consumers in the coordination of economic activities.

**Market price** = the actual price of a commodity, which under the effects of changes in demand and supply, may deviate from its "natural price" (or "value") as defined in some way by various price theories.

**Mergers and acquisitons (M&A)** = fusions of formerly separate enterprises into a single entity and purchases of shares of an enterprise thereby acquiring an "equity capital" stake.

**"Monetary (monetarist) counter-revolution"** = a rejection of and general attack against the Keynesian theoretical "revolution" and policy recommendations by neo-liberal monetarists, who accuse the latter for inviting State interventions, and causing inflation and other disturbances by mistaken fiscal and monetary policy, by excessive budget expenditures financed by inflationary methods (such as irresponsible emmission).

**Monetary phenomena of economic life** = all those phenomena, changes and processes manifested in terms of money, prices and monetary transactions, such as saving and accumulation, marketing of priced products (commodities), services and factors of production, exchange of currencies, lending and borrowing of money, investment of capital and the resulting surplus in money, incomes of the owners of factors of production, emission (supply) of and demand for money, speculation with money, functioning and circulation of money, costs and benefits, losses and gains, productivity, efficiency calculated in money, etc.

**Money as a means of accumulation** = money as a valuable asset which functions as a store of wealth and potential investment fund.

**Money as a means of exchange** = a function of money serving to facilitate the exchange of commodities (in which function a "paper money" can substitute for it).

**Money as a means of measuring "value"** = "real money" which having its own "value" is able and used to measure, even in an abstract comparison, the "value" of all commodities according to the Marxian view, i.e. insofar as "value" is supposed to be determined by labour.

**Money as a means of payment** = money when being payed not at the same time when a delivery of a purchased good or the performance of labour, etc. is made, but in advance or after, or even without any real transaction.

**Money as a means of speculation** = money as a liquid asset which can be used for speculation.

**"Money multiplier"** = a multiplier (applied by the monetarist theory), which shows by how much the national income is changing due to a unit change in the quantity of money, or more precisely: how much the national income should change then in order to reach again a monetary equilibrium in the economy. (The multiplier effect of an increase by one unit of the money supply is attributed to its spread effect in the banking system which follows, like the case of the investment multiplier, a declining geometrical series.)

**Official reserve account** = see under (B).

**Official reserve assets** = see under (B).

**Open economy** = see under (B).

**Opportunity cost** = the cost of sacrificing one alternative for another. In economics it usually refers to a choice between two products, more precisely to the ratio of the sacrificed quantity of a product (a decrease in its output) to the increase in the quantity of the other one (an increment in its output) that can be gained by such a sacrifice.

**"Organic composition of capital"** = a Marxian term which implies the ratio of "constant capital" (i.e. the costs of raw material, energy, machinery, etc. produced in an earlier process of production) to "variable capital" (representing the cost of labour which creates "new value" in the given production process).

**"Pareto optimum"** = such an allocation of resources in the economy as providing everybody the maximum possible welfare, which excludes the possibility to increase the welfare, income or benefits of anybody, by reorganizing production and distribution, without decreasing at the same time the welfare of others.

**Partial equilibrium** = an equilibrium between demand and supply only in one or a few of the "partial markets" (the separate markets of individual products and services, and also of the factors of production, capital, labour and land).

**Perfect/imperfect equilibrium** = an equilibrium in the economy which excludes/involves underutilization of factors of production. In other words, in a "perfect equilibrium" there can be no unemployment and idle capital or other underutilized production resource or capacity, while equilibrium is "imperfect" if any of the factors of production is not fully utilized.

**Portfolio investments** = purchases of financial assets (stocks, bonds, securities, debt notes, etc.) which are sold in stock and money markets).

**Price elasticity of demand** = the percentage change in the quantity of demand for product "x" divided by the percentage change in the price of the same product ("x").

**"Price of production"** = A Marxian term which, as a modified variant of "value", implies the sum of "constant" plus "variable capital" plus "average profit" (instead of the actually created "surplus value"). It is the assumed result of the equalisation tendency, due to capital mobility, of the profit rates, and insofar as it becomes the centre of price formation, thus causes an income-redistribution (in a disguised way, via the price formation) between various industries, according to the rule: "equal profits for equal investment", namely at the expense of those branches of the economy with a lower than average "organic composition of capital" (i.e. the relatively "labour-intensive" ones) and in favour of those with a higher than average "organic composition of capital" (i.e. the relatively "capital-intensive" ones).

**Primary commodities** = unprocessed products, crops, minerals and other raw materials produced in the primary sectors of the economy, i.e. in agriculture (including farming, forestry, fishery) and mining.

**"Production contract curve"** = a curve in the "Edgeworth box diagram" which connects all those points showing both the optimum output and optimum input combinations, i.e. the common tangent points of the "isoquant curves" of (only) the two products and the "isocost lines" reflecting (according to the neo-classical factor price theory) the available quantities of (only) the two factors of production within the country concerned.

**Production possibility curve** (or Production possibility frontier curve) = see under "Transformation curve".

**Quantity theory of money** = a Classical concept which derives the value, the purchasing power of money from its quantity (if its velocity is constant) under a given available volume of commodities (normally, in a closed economy, supposed to correspond to the possible maximum output), and determines the changes in the price level (quite contrary to the labour theory of value) by changes in the quantity of money (and/or in the quantity of output).

**"Rate of surplus value"** = a Marxian term which means the ratio of wages to "surplus value".

**"Real money"** = commodity money, which is distinguished from "paper money" in the sense that it can also be used as a commodity and it is a valuable asset in itself, such as gold or silver, even if not functioning as money, while "paper money" has got a negligable value of its own, as a piece of paper, if not used and functioning as money.

**Real phenomena of economic life** = all those phenomena, changes and processes manifested in kind, in their physical nature, such as production and consumption in physical terms, the products, services, and factors of production in their physical appearance, the exchange of products and services in kind (i.e. barter trade), investment and the resulting surplus in material sense, productivity and efficiency calculated in terms of the physical output per input units, etc.

**Reciprocal (price) elasticity of demand** = the percentage change in the quantity of demand for a certain product ("x") divided by the percentage change in its relative price (the price of "x" divided by the price of another product, "y", or vice versa).

**"Relation approach"** = a view-point seeking for the lasting relations between members or classes of society or between nations, countries behind their position, action or behaviour.

**Revaluation** = a deliberate increase, by an action of the monetary authority, in the relative value of the national currency, i.e. a decrease in the domestic price of foreign currencies, under a peg exchange rate system.

**"Say's dogma"** = the assumption that supply creates its own demand because all those incomes created in the production of the commodities which constitute supply, are always going to appear as effective demand for, i.e. will be spent on, these commodities.

**Self-sufficient economy** = an economy which (along with a maximum import-substitution) is supposed to exchange products and services with foreign partners only if it is necessary (because of the lack of the required, particularly natural resources).

**"Social relations of production"** = those relations between people, based on or determining their position in the system of (re)production, as according to the Marxian concept, which involve, first of all, their "ownership relations", namely the pattern of ownership over the main "means of production" (including the land, and "physical capital"), and the "relations of division of labour" within the society or internationally, i.e. the pattern of occupation, trade, activity, specialization, and last but not least, "distribution relations", i.e. the pattern of income distribution.

**"Speculation demand for money"** = the demand for money as a liquid asset for the sake of speculation.

**Stock approach** = A view-point which focusses on the changes in the stock (the quantity, the supply or store of goods, money, assets, manpower, people, animals, etc.).

**Surplus product (or surplus value)** = that part of the total output or value which exceeds what is required for the subsistence of producers or the repetition of production on the same level. (See also under "Surplus value").

**"Surplus-value"** = a Marxian term which marks out the source of profit, and means the difference between the "new value" created by live labour of the hired workers, and that part of it received by the latter in the form of wages (which can be equal to the value of their labour power). Its source is (what Marx called:) "surplus-labour", implying that "extra" part of the labour actually performed which exceeds the one covering the wage cost, thus required for the reproduction of the labour power (the physical and intellectual ability to perform labour) of the workers.

**"Technical composition of capital"** = a Marxian term which implies a ratio of the number of units of "live labour" to that of "dead" or "past" labour materialised in the means of production, which, insofar as the "value-composition of capital" does not differ from it, is the same as the "organic composition of capital".

**"Total factor productivity"** = the aggregate productivity of all the factors of production used in the process of production, i.e. the ratio of total output to the sum of all the units of factors used. Its increase results mainly from technical change and improved quality and discipline of labour.

**Trade openness of a country** = see under (B).

**Trade policies** = see under (B).

**"Transaction demand for money"** = the demand for money as a medium (or means) of exchange needed for the exchange of goods.

**Transformation (production possibility frontier) curve** = a curve (with a downward, or negative slope) in the coordinate system, which shows, in various alternative combinations, the maximum aggregate output of (only) two products that can be produced (in a country) under the conditions of a full utilization of all the available resources, namely factors of production, i.e. when the economy is in "perfect equilibrium". Production above the curve is impossible, while below the curve it is less efficient. Each point on the curve represents a particular combination of the output of the two products. The (absolute) slope of the curve at each point of the combined production of the two products indicates their "opportunity cost", i.e. the "marginal rate of transformation" (how much of one of the products is to be given up in order to gain one more unit of the other one by transforming the production structure, thereby releasing resources from the production of the sacrificed product for that of the other one). The actual slope of the curve reflects whether the opportunity costs are constant (shown by a straight line), increasing (shown by a concave curve) or decreasing (shown by a convex curve). Increasing opportunity costs may follow from "diminishing returns" at a given level of technology, while decreasing opportunity costs may result from "internal economies", i.e. "economies of scale". An optimum combination of (only) the products is assumed to appear at a point where the highest "community indifference curve" is tangent to the given transformation curve, i.e. where the latter just reaches the highest "indifference curve".

**Transnational corporation (TNC)** = see under (B).

**Utility/use value of a product** = its quality of being useful, consumable or usable in its physical, material nature.

**"Variable capital"** = the term (introduced by Marx) to mark out that part of total capital being spent on hiring the wage workers (who are supposed to produce all the "new value" over and above the "old" one represented by "constant capital"), the value of which turns into a greater "new value" including the "surplus" over the wage cost.

## Key terms, concepts and methods of international economics

**Absolute advantage** (in international trade) = a higher labour productivity (i.e. a bigger output of the unit input of labour) that a country may have in the production of a certain product, as compared to that in another country, which implies a lower labour cost of producing one unit of the product concerned. ("Absolute disadvantage" refers to the opposite.)

**Absolute purchasing-power parity theory** = one of the theoretical conceptions determining the exchange rates of currencies, which postulates that the nominal exchange rate ensuring equilibrium between the demand and the supply of the currencies concerned is (should be) equal to the ratio of the price levels in the two countries. In other words, the same commodities should have the same price expressed in the same currency ("the law of one price") in both countries.

**"Absorption approach" to balance-of-payments adjustment** = a restrictive economic policy (involving certain elements also of the Keynesian "recipe" for adjustment), suggested by Alexander, which implies a reduction of both investment and consumption expenditures in order to improve the balance of trade and thereby the balance of payments of the country suffering deficit in it. Its logic is based upon the following formula:

**Y** = **C** + **I** + **[X – M]**, where **Y** marks national income, **C** the consumption expenditures, **I** investments, **X** export and **M** import. Thus an active balance of trade (**X** - **M**) can be achieved (either by increased national income, which seems to contradict the Keynesian concept of marginal import propensity, or, and under the conditions of perfect equilibrium) by the reduction of both investment and consumption expenditures (which can release capacities for export production).

**"Backwash effects" of trade** = see under (C).

**Balance of (foreign) trade** = the registration, on a balance sheet, of all the exports and imports of a country in value (i.e. volume times unit price) during a particular period of time, usually a year. If the total value of all exports exceeds that of imports the balance of trade is qualified as "active" (with a surplus), while in the opposite case, when import exceeds export, it is "passive" (with a deficit).

**Balance of (international) payments** = the registration in a summary statement of all the international monetary transactions of a country (its residents) with all other countries (their residents) during a particular period of time, usually a year. It consists of two sides (credits and debits) and usually, or in principal, three parts, current account, capital account, and official reserve account.

**Balance of payments adjustment policies** = those measures taken by the government or the monetary authorities which aim at improving the balance of payments of the country concerned, particularly at reducing (or avoiding) its deficit. The related variants, such as the "elasticity approach", the "income approach", the "absorption approach" and the "monetary approach" to balance-of-payments adjustment are rooted in and reflect different theoretical concepts.

**Balassa's test and concept of "revealed comparative advantages"** = an empirical test of the Ricardian concept by calculating RCA indexes (indexes of "revealed comparative advantages"). The latter has (at least) 2 variants: (a) an RCA index measuring the ratio of the share of a particular product (or industry) in the country's total exports to that in its total imports; (b) another RCA index which measures the share of a particular product (or industry) in the country's total exports relative to the share of the same products (or industry) in total world exports.

If the ratio (calculated according to the above variants) is greater than unity it is supposed to mean that the country realizes comparative advantage in the trade of the product (or industry) in question.

**"Basis" for international trade** = those conditions or opportunities inducing international trade and division of labour between countries. Its main variants are: "trade based on" (1) differences in natural conditions, (2) differences in labour productivity, i.e. the Smithian "absolute advantages", (3) differences in relative labour productivity, i.e. the Ricardian "comparative advantages", (4) relative factor abundances (i.e. the H–O type of "comparative advantages"), (5) "technological gap" (as according to Posner), (6) the differences in input requirements during the "product life cycle" (as according to Vernon), (7) "internal economies", (8) "external economies", (9) differences in "tastes", (10) product differentiation, (11) "created competitive advantages" (as according to modern eclectic theory).

**Bretton-woods system** = the international monetary system called "Gold-Exchange standard", which was created at the end of the Second World War by a conference in Bretton Woods.

**Calculation of "comparative advantages" in classical sense** = measuring and comparing two ratios either (1) as according to the original method of the Classical economics, namely according to one of the following two variants: (1a) the relative labour productivities (i.e. the ratio of the labour productivity in country "A" to that in country "B" first in the production of product "x" and then of product "y"; or the ratio of the labour productivity in the production of product "x" to that of product "y" first in country "A" and then in country "B"), as follows:

$$\frac{\mathbf{Pr}_A}{\mathbf{Pr}_B}\,x \text{ and } \frac{\mathbf{Pr}_A}{\mathbf{Pr}_B}\,y; \quad \frac{\mathbf{Pr}_x}{\mathbf{Pr}_y}\,A \text{ and } \frac{\mathbf{Pr}_x}{\mathbf{Pr}_y}\,B$$

or

(1b) the relative labour costs (i.e. the ratio of the labour cost in country "*A*" to that in country "*B*" first in the production of product "*x*" and then of product "*y*"; or the ratio of the labour cost of product "*x*" to that of product "*y*" first in country "*A*" and then in country "*B*"), as follows:

$$\frac{\mathbf{Pc}_A}{\mathbf{Pc}_B}\,x \text{ and } \frac{\mathbf{Pc}_A}{\mathbf{Pc}_B}\,y; \quad \frac{\mathbf{Pc}_x}{\mathbf{Pc}_y}\,A \text{ and } \frac{\mathbf{Pc}_x}{\mathbf{Pc}_y}\,B$$

where **Pr** stands for labour productivity, and **Pc** for labour cost;

or

(2) as according to a method introduced later and suggested by the standard textbooks, namely: the "opportunity costs" of the two products in the two countries (i.e. the ratio of the sacrificed amount of product "x" to the resulting increment in the output of product "y", or vice versa, first in country "A" and then in country "B", or vice versa, which is called as the "marginal rate of transformation", and represents as its equal inverse the relative price/cost of the product concerned):

$$\mathbf{MRT}_{xy} = \frac{-\Delta \mathbf{x}}{\Delta \mathbf{y}}\,A \;\Big|\; = \frac{\mathbf{P_y}}{\mathbf{P_x}}\,A \qquad \text{and} \qquad \mathbf{MRT}_{xy} = \frac{-\Delta \mathbf{x}}{\Delta \mathbf{y}}\,B \;\Big|\; = \frac{\mathbf{P_y}}{\mathbf{P_x}}\,B$$

where $\mathbf{MRT}_{xy}$ stands for the opportunity cost (marginal rate of transformation) of *y*, and $\mathbf{P}_y$ stands for its relative price. ($\mathbf{MRT}_{yx}$, i.e. $-\mathbf{\Delta y} / \mathbf{\Delta x}$ would be the opportunity cost of *x*, and $\mathbf{P}_x$ would stand for the ralative price of *x*.)

"Comparative advantage" appears where relative productivity is higher or relative cost/opportunity cost is lower. There is no "comparative advantage" if the two ratios are equal.

**Calculation of "comparative advantages" according to the H–O theorem** = measuring and comparing the factor endowments of two countries and the factor intensity of two products.This calculation thus requires information on (a) the factor endowments of the two partner countries (or country groups, perhaps) trading with each other, namely either

(a1) the data of the total quantity, i.e. of the total number of all the available units, of both factors of production (labour and capital) within both countries, or

(a2) the data of the price of these factors of production there (which corresponds to the income of their owners), i.e. the average rate of interest and that of wages, and also on

(b) the factor intensity of the two products, namely the number of labour units as well as that of capital units needed as inputs to produce one unit of output of both products.

When such data are available, two ratios have to be calculated both in the case of (a) and (b). If the capital/labour (K/L) ratio is bigger or the interest/wage (i/w) ratio is smaller in country *A* than in country *B*, then the former is qualified as relatively capital abundant, the latter as relatively labour abundant country. (The same is, of course, the conclusion if the L/K ratio is smaller and the w/i ratio is bigger in country *A* than in *B*, or if the ratio of the quantity of capital in country *A* to that in country *B* is bigger than the ratio of the quantity of labour in country *A* to that in country *B*, and the ratio of interest rate in country *A* to that in country *B* is smaller than the ratio of wages in country *A* to that in country *B*.)

In a similar way, two ratios have to be calculated in regard to the two products (*x* and *y*). If the ratio of the required quantity of capital to that of labour (K/L ratio) in the production of *x* is bigger (or the L/K ratio is smaller) than in that of *y*, the former is relatively capital intensive, the latter is relatively labour intensive product.

There is no comparative advantage (and thus no "base" of trade) if the ratios for the countries or for the products are equal, i.e. if the relative factor abundance of the two countries or the relative factor intensity of the two products is the same.

It is to be emphasized that what matters is not the absolute but the relative factor abundance and the relative factor intensity.

**Capital account** = a part of the balance of payments which registers all capital inflows and outflows, i.e. all those inflows of money as capital to the country concerned, which result an increase in the stock of all (non-reserve) foreign financial assets in the country or the reduction of the stock of its financial assets abroad, and also all those outflows of money as capital from the country concerned, which result in a reduction in the stock of foreign (non-reserve) financial assets in the country or an increase in the stock of its assets abroad.

**Capital export** = the transfer of capital (in money form) to a foreign country, either in the form of "direct investment", or "portfolio investment", or "loan".

**"Capital flight"** = the escape of foreign capital and/or the outflow of domestic savings from a country where the economy is in recession or suffers deep imbalances, and the risks of investment are, for whatever reason (e.g. for political disorder), too high. It also includes the transfer of wealth of dictators and other privileged elements to safer foreign banks in case they are afraid to lose their position.

**"Competitive advantage" of firms** = the advantage vs. competitors, which (according to Porter) is manifested in a lower cost level and/or in the "premium prices" of differentiated products, resulting from the ability to provide unique and superior value to the buyer in terms of product quality, special features, or after-sale service.

**Cross exchange rate** = the exchange rate between the currency of country "*A*" and that of country "*B*", as expressed through the exchange rate of each of these currencies and the currency of a third country "*C*". If the exchange rate (**Ne**) of the two currencies is expressed as $\mathbf{C_A/C_B}$, and the exchange rates of these currencies and that of the country "*C*" (namely $\mathbf{C_C}$) are expressed as $\mathbf{C_C/C_A}$ and $\mathbf{C_C/C_B}$, respectively, then the cross exchange rate (**Ce**) is calculated as follows:

$$\mathbf{Ce} = \frac{\mathbf{C_C/C_B}}{\mathbf{C_C/C_A}} .$$

**Common (or single) market** = see under "International economic -integration".

**Conditionalities** = the set of those preconditions, prescriptions or advices the major international creditors (such as IMF and World Bank) expect from the debtors or aid-recipients to meet in order to remain or become eligible for financial assistance.

**Current account** = a part of the balance of payments which includes practically all international monetary transactions other than capital flows, such as the payments (of foreign countries, their residents) for the export of products and services, and the payments (of the country concerned, its residents) for the import of products and services, i.e. the monetary transactions of "merchandise trade", and the inflow and outflow of factor incomes (the transfer of capital incomes: repatriated profits, dividends, interest, and also the transfer of labour incomes: remitted wages and salaries from or to abroad, as well as rents, if any, payed from or to other countries), and various unilateral transfers of money (such as gifts, membership fees, etc.)

**Customs union** = see under "International economic integration".

**Debt ratio** = the ratio of the amount of (net) debt of a country to its annual national income.

**Debt service** = repayment of the due part of the "principal" (i.e. the sum of money received as loan) plus payment of the interest on the latter.

**Debt service ratio** = the ratio of the annual amount of debt service to be paid by a country, to its annual national income or to its net export revenue (total export revenue minus total costs of import).

**Eclectic theory of foreign investments** = Dunning's theory on the foreign investment and business policy of multinational (transnational) companies. It specifies their major motivations, such as "resource-seeking", "efficiency-seeking", "market-seeking" and "strategic-asset-seeking" motives, and their various benefits from ownership-, location- and "internalization"-advantages (as formulated in the "OLI paradigm".

**Economic union** = see under "International economic integration".

**Effective rate of exchange** = the ratio of the amount of a certain currency to an equivalent weighted average of all the other currencies, practically of those of the main partners only of the country concerned, where the weights correspond to the relative importance of each of the partners in the economic (primarily trade) relations of the latter. In other words, it is the weighted average of the exchange rates between the national currency of the country concerned and a number of other currencies. It can be calculated either as (a) national currency of country "*A*" divided by the weighted average of the national currencies of the main partner countries or (b) the weighted average of the national currencies of the main partner countries divided by the national currency of country "*A*".

**Effective rate of protection** = an effective rate of import tariff, as distinguished from the "nominal rate of tariff", which relates the "ad valorem" customs duty to that part of the price of the import substitutive product, representing the domestic value added. It is calculated by dividing the actual customs duty by the domestic value added only in the price of the product concerned, instead of its total price which may include imported input components, too.

**Effects of import tariffs** = the (assumed or real) main consequences of government measures imposing customs duties on imported goods, which affect (a) the domestic producers who are protected thereby versus more competitive imports, (b) the domestic consumers who pay higher prices for imports, (c) the revenue of the central budget which may increase thereby, and (d) the foreign trade of the country concerned, the volume of which is likely to decrease while its terms of trade may improve. Accordingly, the following effects of import tariffs are distinguished: (a) production effect, (b) consumption effect, (c) budget revenue effect, and (d) a double trade effect, i.e. an unfavourable one, reducing the volume of trade, and a possible favourable one, improving the terms of trade of the country.

**"Efficiency-seeking" (motive of TNCs' FDI)** = a motivation of transnational companies which refers to how the aggregate profit rate of the company can be increased by operating affiliates abroad, by getting access to modern technologies, know-hows, research results, highly qualified (but relatively cheaper) labour, etc. abroad, and by benefitting from economies of scale and scope, or from other advantages.

**"Elasticity approach" to balance-of-payments adjustment** = a neo-classical concept suggesting the deficit countries devaluation, and the surplus countries revaluation of their currencies, respectively, i.e. a counteracting exchange rate policy in case the automatic exchange-rate mechanism does not work because of the lack of the required conditions, namely of an "ideal" currency market with freely floating exchange rates. In such a case it is thus the monetary authority, the government or the central bank which must adjust the exchange rate. The name of such a balance-of-payments adjustment by means of exchange rate policy follows from the reference to the necessary (but not sufficient) condition of its success, namely to the "Marshall-Lerner condition", which concerns the elasticities of demand.

**Elasticity of demand** = see under (A).

**Equilibrium/disequilibrium in international trade** = an equal/unequal value of the export and import in the trade between the partner countries.

**Exchange rate mechanism of international equilibrium** = an assumed automatic adjustment of the exchange rates of the currencies of the partner countries trading with each other, which restores equilibrium in their balance of trade. This neo-classical concept is a modified variant of the classical "price-specie-flow mechanism", which in view of the prices being expressed in different national currencies (instead of the same gold-money or money representing a certain weight of gold) postulates perfectly flexible changes in exchange rates when disequilibrium appears in international trade, provided that exhange rates are exclusively determined by the supply of and the demand for the currencies concerned.

If such a perfect currency market exists, i.e. if exchange rates are not fixed, nor government interventions take place in the currency markets, the trade deficit of a country and the trade surplus of its partner (in a two-country model) are supposed to immediately result in a depreciation of the former's currency and appreciation of the latter's, because the supply of the currency of the deficit country and the demand for the currency of the surplus country exceed the demand for the former and the supply of the latter. Depreciation of the currency makes the exports of the deficit country cheaper abroad, i.e. for the surplus country, while appreciation of the currency makes the exports of the latter more expensive abroad, thereby reducing the import of the former. Thus an imbalance in their international trade will result in an opposite tendency: the former (trade deficit) country with its depreciating currency will be able to export more and import less than before, while the other (trade surplus) country with its appreciating currency will import more and be able to export less than before. The preconditions of such an automatic mechanism include, of course, a perfect equilibrium within the partner national economies and free international trade.

**Exchange rate of currencies** = the ratio of the amount of a certain currency to an equivalent amount of another currency, i.e. the amount of the former which is to be paid for one unit of the latter, or vice versa. Accordingly it can be expressed either as (a) national currency (*C*) of country "*A*" divided by the national currency (*C*) of country "*B*", or (b) national currency (*C*) of country "*B*" divided by the national currency (*C*) of country "*A*", i.e.:

$$(a)\ \frac{C_A}{C_B}, \quad \text{or} \quad (b)\ \frac{C_B}{C_A},$$

**Export and import coefficients** = the ratio of the annual value of export and import, respectively, to the annual national income, i.e. the percentage share of the value of export and of import in national income (or in the GDP and in the total domestic consumption or final use, respectively).

**Export multiplier** = the ratio of the absolute change in national income to the absolute change in total export, which manifests an assumed direct cause-effect relationship (in the Keynesian concept) between changes in export and changes in national income (the latter being a function of the former).

**Export orientation** = development/promotion of export sectors in the economy, i.e. industries and other activities producing for export or providing services for foreign countries.

**Export tariffs** = customs duties or taxes charged (rather exceptionally) on exports.

**Factor endowments of a country** = the available (total and relative) quantities of factors of production in a country, i.e. its factor proportions, the relative abundance or scarcity of each factor in the country (to be compared with other countries').

**"Factor intensity reversal"** = the case when the same product appears as relatively capital intensive in one country while it is relatively labour intensive in the other.

**Financial assistance (or aid)** = grants, donations in money form as well as concessional loans (i.e. loans with more favourable terms than commercial loans).

**Forms (stages) of international economic integration** = see under "International economic integration".

**Forms of international capital flows** = (a) direct capital investments, (b) portfolio investments, and (c) loans (including concessional ones which are qualified, together with donations, also as "international financial aid").

**Forward premium and discount** = a percentage (plus/minus) difference, calculated per year, between the forward and the spot rate of exchange. "Forward premium" refers to a forward rate better than the spot one of the currency concerned, which implies expectations on its appreciation (or revaluation), while "forward discount" refers to a forward rate worse than the spot one, implying expectations on depreciation (or devaluation).

**Forward rate of exchange** = the expected nominal rate of exchange which the business partners include in their contract concerning a future exchange of currencies, i.e. deliveries of foreign exchange ususally one, three or six months after the contract is made.

**Free trade association** = see under "International economic integration".

**"Freely floating"** = an exchange rate system in which it is only spontaneous operation of the money markets which, without any regulation or intervention of the governments or monetary authorities, determines the exchange rates of the national currencies. In other words, the latter are shaped only by and change because, and in accordance with, changes in the demand for and the supply of the currencies concerned.

**Gold-Exchange System** = the monetary system (between 1944 and 1971) involving an "adjustable peg" exchange rate system (i.e. with fixed but if necessary adjustable, occasionally modified exchange rates expressed in US dollar the value of which was fixed in gold) and both gold and the US dollar being convertible to gold, as official reserve assets.

**Gold Standard** = the monetary system vith a fixed ("peg") exchange rate regime and gold as official reserve asset.

**Graham paradox** = a conclusion referring to the increasing disadvantage of the country, out of two countries engaged in international division of labour and exchange relations with each other, which specializes on a product whose production is subject to the "law of diminishing returns" as against its partner country specializing on another with increasing returns.

**"Green-field investments"** = see under (A).

**Gross (foreign) debt** = the total amount of all those loans received of the country from foreign creditors.

**Heckscher–Ohlin theorem** = a revised concept of specialization according to "comparative advantages", which is based on the consideration of factor endowments. It makes distinction between countries in terms of their relative factor abundance and between products in terms of their relative factor intensity. It states that a relatively capital abundant country enjoys comparative advantage in the production and export of relatively capital intensive product, while a relatively labour abundant country in that of relatively labour intensive one. This is because capital (as a factor of production) is supposed to be relatively cheaper in the former and labour in the latter country, respectively, due to the lower marginal productivity of these factors of production there, determined by their relative abundance.

This concept is thus based on the marginal productivity theory used in neoclassical economics as a macro-economic price and income theory.

**Heckscher-Ohlin-Samuelson thesis** = a logical conclusion drawn from the H-O theorem, made explicit by Samuelson, which attributes an international equalizing effect to specialization according to relative factor abundance, namely an equalization of factor prices, factor incomes and thus the national income levels, too, because in the course of specialization, i.e. a transformation of the production structure in both partner countries, the price and income of the relatively abundant factor tends to increase (at the expense of the relatively scarce one) due to the shift in the relative demand and supply in favour of the former.

**"Home base" of transnational companies** = the centre of their network operation, which involves the bulk of their research and development capacities, and (according to Porter) the location of many of the most productive jobs, the core technologies, and the most advanced skills.

**Import dependence (or import intensity)** of a national economy = an assumed or real cause-effect relationship between changes in import and a change in GDP, which is calculated as a ratio of an (absolute or percentage) change in GDP to the (absolute or percentage) change in import.

**Import substitution** = development/promotion of domestic production of imported goods, and of domestic services, i.e. those substituting for imports.

**Import tariffs** = customs duties or taxes charged on imports.

**Income adjustment of the balance of payments** ("balance-of-payments adjustment by income effects") = a policy of "balance-of-payments adjustment" by means of reducing investments. It follows from the logic of the Keynesian "income mechanism of automatic equilibrium" and is based on the consideration that while an increase in export obviously depends on the behaviour of foreign markets which can hardly be influenced by the government of the deficit country, investments can be discouraged by the latter, and thereby a (preferably temporary) decline in national income (or in its growth) can lead to a decline in import (or in its further growth), in view of the assumed cause-effect relationship between investment and national income and between the latter and import.

**Income elasticity of import** = an assumed or real cause-effect relationship between changes in national income and changes in import, calculated as follows: the percentage change in the total import divided by the percentage change in national income.

**Income mechanism of automatic international equilibrium** = an equilibrium mechanism based upon the assumed cause-effect relationship between changes in export and in the national income as well as between changes in the latter and in import, as expressed in the Keynesian "export multiplier" and "marginal propensity to import".

In the conventional two-country model, in which two countries are only trading with each other, if one of them achieves an active balance of trade, which corresponds to a trade deficit for the other, then the increase in the national income of the former, resulting from its export growth, is supposed to lead (ceteris paribus, when all the other conditions of equilibrium remain the same) to an increase in its import, while the decrease in the national income, caused by increased "leakage" (import), in the country suffering trade deficit is supposed to lead to a reduction of import. In this way both the export surplus of the first country and the trade deficit of the second may automatically disappear.

The above concept follows from the simplified variant of the Keynesian formula, namely from the assumed equation between investment plus export and saving plus import:

**I + X = S + M**, where **I** represents investment, **X** export, **S** saving and **M** import, respectively.

The two sides of theequation are linked through the national income (Y), as following from the income generating effects of both investment and export (manifested in the related "multipliers") and from the "leakage" role (reducing income generation) of saving and import, while both depending on changes in national income (as manifested in the related "marginal propensities").

**"Infant industry" (and "infant economy") argument** = an argument (attributed to Friedrich List) for the temporary protection (by import tariffs) of those industries in the less developed countries, the products of which are not yet competitive enough versus the imported ones.

**Interest parity ("covered interest arbitrage) theory** = another variant of the theoretical conceptions determining the exchange rates of currencies, which postulates that the difference between the interest rates of the two countries should be equal to the percentage forward discount or premium of the currencies concerned in such a way as counterbalancing the effects of each other in the foreign exchange markets (covering the foreign exchange risk). The currency of the country where the interest rate is higher is at a forward discount (reflecting expectations on its devaluation or depreciation in the future), while the currency of the country with a lower rate of interest has got a forward premium (reflecting expectations on its future appreciation).

**"Internalisation advantage"** = see "OLI paradigm".

**International economic integration** = the elimination or substantial reduction of the barriers of trade and other economic relations between the member-states entering one or another form of economic integration. The related literature distinguishes the following main forms (and also "stages") of international economic integration: (a) "preferential trade arrangement" (i.e. intergovernment agreement concerning the promotion of trade between two or more countries), (b) "free trade association" or area (i.e. elimination of trade barriers among the member countries which keep their independent trade policy vis-a-vis third parties, those countries outside the free trade area), (c) "customs union" (i.e. a common trade policy of the member states vis-a-vis the non-members, in addition to the established free trade area among themselves), (d) "common (or single) market" (i.e. an integrated market of the member countries not only for products and services but also for labour and capital, which implies free flows of labour and capital among themselves, in addition to their customs union), and (e) "economic union" (i.e. the completion of a common market by certain "supra-national" institutions, harmonization of economic policies, and a common currency).

**International monetary systems** = internationally established systems involving, and distinguished according to, (a) the agreed exchange rate system and (b) the accepted system of official reserve assets. The main variants of the former are: "peg", "adjustable peg", "crawling peg", "managed floating" and "freely floating" exchange rate system. The latter's variants are "gold", "gold-exchange" (i.e. gold and a key currency convertible to gold), and "fiduciary" system (one or more currencies or artificially created accounting units which are internationally trusted but not convertible to gold).

**International resource flows** = cross-border flows of factors of production.

**International trade based on "created competitive advantages"** = an increasingly important "basis" for international trade (particularly its "internalized" part) which is shaped by the TNCs not only using the given local advantages in the host countries but also creating new ones there in order to improve their competitiveness, and/or by the purposeful policy of the governments (and other national agents) to increase efficiency of their national economy and its capability to become the "home base" of the latter.

**International trade based on differences in factor endowments** = (See the neo-classical H–O theorem.)

**International trade based on differences in labour productivities/costs** = See classical concepts of "absolute" and "comparative advantages".

**International trade based on external economies** = a possible "basis" for trade and specialization in the case of opportunities for economizing on the costs of infrastructure or enjoying benefits from other "externalities".

**International trade based on internal economies** = a possible "basis" for trade and specialization in the case of economies of scale in production, even if no considerable differences appear in factor endowments between countries.

**International trade based on differences in natural conditions** = an old "basis" for trade between those countries with certain natural resources and those without but needing them, i.e. between countries which owing to their natural conditions are able to produce some products that other countries need but are unable to produce.

**International trade based on differences in "tastes"** = a possible "basis" for trade in the case of differences in consumer preferences between countries, even under the conditions of their identical but concave transformation curves, i.e. when opportunity costs are increasing in both countries.

**International trade based on product differentiation** = a possible "basis" for (intra-industry) trade between countries in the case of differences in consumer preferences also within them, providing opportunities to enjoy economies of scale and also economies of scope.

**International trade based on "product cycle"** = a possible "basis" for trade and specialization in the case of differences in input (and marketing) requirements during the "life cycle" of products and also of differences in R & D capacities (and marketing conditions) between countries.

**International trade based on "technological gap"** = a possible "basis" for trade and specialization in the case of differences in technological level between countries and the resulting temporary monopoly of the most advanced countries introducing new products and production processes which the less developed ones need to import.

**Inward foreign direct investment** = foreign capital flowing into the country concerned and invested in direct form.

**Leontief paradox** = the unexpected result of Leontief's investigation on the labour- and capital-intensity of the US exports and imports in a year, which seemed to contradict what would have followed from the H–O theorem (namely that such a capital-abundant country should export mostly capital-intensive products and import mainly labour-intensive ones).

This paradox can, however, easily be explained if some of the simplifying abstractions of the H–O theorem are released: if e.g. the fact of tariffs imposed on labour-intensive products, i.e. the protection of labour-intensive US industries is taken into account; if a "third" factor of production, which has no place in the H–O model, is not neglected in qualifying some of the export products, namely the natural-resource-intensive goods; and if, particularly, the difference in the quality of labour behind "labour-intensity" is also considered, i.e. the high skill-intensity or "human capital intensity" of many US export products is taken into account.

**Limitations of the applicability of the Classical theory of "comparative advantages"** = those following from its basic premises and simplifications, such as:

- the narrowness of the model presented by it, which is limited to 2 countries and 2 products only (despite the reality of many countries and many products and also static (neglecting technological development and improvement in the quality and efficiency of labour), in other words: limited both in "space" and "time";
- the assumption of various perfectnesses, namely: perfect equilibrium of the economy within both countries; perfect (perfectly competitive) market both within the countries and internationally, i.e. without any "market imperfections" (monopolies, state interventions, tariff and non-tariff barriers to trade, etc.), implying free trade; perfectly balanced trade between the two countries; perfect substitutability of any unit of labour for any other unit, i.e. of labour consisting of homogeneous units (which implies a neglect of any difference in its quality, level of education, skill, experience, culture, i.e. of those features of labour and "human capital" playing the most decisive role in economic development and competitiveness); perfect labour mobility but only inside the two countries;
- together with the exclusion of international labour mobility from the model; and also a complete abstraction from the international flows of capital and foreign direct investments, which are the most decisive determinants in shaping the pattern of international trade; the assumption of constant returns to scale, i.e. a neglect both of the possibility of increasing and of decreasing returns to scale); the disregard for the costs of infrastructure (transport, com-

munication, banking, insurance and other services) required for trade, thus a neglect also of the role of distance and location, and of the possibility of utilizing "external economies"; the disregard also for the differences in consumer habits, preferences, "tastes" between and within the partner countries, thus also for the possibility of intra-industry trade and product differentiation; the assumption that all costs of production can be measured by (as traced back to) labour inputs which determine the "natural price" of all products within the countries, while prices in international trade are not determined accordingly; and the lack of considering the differences between various export products, various branches of export production in their effects on the future development of the national economy concerned, namely on the development of human capital, technology and input-output linkages.

**Limitations of the applicability of the H–O theorem** = those following from its basic premises and simplifications, such as:

- the narrowness of the model presented by it, which is limited to two countries, two products and two factors only (despite the reality of many countries, many products and more than two factors) and also static (neglecting not only changes in factor endowments and intensities, but also technological development and improvement in the quality and efficiency of factors), in other words: limited both in "space" and "time";
- the assumption of various perfectnesses, namely: perfect equilibrium of the economy within both countries; perfect market both within the countries and internationally, i.e. free international trade; perfectly balanced trade between the two countries; perfect substitutability of any unit of both factors of production, i.e. the assumption that each factor consists of homogeneous units (which implies a neglect of any difference in the quality of labour, its level of education, skill, experience, culture, and also of the indivisible nature of physical capital, i.e. equipments and machineries); perfect factor mobility but only inside the countries;
- the exclusion of international factor mobility from the model, i.e. a complete abstraction from international flows of capital and foreign direct investments, thus also of the activities of transnational corporations, which are, as a matter of fact, the most decisive determinants in shaping the patterns of international trade; the simplification about constant opportunity costs, i.e. a neglect both of the possibility of their decline (due to economies of scale) and their increase (caused by diminishing returns); the neglect of the impact of natural conditions (resources, soil fertility, etc.) and environment on factor productivities and production costs; the disregard for the costs of infrastructure required for trade, thus a neglect also of the role of distance and location, and of the possibility of utilizing "external economies", too; the disregard also for the differences in consumer habits, preferences, "tastes" between and within the partner countries; thus also for the possibility of intra-industry trade and product differentiation; the assumption of sovereignty of those making deci-

sions on trade and specialization; the assumption of equal partners as independent countries entering trade relationship with each other at a relatively identical development level, i.e. the neglect of the "international development gap"; the exclusion (of course and necessarily) from the model of the case of "factor intensity reversal"; and last, but not least, the lack of considering the differences between various export industries in their effects on the future development of the national economy concerned, namely on the development of human capital, technology and input-output linkages.

**Location advantage"** = see "OLI paradigm".

**MacDougal's test of the Ricardian concept of "comparative advantages"** = an empirical comparison of the relative labour productivities (output per worker) and the relative export shares between US and British industries in a given year, showing a positive correlation between a higher ratio of the US productivity to the British one in a given industry and a higher US share in the world export of the latter.

**Maizels-index** = a calculation measuring the rate of growth of the share of the individual industries of a country in the total value added in such a way as weighting it by their share in total export. In other words, it is a calculation of the weighted growth rates of sectoral shares in total value added, making use as weights, of the shares of each sector of production in total exports of the country concerned.

**"Managed floating"** = an international exchange rate system (introduced by the most developed countries in 1976) which allows the currency markets to operate spontaneously and modify the rates of exchange according to changes in the supply of and the demand for those currencies involved as long as the fluctuations and the resulting appreciation or (particularly) depreciation of any of the currencies concerned does not go beyond an acceptable measure, thereby undermining the required monetary stability and normal conditions of international monetary transactions for the partner countries, too. In the case of the latter, coordinated interventions are made in the money markets (by decreasing or increasing demand for the currency concerned) in order to bring back the exchange rates to the area of acceptable fluctuations.

**Marginal propensity to import** = an assumed or real cause-effect relationship between changes in national income and changes in import, calculated as follows: the (absolute) change in the total import divided by the (absolute) change in national income.

**"Market-seeking" (motive of TNCs' FDI)** = a motivation of transnational companies which refers to the role of capital export in promoting the export of products, i.e. to the effect of FDI on the marketing facilities of the company concerned.

**Marshall-Lerner condition"** = the (minimum) condition under which devaluation may be (if at all) successful, which requires that the sum of the elasticities of the demand abroad for the exported products and of the demand at home for the imported products be more than one.

**Mergers and acquisitons (M&A)** = see under (A).

**Monetary approach to balance-of-payments adjustment** = a policy aiming at the prevention rather than ex post adjustment of the balance of payments, by keeping the "golden rule" of emmission (and credit creation) and the central budget in order, i.e. by avoiding a large and/or growing deficit in the latter. It is based upon the equilibrium concept of the Monetarist school which assumes that an equilibrium is automatically ensured between the supply of and the demand for money, unless an irresponsible monetary policy disturbs it suddenly and to a large extent increasing the supply of money. Such an irresponsible policy of the monetary authorities is most often aimed at "deficit financing", i.e. to finance by emission the growing deficit in the central budget, which usually follows from a squandering fiscal policy of the government. Insofar as the demand for money cannot cope with the increased money supply, the consequence is (besides inflation) the outflow of money, deteriorating the balance of payments of the country concerned and disturbing the monetary equilibrium also in the partner countries. The Monetarists call for a prevention of such consequences, take as neoliberals a stand against government interventions in the economy and particularly a "soft" and excessive fiscal policy with large-scale budget expenditures. They suggest a strictly balanced budget. In case the growth of the economy cannot increase the demand for money as much as equalizing it with the supply of money, they recommend a radical cut of budget expenditures.

**Monetary approach to exchange rate determination** = another variant of the theoretical conceptions determining the exchange rates of currencies, which postulates that the percentage change of the exchange rate (**+** or **– %$C_1/C_2$**) should be equal to the sum of the percentage changes in the supply of the two currencies concerned (**+** or **– %$S_{C1}$** and **–** or **+ %$S_{C2}$**) and in the demand for them (– or **+ %$D_{C1}$** and **+** or **– $D_{C2}$**) in the exchange market.

**Monetary mechanism of automatic international equilibrium** = an assumed equilibrium mechanism in the international economy, which according to the monetarist theory may operate either under the conditions of flexible exchange rates (in the same way as the automatic exchange rate mechanism) restoring equilibrium between the supply of, and the demand for money in the partner countries, or even under fixed exchange rates. But in the case of the latter, only if the excess supply of money stemming from its inflow from abroad or increased export (and not from "deficit financing" emmission policy) leads to a decline of interest rates and/or increased import, thereby causing money outflow, and thus compensating the short supply of money in the partner country and equating money supplies and demands in both countries (in the conventional model of two countries).

According to the monetarist theory an automatic equilibrium between money supply and demand for money can be ensured within a national economy if the supply of money is properly adjusted to the needs of economic growth (by a monetary policy keeping a "golden rule" of emmission, which increases it only slightly, gradually and in a foreseeable way) and the demand for money, basically determined by the growth of GDP, can easily catch up with the gradually increased money supply, owing to the demand generating effect of increased nominal incomes and the concomitant impulse to the growth of production and investment.

**"Natural" direction of international capital flows** = capital flowing, as assumed by the neo-classical school, from the relatively capital abundant to the relatively capital poor countries where the marginal productivity of capital, supposed to determine its price (interest rate) and reward, is higher than in the relatively capital abundant countries.

**Net (foreign) debt** = the difference between the amount of loans received by the country (its residents) from and that of the loans given by it to foreign countries (their residents), the plus or minus sign of which actually shows the country's debtor or creditor position internationally.

**Nominal rate of exchange** = the actual exchange rate (the domestic price of one unit of a foreign currency or the price of one unit of the national currency in a foreign currency), which is announced officially and/or by the banks and exchange offices.

**Non-tariff trade measures (barriers)** = all those various administrative and procedural measures, restrictions and regulations, other than (import and export) tariffs, imposed by the government on foreign trade, mainly on imports, which include quantitative restrictions (quotas), various quality requirements (such as health and environment protecting regulations, technical standards), export subsidies, "voluntary export restraints", dumping amd anti-dumping measures, etc.

**Official reserve account** = a part of the balance of payments (or a separate account) which registers the changes in the official reserve assets of the country and counterbalances the deficit (a net debit balance) or the surplus (a net credit balance) of the current and capital accounts. If there is a net debit balance (i.e. the total debits exceed total credits) in the current and capital accounts, which is qualified as a deficit in the balance of payments, then it is to be settled with an equivalent credit balance in the official reserve account. If there is a net credit balance in the current and capital acoounts (i.e. a surplus in the balance of payments), then it is settled by an equivalent net debit balance in the official reserve account.

**Official reserve assets** = those valuable assets (gold, certain convertible foreign currencies, and/or artificially created accounting units and common currencies) which are used by all or a number of countries in their official reserves and also accepted as means of payment by them, depending on the prevailing international monetary system.

**OLI paradigm** = Dunning's famous concept, which refers to (1) ownership advantages, (2) location advantages, and (3) internalization advantages. Since ownership may ensure the most direct control over the operation of a foreign subsidiary, transnational companies drive for and make use of such an advantage whenever and wherever their business interest prescribe such a strong control over important resources or the quality of inputs and the final product, for the protection of copyright, brand names etc., as not available by other methods. The "location advantages" may include, of course, all those specific conditions of a given country or region, as distinctive from others', providing "comparative advantages" and "base" for international trade (such as considered in the classical and neo-classical trade theories), but also many other, objective or created circumstances (for example, the geographic position as related to the contemporary centre of gravity of the world economy, the "economic" and "cultural distance" from, in fact the closeness rather to the home base of the company, the hospitable, TNC-friendly atmosphere, "free trade zones", tax and other allowances, etc.). "Internalisation" implies the organization, within the same company, of cross-border transfers of products and services among its subsidiaries located in different countries. Its great advantage follows not only from saving such transactions from market fluctuations and uncertainties, but also from making possible to use special, manipulated or even artificial prices, the so-called "transfer prices" in accountancy, and thus, by means of over-invoicing or under-invoicing the imports or exports, to reduce the local tax burden.

**Open economy** = the economy of a country which has got various regular economic transactions (export and import of products, services, factors of production, transfers of money, technologies, information, etc.) with other countries. "Trade openness" refers to trade relations (and the resulting money flows) only, while "economic openness" in general refers to other economic relations, such as, particularly, capital flows, as well.

**Outward foreign direct investment** = foreign capital flowing out of the country concerned and invested in a direct form abroad.

**"Ownership advantage"** = see "OLI paradigm".

**Patterns of international trade** = (a) the pattern showing the commodity composition of export and import, i.e. the percentage share of the various products or product groups in them, which is called the "commodity pattern", and (b) the pattern showing the directions of trade, the destiny of exports and the origin of imports, i.e. the percentage share of the individual countries or country groups in the export and import, which is called "geographical" or "relational" pattern of trade.

**"Perverse" direction of international capital flows** = an "abnormal" direction of capital flows, observed in reality and postulated, in general, by Thomas Balogh, which implies the orientation of capital towards capital-rich, already developed countries (instead of relatively capital-poor, less-developed countries). It is explained by higher risks for capital in the less developed countries and by their lower level of technological development (i.e. by taking technological development and its international unevenness into account, which the neo-classical derivation of factor prices and rewards from their relative abundance determining their marginal productivity, has disregarded from).

**Preferential trade arrangement** = see under "Forms (stages) of international economic integration".

**"Price-specie-flow" (or "gold-flow" or "price level") mechanism of international equilibrium** = an assumed automatic adjustment of the price levels in the partner countries trading with each other, which restores equilibrium in their balance of trade. This classical concept (of David Hume) is based upon

(a) the premise of "perfect" (full employment) equilibrium within the partner national economies,

(b) free trade conditions, i.e. the possibility of free flow of products and money between countries without tariff or non-tariff barriers or other state interventions,

(c) the operation of the same (golden) money within the partner countries and in their international exchange relations (or of a money perfectly convertible to gold in fixed exchange rate, i.e. of a "gold standard"), which makes all the prices and price changes directly (or indirectly) expressed in the same money, and

(d) the assumed validity of the "quantity theory of money", according to which a change in the quantity of money as well as a change in the quantity of supplied products leads to a proportional change in prices, and vice versa (if the velocity of money does not change).

Accordingly, if, for any reasons, in the trade relations between two countries a disequilibrium appears, i.e. one of the countries imports more from the other than exports into it, which means that the latter exports more than imports, then the prices (measured in the same money) will decline in the former and rise in the latter (because the quantity of available products has increased, due to a greater inflow of products, and the quantity of money has decreased, because of its greater outflow from the former country, while the opposite is the case in the latter). Such a change in the prices in both countries will result then in an opposite tendency: the former (trade deficit) country where prices decline will be able to export more and import less than before, while the other (trade surplus) country where prices increased will import more and export less than before.

**Protectionist trade policy** = a trade policy aimed at the protection (by tariff and/or non-tariff measures) of domestic production.

**RCA (Revealed Comparative Advantage) index** = see under "Balassa's test and concept of 'revealed comparative advantages'.

**Real exchange rate** = an adjusted variant of the nominal (or effective) exchange rate, which corrects the latter by the changes in the relative price levels, i.e. the ratio of the price indexes, of the countries concerned, in such a way as expressing the purchasing power of their currencies abroad under the given nominal exchange rate. It is calculated as follows:

(a) if nominal exchange rate (**Ne**) is expressed as $\mathbf{C_A/C_B}$, then real exchange rate (**Re**) is equal to **Ne** times the ratio of price index (**Pi**) of country "*B*" to that of country "*A*", or

(b) if **Ne** is expressed as $\mathbf{C_B/C_A}$, then **Re** is equal to **Ne** times the ratio of price index "*A* to price index "*B*", i.e.

$$(a)\ \mathbf{Re}\ \frac{\mathbf{C_A}}{\mathbf{C_B}} = \mathrm{Ne} \times \frac{\mathbf{Pi_B}}{\mathbf{Pi_A}}\ -\text{, or (b) }\mathbf{Re}\ \frac{\mathbf{C_B}}{\mathbf{C_A}} = \mathrm{Ne} \times \frac{\mathbf{Pi_A}}{\mathbf{Pi_B}}$$

**"Reciprocal demand/supply curves"** = the (Marshallian curves, often called also as "offer curves") which express, in the usual "two-country, two-product model", the changes in those relative quantities of the two products the two countries are mutually wishing to exchange with each other or still ready to accept in exchange. Since in both countries the increase in the production of own product (which is partly or fully exported) implies decreasing "marginal productivity", i.e. increasing costs, while the increase in the available supply of the imported product implies decreasing "marginal utility" for the domestic consumers, consequently both countries are willing to export more own product in exchange for less imported product at the beginning of developing international trade relations between each other and less and less when their exports and imports grow. Correspondingly, the demand and supply curves of both countries gradually turn towards each other, expressing the above change in their desired ratio of exchange, until they finally intersect, thereby determining the point of an (assumed) equilibrium in international price formation, representing an "equilibrium terms of trade" (as relative prices and quantities).

**Relative international wage differences** = see under (C).

**Relative purchasing power parity theory** = another (more applicable) variant of the theoretical conceptions determining the exchange rates of currencies, which postulates that the nominal exchange rate is changing (should be changed) according and proportionally to the change in the relative price levels of the two countries. Since the latter may be expressed either (a) as a ratio of the price index of the two countries, or (b) as a difference between the % rate of inflation in the countries concerned, the calculation of the new nominal exchange rate reflecting the changes in relative price levels can imply two alternative ways (resulting almost the same), namely:

$$\text{(a) }\mathbf{NE_t} = \mathbf{NE_0} \times \frac{\mathbf{Pi_A}}{\mathbf{Pi_B}}\ -\text{, or (b) }\mathbf{NE_t} = \mathbf{NE_0} \times \mathbf{1} + \frac{\mathbf{R_B\text{-}R_A}}{\mathbf{100}}\text{, where}$$

$NE_t$ marks the new nominal exchange rate, $NE_0$ the present one, $Pi_A$ the price index in country "A", $Pi_B$ the price index in country "B", $R_B$ the rate of inflation in country "B", and $R_A$ the rate of inflation in country "A".

**"Resource-seeking" (motive of TNCs' FDI)** = a motivation of transnational companies which may practically refer to all the possible resources (natural, labour, capital resources, including physical and human capital, technologies, know-hows, management, administration, organization and marketing skill, credit and loan facilities, etc.) which are needed for the operation of the company.

**Rybczynski theorem** = a concept suggesting that if the available quantity (and relative abundance) of one of the factors of production grows in a country under the conditions of unchanged product prices, then it results in a more than proportionate increase in the output of the commodity (at the expense of others') the production of which requires a more intensive use of the factor concerned.

**Self-sufficient economy** = see under (A).

**Specialization according to "absolute advantages"** = an export-oriented production of a product (or products) which can be produced with an "absolute advantage" (by a higher productivity, i.e. at lower cost) within the country concerned, than abroad, coupled with the import of such product(s) which can be produced more cheaply by the partner country (or countries). In the conventional model of 2 countries – 2 products, such as already applied by Adam Smith, both countries can benefit from trade and division of labour "based" on the differences in labour productivity (or labour cost), if one of them enjoys absolute advantage in the production of one of the products while the other has got absolute advantage in that of the other product.

**Specialization according to "comparative advantages"** = an export-oriented production of a product (or products) which can be produced with "comparative advantage" (i.e. at a level of productivity/cost which is relatively higher/lower, respectively) within the country concerned, than abroad, coupled with the import of such product(s) which can be produced at a level of productivity/cost which is relatively lower/higher there, than in the partner country or countries. In the conventional "2 countries – 2 products" model both countries ("A" and "B") can benefit from trade and division of labour "based" on the differences in relative labour productivity (or relative labour cost), even if one of the countries enjoys "absolute advantage" in the production of both products ("x" and "y"), provided that its absolute advantage is not equal in both products, nor is the "absolute disadvantage" of the other country, and both countries specialize in the production of that product where their "absolute advantage" is bigger or "absolute disadvantage" is smaller.

In the classical Ricardian theory "comparative advantages" are to be measured either in relative labour productivity or relative labour cost (both representing a higher relative economic efficiency, as the difference in the productivity of labour is assumed to express also that in natural conditions (e.g. land fertility), and in technologies, i.e. contributions of "Nature" and capital as well, while labour costs include also labour inputs used in the past to produce capital goods or to make land cultivable or more fertile.

**Spot exchange rate** = the actual nominal rate of exchange which is valid at the presence (and also for all those contracted transactions taking place within two business days, which involve exchange of the currencies concerned.

**Stolper-Samuelson theorem** = a thesis which suggests that if the relative price of a product increases, then it results in an increase also in the income of the owners of the factor of production used intensively in its production. (What follows, e.g., is that the owners of the relatively scarce factors are heavily interested in protective import tariffs.)

**"Strategic-asset-seeking" (motive of TNCs' FDI)** = a motivation of transnational companies which refers not only to the strategic aim of pushing the rivals in competition out of the market but also to the possible rationality of establishing "strategic alliances" with them in certain fields of operation (such as R & D).

**Terms of trade indicators** = those indicators showing the changes in the ratio of exchange either in terms of quantities or in terms of prices in international trade. Their main variants are the following:

(a) "Simple commodity" or "net barter" terms of trade, which is equal to: export price index divided by import price index;
(b) "Gross barter" terms of trade, which is: export volume index divided by import volume index;
(c) "Income" terms of trade, which is: net barter terms of trade times export volume index or export value index divided by import price index;
(d) "Single factoral" terms of trade, which is: net barter terms of trade times labour productivity index (in the export sector);
(e) "Double factoral" terms of trade, which is: net barter terms of trade times the ratio of labour productivity indices of export and import-substitutive sectors.

**Theoretical concepts of (approaches to) exchange rate determination** = those concepts or approaches explaining in one or another way the spontaneous formation and changes of exchange rates (appreciation or depreciation of currencies) or the need for, and required extent of, changes in exchange rates (revaluation or devaluation of currencies), such as the concepts of "absolute" and "relative purchasing parity", the interest parity" concept and the "asset market" or "portfolio balance approach" and the most general "monetary approach".

**"Tradeable"/"non-tradeable goods"** = those goods which can and those which cannot be object of international trade. Mostly the services tied to localities (particularly personal and certain public services, including information) have been qualified as "non-tradeable goods". Today, such a distinction is increasingly irrelevant or vague in view of e.g. cross-border data-flows and international tourism.

**Trade openness of a country** = its link by trade with other countries, measured by the export and import coefficients.

**Trade-creating effect** = an effect, stemming mostly from the entrance to a customs union or inward foreign investments of transnational companies, which replaces certain products of domestic production by imports.

**Trade-diverting effect** = an effect, stemming mostly from the entrance to a customs union or inward foreign investments of transnational companies, which shifts the geographical (relational) pattern of trade of the country concerned (its import and export) away from some countries as former partners (e.g. those remaining outside the customs union), in favour of new partners, other countries within the customs union or the business network of transnational companies.

**Trade liberalism** = a trade policy serving free international trade by eliminating or reducing tariffs and non-tariff barriers of trade.

**Trade policies** = various regulations governing foreign trade. Namely, and in a narrower, conventional sense: the tariff and non-tariff measures (trade barriers) only, but in a broader sense: all those government measures, too, (such as taxation, subsidizing, emission and exchange rate policy, trade related investment measures, etc.) affecting the international trade of a country in one way or another.

**Transnational corporation (TNC)** = a company operating affiliates outside its "home country" and usually involving a multinational pattern of equity capital.

**Transnationalization index** = an index of transnationality which can be constructed in various ways, such as by measuring the ratio of foreign assets to the total sum of assets of the companies (i.e. choosing a single key variable only) or by combining several variables (like assets and also sales, employment, etc.). The UN World Investment Report applies a composite index which consists of three ratios: foreign assets/total assets, foreign sales/total sales and foreign employment/total employment.

**Types of (import) tariffs** = "ad valorem" customs duties (levied on imports proportionally to their price), "specific" customs duties (levied on particular imports, selectively) and import and "compound" customs duties (combining the former by selective "ad valorem" customs duties, i.e. different import tariffs prescribed for distinguished groups of imports).

## Key terms, concepts and methods of economics of development, competitiveness and comoparative systems

**Aid** = donation, grant or concessional loan. (See "Financial assistance" under (B).

**"Aid fatigue"** = the (assumed or real) decline in the willingness of the majority of tax-payers in the advanced countries to sponsor by means of international financial assistance the developing countries, because of the frustration caused by the misuse of aid.

**"Backwash effects" of trade** = the concept (of Myrdal) postulating a harmful effect of international trade on economic development in the case of those developing countries specialized in primary production and suffering regular deterioration of the terms of trade.

**"Basic needs" orientation** = a concept and recommendation for development policy which suggests to devote the available resources to meet the real human needs of the masses of population (or, at least, their demands for basic necessities), instead of wasting them for military expenditures, environment polluting activities, unnecessary luxurious items, etc.

**"Capitalist world-economy"** = the second variant of "world-systems" (according to the concept of Immanuel Wallerstein), which is based upon the operation of the market, involving "unequal exchange" between the dominant "core" and the dependent "periphery" within the framework of division of labour, and (unlike the preceding "world empires") does not have a central power able to regulate economic activities.

**"Centrally planned economy"** = an euphemistic term used (before the collapse of the Soviet-type systems in Eastern Europe) to distinguish the type of economic system (actually a "war-economy" type) from the market-economies.

**Choice of technique** = a choice between "capital-intensive" or "labour-intensive" technology (considered, by conventional development economics, as alternatives excluding each other, on the basis of the false assumption that both factors of production consists of "homogeneous units", i.e. have no differences in quality).

**"Colonial pattern of international division of labour"** = the historically developed international division of labour , characteristic, particularly, of the colonial empires, between the more advanced industrial (metropolitan) countries and the underdeveloped primary producing ones.

**"Colonial-type of direct investment"** = direct investment made by foreign capital in the export-oriented primary producing sectors.

**"Competitive advantage" of firms** = see under (B).

**Concept of "convergence"** (of socio-economic systems) = a concept which originally expressed the prediction or expectation, particularly in the 1960s, in the light of the reformed system of both "capitalism" as manifested in the "welfare states" in the advanced countries, and "existing socialism" as manifested in the rise of (at least the germs of) "market socialism" in some of the Eastern and Central European countries, that the two opposite systems would finally converge.

**"Conspicuous consumption"** = a squandering way of spending the income on luxurious items in order to demonstrate a higher position in the society, or, in general, a wasteful use of the available resources and produce for the purchase or possession of various goods or assets representing the symbols of social status (as in a traditional society).

**"Contrast approach"** = the approach, applied by conventional theories of the economics of comparative systems, to the classification and characterisation of different socio-economic systems, which involves a comparison between "capitalist" and "socialist" (or "communist") systems by means of "contrasting" one to the other as representing opposites, and leads to the conclusion that whatever is found on one side, its diametrically opposite is to be found on the other side. Consequently various pairs of contradicting features have been used to describe and characterize the two predominant, opposite systems (for example, the predominance of private vs. that of state ownership; the primary role of the market vs. that of the State; "demand constraints" vs. supply shortages; "hard" vs. "soft budget barriers", etc.).

**Convergence of economic systems** = see under "Concept of convergence".

**"Critical minimum efforts"** = the assumed requirement, in Leibenstein's concept (similar to that formulated in the concept of "big push"), for the developing countries to break out of the "vicious circle" or "quasi-stable equilibrium system" of underdevelopment.

**CSPC** = calorie supply per capita, daily.

**"Cultural dualism"** = a sociological phenomenon, assumed to be characteristic in developing countries, which is manifested in a gap between the traditional cultures, lifestyles and consumption patterns, on the one hand, and the imported ones of a narrow elite stratum, on the other, which imitates, under "demonstration effects", those of the advanced industrial societies.

**Cumulative indebtedness** = When countries need to resort to new loans in order to be able to service their debt (i.e. to repay with interest the loans they had received earlier).

**Debt ratio** = see under (B).

**Debt service** = see under (B).

**Debt service ratio** = see under (B).

**Delinking** = see "Delinking policy" and also "Policy of delinking".

**"Delinking" policy** = an economic policy suggested to the developing countries (by scholars who blame the developed countries for the "international development gap" and "unequal exchange") which implies an individual or collective economic isolation and "self-reliance", i.e. a cut or reduction of trade and other economic relations with the the advanced part of the world economy.

**"Demand-constrained economy"** = the state of the economy (assumed, by the Keynesian school, to be characteristic of the advanced market economies) in which the aggregate demand is not sufficient for inducing so much investment as resulting in a "perfect equilibrium".

**"Demographic explosion"** = a rapid growth of population caused by the divergence of the mortality and fertility rates.

**Demonstration effects** (of consumption) = those effects radiating and spreading from the more advanced countries (or more wealthier strata of society) and reaching the less developed (or poorer) ones, which by showing, demonstrating (through various channels of contact, such as tourism, TV, films etc.) the level of consumption and lifestyle of the former, their consumer habits and preferences, induce the latter to copy the type of consumption, to imitate the lifestyle of the former.

**Development indicators** = various quantitative and qualitative indicators measuring the level and/or the rate of development, such as the per capita national income, the rate of growth of per capita income or GDP (or GNP), the structure of the economy and its change (e.g. the percentage share of different branches of economy in total GDP and/or total employment), various non-economic indicators (e.g. the ratio of literacy, the PEDU, the headcount index of poverty, the size of relative poverty, i.e. the "poverty gap" or "income gap", the Lorenz curve and Gini coefficient, LEB, IMOR, CSPC; and some composite indicators like HDI, the "level of living" index, etc.)

**"Development index" (of UNRISD)** = another composite index which is based on 18 physical indicators, namely: (1) life expectancy, (2) population in localities of more than 20,000 persons as a proportion of the total population, (3) per capita consumption of animal proteins per day, (4) combined primary and secondary enrollment as a percentage of the related age groups, (5) enrollment in vocational training as a percentage of the 15-19 age group, (6) accomodation facilities, calculated as an average number of persons per room, (7) average circulation of daily newspapers per thousand inhabitants, (8) number of telephones per thousand inhabitants, (9) number of radio receivers per thousand inhabitants, (10) percentage share of economically active population in the service sector, (11) average labour productivity in agriculture, measured in 1960 US dollars, (12) percentage ratio of the number of adult male labourers in agriculture to the total number of adult male laboureres, (13) per capita electricity consumption measured in kwh, (14) per capita steel consumption in kg, (15) per capita energy consumption in kg of coal, (16) percentage share of manufacturing industries in GDP, (17) per capita value of foreign trade (sum of exports and imports) measured in 1960 US dollars, (18) percentage ratio of the number of salary- and wage-earners to the total economically active population.

**"Development of underdevelopment"** = the concept (introduced by Gunder Frank) which implies that "underdevelopment" of the developing countries is not an original "backwardness" of traditional societies, but a historical product of the uneven development of the world economy, reproduced by the latter and/or the mistaken "development policy" of the local elite which following its selfish interest actually serves the dominant powers of the world economy.

**"Diffusion" concept** = the concept the essence of which lies in the assumption that the underdevelopment of the developing countries could easily be overcome in such a way that an increasing volume of capital, technology and entrepreneurial skill would be transferred to them from the developed countries.

**"Dirigiste Dogma"** = the term used by Deepak Lal to describe and criticise those concepts manifesting the belief that the price mechanism, or the working of a market economy, needs to be supplanted by various forms of direct government control.

**"Divestment" policy** = A policy (suggested by Hirschman) which implies a selective and gradual winding up of foreign private investments, which could be implemented by means of an international financial body monitoring that all the equity capital of foreign companies would, indeed, be gradually passed into national ownership.

**"Drive to maturity" in Rostow's stages theory** = the fourth "stage" of growth in the unilinear process of historical development, which is characterized by the spread of growth from the leading sectors to the other sectors and the wider application of modern technology, an improvement in the structure and quality of the labour force, the rise of higher consumption demands, the apperance of professional managers, new social objectives beyond industrialization, etc.

**Dual structure of the economy** = the coexistence of a "traditional" sector (with primitive technologies and involving mostly subsistence economies) and a "modern" sector of export-oriented (mostly primary producing) economies, which manifests a disintegration of the economy.

**Emmanuel's theorem of "trade imperialism"** = a variant of the conceptions of "imperialism" which, as distinguished by its author from (Lenin's) "investment imperialism", postulates a regular exploitation of all the developing countries by the working class of the few developed countries through an unequal exchange which follows from the fact that the prices of the products produced by the latter regularly increase because of the rising wages determined by the strength of trade unions there, while the prices of exports of developing countries with low wage level and weak (if any) trade unions remain low or even decline. While international capital mobility tends to equalize the rates of profits, the international wage differences, which accordingly measure the extent of "exploitation", are lasting ones because of the constraints of international labour mobility.

**"Enclaves" (in the economy)** = those, mainly primary producing export sectors in the economy (of the developing countries) which have been more or less isolated from the other parts of the economy, like alien bodies and tied directly to the economy of foreign (developed) countries.

**"Existing socialism"** (or "Real socialism") = the term (originating in a self-definition of the Soviet-type regimes) used before the collapse of the Soviet bloc, to define the socio-economic and political system which had come into existence either by a revolution or as imposed from outside, and survived for a few decades in countries being isolated from and confronting the outside world, thus establishing a more or less militarized order of society.

**"Externalist" theories** (of underdevelopment) = those theoretical concepts explaining the underdevelopment of developing countries merely by their dependence on outside forces, and their exploitation by the latter, by the unfavourable impact of the international environment, of the world economy and its advanced, dominant part, by the disadvantages and losses caused by the latter through colonialism, imperialism, unequal exchange and income drain, without taking account of those domestic conditions, endowments of their economy, social attitudes, political forces, interests and choices which have also hindered or distorted the process of development and/or paved the way for external dependence and unfavourable effects from outside.

**"Flat-earthers"** (in development economics) = those scholars believing (unlike "round-earthers") in the harmonious operation of the world economy, in the mutual interests of the developing and developed countries.

**"Free market capitalism"** = the term, applied in the economics of comparative systems to distinguish such a variant of the capitalist system of market economy from other variants, which describes the economic system in question (on the basis of the assumed example of the US economy) as involving a relatively spontaneous market mechanism, a very limited role of the State in the economy, mainly restricted to make legal regulations, such as anti-trust laws, consumer protection laws, etc., rather than redistribution, and the main concern is the freedom of the individual, and free competition.

**"Gini coefficient"** (Gini concentration ratio) = the ratio of the area (of inequality) between the diagonal (expressing total equality) in the coordinate system and the Lorenz curve, divided by the total area of the half-square (under the diagonal) in which the curve lies. The Gini coefficient ranges from 0 to 1, thus the larger the coefficient, the greater the inequality.

**Globalisation** = A process which has started long time ago, has been accelerating in the last decades, and tends to bring the members of humankind closer to each other and interdependent. In economic sense globalization means the development of the world economy into an "organic system" with lasting relations between more and more countries and interdependencies among them, i.e. a horizontal extension of international economic relations and a vertical deepening of economic interdependencies.

**"Government imperfections"** = corrupt governments with their clientele and client-patronage-system, irresponsible measures, adverse interventions in the economy, and the resulting spread of corruption, rent-seeking activities, squandering, etc.

**Growth rate of "real" per capita income** (GDP or GNP) = the nominal/monetary increase in per capita GDP/GNP minus the rate of inflation.

**"Growth without development"** = the term used to describe the (frequent) case when parallel with increasing GDP the quality of life worsens and income distribution become more unjust.

**Harrod-Domar model** = a growth model (built mainly on the Keynesian theory) in which saving is proportional to income, capital depreciation and technological changes are (for simplification) neglected, and the growth of the labour force is an exogenous variable which is supposed to be constant, while the aggregate output depends on the labour to output and the capital to output ratios. Insofar as the latter are fixed, output is determined by the quantity of labour or the available quantity of capital. It follows, for practical purposes, that once an aggregate capital/output ratio is determined, and the expected rate of population growth is known, it is possible to calculate how much capital is needed (from domestic savings or from abroad) to achieve a certain rate of growth in per capita income.

**"Hayek situation"** = the state of an economy where resource constraints increase competition for the available factors of production.

**Headcount index of poverty** = the percentage share in the total population, of the poor who live below the "poverty line".

**"Home base" of transnational companies** = see under (B).
**Human Development Index** = a composite development indicator which ranks the countries on a scale of 0 (lowest) to 1 (highest human development) based on three criteria: (a) longevity (measured by life expectancy at birth), (b) knowledge (measured by a weighted average of adult literacy as two-thirds, and mean years of schooling as one-third, and (c) standard of living (measured by real per capita income adjustted for the differing purchasing power parity of each country's currency to reflect cost of living).
**"Immiserizing growth"** = an unfavourable type of growth of an "open" economy which (according to Bhagwati) is characterized by the harmful effects of international trade on "welfare" because of the simultaneous deterioration of the three main terms of trade indicators, i.e. the "net barter", the "income", and the "single factoral" terms of trade. This concept refers to the case of many primary exporting developing countries.
**IMOR** = infant mortality rate: per thousand life births and/or per thousand mortality under 5 years.
**"Income drain mechanism"** = a mechanism (presented in different variants in the Post-Keynesian reformist school) by which incomes are supposed to be transferred, through international trade, from the primary producing developing countries to the advanced industrial ones, and thereby the benefits of increased productivity in the export sectors of the former are practically enjoyed by the latter because in the world market the price ratios (relative prices) of the various products do not adjust themselves to the ratios of labour productivities in those economies producing them. The resulting income loss is manifested in the regular deterioration of the terms of trade of the developing countries, which appears (in the different variants) as the consequence either of the inelastic world demand for their primary products, or the dual structure of their economy with "unlimited supply of labour", or the weakness of their labour organisations, etc.
**"Industrial society"** = a modern society with an industrialised economy which (according to the concept of unilinear development) follows the rural or agricultural one, and naturally leads to a "post-industrial" and then to a "post-material society" or (according to new concepts) to the "information society" and "knowledge-based" or "science-based society".
**"Information society"** = a newly arising modern society in a growing number of countries where the use of modern information technologies is wide-spread.
**Input-output linkages** = those organized or unorganized relations of production cooperation between the various producing units of the economy, between its various sectors, branches or enterprises, which are manifested in the use as inputs, of some parts of the output of each other in the production process.
**"Internalist" theories** (of underdevelopment) = those theoretical concepts characterising conventional economics of development and reflecting the assumption of a "unilinear process of development", which explain the underdevelop-

ment of developing countries merely by domestic conditions, by means of a summary of certain "typical" features, factors and circumstances hindering or limiting the process of development, without taking account of the global context of world economy and international forces.

**International development gap** = the (still widening) gap in the level of per capita income and welfare, between the samll group of advanced countries, the so-called "North", and the great number of developing countries, the so-called "South".

**International resource flows** = see under (B).

**"Knowledge-based" or "Science-based society"** = the assumed future type of society based on a high level of mass education, in which the labour force becomes highly qualified, the decisions on all levels are shaped by expertise, science directly influences human activities, the people get an acces to new knowledge and use of new results of science, the top elite of soeciety consists of scholars, researchers and educationists.

**"Late-comers"** = the term used to distinguish those countries making efforts or proved successful in the process of catching up with the advanced ones (particularly by means of industrialisation), from the "pioneering" countries, i.e. from those being the first and are already the most developed.

**"Late-late-comers"** = the term used to distinguish those underdeveloped countries having serious obstacles under unfavourable international conditions to be successful in catching up with the already developed ones, from those "late-comers" which still had some advantages in following the "pioneering" ones.

**"Latin American school of dependencia"** = a theoretical stream, stemming mainly from an earlier, inter-war stream, namely "structuralism", but including a few Marxist or Neo-Marxist scholars, too, which explains the rise and reproduction of "underdevelopment" of the Latin American (and other developing) countries primarily by their dependent position in the world economy and the resulting "unequal exchange".

**LEB** = life expectancy at birth, measured in years.

**"Level of living" index** (of UNRISD) = = a composite index which involves six physical indicators of development, measuring the level of nutrition, education, housing, leisure and recreation, health, and security, and also one monetary indicator reflecting incomes above subsistence to meet higher needs.

**Lewis' concept of "unlimited supply of labour"** = a thesis of Arthur Lewis, referring to the "dual" structure of the economy of underdeveloped (developing) countries which consists of a "modern", export-oriented sector and a "traditional" one being an unlimited source of cheap unskilled labour for the "modern sector", thereby keeping the wage level under pressure there even if labour productivity increases. As long as this mechanism survives an increase in labour productivity in the modern sector may lead not only to increased profits there but also to deterioration of the terms of trade because of increased output of exports competing with those of other developing countries in the market of developed countries.

**Lewis-model** = see "Lewis' concept of 'unlimited supply of labour'.

**Lorenz curve** = a curve in the coordinate system, which shows the quantitative relationship between the percentage of income recipients and the percentage of the total income they receive. (In the coordinate system both the horizontal and the vertical axes are divided into 10 equal segments corresponding to each of the 10 decile groups. The more the Lorenz line curves away from the diagonal which shows perfect equality, the greater the degree of inequality.)

**"Lumpen-bourgeoisie"** = the term (introduced by Gunder Frank) to prescribe and characterise the type of bourgeois class arising in underdeveloped countries, which, instead of making productive investments and modernising the entire economy as a progressive class should do, behaves as a parasitic, rent-seeking and corrupt social stratum, setting increasing demand for luxurious consumer goods and wasting national resources.

**"Lumpen-development"** = the type of development resulting in deepening dependence on the developed countries, which may also follow (as according to Gunder Frank) from the policy of a "lumpen-bourgeoisie".

**"Marginalization"** = a social and/or international phenomenon which marks the exclusion of certain (often the major) part of the society of a country or the world population, from the process of development and the benefits therefrom.

**"Market-friendly" approach** (of the State) = such a regulatory activity of the State as not hindering or disturbing the normal operation of the market, i.e. an appropriate combination of market spontaneity and government interventions.

**"Market socialism"** = see under "Reform-socialism".

**"Mini-systems"** = the name (applied by Immanuel Wallerstein to distinguish the earlier societies from the "world systems") of those primitive agricultural, or hunting and gathering societies within which there already existed a certain division of labour (at least according to sex and age or already also according to the main spheres of activities), demonstrating the social substance of human existence, and the inevitably social implications of production, but without exchange between the producers as a condition for the operation of these "systems".

**"Mono-economics"** = the belief in the relevance of the same economics both for the developed and the developing countries.

**"National diamond"** = Porter's term with an illustrative model which includes four major poles (determinants): (1) the "factor conditions" (particularly "the nation's position" in respect of "skilled labour" and infrastructure), (2) the actual "demand conditions" ("the nature of home demand for the industry's product or service"), (3) the presence and development of "related and supporting", supplying industries (which are also internationally competitive), and (4) the "strategy, structure, and rivalry" of firms ("the conditions in the nation governing how companies are created, organized, and managed, and the nature of domestic rivalry."

**"Particularists" or "exceptionalists"** (in development economics) = those scholars rejecting the assumption and prediction about a unilinear process of development, i.e. sharing, unlike "universalists", the view that the present developing countries can by no means follow the same path of development as the already advanced ones.

**"Peasant society"** (in Hagen's concept) = the type of society attributed to the underdeveloped countries in general, which is characterised by a low social mobility, by underdevelopment of the middle classes, by primitive production techniques, and in regard to the individual motivations, by a high need-conformity (need to conform, placing high value on conformity), a high need-dependency (need to feel inferior to someone), and a high need-affiliation (need to please friends).

**PEDU** = the percentage of age group enrolled in primary education, i.e. net primary enrollment.

**"Perverse" direction of international capital flows** = see under (B).

**Policy of "delinking"** = an economic policy suggested by some theoretical schools for the developing countries, which would imply an individual or collective isolation of them economically (i.e. in trade and capital flows) from the advanced part of the world.

**"Population explosion"** = see under "Demographic explosion".

**"Post-industrial society"** = see under "Industrial society".

**"Post-material society"** = a society which has developed further than the "industrial" or other societies, and follows, on the basis of social welfare, such new objectives as being superior to material ones.

**Poverty gap** = the transfer needed to lift all people above the "poverty line".

**"Poverty line"** = the costs of basic necessities, including the cost of minimum adequate caloric intakes and other components of subsistence minimum, which are internationally compared in PPP dollars, and, in pricipal, also the historically and culturally varying cost of participating in the everyday life of society.

**PPP** = purchasing power parity (between national currencies).

**"Prebisch-Singer thesis"** = a thesis attributed to Prebisch and Singer which points to the (assumed) regular loss of the primary producing developing countries from international trade because of their deteriorating terms of trade, and to the role of such a regular "income drain" from these countries in their lasting "underdevelopment". In the explanation of the income loss of the latter and of the transfer also of the benefits from increased labour productivity in their export sector to the developed countries importing primary products, the (generally assumed) inelastic demand for the latter and the weak bargaining power of workers in the developing countries were mostly emphasized, together with the unfavourable type of specialization.

**"Preconditions for the take-off" in Rostow's stages theory** = the second "stage" in the unilinear process of historical development, which is characterized by radical changes in three non-industrial sectors, namely: transport (connected with the marketing of raw materials abroad), agriculture (producing also for export) and foreign trade (financed also by capital import), by a gradual development within society, of a new mentality (coming also from abroad), and the rise of a new class of businessmen, etc.

**"Pre-eminence of world values"** = a thesis (of Samir Amin) according to which the "value" of all the products of the capitalist mode of production are determined on a global level since the they are internationalized, (global) world commodities.

**"Quasi-stable equilibrium system"** = the term (introduced by Leibenstein) to descibe the economic system of the underdeveloped countries as a self-reproducing one (just like in the concept of the "vicious circle" of underdevelopment, but contrary to the latter:) through such permanent changes in the variables as bringing back the system to its original state.

**Relative international wage differences** = differences in wage levels greater than those in labour productivites.

**"Re-linking"** = the restoration of economic relations (after a period of "delinking") with foreign countries, i.e. reintegration in the world economy.

**Rostow's theory of the "stages of growth"** = a general historical theory outlining a unilinear process of development which is assumed to consist of five "stages of economic growth". Namely: (1) the stage of the "traditional society", (2) the stage of the "preconditions for the take-off", (3) the "take-off" stage, (4) the stage of the "drive to maturity", and (5) the stage of "high mass consumption".

**"Round-earthers"** (in development economics) = those scholars doubting (unlike "round-earthers") the harmonious operation of the world economy, the mutual interests of the developing and developed countries, and emphasising, instead, conflicts and struggle between them.

**"Self-reliance"** = an idea and policy, originating from the famous slogan of the first government of the independent India and also of the Tanzanian leadership after the "Arusha Declaration", etc. which has been interpreted in various ways. One of the variants calls for "self-help" only, i.e. besides the claim for international assistance it suggests concentrated domestic efforts only within the countries concerned. Another variant, as manifested in the above-mentioned Indian and Tanzanian perception, urges a reduction of dependence on foreign powers and international relations, while an extreme version suggests a full "economic independence" even at the price of cutting off all economic relations with the developed countries, i.e. "delinking".

**"Self-sustained growth"** = a continuous growth of the economy which does not require substantial changes in the structures and institutions. (In conventional development economics it is supposed to appear once the "take off" is over.)

**"Semi-periphery"** = the term for distinguishing those countries belonging neither to the dominant "core" (the "centre") of the world economy, nor to its underdeveloped periphery, but moving upward or downward between the two. (According to Immanuel Wallerstein the "semi-periphery" has got a political role in the smooth operation of the system, namely the role of a kind of buffer between the dominant and the subordinated parts of the world-system.)

**"Shortage economy"** = the term (applied by Kornai to characterize the former "socialist" economies in general) which refers to a permanent shortage of supply in the economy (as contrasting the "demand-constrained" one).

**"Social formation"** = a Marxist term distinguishing the major forms of socio-economic systems in the assumed historical process of development, which involve both an "economic base", i.e. a certain "mode of production" characterized by the level of the progressing forces of production and a certain pattern of "social relations of production", and a corresponding political, institutional, legal, moral, religious, and cultural "superstructure".

**"Social (or sociological) dualism"** = a split of the society into two different parts, namely the "traditional" (or "national") major part and a "modern" (or "alien") minor one, which is a consequence (assumed to be characteristic of the develooping countries) of the "dual structure of economy" or "cultural dualism".

**"Social market capitalism"** = the term, applied in the economics of comparative systems to distinguish such a variant of the capitalist system of market economy from other variants, which describes the economic system in question (on the basis of the assumed example of the economy of Germany and other European countries) as involving a "social market economy", i.e., a well-developed welfare system with social welfare programs, tax-financed social security system, and income redistribution, unemployment compensation, workers' representations in boards and ownership-sharing, state subsidies, and indicative planning, etc.).

**"Social market economy"** = the type of (reformed) capitalist market economy in which the unfavourable effects of the spontaneous operation of the market (such as mass unemployment) are avoided or cured and compensated by the social policy of the "welfare state".

**"Socialist world government"** = the third variant of world-systems, following the first two, namely "world-empires" and "world-economy" (according to the concept of Immanuel Wallerstein), which - in contrast to the anarchic and disequalizing system of the market - would implement "socialist planning".

**Sociological "pattern variables"** (in Talcott Parsons' concept) = the assumed general characteristics of the society of the advanced countries, namely: "universalism, achievement orientation and functional specificity", as distinguished from those of the backward society of the developing countries, namely: "particularism" (domination of particular interests), "ascription" (of the roles in the society, in recruitment and reward) and "functional diffuseness" (the mixing up of social roles).

**Stage of "high mass consumption" in Rostow's stages theory** = the fifth "stage" of growth in the unilinear process of historical development, which can be reached only by a technically and technologically "mature" society after having attained a certain level of national income if it is able to resist the attractions of world power and chooses the alternative of increased private consumption including automobiles, durable consumer goods, family homes with gardens in suburbs, etc.

**"State-directed market economy"** = the term, applied in the economics of comparative systems to distinguish such a variant of the capitalist system of market economy from other variants, which describes the economic system in question (on the basis of the assumed example of the economy of Japan and South-East Asian NICs) as involving a close relationship between the State and business, i.e. an efficient cooperation between the government and the companies, the practice of indicative planning based on consultations with the latter and a government industrial policy, a State support to industrial development, the operation of group-oriented forms of economic organizations, etc.

**"Stationary state"** = an assumed final state of the most advanced society, visualised by Classical economists, which has already reached, because of the "law of diminishing return" (and the fall in the average rate of profits) the limit of further growth.

**"Structural adjustment"** (trade-related) = such a structural change in the economy as made consistent with comparative advantages (or the so called "revealed comparative advantages", i.e. with an increasing ratio of the share of the export product in total exports and that in total imports of the country or in the total world exports).

**"Structural change"** = in general, a shift in the proportions of the contribution to GDP of the various branches of production or in their share within total employment (in other words: changes in the relative importance of different sectors in total output and employment).

**"Structural deficit"** (in the balance of payments) = a manifestation and assumed consequence of "unequal exchange" (according to Oscar Braun) which is suffered by the primary producing developing countries, and caused primarily by the trade barriers set up by the developed countries, preventing them from breaking off their relations of dependence with the latter.

**"Subtraction approach"** (or "ideal typical index approach", or "gap approach") = the approach, applied by conventional development economics, to the explanation of the "international development gap", which involves a comparison between developed and underdeveloped (developing) countries by means of "subtracting" the model of a "typical" underdeveloped country from the idealized model of the "typical" developed country, and leads to the conclusion that what appears as a plus (on the side of the latter) may explain the high level of development while the minus represents and explains underdevelopment. (If, for example, a developed country is characterized by a slow population growth, a relative abundance of capital, an expanded and more or less "perfect" market, large-scale supply of skilled labour, well-developed human capital, entrepreneurial spirit, market-friendly institutions, etc. then a typical "underdeveloped", developing country suffers a too rapid growth of population, a kind of "demographic explosion", serious shortage of capital, great many market imperfections, scarcity of skilled labour, poor quality of the working population, i.e. undeveloped "human capital", lack of entrepreneurs and entrepreneurial spirit, obsolete institutions and market-distorting state interventions, etc.

**"Sustainable development"** = a desired or rather required type of development which does not deteriorate the conditions of development (by polluting the environment, disturbing the ecological balance, exhausting the non-renewable natural resources) for the future generations, nor is accompanied by marked or even increasing social and international inequalities, by "marginalisation" of people or nations, by the survival of the "international development gap" making the conflicts sharper and threatening the security of the human society.

**"Take-off" in Rostow's stages theory** = the third, crucial "stage" of growth in the unilinear process of historical development, which is characterized by industrialisation, a rapid expansion of a few leading sectors in the economy, and such a minimum rate of productive investments over 10 per cent af annual national income which is achieved not only once but has been kept up permanently by society, and a definitive social, political and cultural victory of those who modernize the economy, etc. The "take-off" requires all three of the following related conditions: (a) a rise in the rate of productive investment from 5 per cent or less to over 10 per cent of the national income; (b) the development of one or more substantial manufacturing sectors, with a high rate of growth; (c) the existence or quick emergence of a political, social and institutional framework which exploits the impulse to expansion.

**"Take-off" of wages** = the departure of the wage level from a (Ricardian) subsistence minimum level, owing to the rise, for some reasons, of new demands and "claims" of the working class and its organized trade unions.

**"Technological dualism"** = a phenomenon (assumed to be characteristic of the developing countries with "social" and "cultural dualism") which is manifested in the coexistence of very primitive traditional technologies in the major part of the economy and very modern, "capital intensive" ones in its small import-substituting industrial sector, which is due to import substitution mostly in the fields of manufacturing locally those luxurious goods demanded by the ruling elite.

**"Trade imperialism"** = a variant of "imperialism", i.e. dominance coupled with exploitation, which involves - according to certain theories - a permanent practice of "unequal exchange" in international trade between developed and underdeveloped countries, manifesting the dominance of the former and the exploitation of the latter and also explaining the perpetuation of the "international development gap".

**"Traditional society" in Rostow's stages theory** = the first "stage" in the unilinear process of historical development, which is characterized by a lack of systematic understanding of the physical environment, low level of technology and productivity, predominance of food production, wastages for unproductive ends, a hierarchical structure of society, concentrated political power, etc.

**"Transition economy"** = a term which was introduced, on the basis of an over-simplified perception (as a simple "transition from socialist to capitalist economy") of the complex process of transformation in the former "socialist" systems, to distinguish those countries where a return to or the construction of a Western-type market economy came on the historical agenda.

**Transnational corporation (TNC)** = see under (B).

**Transnationalisation index** = see under (B).

**"Two-gaps model"** = a model of those countries suffering "foreign-exchange bottleneck" (because of deficits in the balance of trade and/or payments) and "saving bottleneck", which suggests the conclusion that capital inflows from abroad are required to ease these bottlenecks.

**"Unequal exchange"** = an exchange of products between unequal partners and/or "non-equivalent" products, which does not involve a mutual or equal distribution of benefits from trade. It has several different and heavily debated interpretations and explanations (such as the Marxian which postulates a necessary inequality even in "equivalent" exchange, the "Prebisch-Singer" variant which derives "unequal exchange" mainly from a type of specialization and demand behaviour, the Lewis-vraiant which links it with the "dual structure" of economy, etc.), among which the most well-known is Emmanuel's concept.

**"Universalists"** (in development economics) = those scholars accepting the assumption and prediction about a unilinear process of development, i.e. sharing, unlike "particularists" the view that each country goes through the same path, with the same "stages", of development.

**"Value chain"** (of a firm) = Porter's term which refers to an interdependent system or network of activities, connected by linkages, namely input- and output linkages. Linkages occur when the way in which one activity is performed affects the cost or effectiveness of other activities.

**"Value system"** = Porter's term which refers to a system including not only the firm's own "value chain" but also that of the supplier, the intermediary and the buyer.

**"Vicious circle of underdevelopment"** (or poverty) = a theoretical concept explainimg underdevelopment by itself, in a way of circular (tautological) reasoning, namely by postulating such a vicious circle as spontaneously repeating itself on the same level and with the same results, i.e. a low level of per capita national income is not only a cause of the subsequent elements of the circular motion (such as, e.g., the low level of savings, and the resulting low level of productive investments, or the low level of education and the resulting poor quality and low productivity of labour, etc.) but also their very consequence.

**"World empires"** = the first variant of "world-systems" (according to the concept of Immanuel Wallerstein), which involved (unlike the subsequent "capitalist world economy") a central power regulating economic activities and redistributing incomes.

**"World-system approach"** (of Wallerstein and Hopkins) = an approach in the analysis of the contemporary societies, which is based on the concept suggesting that the world-economy is the only appropriate unit of analysis of the system of capitalism, and the national economies are merely fictitious phenomena.

# REFERENCES

**Ackley, G.** (1961), *Macroeconomic Theory*. Macmillan. New York.

**Agarwala, A. N.–Singh, S. P.** eds. (1958), *The Economics of Underdevelopment*. Oxford University Press, London.

**Ahluwalia, M. S.–Chenery, H. B.** (1974), "The Economic Framework", in: *Redistribution with Growth*, Oxford Univ. Press, pp. 38–39.

**Altvater, E.** (1993), *The Future of the Market.* Verso, London.

**Amin, S.** (1970), *L'accumulation a l'échelle mondial*. Anthropos, Paris.

**Amin, S.** (1973), *L'échange inégal et la loi de la valeur. La fin d'un débat*. Anthropos–IDEP, Paris.

**Amin, S.** (1974a), *Accumulation on a World Scale. A Critique of the Theory of Underdevelopment.* Monthly Review Press. New York–London. Vol. 2.

**Amin, S.** (1974b), "In Praise of Socialism", *Monthly Review*, Sept. pp. 1–16.

**Amin, S.** (1976), *Unequal Development*. The Harvester Press, Sussex.

**Amin, S.** (1978), "The law of value and historical materialism", *IDEP Papers,* R/006/78. Dakar.

**Amin, S.** (1993), "The Challenge of Globalisation: Delinking", in: The South Centre (1993), Facing *the Challenge*. ZED Books, London. Pp. 132–138.

**Anderson, J. O.** (1976), *Studies in the Theory of Unequal Exchange between Nations*. ABO, Helsinki.

**Aron, R.** (1962), Dix-huit lecons sur la société industrielle. Gallimard, Paris.

**Arrighi, G.** (1967), *The Political Economy of Rhodesia.* Mouton and Co., The Hague.

**Arrighi, G.** (1973), "International Corporations, Labour Aristocracies and Economic Development in Tropical Africa", in: Arrighi, G.–Saul, J.S. (1973), *Essays on the Political Economy of Africa.* Monthly Review Press, New York.

**Baade, F.** (1964), *Der Wettlauf zum Jahre 2000. Unsere Zukunft: Ein Paradies oder Selbstvernichtung der Menschheit*. Gerhard Stalling Verlag, Oldenburg .

**Bacha, E.L.** (1978), "An interpretation of unequal exchange from Prebisch-Singer to Emmanuel", *Journal of Development Economics*, Vol. 5, No. 4.

**Balassa, B.** (1965), "Trade Liberalization and 'Revealed' Comparative Advantage", *The Manchester School of Economic and Social Studies*. Vol. 33. pp. 99–124.

**Balasubramanyam, D.–Lall S. eds.** (1991), *Current Issues in Development Economics*. MacMillan, Houndmills.

**Balogh, T.** (1963), *Unequal Partners*. I–II. Basil Backwell, London.

**Balogh, T.** (1963), *Unequal Partners*. I–II. Basil Backwell, London.

**Baran, P.–Hobsbawm, E.** (1961), "The Stages of Economic Growth". *Kyklos*, Vol. XIV, No. 2.

**Bauer, P.T.–Yamey, B. S.** (1957), *The Economics of Underdeveloped countries*. Cambridge.

**Baran, P.** (1957), *The Political Economy of Growth*. Monthly Review Press, London–New York.

**Baran, P.** (1958), "On the Political Economy of Backwardness", in: Agarwala, A. N. and Singh, S. P. eds.(1958), *The Economics of Underdevelopment*. Oxford University Press.

**Baran, P.** (1960), *The Political Economy of Growth*. Prometheus, New York.

**Baran, P.–Hobsbawm, E.** (1961), "The Stages of Economic Growth", *Kyklos.* Vol. XIV. No. 2.

**Barnett, J. and Morse, C.** (1963), *Scarcity and Growth. The Economics of Natural Resource Availability.* John Hopkins Press, Baltimore.

**Batten, T. R.** (1947), *Problems of African Development*. London.

**Bauer, P. T.–Yamey, B. S.** (1957) *The Economics of Underdeveloped Countries*. London.

**Bauer, P. T.** (1957), *Economic Analysis and Policy in Underdeveloped Countries*. N. C., Durham.

**Berend, I. T.–Ránki, Gy.** (1974), *Economic Development in East-Central Europe in the 19th and 20th Centuries.* London.

**Berend, I. T.** (1979), *Gazdasági elmaradottság, kiutak és kudarcok a XIX. századi Európában*. (Economic underdevelopment, successes and failures in the 19th century Europe) Közgazdasági és Jogi Könyvkiadó, Budapest.

**Berend, I. T. ed.** (1994a), *Transition to a Market Economy at the End of the 20th Century*. Südosteuropa-Gesellschaft, Munich.

**Berend, I. T.** (1994b), *"End of Century Global Transition to a Market Economy: Laissez-Faire on the Peripheries?"*, in: Berend, ed. (1994), pp. 9–54.

**Berlage, L.–Legesse, H.** (1990), "Classification of Countries on the Basis of Different Sets of Socio-Economic Variables". *EADI Conference Paper*, Oslo.

**Bettelheim, C.** (1972), "Theoretical Comments", in: *Emmanuel, A.* (1972a)

**Bhagwati, J. N.** (1958), "Immiserizing Growth", *Review of Economic Studies*, June.

**Boeke, J. H.** (1953a), *Economics and Economic Policy of Dual Societies*. New York.

**Boeke, J. H.** (1953b), "Three Forms of Disintegration in Dual Societies". Lecture delivered for the course on Cooperative Education of the *ILO*, Asian Cooperative Field Mission. October.

**Boeke, J. H.** (1954), "Western Influence on the Growth of Eastern Population". *Economia Internazionale*, Vol. VII, No. 2.

**Bonne, A.** (1957), *Studies in Economic Development*. London.

**Bose, A.** (1979), "Concept of Unequal Exchange in International Trade: A Note", *Economic and Political Weekly,* Bombay, Vol. XIV, No. 29.

**Bose, A.** (1987), "Development Theories Revisited: Requiem or Rethinking?" UNESCO, *Etudes et documents*, BEP/GPI/5, Paris.

**Bradford, C. I.** (1986), "East Asian 'models': Myths and lessons", in: Lewis, J. P.–Kallab, V. eds. (1986), *Development Strategies Reconsidered*. Overseas Development Council, Washington.

**Brandt Commission** (1980), *North-South–A Programme for Survival*. The Report of the Independent Commission on International Development Issues under the Chairmanship of Willy Brandt. Pan Books, London.

**Brandt Commission** (1983), *Common Crisis–North-South: Co-operation for World Recovery*. Pan Books, London.

**Braun, O.** (1973), "On 'unequal exchange and the law of value", *IDEP papers*.

**Braun, O.** (1977), *Commercio International e Imperialismo*. Singlo XXI, Buenos Aires. Translated in English: "International Trade and Imperialism", mimeographed manuscript.

**Brown, K.** (1959), *Land in Southern Rhodesia*. Africa Bureau, London.

**Brown, O.** (1946), *Labour Conditions in East Africa*. London.

**Buchanan, N. S.–Ellis, H. S.** (1955*), Approaches to Economic Development*. The Twentieth Century Fund, New York.

**Buchanan, N. S.** (1946), "Deliberate Industrialization for Higher Incomes". *Economic Journal*, Vol. 56, No. 4.

**Cairncross, A. K.** (1961), "Essays in Bibliography and Criticism, XLV: The Stages of Economic Growth". *Economic History Review*, April. Reprinted in: *Meier, G.M.* (1964)

**Camps, M.–Diebold, W.** (1986), "The New Multilateralism", *Council on Foreign Relations.* New York. (referred by Simai, 1992)

**Cardoso, F. H.–Faletto, E.** (1969), *Dependencia y Desarollo en America Latina*, Siglo XXI, Mexico.

**Checkland, S. G.** (1960), "Theories of Economic and Social Evolution: the Rostow Challenge". *Scottish Journal of Political Economy*, November.

**Chenery, H.–Strout, A. M.** (1966), "Foreign Assistance and Economic Development", *American Economic Review*, September.

**Chew, Sing C. ed.** (1996), *The Underdevelopment of Development. For Andre Gunder Frank and Beyond.* Sage Publ. London, New York.

**Clark, C.** (1953), "Population Growth and Living Standards", *International Labour Review*, August, in: Agarwala, A. N. and Singh, S. P. eds. (1958), pp. 32–53.

**Clark, C.** (1957), *Conditions of Economic Progress*. Macmillan, London.

**Cox, R. W.** (1979), "Ideologies and the New International Economic Order: reflections on some recent literature", *International Organizations*, 33. 2. Spring,

**Dandekar, V. M.** (1980), "Unequal Exchange: Imperialism of Trade", *Economic and Political Weekly,* Bombay, Vol. XV, No. 1.

**Dasgupta, S.** (1964), "Underdevelopment and Dualism–A Note". *EDCC*, Vol. 12, No. 2.

**Dawson, A. A.** (1962), "The Place of the Traditional Sector in Economic Development". *Lectures on Economic Development.* International Institute for Labour Studies, Geneva

**de Briey, P.** (1955), "The productivity of African labour", *International Labour Review,* August-September

**de Castro, J.** (1952), *Geography of Hunger*. London.

**Diouf, M.** (1977), *Exchange inégal et ordre économique international*. Abidjan, Dakar.

**Doney, A.** and **Feldheim, P.** (1956), "Social Implications of Industrialization and Urbanization in Africa, South of the Sahara". *UNESCO Paper*, Paris.

**Dunning, J. H.** (1993), *Multinational Enterprises and the Global Economy.* Addison–Wesley Publishing Company, Wokingham, England.

**Eckhaus, R. S.** (1965), "The Factor-Proportions Problem in Underdeveloped Areas". *The American Economic Review*, September.

**Eckstein, A.** (1973), *Comparison of Economic Systems. Theoretical and Methodological Approaches*. University of California Press, Berkeley–Los Angeles–London.

**Elkan, W.** (1959), "Migrant Labour in Africa: An Economist's Approach". *The American Economic Review*, No. V.

**Elkan, W.** (1963), "The Dualistic Economy of the Rhodesias and Nyassaland". *EDCC*. Vol. 11, No. 4.

**Ellis, H. S.** (1962), "Dual Economies and Progress". *Revista de Economica Latino-americana*

**Ellsworth, P. T.** (1962), "The Dual Economy: A New Approach". *EDCC*, Vol. 10, No. 4.

**Emmanuel, A.** (1972a), *Unequal Exchange. A Study of the Imperialism of Trade*. Monthly Review Press, New York.

**Emmanuel, A.** (1972b), "White-Settler Colonialism and the Myth of Investment Imperialism", *New Left Review*. No. 73.

**Emmanuel, A.** (1976), "The multinational corporations and the inequality of development", *International Social Science Journal*, Vol. XXVIII. No. 4.

**Emmerij, L. ed.** (1997), *Economic and Social Developments into the Twenty–First Century.* Baltimore, John Hopkins Press, Wisconsin

**Enke, S.–Salera, V.** (1951), *International Economics*. New York–Evans, H.D. (1980), "Emmanuel's theory of unequal exchange: critique, counter-critique and theoretical contribution", *Discussion Paper*, No. 149. Institute of Development Studies, University of Sussex.

**Evans, H. D.** (1984), "A Critical Assessment of Some Neo-Marxian Trade Theories", *Journal of Development Economics*, Vol. 20, No. 2.

**Fanon, F.** (1961), *Les damnés de la terre*. Maspero, Paris.

**Fay, C. R.** (1940), "Stages in Economic History", *English Economic History*, Cambridge.

**Frank, A. G.** (1963), "Not Feudalism: Capitalism", *Monthly Review*, New York, Vol. 15. December.

**Frank, A. G.** (1966), "The Development of Underdevelopment", *Monthly Review*, September. New York.

**Frank, A. G.** (1967), "Sociology of Development and Underdevelopment of Sociology", *Catalyst,* No. 3. University of Buffalo. (Published also by Pluto Press, London, in 1971)

**Frank, A. G.** (1972), *Lumpenbourgeoisie: Lumpendevelopment*, Monthly Review Press, New York.

**Frank, A. G.** (1977), *L'accumulation mondiale, 1500–1800*. Calman-Levy, Paris.

**Frank, A. G.** (1978a), *World Accumulation: 1492–1789*. Monthly Review Press, New York, and Macmillan Press, London.

**Frank, A. G.** (1978b), *Dependent Accumulation and Underdevelopment*. Macmillan Press, London.

**Frank, A. G.** (1980), *Crisis: In the World Economy.* Holmes & Meier, New York.

**Frank, A. G.** (1988), "The Socialist Countries in the World Economy: the East-South Dimension", in: Lelio Basso Foundation, ed. (1988), *Theory and Practice of Liberation at the End of the XXth Century*. Bruylant, Bruxelles.

**Frank, A. G.** (1991), "The Underdevelopment of Development", *Scandinavian Journal of Development Alternatives*, Vol. X. No. 3. September, pp. 5–72.

**Friedman, M.** (1969), *The Optimum Quantity of Money and Other Essays*. Chicago.

**Fukuyama, F.** (1991), *The End of History and the Last Man*. Basic Books, New York.

**Furtado, C.** (1958), " Capital Formation and Economic Development", in: *Agarwala A. N.–Singh, S. P.* eds. (1958), pp. 312–313.

**Furtado, C.** (1964), *Development and Underdevelopment*. University of California Press.

**Furtado, C.** (1970), *Obstacles to Development in Latin America.* Doubleday and Co., New York.

**Furtado, C.** (1971), "External Dependence and Economic Theory", *IDEP Papers*, Repr. 272. Dakar.

**Furtado, C.** (1973), "Underdevelopment and Dependence: the Fundamental Connection", Centre of Latin American Studies, University of Cambridge. *Working Papers*, No. 17.

**Gannagé, E.** (1962), *Économie du développement*. Paris.

**Gaia** (1985), *The Gaia Atlas of Planet Management*. Pan Books, London and Sydney.

**Gerschenkron, A.** (1955), "Economic Progress", Paper for a Round-Table Conference. *International Economic Association*. Louvin.

**Gerschenkron, A.** (1962), *Economic Backwardness in Historical Perspective*. Cambridge, Mass.

**Giersch, H.** (1955), "Stages and Spurts of Economic Development", in: Dupriez, L. H. ed. (1955), *Economic Progress*. Louvain.

**Gill, R. T.** (1963), *Economic Development. Past and Present*. Prentice-Hall.

**Grabowski, R.–Shields, M. P.** (1996), *Development Economics.* Blackwell Publ., Cambridge, Mass.

**Gras, N. S. B.** (1930), "Stages in Economic History" in: *Journal of Economic and Business History,* No. II.

**Gregory, P. R.–Stuart, R. C.** (1989), *Comparative Economic Systems*. Third edition. Houghton Mifflin Co., Boston.

**Griffin, K.–Enos, J.** (1970), "Foreign Assistance: Objectives and Consequences", *Economic Development and Cultural Change.* April.

**Griffin, K. – Knight, J.** (1989), "Human Development: The Case for Renewed Emphasis", *Journal of Development Planning,* Meier–Rauch (p. 30)

**Grossmann, G.** (1967), *Economic Systems*. Englewood Cliffe, New York.

**Habakukk, H. J.** (1961), "The Stages of Economic Growth". A review of Rostow's book. *Economic Journal*, September – Reprinted in Meier, G. M. ed. (1964).

**Haberler, G.** (1957), "Critical Observation on Some Current Notions in the Theory of Economic Development", *L'industria*, No. 2.

**Haberler, G.** (1964), "Integration and Growth of the World Economy", *The American Economic Review*. No. III.

**Hagen, E.** (1980), *The Economics of Development*. Richard D. Irwin, Homewood. 3rd edition.

**Hagen, E. E.** (1957a), "The Theory of Economic Development". *EDCC*, Vol. 6, No. 3, April.

**Hagen, E. E.** (1957b), *An Analytical Model of the Transition to Economic Growth*. M. I. T., CIS. Document C/57.12.

**Hagen, E. E.** (1962), *On the Theory of Social Change*. Dorsey Press, Homewood.

**Harbison, F.–Myers, C. A.** (1964), *Education, Manpower and Economic Growth*. New York

**Hayek, F. A.** (1931), *Prices and Production*. Routledge, London.

**Hayek, F. A. ed.** (1935), *Collectivist Economic Planning*. Routledge, London.

**Heckscher, E. F.** (1919), "The Effects of Foreign Trade on the Distribution of Income", *Economis Tidskrift*. Vol. 21.

**Helleiner, G.** (1972), *International Trade and Economic Development*. Penguin Books, London.

**Hettne, B.** (1990), "The Globalization of Development Theory", *Studies on Developing Countries,* Institute for World Economics of HAS, Budapest.

**Hettne, B.** (1991), "The Voice of the Third World", *Studies on Developing Countries*, Institute for World Economics of HAS, Budapest.

**Higgins, B.** (1959), *Economic Development*. W. W. Norton and Co., New York.

**Higgins, B.** (1964), "The Dualistic Theory of Underdeveloped Areas". *Economic Development and Cultural Change,* January 1959, reprinted in: Meier, G. M. ed. (1964), *Leading Issues in Development Economics.* New York.

**Hirschman, A. O.** (1945), *National Power and the Structure of Foreign Trade*. University of California Press, Los Angeles.

**Hirschman, A. O.** (1951), "The Rise and Decline of Development Economics", in: *Essays in Trespassing Economics to Politics and Beyond,* Cambridge University Press, Mass.

**Hirschman, A. O.** (1957), "Investment Policies and Dualism in Underdeveloped Countries", *American Economic Review*, September.

**Hirschman, A. G.** (1958), *The Strategy of Economic Development*. New York.

**Hirschman, A. O.** (1964), "How to Divest in Latin America and Why?". *Essays in International Finance,* No. 76. Princeton University, Princeton.

**Hirschman, A. O.** (1981), *Essays in Trespassing-Economics to Politics to Beyond*. Cambridge University Press.

**Hopkins, T. K.–Wallerstein, I.** (1977), "Patterns of Development of the Modern World-System. Research Proposal", *Review,* Vol. I., No. 2., Fall. Fernand Breudel Center, New York .

**Hoselitz, B. F.** (1953), "Social Structure and Economic Growth". *Economia Internazionale*, Vol. 6, No. 3, Aug.

**Hoselitz, B. F.** (1960a), "Theories of Stages of Economic Growth", in: Hoselitz, B. F. ed. (1960), *Theories of Economic Growth*. Glencoe.

**Hoselitz, B. F.** (1960b), *Sociological Factors in Economic Development*. The Free Press, Glencoe.

**Hoselitz, B. F.** (1960c), "Economic Growth in Latin America". Contributions to the *First International Conference in Economic History.* Stockholm, Mouton and Co., The Hague.

**Hoselitz, B. F.** (1963), "Role of Incentives in Industrialization". *Economic Weekly*, Vol. 15, Nos. 28, 29, 30. (Special Number, July) Bombay.

**Hoselitz, B. F.** (1964), "Social Stratification and Economic Development". *International Social Science Journal,* Vol. 16, No. 2.

**Hume, D.** (1802), *The History of England*. Strahan, London. Vol. IV.

**Hunton, W. A.** (1956), *Decision in Africa*. London

**Hveem, H.** (1977), *The Political Economy of Third World Producer Associations*. Universitetsforlaget, Oslo.

**ILO** (1961), *Employment Objectives in Economic Development*. Report of the meeting of experts. Geneva. – Reprinted in Meier, G. M. ed. (1964)

**Kamarck, A. M.** (1967), *The Economics of African Development*. F. A. Praeger.

Keiskammahoek (1952), *Rural Survey*. UN, New York.

**Keynes, J. M.** (1926), *The End of Laissez-Faire.* Hogarth Press, London.

**Keynes, J. M.** (1930), *A Treatise on Money*. Macmillan, London.

**Keynes, J. M.** (1936), *The General Theory of Employment, Interest and Money*. Macmillan, London.

**Knies, K.** (1930), *Die politische Ökonomie vom geschichtlichem Standpunkte*. Leipzig.

**Koopmans, T. C.–Montias, J. M.** (1973), "On the Description and Comparison of Economic Systems", in: *Eckstein, A. ed.* (1973), pp. 27–78.

**Kornai, J.** (1980), *Economics of Shortage*. North–Holland Amsterdam.

**Kornai, J.** (1992), *The Socialist System. The Political Economy of Communism*. Clarendon Press, Oxford University Press, Oxford, New York.

**Koshla, A.** (1995), "Trade Not Aid?". *South Letter,* No. 23. Summer 1995. (Reprinted from Development Alternatives).

**Krugman, P. R.–Obstfeld, M.** (1991), *International Economics. Theory and Policy*. Second edition. Harper Collins Publishers, New York.

**Kunkel, J. H.** (1965), "Values and Behaviour in Economic Development". *EDCC*, Vol. 13, No. 3.

**Kuznets, S.** (1958), "Underdeveloped Countries and the Pre-Industrial Phase in Advanced Countries", in: Agarwala, A. N. and Singh, S. P. eds. (1958), *The Economics of Underdevelopment*. Oxford University Press. Pp. 149–151.

**Kuznets, S.** (1960), "Notes on the Take-Off". Paper presented at the International Economic Association's Conference at Konstanz in September 1960. Reprinted in: Meier, G. M. (1964), *Leading Issues in Development Economics*. New York.

**Kuznets, S.** (1966), *Six Lectures on Economic Growth*. Frank Cass and Co.

**Kuznets, S.** (1973), "Notes on Stage of Economic Growth as a System Determinant", in *Eckstein, A*. (1973), Ch. 8.

**Lal, D.** (1980), "A Liberal International Economic Order: The International Monetary System and Economic Development", *Princeton Essays in International Finance*, No. 139. Princeton University Press.

**Lal, D.** (1983), *The Poverty of 'Development Economics'*. The Inst. of Economic Affairs, Hobart Paperback. London.

**Landes, D. S.** (1969), *The Unbound Prometheus.* Cambridge University Press, Cambridge

**Lange, O.** (1936), "On the Economic Theory of Socialism", *Review of Economic Studies*. (Also in Lippincott, B. E. ed. (1938).

**Leibenstein, H.** (1957), *Economic Backwardness and Economic Growth*. New York.

**Leibenstein, H.** (1960), "Technical Progress. The Production Function and Dualism". *Quarterly Review,* Banca Nazionale del Lavoro. December.

**Lenin, V. I.** (repr. 1948), *Imperialism: The Highest Stage of Capitalism*. Lawrence and Wishart, London.

**Lenin, V. I.** (repr. 1967), Selected Works. Vol. I. Moscow.

**Leontief, W. W.** (1953), "Domestic Production and Foreign Trade: The American Position Reexamined", *Proceedings of the American Philosophical Society*. Sept.

**Lerner, A. P.** (1944), *Economics of Control*, New York.

**Levin, H. S.** (1971), "On Comparing Planned Economies (A Methodological Inquiry)", in: *Eckstein, A*. ed. (1971), Part II. Ch. 5.

**Lewis, W. A.** (1952), "World Production Prices and Trade, 1870–1960". *The Manchester School of Economic and Social Studies*, Vol. XX.

**Lewis, W. A.** (1955), *The Theory of Economic Growth*. London.

**Lewis, W. A.** (1958), "Economic Development with Unlimited Supplies of Labour", in: Agarwala, A. N. and Singh, S. P. eds. (1958), *The Economics of Underdevelopment*. Oxford University Press, London. Pp. 400–449.

**Leys, C.** (1977), "Underdevelopment and Dependency: Critical Notes", Journal of Contemporary Asia, No.1.

**Lippincott, B. E. ed.** (1938), *On the Economic Theory of Socialism*. Minneapolis.

**List, F.** (1841), *Das nationale System der politischen Oekonomie*. Stuttgart.

**Little, I. M. D.** (1950), *A Critique of Welfare Economics*. Oxford.

**Little, I. M. D.** (1964), *Aid to Africa*. Overseas Development Institute. London.

**Little, I. M. D.** (1982), *Economic Development: Theory, Policy, and International Relations.* Basic Books, New York

**Lukács, G.** (1968), "The Marxism of Rosa Luxemburg", in: *History and Class Consciousness*. Merlin Press, London.

**Lutz, V. C.** (1958), "The Growth Process in a Dual Economic System". *Quarterly Review*, Banca Nazionale del Lavoro. September.

**MacDougal, G. D. A.** (1951), "British and American Exports: A Study Suggested by the Theory of Comparative Costs", *Economic Journal*, December.

**Maizels, A.** (1982), "The industrialization of the developing countries", in: Frowen, S. F. ed. *Controlling Industrial Economies: Essays in Honour of C. T. Saunders*. Oxford University Press.

**Malthus, A.** (1914, 1952), *Essay on Population*. 2nd ed. J. M. Dent, London.

**Marshall, A.** (1879), *The Economics of Industry*. Macmillan adn Co. London

**Marshall, A.** (1890), *Principles of Economics.* Vol. 1. Macmillan & Co., London

**Marshall, A.** (1907), *"Social Possibilities of Economic Chivalry"*, in: *Memorials.*

**Marshall, A.** (1923), *The Pure Theory of Foreign Trade. Money, Credit and Commerce*. Macmillan, London.

**Marshall, A.** (repr. 1930), *Principles of Economics*. 8th edition, Macmillan, London.

**Malthus, T. R.** (1951), *Principles of Political Economy*. 2nd edition. Augustus Kelley, New York

**Marini, R. M.** (1973), *Dialectica de la Dependencia*. Era, Mexico City.

**Marx, K.** (1853), "The British Role in India", *New York Daily Tribune*, 25 June, in: Avineri, S. ed. (1969), *Karl Marx on Colonialism and Modernization*. Anchor Books, New York.

**Marx, K.** (repr. 1964), *Pre-Capitalist Economic Formations*. Lawrence and Wishart, London.

**Marx, K.** (repr. 1965), *Capital*. Vol. I. Progress Publishers, Moscow.

**Marx, K.** (repr. 1966), *Capital*. Vol. III. Progress Publishers, Moscow.

**Marx, K.** (repr. 1967), *Capital*. Vol. II. Progress Publishers, Moscow.

**Mátyás, A.** (1963), *A gazdasági fejlődés feltételei. Bevezetés* (The conditions of economic development. Introduction). Közgazdasági és Jogi Könyvkiadó, Budapest.

**Mátyás, A.** (1979), *History of Modern Non-Marxian Economics*. Akadémiai Kiadó, Budapest.

**Mátyás, A.** (1993) and (1999) *A modern közgazdaságtan története*. (History of modern economics) Aula, Budapest.

**McClelland, D. C.** (1957), *"Community Development and the Nature of Human Motivation: Some Implications of Recent Research"*. Conference on Community Development and National Change. Massachussetts Institute of Technology. December.

**McClelland, D.** (1961a), *The Achieving Society*. Van Nostrand, Princeton.
**McClelland, D.** (1961b), *The Achievement Motive*. Appleton–Century-Crofts, New York
**McClelland, D.** (1964), "A Psychological Approach to Economic Development". *EDCC,* Vol. 12, No. 3, April.
**McCulloch, J. R.** (1888), *The Works of David Ricardo*. John Murray, London.
**McKinnon, R. I.** (1964), "Foreign Exchange Constraints in Economic Development", *Economic Journal,* June.
**Meadows, D. and D.** (1972), *The Limits to Growth*. Universe Books, New York.
**Meier, G. M.–Baldwin, E.** (1957), *Economic development. Theory, History, Policy*. New York.
**Meier, G. M.** (1958), "The Problem of Limited Economic Development", in: *Agarwala, A. N.–Singh, S. P.* eds. (1958), pp. 149-151.
**Meier, G. M.** (1964) and (1995), *Leading Issues in Economic Development*. Oxford University Press. Oxford and New York.
**Meier, G. M.–Rauch, J. E.** (2000), *Leading Issues in Economic Development.* Seventh Edition. Oxford Univ. Press, Oxford and New York
**Mill, J. S.** (1896), *Principles.* Green Longman, London.
**Mill, J. S.** (repr. 1924), *Autobiography.* Columbia Univ. Press, New York.
**Mill, J. S.** (repr. 1965), *Principles of Political Economy*. Univ. of Toronto Press, Toronto, and Routledge and Kegan Paul, London.
**Millikan, M. F. ed.** (1967), *National Economic Planning.* New York.
**Munn, T.**, *England's Treasure by Foreign Trade*. Reprinted in 1928, Basil Blackwell, London
**Mushakoji, K.** (1988), *Global Issues and Interparadigmatic Dialogue. Essays on multipolar politics.* Albert Meynier, London.
**Myint, H.** (1958), "An Interpretation of Economic Backwardness", in: *Agarwala, A. N.–Singh, S. P.* eds. (1958)
**Myint, H.** (1963), "Economic Theory and the Underdeveloped Countries", *Journal of Political Economy,* No. 5. Chicago.
**Myint, H.** (1964), *The Economics of the Developing Countries*. Hutchinson, London.
**Myrdal, G.** (1953), *The Political Element in the Development of Economic Theory*. Routledge and Kegan Paul, London.
**Myrdal, G.** (1956), *An International Economy*. Harper, New York.
**Myrdal, G.** (1957), *Economic Theory and Underdeveloped Regions*. University Paperbacks. Methuen, London.
**Myrdal, G.** (1968), *Asian Drama: An Inquiry into the Poverty of Nations*. Vols. I–III. Pantheon, New York.
**Nash, M.** (1963), "Introduction, Approaches to the Study of Economic Growth", in: Nash, M.–Chin, R. eds. (1963), *Psycho-Cultural Factors in Asian Economic Growth*. Special issue of the Journal of Social Issues, 29, No. 1, January.
**Nerfin, M.** (1987), "Neither prince nor merchant: citizen – an introduction to the third system", *Development Dialogue*, No. 1.

**Nerfin, M.** (1990), "Is Global Civilization Coming?". *Council of Europe. East-West-South Encounter.* Working Document No. 11. Budapest.

**North, D. C.** (1958), "A Note on Professor Rostow's Take-Off into Self-Sustained Economic Growth". *The Manchester School*, January

**Nurske, R.** (1952a), "Some International Aspects of the Problem of Economic Development", *The American Economic Review*, May.

**Nurske, R.** (1952b), *Some Aspects of Capital Accumulation in Underdeveloped Countries*. Cairo

**Nurkse, R.** (1953), *Problems of Capital Formation in Underdeveloped Countries*. Oxford Univ. Press.

**Nurkse, R.** (1957), "Excess Population and Capital Construction". *Malayan Economic Review*, Oct. (Reprinted in Meier, G. M. (1964), *Leading Issues in Economic Development*. Oxford University Press. Pp. 74–77.

**Nurkse, R.** (1958), "Some International Aspects of the Problem of Economic Development". *The American Economic Review*, May, 1952. Reprinted in: Agarwala, A. N.–Singh, S. P. eds. (1958)

**OECD-DAC** (1995), *Development Co-operation*. Paris.

**Ohlin, B.** (1933), *Interregional and International Trade*. Cambridge, Mass.

**Ohlin, G.** (1961), "Reflections on the Rostow Doctrine". *Economic Development and Cultural Change.* July.

**Pajestka, J.–Kulig, J.** (1979), "The Socialist Countries of Eastern Europe and the New International Economic Order", *Trade and Development, UNCTAD Review*, No. 1. UN, Geneva.

**Paukert, F.** (1962), "The Place of the Traditional Sector in Economic Development", *Lectures on Economic Development*. International Institute for Labour Studies, Geneva.

**Pen, J.** (1965), *Modern Economics*. Pelican Books. Penguin. Harmondsworth.

**Perroux, F.** (1964), *L'économie du XXième siècle*. University Press, Paris.

**Perroux, P.** (1966), "Blocages et freinages de la croissance et du développement", *Tiers Monde*, April–June.

**Perroux, F.** (1969), *Indépendance de l'économie nationale et interdépendance des nations*. Editions Aubier Montaigne, Paris.

**Perroux, F.** (1975), "Lés unitransnationales et la renovation de la théorie de l'équilibre général (intérieur et extérieur)", *Mondes en Développement*, No. 12.

**Perroux, F.** (1978), "Lés firmes transnationales et l'Amerique Latine", *Revue de la Défense Nationale.*

**Perroux, F.** (1979), "The Concept of Global, Endogenous and Integrated Development", Working paper for the UNESCO meeting of experts concerning "Research on the Concept of an Integrated Development", Quito, Ecuador, 27–31 August. *UNESCO*, SS-79/Conf. 612/5. Paris.

**Porter, M. E.** (1990), *The Competitive Advantage of Nations*. Free Press, New York.

**Prebisch, R.** (1950), *The Economic Development of Latin America and Its Principal Problems*. UN. New York.

**Prebisch, R.** (1959), "Commercial Policy in Underdeveloped Countries", *The American Economic Review*, Papers and Proceedings.

**Prebisch, R.** (1962), *Economic Development of Latin America and Its Principal Problems*. ECLA, No. 1., UN, New York.

**Prebisch, R.** (1964), *Towards a New Trade Policy for Development*. Report by the Secretary-General of the United Nations Conference on Trade and Development. United Nations, New York.

**Prebisch, R.** (1972), "Change and Development – Latin America's Great Task". *IDEP Papers*, ET/Cs 2367-21. Repr. Dakar.

**Pronk, J.** (1991), *Towards a System of Responsible Global Governance for Development*. Development Cooperation Information Department of the Ministry of Foreign Affairs, The Hague

**Raffer, K.** (1987), *Unequal Exchange and the Evolution of the World System. Reconsidering the Impact of Trade o North-South Relations*. Macmillan Press, London.

**Rao, V. K. R. V.** (1964), *Essays in Economic Development*. Asia Publishing House, Delhi–London.

**Reich, R. B.** (1991), *The Work of Nations*. Alfred A. Knopf, New York.

**Ricardo, D.** (1821), *Principles of Political Economy and Taxation*. London.

**Ricardo, D.** (repr. 1887), *Letters of David Ricardo to Thomas Robert Malthus 1810–1823*. Ed. by J. Bonar. Clarendon Press, London.

**Robinson, J.** (1966), *Economic Philosophy*. Pelican, New York.

**Robinson, J.** (1979), *Aspects of Development and Underdevelopment*, London.

**Rodney, W.** (1974), *How Europe underdeveloped Africa*. Howard Univ. Press, Washington.

**Rodrik, D.** (1982), "Comparative Advantage and Structural Change: A Quantitative Analysis", *UNCTAD Discussion Papers*, No. 8.

**Roscher, W.** (1843), *Ansichten der Volkswirtschaft aus dem geschichtlichen Standpunkte*. Leipzig–Heidelberg.

**Roscher, W.** (repr. 1900), *Grundlagen der Nationalökonomie*. Stuttgart.

**Rostow, W. W.** (1958), "The Take-Off into Self-Sustained Growth", in Agarwala, A. N.–Singh, S. P. eds. (1958), *The Economics of Underdevelopment*. Oxford University Press, London.

**Rostow, W. W.** (1960a), *The Stages of Economic Growth. A Non-Communist Manifesto*. Cambridge University Press, Cambridge.

**Rostow, W. W.** (1960b), *The Process of Economic Growth*. Oxford University Press.

**Rostow, W. W.** (1990), *Theorists of Economic Growth from David Hume to the Present*. Oxford University Press, New York–Oxford.

**Rotwein, E. ed.** (1955), *David Hume, Writings on Economics*. University of Wisconsin, Madison.

**Routh, G.** (1969), "Methodology", *The Teaching of Economics in African Universities*. (1969). Univ. of Dar es Salaam. (Edited by: Livingstone).

**Roxborough, I.** (1979), *Theories of Underdevelopment*. The Macmillan Press Co., London.

**Sachs, I.** (1964), *Patterns of Public Sector in Underdeveloped Economies*. Asia Publishing House, New Delhi.

**Saigal, J. C.** (1973), "Réflexion sur la théorie de 'l'échange inégal'", in: *Amin, S.* (1973a).

**Salvatore, D.** (1990), *International Economics*. Macmillan, New York.

**Samuelson, P. A.** (1948), "International Trade and Equalization of Factor Prices", *Economic Journal,* June.

**Sau, R.** (1978), *Unequal Exchange, Imperialism and Underdevelopment. An Essay on the Political Economy of World Capitalism*. Oxford University Press, Calcutta.

**Sauvy, A.** (1956), *Théorie générale de la population*. Vol. I. Paris.

**Schackle, G. L. S.** (1962), "The Stages of Economic Growth". *Political Studies*, February.

**Schatz, S. P.** (1967), "The Capital Shortage Illusion: Government Lending in Nigeria". In: Whetham, E.–Currie, J. J. eds. (1967), *Readings in the Applied Economics of Africa*. Vol. I. Cambridge Univ. Press, Cambridge.

**Schmoller, G.** (1923), *Grundriss der allgemeinen Volkwirtschaftslehre*. I. München–Leipzig

**Schnitzer, M. C.** (1994), *Comparative Economic Systems*. 6th edition. College Division. South-Western Publ. Co., Cincinnati–Ohio

**Schumpeter, J. A.** (1951b), The Sociology of Imperialism and Social Classes. Meridian, New York.

**Schumpeter, J. A.** (1951a), *The Theory of Economic Development*. Harvard University Press.

**Seers, D.** (1963), *Economic Philosophy*. Pelican, New York.

**Sen, A.** (1983),"Development: Which Way Now?", *Economic Journal*, December.

**Sen, A.** (1984), *Resources, Values and Development*.

**Sen, A.** (1985), "A Sociological Approach to the Measurement of Poverty. A Reply to Professor Peter Townsend", *Oxford Economic Papers*, Dec. pp. 669–70.

**Senghaas, D.** (1985), *The European Experience. A Historical Study of Development Theory*. Berg Publishers, Leamington Spa/Dover, New Hampshire

**Senghaas, D.** (1993), "Global Governance: How Could It Be Conceived?", *Security Dialogue*, Vol. 24., No. 3. (pp. 247–256)

**Simai, M.** (1992), *A világgazdasági rend és az új multilateralizmus*. (The world economic order and the new multilateralism). Aula, Budapest. (In Hungarian)

**Simai, M.** (1994), *The Future of Global Governance. Managing Risk and Change in the International System*. United States Institute of Peace Press. Washington, D. C.

**Singer, H. W.** (1949), "Economic Progress in Underdeveloped Countries". *Social Research*, Vol. XVI, No. 1.

**Singer, H. W.** (1960), "Distribution of Gains between Investing and Borrowing Countries", *The American Economic Review,* May.

**Singer, H. W.** (1964), *International Development: Growth and Change*. McGraw–Hill.

**Singer, H. W.** (1971), "Distribution of Gains from Trade and Investment–Re-visited". First Interpag Conference. IDS. May 28th 1971. *IDEP Papers*, Repr. No. 270. Dakar.

**Skinner, A. S.** (1996) "Analytical Introduction" in Smith, A. (repr . 1997), pp. 8–96

**Smith, A.** (1759), *The Theory of Moral Sentiments*. London.

**Smith, A.** (1776), *An Inquiry into the Nature and Causes of the Wealth of Nations*. MacCulloch, Edinburgh. Reprinted: in 1937 as: *The Wealth of Nations.* Canan, E. ed. Random House; in 1961. Methuen and Co., London; in 1997 "Penguin Books" London.

**Smith, S.** (1980), "The Ideas of Samir Amin: Theory or Tautology?", *Journal of Development Studies,* October.

**Social Science Research Council** (1946), "Theory and Practice in Historical Study: A Report of the Committee on Historiography", *Social Science Research Council Bulletin*, No. 54.

**South Commission** (1990), *The Challenge to the South*. Oxford University Press.

**Spybey, T.** (1992), *Social Change, Development and Dependency*. Polity Press, Cambridge, UK

**Sraffa, P.** (1960), *Production of Commodities by Means of Commodities*. Cambridge

**Stammler, R.** (1906), *Wirtschaft und Recht nach der materialistischen Geschichtsauffassung*. Leipzig

**Stiglitz, J. E.** (1989), "Markets, Market Failures and Development", *American Economic Review, Papers and Proceedings*, May.

**Stolzmann, R.** (1896), *Die Soziale Kategorie in der Volkswirtschaftslehre*. Berlin.

**Streeten, P.** (1977), "L'évolution des théories au développement économique", *Problemes Économiques*, No. 1546. 9 Nov. pp. 2–5.

**Streeten, P.** (1985), "Development Economics: the Intellectual Divisions", *Eastern Economic Journal*, Vol. XI. No. 3. July–Sept. pp. 235–247.

**Sunkel, O.–Zuleta, G.** (1990), "Neo-Structuralism versus Neo-Liberalism in the 1990s", *CEPAL Review*, No. 42. December.

**Sunkel, O.** (1969), "National Development Policy and External Dependency in Latin America", *Journal of Development Studies*, No. 1.

**Szentes, T.** (1964), "Migrant Labour System in Black Africa". *Indian Journal of Labour Economics,* Vol. VII, Nos. 1–2.

**Szentes, T.** (1971), *The Political Economy of Underdevelopment*. Akadémiai Kiadó, Budapest (Fifth edition in 1988)

**Szentes, T.** (1976) "The Structural Roots of the Employment Problem", *International Social Science Journal*. UNESCO. Vol. XXVIII. No. 4. Paris. pp. 789–807.

**Szentes, T.** (1981), "The TNC issue: naive illusions or exorcism and lip service?", *Review*, A Journal of the Fernand Braudel Center. State University of New York. No. 34.

**Szentes, T.** (1985), *Theories of World Capitalist Economy. A critical survey of conventional, reformist and radical views.* Akadémiai Kiadó, Budapest.

**Szentes, T.** (1986), "Delinking from the capitalist world economy: how possible a strategy for the periphery?", *Scandinavian Journal of Development Alternatives*. No. 4. Oslo. pp. 60–80.

**Szentes, T.** (1988), *The transformation of the World Economy. New Directions and New Interests,* The United Nations University–ZED Books, London.

**Szentes, T.** (1990), "Analogies – if any – between East and South: A sketch of comparative system analysis", *The European Journal of Development Research*. Vol. 2. No. 2. Dec. London. pp. 163–175.

**Szentes, T.** (1993), "The Challenge to the South? A Challenge to Humankind as a Whole!", in: *The South Centre* (1994), pp. 100–116.

**Szentes, T.** (1994), "The Transformation of Central and Eastern Europe: A Study on the International Context of the Process". In: *Berend, I. T.* (1994), pp. 101–114.

**Szentes, T.** (1995), "A few thoughts on the political economy of 'transition' in Eastern Europe". Discussion paper. *International Colloquium on the World Economy*, Nov. 10–14. Vienna

**Szentes, T.** (1996), "'Structural adjustment' in the contemporary world economy: the case of Hungary", *El Mundo Actual*, Collection, Mexico.

**Szentes, T.** (1999), *Világgazdaságtan I. Elméleti és módszertani alapok*. (World Economics. I. Theoretical and Methodological Fundaments) Aula, Budapest.

**Thurow, L.** (1992), *Head to Head: The Coming Economic Battle Among Japan, Europe, and America.* William Morrow, New York.

**Tinbergen, J.** (1963), *Lessons from the Past*. Elsevier Publishing Company, The Hague.

**Tinbergen, J.** (1964), Central Planning. New Haven.

**Todaro, M. P.** (1997), *Economic Development*. Sixth edition. Longman Publ., London and New York.

**Toye, J.** (1987), Dilemmas of Development. Blackwell, Oxford .

**UN** (1951), *Review of Economic Conditions in Africa*. New York.

**UN** (1953), *Aspects of Economic Development in Africa*. UN Document E/2377, New York.

**UN** (1958), *Economic Survey of Africa since 1956*. New York.

**UN ECE** (1965), *Economic Planning in Europe*. Geneva.

**UNCTAD** (1979), *Handbook of International Trade and Development Statistics*. New York–Geneva.

**UNCTAD** (1992), *International Monetary and Financial Issues for the 1990s*. UN. New York, "The World Development Report 1991: A Critical Assessment". Pp. 1–29.

**UNDP** (1992), *Human Development Report 1992*. Oxford Univ. Press, Oxford, New York

**UNRISD** (1966), *The Level of Living Index* (prepared by Drewnowski, J. and Scott, W.). UN, Geneva.

**UNRISD** (1970), *Contents and Measurement of Socio-Economic Development: An*

*Empirical Enquiry* (prepared by McGranahan, D.–Richard-Proust, C.–Sovani, N. V.–Subramamian, M.) Report No. 70.10, Geneva.

**Vaitsos, C. V.** (1989), "Radical Technological Changes and the New 'Order' in the World Economy", *Review*, Fernand Braudel Center, Vol. XII. No.2, Spring. Pp. 157–190.

**Vajda, I.** (1965), *The Role of Foreign Trade in a Socialist Economy*. Corvina Press, Budapest.

**Vernon, R.** (1966), "International Investment and International Trade in the Product Cycle", *Quarterly Journal of Economics*. May.

**Viner, J.** (1953), *International Trade and Economic Development*. Clarendon Press, Oxford.

**Viner, J.** (1958), "The Economics of Development", in: *Agarwala, A. N.–Singh, S. P.* eds. (1958)

**Waelbroeck, J.** (1998), "Half a Century of Development Economics: A Review Based on the Handbook of Development Economics", *The World Bank Economic Review*, Vol. 12, No. 2, pp. 322–352.

**Wallerstein, I.** (1972), "The Rise and Future Demise of the World Capitalist System: Concepts for Comparative Analysis". Paper presented to the Annual Meeting of the American Sociological Association, New Orleans, 28–31 August.

**Wallerstein, I.** (1974), *The Modern World-System. Capitalist Agriculture and the origin of the European World-Economy in the Sixteenth Century*. Academic Press, New York–San Francisco London.

**Wallerstein, I.** (1975), "Semi peripheral Countries and the Contemporary World Crisis", A paper prepared for the *CENDES Seminar*, May. Mimeographed

**Wallerstein, I.** (1976), "A world-system perspective on the social sciences", *The British Journal of Sociology*, Vol. 27, No. 3.

**Wallerstein, I.** (1977), "Civilizations and Modes of Production: Conflicts and Convergences". Paper for the *Sixth Annual Meeting of the International Society for the Comparative Study of Civilizations.* Bradford College, Haver-Hill, Mass., April 15.

**Wallerstein, I.** (1978a), "Societal Growth: World Networks and the Politics of the World-Economy". Paper for the Plenary Session of *1978 Meetings of the American Sociological Association,* San Francisco, Sept 5.

**Wallerstein, I.** (1978b), "Contra Historical Myths: The Persistent Debate between the Developmental and World-System Paradigms". Keynote address. *Conference on Exports and Change in Third World Societies*, Duke University, January 20–21.

**Wallerstein, I.** (1978c), "The Dialectics of Civilizations in the Modern World-System". Paper for the *IX. World Congress of Sociology.* Uppsala, aug. 14–19.

**Wallerstein, I.** (1993), "The World System After the Cold War", *Journal of Peace Research*, Vol. 30. No. 1. (pp. 1–6)

**Ward, B.** (1967), *The Socialist Economy*. New York.

**Warren, B.** (1980), *Imperialism: Pioneer of Capitalism*. New Left Books, London.

**Weisskopf, T. E.** (1972), "The Impact of Foreign Capital Inflow on Domestic

Savings in Underdeveloped Economies", *Journal of International Economics*, February.

**Whitaker, J. K. ed.** (1975), *The Early Economic Writings of Alfred Marshall, 1867–1890*. Macmillan, London.

**Williamson, J.** (1997), "The Washington Consensus Revisited", in: *Emmerij, L. ed.* (1997), *Economic and Social Developments into the Twenty-First Century*. Baltimore, Johns Hopkins Press Wisconsin, pp. 257–302.

**Woddis, J.** (1961), *Africa. The Roots of Revolt*. London.

**World Bank** (1990), World Development Report. New York.

**World Bank** (1991), *Development Report 1991*. Oxford Univ. Press, New York.

**World Bank** (1995), *Global Economic Prospects and the Developing Countries*. A World Bank Book. IBRD, Washington.

**Yeats, A. J.** (1985), "On the Appropriate Interpretation of the Revealed Comparative Advantage Index: Implications of a Methodology Based on Industry Sector Analysis", *UNCTAD Reprint Series,* No. 54. Geneva.